CONTENTS

PREFACE TO THE SECOND EDITION

More than a decade on and I'm still finding more to say about *The Castles of Glasgow and The Clyde*. Many more sites have been rediscovered, though I'm sure that as many remain lost in the ground. Partly as a result of the development of more detailed internet resources and the improved availability of older resources via republication, the original list has expanded considerably. I have already submitted a number of these sites to subsequent editions of Martin Coventry's *The Castles of Scotland*; however there is still scope in this volume to bring you more.

Learning is a life-long process they say, and I have certainly added a great deal to my knowledge in the intervening years. I have been able to confirm most of the additional sites listed in the original volume and more clarity has emerged about many of the original entries.

When Martin published his first edition of *The Castles of Scotland* back in 1995, it quickly became obvious that the initial aim of producing a complete list of castles which had existed in Scotland was an impossible goal. Always there are more facts to find, and no comprehensive record could be borrowed from a library giving details on the buildings or their nature. As a result his list expanded to prompt second, third and fourth editions and no doubt there will be others.

My original aim was to provide more detail of the sites on a local basis. At the time I felt that I'd achieved that aim, but now it is time to revise, update and supplement what appears to me now to be an outdated work. Researching castle sites is a process that I will continue for as long as my senses and interest can be maintained. This is a hobby after all, my professional interests lie elsewhere. I started 'collecting' sites at a young age and now over 40 years later I still strain my eyes at old maps and texts. Glasses help nowadays, but so does my younger daughter Rebecca, who through questioning her old dad has reinvigorated my research for fear that I don't have answers to her very many questions.

For that reason alone, this book is for her, Rebecca Elizabeth Mason.

ACKNOWLEDGEMENTS

Thanks are due to;

Martin Coventry at Goblinshead for giving me the opportunity to produce this second edition and for creating the finished article from the raw materials of my text and photographs.

Paul Fox for digging me out of a rut. Well that's what archaeologists do!

Graham at Microlight Scotland based at Strathaven Airfield, for his piloting skills and patience which allowed me the opportunity to take a few aerial photographs for this book. Not as unnerving an experience as it sounds.

Robert Letham, for showing an interest and providing a welcome distraction. A genuine £12 note is certainly a distraction!

Sandy and Seonaid Edgar at Lamington Mains for the offers of tea, warm welcomes and hospitality.

Bruce Dick, owner of Busby Peel, who provided access to original missives which have shed new light on the history of his home.

The many landowners who allowed access to their fields, yards and gardens, thank you for your patience.

My wife Janette, who has been tolerating my abandonment for the PC and senseless chatter about castle sites for many years.

MEMORIAM

RQMS Thomas Wilson Mason (Scotty), born 1st July 1911, died 14th November 1978. A proud though modest hero of Dunkirk, El Alamein, the Invasion of Italy, D-Day and the push into Germany.

His greatest achievements were as my father. Had he lived he would have become a centenarian whilst this book was being written. Much loved and sadly missed.

GWM
Drumsagard 2013

PREFACE TO THE FIRST EDITION

As an eight-year-old, I became absorbed by stories of Robert the Bruce. One day I read in an old history book that he had died at Cardross. I was taken with this idea. My Gran lived at Craigendoran, and every Saturday my parents and I got on "The Blue Train" to gran's and the penultimate stop was Cardross. Robert the Bruce died near my Gran's house, wow!

Thereafter my weekends down the Clyde took on new meaning and from Dalreoch to Craigendoran my gaze, formerly fixed on the beautiful Firth, turned inland. I started taking my bike on the train, spending whole summer holidays searching for Bruce's Castle, finding others, but not his. 30 years later, I've a pretty good idea where it was, and wasn't, but I've learned about a few others on the way. This book contains much of that, within the area described.

I would like to thank Martin Coventry for the invitation to expand the descriptions and material for this area from his own *The Castles of Scotland*.

Thanks also to my wife, Janette for her patience and for allowing me to indulge in this second of my obsessions (the first is fishing), and my daughter Nicola, for her own special contributions.

Finally, as thanks for their encouragement and inspiration, may I dedicate this book to my late parents, Tom and Ina.

INTRODUCTION

This book was originally derived from *The Castles of Scotland* by Martin Coventry. Martin conceived the idea of writing another, larger book containing as much detail as was available on each site. This would not have been viable due to the probable encyclopaedic proportions involved in covering the whole country, and so the idea was mooted of producing local guides. My first edition was devised to provide greater detail of the sites within the watershed of the River Clyde and its tributaries.

In this second edition I have expanded both the lists and each individual entry to provide further information. There is only so much you can say about stone and mortar, particularly when the bulk of it has been robbed away. The real story of a castle is that of the people who lived in it. I have attempted to provide more generous family histories, but within the remit of producing a local guide as opposed to a comprehensive history.

At times I have found myself at odds with official records, either in providing a location, or in the nature or status of the building. Gilbertfield, for instance, has not been demolished and is still standing despite its poor condition. The availability of old maps on line has also allowed me to be more exact as regards location than the estimates given elsewhere. This in the case of Whiteford, as an example, has identified the location half a mile to the west of that given by the RCAHMS.

History they say is written by victors, and there is no doubt that over the centuries written interpretations of events have been coloured by the needs of the audience of that time or the classical education of writers who produced work which reflected the standards prevalent in their own age and society. As you read more old texts, whether ancient or relatively modern, the variations can be quite startling. It becomes obvious that history, like beauty, is in the eye of the beholder.

Over the last 30 years or so, modern historians have been revising the traditional interpretations of history, reanalysing what was the accepted rationale for events and attempting to establish history without the encumbrances of current society. In short, they are trying to understand what happened within the context of the original era, and not in present day terms. Since the first edition of this book, much of this revisionist thinking has pushed its way onto the bookshelves, challenging traditional attitudes to Scottish history and giving a more accurate understanding of the great events and day-to-day moments that make up our history. This inevitably has had an effect on the interpretation of our ancient architecture, an art which reflects the culture of its time, and which when analysing Scottish castles, has produced a greater degree of clarity as regards the functions of these buildings. Architectural historians have also adopted the revisionist ideal, and in reappraising our historic buildings, are also promoting alternative views on the role and design of late medieval and Renaissance residences. Reflecting on all of this, I have revised the chapter on the development of castles, taking several of their points on board.

That brings us to the vexed question of which sites warrant inclusion in this book? Marc Morris in his excellent TV series and subsequent book *Castle* attempted to define what is meant by the term, albeit within the English model. When discussing an apparent lack of defensive ability at Bodiam, one of England's most famous and iconic castles for which a license to crenellate had been granted, he came to the conclusion that if the owner and his peers believed it to be a castle, then it must be. Plantagenet Somerset Fry in his *Castles, England, Scotland, Ireland, Wales*, questioned the validity of categorising Crookston as a fortress since it has a dearth of obvious *active* defensive features, such as arrow loops, and it's defences appear to be entirely passive. These points serve to highlight the traditional view of a castle as being a defensive structure. But in Scotland many buildings which we now accept as castles were not called castles in their own time and might be excluded, and many which are included have no defensive features at all. Many authorities traditionally define castles simply as the seats of great medieval lords, where military and defensive strength was paramount and domestic comfort was secondary to the administrative functions of the barony. That would exclude many buildings for which common usage determines an acceptance as such, and within our own culture are identified as iconic representations of the genre, again highlighting Scotland's unique cultural heritage.

Whilst defensive intent remains the primary criteria for inclusion, this edition is a gazetteer of the homes and strongholds of the landholding classes within the period 1058-1700 and, as such, you will often find me use phrases like 'old or fortified house' where the defensive quality or nature of the building cannot be determined. Where it can, I have tried to categorize the building when evidence indicates a style. You will find me use terms like 'tower house', 'hall-house', 'bastle', 'fortified house' and 'castle'. I have also included the early earth and timber castles. There are still a few transitional houses included, illustrating the trend away from defence as a primary design feature.

The castles appear within an alphabetical gazetteer and on a series of maps covering the area. This consists of the entire shire of Renfrew, the City of Glasgow, North Lanarkshire and South Lanarkshire. Circuiting the north of the city I describe the sites which stood within the former domain of the Earls of Lennox combined with the area which was formerly East Dunbartonshire. You may notice that in defining each area I have not necessarily followed conventional boundaries. I have used a mixture of the ancient and the modern, often providing variance where I felt that local contacts could not separate a group of sites. The Lennox and East Dunbartonshire, for instance, takes in parts of the present council areas of Stirling, Dunbarton, North Lanarkshire, and Argyll and Bute – and I have included a single site from Falkirk because it is more readily identified with Cumbernauld, and two sites from Ayrshire and Dumfries and Galloway, which sit very close to the head waters of Clyde tributaries. I have tried to reflect local identity and traditional associations. I trust that most readers will find the result satisfactory.

There are many 'castles' which are red herrings, the word castle in a name does not guarantee inclusion in this book. One or two sites included in the first edition have since been identified as being unqualified for inclusion though remain in the text in order that the reader is informed. These entries stemmed from the wider use of the word 'castle' in earlier eras, when it was used to describe Prehistoric, Dark Age and Roman sites.

Wealthy Victorians were particularly fond of romanticising their mansions by describing them as castles and adopting the architectural motifs through which their landed predecessors had proclaimed their status. Sites such as Craigrownie Castle or the second Balloch Castle can prove disappointing for those seeking defensive sites. They have some apparently defensive features which are purely decorative in function. For me, the earthwork which represents the last vestige of the original castle at Balloch is a much more rewarding visit than the adjacent 'modern' house, since it lends a greater sense of history and atmosphere to the area.

The reverse situation may also mislead. A great pile such as Finlaystone House appears to all intents and purposes to be an altered Georgian mansion, but in discounting it you would be ignoring hundreds of years of history, and confirmation that a castle is incorporated within the present house.

You will find, as you read on, that the concentration of known sites is very uneven. North Lanarkshire has the least, and South Lanarkshire by far the most. Other than surface area, there are several reasons for this. The first was the predominant ownership of land by the pre-reformation church in Scotland. In most areas of the country the reformation meant a large increase in land ownership for those who had supported the Protestant cause. There was a resultant increase in castle building on former church land throughout the second half of the 16th and early 17th centuries. Understandable, since the church had owned the greater share of the most fertile lands in the country and the new owners sought to protect and display their newly won wealth.

The scene in Glasgow and North Lanarkshire differed though. Merchants from the city were discovering their own source of wealth via a developing trade with the Americas. These merchants, rather than adopting the architecture of the *Aul' Regime*, often opted for the comparative luxury of purely domestic architecture. The result was a rash of country mansions such as Ibrox, Ibroxholm, Dalmarnock, Plantation, Westthorn, Bellahouston and so on. These are not included. In the Monklands, a few similar properties began to appear, such as Drumpellier House. But the Monklands were ripe for other development and in the centuries that followed entrepreneurs began to invest in digging up the countryside. Coal production, begun on a small scale by the clerics, was rapidly expanded to fire the furnaces of new iron works and to fuel the mansions of the city. This destroyed much of the surrounding countryside, as did the expansion of the city and towns which accommodated the workforce. Numerous properties of possible interest were lost and, since most were of little historical importance, only names survive with little in the way of written record to verify the nature of the buildings.

Elsewhere agricultural land and country estates survived the onslaught of industry. Stirlingshire, Renfrewshire, the Lennox, East Dunbartonshire, and South Lanarkshire had considerable localised mineral wealth, but retained importance as areas of farming activity. Hence the survival rate of the buildings was higher out with the industrial heartland, despite the widespread use of ruins as convenient sources of good building stone.

As we look to the future, we have to ask if the remaining buildings will survive. As the most characteristic examples of our own brand of architecture, their importance cannot be underestimated. The attractiveness of sites such as Edinburgh or Eilean Donan to the tourists who have become an enormously important part of our economy is obvious. However the smaller houses and ruins around the country add romance, mystery and atmosphere which must to these important guests be a lure to return. They spread the interest across the land, adding character to scenery so often devastated by our industrial past.

'An Englishman's home is his castle' goes the saying and, in terms of the landholding classes of the era discussed, the same could be said of a Scot. It could also by now be his barn, his midden wall, the gable end of his cottage, the stony patch in his field, the attractive carved stonework in his dyke, or a complete mystery to him. I know that the first edition of my book helped one or two individuals identify that they had once had a castle on their land, or in one case identify that they were actually living in a small tower house, albeit extended, adapted and remodelled beyond recognition. I hope that this second edition can provide a greater appreciation of the history behind many of the place-names in the area, of the buildings that once stood there, and make you wonder what might lie hidden on your wee plot of land!

HOW TO USE THIS BOOK

An introductory chapter describes my own opinions on the development of castles from the earliest times. It is written from a historical perspective, relating the fashions and requirements of castle building in relation to national events.

Maps illustrate the dispersal and locations of castle sites This is the place to start if touring and exploring sites within a particular area. The gazetteer section can then be used to discover the history, architecture, ownership and legend associated with your site of choice. Each entry provides simple directions to the site, and a position in reference to an Ordnance Survey sheet number and grid reference. These correspond to the Landranger 1:50,000 series. Grid references are given in six digits, providing a location usually accurate to a few tens of yards.

An architectural description, with historical narrative and legend complete the entry. If you are interested in a particular family, go to the index. If an individual or family branch owned more than one site, I have endeavoured to allocate the history in terms of the period they occupied a particular castle. Some castles were occupied simultaneously by the same family, as they moved around different residences. In this case I have tried not to be repetitive, and you may find all of the history allocated to the larger or more important site.

The inclusion of a castle site in this book does not authorise access, many are on private ground, and others are still used as homes. For many sites access is denied. Please respect other people's property when going exploring: it only takes one visitor to upset a landowner and no one else will be allowed to the site. In such circumstances, the presence of visitors is often only tolerated on the basis of their manners and appreciation that their presence may be an intrusion.

I have checked my data as far as is possible, and visiting arrangements are described where they exist. Many of these sites, however, are not worth going to, either because of the defensive nature of the site making visiting dangerous or because nothing of interest remains The very nature of castle design was to make access difficult, and so disabled access is often impossible even on well maintained and managed sites. Many of the surviving buildings are abandoned crumbling ruins, and this can make them very dangerous places indeed. Castle ruins are alluring, can encourage a sense of adventure and stir the imagination, but they are far from being play areas for children. Sites such as Polnoon and Duchal are particularly treacherous and neither the author nor publisher can accept responsibility for any injury or difficulty you sustain in visiting any of the sites.

Please adhere to the Scottish Outdoor Access Code, available online at:
http://www.outdooraccess-scotland.com/

LIST OF ILLUSTRATIONS

Photographs by Gordon Mason, drawings from MacGibbon and Ross: *Domestic and Castellated Architecture of Scotland*, and other illustrations from collections of Gordon Mason and Martin Coventry.

THE DEVELOPMENT OF CASTLES IN SCOTLAND

From early times the peoples of Scotland have created defendable buildings which acted as hubs for their communities. There is a rich archaeological heritage in these structures. These appeared in a variety of forms, some styles appearing nationwide and others only in regions. Hill forts, duns, brochs, crannogs and timber hall houses were common in their own particular areas and many of these structures continued in use into the medieval period, albeit often adapted or modernised. For some, on a local basis, the symbolism of lordship represented by these traditional residences may have lingered on. In short, it took a while for some of the peoples of Scotland to fully adopt the lifestyle and cultural motifs of the Norman immigrants who brought with them the concepts of castle and feudalism. Indeed the peoples of the highlands never fully did and drew their influences from their own tradition, or from Scandinavian contacts. On the other hand, there were those for whom adopting these styles was an attractive and desirable development as they grasped the nettle of feudalism with both hands.

It is very easy to follow the traditional model of incoming Norman aristocracy building motte-and-bailey castles to enforce military and social obedience on the local inhabitants, but it must also be remembered that in some areas local lords remained in power and adapted to the new culture voluntarily. In this book, that point is particularly relevant to the Lennox, where the earls and the local clans balanced traditional Gaelic culture with that of feudalism as their territories straddled the natural boundary formed by the Great Highland Fault. The reverse is also true, where immigrants to all parts of the country adopted local culture to a greater extent as they blended in to their new environment. It can be seen then that the process of integration could vary. It was simply a case of developing effective local systems within a legal framework which was adaptable enough to honour cultural differences.

In the 12th century Scotland was not as well defined a nation as it is now. The writ of the kings of Scots based in the lowlands and borders was ineffective in areas such as the west highlands, Moray, Sutherland, the Firth of Clyde, Caithness and Galloway. One aspect of a deliberate policy enacted by the Canmore dynasty was the recruitment of Norman and Flemish knights, renowned as the most efficient and feared warriors of their day. Their role was to assist in extending areas of Royal influence and to strengthen the military and administrative structures of the nation. The immigration began as Malcolm III introduced a few Norman mercenaries into Scotland, but the policy was developed by his son David, Earl of Cumbria, later enthroned as David I, who was educated in England and raised at their court.

There were two distinct waves of settlement as the Normans came north. The first wave brought Flemish and Norman settlers to south western Scotland, though David retained the royal demesne lands of Clydesdale. A second wave from about 1160 settled mainly north of the Forth, particularly on the coast of Moray, but at this time Malcolm IV actively settled Clydesdale with Flemish settlers. This process provided Scotland with many now traditional surnames. The Stewarts were descended from Walter Fitzallan, recruited as the High Steward and based at Renfrew and later became the Royal House. De Brus become Bruce and were settled in Annandale. Comyn, the enemy of the Bruces, later named Gunning, Commons, Cummin, Cumming and possibly Stirling. The Flemish families who settled in Biggar and Upper Clydesdale became the Flemings. Others adopted territorial names from their property, de Moravia for instance becoming Murray, who with Douglas and Maxwell, are among the better known.

In some areas the established local nobility adopted cultural change by integrating with the feudal styles of habitation and government. The Lords of Galloway seem to have readily adopted the motifs of the new culture, despite Galloway remaining virtually independent for another two centuries or so. Galloway still supported the indigenous nobility who began to build earthwork castles, mostly of the motte-and-bailey type. They seem to have been very enthusiastic in integrating with Norman-French culture, building a close association with the court of William the Conqueror, using Norman-style Christian names such as Roland and Alan, and marrying into the Norman aristocracy of the de Morville family at an early stage.

In Clydesdale there is little or no evidence for a local aristocracy due to its royal patronage and because many of these estates were originally held by the church of Glasgow. It has been suggested that the leader of the Fleming immigrants was a crown appointed 'populator', who later took on an increasingly judicial role as Sheriff of Lanarkshire. Baldwin of Biggar appears to have used family connections to assemble a close-knit group within the area. The suggestion continues that another Fleming, Freskin of Moray, carried out the same role in the north once the locally based rival claimants for the throne had been fully subdued. It is interesting that the Douglases of Lanarkshire and the Murrays shared similar devices in their early coats of arms, indicating similar ancestry or a close familial relationship. Through marriage, Freskin's descendants eventually inherited the vast estates of the Barony of Bothwell, which in turn were gained by the Douglases, also through marriage. This type of familial networking was common practice throughout the period covered by this book.

The administrative centre and residence of each settler was the earth-and-timber castle, of which the motte-and-bailey was the most common variety. These were rapidly built and readily defended structures in the days when Norman knights on heavy horse, armoured and equipped with sword, mace, shield and lance were the most advanced and powerful tools of war available. The motte consisted of a steeply built earthen mound, often layered alternately with stones to provide stability, within the perimeter of a deep ditch. Atop this mound would have been a wooden tower which provided the main residence of the Lord. The whole was adjacent to a larger area known as the bailey. This contained a living area for the garrison and livestock supporting subsidiary buildings such as a hall, chapel, bakehouse, brewery, and stables. This was also protected by a ditch. The defences were supplemented by palisades, or wooden walls surrounding both the motte and the bailey, the ditches filled with water creating a moat, or heavy spikes set into the ground so thickly as to provide an impenetrable barrier to charging heavy cavalry.

There were many variations to earth-and-timber castle design. For instance, an early reference tells us that the motte of the Somervilles at Carnwath had what appeared to be a spiral stairwell descending through the summit. This led to a suggestion that the tower was accessed via a radial tunnel through the base of the motte, and thence by a central well and ladder to the centre of the block house. The 'motte' at Cadder was described as being almost square. Maiden Castle at the foot of the Campsie Fells, near Lennoxtown, was of the traditional Christmas-pudding shape with relatively small summit area which would have been accessed by removable ladder. Along the road at Kilsyth is Balcastle, a large earthwork shaped like an upturned frying pan which has a circular summit of about 90ft diameter. At Crookston we have a well-preserved ringwork, a continuous ditch which enclosed a central area occupied by timber buildings. This ditch would have been supplemented by a palisade and probably a rampart, with an entrance probably guarded by a timber gatehouse. Crogals Castle and Drumsagard were ditches which isolated partly manufactured level platforms on the end of promontory sites, which were naturally defended on their other sides by the surrounding terrain. These may not have supported the traditional motte-style mound, though several similar sites such as Ringsdale probably did.

Nowadays the remains of these earth-and-timber castles provide unusually contoured, though attractive, additions to the landscape, mellowed by nature over the centuries and having lost their timber buildings and palisades, of which only archaeological traces may survive. In their heyday their appearance would have been offensive, the mounds of raw black earth contrasting a gentle green countryside. Add to this the foreboding array of spikes, aimed to threaten those outside from every angle. This combined with the stench of rotten corpses and the cackle of a variety of carrion-eating birds on the nearby Gallowhill, presented a fierce and sinister symbolism of the power of the lord within.

These men had to earn their lands. They were held from a superior in return for military service in the national cause, but they were also to provide stability and administrative structure within the country itself. The upper wards of Lanarkshire typify the traditional model. A grant of land was made to an incoming knight who was granted baronial control of a large area and its populace by the king. In return he gives military service and feus out portions of his land to a number of lesser landowners, who in turn are required to support his jurisdiction and military contribution. The names of some of these men remain as those of villages, Thankerton and Symington from the brothers Tancard and Simon Loccard, Lamington from Lambin Asa, Roberton from his brother Robert, Wiston from Wice, while other settlers took the names of the lands – Coulter, Douglas, and Carmichael are examples.

A note of caution though, there is evidence that at least in the Clydesdale area, mottes were built as temporary residences at least until the 14th century. The motte at Moat, two miles south of Roberton, has been shown to have been built at this time. When excavated it gave up pottery of that date from the ground below and cannot, as originally thought, be attributed as Robert's seat. It is thought to have been built by Mary of Stirling, who had supported the anti-Bruce faction throughout the reigns of Robert I and David II. She had been compelled to provide herself and her retinue with safe lodgings in the area.

As the Clyde moves toward the Firth is an area traditionally threatened from the Western Isles, (another independent lordship), harried by highlanders from north of the great fault line, and assailed from the sea by Vikings. They, until the Battle of Largs a century later, ruled much of the western seaboard from Ireland, the Isle of Man, and through the west highlands and isles to Sutherland, their very own south land, now the northern part of Scotland.

David I and his heirs extended his policy of settlement, utilizing both native and immigrant nobles. The Earls of Lennox created a defensive line of earthwork castles stretching from the Royal fortress at Dumbarton, to that at Stirling. This mediaeval Maginot Line included Faslane, Balloch, Catter, Balfron, Fintry, Graham's Castle or Dundaff, Maiden Castle, Balcastle and Colzium. These guarded the natural travel ways from north to south, routes later used as drove roads by the cattlemen of the highlands. The Firth itself was guarded by the High Steward, with properties at Dundonald, Inverkip, Renfrew, then later Rothesay Castle on Bute then Dunoon Castle as he began to make inroads into Norse territory. The great Somerled, King of the Isles and ancestor of the Lords of the Isles, had met his death in treacherous circumstances close to Renfrew while leading his followers in a major assault on the area. In those days the lands around the Firth of Clyde were still a frontier zone.

Compare this to the rich, fertile regions of the Lothians, where evidence of mottes is rare. Set to become the traditional killing fields of the wars between Scotland and England, in David's day there was peace. David's sister was married to Henry I, the men had been reared and educated at the English Court, and David had been one of Henry's earls, of Huntingdon. Prior to his accession to the throne he had been based in Carlisle under Henry's authority, with a remit to quell the troublesome northern lands. The two then were understandably close, and no threat would have been perceived in the settled counties, with little need for demonstrations of military power at least until Henry's death in 1135. Indeed, after the Battle of the Standard in 1138, the border was considerably further south of Lothian than the modern counterpart, the modern English shires of Cumbria and Northumberland essentially being part of the Scottish kingdom.

But Norman settlement was only part of his master plan. Their introduction redesigned the military and judicial structures of the country along feudal lines. But at the same time he introduced the first coinage since the Roman period and devised the parish system of local government, building many of our famous abbeys and priories. He made generous grants of land in Lanarkshire and elsewhere to various sects of the Roman Church. Their clergy had initially been introduced by his mother Margaret, who was later made a saint, to replace the traditional Celtic form of worship. Expansion of the church's influence provided both national and local administrative structures alongside rapid economic development and diversification as the various sects of churchmen put their own specialist skills to work in building the economy. David I had set the scene for Scotland and its administration for the next 450 years, barring a few enforced English incursions.

The first stone castles began to appear in the second half of the 12th century. The earliest confirmed dating of a surviving stone castle on the mainland is Castle Sween, built around 1200. Any earlier examples have probably been lost though it is likely they were rare. David I was, however, actively building some castles in stone, such as at the great keep at Carlisle, and very probably at his preferred residence in Roxburgh, where he may have built a large donjon. The early Scottish baronial stone castles consisted simply of a high, thick, curtain wall or enceinte, which supported a parapet from which the entry and walls could be defended. In these earliest structures, the buildings within would initially have consisted of lean-to wooden buildings with the largest functioning as the main hall and lord's residence. These simple structures were added to as new defensive features were developed and incorporated in response to the increasing sophistication of assault weapons and tactics, a process continuing even today in modern warfare. Initially corner towers would have been added, gatehouses, and then stone keeps, with the result that the remaining examples require close study to reveal how the surviving structure came about over the centuries. These additional features became part and parcel of the design of each new castle, individual buildings reflecting the wealth and social standing of its lord.

Bothwell Castle is an excellent example of this, despite having never been completed to its original plan. Stone castles took a great many man hours to build, accumulating to years of construction time. A period of peace was therefore required in order that the structure could be completed without the threat of attack in the interim. It would have been a great investment for a lord to contemplate, peace allowing him to accrue the necessary resources and to build without interference by belligerent enemies. The actual workforce would have included a number of expensive and highly skilled tradesmen, masons, carpenters and armourers, backed by a multitude of labourers. In the original planned form, Bothwell would have become one of the grandest residences in the land. The great keep, or donjon, displays stonework of great quality, and the sheer size is a statement of the status of the de Moravia family. If the Wars of Independence had not interceded, the intended internal area would have exceeded any contemporary Scottish baronial castle. Much of it had reached only foundation level at the time of the English invasion of 1296. By then all that had been completed was the donjon and adjacent prison tower, with interceding wall. Even in this incomplete condition it took a siege of 14 months for the Scots to regain Bothwell from English hands in 1298.

The Wars of Independence resulted in the deliberate policy of rendering indefensible all castles which could be held by an invader against the Scots. This policy was conceived by Robert I, the Bruce. Dumbarton and Berwick were to be the only exceptions among the Royal castles, although he also built or strengthened a few castles such as Tarbert in Kintyre. The consequence is that only the sections of buildings which were left in a repairable state survive as testament to the skill of the early medieval tradesmen. It has been suggested that moated sites and other forms of earthwork castle may have become the normal style of residence for the landed gentry during the years of the Bruce kings. Robert himself may have set the tone by building his manor at Cardross. Since the majority of these sites have not been excavated or dated, the assumption that they were all early Norman work has to be questioned until adequate archaeological work is carried out to clarify if there had been resurgence in motte building in the first half of the 14th century.

Following the death of 'Good King Robert' in 1329 and the subsequent attempt to re-establish a Balliol monarchy during the reign of David II, the Scots appear to have gradually relearned the value of fortified stone residences. Simple keeps became the order of the day in the late 14th to early 15th centuries. These consisted of a large main block of cube-like proportions, normally within a courtyard, with exceptionally thick walls and battlements. There were usually three storeys, the basement having no communication with the other floors. The main entrance was by removable stair from the courtyard to the main hall on the first floor, the private quarters on the floor above were accessed by a narrow stair built within the structure of the wall. Often additional rooms were created within the walls, these mural chambers serving as smaller guest rooms or as garderobes. The roofs were of stone, a parapet providing a fighting platform around the wall tops, and the remainder was protected by flagstones against attack with fire. As always, the grander the house the greater the lord, with later additions often masking the original building. Mearns, Levan and Covington represent three excellent examples within the area, while Crookston is an exception, illustrating aptly that as symbols of power, the lord's castle tended to reflect the wealth available to him.

It is worth mentioning at this point that wealth was not purely a monetary commodity in these early days, but a direct reflection of political influence and the fighting manpower and resources available under the lord's superiority. Crookston is unique amongst the castles of this period, having had a massive main central block of at least three storeys, further strengthened by four corner towers, providing a rough X-plan. It does not appear to have had a courtyard as such, any subsidiary buildings being within the perimeter of the deep and wide ditch which protected its predecessor, the ringwork of Robert Croc of Neilston.

Until 1400, the expense in resources of building stone castles limited their construction and ownership to the upper echelons of society. However, as part of a systematic reduction of the power of the great lords, the Crown passed an Act of Parliament in 1401 which took the baronies directly under Royal control whenever the superior earldom fell to the Crown. The division of these great properties allowed the granting of smaller though substantial parcels of land to lesser men, and heralded an explosion of activity in the construction of lesser houses as these new 'bonnet lairds' felt the need to impress their new-found wealth.

The hall house was a common design. A two- to three-storey block, longer than it was tall, generally with service rooms on a vaulted ground floor, hall and solar taking up the first floor, with bedrooms above, often in the garret. Provanhall provides an excellent example. The design persisted through the centuries, but for some it was not ideal. It was realised that defensive quality could be improved by upending the design. Decreasing the footprint of the building allowed a more compact site, and by placing rooms one above the other as with the earlier simple keeps, the additional height gave a defensive advantage. The result was the birth of the traditional Scottish tower house. This became the most frequently occurring variety of Scottish castle. Usually of three to four storeys, early access was to a basement with vaulted ceiling, often with no access to the floors above. The main entrance to the simple tower would, like the stockier keeps of previous years, have been to the first floor by a removable stair. The standard arrangement provided one room per floor, the first floor as the hall, and private quarters above. Each tower was surrounded by a barmkin which supported lesser buildings such as stables, stores etc. A good example was Drumry Peel, now sadly demolished.

In 1455 the campaign by James II against the Black Douglases saw the destruction of their power. In the aftermath of his victory at Arkinholm, James attainted the family, destroying their castles and dividing their estates. It is likely that several castles in this area were lost as a result, possibly including two in Carmunnock Parish.

In 1535 another Act of Parliament obliged each landholder 'on the borders or inland' to build a barmkin, with a tower within if required as residence. The result was a two-year flurry of activity on the building front.

L-plan towers provided better defensive ability and improved domestic planning. They began to appear in the early 16th century, either as new builds, or extended simple towers. The position of the main entrance within the re-entrant made it possible to place the door at ground-floor level, covering fire being given from gunloops at strategic positions on the adjacent walls. Additional defensive features were various: caphouses, bartizans, parapets and open rounds. A latticed iron gate known as a yett protected the door. The hall would have remained on the first floor, though a more complex arrangement of numerous rooms to each storey was now possible. The increasing sophistication and tastes of the gentry now demanded wine cellars, numerous bedrooms, kitchens, food stores, and separate stair towers. There were many superb examples within the area, such as Jerviston, Jerviswood and Haggs.

As these tastes developed, by the latter part of the 16th century, extensions were added to create the more complex structures of E-, Z- and T-plan, each geometrically enhancing the apparent defensive ability of the building. Around 1550-60, the Scots more frequently expressed their continental influences in the architecture of their domestic buildings. This was in part due to the French influences brought into Scotland by Mary of Guise, Queen to James V, and then by their daughter Mary, Queen of Scots. New building projects often incorporated or adapted older work to save on building costs, while developing the model of country residences as opposed to baronial strongholds. They became more chateaux than fortified residences. This signified a change of emphasis where announcing the status and lineage of the owner gained greater dominance over an apparently diminishing need for defensive ability. Features such as battlemented parapets, machicolations and gunloops obtained a more ornamental than functional purpose, simply proclaiming the status of the owner as they were transformed from 'warlike apparatus' to architectural badges of rank. The term castle was rarely used at this time, being reserved mainly for places of great strength. Place, palace, tower, hall, fortalice, mansion and house were poorly defined terms describing the various forms of fortified house. More often, no term was used, the buildings simply being known by their name, so Craigbarnet or Newark would specifically refer to the main building of the estate, though 'castle', 'tower' or 'hall' were added to many by later commentators or owners.

Several sites may have been lost to the area in the aftermath of the Battle of Langside in 1568, as the Regent Moray conducted a campaign against those who had supported the deposed Mary, Queen of Scots. There was then a more vigorous campaign by the Regent Lennox, assisted by English troops with artillery, following Moray's assassination in 1570. Buildings were destroyed across Lanarkshire as the Hamiltons paid a heavy price for their loyalty to the defeated faction. Some say Lennox attacked every Hamilton property, which would make a long list and perhaps explain the demise of sites like Drumsagard, Cadzow and Dalserf. The former Regent Morton then attacked and dismantled Craignethan and Hamilton in 1579 as the family remained on the wrong side of the regime.

One development of the 15th-early 16th centuries was improved access to gunpowder and associated weaponry. Financially the viability of defending against artillery was limited. For the vast majority to reflect this new destructive power in the nature of their buildings meant defence by use of small arms, muskets and small cannon or mortars. A few wealthy individuals were able to afford defence against larger cannon, creating a new challenge in castle design. Craignethan stands out as an outstanding local example.

The defensive works of Sir James Hamilton of Finnart at Craignethan were built as a showpiece. In his role as Master of Works to James V he was in a position of considerable influence and power, and his name will crop up frequently in this book. Sir James designed and built Craignethan from the old castle of Draffane to create a state-of-the-art fortress with many unique design features. Curiously he chose a site where all of these defences were apparently vulnerable to artillery. The ridge across the approach would have provided a perfect platform from which the bombards of the day could have strafed the entire site were it not for the massive proportions of the defensive wall and the squat nature of his keep. Craignethan was built not only for its functionality, but to illustrate Hamilton's personal abilities as an architect and enhance his reputation by defending a difficult site as this entrepreneurial character endeavoured to amass a personal fortune.

The period 1560-1650 brought what is now known as the bastle house, a simple fortified farmhouse which defended stock and inhabitants against the reivers of the borderland and Clydesdale. These structures varied in their detail and so any description is bound to be a generalisation. Their purpose was to provide an element of defensibility against lightly armed raiding parties, inhibiting the theft of livestock and stores, while also putting a roof over the head of the landholder and his family.

The ground floor was an animal shed accessed by a single door, usually wooden, which could be defended from the floor above. In most there was a vaulted ceiling. The upper floor consisted of the living quarters, reached by an internal stair. A garret was standard. There was not normally a courtyard, though a collection of outbuildings clustered around would have formed a yard of sorts. Often there were earthworks or dykes around the whole. The bastle was the best building in the farmstead, representing the working core and main residence. Many have disappeared, though ruins survive in some of the far-flung corners of the upper ward of Clydesdale. Glendorch is one of the more substantial ruins, and had a vaulted ground floor. An example was uncovered at Thorril during the M74 fieldwork project in 1990. Others stood at Snar, Nemphlar, Glenochar and Windgate.

Following the Union of the Crowns in 1603, defensive features should have become even less necessary. Wisely, or because of the added expense, some Scots had been slow to give up the main design motive of their homes, opting to adapt older structures rather than build anew. It proved to be a positive asset, as religious conflict and civil war illustrated. However, Cromwell's occupation following the Scots transfer of allegiance to the Royalists saw the destruction of many more castles, Kilsyth being a prominent local example.

By the early part of the 18th century features of fortification gradually fell into misuse as comfort and spaciousness became the primary driving force. The Act of Union brought increased prosperity to the country as a whole. As Scotland entered the 'enlightenment' many castles were abandoned, replaced or extended until they eventually became the lesser part of great mansions, or survived as ornamental garden features. The later editor of Hamilton of Wishaw's *Descriptions of the Shires of Lanark and Renfrew* summed it up well when referring to Castlemilk: 'The fortalice of Castleton still remains, though quite hid by large additions, in the castle style, which have lately been made to it – the old tower itself being remodelled that it may assimilate with these preposterous and garish extensions.'

As the period of the fortified house closed, the creation of fortresses built to sustain a full-time garrison from the standing army became necessary. The example of Dumbarton stands out, losing much ancient stonework and character in favour of a more martial design. Gun batteries, barracks and cell blocks replaced the personal touch of the Governor who had on occasion to provide comfortable lodging for his Royal patron. In short, it became less of a home and more of a military installation.

MAPS

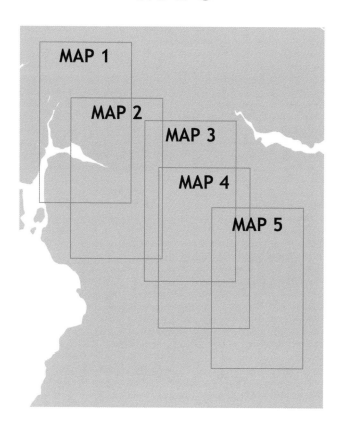

MAP 1

MAP 2

MAP 3

MAP 4

MAP 5

MAP 1

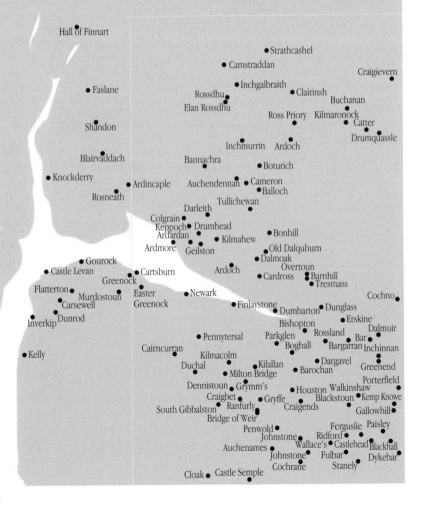

MAP 2

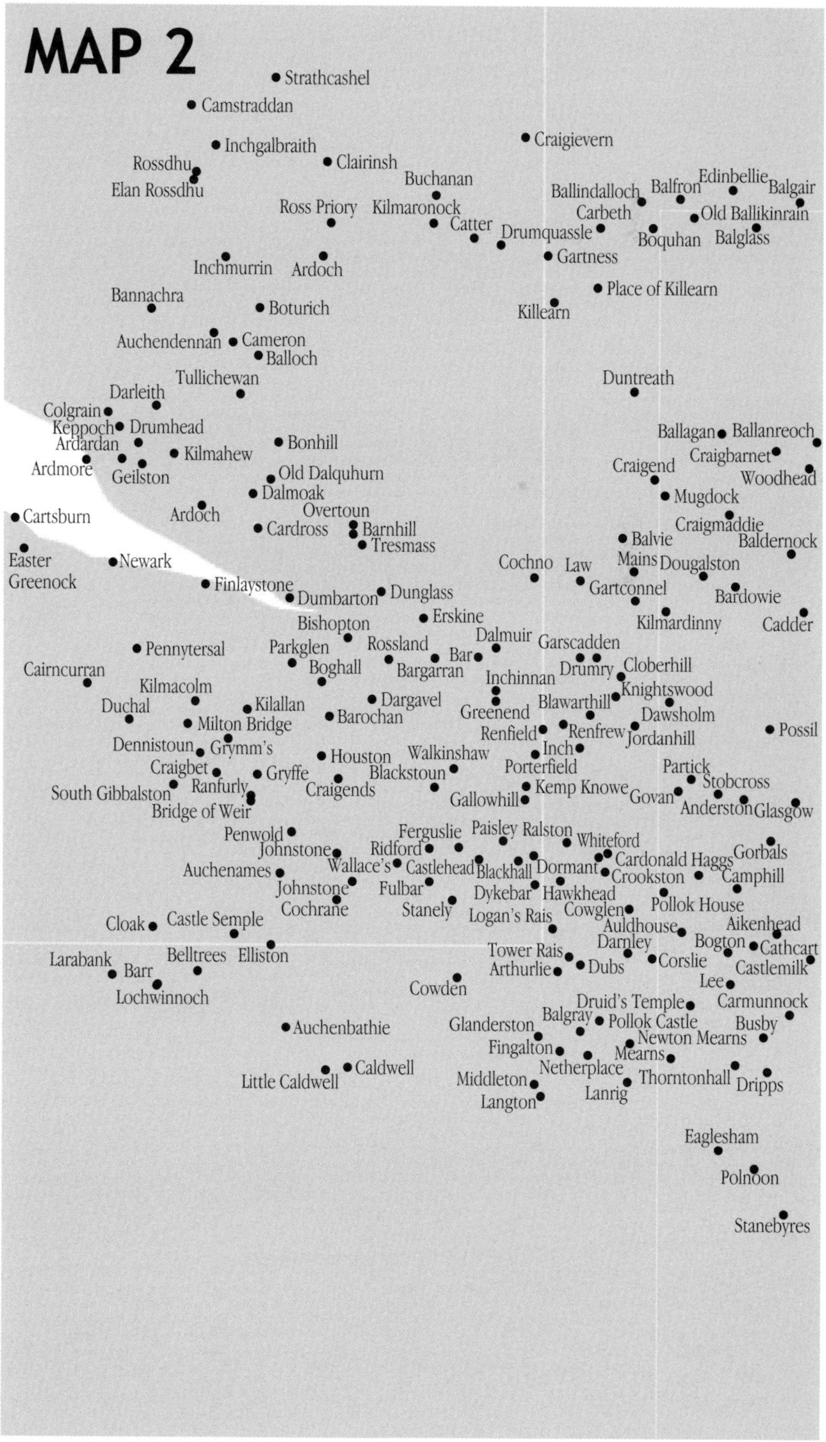

Strathcashel

Camstraddan

Inchgalbraith

Craigievern

Rossdhu
Elan Rossdhu

Clairinsh

Buchanan

Ballindalloch Balfron Edinbellie Balgair

Ross Priory Kilmaronock

Carbeth Old Ballikinrain

Catter Drumquassle Boquhan Balglass

Inchmurrin Ardoch

Gartness

Bannachra

Boturich

Place of Killearn

Killearn

Auchendennan Cameron

Balloch

Tullichewan

Duntreath

Darleith

Colgrain
Keppoch Drumhead
Ardardan Kilmahew Bonhill

Ballagan Ballanreoch

Ardmore Geilston

Craigend Craigbarnet

Old Dalquhurn

Woodhead

Dalmoak

Mugdock

Cartsburn Ardoch Overtoun

Craigmaddie

Cardross Barnhill

Balvie Baldernock

Tresmass

Easter Newark
Greenock

Cochno Law Mains Dougalston

Finlaystone

Gartconnel

Bardowie

Dumbarton Dunglass

Bishopton Erskine

Kilmardinny Cadder

Pennytersal Parkglen Rossland

Dalmuir Garscadden

Cairncurran

Boghall Bargarran Bar

Drumry Cloberhill

Kilmacolm

Inchinnan

Knightswood

Duchal Kilallan Dargavel

Blawarthill

Milton Bridge Barochan

Greenend Dawsholm

Renfield Renfrew Jordanhill

Possil

Dennistoun Grymm's

Houston Walkinshaw

Inch

Craigbet Gryffe Blackstoun

Porterfield

Partick

Ranfurly Craigends

Stobcross

South Gibbalston

Gallowhill Kemp Knowe Govan

Anderston Glasgow

Bridge of Weir

Penwold Ferguslie Paisley Ralston

Whiteford

Johnstone Ridford

Gorbals

Auchenames Wallace's Castlehead Blackhall Dormant Cardonald Haggs

Johnstone Fulbar Crookston Camphill

Cochrane Stanely Dykebar Hawkhead

Cloak Castle Semple

Logan's Rais Cowglen Pollok House

Auldhouse Aikenhead

Larabank

Belltrees Elliston

Tower Rais Darnley Bogton Cathcart

Barr

Arthurlie Dubs Corslie Castlemilk

Lochwinnoch

Cowden

Lee

Druid's Temple Carmunnock

Auchenbathie

Glanderston Balgray Pollok Castle Busby

Fingalton Mearns Newton Mearns

Little Caldwell Caldwell

Middleton Netherplace Thorntonhall Dripps

Langton Lanrig

Eaglesham

Polnoon

Stanebyres

9

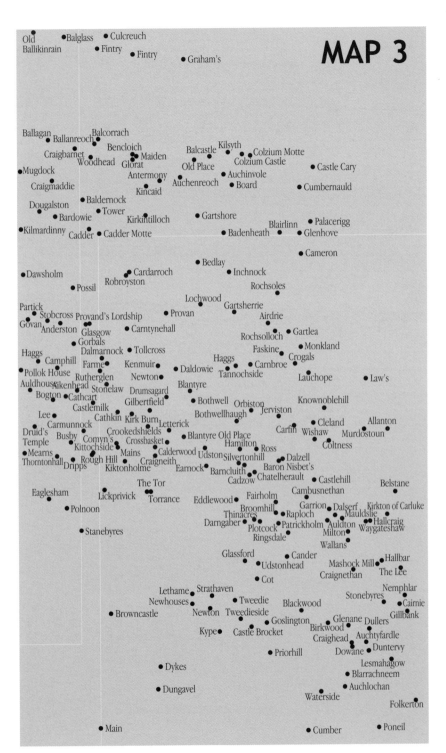

MAP 3

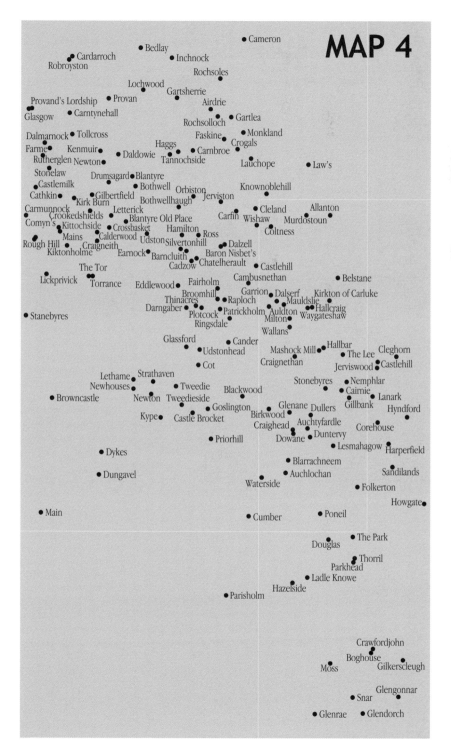

MAP 4

Cameron
Bedlay
Cardarroch
Robroyston
Inchnock
Rochsoles
Lochwood
Gartsherrie
Provand's Lordship
Provan
Airdrie
Glasgow
Carntynehall
Gartlea
Rochsolloch
Dalmarnock
Tollcross
Faskine
Monkland
Farme
Kenmuir
Haggs
Crogals
Daldowie
Carnbroe
Rutherglen
Newton
Tannochside
Lauchope
Law's
Stonelaw
Drumsagard
Blantyre
Castlemilk
Bothwell
Orbiston
Knownoblehill
Cathkin
Kirk Burn
Gilbertfield
Bothwellhaugh
Jerviston
Carmunnock
Letterick
Cleland
Allanton
Crookedshields
Blantyre Old Place
Carfin
Wishaw
Murdostoun
Comyn's
Kittochside
Crossbasket
Hamilton
Coltness
Mains
Calderwood
Udston
Silvertonhill
Ross
Rough Hill
Craigneith
Dalzell
Kiktonholme
Earnock
Barncluith
Baron Nisbet's
Cadzow
Chatelherault
Castlehill
The Tor
Cambusnethan
Lickprivick
Torrance
Eddlewood
Fairholm
Belstane
Garrion
Dalserf
Kirkton of Carluke
Broomhill
Thinacres
Raploch
Mauldslie
Darngaber
Plotcock
Patrickholm
Auldton
Hallcraig
Ringsdale
Milton
Waygateshaw
Wallans
Glassford
Cander
Udstonhead
Mashock Mill
Hallbar
The Lee
Cleghorn
Cot
Craignethan
Jerviswood
Castlehill
Lethame
Strathaven
Stonebyres
Nemphlar
Newhouses
Tweedie
Blackwood
Cairnie
Lanark
Browncastle
Newton
Tweedieside
Glenane
Dullers
Gillbank
Hyndford
Goslington
Birkwood
Kype
Castle Brocket
Craighead
Auchtyfardle
Corehouse
Priorhill
Dowane
Duntervy
Lesmahagow
Harperfield
Dykes
Blarrachneem
Dungavel
Auchlochan
Sandilands
Waterside
Folkerton
Howgate
Main
Cumber
Poneil
The Park
Douglas
Thorril
Parkhead
Ladle Knowe
Hazelside
Parisholm
Crawfordjohn
Boghouse
Gilkerscleugh
Moss
Glengonnar
Snar
Glenrae
Glendorch
Stanebyres

11

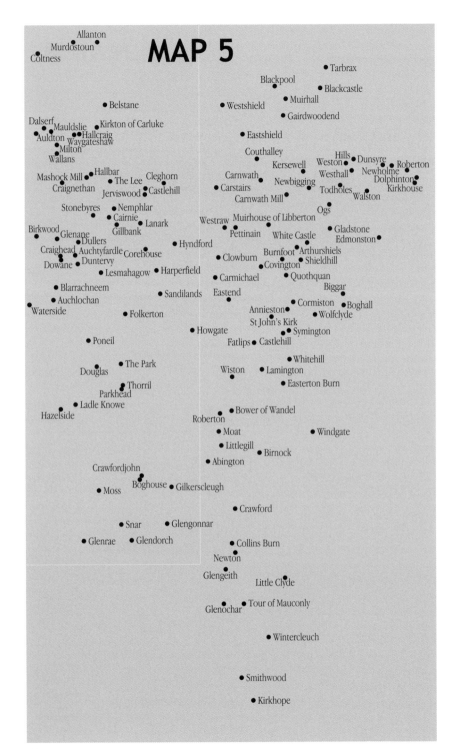

MAP 5

Allanton
Murdostoun
Coltness

Tarbrax
Blackpool
Blackcastle
Muirhall
Westshield
Gairdwoodend

Belstane

Eastshield

Dalserf
Mauldslie   Kirkton of Carluke
Auldton   Hallcraig
Waygateshaw
Milton
Wallans

Couthalley
Kersewell   Hills   Dunsyre
Weston   Roberton
Westhall   Newholme
Carnwath   Newbigging   Dolphinton
Carstairs   Todholes   Kirkhouse
Carnwath Mill   Walston

Mashock Mill   Hallbar
The Lee   Cleghorn
Craignethan   Castlehill
Jerviswood

Stonebyres   Nemphlar
Cairnie   Lanark
Birkwood   Gillbank
Glenane   Dullers   Hyndford
Craighead   Auchtyfardle   Corehouse
Dowane   Duntervy
Lesmahagow   Harperfield

Ogs
Westraw   Muirhouse of Libberton
Pettinain   White Castle   Gladstone
Edmonston
Clowburn   Burnfoot   Arthurshiels
Covington   Shieldhill
Carmichael   Quothquan

Blarrachneem
Auchlochan
Waterside

Sandilands   Eastend
Folkerton

Poneil

Annieston   Cormiston   Biggar
St John's Kirk   Wolfclyde
Symington
Fatlips   Castlehill

Howgate

The Park
Douglas
Thorril
Parkhead
Ladle Knowe
Hazelside

Whitehill
Wiston   Lamington
Easterton Burn

Bower of Wandel
Roberton
Moat   Windgate
Littlegill
Birnock
Abington

Crawfordjohn
Moss   Boghouse   Gilkerscleugh

Crawford

Snar   Glengonnar
Glenrae   Glendorch

Collins Burn
Newton
Glengeith
Little Clyde

Glenochar   Tour of Mauconly

Wintercleuch

Smithwood

Kirkhope

ALPHABETICAL GUIDE
TO THE CASTLES
(A-Z)

ABINGTON MOTTE

South Lanarkshire   Ruin or site   OS 72   NS 932250
East of M74 and A702, 0.5 miles north of Abington, just east of Abington Services at Nether Abington

Impressive earthworks remain of Abington Motte, the best preserved motte and bailey castle in the region.

Guarded on the east by the Clyde, on the south by a pair of deep natural gullies, and on the west and north by a horseshoe shaped ditch and rampart, both the motte and the bailey are well defined. The motte stands at the southeastern corner of the bailey to a height of 36ft above the river and has an oval summit 70ft by 35ft. It has its own 5ft deep ditch which runs around the base of the motte to meet the gully at each end. The bailey sits 30ft above the river and is protected by a 5ft high rampart which runs from the head of the gully at the southwestern corner in a broad arc to the far northeastern corner. There it meets the river bank some 180ft from the motte. A ditch which once followed the rampart is now silted up. A track enters the bailey on the north breaking through

the rampart and may be relatively modern. On the southwest is a 13ft gap where the edges of the rampart have been rounded. This seems to be the original entrance. The surface of the bailey is uneven and early excavation of the motte summit revealed habitation remains in the form of animal bones and charcoal. The summit of the motte is now occupied by a monument to enthusiastic angler, and local postmaster, Matthew McEndrick.

In the 12th century Abington was the seat of John, the stepson of Baldwin of Biggar. It is likely that the motte was built by him. John allegedly added his name to this portion of Crawford to distinguish it from the lands held by Galfridus, hence Crawfordjohn. John of Crawford witnessed a charter by Baldwin in 1160 and is known to have held his estate as early as 1159.

AIKENHEAD

The City Of Glasgow   Private   OS 64   NS 596603
In King's Park, Glasgow, 0.5 miles east of B766, in the King's Park, at Aikenhead House.

Site of a tower house which was replaced by a mansion. The tower house appears on Pont's map of Renfrewshire, dated c.1583-96, and in Blaeu's *Atlas Novus* of the 17th century.

Gilbert de L'Akenheud appears on the Ragman Roll rendering homage to Edward 1 in 1296. Robert II granted Aikenhead to the Maxwells in 1372, but at some point the estate was divided and in 1611 this portion was sold to James Hamilton of the Torrance family. He was Provost of Glasgow on three occasions between 1614 and 1628. When he died in 1633 he was a wealthy merchant and had begun building a new house here. He left £4,000 to his son Robert to complete the work. His great-grandson, also James, was twice rector of Glasgow University. The Hamiltons sold the estate to the Rae family in the 18th century who built the present neo-classical mansion in 1806. It was extended by the addition of wings to the plans of the architect David Hamilton in 1823. It then it passed to a Mr Scot, a Glasgow banker, and then to the Gordons. The house was subdivided into flats in the 1980s and is a category 'A' Listed Building.

Other reference: Aitkenhead

AIRDRIE HOUSE

North Lanarkshire Ruin or site OS 64 NS 749656
North of A89, at Monklands General Hospital, Airdrie.

Site of an old or fortified house originally owned by the Cleland family and from 1490 by the Hamiltons. The old house was 'much decayed' by the early 18th century.

Airdrie House, a Scots Baronial mansion was built on the site, possibly incorporating part of an earlier structure.

One of the earliest stories emanating from local legend tells that a Cleland (Keuland or Kneland) of Airdrie was brother-in-law to William Wallace. While marshalling his forces the night before the disastrous Battle of Falkirk in 1298, Wallace and his army allegedly camped beside the house.

John Hamilton of the Fingalton and Preston family gained Airdrie in 1490 and died at Flodden in 1513. His son Methusalem was a foremost reformer and cousin to Patrick Hamilton, 'the first Scottish martyr' who was burned at the stake for heresy at St Andrews in 1528. Gavin Hamilton of Airdrie was in the party involved in the attempted capture of the young James VI from Stirling Castle in 1571. Robert Hamilton of Airdrie supported the Covenant, and fought at the Battle of Drumclog. After the battle Airdrie House was captured and used as a barracks for Claverhouse's dragoons.

Hamilton fled into exile, and on his return was imprisoned in the tollbooth of Edinburgh. On his release in 1693 he planned the town as a weaving centre. The estate passed to Lord Elphinstone and then to an American named Aitchison in 1769. Later it was owned by the Alexanders and then the Wilsons from 1896. Sir John Wilson was a career politician and coal master of one of the largest mining firms in the UK. He was created a baronet in 1905.

The house was then used as the local maternity hospital. It was demolished in 1964, when the new Monklands General Hospital was to be built. The Wilsons of Airdrie now live in Buckinghamshire.

ALLANTON HOUSE

North Lanarkshire Ruin or site OS 72 NS 844573
1.5 miles northeast of Newmains, by A71, at or near Allanton.

Site of a castle, which may have been incorporated into a large mansion designed by James Gillespie Graham. There was an extensive garden with picturesque lake. The building was completely demolished in the 20th century.

Originally an estate of Arbroath Abbey, it is said that Allanton was granted to Sir Allan Stewart of Daldowie in 1421. His family claimed descent from Alexander, 4th High Steward of Scotland, via the Stewarts of Bonkyll (Dumfriesshire), though it has been alleged that this lineage is fictitious. Alternatively it is suggested they descend from another Alan Stewart of Daldowie, a son of Robert Stewart of Minto, who lived in the early 16th century.

There is a legend that the Protestant martyr George Wishart often sought refuge within the walls of Allanton, Sir Alan Stewart of Allanton being a close friend and supporter. When Sir Alan died, the estate passed to his nephew, James of Daldowie, who fought with the Regent Moray at Langside in 1568. The house was visited by Cromwell in 1650. In 1787 Henry Stewart married Lilias Seton a daughter of the Laird of Touch. The family combined their names becoming the Seton-Stewarts of Allanton and Touch. The old tower house was considered to be too cold and damp for his new wife, so Henry built the new house. It remained with their descendants until the estate was divided and sold in 1932.

ANDERSTON

City of Glasgow   Ruin or site   OS 64   NS 582653
1.5 miles west of Glasgow Cathedral, east of M8, at or near Bishop Street, Anderston.

This may be the location of a manor of the Bishops of Glasgow. The area was known as Bishops Forest, a forest in medieval times being a managed hunting ground and not necessarily a large wooded area. Traditionally though it was known as Bishop's, or Parson's Croft, indicating a small productive landholding.

The area had been church land since 1450, when James II granted the property to the Bishops. In 1603, it is said, James VI gave 13 acres to the clerk of his Privy Council, John Andrew. It later belonged to the Incorporation of Tailors. The Anderson family had held a portion of the property from the late 16th century and built their mansion at Stobcross. A small village developed, and was known as Anderson's Town, later contracted to Anderston (compare Stobcross).

ANNIESTON CASTLE

South Lanarkshire   Ruin or site   OS 72   NS 997366
3 miles southwest of Biggar, south of the Clyde, on minor road north of A72, 1 mile north of Symington at Annieston.

Little remains of a tower house which once had 3ft thick walls, a vaulted basement and a turnpike stair. Only a right-angled wall fragment still stands. Recent survey prior to building work showed evidence of a shallow ditch.

The name Annieston apparently derives from Agnes de Brus, who owned lands here in 1185. She appeared as Anneis de Brus when she donated the Church of Thankerton to Kelso Abbey in 1180. Simon of Annieston paid homage to Edward I in 1296.

The Mures of Annieston are recorded as early as 1493, and were still in possession in 1662. James Lockhart of Annieston appears on record in 1690 and there was a family named Muir in Annieston by 1760. The Rait family seem to have been in possession by the end of the 18th century and in the 19th century it belonged to David Dickson of Hartree.

ANTERMONY CASTLE

The Lennox & East Dunbartonshire   Ruin or site   OS 64   NS 662765
1 mile east of Milton of Campsie, on minor roads north of A891, west of Antermony Loch, at Antermony.

Site of a tower house of the Flemings, who held the estate from 1424. It was purchased by the Lennox family, but the castle was demolished in the 18th century to clear the site for a new mansion, itself now demolished. It passed to the Bell family.

Close to the house, a mound known as King's Hill was recorded in the 18th century. It had already been partly quarried away but there was a suggestion that it had been a motte. It is more likely to have been an ancient burial cairn. Whichever, it was remarkable enough to be recorded and illustrated in Alexander Gordon's *Itinerarium Septentrionale* in 1726.

My ancestor Andrew Mason was recorded in Campsie Parish in 1661. He was listed as being born 'at Antermony'. Presumably the family were in service, since there are no records of us owning the place, despite my best efforts to find them! A branch of the family is recorded in various trades in Campsie Parish in the 18th and 19th centuries.

ARDARDAN

The Lennox & East Dunbartonshire   Ruin or site   OS 63   NS 331785
2 miles west of Cardross, south of A814, by track and minor road, at neck of Ardmore Point, at Ardardan.

Site of a tower house of the Nobles who held the lands in the mid 16th century and possibly earlier. They sold the estate in 1798 to their near relatives, the Geils. The family designation in the 18th century was Noble of Ferme and Ardardan, possibly indicating that Ferme and Ardardan were two separate properties. There were close family ties around this time between the Browns of Cathkin, the Nobles, and the Dennistouns of Colgrain. By 1921, the Ferme title had been dropped in favour of Ardmore hence, Noble of Ardmore and Ardardan Noble.

Other reference: Ferme

ARDINCAPLE CASTLE

The Lennox & East Dunbartonshire   Ruin or site   OS 56   NS 282830

Northwest of Helensburgh, south of Rhu, on minor roads east of A814, east of Cairndhu Point, on hillside above the junction of Ardencaple Drive and Castle Avenue.

Ardincaple (or Ardencaple) Castle, once a large castellated mansion, incorporated an early castle of the MacAulays. Some of the work was allegedly from as early as the 12th century and it is said to have had a moat and outworks. It was pulled down in 1957, save a single tower utilised as a navigation beacon for the Royal Navy.

The family held the estate from the 13th century and were principal vassals of the Earls and Dukes of Lennox. Originally known as Ardincaple of that Ilk, the family adopted the patronymic MacAulay in honour of a 16th century chief. The family are said to descend from the early Earls of Lennox and/or the royal house of MacAlpin.

In 1489 Robert of Ardincaple was granted a remission for his part in the holding of Dumbarton Castle against the king. In 1567 Walter MacAulay of Ardincaple signed a bond of protection for the young James VI following the abdication of Mary, Queen of Scots. There were running feuds involving the MacAulays, Galbraiths, MacGregors, Colquhouns, Campbells and Buchanans. In 1590 during a clash with the Buchanans on the High Street of Dumbarton, Walter MacAulay was killed. A number of other local notables were injured, including Walter's brother, Thomas, who was wounded 'through the brain', though he seems to have survived. A number of Buchanans were charged with Walter's murder but the case was not satisfactorily resolved. The feuds rumbled on for more than a decade, involving legal actions, clans and magnates throughout the region. The MacAulays had entered into a Bond of Manrent with the MacGregors for their mutual aid. In doing this they identified the MacGregors as their chiefly line, harking back to their MacAlpin ancestry. The ongoing unrest in the region ultimately led to the Battle of Glenfruin in 1603 and the proscription of the MacGregors. The MacAulays did not come out of events entirely unscathed, periodically being outlawed. They survived due to the interventions of the Duke of Lennox.

In 1603 the chief was with the Duke of Lennox as he accompanied James VI on the journey south to his English coronation. The king had apparently written, requesting MacAulay's company. In 1639 Walter MacAulay of Ardincaple was made Keeper of Dumbarton Castle for the Covenanters. In 1688 the Glorious Revolution saw the clan raised to fight alongside the Earl of Argyll for William and Mary.

Financial troubles in the 18th century saw the MacAulays sell off the majority of their estates in small lots. By 1750 they had abandoned Ardincaple as a roofless ruin and moved to Laggarie. They finally sold out to the Campbells in 1767. Ardincaple was remodelled and extended in 1772 and earlier. Robert Adam had been involved, though his initial plans were abandoned and his second draft seems to have been implemented in part only. The property was sold to the Colquhouns of Luss before 1890 but had been demolished by 1957 to allow development of the site for naval housing. The surviving tower is a 'B' Listed Building.

ARDMORE

The Lennox & East Dunbartonshire   Private   OS 63   NS 317785

2 miles west of Cardross, south of A814, by track & minor roads, Ardmore Point, north shore of the Firth of Clyde.

A castle here was rebuilt or replaced in 1654. It was then remodelled and extended as a mansion with a central battlemented tower in 1806. Three towers of the 16th to 17th centuries survive, one with gunloops. Ardmore was an island in prehistoric times.

Ardmore may have been held by the Napiers at some point in the 17th century. This was then a property of the Noble family, until sold to their near relatives the Geils in 1798. The Nobles repurchased it in 1890 and, although still in private ownership, a nature trail here is managed by the Scottish Wildlife Trust. The present house is a category 'B' Listed Building.

Other reference: Hill of Ardmore

ARDOCH

The Lennox & East Dunbartonshire   Ruin or site   OS 63   NS 412864

4 miles northeast of Balloch, by minor roads and foot north of A811, on southern shore of Loch Lomond, 0.3 miles west of Ardoch.

Site of an old fortified house or mansion. The present ruins are of a thin-walled one-storey thatched property with corbiestepped gables. Early map references indicate a more substantial house stood here. It is also referred to as 'Old Place of Ardoch' in one reference, suggesting a hall house. It was a property of the Bontines, Buchanans, and the Findlays.

ARDOCH HOUSE

The Lennox & East Dunbartonshire   Ruin or site   OS 63   NS 363768
1.5 miles southeast of Cardross, on minor road north of A814, north of Ardoch, at Ardochmore Farm.

Nothing remains of the tower house of the Bontines, although ruins were still evident in 1856. Ardoch passed by marriage to the Grahams of Gartmore, and the tower was replaced by a mansion, itself demolished around 1874. The Grahams built Ardoch House to the south, a small mansion of 1840 with a round stair tower at one corner. An occupant was Robert Bontine Cunninghame Graham, first president of the Scottish Labour Party in 1888, and president of the National Party of Scotland in 1928.

Other reference: Tower of Ardoch

ARROCHAR

The Lennox & East Dunbartonshire   Ruin or site   OS 56   NN 296039
In Arrochar, just east of Loch Long and A814, south of A83, at Claymore Hotel.

The Claymore Hotel has a date-stone of 1697 with a Gaelic inscription relating to the MacFarlanes. This represents the last remnant of a castle of the MacFarlanes which had previously occupied the site. Down the years it has been known as Inveriach, New Tarbert, Arrochar House, the Arrochar House Hotel, and the Cobbler Hotel.

The MacFarlanes claim descent from Gilchrist, son of Ailin Earl of Lennox. Gilchrist was granted the lands of Arrochar in the 12th century. The chief appeared in the Ragman Roll of 1296 as Duncan MacGilchrist of the Lennox when he gave homage to Edward I of England. Early chiefs had used the patronymic MacGilchrist; however they adopted MacPharlain after their 14th-century chief. He provided refuge, then men for Robert the Bruce in the years after 1306 and fought alongside him at Bannockburn in 1314. In 1488 , many years after the execution of the Earl of Lennox, the MacFarlane chief submitted an excellent claim to succeed to the Earldom. The title, however, was given to John Stewart, Lord Darnley.

MacFarlane of Arrochar sacked Boturich Castle in the early 16th century. The 11th chief died at the Battle of Flodden in 1513, and the clan was on the losing side with the Earl of Lennox at the Battle of Glasgow Muir in 1544. They were forfeited as a result, though quickly gained a remission. The 13th chief died at the Battle of Pinkie in 1547. They fought on the victorious side at Langside with the Regent Moray in 1568 and at Inverlochy in 1645 with Montrose. Their island stronghold at Inveruglas on Loch Lomond was destroyed by Cromwell in the 1650s. They did not fight in the Jacobite rebellions, though many of the clan had moved to Ireland by the reign of James II and VII.

Locally a full moon is known as MacFarlane's Lantern, providing enough light to thieve cattle. Another version is that when on military service, they were exceptional in night raids, particularly against the English. Perhaps one skill led to the other.

It is said that when Walter, 20th chief, died in 1767 the family sold their Arrochar estate to Colquhoun of Luss, one of their local adversaries. It is more likely that this happened after the death of William, 21st chief, in 1784, when the lands were sold to Fergusson of Raith who leased them out to the Duke of Argyll. He added an extension to the house. In 1821 the estate was sold to the Colquhouns who extended the building for a second time. They renamed it Arrochar House.

The old building is apparently haunted by a 'Green Lady', although there are different stories about the origin. One is that this unfortunate soul is the ghost of the daughter of a chief. The girl had fallen for a Colquhoun, ancient enemies of the clan, and ignoring her father's warnings not to see her lover, was locked in a room where she was starved to death.

Other references: Inveriach, New Tarbert

ARTHURLIE HOUSE

Renfrewshire   Private   OS 64   NS 507588
Arthurlie Street, Barrhead, Renfrewshire.

Site of an old or fortified house. This mansion of 1818 was successor to a series of earlier structures.

In 1372 Robert II granted the Arthurlie estate to a son of Pollok of that Ilk. He lost the estate, and in 1439 the lands were divided into West Arthurlie and Arthurlie. They were given to Ross of Hawkhead and Stewart of Castlemilk respectively. One source indicates that Arthurlie was retained by the Stewarts of Castlemilk until the 18th century; however this may pertain to the superiority of the property. Arthurlie was again a Pollok possession by the 16th century. Thomas Pollok, a son of Allan Pollok of Arthurlie who appears in 1695, built another house known as South Arthurlie. The Pollok line died out and it came by marriage to the Ralstons of that ilk sometime in the 18th century. When it became a Dunlop property in 1808, they demolished the old house and built the present edifice in c.1810. There is an armorial stone bearing the arms of Dunlop. The house now operates as a community centre. There may also have been a castle at West Arthurlie.

Other references: Nether Arthurlie, East Arthurlie.

ARTHURSHIELS

South Lanarkshire Ruin or site OS 72 NT 004414
2 miles northwest of Biggar, off minor roads west of the B7016 and A721, at Arthurshiels.

A tower appears here on Pont's map of 1596, and Arthurshiels is known to have been the property of the Gladstone family. As the family fortunes deteriorated in the early 17th century, the family made this their main residence by moving from nearby Gladstone.

AUCHENAMES CASTLE

Renfrewshire Ruin or site OS 63 NS 395625
2 miles south of Bridge of Weir, on minor roads to the south of the A761, 0.5 miles southwest of Kilbarchan, at Auchenames.

Site of a much altered 14th century castle of the Crawfords. The keep was described in the 18th century as standing to six or seven storeys. It appears on both Pont's map of c.1596 and Blaeu's *Atlas Novus* of the 17th century, but in neither does it appear to be as massive as described. It was demolished in 1782, the last remnants being removed in 1825.

The family were granted the lands in 1320 by Robert I. The Crawfords of Auchinames were a branch of the Crawfords of Loudoun, who were hereditary Sheriffs of Ayr from the reign of Alexander II to that of Robert I. Robert Crawford of Auchenames was killed at the Battle of Flodden in 1513 and John Crawford was the eldest of three brothers killed at the Battle of Pinkie in 1547. In the 18th century, Patrick Crawford feued off the majority of the estate in small portions. His son John was MP for the burghs of Glasgow, Rutherglen, Renfrew, and Dumbarton. The estate was sold to the Barbours in 1762, who built a new house 0.25 miles to the north in 1779. The stones of the castle were then gradually removed for dyke building.

Other reference: Auchinames

AUCHENBATHIE CASTLE

Renfrewshire Ruin or site OS 63 NS 397565
3.5 miles north of Beith, near the junction of the B776 and a minor road, just east of Barcraig Reservoir.

Rubble and wall fragments to a height of 1.5ft remain of this tower house of the Wallaces.

Auchenbathie was held by Sir Malcolm Wallace, who was said to be the father of Sir William. John Wallace of Elderslie resigned his lands of Auchenbathie to his son Thomas in 1398. He was the ancestor of the Wallaces of Johnston.

Near Barcraig is Auchenbothie House, a rambling harled and castellated mansion of 1898, with towers, corbiesteps, turrets and dormer windows. 'Auchinbothie' appears as a large tower to the west of Caldwell and Little Caldwell on Pont's map of the late 16th century.

Other reference: Barcraig

AUCHENDENNAN CASTLE

The Lennox & East Dunbartonshire Private OS 56 NS 368835
2 miles northwest of Balloch, by minor road west of the A82, west of Loch Lomond.

Auchendennan was part of Robert the Bruce's hunting forest, used when resident at his manor of Cardross. In the early 15th century it said to have been feued to the Dennistouns and later to the Napiers of Kilmahew. There is no record of an earlier house here.

The present Auchendennan Castle is a large 19th century mansion, which replaced an earlier villa known as Belretiro. Belretiro was built and owned by the Rouet family. Auchendennan was designed by the architect John Burnett, and owned by George Martin, a Glasgow merchant. He sold it to the Chrystal family, who extended it.

In World War II it was requisitioned and used as the Searchlight Headquarters of the 12th Anti Aircraft Division. It now operates as a youth hostel and conference centre, and is a category 'A' Listed Building.

The castle reputedly harbours a ghost, known as Veronica.

AUCHENREOCH CASTLE

The Lennox & East Dunbartonshire   Ruin or site   OS 64   NS 678767

3 miles southwest of Kilsyth, just east and south of the junction of A803 and A891, at or near Auchenreoch Mains.

Site of a 16th century tower house of the Kincaid family. It passed by marriage to the Buchanans in the 18th century and in the 19th century to a Miss MacInnes. It was apparently known as 'The Prince's House', since it was occupied by the heir to the Kincaid chief. A small tower here appears on Timothy Pont's manuscript map of 1583–96, and in Blaeu's *Atlas Novus* of the 17th century.

Other References: Auchinreoch, The Prince's House.

AUCHINVOLE CASTLE

The Lennox & East Dunbartonshire   Private   OS 64   NS 714769

On south bank of River Kelvin, 0.5 miles south of Kilsyth, west of B802, just north of B8023, at Auchinvole Castle Yard.

Site of a tower house, which was demolished in the 1960s.

Much altered and extended, Auchinvole was a late 16th or early 17th century L-plan building with a vaulted basement. There was a very small stair turret corbelled out above third-floor level, which led to a watch tower in the re-entrant. The basement contained a wide-arched fireplace recessed into the gable. A wide turnpike stair led

to the second floor. The upper floors were accessed via the stair turret. A bartizan topped one corner. This entire structure was demolished, leaving only three sides of a wall which enclosed a large rectangular yard, possibly the remains of a walled garden. This reaches no great thickness, maximum 3ft, though on the southern wall there remains a roofless round doocot tower, probably of a later date than the original house. On the eastern and thicker portion of wall, there is a bricked-up side gate guarded by an arrow slot. This may be ornamental and of later date and appears intact to its original height of about 10ft. One reference states that this was the site of an early castle with drawbridge and moat.

The castle was built by the Stark family, and may have passed later to a family of Wallaces. Legend asserts that the first Stark was John Muirhead, second son of the Laird of Lauchope. He was apparently hunting with James IV at Cumbernauld when he realised that the king was in danger from an angry bull. Rushing at the bull, John grabbed it by the horns and turned it so suddenly that he broke its neck. In gratitude, he was awarded the surname Stark, meaning of great strength, and the lands of Auchinvole. There are however records pertaining to the surname in the 14th century, when Richard Starke was given a lease of the lands of Estirbalbriteane. It seems the Muirheads were fond of tales of great derring-do!

Auchinvole was evidently haunted by a lady whose lover was murdered. He was reputedly buried by a tree stump on the bank of the River Kelvin, a spot at which her spectre stared.

In recent decades the yard has been owned and used by a haulage contractor and plant hire company. Permission should be sought from the office before approaching the site. Parts of the wall are in a dangerously dilapidated state, and risk of injury enhanced by poor ground conditions and debris.

Other references: Auchenvole, Auchenvoil

AUCHLOCHAN CASTLE

South Lanarkshire   Ruin or site   OS 71   NS 809375
Off minor roads, 0.5 miles south of New Trows, Lesmahagow.

A tower at Auchlochan appears on Pont's manuscript map of 1596, and subsequently in Blaeu's *Atlas Novus* of the 17th century. Nothing remains. Both Over and Nether Auchlochan are depicted, 'Over Auchlochan' being the larger.

The family of Broun, or Brown, were church vassals from an early date and appear to have held the castle here until it was demolished. The Browns of Auchlochan were Covenanters, Thomas Brown fighting at both Drumclog and Bothwell Bridge in 1679. After the latter, dragoons pursued him to his door and left him for dead after a struggle. He was however only stunned and lived to a ripe old age. The sword that he had used that night was preserved in the house at least until the 19th century. The present mansion replaced their castle about 1814 and is reputedly haunted by a 'Black Lady', the beautiful wife of one of the lairds.

The estate now forms a retirement village and the house has been converted into flats. The walled garden is open to the public as part of the Scotland's Gardens scheme.

AUCHTYFARDLE CASTLE

South Lanarkshire   Ruin or site   OS 71   NS 826409
1 mile east of M74 at Lesmahagow, off minor roads, at or near Bogside.

Site of a large tower house or castle, marked on Pont's map of c.1590s. Between 1180 and 1203 the lands of Dowane were granted by the Abbot of Kelso (Superior of Lesmahagow) to one Constantine. He took the name 'de Dowane' and was son of a priest at Lesmahagow named Gilbert. He was granted the right to hold court over his own tenants. By 1240, Robert de Dowane had built a 'house' on the property. The estate became the subject of litigation between the monks of Kelso and the de Dowane family, the monks claiming that some of the land had been taken illegally. The family retained both the Auchtyfardle and Dowane portions with concessions to the clergy. This involved the construction of a mill. The lade was to run through the Dowane lands close to the confluence of the Dowane (Devon) Water and the Nethan.

In 1301 the estate was formally divided into two, Dowane and Auchtyfardle, these always having been two separate portions. The family had come into debt and had temporarily resigned part of their lands to the abbot in exchange for cash in 1294. They resigned Dowane 'in excambion' for 'Hautiferdale'.

Both Dowane and Auchtyfardle came to the Weirs, as did much of the area. However in 1546, Auchtyfardle became a Kennedy holding, and sometime in the 18th century belonged to Hugh Mossman.

AULDHOUSE

City of Glasgow   Private   OS 64   NS 556605
Just west of B769, 2 miles north of A726, at Auldhouse Court, Glasgow.

Auldhouse is a much altered, early 17th century tower house of the Maxwells. There was probably some sort of residence here from an early date, either fortified or otherwise, the name itself implying some antiquity.

Originally part of the Steward's Renfrewshire estates, Auldhouse was granted to Paisley Abbey. The monks rented it out and Roger son of Reginald de Auldhous is on record in 1265. In 1284 John, the son of Roger, renounced his rights in return for a charter in favour of both himself and his wife for the duration of their lives. Auldhouse was granted to the Maxwells with other local properties in 1344. Around the mid 15th century it was given to a younger son of Maxwell of Pollok. 'Oldhouse' appears as a small property in Pont's map of the late 16th century.

Auldhouse has been greatly altered over the years, having been used as a children's home. In the 20th century it was converted to flats and extensions of 1800 and earlier removed to reveal the nature of the building. On an L-plan, this three-storey house has a stair tower in the re-entrant, at the top of which is a watch room. It has crowstepped gables and is fairly compact when compared to similar houses. All the windows have been altered, those to the front giving a Georgian feel to the building. Those to the rear have been blocked up, with the exception of two tiny ones in the watch room. Stonework above the second floor appears to be of a slightly different date to that below, though later alterations may be partly responsible.

Many original features may have disappeared, though an original fireplace apparently retains a lintel inscription of 1631:

THE BODIE FOR THE SAUL WAS FRAMED; THIS HOUS THE BODIE FOR;

IN HEAVNE FOR BOTH MY PLACE IS NAMD IN BLISS MY GOD T'ADOR.

George Maxwell, Minister of Mearns, and his son John, Minister of Eastwood and the High Church of Glasgow, built the present house. The next Auldhouse Maxwell, George,

inherited the lairdship of Pollok. He zealously pursued witches and was involved in a witch trial at Gourock in 1676. For that story and further family history see the entry for Pollok House.

AULDTON

South Lanarkshire Private OS 64 NS 795502
2 miles southeast of Wishaw, by minor road southwest of A72 at Dalserf, at Auldton.

This house has been adapted, and retains none of its defensive features, although it apparently has a date-stone of 1610 at the northeast corner. A roofless ruin in 1914, it now forms part of a farm complex. The original building was described as being of two storeys in 1954, and as the ancient seat of the Hamiltons of Dalserf.

The Hamiltons were granted the Barony of Dalserf, or Machanshire as it was then known, by Robert I in 1312. In the reign of Robert III, it was granted by Sir John Hamilton, 4th of Cadzow, to his son David. Auldton does not appear on the earliest maps; however a small tower named Bruntsfield is illustrated in this vicinity and may be the same building.

It is said that Auldton became the residence of the Hamiltons of Millburn until the turn of the 18th century. They built a new house called Millburn, just to the northeast, which dates from c1780 and is a category 'B' Listed Building. Millburn, and presumably Auldton before it, is known to have been the dower house of Dalserf.

Other reference: Bruntsfield

BADENHEATH CASTLE

The Lennox & East Dunbartonshire Ruin or site OS 64 NS 713724
Mollinsburn, north of M80/M73 Mollinsburn Intersection, west of Mollins Road, eastern corner of Badenheath Farm.

All that remains of this 15th century keep is a carved stone which was set upon a plinth within the precincts of the sewerage works. The stone carried the date 1661 and the initials E.W.K. and I.C.K. (Earl William of Kilmarnock and Jean Countess of Kilmarnock, probably commemorating the 1661 award of the earldom.). There are reported to be further decorated stones set into the wall of a barn at Badenheath Farm.

The castle consisted of a rectangular keep 42ft by 30.5ft of fine ashlar blocks, later pillaged by local builders. There were four storeys, over walls between 6 and 7ft thick, with two vaulted rooms on the ground floor. A spiral staircase led from the entrance to the hall on the first floor. The quality of the fine mouldings around the main entrance, hall fireplace, remaining windows and the corbelling for corner turrets caused MacGibbon and Ross to conclude in 1887 that it had been 'a superior tower of its class', although by their time only about half of the building remained. In its original state there was a moat and a deer park, from which the nearby area of Deerdykes takes its name. Around the turn of the 19th century it is known to have had a 'leaden roof' and was being plundered for its stone.

The Lords Boyd built the castle, possibly as early as 1405, when they gained the estate by marriage. Robert Boyd of Badenheath was a member of Mary, Queen of Scots's bodyguard at the Battle of Langside in 1568 and was exiled by the Regent Moray for his trouble. He had returned by 1579 when he destroyed the Bishop's Palace at Lochwood.

By 1900 parts of Badenheath were still habitable and appear to have been used to house farm workers. While a Miss Boyd of Badenheath is on record around 1900, this probably relates to the farm. The castle may have been owned, occupied or leased by a family named Couper in the 17th century and in 1647 there is a 'James Cleland in Banheith'. From 1708 it was owned by the Keiths. The tower was completely demolished in 1953. The site now lies below the garden of the modern farmhouse.

Other references: Banheith, Bonheith

BALCASTLE

The Lennox & East Dunbartonshire   Ruin or site   OS 64   NS 702782
0.75 miles west of Kilsyth, off minor roads north of A803, west by foot from Balcastle Farm.

An impressive earthwork remains of an earth and timber castle. Balcastle stands within the confluence of two streams which descend the hills from the north. It was protected on this side by a deep ditch, 19ft wide, of which only a trace remains. It is a partly natural feature, a knoll having been enhanced by earthworks. The summit is a rough oval of about 120 by 85ft and varies in height from 12 to 40ft above the surrounding terrain. It has been damaged by agricultural activity and it is thought the track leading to the summit from the northeast may be relatively modern. The summit has been cultivated in the past.

This was one of a series of 12th century strongholds of the Earls of Lennox, who also built the motte at Colzium nearby. The de Callendar family held Balcastle until an heiress carried the estate by marriage to the Livingstones. They continued to use Balcastle for several centuries. Its original name was Kelvesith, later Kilsyth, a name which they transferred to their 15th century castle at Allanfauld Farm.

The original name of the parish and village was Moniebroch, the name Kilsyth not being used for other than the castle until 1620, when Sir William Livingstone of Kilsyth acquired the status of burgh for his newly planned town.

Baile means 'place' or 'township' in Gaelic, so 'place of the castle' in a mixed Gaelic/English name source. The name probably relates to the later farmstead only. It appears as a small building in both Pont's map of the late 16th century and Blaeu's *Atlas Novus* of the 17th century.

Other references: Ba' Castle, Kelvesith, Kilsyth

BALCORRACH CASTLE

The Lennox & East Dunbartonshire   Ruin or site   OS 64   NS 613797
1 mile west of Lennoxtown, north of A891 at Balcorrach, just northeast of Clachan of Campsie.

Site of an old castle of the Lennox family, of which nothing remains. In 1421 Duncan, Earl of Lennox, granted Donald, his son from his second marriage, the lands of Balcorrach, Balgrochan, Bencloich, Thornbay, and others, in the parish of Campsie. Donald's descendants adopted the surname Lennox. There was already a castle on the site when the grant was made, but the family moved to Woodhead in 1570.

Other reference: Ballecorrauch

BALDERNOCK MOTTE

The Lennox & East Dunbartonshire   Ruin or site   OS 64   NS 600751
1 mile northeast of Torrance, by minor roads north of A807, just west of Castlehill Farm, south side of Tower Road.

Described as a scarped mound and a probable motte, this site lies within the parish of Baldernock which was granted to the Galbraiths by the Earl of Lennox in 1238.

Other reference: Castlehill, Baldernock

BALFRON MOTTE

The Lennox & East Dunbartonshire Ruin or site   OS 57   NS 555887
Just east of Balfron, east of A875, just south of junction of Dunmore Street and Roman Road.

This motte consists of a partly natural mound, which averages between 6 and 10ft above the surrounding land, except on the southeast corner where it reaches a height of 33ft above falling ground and the intersection of two gullies. The ground between these was protected by a ditch around the northern perimeters. This is now almost entirely silted up. The summit is oval, being approximately 130ft by 110ft. It has been planted with trees. This may be one of the series of mottes constructed by the early Earls of Lennox, or by the Grahams who were granted estates here in the 13th century.

Other reference: Woodend Motte

BALGAIR CASTLE

The Lennox & East Dunbartonshire Ruin or site   OS 57   NS 603886
1 mile west of Fintry, by minor road west of B822, north of Endrick water, west of Overglinns Farm.

Balgair Castle is a ruined 18th century mansion, which may never have been occupied and probably replaced an older house or hall. The estate was a property of the Cunninghames, which they gained in 1467. They had been granted the neighbouring estate of Ballindalloch in 1362.

The family of a John Galbraith were tenants here by 1534. John is on record as an accomplice of Humphrey Galbraith, tutor of Culcreuch, in the murder of William Stirling of Glorat, Keeper of Dumbarton Castle.

In 1563 Balgair was occupied or owned by Humphrey Galbraith and his wife, Isabel Cunninghame. Humphrey is thought to be a younger son of the Galbraith chief, or possibly of the John mentioned above. This branch of the family moved to Ireland in the early 17th century when James VI colonised Ulster with Scottish and English Protestants.

It has been said that in 1605 Balgair was granted to the Buchanans by James VI. However the Galbraiths seem to have retained possession through other branches of the family. The estate was purchased by an Edinburgh-based family named Galbraith in 1687, who may also have been descended from those who went to Ireland.

The mansion of 1721 was built by James Galbraith, 2nd of Balgair. It may never have been finished or occupied due to early subsidence of the foundations and James's death in 1728. By 1963 it was a roofless ruin which now, in a dilapidated state, is a central feature within a caravan park.

This property is marked on Blaeu's *Atlas Novus* of the 17th century as 'W.Bag'.

Other references: Old Place of Balgair, Overglinns

BALGLASS CASTLE

The Lennox & East Dunbartonshire Ruin or site   OS 64   NS 585876
4 miles east of Killearn, on minor roads south of A818, near Place of Balglass.

Only earthworks remain on the site of this once strong 13th century castle. The lands belonged to the Stirlings of Craigbarnet, passing to the Bontines by the 17th century.

A reset date-stone of 1602 bearing the initials of Michael Stirling was reported on the wall of a ruinous farmhouse. There is now no trace of either the castle or date-stone. A tower here is illustrated in Blaeu's *Atlas Novus* of the 17th century. A 'large dwelling-house or castle, of an antiquated construction' still stood on the site in 1795.

The site noted above is an artificially steepened knoll, with a revetment to the north side, which is possibly of 18th century date, indicating reconstruction or the building of a new house. A modern house and ruined farm buildings now occupy this site. It is possible the castle site lay at Mount (NS 581869) on the site of the 'old farm'.

William Wallace is said to have sheltered here during the Wars of Independence. A grant was issued to John Stirling of Craigbarnet for the lands of Balglass in 1486. Sometime after 1602, Balglass passed to the Bontines and by the 18th century belonged to the Dunmores.

One of the Bontines of Balglass murdered the Reverend John Collins on his way home from a presbytery meeting in his parish of Campsie in 1648. The story goes that Bontine had eyes for the minister's wife, but knowing that she could not consider him while her husband was alive, killed him in the hope that they might then become involved. Sometime after the murder, the widow and her husband's murderer were married; however after several months she discovered him in possession of her late husband's pocket watch. The truth was out and Bontine apparently left the house never to be seen again.

Other reference: Baron's Place

BALGRAY HOUSE

Renfrewshire Private OS 64 NS 513566

2 miles southwest of Newton Mearns, by minor roads west of B769, south of Balgray Reservoir, Balgray House.

Site of an old or fortified house of the Polloks. The present building is a small late 18th century Georgian-style house of two storeys, which stands on the site.

Houses at Nether and Over Balgray appear in Pont's map of the late 16th century and in Blaeu's *Atlas Novus* of the 17th century. Balgray was a property of the Park family, who alienated the estate to David Pollok of Lee in 1603. The Polloks of Lee and Balgray were a cadet branch of the Polloks of that Ilk. In 1684 the old house was purchased by Thomas Pollok, a Glasgow merchant, who was also a descendant of the Polloks of that Ilk.

BALLAGAN CASTLE

The Lennox & East Dunbartonshire Ruin or site OS 64 NS 572796

3.5 miles north of Milngavie, just north of A891, 0.5 miles east of junction with A81 at Strathblane, at Ballagan House.

Site of a large 12th century castle of the Earls of Lennox, later held by the Stirlings, originally known as 'Camsi', or Campsie Castle, and then Strathblane.

The castle provided the building materials for the garden walls of the 18th century Ballagan House. Excavation late in the 19th century revealed the plan and dimensions of the castle. The main building had a total perimeter of 140ft, within an internal courtyard measuring 82ft by 72ft. The external walls of this building were 5ft thick, and the internal walls 3ft thick. The main entrance to the internal courtyard was centrally placed on the west wall, with entry to the larger outer courtyard placed on the north side. There was a moat around it all 14ft wide and 11ft deep, traversed by two drawbridges, one at this main entrance, and a larger second one for horse and cart set to one side. This original site lies slightly north of the present house and the walled garden.

The Earls held the castle until granting the Kirklands of Strathblane to the Stirlings of Glorat in 1522, allegedly in return for their assistance in battle. William Stirling initially gave the western portion, including Dunglass, to his brother and kept the remainder. The two halves of the estate were reunified in 1657. The Stirlings became immersed in debt due to their support of the Jacobites and sold the lands to the Glasgow merchant, Thomas Graham, in 1746. He built the new house about 1760, which incorporated a date-stone of 1648, apparently taken from an older building nearby. The Grahams died out in 1891, when the house was sold to the Stephens and then to the Craigs. It was they who extended the house to create the present entrance and facade. It was sold again, this time to Glasgow ship owner Colonel Peter MacFarlane. His family retained the house until selling to a developer in 1973 and it was then converted into flats.

The site is picturesque, set at the southwestern base of the Campsie Fells, with a glorious waterfall known as the 'Spout of Ballagan' providing a backdrop as it falls from the precipice behind. There is also an ancient yew tree in the garden, perhaps a survivor from the days of the castle.

Other references: Campsie Castle, Strathblane Castle

BALLANREOCH CASTLE

The Lennox & East Dunbartonshire Private OS 64 NS 610794

1.5 miles northwest of Lennoxtown, just north of A891 at Haughead, just west of Clachan of Campsie.

Site of a tower house built by the Brisbanes, known as Ballanreoch or Ballancleroch.

The Grahams had been granted these estates by the Earl of Lennox in the 13th century. They granted the lands to the Brisbanes as early as 1423. In 1523 John Brisbane, as heir to his father, was granted a charter of confirmation of the lands by John, Earl of Lennox. In 1652 the property was sold to MacFarlane of Keithton, a descendant of the early Arrochar-based chiefs. They built anew.

The northeast section of the castle is the oldest, being built by the MacFarlanes in 1655, and was extended in 1852-3 to the south and the west. The MacFarlanes sold the estate in 1921. Further renovations and alterations were made when it was converted into a hotel and then after a major fire in the 1980s. It lay derelict for a number of years before being restored for use as a religious retreat and conference centre, being operated by a German branch of the Catholic Church.

A tower named 'Bancleyrach' appears in Blaeu's *Atlas Novus* of the 17th century.

'Schoenstatt' means 'beautiful place' in German, the nuns certainly got that right when they moved here.

Other references: Ballancleroch, Kirkton Hall, Schoenstatt

BALLINDALLOCH CASTLE

The Lennox & East Dunbartonshire Private OS 57 NS 540885
On minor roads 0.5 miles west of Balfron, at Ballindalloch.

Only a sundial of the early 17th century survives of Ballindalloch Castle, which appears on Blaeu's *Atlas Novus*.

The Cunninghames of Kilmaurs were granted the Barony of Ballindalloch in 1362 by Malcolm Fleming. In 1488 Sir Alexander Cunninghame was made Earl of Glencairn after helping James III defeat the rebels at Blackness. He died with the king at the Battle of Sauchieburn in June of that year. James IV revoked all titles given by his father and so the 2nd Earl, Robert, lost his earldom. His son regained it in 1503, becoming the 3rd Earl.

The Cunninghames had a 213-year feud with the Montgomeries and positions such as Baillie of Cunninghame, which had been held by one party, were given to the other as favour with the ruling party ebbed and flowed. This led to the burning of the Cunninghame's castle at Kerelaw in 1488 and an attack on Irvine by Cuthbert, 3rd Lord Kilmaurs, in 1499. The 4th Earl attacked and burned the Montgomery's castle at Eglinton in 1528, and in 1586 a Cunninghame murdered the Montgomery 6th Earl of Eglinton. The feud ended amicably with the marriage of the 9th Earl of Glencairn, Chancellor of Scotland, to the daughter of the 6th Earl of Eglinton. The 9th Earl tried to raise an army for Charles II in a bid to restore the Crown, but his rising against Cromwell failed, though he did mange to avoid the axe.

The Cunninghames held possession of Ballindalloch until the 18th century, when it passed to the Dunmore family. By the 19th century it belonged to the Coopers.

There was a mansion of 1745, which was demolished in 1868, and replaced by the present house of which large parts were demolished in 1967-9. In addition to the remaining portion of the house, there are a number of 'B' listed features and buildings including a 17th century sundial, a walled garden, the north and south lodges and the stables. The stables and lodges have been converted into modern homes.

BALLOCH CASTLE

The Lennox & East Dunbartonshire Ruin or site OS 56 NS 388826
North of Balloch, east of A82 and north of A811, in Balloch Castle Country Park, on east shore of Loch Lomond.

Only earthworks and a ditch remain of this 13th century castle of the Earls of Lennox. It was their main seat until the completion of Inchmurrin by 1393.

The earthworks consist of an irregular mound measuring approximately 165ft by 150ft. It is surrounded on three sides by a ditch 16ft wide and 6ft deep. The fourth side was protected by a marsh. There are traces of a broad outer bank on the northeast. When the ditch was drained in about 1869, the remains of an oak causeway leading to the remains of a bridge or drawbridge were apparently found. No trace of these remain.

The castle was held by the Earls of Lennox until their forfeiture in 1425, when it went to the Stewarts of Darnley, who later became Earls of Lennox. The estate was purchased by Sir John Colquhoun of Luss in 1652 and then by the Buchanans of Ardoch, who owned it in the 19th century.

A castellated mansion designed by Robert Lugar, dated 1808 and also called Balloch Castle, stands on the hill above. This contains a visitor centre for the park and walled gardens. It is alleged that stone from the old castle was used in the construction of the mansion, though this is not apparent.

Park open all year, visitor centre April to October (tel 01389 758216).

BALVIE

The Lennox & East Dunbartonshire Ruin or site OS 64 NS 536753
1 mile northwest of Milngavie, off minor road east of A809, north of Mains housing estate, at or near Douglas Academy.

Site of a tower house of the Logans of Balvie. Balvie is drawn on Charles Ross' map of 1777 as a particularly lofty tower, possibly with round corner towers. It appears in Blaeu's *Atlas Novus* as 'Bauei'.

The estates of Balvie and Mains, with other local properties, were granted to Maurice Galbraith by Maldouen, Earl of Lennox, in the 13th century. He died toward the end of the 14th century when the estate was divided among his daughters. One of these brought Balvie to the Logans.

The Logans carry a heart in their coat of arms. This, as with Douglas, commemorates the taking of the heart of Robert I (the Bruce) on crusade. Two Logans, Robert of Restalrig and Walter of Lanark, were in the party of Sir James Douglas when they were killed by Saracens at the Battle of Teba in 1330.

In 1526, John Logan and his two sons killed John Hamilton of Bardowie at nearby Blairskaith. The Logans of Balvie were for a time hereditary Baillies of Dumbarton.

About 1600 the estate was purchased by a son of Colquhoun of Luss and then passed through the ownership of Sandersons, Campbells, Glassfords and MacNairs.

The estate was purchased by the Douglases of Mains sometime after 1819. By that time the estate was much smaller than that left by the Logans since various portions had been sold over the years. They built a new mansion on the site, naming it Mains, and moving from their own property, which then became Old Mains. The mansion was subsequently demolished in the 20th century and Douglas Academy built on the site.

Other Reference: Mains

BANNACHRA CASTLE

The Lennox & East Dunbartonshire   Ruin or site   OS 56   NS 343843

3 miles east and north of Helensburgh, on minor roads south of the B832, 1 mile west of A82 at Arden, just south of Fruin Water, at Bannachra House.

A ruined rectangular tower house of the 16th century, measuring about 45ft by 23ft, Bannachra had three storeys, corbie stepped gables and shot holes below the windows. The west wall stands to a height of 30ft, while the remains of the east wall are only 6ft long and in places reach only 2.5ft in height. The north and south walls vary in height from 6 to 25ft and all walls are 3.5ft thick. There is the outline of a fireplace in the east wall, others having arrow slots, corn drying kilns, gunloops and narrow windows. Victorian landscapers apparently utilised the castle as a source of stone when creating the garden for the present house.

Bannachra was a property of the Galbraiths until gained by the Colquhouns, and they built the castle in about 1512.

Maldouen, Earl of Lennox, granted the lands of Colquhoun east of Dumbarton, to Humphrey de Kilpatrick in the 13th century. His son, Ingelram, first used the name of the lands as his own in the reign of Alexander III. About 1368, Robin (Robert) de Colquhoun married the heiress of Godfrey of Luss, known as the 'Fair Maid of Luss' and so the family connection with the estate was established and is maintained to this day.

The opportunistic Iain (John) Colquhoun of Luss had married the daughter of the Earl of Lennox by 1424, the time of the release of James I from English captivity. As James began to take his revenge on those who had obstructed his earlier release, he targeted the Earl of Lennox. Seeing an opportunity, Iain seized Dumbarton Castle from Lennox on behalf of the king. By 1427 he was Sheriff of Dumbarton and then Governor of the castle. In 1439 he was killed at Inchmurrin, apparently by the MacLeans of Duart. In 1457 James II granted Luss as a Free Barony to Iain's son, Sir Iain, who had become Comptroller of the Royal Household. Sir Iain died at the siege of Dunbar Castle in 1478, apparently by cannon fire. Another chief died at Pinkie in 1547.

Tradition tells that Sir Humphrey Colquhoun was murdered at Bannachra by the MacFarlanes or MacGregors in 1592. A servant illuminated him by holding up a lamp as he retired to bed, allowing a bowman to shoot him through a window. It has been suggested that this was a cover story. Another source informs that John Colquhoun, Sir Humphrey's brother, was responsible, and was as a result beheaded in Edinburgh on the 30th November. That left Alexander the third brother to inherit. The castle was destroyed that year, the chief's main residence by then being at Rossdhu.

The MacGregors and Colquhouns battled in nearby Glenfruin (Glen of Weeping) in 1603. Less of a battle and more of a massacre, the MacGregors killed 200 of the people of Luss in an infamous meeting which subsequently led to 35 of their number being hanged with their chief and partly contributed to the proscription of the Clan.

The castle is a category 'B' Listed Building and a Scheduled Ancient Monument.

BAR

Renfrewshire   Ruin or site   OS 64   NS 469709

North of Erskine, on minor roads west of A726, west of Rashilee in North Bar.

Site of a large tower, which appears on Pont's map of the late 16th century, and probably as 'Kraiged' in Blaeu's *Atlas Novus* of the 17th century.

Bar, or Old Bar, was an estate of the Stewarts from 1490 to 1673. The castle stood in the southeast corner of a stone walled enclosure measuring 330ft by 150ft. The foundations of a rectangular building, with traces of a wing and a round stair tower, were excavated. The main part of the building measured 38ft by 14. 5ft. There was a well 33ft to the west which was built of dressed ashlar. It was blocked with rubble including steps from a spiral staircase. This was excavated to a depth of 18ft. Pottery fragments from the 15th, 16th and 17th century were recovered.

This was the seat of the Stewarts of Barscube, descended from the Stewarts of Darnley. Matthew, Earl of Lennox, granted a charter of North Bar, Barscube, Craigtoun and Rashielee to Thomas Stewart at Crookston in

1497. The family died out with another Thomas Stewart in the Irish wars of the late 17th century. He 'alienated' the estate to a Glasgow merchant Donald MacGilchrist in 1670, and he built the first North Bar House in 1676. This was situated on the south shore of the Clyde where he constructed a harbour next to the house (NS 466714). The estate was acquired by Lord Semple in 1741. The Semples sold it on to the Buchanans in 1798 and it was then purchased by the Stewart, Lords Blantyre, in 1812. They connected this estate to their Erskine estate by means of a 'bridge over the road' near Erskine Ferry. North Bar House is long gone, but the sundial survives having been transported to the garden at Lennoxlove Castle. A housing development now occupies the site.

Other references: Barscube, Rashielee

BARDOWIE CASTLE

The Lennox & East Dunbartonshire   Private OS 64   NS 578737
1.5 miles east by south of Milngavie, on minor roads north of A807, on north bank of Bardowie Loch, at Bardowie.

Bardowie consists of a simple rectangular tower house of the early 16th century, extended in the late 17th century by the addition of a two-storey block. Further additions and remodelling of the 18th and 19th centuries have created a mansion.

The original tower is 33ft by 27.5ft, with three storeys and a garret. The corners are rounded. There is string coursing at second-floor level on the southern wall. The gables are corbiestepped at the eastern and western ends. The entrance stands centrally in the thicker south wall facing the loch. This leads to a vaulted basement and a straight stair to the first floor. Another stair continues within the thickness of the north wall to the second floor. Thereafter a turnpike stair leads to the northern battlements. From the southern side of the second floor a mural stair leads to the battlements on that side.

The first floor consisted of a vaulted main hall with plain fireplace and the second floor of a large single room. Unusually, the garret space has been filled with another hall, covered by the wide sloping roof which extends over the battlements on both sides. This extra hall and extended roof may be a later alteration allowed by heightening of the gables. There are three openings in the southern wall at this level, which would correspond with an original parapet. Small windows in the end walls provide additional illumination. The roof is of open timber over this hall. It has no fireplace. Part of the building carries an initialled stone of John Hamilton and his wife Marion Colquhoun, and the date 1566, which may signify early alterations, or simply their marriage.

Bardowie was originally part of the estate of the Galbraiths of Baldernock granted by Maldouen, Earl of Lennox, in the 13th century. They had other local castles at Gartconnel and Craigmaddie. They were chiefs of their clan; however they died out at the beginning of the 15th century. Janet Keith was heiress and inherited through her Galbraith mother. She took the property by marriage to her husband, David Hamilton of Cadzow. Craigmaddie appears to have been the main seat until the family moved to Bardowie, leaving the old house to fall into ruin.

The Hamiltons of Bardowie were an argumentative lot and had their share of feuds with neighbours. In 1526 John Hamilton of Bardowie was killed at nearby Blairskaith fighting with the Logans of Balvie. In 1531 Bardowie and other local lands were granted to Sir James Hamilton of Finnart.

In 1532 Finnart resigned his rights and Sir John Stirling of Keir was granted Bardowie and all the lands which Alan Hamilton of Bardowie had rented from

Sir James. Alan was killed by a neighbour, Colin Campbell of Auchenbowie and Dowan, and then, in 1591, another laird had a serious quarrel with Walter Graham of Dougalston. A James Stirling of Baldernock, Laird of 'Pardowie' appears in Scottish parliamentary records in 1647-49.

In 1707 Mary Hamilton, sister of the laird, married Gregor 'Black Knee' MacGregor. He was nephew and chief to Rob Roy who had been his guardian in childhood. During the 1745 Jacobite rebellion he was a colonel in Bonnie Prince Charlie's army and was in charge of the garrison at Doune Castle, having captured it for the Prince. He missed Culloden as he was in command of a division tracking Hanoverian troops through Sutherland.

When the 16th Hamilton laird died, the estate passed via his sister to Thomas Buchanan of Spittal and Leny.

Other reference: Pardowie

BARGARRAN

Renfrewshire   Ruin or site   OS 64   NS 457709?
East of M898, and south of A726, on or near Bargarran Road

Site of a tower of the Shaw family, who had held the estate of Bargarran since the 15th century. They were a cadet branch of the Shaws of Sauchie. The first on record is John Shaw, who in 1454 resigned the lands in favour of his son John.

On Pont's map of the late 16th century the tower appears almost superimposed upon that of Erskine, which lay just a little to the north. The name Bar appears twice, once for this entry, and once for Old Bar. On Blaeu's *Atlas* of the 17th century it is the only entry of Bar.

This was the home of 11-year-old Christian Shaw, daughter of another John Shaw of Bargarran. She was central to an infamous trial of witches at Paisley in 1696. Christian claimed to be tormented by witchcraft after being cursed. It has been suggested that Christian did not live up to her name, and had manufactured the evidence, or was simply hysterical. Nevertheless, the outcome was fatal for the seven accused. One committed suicide, the other six were hanged and then burned at the Gallowhill in Paisley on the 10th of June 1697.

Christian introduced a method of spinning fine thread, her product becoming known as Bargarran Thread. It apparently fetched a high price. She founded the Bargarran Threadmill to keep up with demand.

Other reference: Bar

BARNCLUITH CASTLE

South Lanarkshire   Private   OS 64   NS 730545
Above west bank of River Avon gorge, 1.5 miles southeast of Hamilton, on minor road south of A72, at Barncluith.

Barncluith from Baron's Cleugh (a cleft or gorge).

Barncluith is a small rectangular 16th century tower house of three storeys and a garret. Due to its site on a steep slope, the basement is subterranean. There are twin doors on the northern wall, one leading down a stair to the basement, the other via a turnpike stair to the first floor.

While the upper storeys remain in their original state, the two lower floors were restructured internally to house a heating system for Barncluith House. The original small windows remain unaltered. There was an extension to the north which has been demolished.

The 16th century terraced 'Dutch' gardens had summer houses and a walkway to the River Avon in the gorge below. The property was substantially renovated and altered in 1909 when purchased by local solicitor, James Bishop. More recently it had been the home of the late Bill Fleming, a well-known businessman, who had spent considerable time restoring the gardens following a period of neglect and vandalism. In the garden is a grand armorial stone, a remnant of Hamilton Palace.

William Hamilton of Rossmoor gained the estate through marriage to the heiress of Machan in 1507. The tower house was built in 1538 by the ancestor of the Hamilton Lords Belhaven, John Hamilton. He died in 1568 at the Battle of Langside fighting for Mary, Queen of Scots. His son, John, returned to Barncluith in 1583 having lived on the continent in exile. He restored and extended the tower house, and laid out the gardens. John Graham of Claverhouse allegedly spent the eve of the Battle of Bothwell Bridge in the house in 1679. He awoke to see the Covenanters defeated by the Duke of Monmouth. In 1707, just after the Treaty of Union, John Hamilton of Barncluith was considered deputy to the Duke of Hamilton. As such he held the position of Sheriff of the Lower Ward of Lanarkshire. In this capacity, he brought the court to Barncluith and sat in judgement in his own garden. There, so the legend tells, he carried out executions on an old oak tree nearby.

Barncluith House originated in the 18th century and was extended in Victorian times. It was leased out during the 18th century and by 1745 was home to a local magistrate named Campbell. In the 19th century, it was inherited from the Hamiltons by Lady Ruthven, before being sold to the Bishop family in 1908. It was during this period that Hamilton Palace was demolished and a variety of pieces of fine stonework found their way into the garden. The estate then passed to the Stewarts and Grahams before being bought by Bill Fleming. The house is an 18th century mansion with Victorian alterations, which now provides the accommodation on this site. The building is 'B' Listed, as is the tower house, while the summer houses and garden terraces are 'A' Listed.

BARNHILL HOUSE

The Lennox and East Dunbartonshire Private OS 64 NS 425756
1 mile north of Milton, to the north of Loch Bowie, Dumbarton.

Site of an old house or tower, the home of the Colquhouns of Milton since before 1543.

In 1543 Sir John Colquhoun resigned his two merk land of the west half of Barnhill to facilitate the re-grant of the whole of Barnhill by John Colquhoun of Luss. The grant was to Sir John and the 'heirs male of his body'. Failing that, the estate was to return to Colquhoun of Luss. In 1555 a grant of the estate in 'life rent' was made to Janet Laing, spouse of Barnhill. It was to follow to her son, Walter Colquhoun, 'in fee' thereafter. It is believed that Colquhoun of Barnhill was descended at some point from a younger son of Colquhoun of Luss, and it is known that the family had moved from Milton about this time. The Colquhouns of Barnhill are on record at least as late as the 19th century.

Barnhill appears in Blaeu's *Atlas Novus* of the 17th century. The present house is largely of 19th century origins, but may incorporate parts of the older structure.

BAROCHAN HOUSE

Renfrewshire Private OS 64 NS 415686
2 miles northeast of Bridge of Weir, on minor roads east of B789, at Barochan

The earliest castle at Barochan is thought to have stood on Castlehill (NS 406690). This structure may have burned down during the Wars of Independence. The castle occupied a strong defensive position on a summit, which may have been partly artificial and surrounded by a ditch. Aerial photography in the 1990s has shown that in fact there had been three ditches around the site, suggesting that it may have originated much earlier as a fort. Field walking produced a little pottery of medieval style and later, but no evidence of earlier use; however archaeological opinion is that this is a multi-phase site.

Barochan House is a mansion of the 19th century, which incorporated a corbiestepped tower at the centre of the complex. This stood about 20ft proud of the rest of the building. Much of the house, including the visible older structure, was pulled down in 1947 and at some earlier stage may have been burned. In 1951 the house was described as having the appearance of having been recently renovated. The tower may have been erected in the late 16th century by Janet Sempill, widow of Fleming of Barochan.

Alexander III granted Barochan to the Flemings. William Fleming of Barochan witnessed a charter by Malcolm, Earl of Lennox, to Walter Spreull of the lands of Dalquhurn around this time. In 1488 another William Fleming of Barochan was Sheriff of Lanark, and he died at Flodden in 1513, while the estate passed to his son James. Malcolm Fleming is on record at Barochan in 1780, when he inherited the estate of Doonholm in Ayrshire by marriage. He sold Doonholm, but the family regained the property in 1790. The spinster heiress of Barochan died in 1863, and the lands appear to have been divided. There may have been other families associated with this estate, there being references to an Alan Erskine of Barochan in the 13th century and Sempills in the 16th century, though this probably relates to the Janet mentioned above. By the 19th century part of the estate had been alienated to Archibald Speirs of Elderslie.

The Barochan Cross, an intricately carved 8th century Celtic cross, originally stood nearby. It was removed to Paisley Abbey to help protect it from the elements, and has been restored and is on view.

BARONIAL HALL, Gorbals

City of Glasgow Ruin or site OS 64 NS 592640
South of Gorbals Cross, on Gorbals Street, at or near the Procurator Fiscal's Office.

Nothing remains of this tower extended to form a C-plan mansion of the 16th century. The top storeys were removed in 1849 and the remainder removed in 1870 as part of local redevelopment.

In the early years the Gorbals constituted part of the Govan Ward of the Barony of Glasgow and as such belonged to the church. At this time the village was known as Bridgend and became world famous as a manufacturing centre for quality swords and small firearms.

By 1512 the lands had been leased by the merchant George Elphinstone and were subsequently passed through his family. The third of his name had dropped the 'e' from the surname by 1563, when he acquired the lands of Blythswood in the west of the city. His lease was then granted as a feu holding by Bishop Boyd in 1579. A leper hospital (NS 591644) serving the City had stood close to the site, but had fallen into misuse by this time. Elphinston converted its chapel (NS 590643) into a place of worship for his family. He began construction of a C-plan mansion with courtyard incorporating a castellated tower, effectively a keep, which faced onto the main street.

James VI knighted Elphinston in 1594 and granted the status of Free Barony to his lands, hence the Barony of Blythswood. He was elected as Provost of the City in 1600 and later sat in the Scottish Parliament. He fell into debt and in 1634 sold the estate to Robert Douglas, Viscount Belhaven, who extended the house.

Robert was the second son of Malcolm Douglas of Mains and had been Page of Honour to Prince Henry of Scotland. Later he was Gentleman of the Bedchamber to James VI and then Charles I. He was granted the title Viscount Belhaven in 1633. He died in 1639 and the title became extinct. The estate passed to his nephew, Sir Robert Douglas of Blackerstone, and in 1650 he transferred the Gorbals estates to the City Magistrates for the benefit of the City, the Trades House and Hutcheson's Hospital. The tower was subsequently used as a gaol and town hall. It survived the remainder of the mansion by many years, as did the chapel, which was demolished early in the 20th century.

Other reference: Elphinston Tower

BARON NISBET'S HALL

North Lanarkshire   Ruin or site   OS 64   NS 757548?
1.5 miles south of Motherwell, by minor roads and foot south of A721, east of Dalzell Burn, and north of River Clyde in Baron's Haugh Nature Reserve.

Site of an old or fortified house of the Nisbet family. John de Nisbet is noted as joint proprietor of a portion of the Barony of Dalzell when Robert II became king in 1371. Foundations still existed in the 19th century. A stone cross stood close to the site, but was later re-sited to Dalzell House.

BARR CASTLE

Renfrewshire   Ruin or site   OS 63   NS 347582
0.5 miles southwest of Lochwinnoch, 0.25 miles west of the Barr Loch, just south of the A760.

Barr is a ruinous rectangular tower of the 15th century. Little now survives of the courtyard drawn by MacGibbon and Ross and, since their time, a gable has collapsed. No internal access can be gained due to the damage caused.

The courtyard was entered via a round arched gateway in the northern wall and guarded by gunloops in the adjacent wall. The courtyard supported various subsidiary buildings, including a wing attached to the southern wall of the tower, all long gone.

The main building itself measures 35.5ft by 26ft, and was of four storeys and a garret. The wing was probably added later in the 16th century. Entry was via a porch of later date at the northwestern corner of the house. Above this the original entrance at first floor level is closed up. The ground floor contained a corridor accessing two vaulted chambers. One of these functioned as the kitchen and has an arched fireplace 11ft wide and 4.5ft deep. From the north end of the corridor a turnpike stair leads to the floors above.

The first floor consisted of a hall of 24ft by 17ft. Illumination was by four windows, one to each wall. There is a large fireplace in the western wall. In the northeastern corner there is a small mural chamber with ventilation slots. There were various cupboards and a sink within the wall. A continuous corbel supported the floor above. A small stair ascends from the southwestern corner to the floors above.

Subsequent floors consisted of two rooms to each, with garderobes and a variety of mural chambers.

The battlement was continuous around the roof, interrupted by roofed corner turrets. A series of continuous corbels project from the walls to support it. There are various water spouts around the circumference. Little now remains of the garret.

Various initialled and dated stones are incorporated into the structure, possibly indicating dates of renovation or alteration. These are I.W. and M.H. over the porch, L.H.I.C. 1680, over the lintel at the stair foot, and W.O. 1699 on the battlements. It has been suggested that these later developments in the structure are responsible for the lack of a defensive wall around the building, the stone having been used during building.

In the 12th century Walter the Steward granted the lands of Moniabrock around Lochwinnoch to the monks of Paisley Abbey. They rented portions out including the lands which became Barr and the Lordship of Glen.

In 1180, Henry de Ness, a retainer of the High Steward, founded a chapel within his court. It is said that he was the lord of the Barony of Glen and held a number of estates including Barr. His descendants are said to have been known as 'de le Glen', or simply Glen. The first of the Glens of Barr who appears on record is John, who paid homage to Edward I in 1296. The next is Alan, who witnessed a gift of the fishing of Crockat-Shot by Robert Lord Lyle to Paisley Abbey in 1452. James Glen of Barr and his sons were members of Mary's party following Langside in 1568 and were imprisoned for a period in Spynie Palace. James was forfeited, but his lands were restored by the Treaty of Perth in 1573. The Glen family died out with the death of Alexander Glen in 1616.

Barr is believed to have been built by the Glens and they retained it until it was acquired by the Hamiltons of Ferguslie at the close of the 16th century. The estate passed to the MacDowells of Castle Semple and then the Adam family in the late 18th century. The old castle was abandoned for a new mansion around that time, itself likewise abandoned for a successor in the 19th century. The building is 'B' Listed. It appears on both Pont's map of the late 16th century and in Blaeu's *Atlas Novus* of the 17th century.

BEDLAY CASTLE

North Lanarkshire Private OS 64 NS 692701
0.25 miles east of Chryston, and 0.5 miles west of Moodiesburn, on the north side of the A80 at Bedlay.

Bedlay sits on the end of a long ridge and prior to the construction of terraces around the house, was protected by steep escarpments on three sides. At the foot of these slopes, on the north and west sides, the Bothlyn Burn and a tributary provided added protection.

The castle is of two periods, the older section at the eastern end being of the late 16th century. This consisted of a rectangular keep with offset square stair tower at the northeastern corner. The keep is of two storeys and an attic, with two vaulted chambers on the ground floor. One of these acted as the kitchen, the other as a store later adapted as a bedroom. Along the northern side of these a vaulted corridor runs the full length of the building, providing a link from the entrance at the base of the stair tower to the later western portion. Above this on the first floor are two rooms, created from what was once the hall. One of these contained the old fireplace, now altered. A similar link corridor to that on the ground floor has been created. The northeastern stair tower has an additional storey and provides the entrance on its south face. A turnpike stair which formerly gave access to attic level, now reaches only the first floor, a later stair tower having been corbelled out in the re-entrant from first-floor level. The space within the stair tower released by this adaptation has provided additional rooms, that at the head of the stair acting as a vestibule. Each of these towers has corbiestepped gables. The stair tower widens at corbelling above the first floor.

The western portion of the house was added about 100 years after the initial construction. It consists of a square block of two storeys and an attic, with round towers at the northwestern and southwestern corners. These provide additional space with a storey below the ground floor level of the main building, since they were constructed down the escarpment. Each floor of this block consists of a single room, accessed from the link corridors of the old block. The extra cellar spaces of the round towers are accessed by floor hatches from the rooms above.

At the junction of the two main blocks, another square stair tower is built out from the north face. This may represent part of the original building, since it has similar fittings. It provides access to all floors at the western end of the link corridors.

Between this and the northeastern stair, the space has been filled by a two-storey block of the 18th century, giving the existing structure a continuous facade.

Various portions of the building have been altered to provide more modern amenities; however features, such as the garderobe flue have been utilised to carry water pipes, and so they survive. The windows have been enlarged. There were a few interesting features remaining when MacGibbon and Ross surveyed it, such as the garderobe within the north wall, the 16th century fireplace, and Tranter noted the 'squinch arch' upon which the corbelling for the stair turret is built.

Bedlay (or Ballayn) was a property of the Archdiocese of Glasgow from early times. David I restored the lands to the church in his 'Inquisition' following their despoilation. In 1180, William the Lion confirmed the grant to Bishop Jocelyn. Bishop Cameron is known to have had a castle here in the 15th century. In 1507 Peter Colquhoun of Glins was renting the property from the church. In 1535, George Colquhoun and his wife Marion Boyd agreed to the rental being taken over by Robert, son of Lord Boyd, though by recompense they were granted the profits of the property for their lifetime. In 1580 James Boyd, titular bishop, gave them to his kinsman Robert, 4th Lord Boyd. It is thought that Thomas Boyd of Bedlay, second son of 5th Lord Boyd, built the earliest portions of the present castle upon older foundations. In 1642 the Boyds sold the property to the advocate James Roberton, later

Lord Bedlay. The sale was the result of a £15,000 fine imposed by Cromwell due to Boyd's consistent support of the Royalists. About this time the western extension was added. The Boyds initially retained superiority of the estate, though sold it to Roberton's successors in 1740. The Earl of Kilmarnock was beheaded for his part in the Jacobite rising of 1746.

Bedlay was sold in 1786 to the Dunlops of Garnkirk, who then sold their Bedlay and Garnkirk estates to Glasgow merchant, John MacKenzie. He sold Bedlay to James Campbell of Petershill in 1804. It passed by marriage of a grand daughter to the Christies. Since 1959 it has been the property of the family of Captain MacAdam.

To the rear of the property a remnant of the old Glasgow to Stirling coach road survives as a lane following the Bothlyn Burn from Chryston to Bedlay Cemetery. A gate from the garden opens on to this, and it is said that on a summer's evening, a coach and horses can be heard. The spectre of a young girl follows, then a scream, and complete silence overcomes even the rustling of the trees in the wind.

In the 1970s the apparition of a large bearded man was reported moving around the castle. Another spectral visitor is believed to represent Bishop Cameron, who in 1350 (according to the story), was discovered face down in Bishop Loch in suspicious circumstances. There was, however, no bishop of that name in 1350, although it perhaps refers to John Cameron, who was bishop from 1426-46.

When the Campbells moved in, they built themselves a mausoleum in the gardens. This was built of stone taken from the ruin of the Bishop's country residence at Lochwood. Spectral appearances were reported and associated with the hooting of owls. The ghosts apparently left when the family had the mausoleum relocated to Lambhill Cemetery.

The house was recently put up for sale, and was described as being in need of refurbishment, although it no longer appears to be on the market.

BELLTREES PEEL

Renfrewshire Ruin or site OS 63 NS 362588
0.5 miles east of Lochwinnoch, west of A737, on peninsula in Castle Semple Loch.

Belltrees Peel stands on what was once an island, the level of the loch having been lowered exposing what may once have been a causeway leading to the island. It was built between 1547 and 1572.

The present remains are those of a small tower house, rectangular in plan, measuring 43ft by 33ft with wide-mouthed gunloops on the ground floor. There is a portion of a circular stair which led to the floors above. The ground floor was vaulted. The highest portion of the tower now stands to 16.5 ft. It may once have stood within a courtyard of an irregular hexagon shape.

The lands of Belltrees were granted by James III to William Stewart and his wife Alison Kennedy in 1477. The family died out in 1559 and the estate passed to Robert, Lord Semple, who apparently built the tower and granted it to his son, John. He married Mary Livingstone, one of Mary Queen of Scot's 'Four Maries', who accompanied her to exile in France as a child. The others were Mary Beaton, Mary Seton, and Mary Fleming.

Robert and Mary's son was Sir James Semple of Belltrees, who was educated with James VI by George Buchanan and in 1601 acted as Ambassador to France. Later the Semples used the Peel as a shelter when sailing on Castle Semple Loch.

The lands of Belltrees were sold in the 17th century to Crawford of Cartsburn, and then in 1758 to MacDowell of Castle Semple. They were then acquired by John Orr, who died in 1770, and is body was placed in a tomb in the garden. The lands thereafter passed to his wife's family, the Cochranes of Ladyland.

Two fine cannon were found submerged nearby, one made of 'brass', discovered prior to 1791, and the other made of bronze, found in 1850. The first is described as very fine and of French make, and the other bore the Royal coat of arms with the initials JRS which would equate to Jacobus Rex Scottorum, James, King of Scots. Apparently six such cannon were lost when Castle Semple was besieged in 1560. One of them is apparently in the collection of the Glasgow Art Galleries and Museum at Kelvingrove.

Other references: Beltrees, The Peel

BELSTANE CASTLE

South Lanarkshire Ruin or site OS 72 NS 850525
About 2.5 miles north of Carluke, off minor roads east of A73, at Belstane Racing, Belstane Place.

Site of a 16th century tower house of the Livingstones, mentioned in 1585.

Belstane is first mentioned in a grant of lands by Robert I to Ellen de Quarantly. She gained the manor of Belstane and an orchard which were enclosed by a wall. This was part of an exchange as he attempted to gather land to found Greyfriars Monastery at Lanark. It was the first portion of the Royal hunting forest of Mauldslie to be granted away.

It later became part of the Barony of Mauldslie. At the end of the 14th century, this was Dennistoun property. The line died out, and their estates were divided among heiresses, Mauldslie going to the Maxwells of Calderwood in 1400.

By 1572 Belstane was Livingstone property. In that year, John Livingstone of Belstane was one of those arraigned as accessory in the murder of Henry, Lord Darnley. In 1585 he complained to the Privy Council, having been 'suddenly beset' as he left Belstane by about 40 men dressed as though for war. They were led by William Hay, Master of Yester. Livingstone narrowly evaded them as he ran back into the house under a shower of musket balls, and he was trapped in the house for about three hours while his attackers fired through every aperture. As they left, they apparently abused his wife and daughter. Hay apparently was a notorious troublemaker, being at feud with the Stewarts of Traquair and any of their associates. He was eventually imprisoned in Edinburgh Castle for a time, having carried out numerous attacks with apparent disregard to the interventions of the king.

By 1626 Belstane had passed to the Lindsays. James Lindsay of Belstane was summoned before the Presbytery for burying his child within the church without consent. He admitted the offence and undertook to build an aisle for his family.

In 1643 Lindsay of Belstane was involved in the commission of supply for the Irish wars at that time, and in 1644 was created Governor of Berwick. His son, William Lindsay of Belstane, led a force which attacked the Earl of Queensberry at Drumlanrig, burning the gates of the castle. He paid his share of £2,000 in compensation.

In 1671, Charles II issued a grant of confirmation of Belstane to Lindsay, who quickly sold it to the Marquis of Douglas. It may have come back to the Maxwells at some stage. By 1710 Belstane was a Carmichael property, though a Douglas, Lord of Belstane, is recorded in 1839. The old tower was demolished in the 1840s to extend a kale yard, the description of the time recording that it had a turnpike stair. In 1857 it was the property of James Gibson.

A tower at 'Bellstain' appears on Timothy Pont's map of the late 16th century and subsequently in Blaeu's *Atlas Novus* of the 17th century. They both depict the tower as standing on a site which corresponds more readily with Belstane Place. Roy's map of the 18th century names it Belstane Mains, while slightly later maps use the name Belstane Place. These names are both indicative of a castle site and so the location has been revised. This site is now occupied by a well-known horse racing stable.

BENCLOICH CASTLE

The Lennox & East Dunbartonshire   Ruin or site   OS 64   NS 640785
Just north of Lennoxtown, on minor roads and foot north of A891, 0.5 miles east of Bencloich Mains.

Site of a tower house of the Livingstones, and earlier strongholds. The oldest castle on this estate was Maiden Castle, a motte built by the Earls of Lennox, which lies just east of Bencloich. It is described in a separate entry.

In 1421, Duncan, Earl of Lennox, granted Donald, his son from his second marriage, the lands of Balcorrach, Balgrochan, Bencloich, and Thombay, among others, in the parish of Campsie. Donald's descendants adopted the surname Lennox. They may have managed both estates from Balcorrach to the west until they moved to Woodhead in 1520, but they had built a separate house at Bencloich.

A Robert Callendar of Bencloich is on record in the 16th century. He married a daughter of Lord Livingston, and their granddaughter married James Livingston of Inches, of the Kilsyth family.

In 1660 part of Bencloich was sold to the Edmonstones of Duntreath, who then sold it to Charles Mackintosh, inventor of the famous Mackintosh overcoat, who had alum works here in the 19th century. This refers to land close to the Glazert Water. There is also mention of a Mr MacFarlane of Bencloich, which probably refers to Bencloich Farm.

It is said that Bencloich was a Barony, and that Lord Kilsyth hanged one of his servants at the Gallowhill in 1639. Sir James Livingstone built Bencloich Tower in 1659, or alternatively purchased the estate in 1662 and built the tower in 1667. The former is more likely since Sir James is on record as using the title in 1661. The Livingstones were forfeited in the wake of the 1715 Jacobite rebellion. Bencloich Tower came to the York Building Company, who were guilty of neglecting forfeited estates, and Bencloich quickly fell into disrepair. Nothing remains of the tower, other than a level platform which has been partly covered by the spoil heaps of old limestone workings. 'Bandcloich' appears on Pont's late 16th century map of the area, and as Bandoich in Blaeu's *Atlas Novus* of the 17th century. It appears as 'Tower of Bencloich' on General Roy's map of 1746, but had disappeared before the early 19th century.

Other references: Bandcloich, Bandoich

BIGGAR CASTLE

South Lanarkshire   Ruin or site   OS 72   NT 039377

In Biggar, just west of Junction of A702 and B7016, in garden of Parkmanse.

Only a motte remains of Biggar Castle. It stands 20ft above the surrounding ground and would have provided excellent views across the countryside. There are slight remnants of a ditch, and the summit is almost rectangular, measuring 66ft by 120ft. Over the years building work around the base of the motte has obliterated any trace of a bailey or later development of the site. It has obviously had an effect on the ground level at the base, since in 1854 the motte was described as being 36ft high. A variety of Roman coins have been found at the site.

Biggar was first settled c.1160 by Baldwin the Fleming, who had a large motte and bailey castle here. His descendants later developed it into a more substantial stronghold, before moving to Boghall in the 14th century.

Baldwin was the leader of a group of Flemish immigrants granted estates in this region by Malcolm IV. Abington was held by his stepson, John. Others of his followers built mottes at Wolfclyde, Roberton and possibly the site now occupied by the remains of the Bower of Wandel, among others. It has been suggested that he was a 'locator' or 'populater', a man charged with finding suitable colonists for a particular block of land for a feudal superior. Baldwin was also Sheriff of Lanarkshire, which in those days included what is now Renfrewshire. He founded a powerful family dynasty who remained, initially at any rate, hereditary Sheriffs. They held lands throughout the country, particularly in Lanarkshire, Renfrewshire and at Cumbernauld. The Fleming name repeatedly crops up as important office bearers at the Royal court and as players in many of the most famous events in Scottish history. They were involved in the slaying of the Red Comyn by Robert the Bruce, Mary Queen of Scots's childhood in France, and played their part in the story of Montrose. More of the history of the Flemings can be found in the entries for Cumbernauld, Boghall, Dumbarton and others.

William Wallace is said to have defeated the English army nearby in 1297, though Blind Harry's estimate of 60,000 men in the vanquished force seems to be a typical exaggeration. Biggar, like the other Fleming village at Cumbernauld, retains its medieval plan, grouped around the castle and kirk with a wide main street and narrow strips of land behind each property.

The site came to a Reverend Livingstone in 1659 and was occupied by an inn, a slaughter house, a school, and a manse.

Other reference: Gillespie Motte

BIGGAR KIRK

South Lanarkshire   Private   OS 72   NT 040379

Off A72/A702, on Biggar High Street.

The Collegiate Church founded by Malcolm, Lord Fleming, in 1545 possibly includes older work. Part of the structure is a crenellated tower with gunloops. The building was restored in the 1870s and again in the 1930s, and is still in use as the parish church, with a fine collection of modern stained glass. In the 19th century, mention is made of branks and jougs attached to the walls, indicating that justice of some kind was meted out here.

BIRKWOOD

South Lanarkshire   Ruin or site   OS 71   NS 795424

0.5 miles south of Kirkmuihill, 1.5 miles northwest of Lesmahagow, by minor roads immediately west of M74, at Birkwood.

Site of a small tower, depicted on Pont's map of 1596, and subsequently appears in name only in Blaeu's *Atlas Novus*. In the late 18th century, there were remains of a building on 'Castlehill'. Birkwood was a property of the Weirs of Blackwood.

There is a story which tells of the disinheritance of the eldest son of George Weir of Birkwood. George held Birkwood and was also heir to the senior line of Weir of Blackwood. He had two sons, the eldest was weak and unpromising, while the younger brother was strong, sharp and brisk. George developed a stronger affinity with his younger son and so left him the entire Blackwood estate at the expense of the elder brother. He was granted only the original Birkwood portion of his inheritance.

On the death of another George, the last of the Weirs of Birkwood, the property was divided and sold in two portions. The Upper Birkwood portion was purchased by James McKirdy and stood to the south of Lesmahagow at the former Birkwood Hospital site. The remaining portion is the site given and is that of the original house, which was purchased by a Dr Tod of Lanark.

BIRNOCK

South Lanarkshire   Ruin or site   OS 72   NS 973256

3 miles northeast of Abington, east of A702 at Wandel by minor road and track.

Site of a tower, illustrated on Pont's manuscript map of the late 16th century. No trace remains.

This was a Jardine property. Thomas Jardine of Birnock seems to have gained some notoriety. In 1582 he was one of the accomplices of his superior Jardine of Applegarth when they had to answer charges of treason and *lese-majesty*. They failed to appear. Part of the charge included 'fire raising and slaying and hocking of hors and oxin of which they are said to be guilty'. In 1596 by 'shots of hackbuts and pistolettes' Thomas and his sons had taken the life of Robert Browne of Coulter. Thomas also killed William Campbell of Over Wellwood at the Kirk of Douglas in 1597. On the 9th of August 1609 he and his sons, Humphrey and Alexander, were beheaded for murder on 'The Maiden', a Scottish guillotine. He and his sons had been acquitted on the Browne murder, but were condemned to death for their other crimes.

By 1662 Birnock was a Laidlaw property.

BISHOP'S HOUSE, LOCHWOOD

City of Glasgow   Ruin or site   OS 64   NS 694670

3.5 miles northwest of Coatbridge, and 1 mile northeast of Easterhouse, off minor roads west of A752, east of Bishop Loch.

Site of the country residence and hunting lodge of the Bishops of Glasgow. It was destroyed by Robert Boyd of Badenheath in 1579. Its foundations were still visible in the field between the present house and the loch until just over 100 years ago.

Recent excavation has confirmed the location of the site and revealed the remains of a moat around the southern edge of a central mound of rubble and slate. Some of this slate was shaped in a way which suggests that it had once covered the roof of a round turret. The moat contained the remains of a collapsed barmkin wall. Sections of wall, 3ft thick, were uncovered, with coins dating from the 13th to the 14th century. The roofing slate and lead, plus pieces of imported pottery, confirmed the high status of the remains.

Bishop John Cameron died at Lochwood in December 1446. One local tale says that he was found face down in the waters of Bishop Loch. He had been a close advisor to James I, and was Keeper of the Privy Seal then Lord Chancellor.

The bishops are reputed to have dug a narrow canal linking the Molendinar Burn, Hogganfield Loch and Frankfield Loch to the Bishop Loch in order that they could sail by barge from Glasgow. This would explain the remarkably straight waterways hereabouts, although similar work was carried out to supply water to the Monkland Canal from various lochs.

Lochwood passed to the Main family at the Reformation. The later mansion house on the hill to the south was rebuilt by the Bairds of Gartsherrie. The eastern end of Bishop Loch is badly silted up and is now a bog. Effectively the size of the loch has halved since the days of the bishops, and consequently the site is to the east of the loch, having once been on the shore.

BISHOPTON HOUSE

Renfrewshire   Private   OS 64   NS 419726

3.5 miles northeast of Bridge of Weir, 0.5 miles west of Bishopton, on minor roads south of the M8, and north of the A8, at Cora House.

Bishopton House consists of a tall 17th century tower house with corbiestepped gables, incorporating an earlier L-plan structure which was extended at each end and upwards. The older block has three storeys and a garret.

The original L-plan tower has two vaulted chambers on the ground floor. One of these functioned as the kitchen and has a wide fireplace. These rooms have slim arrow slot windows, indicating an early construction date. The entrance is guarded by one of the arrow slots and lies at the base of the stair wing. It gives access to the vaulted chambers of the main block and to a wide scale and platt stair to the upper floors. The core has been extended upward with additional floors. The main block has also been extended to the west by a two storey block containing a new kitchen at ground floor level. Similarly a two storey extension has been added to the north of the stair wing. A large, early 20th century extension has been added to the south.

The property belonged to the Brisbane family, probably long before 1332 when William Brisbane was Chancellor of Scotland. Matthew Brisbane of Bishopton fell at Flodden in 1513 and John Brisbane of Bishopton

died at Pinkie in 1547. The family moved to Kelsoland in North Ayrshire at the close of the 17th century, renaming that property Brisbane House.

Bishopton then came to the Walkinshaws of that Ilk and subsequently to the Dunlops, Semples, and Maxwells of Pollok. In the 19th century it went to the Stewart, Lords Blantyre. It came into use as a farmhouse, until converted and altered to become the Convent of the Good Shepherd. This now operates a residential home for girls with social, emotional, and behavioural difficulties in a newer building. They have a secure unit. The Cora House Learning and Conference centre utilises the old house on the same campus.

Other reference: Old Bishopton

BLACKCASTLE

South Lanarkshire Ruin or site OS 72 NT 022534
Off minor road west of A70, 7 miles north of Carnwath, at or near Blackcastle Farm.

Site of a tower which is illustrated on Pont's map of the late 16th century, and denoted in Blaeu's *Atlas Novus* of the 17th century. Sometime before 1347, Blackcastle was granted by John, Lord Somerville, to his son David. A Thomas Somerville of Blackcastle is recorded as one of the guardians of Lord Somerville in the early 16th century. In 1550 James, Lord Somerville, resigned the lands of Blackpool, Blackcastle and half of Auchengray in return for a new grant to himself and his wife, Agnes Hamilton, daughter of Sir James Hamilton of Finnart.

A William Somerville occupied Blackcastle in 1678, and in 1717 someone of the same name is listed as a tenant here. In 1741 William Bertram of Nisbet petitioned the baillie of Carnwath, alleging encroachments onto his land of Blackcastle by William Nimmo, Thomas Somerville and Adam Somerville, portioners of neighbouring Tarbrax. By the 19th century the farm was in the possession of the Sanderson family.

BLACKHALL MANOR

Renfrewshire Private OS 64 NS 491631
0.25 miles south of Paisley Abbey, just south of Cart Water, and north of A726, at Blackhall.

Blackhall is a restored 16th century house of two storeys and an attic. It is roughly T-plan, though the projecting wing on the southern wall is small. It holds a turnpike stair. The gables are corbiestepped, as are those of the stair tower. There are numerous small windows on each floor. Three shot holes are evident, one guards the door, another is in the stair tower. Close to this is a carved stone bearing three hearts. A worn armorial stone is fixed to the gable wall.

The original round arched doorway is adjacent to the stair tower and accessed a lobby. From this three vaulted chambers can be entered. One of these is the kitchen which has a slop drain. A later door had been opened from here through the eastern gable. There was a garderobe on this floor.

The first floor contained the hall and a private room, each entered from the stair head. There was a separate connecting door to the north. The hall had a large fireplace and an inverted heart carved into the west wall. The garret had its own windows and provided sleeping quarters.

Blackhall Manor originated in the 12th century. It appears in the foundation charter for Paisley Abbey in 1163 when it is mentioned as having been built on a rock by Walter Fitzalan, the High Steward. His son, Alan, confirmed his father's grants to the abbey and again mentions the hall which his father had built. In 1396 Robert III granted this part of the Steward's ancient estate of Renfrew to Sir John Stewart, his 'natural son'. Sir John had previously been granted Achingoun in 1390 and gained the estate of Ardgowan in 1404. Sir James Stewart of Auchingoun, Blackhall and Ardgowan was murdered by Robert Boyd of Kilmarnock on 31 May 1445. A charter

of 1576 by James VI erected the three estates into a single barony named Blackhall for his namesake James Stewart of Achingoun. Archibald Stewart of Blackhall was knighted by Charles I and joined his Privy Council, a role he also took up for Charles II when he came to Scotland in 1650. He was made a Baronet of Nova Scotia in 1657

The present house was built in the 16th century. It came into use as a farmhouse by 1710 and was roofless by the 1840s. This was because the farmer had a new house and wished to avoid paying rates on the old one. It was used as a store for the next 100 years until in 1940 the family, by now Shaw-Stewarts, donated it to the Burgh of Paisley. By 1978 the council were considering demolition due to the poor state of the building, precipitated by vandalism and neglect. Public protest saved it until it passed into private ownership. It was restored with great care in the 1980s, a process which involved rebuilding the roof, upper storeys complete with windows, and replacing the kitchen chimney. Some of the ornate stonework used in the restoration was salvaged from Ferguslie House, including the thistles above the dormer windows and the lions at the gates. Blackhall is a category 'B' Listed Building. The family now live at Ardgowan House, near Inverkip.

The Stewarts had a chapel just to the west of the manor house. It existed by 1272 when its chaplain witnessed a charter. There were some remains in about 1810, but now all that survives is the name of nearby Chapelhouse, a mansion close to the site.

BLACKPOOL

South Lanarkshire Ruin or site OS 72 NS 986538
7 miles north of Carnwath, west of A70, by minor roads, 1 mile southwest of Auchengray, at or near Pool.

Site of a small tower, recorded as Blackpool or Blackpot, which is illustrated on the east bank of Dippool Water on Pont's map of the late 16th century and denoted in Blaeu's *Atlas Novus* of the 17th century. Pall and Pall House appear on Roy's map of the 18th century.

In 1550 James, Lord Somerville, resigned the lands of Blackpool, Blackcastle and half of Auchengray in return for a new grant to himself and his wife, Agnes Hamilton, daughter of Sir James Hamilton of Finnart.

Other references: Pall, Pool

BLACKSTOUN

Renfrewshire Ruin or site OS 64 NS 457660
1 mile northwest of Paisley, by minor roads north of the A737, and west of the M8, on west bank of the Black Cart Water, at Blackstoun.

Site of a large and obviously important castle, known as Blackstoun or Blackston, which appears with some prominence on Pont's map of the late 16th century. Pont's sketch illustrates two large towers within a courtyard, with a centrally placed gatehouse. The site retains some degree of importance on later maps.

This was the site of a grange of the Abbot of Paisley, which appears in records as early as 1460. It developed into a summer residence, built by Abbot George Shaw between 1471 and 1499. At the Reformation it became the property of Claud Hamilton, Commendator of Paisley Abbey and later Lord Paisley. His son became 1st Earl of Abercorn in 1603. He or subsequent earls improved and altered the building. It burned down in the 1730s, by which time it belonged to Alexander Napier. A mansion house was built a little to the south, which is recorded by Ainslie in 1796 as belonging to Napier Esq. This appears in the OS map of 1950 but had been demolished by 1953.

By 1855 the present complex of farm buildings had been built upon the site of the grange. These have since been extended. In 1993, the farmer at Middleton reported that his plough had pulled up a wooden trap door, exposing a 6ft deep tunnel which he filled in. This event took place on the line of a crop mark which runs between

Blackstoun and Middleton Farms, then down to the Cart. The feature is thought to be a drain, possibly related to the grange.

Other references: Middleton

BLACKWOOD CASTLE

South Lanarkshire   Ruin or site   OS 71   NS 773433
At or near Blackwood House, off minor roads, 2 miles west of B7078/M74 junction, at Blackwood.

The Weirs appear to have had a castle here from an early date, passing it later to the Lawries and from the 19th century to the Hope-Veres. It developed into a mansion, which was demolished to be replaced by a timber bungalow-style house.

The Weirs are on record in the area from 1276, when Thomas Wer was witness to a resignation of Hautillet to the Abbot of Kelso by Phillip de Greenrigs. A Richard Were of Lanarkshire rendered homage to Edward I in 1296. In 1400 Rotaldus Were, the 'well beloved and faithful' baillie of Lesmahagow, was given a grant by the Abbot, to him and his male heirs of the lands of 'Blackwodd and Dermoundyston with the whole of Mossmynyne'. Evidently these had belonged to his father. He is said to have split the property between his two sons, creating the dynasties of Weir of Blackwood and Weir of Stonebyres.

In 1572 James Weir of Blackwood is recorded as being one of the supporters of Mary, Queen of Scots, and was indicted as an accessory in the murder of Henry, Lord Darnley. There was apparently a 100-year feud between the Weirs of Blackwood and those of Stonebyres. It ended in 1592 when the Stonebyres branch swore fealty to the Blackwoods and acknowledged them as the chiefly line.

William Lawrie of Blackwood was put on trial in 1683 for harbouring Covenanters. The legal process seems to have lasted for over a year, ending with a sentence of death being pronounced. However, while awaiting execution, he received a pardon due to the intervention of the Marquis of Douglas. At the Glorious Revolution of 1688 he seems to have won favour with William and Mary, being knighted and gaining a variety of lucrative positions. In 1690 an Act of Parliament was passed specifically to declare his previous conviction null and void, despite having been included in the act which had rescinded all fines and forfeitures of that time.

Blackwood appears as a large tower house on Pont's manuscript map of 1596, and again in Blaeu's *Atlas Novus* of the 17th century.

BLAIRLINN

The Lennox & East Dunbartonshire   Ruin or site   OS 64   NS 758730
2 miles southwest of Cumbernauld, east of A73 by minor roads, east of Luggiebank, on south bank of Luggie Water in northern corner of Blairlinn industrial estate.

Possible site of an early castle. The estate of Blairlinn was the seat of a cadet branch of the Clelands.

The crop mark of a ditch was recorded on aerial photographs of 1947. Once within a field and now covered by an industrial area, the feature cut across the neck of a triangular promontory created by an acute bend in the burn below. On the west and north sides above the burn, there are cliffs protecting the site. The ditch protected the only viable approach and was approximately 16ft wide and 265ft long. It enclosed an area 200ft by 250ft.

Interestingly a few hundred yards southwest stood a flax mill and later farm known as Petty Castle or Wester Blairlinn, and on the north bank near Auchenkilns an early settlement known as Chapleton. In the 19th century human remains, suggestive of an old graveyard, were unearthed when houses were demolished there. At that time it was generally believed that there had been an old chapel here. The name persists in Chapleton Road.

The north bank opposite the Blairlinn site was occupied by Lenziemill, and the waters below the site were diverted by a dam and sluice to feed a mill lade on the opposite bank. The mill and lade were still evident as late as the first edition OS maps of the late 19th century.

Other references: Petty Castle, Pettie Castle

BLAIRVADDACH

The Lennox & East Dunbartonshire   Private   OS 56   NS 263853
In Rhu, 1 mile northwest of Helensburgh, east of A814, on Shore Road at Blairvadach.

The present modern mansion house stands on the site of an earlier structure mentioned in 1558. It is thought to have resembled a border keep or peel. There are various spellings, including Blairvadic, Blairvadick and Blairvadoch.

This was a MacAulay estate, a gravestone of Alexander MacAulay 'late in Blairvadick' can be found in the old churchyard in Rhu, dated 1780. The death of Robert Shannon of Blairvadick is recorded in 1789. The property was owned by the Buchanans in 1805 when James, 2nd of Blairvadick, married Janet Sinclair. This family also owned Craigend at Mugdock at the time.

The old 'mansion' was described in the 19th century as having been an old-fashioned, square, two-storey house with attics, which had been enlarged by James Buchanan of Ardenconnell. It was demolished to make way for the new house, a Scots baronial mansion built in 1850 by the architect J.T. Rochead for Sir James Anderson, Lord Provost of Glasgow. It passed to the Donaldson family and then to the MacLellans. It was purchased by the Corporation of Glasgow in the 20th century. It was used as a POW camp during World War II, as a Children's Home, and is now an outdoor education centre.

BLANTYRE FARM

South Lanarkshire   Private   OS 64   NS 686603

1.5 miles north and west of Blantyre, 1 mile north of junction of Blantyre Farm Road with A724, east of Blantyre Farm Road, at Blantyre Farm.

Site of an old or fortified house of the Hamiltons of Blantyreferme. Blantyre Farm was one of the original fermtouns of the barony. It has been suggested that it was the orchard of Blantyre Priory, and has been recorded as Blantyrefarm, Blantyre Ferme and Blantyrfarm, as well as Blatyrferme and Fremblantyre.

Thomas Hamilton purchased 'Fremblantyre' from the Dunbars of Enterkin c,1400. William Hamilton of Blantyre Ferme was son-in-law of John Dunbar of Knockshinnoch near Cumnock and was an executor of his will in 1551. James Hamilton of Blantyreferme is mentioned in Parliament in 1696. In 1773 the family died out and the estate passed to a nephew, James Coats. It belonged to a family named Scott in 1866 and to a MacPherson by the end of the 19th century. A later mansion stood on the site; however this was demolished in the early 20th century.

Other references: Blatyrferme, Fremblantyre

BLANTYRE OLD PLACE

South Lanarkshire   Site or ruin   OS 64   NS 680568

In High Blantyre, off minor roads north of A725, near junction of B7012 and B758, in Janefield Place.

This is almost certainly the site of the 'tower of the fortalice' of Mains of Blantyre. A tower here was surrounded by a moat, and demolished around 1800. The present house dates from the mid 18th century and has recently been restored.

While the history of Blantyre is overshadowed by that of Blantyre Priory, the Dunbars continued as barons within the parish. It is said that an ancient charter granted the right of a weekly fair to the tower and fortalice at Blantyre.

Sometime between 1234 and 1241 Maldouen, Earl of Lennox, granted a half ploughgate of land in Killearn to Stephen of Blantyre. In 1263 an inquest into these lands was held to ensure that Stephen's son Patrick was entitled to inherit, which was confirmed.

Patrick, Earl of Dunbar, and his wife dedicated Blantyre Priory to the Holy Rood before 1272. The Dunbars retained superiority of the remaining lands and probably had a castle near High Blantyre. If traditional medieval practice were followed, it would have been close to the site of the original village and church, in the vicinity of Old Place.

The Dunbars lost the property in the years after Bannockburn, when Robert the Bruce granted it to his nephew Thomas Randolph, Earl of Moray. It came to his daughter, the famed 'Black Agnes', who successfully withstood a five-month siege of Dunbar Castle by the English in 1338. She was the second wife of Patrick, 8th Earl of Dunbar or March. He died in 1368 without a male heir.

Blantyre then came to the family of Patrick's second son, one of whom had married Agnes's sister, Isobel. Her first son John inherited the Earldom of Moray, while her second son, George, became 9th Earl of March and passed Mochrum, Cumnock and Blantyre to the Dunbars of Enterkin. Patrick Dunbar of Cumnock granted the three baronies to his brother Cuthbert in 1472. However, this appears to have been rescinded and by charters of 1474 and 1479 his daughter Janet and her spouse Patrick Dunbar were granted Blantyre. Other members of the family received the remaining estates. In 1537 Gilbert Kennedy, Earl of Cassillis, and accomplices 'found surety to underly the law' at the Justice-Aire in Ayr, for their part in an attack upon John Dunbar of Blantyre and his four servants. The attack was conducted by a party of 50 men 'armed in warlike manner', who severely wounded three of John's servants.

In 1557, William Hamilton the Rector of Cambuslang, produced a charter whereby John Dunbar of Blantyre charged James Clerk, Baillie of Blantyre, to give Hamilton sasine of the Mains of Blantyre 'with half of the tower of the fortalice of Blantyre, with its yards orchards and pertinents, extending to the 20 shilling land of old extent' and half of John Dunbar's mill at Blantyre

In 1588, Hugh Campbell of Loudoun had a grant of lands from William Dunbar of Blantyre. In 1596, Walter Stewart, Commendator of Blantyre Priory, became Lord High Treasurer, and in 1598 he purchased the estate from John Dunbar of Enterkin. James VI then granted him the portion formerly owned by David Dunbar of Dunderk, though by this time the estate had been entirely feued out in small portions. In 1599 the king then had the Priory dissolved from the monastery at Jedburgh, and erected the entirety of the 'Burgh of Blantyre' into a free barony in Walter's favour. Sir John Hamilton of Lettrick, Sheriff Depute of Lanarkshire, gave sasine to Walter at the tower and fortalice of Blantyre. In 1606 Walter became Lord Blantyre. He adopted Blantyre Priory as his home.

In the 18th century Old Place became the property of the Coats family, who probably built the present house.

The 1557 division of the Mains of Blantyre is reflected in General Roy's map of 1747-56. It clearly shows Old Place, recorded elsewhere as Mains, with Newmains just to the east. Occasionally large worked stones, presumably from foundations, have been unearthed in the vicinity of the present house.

Other references: Blantyre, Mains of Blantyre

BLANTYRE PRIORY

South Lanarkshire Ruin or site OS 64 NS 686594
1 mile north of A724, by B758, at Priory Playing Fields, 0.25 miles east of car park by foot.

Sections of wall stand to a maximum height of about 5ft. The foundations of various rooms and buildings are hidden below heavy undergrowth in woods on the edge of a precipice above the west bank of the Clyde.

The Priory consisted of a perimeter wall of 115ft by 150ft, up to 10ft high and 3ft thick. This was surrounded by a ditch on two sides, the north side being protected by a deep gully, and the east being the precipitous drop to the River Clyde. Within the wall were a series of buildings, including the prior's house in the northeast corner, and another structure south of it which was at one time thought to be the chapel since there was a stoup. Secular style windows indicate that this building may have been adapted. Toward the end of the 19th century, gables and a vaulted basement of the prior's house survived. The most visible section of what remains is on the north side, where a section of wall forms a revetment on the edge of a vertical drop into the gully.

All of the remains indicate that the buildings were built of the same red sandstone as Bothwell Castle, which stands on the opposite bank of the Clyde, and of which the cliffs below are composed.

The Augustinian Priory of Blantyre was an outpost of Jedburgh Abbey. Its founders, Patrick Earl of Dunbar and his wife, dedicated it to the Holy Rood in about 1239. It is first mentioned in 1275, where it appears in the 'Bagimund Roll', a list of ecclesiastical establishments taxed by the Pope to fund a crusade. It is thought to have been mentioned in an earlier list of 1254 for a similar purpose. William de Cokeburne, the first prior in surviving records, submitted to Edward I at Berwick in 1296. Most of his successors appear in the records of Scottish Parliaments. The last Prior, William Chirnside, converted to Protestantism and became the first Protestant minister of Blantyre Kirk after the Reformation.

In 1580, Walter Stewart, who had been educated alongside James VI by George Buchanan, was appointed Commendator of the Priory of Blantyre. By 1582 he was a member of the Privy Council, and Keeper of the Privy Seal. He subsequently gained the title Lord Blantyre and adopted the priory as his home. His wife however, could not tolerate the strange noises and eerie goings

on in the priory, and left her husband to live in it alone. Meantime, she and her daughters moved into another recently acquired property at Cardonald.

One of their grandchildren was Frances Stewart, 'La Belle Stewart', who is mentioned in the entry for Cardonald. Contrary to a story that she had been born in Blantyre, she was in fact born in Paris while the family were in exile. This was as a result of their Royalist sentiments during the Civil War. They returned at the restoration of Charles II, when Frances was 14.

In her tour of 1803, Dorothy Wordsworth said of the priory 'nothing can be more beautiful than the little remnants of this holy place'.

At the foot of the cliff below the priory are a series of impressive rock carvings depicting scenes from the crucifixion and the faces of local worthies, such as David Livingstone. Their discovery prompted some excitement in the press and evaluation by archaeologists, the speculation being that the crucifixion scenes dated from the time of the Priory and had lain undiscovered for centuries. It would seem however that they were carved by local man Tommy Hawkins in the 1950s and 60s.

There is also (an inevitable) legend regarding William Wallace. The great patriot apparently took refuge within the priory. Being aware of the approach of English soldiers and having no other means of escape, he jumped from a window into the Clyde, some 70ft or so below.

Another local story which has caused great speculation is the rumour of a tunnel below the Clyde linking the Priory to Bothwell Castle. There is a similar story regarding a tunnel below the river in the vicinity of the David Livingstone centre. No convincing evidence for either is apparent, although there were extensive mine workings in the area.

Other references: Craig of Blantyre

BLARRACHNEEM

South Lanarkshire   Ruin or site   OS 71   NS 810384?
1.5 miles southwest of Lesmahagow, 2 miles west of M74, by minor roads, just north of New Trows, at or near Woodhead.

Site of a tower depicted on Pont's map of 1596 and subsequently in Blaeu's *Atlas Novus*. It does not appear on any later cartographic or other reference. The site may lie some way to the west where it is depicted on Pont and Blaeu, the location given above having been plotted on a modern map in reference to nearby sites.

BLAWARTHILL

City of Glasgow   Ruin or site   OS 64   NS 520687
At or near Blawarthill Hospital, 2.5 miles east of Clydebank, north of A814, Glasgow.

Site of a tower, which appears on Blaeu's Atlas.

Being within a detached part of Renfrewshire on the north of the Clyde, Blawarthill and Wester Partick belonged anciently to the High Steward. It was granted by charter of James II to the Stewarts of Arthurlie, then went by marriage to the Stewarts of Darnley and then those of Minto. It was part of the Sempills' Renfrewshire estates by the 16th century. It had been held in ward by the Earl of Huntly for the young, John, Lord Sempill. By an Act of Parliament in 1567, Mary, Queen of Scots, restored Blawarthill and his other estates to John. By the 17th century, it was a Maxwell property and in 1732, John Maxwell of Blawarthill inherited his cousin's estates of Pollok. In the 19th century, the family donated the site for use as a hospital and it remains so today.

A tower house is illustrated on a hilltop site on Blaeu's *Atlas Novus* of the 17th century and similarly on Herman Moll's map of 1745.

BOARD

The Lennox & East Dunbartonshire   Ruin or site   OS 64   NS 720761?
1 mile south of Kilsyth, north of A80 and west of B802, just west of Croy, near Girnal Hill.

Probable site of a castle. The lands of Board were a property of the Erskine family until 1339. They were exchanged with Patrick Fleming, the second son of Sir Malcolm of Biggar and Cumbernauld, for Garscadden.

The exact site is not known and it is likely that any in situ remains have been destroyed by the effects of quarrying, coal mining and railway construction. Even Boards Loch has disappeared since the mid 18th century.

On Ainslie's Map of the 19th century, Board appears just south of the point where the road from Auchinstarry passes through the Antonine Wall. Over Croy cottage, which was built c.1800, contained sculpted stone fragments which had obviously been taken from a superior medieval structure. Close by was a subterranean vaulted chamber, built into the side of a bank, although the brick vaulting of this structure indicates a later date. The entrance is low, and there is a hatch in the ceiling. This may simply be an ice house of similar date to the cottage, but was possibly part of or belonged to a much larger residence. Over Croy farmhouse was said to have carried dates of 1618 and 1728 on its door lintels, despite having been built c.1800 with a later extension. According to the official listing document, the latter lintel is now over a window and carries the initials IH and MM, and the former date apparently reads as 1818. The village was built in the 19th century to house quarriers. The name Croy is from the Gaelic *cruaidh*, 'hillside'.

BOGHALL CASTLE

Renfrewshire Ruin or site OS 63 NS 412700

2 miles northeast of Houston, and 3 miles north of Bridge of Weir, by minor roads north of A761, just south of Formakin Mill, at or near Boghall Cottage.

Nothing remains of a large castle named Boghall, which appears in this location on Pont's map of the late 16th century and in Gordon's map of the early 17th century. Boghall was a ruin when mentioned by Crawford in his *History of the Shire of Renfrew* in 1710. Subsequent maps show a house known as Boghall, just south of Formakin Mill. The other mill site nearby, now known as Nether Mill, was once Boghall Mill.

This was a Fleming property, the family being descended from a younger son of one of the Flemings of Biggar. The line died out in 1581 and the estate reverted to John, Lord Fleming. In 1593 he granted it to his second son, James. By 1710 the estate belonged to the Earl of Dundonald.

Just to the north, Formakin House is a grand mansion built in 1903 by Sir Robert Lorimer for J.A. Holm. It was never finished, since the owner ran out of funds before it was completed. It became the property of the local council, who utilized the estate as a country park. This endeavour saved the house and subsidiary buildings for posterity. The house is a category 'A' Listed Building, while no less than 11 subsidiary buildings are category 'B'. Formakin House has now been converted to provide six separate homes.

Other references: Formakin Park

BOGHALL CASTLE

South Lanarkshire Ruin or site OS 72 NT 041370

0.25 miles south of Biggar on minor roads and foot south of A702, southeast of Boghall Farm.

Remains of one square and two almost circular corner towers survive of this 14th century courtyard castle of the Flemings. The scant remains are of 15th and 17th century origin.

MacGibbon and Ross pieced together a fair picture of Boghall, the ruins being only a little more substantial in

their day. From archive material, they described a very large courtyard within a ditch set in the midst of a marsh, hence the name. It was an irregular hexagon shape, of uneven sides, the entrance being at an angle of the northern wall. This was a large gatehouse of 15th century origin, with guardrooms either side, a battlemented parapet and corner turrets.

At either end of this wall were the two round towers, about 17ft in diameter, of which something survives. Gunloops show that they were later additions to the structure. Against the southern wall was a later mansion block with a centrally placed square stair tower. Part of this remains. Just below the eaves was inscribed the date 1670.

Excavations at various times have been carried out by teachers and pupils of Biggar High School. This revealed the foundations of a 15th century L-plan tower house in the western section of the courtyard.

The property passed by marriage to the Flemings of Biggar in the late 13th century. They were descended from Baldwin of Biggar who, in addition to his estate here, held lands at Houston and Inverkip in Renfrewshire. He became Sheriff of Lanarkshire.

Edward II of England stayed at Boghall in 1310. In 1458 the family were made Lords Fleming of Cumbernauld, and more of their history can be read in that entry. James V visited, as did Mary, Queen of Scots, in 1565. In 1568 in the aftermath of Langside, the castle was surrendered to the Regent Moray after a siege.

In 1605 the family became earls of Wigtown. In 1650 the castle was again besieged and then occupied by Cromwell. The 6th and last earl died in 1747, and the castle fell into ruin. Over the years it has been used as a useful supply of stone, and so has deteriorated to the present poor state.

BOGHOUSE CASTLE

South Lanarkshire   Ruin or site OS 71 NS 878236
About 0.5 miles south of Crawfordjohn, just east of the B740, 3 miles southwest of its junction with the A74.

Site of a 16th century castle, probably built by Sir James Hamilton of Finnart, 'the Bastard of Arran'. Nothing remains, though Forrest had drawn the ruins on his map of 1816 and some remnants were extant in 1836. It is said that it was built using stone from the ruins of Crawfordjohn Castle. Pont depicted a large L-plan tower here, naming it 'Boghouse or Crawfordjohn Castle' and Blaeu followed suit. The *New Statistical Account* reports that the barony had at some point been separated in to two halves, which Finnart acquired separately to reunite the estate.

Sir James was granted a licence to build towers within the Barony. It has been suggested that he built Boghouse so that James V could liaise with his mistress, Catherine Carmichael, daughter of the keeper of Crawford Castle. Sir James was known to have encouraged the young king in all 'manly pursuits'. Hamilton had exchanged this estate and another at Kilbirnie with Lawrence Crawford for his own property at Drumry in the Lennox. This was in 1528, but in 1535 he exchanged Crawfordjohn with the king for the Barony of Kilmarnock. Adept property dealing or utmost generosity toward his liege? Either way the king's opinion was shown in 1540 when Sir James was beheaded for treason. His heirs lost everything when forfeiture was imposed. By an Act of Parliament in 1543, the forfeit was reduced and Sir James's estates, excluding Kilmarnock but including Crawfordjohn, were restored to his son, James Hamilton of Avondale.

An alternate history is given by Hamilton of Wishaw, presumably for the other half of the barony. The barony was the property of Lord Monipenny. During the reign of James II, he exchanged it with Lord Hamilton for Kirkinner in Galloway. It remained with the Hamiltons until the Earl of Arran gave it to Sir James Hamilton of Finnart. He exchanged it with James V as stated above, when Lord Boyd was forfeited. The king then built Boghouse for Catherine Carmichael.

James V apparently spent much of the summer of 1541 resident here and hunting with Marie de Guise, his second wife. Catherine eventually married John Somerville of Cambusnethan. James is known to have had at least nine illegitimate children by different mistresses. His offspring included James Stewart, Earl of Moray, later Regent, and Robert Stewart, Earl of Orkney; however his only surviving legitimate heir was Mary, Queen of Scots.

BOGTON CASTLE

City Of Glasgow   Ruin or site OS 64 NS 575596
2 miles west of Rutherglen, just west of B767, and east of Muirend railway station, at Bogton Avenue.

Site of a tower house of the Blairs. They built the castle in 1543, though Crawford in his *History of Renfrewshire* states it was built by John Blair of that Ilk and his wife, Grissel Semple, in 1580, having purchased the lands from Lord Cathcart. It passed to John's nephew, Sir Adam Blair. In 1679 the tower was purchased by James Hamilton of Aikenhead and appears to have been demolished at some point thereafter.

'Boigton' appears as a large tower on Pont's map of Renfrewshire of the late 16th century and as a tower within a park in Blaeu's *Atlas Novus* of the 17th century. By the time Richardson compiled his map of Glasgow in 1796, Bogton appeared as a cluster of minor buildings, with no mansion. Bogton House, a later mansion, appears on the 1890 OS map of Glasgow.

BONHILL PLACE

The Lennox & East Dunbartonshire   Ruin or site   OS 63   NS 394792

About 3 miles north of Dumbarton, on west bank of River Leven, east of A82, off A813, at Vale of Leven Academy.

Bonhill Place was a mansion house of the Smolletts, Burgesses of Dumbarton. It may have had an older fortified house of the Lindsays at its core. It is not known when the building originated, but the mansion was demolished in 1950.

This was the property of the Earl of Lennox, which came to the Lindsays in the 13th century when Earl Malcolm granted the lands of Bonhill to his kinsman, Sir Patrick de Lindsay, and appointed him Forester and Baillie of the Lennox estates. It is said that a David Lindsay of Bonhill was forfeited by Edward I for supporting William Wallace in the 13th century and regained his estates when fighting alongside the Robert I. A Lindsay of Bonhill was killed by the MacGregors at the Battle of Glenfruin in 1603. The estate was still owned by the family in 1622 when Quentin Lindsay of Bonhill obtained a grant of the lands of Pillanflat. Mungo Lindsay of Bonhill was mentioned in an Act of Charles I in 1643.

In 1684 Bonhill was purchased by the Smolletts. They married into the Telfer family, becoming Telfer-Smolletts. The family left Bonhill in 1762 and moved to Cameron House. The Turnbull family moved in after extensive restoration work c.1806.

The house allegedly had a tunnel leading to the River Leven. The entrance was hidden behind the drawing room fireplace and a piper was sent in to explore it. He never returned, though his ghostly pipes could be heard playing within the walls thereafter.

Bonhill was a ferry point across the Leven, anciently used by cattle drovers, as it provided a more economic toll than payment to the garrison at Dumbarton. A dispute raged through the later 17th century as the Duke of Lennox attempted to extend the levy due to the Castle Governor to include the 'Boat of Bonhill'. The case went as far as the Privy Council, before being settled a year after the Duke's death in 1673.

Other reference: Place of Bonhill

BOQUHAN OLD HOUSE

The Lennox and East Dunbartonshire   Private   OS 57   NS 545875

1 mile northeast of Killearn, 1 mile south of Balfron, east of A875, and north of A818 by minor roads, east of Boquhan on west side of Boquhan Glen.

Boquhan Old House is dated 1784 with 19th century extensions, and is thought to have been designed by David Henderson. It stands on the site of a tower marked on Timothy Pont's map of the late 16th century and on Blaeu's *Atlas Novus* of the mid 17th century.

This was a Galbraith property and was occupied by a younger brother of Galbraith of Culcreuch in the late 16th century.

Old House became a seat of the Buchanans by the mid 17th century. Walter Buchanan of 'Balquhan' was tried in 1728, charged with fire raising, poisoning, theft and depredation, the killing and eating of other people's sheep, and harbouring sundry thieves and robbers. The Buchanans of Boquhan were descended from those of Ardoch. The estate passed to an heiress in the 19th century, who died a spinster in 1828.

There is another property of the same name to the east of Kippen, 8 miles to the northeast.

Other references: Balquhan, Bowhan

BOTHWELL CASTLE

North Lanarkshire   His Scot   OS 64   NS 688594

200 yards West of Castle Avenue, 0.5 miles south of Main Street, Uddingston

Set spectacularly above a gorge on a bend in the Clyde, and protected on the landward sides by a deep ditch, Bothwell guards what was once a critically important crossing point of the river. Bothwell's bridge was the point at which an invading army from the south using the west coast route would meet the Clyde. The ruins at Bothwell reflect the importance of the site.

A massive, though partly demolished, donjon or great keep of the 13th century, 90ft to the parapet, 65ft in diameter and with walls 15ft thick, dominates the western end of a massive courtyard castle. Most of the remaining structure is of 14th and 15th century origin. This consists of a massive wall of enceinte, interrupted at various intervals by strong corner towers.

The donjon provided the living quarters of the lord and, despite having been partially destroyed in the early 14th century, it was repaired by building a rectangular block to close its open side and provide an impressive residence. It has its own now dry moat within the courtyard, crossed by drawbridge. Sluices for draining the moat can still be seen through the base of the tower, even these having a defensive format to prevent surreptitious entry.

The keep consisted of three floors above the basement and a fighting platform at parapet level. It has a finely moulded pointed arched entrance. Despite the circular exterior, the rooms within were octagonal and a central stone pillar rose from the basement to support the floors at the first and second storeys. This may have been continued to the other floors in wood. The basement contained the well and an adjacent recess in the wall housed the winding gear and bucket. A mural stair leads to the first floor, where a twisting rib-vaulted corridor accessed the Lord's Hall, mural stair to the second floor, main entrance and a vaulted room which housed the lifting gear for the drawbridge and portcullis. The entrance is guarded from this room by impressive arrow slots. A second or 'common hall' was on the floor above, both halls having a latrine within the thickness of the walls. The third floor is thought to have been the lord's private chamber and provided a separate door leading to the wall-walk providing a means of escape for the lord. The battlemented parapet had machicolations, or slots, through which fluids or objects could be dropped on attackers at the base of the wall 90ft below.

During the Wars of Independence, Bothwell consisted of only this tower and the prison tower. It was nevertheless a formidable building and was occupied by Sir Aymer De Valence, the English Earl of Pembroke. The tower therefore earned the by-name of the Valence Tower. In the south wall, just east of the donjon, stands the lower section of the prison tower, with pit prison. At its eastern base, some 15ft below the level of the yard, is the postern gate. A steep bending slope carries up from the gate to the interior, the embankment to the side allowing defence from above. A further steep slope descends from the exterior of the gate, along a narrow causeway below the walls with a similar purpose. The postern originally had a portcullis. High above the exterior of the gate the arms of Douglas can still be made out carved into the wall.

The southern wall continues to complete the perimeter at this side at the southeastern tower and is punctuated by a series of windows which betray the site of a large accommodation block. The largest again a pointed arch, gave light to the dais of a chapel at the southeastern corner of the yard. The wall at the chapel site shows sockets for flooring at first floor level, stone window seats, fonts for Holy Water, basins within the walling, and the remains of the vaulted ceiling.

The southeast tower is another impressive and decoratively structured building, again machicolated, with hexagonal rooms within a circular exterior. Each floor had a single room with ornate fireplace.

Adjacent, the eastern end of the yard is occupied by a large block of two storeys, the upper storey being the hall. There was a dais and large ornate pointed arch windows, the largest illuminating the dais. There are three vaulted storage rooms at ground level. One of these contains the remnant of a blocked up turnpike stair. The eastern wall runs to almost full height to terminate at the fragmentary remains of the rectangular northeast tower.

This was once loftier than even the great donjon. It represented the main residence of the Douglases. Little now remains, but it had its own portcullis, with drawbridge entry from a position now within the hall. The massive proportions of the foundations impress.

The wall continues to form the northern perimeter, turning back to meet the donjon at the northwestern corner. Midway along this wall the modern entrance was built in 1987, filling a gap where once stood a huge gatehouse. This would have contained the quarters of the Constable, who was responsible for the administration of the castle. The position of the modern shop, just west of the hall in the northern wall, with a fireplace and oven built into the wall above it, indicate the site of the original kitchen-block. A buttress on the exterior of this section of the enceinte supports an impressive example of corbelling, which presumably was once surmounted by a turret. There are latrine chutes at various points on the external wall.

Outwith the surviving structure, foundations were uncovered in the late 19th century. These were those of a latrine tower and a massive gatehouse. It is believed that these structures were never completed but were part of the original plan. Their position outwith the existing walls and just within the deep ditch illustrate that the originally intended scale of the castle was to be about double its present area.

The Barony of Bothwell originally consisted of the lands bounded by the two Calders, the North and South Calder Waters. It was granted to David Olifard (Oliphant) in the 12th century. His son and grandson, both Walter, succeeded in inheriting the estate and the position of Justiciar of Lothian. The daughter of the younger Walter married Walter de Moravia (Moray or Murray), and he inherited in 1242. The site of the original caput of the barony is not known, but was probably close to St Bride's Kirk in the town.

Walter of Moray lost little time in showing off his new found position, and began construction of his new castle. However, by the time of the Wars of Independence, it was not complete. Only the donjon and prison tower represented the defendable structure, the other towers reaching only foundation level. A palisade and the ditch probably defended the rest of the site.

During the invasion of 1296, Edward I of England captured William Murray of Bothwell and took his castle. His nephew, Andrew, took revenge at the Battle of Stirling Bridge a year later, but was fatally wounded. In 1298 the Scots commenced a 14-month siege before successfully recovering Bothwell. Edward I, or 'Longshanks', returned in 1301 and used specially constructed siege engines or towers to retake Bothwell. One particularly successful tower was given the name 'Bothwell', and was subsequently used against Stirling Castle. This may have been the tower, or 'belfry' built at Glasgow, for which the woods of the City were plundered for material. The castle was left under the control of the Earl of Pembroke, who was appointed Governor of Scotland.

The castle remained in English hands until 1314 when, in the immediate aftermath of the Battle of Bannockburn, several English lords sought refuge within the walls. However, on the arrival of their Scots pursuers, the Constable, Fitzgilbert, opened the gates and surrendered the castle and his compatriots. Fitzgilbert was from Homildon in the North of England and as reward was given a grant of land at Cadzow. The family subsequently became known as Hamilton and gave their name to the town.

The English retook Bothwell in October 1336, Edward III making it his headquarters in his invasion to support Edward Balliol's claim to the throne. The Scots by this time had laid it waste and a master mason by the name of John de Kilbourn was charged with repairing the damage. Some of the 14th century work is his.

By March 1337 the posthumously born son of Sir Andrew Murray, another of the same name, arrived with a siege engine called 'Bowstoure' and quickly retook his ancestral home. In accordance with Bruce's old policy he pulled down the western side of the donjon, which fell into the river. The damage caused by his action remains to this day.

The castle remained in a ruinous state until 1362, when Joanna of Bothwell married Archibald the Grim

or 'Black Archibald', later Lord of Galloway and Earl of Douglas. He undertook to rebuild, his work being completed by his son following his death in 1400. The result is substantially what remains today.

The Black Douglases were forfeited in 1455 and the Crown took possession. The property was given in turn to Lord Crichton, then to Sir John Ramsay, who were both also forfeited. However, James IV granted the barony and its castle to Patrick Hepburn of Dunsyre, 2nd Lord Hailes, in 1489. He was created Earl of Bothwell, a title borne by the 4th Earl, his more infamous descendant in the reign of Mary, Queen of Scots. The castle did not stay with the Hepburns as the title did. In 1492, with the permission of the king, Hepburn exchanged it for Hermitage in Liddesdale with another Archibald Douglas, Earl of Angus, this time of the Red Douglases. James IV visited Bothwell in 1503 and 1504. In 1540, the castle and estates of Bothwell were listed among the properties of the forfeited Sir James Hamilton of Finnart. The Crown incurred expenses for the castle in 1544. By 1584 Dame Margaret Maxwell, dowager Countess of Angus, was in residence with her husband, William Baillie of Lamington. Ten years later the couple were accused of conducting a Catholic mass in the chapel, a practice much denounced in those post-Reformation years.

Archibald Douglas, 1st Earl of Forfar, gained possession in 1669 and began to take stone to construct his new mansion. The second Bothwell Castle stood in the park to the east of the original castle. This mansion survived until 1926, when it was demolished due to the effect of coal mining. There are a few peripheral remnants of this unfortified house as Bothwell is approached from the castle, and several surviving subsidiary buildings within the local area. After a lawsuit in the 18th century, the property went to the Stewarts of Grandtully, then by descent to the Earl of Home. In 1935 the castle was taken into state care and is now managed by Historic Scotland.

'Bonnie Jean' supposedly haunts the castle. On Halloween she is said to appear above the donjon. Being a lady, she was forbidden her love for a local peasant, but conceived a plan with a local cleric whereby she would sail across the river to meet her man and elope. Attempting the crossing during a storm, her boat sank and the river swept her to her death.

Tel: 01698 816894 (Historic Scotland); open daily, except Thu and Fri from November to March.

Other reference: Valence Tower

BOTHWELLHAUGH

North Lanarkshire   Ruin or site   OS 72   NS 723579

North of Hamilton, and west of Motherwell, in Strathclyde Park, 0.5 miles southeast of Raith interchange on M74/A725, below surface of Strathclyde Loch north and east of outflow to the Clyde.

Site of an old or fortified house, belonging to Hamilton of Bothwellhaugh, which was still standing in 1851. Other recorded names are Bothwellmuir and Bothwellpark.

In the *Retours of the Shire of Lanark* for 1602, mention is made of Alison Hamilton 'in parte toftae seu mansionis de Boythwelpark', joint owner of the mansion of Bothwell Park. A building complex is illustrated on Pont's map of the late 16th century and again in Blaeu's *Atlas* of 1654, where it includes a small western tower. It sat just west of the former mouth of the south Calder where it met the Clyde. The site later developed as a farm complex and from the late 19th century as a mining village. Both mine and village were deserted in the 1960s, and the site flooded to create Strathclyde Loch in the 1970s. There are some references to 'a village and castle' at Bothwellhaugh, though these may have meant a large house, or be derived from folklore rather than hard evidence.

James Hamilton of Bothwellhaugh is infamous as the man who shot and killed the Regent Moray from a window in Linlithgow in 1570. The attack was precipitated by Moray's determination to destroy the power of the Hamiltons, who were the principal supporters of his half-sister, Mary, Queen of Scots. Mary's army had been defeated at Langside in 1568, from where she fled to captivity in England. In the aftermath of the battle, Moray punished those who had supported her and many Hamilton properties were destroyed or forfeited.

One story, discredited as fictional creation by Sir Walter Scott, has Sir James Bellenden being granted Hamilton's estate at Woodhouselee. In taking possession he turned Hamilton's naked wife and infant child out of their home in winter. The baby died and his wife became insane, dying later. Hamilton took his revenge.

David Hamilton had been granted the lands of Monkton Mains in 1545 and acquired the lands of Bothwellhaugh on the death of his father around 1568. He was the 5th son of Gavin Hamilton of Orbistan. David's son, James, inherited Bothwellhaugh and married one of the Sinclair heiresses of Woodhouselee in Midlothian. Another son, David, inherited Monkton Mains and apparently married the other Woodhouselee heiress. Both are said to have fought at Langside in 1568. It has been suggested that both brothers and their wives lived at Bothwellhaugh and that the later summons were served for both at that house. A third brother became Provost of Bothwell. A daughter, Janet, is said to have married Muirhead of Lauchope. All of the brothers were charged with treason in the aftermath of the murder, along with their mother Christian Schaw, Muirhead and Claud Hamilton Commendator of Paisley Abbey. The charges related to the assistance given to James in his escape to France where he died in 1581.

James's uncle, John Hamilton, the Archbishop of St Andrews, owned the house in Linlithgow used in the assassination. He was captured at Dumbarton and tried and hanged for his part. David was forfeited and excluded from the Treaty of Perth in 1573, but by an act of 1592 was reinstated. He gained his brother's property at Bothwellhaugh from James's daughter, Alison. David is buried at Crosbie Kirkyard in Ayrshire. His tombstone gives a date of 1619 for his death; however Hamilton of Wishaw states that this is erroneous and that he died in 1613. As Wishaw says 'such errors are to be expected in matters of this kind'.

For an interim period from 1581 to c.1586 Captain James Stewart of the King's Guard was granted the Earldom of Arran. A second son of the Ochiltree family and a confidante of Esme Stewart, Duke of Lennox, and James VI, he used his influence to have the incumbent James Hamilton, 3rd Earl, pronounced insane. James Stewart was styled 'of Bothwellmuir' or sometimes 'of Bothwellhaugh'. It may be that during the period of David's forfeiture he had gained Bothwellhaugh, but he was murdered in 1596.

David was succeeded by his son, David, and then by his grandson James, who is mentioned in a deed of 'Clare Constat' for Monkton Mains (later called Fairfield) by the Earl of Abercorn in 1628. Bothwellhaugh remained with the wider Hamilton family until the 20th century.

BOTURICH CASTLE

The Lennox & East Dunbartonshire Private OS 56 NS 387845

1.5 miles north of Balloch, by minor roads north of the A811, on the southern shore of Loch Lomond.

Site of a 15th century castle, now occupied by a castellated mansion of the same name, built by John Buchanan to a design by Robert Lugar in 1830. The stump of an old L-plan tower was apparently incorporated into the house.

The original tower may have been built by the Duchess of Albany and Countess of Lennox, Isabelle, who died in 1450. She was the widow of the Duke of Albany and daughter of the Earl of Lennox. Albany and Lennox were both forfeited and executed for treason on the return to Scotland of James I following his long imprisonment in England. Having been kept in custody at Tantallon for many years, Isabelle was finally released to live out her life at Inchmurrin Castle.

The estate came to the Haldanes of Gleneagles. John Haldane of this family died at Flodden in 1513. Boturich is mentioned in Sir David Lindsay's 16th century poem, 'Squire Meldrum'. In the poem, Haldane's widow was the beautiful Marion Lawson, daughter of Lawson of Humbie. The intrepid squire had gone off to Gleneagles to woo Marion, but while there he received news that the MacFarlanes were taking liberties at Boturich and were sacking the castle. Seeing a chance to impress, he gathered as many men as he could and set out to save his lady's house. He apparently succeeded, driving the MacFarlanes out of the estate. He travelled to Edinburgh and came across Stirling of Keir, a rival for Marion's hand. They fought in Leith Loan, but the Squire was outnumbered. Left for dead, his legs and arms badly injured, he survived to live out his days at his estate of Cleish and Binns.

The estate of Knockour, of which Boturich was part, was sold to the Buchanans of Ardoch in 1792. They had Robert Adam draw up plans for 'Knockour Castle', which was never built. It is possible that these plans were intended to provide an extension at Boturich. In 1830 the Buchanans had Lugar design and build the present house. It was sold again in the 1850s to the Findlays who still own it. Boturich is available for hire as a wedding or conference venue, though overnight accommodation is not available since the property remains a family home (www.boturich.co.uk).

Other references: Baturich, Knockour

BOWER OF WANDEL

South Lanarkshire   Ruin or site   OS 72   NS 952288
About 3.5 miles north of Abington, just west of A73, 1.5 miles north of junction with M74, on east bank of River Clyde, at Bower of Wandel.

The remains of a tower house of the Jardines.
On a rocky eminence part of a basement with gunloops survive of an almost square 15th century tower house. There is an unlikely suggestion in one reference of a secondary tower once attached to the southeastern corner. The knoll is surmounted by a shaped mound which may once have been a motte and is bounded on three sides by a loop of the Clyde. In 1955 the remaining walls were recorded as 6ft high and 6ft thick. At that time the

springing for a vaulted basement was also visible on the northwest wall. The remains are 'B' Listed.
Wandel Parish appears to have been divided into two baronies at an early date. One portion became what is now known as Lamington and remained the site of the parish church. In 1116 this portion then known as Quendal was the property of the Bishops of Glasgow.
Hartside is the name of the property on which the Bower is built and is occasionally mentioned as an alternate name for the Barony of Wandel. It has been suggested that the 'de Hartside' family may have resided at the site now occupied by the Bower.
In 1225 William de Hertesheued is mentioned as Sheriff of Lanark, possibly indicating a family link to the Flemings of Biggar. He had appeared in charters as a witness as early as 1198 and as late as 1250, this longevity possibly indicating a father and son of the same name. David II granted Hartside to William Gardino in 1345. He is noted as the ancestor of the Jardines of Applegarth. Hartside was in ward of the Crown in 1359. In 1573 Sir Alexander Jardine was confirmed his estates at Jardinefield in Berwickshire, Applegarth and Sibbaldbie in Dumfrieshire, Hartside and Wandel in Lanarkshire, and Kirkandrews in Kirkcudbright. George Jardine, Professor of Glasgow University, and pioneer of collaborative learning was born at Wandel in 1742.
By the second half of the 18th century it belonged to Lord Douglas and then the Earl of Forfar.
The Bower is traditionally noted as having been used as a hunting lodge by James V and given his association with nearby Boghouse, the tradition cannot be discounted.

BROOMHILL CASTLE

South Lanarkshire   Ruin or site   OS 64   NS 755507
0.5 miles south of Larkhall, on minor roads west of the B7078, east of Avon Water, south of Millheugh, at Broomhill.

Site of Auld Machan Castle, a Hamilton property described as being of four storeys, each a room wide, surmounted by bartizans.
The parish of Dalserf (until 1690 Machan or Machanshire) was Crown property in earliest times, being a part of the Cadzow estate. It became Comyn property until the reign of John Balliol, when it returned to the Crown. Robert I granted it to Walter Fitzgilbert, the ancestor of the Hamilton family, in 1312, upon whose death the estates were divided.
In 1473 James, 1st Lord Hamilton, granted Machan to his illegitimate son John, by Janet Calderwood. John

was later legitimised. In 1516 John Hamilton of Broomhill was present when the Earl of Arran captured Glasgow Castle from the Duke of Albany. David Hamilton of Broomhill accompanied James V to France for his marriage to Queen Madeleine. David died at the Battle of Pinkie in 1547, while trying to free the captured Lord Semple.

At the Reformation an angry crowd approached intent on burning the Hamiltons nearby chapel. Lady Elizabeth Hamilton shouted to the mob 'If ye dinna burn it doon, I'll mak a guid barn o' it'. This promise was apparently kept and a barn it remained until it fell into disrepair in 1724. The chapel site is given as just beyond a railway bridge, off Broomhill Avenue.

The family supported Mary, Queen of Scots, and Sir John Hamilton of Broomhill was wounded and taken prisoner at Langside in 1568, later dying of his wounds. His son Claud fled to France. The castle was torched in 1572 by Sir William Durie, Governor of Berwick as part of the post Langside attacks on Hamilton properties. Claud Hamilton returned after his exile, building Broomhill House upon the foundations of the old castle in 1585.

In 1647 Sir John Hamilton, eldest son of Sir James Hamilton of Broomhill, was created Lord Belhaven. His brother was Patrick Hamilton, Bishop of Galloway, who acquired Broomhill. Patrick had two sons and a daughter. The eldest son John Hamilton became immersed in debt and his bills were paid by his brother-in-law, John Birnie, who gained the estate.

The property apparently came to the Bruces and finally the MacNeill-Hamiltons. The house was demolished after a fire in 1943, leaving only the cellars.

There was apparently a spectral 'Black Lady', a ghost of more recent years. She is supposed to be the spirit of an Indian lady, who was a servant in the house and disappeared c.1900. She was reputedly the mistress of Captain MacNeil-Hamilton, who died in 1924.

Other references: Castle of Auld Machan, Auld Machan Castle

BROWNCASTLE

South Lanarkshire   Ruin or site   OS 71   NS 621431
About 4.5 miles west of Strathaven, by minor roads north of A71, on north bank of Calder Water just east of the confluence with the Browncastle Burn, at West Browncastle.

Site of a small flat-roofed tower, which is illustrated on Charles Ross's map of 1773. It is on record in 1546 when Browncastle is said to have been in the Parish of Torrance, which later amalgamated with that of Kilbride. The property appears on Pont's manuscript map of the end of the 16th century as 'Over Browncastle'.

The Hamiltons of Browncastle are described as an 'old Lanarkshire family'. Andrew Hamilton received a charter of the estate during the reign of Mary, Queen of Scots, the lands were apparently his Douglas mother's inheritance. In 1684 George Hamilton was fined £2,000 Scots for 'non-conformity'. Shortly afterwards the property passed to the Hamiltons of Dalziel. They were still in possession in 1710. A large house here is denoted on Forests map of the early 19th century, the property of 'Cathcart & Graham Esq'. In 1793 this was described as a 'commodious house…lately built'.

BUCHANAN CASTLE

The Lennox & East Dunbartonshire   Private   OS 57   NS 463886
0.5 miles west of Drymen, off minor roads south of B807, and west of A809, at Buchanan Castle Golf Club.

The present structure is a ruinous mansion. Following the burning of Buchanan Old House, the Duke of Montrose commissioned William Burn to build a new mansion, of which the family took possession in 1855. The castle was sold in 1925, following the death of the 5th Duke of Montrose, and was used as a hotel. In World War II there was a military camp and hospital just west of the castle. Some of the huts survive.

In 1940 Hitler's deputy Rudolf Hess flew a solo mission in an attempt to broker peace between the Germans and Britain. Attempting to reach Dungavel to contact the Duke of Hamilton, whom he had met before the war, he crash landed at Floors Farm near Busby and was brought to Buchanan Castle as a prisoner and to be treated for crash injuries.

In the 1950s, the roof was removed in order to avoid paying rates (an old Scottish tax on buildings). The building deteriorated rapidly, though has now been consolidated. The gardens, once designed by Capability Brown, are now occupied by a golf course. The ruins stand as a centre piece of a 20th century housing estate.

In the 2000s, a planning proposal by developers to construct flats within the shell of the building was rejected, since they proposed to remove the internal structure.

BUCHANAN OLD HOUSE

The Lennox & East Dunbartonshire Private OS 57 NS 457888

1 mile west of Drymen, off minor roads south of B807, and west of A809, at Buchanan Castle Golf Club, west of Buchanan Castle.

Buchanan Old House was an L-plan tower house, later extended to form a long rectangular mansion with wings. It is thought to have been begun in 1595 and was demolished then rebuilt in 1724. References to 'the pele' being demolished in 1724 probably refer to the Old House, and describe an 'old tower and a great many other buildings'. It was extended in 1751 and 1789 then burned down in 1850, when only the 18th century additions survived.

This was a seat of the Buchanans of that Ilk until their estates were purchased by the Duke of Montrose in c.1682. It is presumably the Old House which is sketched on Robert Gordon's map of the early 1600s. It shows a large rambling building with numerous towers on the north bank of the Endrick, opposite Kilmaronock. In Blaeu's *Atlas Novus* of the mid 17th century it again appears as a large tower, albeit a little more to the west.

BUCHANAN PELE

The Lennox & East Dunbartonshire Ruin or site OS 57 NS 457886

1 mile west of Drymen, off minor roads south of B807, and west of A809, at Buchanan Castle Golf Club, south of clubhouse.

The oldest house of the Buchanans on this site was said to have stood about 200 paces in front of Buchanan Old House. They possibly moved here from their traditional island stronghold of Clairinsh, in Loch Lomond. A pond on the golf course in this area is said to have been called the Peel Pond. It is formed from a loop in the former course of the River Endrick. No trace of the building survives, though there are reports of old foundations being uncovered in the area. Castle Park in Drymen is supposed to commemorate the building. The family moved to Buchanan Old House c.1600.

To the northwest the Buchanans built a chapel dedicated to St Mary, the ruins of which lie within woodland at the edge of the golf course. It is said to have been built in 1474, possibly giving some indication of when they moved from Clairinsh. The ancient church of St Kentigerna on Inchcailloch remained the parish church. By the 17th century, the Buchanans found the upkeep of two churches inconvenient and allowed it to fall into disrepair. They preferred St Mary's and were castigated by the church authorities for neglecting Inchcailloch. The Buchanans got their way in the end, and in 1621 St Mary's became the parish church. When the Grahams decided to build the new Buchanan Parish Church in 1764, they used the stone from St Mary's.

BURNFOOT

South Lanarkshire Ruin or site OS 72 NS 992404

South of A721, south of Carnwath, and south of B7016 from Libberton by minor road, immediately north of Burnfoot.

Three aerial photographs taken of a field at Burnfoot Farm display very impressive crop marks which have been interpreted as a motte and bailey and an adjacent settlement. The motte site, the more northerly of two ditched enclosures, is roughly 300ft in diameter, roughly circular, and is double ditched. There is a break in the ditch on the eastern side indicating a possible entrance. The second enclosure sits immediately to its south, between it and the farm. It is polygonal and a little larger. It is suggested that this represents a later settlement, since its ditch intersects that of the 'motte'. Resistivity surveys of this site were carried out in 1999 and apparently provided more information. This, however, has not been posted on Canmore. The double ditch may indicate reuse of an older site.

A further ditched rectilinear feature roughly 240 ft long is recorded to the south of the farm.

These sites are located within mile of Shieldhill and of Quothquan, both properties of the Chancellor family.

BUSBY PEEL

South Lanarkshire Private OS 64 NS 594561

2.5 miles west of East Kilbride, 1 mile south of Carmunnock, just east of Busby, at the north side of the junction of the A726 and B766.

On a defensive knoll above the Kittoch Water, Busby Peel consists of an altered 16th century L-plan tower house of four storeys with numerous later extensions. There is a complicated corbelling pattern supporting an ashlar parapet. The roof has been altered and is not original. The remainder of the old tower is harled. The stair tower extends from the northeastern corner and contains a very wide turnpike. This appears to be of the 17th century and replaced a smaller original stair tower in a similar position. From this, a three-storey 19th century extension runs eastward. On the eastern gable of this block, is a low single-storey extension which has replaced a taller structure. An 18th century extension adjoins the southern face of the tower, the lower storey of which may have older origins than the first floor. Recent research conducted for the owner has narrowed the construction date of the tower to the period 1528-34, based on the introduction of the 'peel' place name element.

The estate of Thornton was part of the Comyn barony of Kilbride, which was granted to Robert the High Steward in the 14th century. Just prior to becoming King Robert II, the monarch, granted it to Lindsay of Dunrod. At times several portions of the estate were occupied by families such as the Colquhouns, Warnocks and Taits. This produced local smallholdings, such as Warnock's Thornton, Tait's Thornton and Colquhoun's Thornton. The lands currently known as Thorntonhall are listed separately.

The Lindsays held Thornton-Peill, Braehead, and Cross for themselves, Thornton-Peill probably being 'The Peel'. It seems likely therefore that they built the original tower.

In 1534 the Lindsay portion of Thornton-Peill was purchased, with its superiority, by Sir James Hamilton of Finnart. In 1539, it was incorporated into his barony of Avondale, but in the following year he was executed for treason. In 1540 it appears to have been in the possession of Robert Lindsay of Crossbasket, though this probably refers to the superiority.

By 1547 The Peel was again occupied by Hamiltons, this time by James Hamilton of the Torrance family. In that year he was designated 'of ye Peill', and it is very probably he who, as 'James Hamilton of Torrens', is recorded as Provost of Glasgow in the following year. In 1587, his son, James Hamilton, was in possession and he outlived both of his sons. When Andrew the elder of these died, his widow married James Hamilton of Kirktonholme who 'took responsibility' for her daughters, Margaret and Beatrix. James took the designation 'of the Peill'. In 1600, Margaret married her cousin James Hamilton of Corsehill, and took up her inheritance.

In 1611 Peill-Thorntoun was erected into a barony for James Marquis of Hamilton, and this seems to coincide with him becoming the superior of the property. In 1620 James Hamilton of The Peill, by this time Margaret's widower, received a remission for the murder of John Lithgow. Despite having two children by Margaret, it was William, his second son from a subsequent marriage, who in 1639 styled himself the second son of James Hamilton of The Peill. By that time the property had passed from their ownership.

From 1633 until at least 1662 it belonged to Archibald Fleming, whose initials can be seen on a sundial high on the southeastern corner. In 1663 it was occupied by Sir Ludovick Stewart of Minto, who seems to have rented the property. In 1701 it was owned by William Somerville of Kennox who may have gained the estate through his wife, Margaret Fleming. It was purchased by the merchant Robert Robertson in 1725 and sold again in 1774 to Alexander Houston of Jordanhill. He purchased both the property, and the superiority. His son, Andrew, held it in 1793 when it was lying vacant and, as the Rev. David Ure pointed out, could be made 'commodious' with a little effort.

In the same year it was sold to John Muir, another Glasgow merchant. The superiority seems to have returned to the Dukes of Hamilton around the time of the Houston's bankruptcy in 1795. The Muir family owned The Peel until at least 1847, but seem to have rented it out. In 1843 the family were living in Peel Farm, while The Peel was occupied by the architect Robert Foote, who had Alexander 'Greek' Thompson as an apprentice.

By the 1860s the Strang family were in residence and seem to have still stayed until at least 1896. They were followed by the Flemings, Stevensons and, for the duration of World War II, the Aitkens. During their tenure The

Peel hosted the Battalion Headquarters for the 5th Lanarkshire Home Guard, after which it was purchased by the Dick family, who still own it. The family run a furniture and interior design business from the property.

Ure, in his *History of Rutherglen and Kilbride*, singled out a particularly unusual feature, 'The Compass, containing the 32 points, is painted on the ceiling of the uppermost apartment; the index, which is fixed to an iron rod that goes through the roof, is directed by the wind in whatever point it blows.' This has long since been removed.

The Peel and stables are category 'A' Listed Buildings, while the lodge is category 'B'.

http://www.johndickandson.co.uk/

Other references: Peel, Peil, Peilhowis, Peill, Peill-Thornton, The Peel, The Peill, Thornton Peill

CADDER CASTLE

The Lennox and East Dunbartonshire Private OS 64 NS 606727

Off minor roads 0.75 miles north of A803, on south bank of River Kelvin, At Cadder House, Cawder Golf Course, Bishopbriggs

The mansion of Cawder House is now a golf club house but dates in part from 1624. It stands slightly north of the site of a castle and close to the line of the Antonine Wall. The northern wall of the west wing incorporates a carved Roman stone from the wall. An earthwork castle of the Stirlings stood close to Cadder Kirk, to the southeast.

In 1815 workmen discovered the foundations of the old tower below the front lawn of the house. They also uncovered a coin hoard said to be of no earlier than 1428. The hoard consisted of 380 gold coins, some inscribed 'Jacobus'. Later accounts state that 118 lions of James I and James II plus 23 other coins were recovered.

The Stirlings of Cadder were given a grant of the parish of Cadder in the 12th century by the Bishop of Glasgow. Allegedly originally Comyns, the family became hereditary Sheriffs of Stirling and adopted the surname. Cadder was the chiefly line and the family were first recorded in 1147. Later, seniority passed to the Stirlings of Craigbarnet and then to those of Glorat. In 1866, Sir William Stirling succeeded to the Maxwell estates of Pollok and adopted the additional surname, creating the line of Stirling-Maxwell of Cadder, Pollok and Keir.

Some old maps refer to the site as Broken Tower. In other reference sources this name is more correctly attached to Tower, at nearby Torrance. The name seems to have strayed a little.

Cadder Castle appears as a particularly tall tower and courtyard within a park on Pont's 16th century map. Cawder House, the stables, doocot, icehouse and a bridge form a group of 'A' Listed Buildings on this site.

Other references: Broken Tower, Calder Castle, Cawder Castle, Cawdor Castle

CADDER MOTTE

The Lennox and East Dunbartonshire Ruin or site OS 64 NS 614725

1 mile northeast of Bishopbriggs, by minor roads northwest of A803, 100yds north of Cadder Kirk, at Cadder.

Site of an earthwork castle, now completely removed by quarrying. It was roughly square and measured 54ft by 52ft. In 1936 it was described as 12ft high, surrounded by a ditch and rampart, which on the northwestern side was about 2ft high on the interior edge, though sloped sharply for about 8ft on the exterior. Early 20th century excavations illustrated that the ditch had been broad and flat bottomed; medieval pottery fragments were found.

This is probably the original seat of the Stirlings, granted Cadder by the Bishops of Glasgow in the 12th century. Thoraldus, Sheriff of Stirling was the 1st of Cadder, and is named in a charter of David I in 1147. John de Striveling, 4th of Cadder, was Sheriff of Stirling in the mid-late 13th century. His third son, Sir William de Striveling, paid homage to Edward I in 1296. It is from William that the Stirlings of Rathoran and Keir were descended. Sir John de Striveling, 6th of Cadder, died at the Battle of Halidon Hill in 1333 and William, 8th laird, was one of the hostages taken for the return of James I in 1424.

By the 16th century the family were using Stirling as the preferred version of their name.

CADZOW CASTLE

South Lanarkshire Ruin or site OS 64 NS 735538

1.5 miles southeast of Hamilton, on minor roads south of the A72, in Hamilton High Parks, on southern side of Avon gorge, opposite Chatelherault.

Cadzow Castle consists of a very ruinous 16th century tower house within a courtyard, extended by the addition of an outer courtyard enclosed on three sides by various buildings. A wide ditch protected the approaches from the south and west, while the deep and precipitous gorge of the Avon Water protected it on the north and steeply

sloping ground protects the east. It is thought that Cadzow was built by Sir James Hamilton of Finnart on behalf of his half-brother, the 2nd Earl of Arran.

Interpretation of the ruins has provided difficulties, as in the mid 18th century and early 19th century stone from the site had been used in an extensive landscaping of Hamilton High Parks, a project which included the remodelling of the ruin itself to provide a romantic and scenic outlook from the later hunting lodge at Chatelherault. This has altered and disguised much of the original layout, particularly within the older inner ward.

Excavations in the years after the millennium have shed some light on the development and structure of the site, though they examined only sections of the ruin and considerable amounts of work are still required. The results to date have altered long held notions that Cadzow, like its contemporary at Craignethan, had been constructed principally with the ability to defend itself with and against artillery. The notion that it occupied a much older site has also been called into question. To date no evidence has been found to support the idea that the site had been developed before the 16th century. Interpretation of the site now indicates that it was constructed as a hunting lodge, later extended to support a larger household and improve the guest accommodation demanded by the Hamiltons' rapidly ascending social status.

The original structure on site is now believed to have consisted of a large almost square tower house with vaulted basements and wooden floors over a minimum of two storeys. There was probably a hall on the first floor. A narrower eastern wing of at least three storeys was later extended into the courtyard on its north. There were at least two large north facing windows here. Fragments of an oriel window were recovered and there was probably a wall-walk or exterior gallery. The vaulted cellars in the northwestern corner of the courtyard occupied a lower terrace of the bedrock which dropped off to the northern side. Their roof provided a level base for a courtyard above. There was a well in the northwestern corner.

The courtyard was bounded on all sides by a wall with two round corner towers on the southern flanks. There was a gateway on the west side accessed by a bascule bridge over the ditch. This area has been badly affected by the later landscaping and may have supported a gatehouse. The exact layout within the courtyard has not been fully determined, since the later aesthetic remodelling of the site completely filled the area of the courtyard, and excavation has not yet penetrated adequately due to the unstable nature of the infill. The corner towers of the courtyard have been excavated, illustrating that gunloops could provide defensive cover down the lines on the ditch, but had been inserted as later adaptations. The inner ward was defended by an original ditch on the south and west sides. Large quantities of monogrammed glazed floor tiles were found here, which are identical to samples at Linlithgow Palace. This could be taken as reinforcing the widely held belief that Finnart was involved in the construction of Cadzow. He was involved in simultaneous work at Linlithgow in his role of Master of Works to James V and it has been postulated that he acquired them from there

The outer ward is protected on the southwestern approach by a ditch 660ft long, up to 5ft deep, and of varying widths of 23 and 34 ft wide. This takes on slightly smaller proportions at its western end where it turns north for a short distance to meet the Avon gorge. It has been suggested that this ditch is a 'pale' designed to retain animals for the hunt within the deer park to the south, though the dimensions indicate defence as the primary purpose. The outer ward sits to the west of the inner ward and consists of the remains of at least two ranges which enclose a yard on the north, west and partially on the south. These have received little attention from the archaeologists. However, a host of windows in the northern wall overlooking the gorge display the facade of an impressive two-storey block.

The ruins are slowly being consolidated. Public viewing is restricted by a perimeter fence due to the unstable, crumbling and dangerous nature of the structure.

Cadzow was the original name of the estate and parish of Hamilton. Both names are used to describe the barony, town and a variety of different sites. This has caused considerable ambiguity in determining the history of a particular site. Many historians had considered this location to be the likely site of an earlier castle, though other sites in the area have also required deliberation. It has also meant that disentangling accounts of the history and attacks on the various Cadzow/Hamilton castles is difficult when using documentary sources.

In 1455 the name of Hamilton was formally adopted for the town and district. This honoured the award of a Lordship of Parliament to Sir James Hamilton. His son's marriage to Princess Mary Stewart, the sister of James III, emphasised the importance that the family had established on the national scene. He gained the title Earl of Arran and in the reign of Mary, Queen of Scots, the 2nd earl was appointed Governor of the Realm. He was then awarded the title Duke of Chatelherault by Henri II of France. Mary, Queen of Scots, stayed in Cadzow during her flight from Lochleven Castle in 1568. The Hamiltons were the leading supporters of Mary. Following her defeat at Langside her opponents, led by her half brother the Regent Moray, and his successors, turned their attention to diffusing the power of the Hamiltons.

In 1570 the Earl of Lennox besieged the castle and it capitulated within two days. In 1579 forces under the direction of the Regent Mar captured and dismantled it.

In the 18th century the ruin became part of the formal landscape of Hamilton Palace, a development conducted by William Adam. Further landscaping and alteration of the ruin was carried out by the 10th Duke of Hamilton in the 19th century.

Hamilton High Parks were purchased by the Scottish Executive to allow renovation of Chatelherault. This was then returned to the local council, though Cadzow was retained under the control of the RCAHMS. The long term plan is to fully consolidate the ruin, and allow public access.

The grounds of Chatelherault and the High Parks are open to the public.

Consolidation of the castle is being conducted by Historic Scotland.

Park open throughout year, excepting Christmas and New Year (tel 01698 426213).

CAIRNCURRAN

Renfrewshire Ruin or site OS 63 NS 318699
About 4 miles west of Kilmacolm, on the B788, at Cairncurran.

Site of an old or fortified house of the Cunninghames. The site is marked on Pont's map of the late 16th century.

William Cunninghame, 1st of Cairncurran, was the second son of William Cunninghame, 2nd of Craigends, and so great-grandson of Alexander Cunninghame, 1st Earl of Glencairn. In 1534 William received the lands of Cairncurran from his mother, Giles Campbell, who had acquired them from John, Lord Lyle, in the same year. His son Gabriel succeeded him, followed by an uninterrupted series of nine Williams. The eighth of these uprooted the family, taking them a few miles from their old house high in the moors to New Cairncurran, which he built afresh in 1722. Now known as Carruth House, this property lies southwest of Bridge of Weir to the south of Quarriers Village. This second house was rebuilt again c.1782. Charles Cunninghame inherited in 1802, and was succeeded by another William in 1861. By that time the family were resident in Glasgow.

CAIRNIE CASTLE

South Lanarkshire Ruin or site OS 71 NS 853438
On the A72, above the south bank of Clyde near Stonebyres Falls, within grounds of Hydro Electric Power Station.

Possible site of a castle. Greenshields in his *Annals of Lesmahagow* tells that above Stonebyres Falls there stood an old castle or stronghold. He cites the *Old Statistical Account* which states that 'a series of narrow archways' were found at a place called Cairny Castle about 1794; the site has also been recorded as Cairns Castle. One had a corbelled roof, was about 3.5ft high, and 7-8ft long. It was found to contain querns, antlers and animal bones. The original description appears in the entry for Lanark Parish and draws comparison with Iron Age structures.

The possible building remains noted at the time are more likely to be the remains of Stonebyres Linn Mill, which had disappeared by the mid 19th century. It was depicted on Roy's map of the mid 18th century.

A tower close to this location does appear on Pont's map of the late 16th century, marked as 'Kilbanck', though this represents Gillbank House.

Other references: Gilbank, Kilbanck

CALDERWOOD CASTLE

South Lanarkshire   Ruin or site   OS 64   NS 662552
1 mile northeast of East Kilbride, on minor roads south of A725, west of River Calder.

Calderwood was a massive keep of 69ft by 40ft, and 87.5ft high. There appear to be no records of the construction of the castle, though it may have been of an early date. Some sources credit Sir James Hamilton of Finnart with the building of Calderwood, though there was certainly some structure on site before his time, and there is said to be evidence of the existence of a tower in 1450. The building collapsed into the Calder in 1773. The remaining outbuildings were later enclosed within a mansion, which was extended in 1840.

The site is on a promontory, the sides of which retain stone revetment and other in situ stonework. This includes a steep though badly-worn staircase. There is a great deal of rubble strewn about the slopes, much of which is now overgrown. The summit of the promontory is now a flat grassy area, though early images of the castle illustrate that the ground was not as level as it is now. There has been extensive landscaping and remodelling of the site to accommodate later development. The original keep seems to have stood considerably higher than the other early buildings, being on a knoll at the eastern end of the promontory.

There are numerous garden features of the later mansion within the nearby woodland. These include the lower courses of a summer house, garden terracing, stairs, and long sections of wall which protects pedestrians from a steep fall into the Calder gorge below. The old gates and lodge at the entry to the drive are some distance to the north on Stoneymeadow Road, opposite Crossbasket. The mansion was mostly demolished for safety reasons in 1947 and the remaining octagonal tower blown up in 1951.

Calderwood was the property of a family of the same name. Isabele de Calderwood rendered homage to Edward I in 1296. Sir John Maxwell of Pollok and his wife were granted a portion of the lands of Badruel in Perthshire by David, Earl of Strathearn, in 1372. They exchanged this with Sir Bernard Haldane for the Barony of Jackton in Kilbride parish in 1398. This presumably included Calderwood. They settled the Calderwood estate on their second surviving son, Sir Robert, in 1401. Sir Robert had married Elizabeth Dennistoun, an heiress who inherited the estates of Nether Finlaystone (Newark), Mauldslie, and Stanley in 1402. Their second son, George, founded the Newark branch of the family. The family seem to have chosen Mauldslie as their home. In 1423 Sir John Maxwell of Calderwood was one of the Scots who negotiated the release of James I from his captivity in England and became one of the hostages for his ransom in 1424. He was one of the escorts of the young Princess Margaret of Scots on her journey to marry the Dauphin of France in 1436. In 1627 Sir James Maxwell of Calderwood was created a baronet of Nova Scotia with the title '1st Baronet Maxwell of Calderwood'. His son, Colonel John Maxwell, died at the Battle of Dunbar in 1650. The last of the line, Sir William, was 9th Baronet. He died without an heir in 1885, though the property probably remained with his widow until 1900. The 1,100-acre estate, including the village of Maxwellton, was purchased by the Scottish Co-operative Wholesale Society (SCWS) who grew oats, fruit and vegetables on one half of estate, renting out the other half. Troops were stationed in the castle from 1940–45 and it was purchased by the East Kilbride Development Corporation in 1947. Since 1982 the castle site and those grounds which lie along the Calder have been part of Calderglen Country Park, which also includes part of the former Torrance estate.

CALDWELL TOWER

Renfrewshire   Ruin or site   OS 64   NS 422551
2 miles north of Lugton, 4 miles southwest of Neilston, on north side of B776, 1 mile west of Uplawmoor, 0.5 miles west of junction with A736.

Caldwell Tower overlooks the valley of the Lugton Water from a lofty position at the end of a ridge. It consists of a small square 16th century tower of three storeys, and probably had a garret in its original form. There is a parapet supported by two layers of chequered corbelling, though the parapet itself may have been replaced.

The basement is entered from its own door in the west front. It consists of a single vaulted chamber with fireplace and slit windows. There is no access to the upper floors.

The main entrance is at first floor level in the north wall, now reached by a stairway built against the walling, though originally there would have been a removable stair. A mural stair gives access to the floor above. The hall on the first floor is also vaulted and has a fireplace and garderobe. There are small windows illuminating each of the floors above basement level. These have sealed up gunloops below and simple roll mouldings above.

The tower was renovated on several occasions, possibly as a folly or as a riding shelter. It may contain elements of an older structure and is very probably the only remnant of a much larger castle.

The estate belonged to the Caldwells of that Ilk, until passing by marriage to Gilchrist Mure in the 14th century. The Mures of Caldwell were a cadet branch of the chiefly line of Mure of Rowallan. After the capture of David II at Neville's Cross in 1346, Sir William Mure of Caldwell was one of the negotiators who bargained for the king's release and was held hostage until the ransom was paid in full. John Mure of Caldwell attacked Glasgow Castle with artillery in 1515 before making off with plunder, including the bishop's personal belongings. He was tried, found guilty and forced to remunerate the bishop. The family were involved in a dispute with the Pollok Maxwells regarding ownership of Glanderston in the 15th century. When Sir John Mure of Caldwell was murdered in 1570, the Cunninghames of Aiket were tried and acquitted.

William Mure was involved in the Covenanter Pentland Rising which ended in defeat at Rullion Green in 1666. This slippery character had intended to join the Covenanters, leading 50 friends, but found his way barred by the king's men. Mure sided with the prosecution against the others to save his own skin. He went into self-imposed exile and his forfeited estate was given to Dalziel of The Binns. The family returned in 1698 to reclaim their estate, though do not appear to have reoccupied the tower. They lived at a mansion on the lands of Ramshead, which they built for themselves in 1712, until moving to their new mansion at Caldwell House in 1773. This was designed by James and Robert Adam and was their home until 1909. From 1927-1985 it was used as a specialist hospital, since when it has suffered serious fire damage and has lost the roof. It is now considered at risk and is ruinous, while plans are being drawn up to convert it into flats.

There is an unlikely local legend which said that a tunnel led from the house to the Lugton Inn.

Other reference: Tower of Caldwell.

CAMBUSNETHAN

North Lanarkshire   Ruin or site   OS 64   NS 779519

1 mile west of Overtown, west of A71, and south of Castlehill Road, by foot, 100yds southwest of Cambusnethan House.

Site of a large tower, which appears in Blaeu's *Atlas Novus* of the 17th century as 'Kawslethead'. Careful examination of Pont's late 16th century map shows a cluttered and indistinct area at this location, out of which emerges the name Cambusnethan.

The Barony of Cambusnethan is said to have been held by William Finnemund at the beginning of the 12th century. Ralph de Clare was in possession in c.1185, when he granted Kelso Abbey the right to grind grain before anyone else at his mill at Cambusnethan. In addition he granted them the church of Cambusnethan and 'the teinds, multure, and exit' of the mill. In the same year we find favour returned and Ralph is granted the right to build a private chapel. Sometime before 1226 he granted the land of Garrion to Paisley Abbey.

The Barony of Cambusnethan was apparently granted to the Bairds by Robert I. Sir Robert Baird erected a large square tower of four storeys in the 14th century and it is said to have remained 'entire' until 1661. Sir Robert was forfeited and executed for treason in 1340, possibly a result of having favoured Edward Balliol in his attempt to take the throne from David II.

King David then granted Cambusnethan to Sir John Edmonstone. His heiress married John, Lord Somerville, who granted it to his son John, whose descendants held it for several

centuries. Many portions of the Barony were feued out to form separate estates, or sold off to such as the Hamiltons, who bought Wishaw, and the Stewarts, who purchased Coltness. In 1520 John Somerville of Cambusnethan backed the wrong side in the Edinburgh skirmish known as 'Cleanse the Causeway'. In defeat he was declared forfeit. The victorious Earl of Arran, on the other hand, saw James V award Cambusnethan to Sir James Hamilton of Finnart in 1524. Somerville was restored to his estate 20 years later. What remained of the estate passed to Somerville of Drum on the death of the last of the Cambusnethan line in 1659. He then sold it to Sir John Harper in 1661, who found the tower in such a state of decay that he had it pulled down and built the first Cambusnethan House. Sir John left the estate to his daughter who had married Lockhart of Castlehill.

In the early 19th century, Cambusnethan House burned down, and the Sinclair-Lockharts commissioned James Gillespie Graham to build anew. The second, splendidly gothic, Cambusnethan House is also known as Cambusnethan Priory and was the family home into the 20th century. It eventually came into use as a hotel. This venture folded in 1984, since when the house has decayed and fallen victim to vandals. It is now on the Buildings at Risk Register.

Other references: Baird's Tower, Kawslethead

CAMERON

North Lanarkshire Ruin or site OS 64 NS 776706
1 mile east of A73, north of B803, by minor roads 0.25 miles west of Greengairs at Cameron Farm.

Site of a small tower house, illustrated on Pont's manuscript of 1596, and subsequently in Blaeu's *Atlas Novus*. On Pont it is labelled 'Kamro' and on later maps there was a place called Yett, a little to the west of the modern farm.

Other reference: Yett

CAMERON HOUSE

The Lennox & East Dunbartonshire Private OS 56 NS 375831
On the west bank of Loch Lomond, east of A82, 1.5 miles north of Balloch.

The Scots Baronial mansion of the Smolletts stands on the site of previous houses dating back to the 15th century. This was part of the estates of the Earls of Lennox, passing to the Dennistouns of Colgrain, who apparently built a house here in about 1480. The Colquhouns acquired it from Walter Dennistoun in 1612. It was feued out to two families named Smith and Shaw, before being purchased from them by Donald Govan in 1696. He sold it to the Glasgow merchant, Hugh MacLachlan, in 1749, who in turn sold it to Colonel Charteris of Amisfield in 1756. From him, it was acquired by the Smolletts in 1763. They moved here from Bonhill, since their old home was falling into disrepair. Tobias Smollett the novelist was entertained in the house in 1766 by his cousin James Smollett. Boswell and Dr Johnson stayed overnight in 1772 after visiting Rossdhu. James died a few years later and Cameron and Bonhill passed to his cousin, Jane, and her husband, Alexander Telfer, who adopted the name Telfer-Smollett. The grounds were opened as a Bear Park in 1972, though by 1986 the venture was failing. The family sold the estate in 1986, when it became a hotel and leisure centre.

The old house had cellars dating back to the 15th century, and drawings of it were apparently retained by the Telfer Smolletts. They renovated and extended the building when they bought the estate, and added a new facade in 1806. The present building was designed by William Spence for the family in 1830. It was burned out in 1865, then renovated and extended. It may still incorporate portions of the old house. The house required further alterations when converted to use as a hotel. It has developed into a renowned 5-star hotel and resort, occasionally frequented by 'A list' celebrities and used as a base by the Scottish national football team before international matches at Hampden Park.

Supernatural objects are said to appear in the house and the freezing over of Loch Lomond was said to herald the death of one of the family in residence.

CAMPHILL

City of Glasgow Ruin or site OS 64 NS 577621
In Queen's Park, Glasgow, west of A77 and north of Langside Avenue.

Camphill is a medieval earthwork which sits on a hill within Queen's Park. It consists of an oval enclosure within a bank, which runs over the summit of the hill and the western shoulder. It measures 390ft by 327ft. The rampart is badly eroded in places. A circuit road within the park covers the position once occupied by a ditch. On the east and southeast the rampart reaches a height of 7-8ft, and 5-6ft internally, being 25-30ft thick. There is a gap on the southeast which was probably the entrance. This is 22ft wide and another of 25ft wide in the southwest was proposed as another possible entrance. Various interpretations had been made as to the nature of the site, stating that there is a Roman connection, or that the earthwork was built in preparation of the site for the Battle of Langside in 1568, since it occupies the hillside chosen by the Regent Moray to array his troops. Excavations of 1951, however, concluded that this was a 'clay castle', within which a portion of paved floor was uncovered. From other sources it is supposed that this may have been the original caput of the barony and family of Cathcart. Excavations revealed a portion of the paved floor was covered by a layer of charred oats and oak pieces, leading to the conclusion that this had been a corn-drying kiln. Excavation of the site of the ditch produced pottery sherds of no later than the 14th century from its base.

A little to the south of Camphill stands a memorial to the Battle of Langside, the estate of Battlefield and the names of local streets also commemorate the final defeat of Mary, Queen of Scots, prior to her flight to England. Legends abound in the park and vicinity regarding the aftermath of the battle. The park is named after Mary, Queen of Scots, and not Queen Victoria as many assume. The pond in the park is known as the 'Deil's Kirkyaird', a reference to the story that when the pond was dug out the bones of dead soldiers were uncovered with their weapons. Similarly bodies are alleged to have been uncovered at the site of a local bowling club and that area has the name 'Dead Man's Lea'.

CAMSTRADDAN CASTLE

The Lennox & East Dunbartonshire   Private   OS 56   NS 360921
On west bank of Loch Lomond, 0.5 miles south of Luss, east of A82, near Camstraddan House.

Sites of castles of the Colquhouns. References dating back to 1600 describe the original seat of the Colquhouns at Camstraddan as having stood on an island in the bay. This island site is listed as a possible crannog, but was apparently large enough to support both the castle and an orchard. It was visible as late as the end of the 19th century in low water conditions. The island apparently 'sank' in the 16th century, though a rise in the level of the loch is a more likely explanation. In the 19th century a heap of stones about 20yds offshore was considered to be a cairn raised upon the former island to mark the shallow for boats. Recent archaeological survey has failed to locate this, although one shallow area in the bay is considered as a possible location.

The Colquhouns relocated to a site on the shore prior to 1600 and in 1684 a three-storey addition, measuring 20ft by 15ft, was made to the tower. It was replaced by a mansion of 1739. The present Camstraddan House is an early 19th century classical mansion with late 19th century additions. It may occupy the site of the tower, of which no trace remains.

Robert Colquhoun, 1st Laird of Camstraddan, was a second son of Sir Robert Colquhoun, 7th of Luss. He gained the estate from his brother in 1395. The 6th Laird of Camstraddan fought at the Battle of Pinkie in 1547. A younger son of the laird fought with the Regent Moray at Langside in 1568. The sons of Colquhoun of Camstraddan were killed at the Battle of Glenfruin in 1603. 1625 saw the creation of a baronetcy of Nova Scotia for the Colquhouns, this title later passed through a son-in-law to the Grants. In 1698 Colquhoun of Luss purchased the Camstraddan estates and rented them back to the Laird of Camstraddan. Camstraddan bought them back in 1713. The arrangement seems to have been made to allow funds for the repayment of debts, but the returned lands did not include the lucrative 'slate crags'. During the 1715 rebellion Colquhoun of Camstraddan led some like-minded allies in the 'Loch Lomond Expedition', whereby they captured all the boats on the loch to prevent their use by the MacGregors, who wished to join up with the Jacobite Earl of Mar. In 1786, under the British system, the family were again granted a baronetcy.

In 1833 Sir Robert Gilmour Colquhoun KCB of Camstraddan purchased Fincastle in Perthshire. He had served for seven years as Consul General in Egypt and was the last of the Camstraddan line. He died at Fincastle in 1870.

Camstraddan at some point returned to the Colquhouns of Luss. It became the home of the Luss Estates factor. Sir Ivar Colquhoun settled his family here shortly after his marriage in 1943, later moving to Rossdhu, then returning in 1972. He died at Camstraddan in 2008, aged 92. He had been chief of the name for 60 years and had successfully reinvigorated the estate. He was succeeded by his second son, Malcolm Rory Colquhoun of Luss, 9th Baronet.

The house, wall, gate piers and sundial are 'B' Listed structures.

Other reference: Castle of Camstraddan

CANDER

South Lanarkshire Site or ruin OS 64 NS 767474
0.5 miles southeast of Stonehouse, south of the A71, and the Avon Gorge, at or near Canderside Mains.

The old castle or tower of Cander stood high above the Cander Water. It was becoming ruinous by 1700 and nothing now remains. It appears as 'Kand' on both Pont's map of the late 16th century and Blaeu's *Atlas* of the mid 17th century.

This was a Hamilton property, and the Hamiltons of Cander are credited by some sources as being one of the four senior lines of the family. In 1473 Cander belonged to James Hamilton of Broomhill, being one of the properties granted to him by his father, the 1st Lord Hamilton. The family appear regularly in records throughout the remainder of the 15th and 16th centuries. In 1595 Margaret Hamilton, the daughter of John Hamilton, married the illegitimate son of Lord Claud Hamilton. She had succeeded on the death of her brother Cuthbert. They had a son, another Cuthbert, who inherited the estate in 1621. In 1632 he granted Cander to the Hamiltons of Broomhill and then in 1662 reversed this and 'wadset' Cander to the Hamiltons of Millburn. There was another Cuthbert Hamilton of Cander listed as heritor in the Parish of Stonehouse in 1712, though by his time the castle was much decayed.

CARBETH CASTLE

The Lennox & East Dunbartonshire Private OS 57 NS 524876
At Carbeth House, Killearn, on minor roads north of the A875/B818 junction.

Carbeth from 'Caer Beath', the fort of life.

A 15th century tower of the Buchanans previously occupied this site. They held the lands by grant of the Grahams from 1476. The Buchanans of Carbeth were an important cadet line of the family, and descended from Thomas, 3rd son of Walter Buchanan of that Ilk, and Isabella, daughter of Murdoch, Duke of Albany. There were 11 Buchanan lairds in all, John the last dying in 1872. His two daughters sold the estate. The Wilsons then had possession and Sir David Wilson was given a baronetcy in 1920 for his services to agriculture. The Wilsons of Carbeth now live in Surrey.

The present mansion dates in part from the 17th century and may incorporate part of the old castle. It was remodelled as a castellated mansion in 1840 and was subsequently altered in 1879. It was converted into flats in the 1980s and is a category 'B' Listed Building.

CARDARROCH HOUSE

City of Glasgow Ruin or site OS 64 NS 638695
2 miles east of Bishopbriggs, and 3 miles southwest of Lenzie, just south of B812, 0.5 miles east of Robroyston Mains, near Wallace's Well.

Nothing remains of this 'transitional' two-storey house with attic, dated 1625. Originally on the L-plan, a small stair tower extended from the northwest corner of the main block. It had comparatively thick exterior walls and the gables were corbiestepped. A wide staircase went to the first floor and then a steep narrow stair led to the attic.

In 1718 an extension was added to the west of the main block, creating a T-plan. The interior of the old block was adapted in the modernisation at that time, altering the appearance of the house from that of a small fortified house, to that of a comfortable 18th century house. This included window enlargement and the construction of a porch.

A building to the north was originally a carriage house with doocot on the upper floor, though this building was converted to provide another house.

This was described by the writer Hugh McDonald in the 19th century as 'a queer-looking old structure, with peaked gables, crowsteps, narrow windows, and a picturesque old doorway'. A painting of Cardarroch, dated 1898 by

1718   1625

William Simpson, is held in the collection of Glasgow Museums and Art Galleries.

The house may have been occupied in the 16th century by the Heriot family, as tenants of the Archbishop of Glasgow. They later sublet to Sinclairs. The house was occupied by William Din in 1627 and was the property of John Fleming in 1634. By 1710 it belonged to the Glasgow merchant, Matthew Cumming. Later in the 18th century it was owned by the Peters of Crossbasket, who had their main residence in Craigmaddie House. One of this family was Thomas Peter, Dean of Guild of Glasgow in 1707-09, who left funds 'for the sustenation of an honest decayed and poor man of the merchants rank, being a burgess, guild brother, and inhabitant of the burgh.' At some point it was occupied by the 19th century poet Walter Watson. By the end of the 19th century it was home to several families of weavers and labourers. Foundations were still visible in the 1970s.

CARDONALD PLACE

City of Glasgow   Ruin or site   OS 64   NS 526635
On minor roads south of A8, in Cardonald, at end of Cardonald Place Road, on north bank of White Cart Water, 0.75 miles north of Crookston Castle, at former Cardonald Place Farm.

Place equates to 'Palace' or 'Palis', an old Scots word for a hall house.

Cardonald Place was a large two-storey hall house of 1565. It was demolished in 1848 to make way for the present 19th century farmhouse, which contains an armorial stone dated 1565 from the original building.

The lands of Cardonald belonged to Johannes Norwald and his descendants until it passed by marriage to the Stewarts of Darnley in 1487. The first laird was Allan Stewart, who was apparently a son of John Stewart, Earl of Lennox, though there remains some doubt as to his legitimacy. He had married Marion Stewart the daughter of William Stewart of Castlemilk and Isabella Norwald. Allan's grandson, James Stewart, built the castle in 1565 and his initials adorn the armorial stone mentioned. This bears the arms of Stewart, crossed by a black diagonal bar signifying illegitimacy, though this may have been added in error at some restoration. The stone also depicts a helmet and the motto *Toujours Avant*, meaning always forward, or always in front.

James Stewart died in 1584 and is buried in Paisley Abbey. His epitaph indicates that he was once Captain of the Scots Guard to the French Royal house. On his death, the estate passed to his nephew, Walter Stewart of Minto, Commendator of Blantyre Priory. He had been a childhood companion of James VI and became Lord Blantyre in 1606. His wife was unhappy living at the priory and moved with her daughters to Cardonald.

One of Walter's grand daughters was Frances Theresa, *La Belle Stewart,* who so infatuated the courtiers at London that Charles II had her model as Britannia. She was willing to marry 'any gentleman of £1500 a year who would have her in honour'. She eventually wed the Duke of Richmond and Lennox. Lennoxlove, near Haddington in East Lothian, is named after her following her generosity to the Stewart Lord Blantyre, who then owned that property. Lennoxlove is currently home to the Duke of Hamilton.

The family purchased the Erskine estates and moved to Erskine House, now the renowned hospital for ex-servicemen. The 12th and last Lord Blantyre died in 1909, the estate passing to the Laird family of Erskine and Lennoxlove.

Cardonald Place Farm was purchased by the City of Glasgow in 1926 and for many years the house and farm functioned as a nursery for the City Parks Department. It was sold, then renovated and is now occupied as a family home.

CARDROSS MANOR HOUSE

The Lennox & East Dunbartonshire   NTS   OS 63   NS 385759
In Dumbarton, 0.5 miles west of River Leven, just north of A814, north of Brucehill, adjacent to Notre Dame School, at Castlehill.

A large mound within a small area of parkland held by the NTS commemorates the death place of King Robert I (the Bruce). The Parish of Cardross once extended as far as the River Leven and the medieval church remains as a ruin within Levengrove Park.

In about 1326 Bruce looked for a suitable site to build a comfortable retirement home after his years of warring with the English. He chose the parish of Cardross and obtained it by exchanging Royal estates with local landowners, principally Sir David Graham. This gained the Grahams the estate of Old Montrose, with which the family are normally associated.

Argument has raged over the years as to whether this was a castle or not; however ancient documentation describes it as a 'manororium', or manor house. No evidence exists to suggest that the structure was fortified. Documentation reveals that it had a single stone wall bordering the king's apartment. It had thatched roofs and some of the windows were glazed. It was a large building, with a separate chamber for the queen, a chapel, a hall, and from 1328 a 'new chamber'. There was a garden and a hunting park with a specially built falcon house surrounded by hedging. The king was known to have kept galleys here to sail the western seas, including one he called his 'great ship'. There are records showing that it was pulled up for repairs into the burn which ran beside the house.

Speculation continues as to the location of the manor which, despite the best efforts of enthusiasts, remains elusive. Only thorough archaeological investigation could confirm the true site, assuming that traces survive. Archaeology could establish the nature of the mound at Castlehill, which may simply be a natural rock outcrop.

Bruce died here in 1329, his heart was removed and taken on crusade as he requested. It was carried in a silver casket by Sir James Douglas. He, with many of his entourage, died in battle against the Moors in Grenada. Bruce's heart was returned to Scotland and interred in Melrose Abbey, while his body was buried at the Abbey of Dunfermline. The manor does not appear to have been used after his death. The estate was absorbed into the castle lands of Dumbarton, remaining Crown property and providing revenues used to maintain the castle.

CARFIN

North Lanarkshire   Ruin or site   OS 64   NS 769575
1 mile south of Carfin and B7029, east of A723 by minor roads and foot, within former site of Ravenscraig Steelworks, a little west of Carfin Bridge.

'Caerfin' appears as a large tower close to a bridge on the west bank of the South Calder on Pont's map of the late 16th century. A mansion named Carfin House was built on the site, although this was demolished in 1937.

This was Baillie property, which was apparently purchased by the Nisbets in 1677. They were certainly in possession by 1710. It is said they sold it in 1787, moving to Holmhead and renaming it Carfin. By the 20th century the estate belonged to the Graemes, a wine merchant family.

The Baillies of Carfin are said to be the most senior of the cadet lines of the family. They claimed descent from Alexander, second son of the first William Baillie of Lamington.

In 1488 Alexander Baillie of Carfin sued William Hamilton over wrongful occupation of Carnbroe. In 1512 Cuthbert Baillie of Carfin was Lord High Treasurer to James IV. In 1556 James Baillie, younger of Carfin, was one of a jury who convicted John Whiteford of that Ilk and others of the 'oppression' of Charles, the tutor of Pollok.

In 1604 John Hamilton of Orbistan is said to have held a charter of various lands, including the Baillie properties of Carfin, Jerviston and Carnbroe. He seems to have been the feudal superior.

William Baillie of Carfin was appointed one of the Lanarkshire Commissioners for War at a Parliament of 1643. In 1650 he, with Baillie of Lamington, co-wrote one of the appendices later included in William Hamilton of Wishaw's *Descriptions of the Sherriffdoms of Lanark and Renfrew*. The Baillies of Parboath and those of Jerviston were said to be descended from the Baillies of Carfin.

Other references: Caerfin, Carphin

CARMICHAEL HOUSE

South Lanarkshire   Private   OS 72   NS 936390
5 miles south of Lanark, on minor roads west of A73, north of Cleuch Burn, at Carmichael.

Site of a 14th century castle. In 1710 Carmichael House was described as 'a good substantious old house, much repaired and well finished of late'. It appears in Pont's map of the late 16th century as a large tower and again in Blaeu's *Atlas Novus* of the 17th century.

The present structure consists only of the walls of two wings, between which are the remains of a central tower and linking corridor. The west wing is dated c.1754, and the east wing from about 20 years later. The central part of the structure was never completed. The buildings were occupied until used to billet Polish soldiers during World War II. Post war, the Carmichael-Anstruthers sold it for use as a nursing home; however this enterprise failed and the property was repurchased by the family. The roofs were removed in 1954 to avoid payment of rates and a demolition sale proceeded when all fixtures, fittings, doors and windows were sold. This left the present empty shell. The remains of the ornamental gardens contain many fine examples of decorative stonework and host regular clan gatherings.

The Carmichaels first appear in record when Robert de Carmilety (Carmichael) resigned his rights to the church at Cleghorn in 1220. The family are said to have devolved their name from that of Kirkmichael Parish and built their home within the bounds of an ancient fort, hence Caer or Carmichael. The church is reputed to be one of the original churches founded by St Margaret. It was dedicated to St Michael in 1058. It is not known if the

family were indigenous or of Norman descent, though one genealogy conducted for the family claimed they were descended from a Norman knight, who took his name from Mon St Michel in Normandy.

A William de Carmichael is mentioned in 1225 in a charter of Lindores Abbey. Sir John Carmichael received a charter of his lands from the Earl of Douglas in 1374–84. John Carmichael slew the Duke of Clarence, brother of Henry V of England, at the Battle of Baugé in 1421. The family crest of a broken spear commemorates this. In 1424 John Carmichael was present at the Battle of Verneuil. On the death of the Bishop of Orleans, he was appointed as the next bishop in recognition of the participation of the Scots and became known to French history as Jean de St Michel.

In 1528 William Carmichael of that Ilk had a charter of the Barony of Carmichael. Sir John Carmichael of that Ilk was Warden of the West marches. In 1566 he was one of the murderers of David Rizzio, secretary to Mary, Queen of Scots. He was Scottish Ambassador to Denmark in 1588 and was himself murdered by the Armstrongs in 1600. His daughter Mary, or Marion, was Lady in Waiting to Anne of Denmark, wife of James VI. His son, Sir Hugh, was also an Ambassador to Denmark, a Privy Counsellor then Master of the Horse in 1593. He gained his father's old position of Warden of the West March by 1602.

In 1633/34 the title passed to a cousin, James Carmichael of Meadowflat and Hyndford. James was created 1st Baronet Carmichael of Westraw and Hyndford in 1627, and served as Chamberlain of Scotland between 1627 and 1630. He was knighted by Charles I in 1632 while Sheriff of Lanarkshire and became a Privy Counsellor in 1634. In 1636 he was Treasurer Depute of Scotland and was a Lord of Session in 1639. He was an 'engager' for the release of Charles I and was created 1st Lord Carmichael in 1647. He held the position of Lord Justice Clerk from 1649 until relieved of office by Cromwell and fined £2,000 by 'The Act of Grace', whereby the people of Scotland were pardoned by Cromwell and absorbed within the Commonwealth.

His son John died at Marston Moor in 1644 fighting for the Royalists. Another son, James, fought at Dunbar in 1650 against the Parliamentarians. His other son, William, Master of Carmichael fought for the Parliamentarians at Marston Moor then against Montrose at Philiphaugh in 1645. William was Lieutenant Colonel in the Clydesdale Regiment. He married the daughter of Lord Douglas and their son, John, succeeded his grandfather. He was created Earl of Hyndford, Viscount Inglisberry and Nemphlar in 1701. He was secretary to King William.

John Carmichael, 3rd Earl, was a British Envoy to the courts of Prussia and Russia in the 1740s and was a Hanoverian. It was he who built the present house on the site of the old castle. He was Lord of the Bedchamber, Member of the Privy Counsel, and Knight of the Thistle. The house is mentioned as being unoccupied in the *Old Statistical Account*.

The estate passed to the Anstruthers in 1817, who changed their name to Carmichael-Anstruther. The present chief, named Carmichael, inherited the estate in 1980 from his cousin allowing the estate and chiefs to be reunited for the first time since 1817. They still own the estate, which operates the Carmichael Clan Association, farm, deer farm, holiday cottages and sawmill. The Carmichael Heritage Centre nearby features family history of the Carmichaels and other lowland families. It has a small wax work featuring characters from Scottish history (www.carmichael.co.uk).

On Carmichael Hill above the house, is a monument to Lord Hyndford, erected in 1774. This, with the house, and a large collection of other structures form a group of 'B' Listed buildings.

CARMUNNOCK

City of Glasgow   Ruin or sites   OS 64   NS 600570, various sites.
At or near Carmunnock village, within Carmunnock Parish, 1 mile east of Busby and north of A726, by B759 or B766.

The name Carmunnock comes from 'Caer Mynnock', the 'monk's fort', which some believe to refer to St Cadoc.

There are a number of sites within the old parish of Carmunnock, including Castlemilk, Cathkin and unconfirmed sites such as a promontory site on the Kittoch. The earliest antiquity in the area is the earthwork which comprises one of the greens on Cathkin Golf Course. It has been suggested that it is the remnant of a medieval ringwork castle. Alternatively it may be the site of an Iron Age settlement, or the site of the now vanished early burial mound known as Queen Mary's Cairn. It consists of a circular enclosure surrounded by a ditch 18ft wide and 3ft deep. A breach in the ditch on the east appears to be the entrance, while the south and west sides are hidden within an area of tree planting. Another possible entrance on the southeast is considered to be later damage to the site. A further circular enclosure attached to the rim has been detected. It has a diameter of 66ft, and a crop mark near its centre 6ft by 3ft has the dimensions of a burial.

Both this site and Castlehill at Kittochside have been suggested as possible seats of the Norman lord, Henry son of Anselm, who gifted the church of Carmunnock to Paisley Abbey before 1189. He had a son, also named Henry, who may have succeeded and is mentioned in a charter granted at Inchcolm in the late 12th century. A Steven de Cormanough appeared in the Ragman Roll of 1296 giving homage to Edward I.

Carmunnock joined Drumsagard, Avondale and Bothwell in becoming part of the estates of Maurice Murray, Sheriff of Clydesdale. His daughter and heiress, Johanna of Bothwell, took it to her husband Archibald the Grim, Earl of Douglas, when they married in 1362. One source cites *The Exchequer Rolls* to indicate that the Douglases had two castles in Carmunnock. It is likely that they were located at the sites later occupied by Cathkin and Castlemilk.

The widow of the 5th Earl, Euphemia Graham, had been granted a 'terce', which included Bothwell. She exchanged this with the 6th Earl, James the Gross, for the baronies of Carmunnock and Drumsagard, taking them to her new husband, James Hamilton of Cadzow. This was confirmed by Royal Charter just prior to the forfeiture of the Douglases in 1455. They divided the estate, and feud the Cassiltoun portion to the Stewarts of Castlemilk, Dumfrieshire. The Hamiltons retained the feudal superiority of the estate until their portion was gained by the Hamiltons of Westburn. The Stewarts became patrons of the church at Carmunnock in the 18th century.

CARNBROE HOUSE

North Lanarkshire   Ruin or site   OS 64   NS 735623
2 miles south of Coatbridge, east of junction of B7070 and A725, above south bank of North Calder Water, west of Carnbroe Mains Farm.

Carnbroe House was a much altered 16th century L-plan tower house of three storeys and a garret, which was demolished in the mid 20th century.

Two round towers projected from the main block. There were three vaulted chambers in the basement and a hall on the first floor. There was apparently an Adam fireplace, indicating a degree of modernisation at some point in the 18th century. The tower at 'Karnbru' appears on Pont's map of the late 16th century and appears again as 'Karnbrun' in Blaeu's *Atlas Novus* of the mid 17th century.

It may seem strange that a name so well known today as an area of Coatbridge was not originally a part of the Monklands, but fell within the Barony and Parish of Bothwell. Some explanation can be given by the location of the house, which was on the south bank of the Calder Water, the parish boundary.

Prior to 1226 the monks of Paisley Abbey had a gift of land from Uctred, son of Pagan, of the lands of Carnbroe. Uchtred had died by 1256 when his grant was again mentioned in a letter from Pope Clement IV to the Abbey and Convent at Paisley.

There is no record of when the Baillies gained Carnbroe, but the William Baillie of Lamington, who married Marion Seaton c.1430, is recorded as being the grandson of William Baillie of Hoprig, Penston and Carnbroe. It is said that in 1488 Alexander Baillie 'of Carfyn' brought a law suit against Christian Inglis and her husband, William Hamilton of Orbistan, for wrongful occupation of 'Carnbro' over a period of six years. The following year William Hamilton complained that Baillie had not proceeded with the summons and a few years later in 1471 Baillie sued Robert Hamilton over the estate.

In 1619 William Baillie of Carnbroe is mentioned as a merchant in Poland, where his lawyers raised a legal action to retrieve payment of debts owed by another Scottish merchant, Alexander Nisbet. Major General Matthew Baillie of Carnbroe was the last of the line to occupy the house. He sold the estate in the early 19th century, and died in Nice in 1825. His son Matthew lived at Cambusnethan.

Carnbroe belonged to John Meiklham (or MacIlwham) by 1816 when Forrest drew his map of Lanarkshire naming it 'Cairnbroe'. The property is now owned by the Miss I.D. Meiklham Trust.

CARNTYNEHALL

City Of Glasgow   Ruin or site   OS 64   NS 636652
A little south of Carntynehall Road at Carntyne Square, Glasgow.

The old or fortified house of the Grays of Carntyne stood here from the late 16th century until Carntyne House was built in 1802. The hall was partly demolished and came into use as farm buildings and as a residence for the estate factor. 'Carntyne' appears in Pont's map of the late 16th century as an indistinct entry, possibly a small tower.

Carntyne is first mentioned in a letter from Pope Urban III to Brother Jocelyn, Bishop of Glasgow in 1186. It was one of the properties listed as belonging to the Church of Glasgow when it was taken directly under Papal authority without intermediary.

The Grays seem to have gained Carntyne at the Reformation. It is said that the family owned Tollcross until about the middle of the 16th century when two brothers had a legal dispute which caused them to sell the estate. James was a lawyer and instigated the suit, while John the heir became the progenitor of the Carntyne family. He is said to have purchased Carntyne with the proceeds of the sale of Tollcross.

The family acquired part of the Dalmarnock estate in 1678 and for a century thereafter were known as the Grays of Dalmarnock. It was about this time that another John Gray began the coal workings on the Carntyne estate. John was a zealous Covenanter and achieved some notoriety for providing shelter and concealment to his proscribed friends. He died in 1687 and was succeeded by his son, another John. He was a Jacobite and prepared himself to join the rebellion in 1715. He had married Elizabeth Hamilton of Newton, who informed on him, leading to his imprisonment until the rebellion had settled. This betrayal does not appear to have adversely affected their relationship, as they produced seven children. Their grandson, James, inherited and also married an Elizabeth Hamilton of Newton. However, the estate later passed to his brother John. He found the estate immersed in debt and sold their lands at Dalmarnock and Newlands in 1784.

Carntyne was famous for the wealth of coal reserves. The family apparently produced enough coal from the Westmuir Pit alone to supply the whole of Glasgow. The pits were notorious for flooding and were drained by means of a windmill, which was eventually destroyed by a storm. They introduced a steam engine to drain the pits in 1768, at that time a unique project for the west of Scotland. There were increasing difficulties in effectively removing water and so production ceased in 1875.

The last Gray of Carntyne was the Reverend John H. Gray, who held a ministry in Derbyshire and managed the estate by letter. When 13 years old, he had been painted Sir Henry Raeburn. On his death, the estate passed to his daughter and her husband, the Anstruther-Thompsons of Charleton and Carntyne. Carntyne came to their 3rd son, who dropped the Thompson in favour of Gray. He was William Anstruther-Gray of Kilmany and Carntyne, who had a distinguished career as a soldier, politician and was well known as an antiquary. He died in 1938.

Carntyne housing estate was built in the 1930s and now covers most of the old property.

CARNWATH HOUSE

South Lanarkshire   Ruin or site   OS 72   NS 976464
At western end of Carnwath, north of A70 opposite church.

Carnwath House contained part of an earlier structure, possibly a castle of the 16th or 17th century. It had been extended in 1820 and the early work hidden within the southeast wing. The new building was a plain two-storey mansion. When portions of the harling fell away, blocked window recesses of an earlier style were found. The house was used as the club house for the local golf club, but was demolished in 1970 when new facilities were built.

The earliest fortification here is represented by the motte of Sir John Somerville, which stands conspicuously on the golf course near the western approach to the town. The Somervilles owned Carnwath from 1140. Gilbert, 8th Lord Somerville, disponed the estate to John Erskine, Earl of Mar, during the reign of James VI. He gifted the estate to his son, James Erskine, Earl of Buchan. In 1630 it was sold to Robert, 2nd Lord Dalzell. He was created Earl of Carnwath in 1639. In 1643 he was accused by the Scottish Convention of betraying them to the king. Found guilty, they sentenced him to death, though commuted this to a fine of £10,000. As a result he had to sell his Dalzell estates to his nephew, James Hamilton of Boggs, in 1649. He fought for the Royalists at the Battle of Naseby in 1645.

The Dalzells retained the title as Lords Dalzell and Earls of Carnwath when they sold the estate to Sir George Lockhart, second son of Lockhart of Lee, in 1681. The Dalzells were a Jacobite family who were forfeited following the rising of 1715, the attainder being lifted in 1826. They had a family home named Carnwath House in Fulham, London. The family died out in 1941 on the death of the 13th Earl.

Sir George Lockhart of Carnwath, mentioned above, was a noted lawyer whose eloquence was famously persuasive. He was MP for Lanarkshire, Lord President of the Court of Session, and became a Privy Counsellor and Commissioner of the Exchequer in 1686. He was shot dead in Edinburgh by John Chiesly of Kersewell and Dalry, against whom he had pronounced judgement in court. He was succeeded by his son George, who became a commissioner of the Act of Union but opposed the bill. In 1713 he attempted to have it repealed and published a list of bribes paid by the Westminster government to procure the passage of the bill through the Scottish Parliament. He was a prominent Jacobite and was imprisoned at the outbreak of the 1715 rebellion. On his release he became James the Old Pretender's principle agent and later fled into exile. He died in a duel in 1731. Later Lockharts did not live in the house, using it as an occasional hunting lodge. The golf course was laid out in 1907 on land then known as Gallowhill. It was opened by Lady Lockhart of Lee, wife of the laird.

CARNWATH MILL

South Lanarkshire   Ruin or site   OS 72   NS 997454
1 mile southeast of Carnwath, off minor road south of A721, at Carnwath Mill.

The farmhouse incorporates part of a much altered bastle house. The basement was not vaulted. Only a few original features survive following extensive adaptation. The external walls are 4ft thick, except on the west where the wall is thinner at 2ft. One of the first floor windows on the north side was once the entrance, originally accessed by an external stair. There are a few other small windows on the upper floor which retain sockets for iron bars and rebates for partly glazed leaded windows. There is a date-stone of 1611 with the initials HF and I or JV. It appears as Carnwath Mill in Blaeu's *Atlas Novus* of the 17th century.

Carnwath Mill features in the verses of the traditional drinking song, 'We're No Awa' Tae Bide Awa'
'So whenever friendly friens may meet,
Wherever Scots foregather,
We'll raise oor glass and shout Huroo!
It's Carnwath Mill forever.'

The present complex was a 19th century water-driven lint mill, later converted for use as a farm. In the modern era it became a stud farm. The workers' cottages have been sold off, and the farmhouse is available for holiday let.

CARNWATH MOTTE

South Lanarkshire   Ruin or site   OS 72   NS 975466
Just west of Carnwath and north of A70, adjacent to first green of Carnwath Golf Course.

From before 1140 this was Sir William de Somerville's caput for his barony of Libberton, later Carnwath. A traditional Christmas pudding-shaped motte, traces of the bailey survived until the laying out of the golf course in 1907. A centrally placed shaft full of stones was evident on the summit. This led to the belief that this had been an entrance, and that it was linked to a radial tunnel through the base. The *Old Statistical Account* mentions a 'rude turnpike sort of stair' within this shaft.

The motte stands to a height of 30ft, with diameters of 132ft at the base and 45ft on the elliptical summit. There remains a ditch around the motte and a counter scarp bank to the south, though the ditch is not original. The MacDonald-Lockhart laird dug out a new ditch and planted a hedge around it in the 19th century. In the 18th century the motte was planted with conifers.

Sir William de Somerville was of Norman descent, and was one of those knights granted estates by David I. The first of five Williams, he was a witness to the charter granted by David to found Melrose Abbey in 1136.

Originally Carnwath was within the Parish of Libberton and William built a more convenient church at Carnwath. The Somervilles at this early date seem to have feued out much of Libberton to a number of vassals, but retained superiority.

His son witnessed grants by David I to Kelso Abbey and other charters of Malcolm IV and William the Lion. Another William was granted the estate of Linton in 1174. Traditionally this was a reward for the killing the 'Linton Worm', a dragon which terrorised Roxburghshire. The village of Wormington is allegedly named to commemorate this, and heraldic panel in the church shows a knight spearing the beast through the mouth. Nearby is a cave known as 'Worm's Hole', where it reputedly lived. William was known as 'the Wode laird'. He was knighted, and later gained the office of Royal Falconer. The family quickly established themselves at Couthalley and are on record there by the mid 12th century.

CARSEWELL

Renfrewshire Ruin or site OS 63 NS 227741
2.5 miles southwest of Greenock, 1 mile northeast of Inverkip, immediately west of A78 at Chrisswell.

Site of an old castle. It was inhabited in 1710 but ruinous by 1796. The ruin appears on several late 18th and 19th century maps. Adjacent to the castle site were Christ's Well and a 14th century chapel. This was all practically destroyed in the early 19th century during the construction of a road which drove through the centre leaving the end walls standing at either side of the road. The chapel ruin was denoted as late as 1857, though by this time the castle site was occupied by farm buildings which utilized the well.

The chapel was founded during the reign of Robert III and was endowed with extensive lands in the area. In 1556 the 'Prebendar' of the chapel, Sir Lawrence Galt, granted the estate and lands to the chaplain Sir James Lindsay and his heirs. At some point Christswell came to the Stewarts of Blackhall. In 1679 James Stewart inherited the estate from his father Robert. By 1890 it was incorporated within the Stewarts Ardgowan Estate.

Other references: Christ's Well, Christwall, Crisswell, Cristiswell, Cresswell, Crosswell, Crysswell, Langhouse

CARSTAIRS CASTLE

South Lanarkshire Ruin or site OS 72 NS 939461
Just east of the A70 south of junction with the A721, at northeast corner of Carstairs Village, just northeast of St Mary's Church.

The remains of Carstairs Castle are shown on OS maps up to the end of the 19th century and are described as standing upon a Roman Station. All of these remains are now believed to be from the medieval period, though Roman origins for the site have not been entirely discounted.

A castle here was granted to the Bishops of Glasgow in 1126 and by 1286 rebuilding had begun in stone. The estate may previously have belonged to a family known as 'de Carstairs'. Bishop Robert Wishart was granted an exemption from prosecution for commencing construction without the permission of Edward I of England in 1292. In addition he was given licence to complete it by adding turrets and crenels. He signed a charter here in 1294, indicating that the castle was habitable by then. In 1535 the castle was rented to Sir James Hamilton of Finnart and passed to the Hamiltons of Avondale.

The castle remains were apparently dismantled to provide material for the parish church, which was built in 1794 to replace the earlier St Mary's. Excavation in 1820 revealed old walls, 'gothic stonework' and a 'paved floor of considerable dimensions'. A 'cannon bullet' was found lodged in one of the walls.

Carstairs was created a Burgh of Barony in 1765, and was planned and rebuilt by Henry Monteith, who purchased the estate in 1819. He built himself a Tudor-Gothic mansion, designed by William Burn, which remains as St Charles Hospital. With the exception of the State Hospital and railways, the village is essentially as Monteith planned.

Other references: Casselterras, Casselterres, Casselterris

CARTSBURN

Renfrewshire   Ruin or site   OS 63   NS 287756
1 mile east of Greenock on minor roads south of A8, 0.5 miles south of Firth of Clyde, At Cartsdyke.

Near the Cartsburn stood a tower of the Crawfords, probably dating from the 16th century. It is drawn on Pont's map of Renfrewshire of the late 16th century, just north of Easter Greenock Castle and closer to the southern shore of the Firth of Clyde. The property was also known as Cartsdyke.

The lands of Easter Greenock, of which Cartsburn was part, belonged to the Galbraiths. They passed by marriage to the Crawfords in the 14th century and were part of their barony of Kilbirnie. Easter Greenock Castle was the original seat.

During the 16th century Cartsburn was given to a second son of the family. Sir Patrick Crawford of Cartsburn was denounced as a rebel after fighting for Mary, Queen of Scots, at Langside in 1568. The family line ended with David Crawford during the reign of Charles I and the property passed to the Crawfords of Newton. It returned to the Kilbirnie Crawfords in 1657.

The estate of Cartsburn was recreated by Lady Kilbirnie for her cousin, Sir Thomas Crawford, the second son of Crawford of Jordanhill. It was formed from the lands of Cartsburn, Crawfurdsdyke, and parts of the lands of Easter Greenock Castle. These were erected into a free barony for Sir Thomas in 1669. At the same time, the remaining portion of Easter Greenock was alienated to Sir John Shaw of Greenock.

Sir Thomas Crawford invested heavily in the development of Port Glasgow then lost much of his wealth in the Darien Scheme. His son, George Crawfurd, wrote the first edition of *A History of The Shire of Renfrew* in 1710. Robert Burns stayed at Cartsburn in the late 18th century as a guest of the 4th Baron, another Thomas Crawford.

The house was still standing in the 19th century, when it was drawn from a photograph for *Views and Reminiscences of Old Greenock*, published in 1891. It appears to have consisted of a three-four storey L-plan tower, with a lower wing creating a T-plan mansion. It had subsidiary buildings at the opposite side of a courtyard. This had an arched entrance through the wall, over which an armorial panel and sculpture provided decoration. In 1856 it was described as being a small two-storey house with outbuildings. The date 1672 was noted above one of the windows.

The house was demolished and the site was occupied by Cartsburn School, itself destroyed by German bombing in 1941.

CASTLE BROCKET

South Lanarkshire   Ruin or site   OS 71   NS 735420
4 miles west of Blackwood, and 4 miles southeast of Strathaven, south of A726 adjacent to B7068 at Castle Brocket.

Site of a tower house, which is recorded with a variety of names. It appears in Pont's map of the late 16th century as 'Castel Bretwood', as 'Castle Bratwood' in Blaeu's *Atlas Novus* of the 17th century and as 'Castle Brocket' when depicted as a ruin on maps thereafter. It seems that the original name was Bradewude, but once ruined the name became corrupted to Castle Brocket. Brocket probably means broken or ruined.

The site is depicted as a large ruin on Forrest's map of 1816. It was marked 'Castle, Site of' on Ordnance Survey maps until the early 20th century. It is mentioned in some old descriptions of Avondale as Castle Bradewude in the 19th century. The farm was occupied by the Allan family in 1770, Abraham Torrance in 1820–45 and J. Stobo in 1895, though there appears to be no record of ownership of the castle itself. Compare the entry for Kype.

Other references: Castle Bradewude, Castle Brocker, Castle Bratwood, Castle Bretwood

CASTLE CARY

Falkirk   Private   OS 64   NS 787775

2 miles northeast of Cumbernauld, on minor roads southeast of A80, south of Castlecary Viaduct, east of Red Burn.

Included due to proximity to Cumbernauld, strictly speaking Castlecary stands in the watershed of the Forth.

Castle Cary is protected on three sides by a very steep drop to the Red Burn. It stands close to the site of one of the principal Roman forts associated with the Antonine Wall. The castle is rubble built and is said to incorporate much Roman stone. It is a 40ft-high rectangular 15th century tower of four storeys and a garret. The basement is barrel vaulted. There is a two-storey 17th century extension with attic to the east, and the castle was once surrounded by a deep ditch, which was filled to support this extension. A further lower building stands on an eastward alignment continuous with the extension. There is a small square tower containing a turnpike stair at the northern angle of the main block and the extension. The tower is reported to date from or before 1475 and has a restored crenellated parapet with a wall-walk which is drained by waterspouts. There is a machicolated projection on the north wall at the eastern end, just below parapet level. This is probably a garderobe chute since it is not sited above the entrance at the western end of this wall. There are a number of projecting stones below this which mark the position of a wing which was either never completed or destroyed. The building retains a yett. A gunloop opens from the basement on the south face. A mural turnpike stair within the wall leads from the entrance to a caphouse on the parapet. The interior of the tower has been greatly altered.

The extension carries the date 1679 over the door and enters the main block at basement level. Like the garret, it has corbiestepped gables. There is a walled garden.

It is said that an earlier castle, possibly a motte, stood on the site and that Edward I ordered the Sheriff of Stirling to gather his forces at 'Chastel Kary' in 1304. Standing within Falkirk parish which was largely owned by the Livingstons of Callander, it is hardly surprising that by 1450 Castle Cary is recorded as belonging to a branch of that family. This is when Robert Livingston is said to have been forfeited for treason. It is also reputed that in 1473 Henry Livingston of Middilbyning was in dispute with others over ownership of the estate. Henry and his wife granted the property to their son Patrick in 1491, when the lands were apparently known as Weltoun or Walton and the charter apparently mentions the castle 'to be built' by Henry. The last of the Livingstons of Castle Cary died around 1657. It seems to have gone to the Nicholsons of Carnock, then to the Browns of Seabegs, and thence to the Baillies. It was burned by Jacobites during the 1715 rebellion.

One of its inhabitants was the noted antiquarian Alexander Baillie, who produced a history of the Baillie family. It was his 'history' which popularised the family legend of descent from Balliols and also from the daughter of William Wallace. It may have been his sister Elizabeth (Lizzie) who apparently eloped with her lover, a Graham from the Lennox. She made her exit from Castle Cary by leaping from the parapet into the safety of his plaid. Her father had other marriage plans for her and died when given news of her antics. Her ghost is said to haunt the castle searching for her father. Her story is commemorated in the ballad 'Bonnie Lizzie Baillie'.

In 1730 Bethia Baillie married James Dundas of Fingask taking the estate to her husband. Their descendants became Marquesses of Zetland (Shetland).

The ghost of the Covenanting General William Baillie is also reputed to haunt Castle Cary. He led the army defeated by the Marquis of Montrose at the Battle of Kilsyth in 1645. Escaping the scene and out riding his escorts, Baillie took temporary refuge at Castle Cary. The castle is privately owned and occupied, and may recently have been restored. It is a category 'A' Listed Building.

CASTLEHEAD

Renfrewshire   Ruin or site   OS 64   NS 475633

In Paisley, west of B775, and south of A761, at Castlehead, just south of junction of Main Road and High Road.

Only slight traces remain of a once impressive ditch and rampart, which are thought to be the remains of a Norman ringwork. Landscaping works for nearby Castlehead House in the 19th century may be responsible for the deterioration. Excavation in the 1970s produced a sherd of medieval green glazed pottery, and a red clay jug recovered in the 19th century is now thought to be of medieval origins. This was once thought to be Roman, as was the site.

The remains consist of an overgrown rampart with external ditch. In the 19th century the ramparts were described as being 20ft high externally and 10ft internally on the southeast, while on the west there were no remains. On the east side it was 12ft high externally, and level with the interior. Study of the 25inch OS map of the period shows a roughly D-shaped earthwork of which the straight side is missing. A path passed through the site midway along the eastern side at a break in the ditch. It is possible that this utilised an original entrance.

CASTLEHILL, Bridge of Weir

Renfrewshire Ruin or site OS 63 NS 385651

0.5 miles south of Bridge of Weir, on minor roads south of A761, on Ranfurly Golf Course.

A partly mutilated motte with ditch, sits to the southeast of the ruin of Ranfurly Castle. The mound is rhomboidal in shape with rounded corners. Damage had been caused by landscaping for the golf course, the creation of a tee destroying the southwestern corner of the ditch. Shallow rectangular depressions once recorded on the summit indicate the site of a building, though this is probably not original and may date from World War II.

The RCAHMS give an average diameter of only about 10ft, though 100ft is more accurate. The summit is flat and about 60ft across. The mound rises to a height of around 16.5ft above a flat-bottomed ditch, which is now 6ft wide and 3ft deep. The ditch surrounded all but the western side where a steep natural slope provided protection. Some early archaeological excavation may be responsible for mutilation on the west. Finds from the beginning of the 20th century included Roman pottery, medieval green glazed ware, a bronze key, bones and charcoal.

Interestingly, a description of 1853 provides an alternate description: 'on an elevated rock, over topping the castle, is a green mound, all of forced earth, named Castlehill. It is of a quadrangular form, the sides facing the four cardinal points. A trench, dug out of the solid rock, surrounds its base, on the east, part of the north and south sides; the west side rests on the edge of this steep rock. This mound is 330ft in circumference at the base, 70ft in diameter at the summit, and 20ft high. The top is hollow. There has been an entrance into it on the eastern side.' If this is accurate, it suggests greater landscaping activity than supposed. The site is a Scheduled Ancient monument.

Other reference: Ranfurly Motte

CASTLEHILL, Busby

Renfrewshire Ruin or site OS 64 NS 589563

0.25 miles north of A726, west of Busby Peel, 0.5 miles east of Busby, on south bank of Kittoch Water.

In 1793 it was stated that the last vestiges of an older castle stood about a quarter of a mile to the west of Busby Peel. The removal of stone is recorded from the ruin. This corresponds with the 'motte' known as Castlehill and is said to have been the site of a castle obtained by the Stewarts of Minto c.1490. The estate is said to have previously belonged to the Semples. The Stewarts held the lands of Busby until the reign of James VI, when they sold them to the Dicksons of Inveresk.

The motte consists of a 33ft-high natural eminence, with a flattened oval summit of 56ft by 80ft. All sides are precipitous. There are uncorroborated suggestions of a rampart, terraces and foundations of a possible gatehouse.

CASTLEHILL, Cambusnethan

North Lanarkshire Ruin or site OS 64 NS 789535

1 mile south of A721, at or close to Castlehill House, Gowkthrapple Road, Wishaw.

John Lockhart of Castlehill gained this estate in the reign of Charles II and had a tower house on this site. He was a second son of Lockhart of Lee, a Senator of the College of Justice and a Lord of the Justiciary. His heiress married a Sinclair of Stevenson and their second son adopted the surname Lockhart on inheriting Castlehill. It was probably he who married the heiress of Sir John Edmonstone, gaining the Cambusnethan estate. Castlehill may have burned down prompting a move to Cambusnethan House, though it seems more likely that they moved there before the first Cambusnethan burned, prompting the building of Gillespie Graham's gothic masterpiece.

The present Castlehill House is a two-storey house with outbuildings. It apparently retains a vault and gunloop from the original house and allegedly has a ghost in the form of a headless horseman.

CASTLEHILL, Cartland

South Lanarkshire Ruin or site OS 72 NS 882459

1.5 miles northwest of Lanark, above the gorge of the Mouse Water, on minor roads and by foot east of the A73, west of A706, and south of A72, south of Castlehill Farm.

The overgrown remains of this tower barely protrude through the turf and sit on a promontory site between the deep gullies of two burns. It is defended from the higher ground to the north by two ditches, which separate the site from its only accessible approach. The ruins stood to a maximum height of 7ft when measured in 1955, and are of a rectangular building measuring 36ft by 53ft approx. The ruins are now considered too overgrown to provide accurate measurement.

This is probably Craiglockhart, which was a property of the Lockharts of The Lee, later passing to the Lockharts of Cleghorn. It appears on Pont's map of the 16th century, but the name is illegible. Robert Scott engraved a view of the building with Lockhart Mill in 1795. It is recorded on Forrest's map of 1816 as 'Castle in Ruin'.

An early castle in this vicinity was apparently held by William Wallace prior to an attack on Lanark. He is said to have hidden in a cave on nearby Cartland Craigs, above the Mouse Water, after killing Hazelrig, the English Sheriff of Lanark. Wallace's Cave is now inaccessible but lies just to the north of Telford's Cartland Bridge.

Other reference: Craiglockhart

CASTLEHILL, Hamilton
South Lanarkshire   Ruin or site   OS 64   NS 729548
1 mile south of Hamilton, off minor roads south of the A74, east of Barncluith Road, just south of Fergus Gardens.

In the 19th century the site of an early castle was considered to have been on an eminence above the Coven Burn, west of the Old Avon Bridge. This site was known as Castlehill and a house of that name replaced a small cottage on the site before 1816. By the dawn of the 20th century, the site had been developed as a housing estate.

Until the reigns of the grandsons of David I, much of Clydesdale was Royal demesne land centred upon a stronghold at Cadzow. An early castle here was used as a hunting lodge by David I in the 12th century. Royal charters were issued here as early as 1139.

The Royal estate was divided in 1222 and Alexander II granted the portion at Rossavon to the monks of Kelso Abbey, while at some point Cadzow came to the Comyns. Following their forfeiture, Robert I granted the estate to Walter Fitzgilbert. He hailed from Homildon in Northumberland and the family name developed as Hamilton.

CASTLEHILL, Kittochside
South Lanarkshire   Ruin or site   OS 64   NS 608555
2 miles west of East Kilbride, north of A726, on north bank of Kittoch Water, just south of Kittochside, east of Stewartfield Way, just southwest of Castlehill Green.

A motte on a promontory site, whose northern approach is guarded by an L-shaped ditch, the arms of which are 22ft and 8ft long. In 1793 the Reverend David Ure described this site as being the end portion of a ridge which has been separated from the main section by a ditch, 57ft wide and 11ft deep.

It has a kidney-shaped summit, which is deteriorating due to the result of land slippage, which is clearly evident toward the southern end. The motte has been formed by the deposition of spoil from the ditch to form a platform at the end of the promontory. At present the base of the ditch varies in width from 2–4ft wide, with a depth of 4–6ft. The motte rises to approximately 20ft above the base of the ditch. Agricultural activity over the years has caused the ditch to infill.

At the southern end of the promontory where there is a slightly raised sub–circular platform. The summit rises to almost 60ft above the Kittoch Water and the haughland known as Castleflat. This height is maintained on both east and west sides as the Kittoch takes a wide loop around the site.

Archaeological test digs were carried out on the ditch and the area to the north of the site in 1994 in advance of housing development. No dating evidence was found though the results did confirm that the area had been subject to intense cultivation. This site has often been associated with Henry son of Anselm, Lord of Carmunnock, in the 12th century, despite now lying within Kilbride Parish. A number of complex early boundary changes may account for this, though it seems likely that the site has always lain just outside the affected area and has consistently been within Kilbride. The site is a Scheduled Ancient Monument. Only 200yds away on the opposite side of the Kittoch is Rough Hill, another motte which once supported a stone tower. Compare: Carmunnock and Comyn's Castle for historical background.

CASTLEHILL, Symington

South Lanarkshire   Ruin or site   OS 72   NS 993345
4.5 miles west of Biggar, 0.5 miles southeast of Symington, east of A73, and south of its junction with the A72, south of Castlehill Farm, by foot.

This wooded knoll supports an oval enclosure within a bank of earth and stone, which varies between 13 and 26ft thick. It covers an area measuring 171ft by 141ft and has an entrance 12ft wide on its east side. The embankment has been cut through on the southwestern side. Early reports of mortared stone within the embankment have now been dismissed as natural deposits with concretion. It is overlooked on the north by the slightly higher summit of the knoll. To the east on the sloping ground below the site, another slightly smaller oval enclosure has been detected by aerial photography. Symington Mains Farm sits a little way to the south, which gives tentative place-name support to a medieval origin for this earthwork. This is one of the sites in the area which is said to have been the original manor of Simon Loccard, who gave his name to the settlement in the late 12th century.

Castlehill is a Scheduled Ancient Monument, but as yet has not been dated or classified by excavation.

CASTLE LEVAN

Renfrewshire   Private   OS 63   NS 216764
1.5 miles southwest of Gourock, on minor roads south of A70, just south of Firth of Clyde, at Levan.

Castle Levan stands high above a ravine in a strongly defensive position overlooking the Firth of Clyde. At variance with the L-plan, it consists of two blocks of separate dates linked at one corner. The older main block, to which the owners attribute a date of c.1457, certainly dates from the late 14th or early 15th century. It has been altered when the extension was added. This is a little smaller and dates from the 16th century. Each is of three storeys and a garret, with a parapet, wall-walk and open rounds at the corners, all supported on chequered corbelling. The walls reach 5ft in thickness and have many arrow slots and small windows. The corbelling and parapet of the older block was altered to match the style of the extension.

There are three entrances, all on the north in the re-entrant. One is more recent and enters the extension at the ground floor. Two are original and are in the main block. The first at ground level would originally have only accessed the ground floor. It now leads to a mural stair and thence the first floor of the main block. Two vaulted cellar rooms can be entered from a linking corridor between the stair and door. The original main entrance was at first-floor level, accessing the hall and has been enlarged. The recessed windows of the hall have stone seating. Mural stairways access the floors above.

The smaller block has been added to provide additional amenities, the vaulted basement providing storage and the first floor hosts a kitchen with large fireplace. A mural turnpike has been carved out within the adjoining wall between the two blocks. It provides access to both at ground and first floor level.

Levan was a property of the Morton family, and there may have been an earlier building on the site. It was sold to the Semples by Adam Morton 'of Levane' before 1539, although other sources say Adam alienated the lands to Lord Semple in 1547 the year of his death. At this time Semple had the property absorbed into his own barony. James Morton, son of the previous laird, was not happy and took out an interdict forbidding Semple from collecting his revenues from the estate. Semple eventually won a prolonged legal battle. In 1649 the Stewarts of Inverkip, later known as Shaw-Stewart, gained the estate.

Parts of the upper floors collapsed as the structure fell into ruin. It has been sympathetically restored and has been occupied since the late 1980s. It stands close to a 19th century mansion of the same name, which is now used as a hotel.

There is apparently a 'White Lady' who haunts Levan. She is said to represent Lady Montgomery, who mistreated the peasantry and as punishment was starved to death by her husband.

Levan can provide Bed & Breakfast accommodation (www.castle-levan.com).

CASTLEMILK

City of Glasgow   Ruin or site
OS 64   NS 609595

In Castlemilk, just East of Machrie Drive, and south of Oak Tree Gardens, on knoll above pond, at children's' play area.

The stump of a 15th century tower is all that remains of Castlemilk, a much-altered castle which was extended to form a grand mansion of the 18th and 19th centuries. The original keep latterly formed the entrance block and was of three storeys with an added parapet and garret. The knoll was once separated from the top of the ridge by a deep ditch, filled in the 19th century.

There are many remnants of post-medieval estate buildings scattered around the area, such as the stables, estate offices, bridges, dams etc. Preserved within the stables is a hugely impressive 19th century carved oak fireplace, which depicts scenes from the Siege of Orleans in 1429. It had been saved at the demolition of the castle and had been a feature of the main hall.

Originally these lands were known, as 'Cassiltoun', being the castle town of the parish of Carmunnock. An ancient motte in the woodland to the east of Tormusk Road is one of several early fortified sites within the old parish. See the Carmunnock entry for the earlier history of the estate. The Hamiltons of Cadzow had a grant of confirmation of the estate of Carmunnock in 1455. They feud out the 'Cassiltoun' portion to the Stewarts of Castlemilk (in Dumfriesshire).

This family were descended from Alexander, 4th High Steward of Scotland, via his son Sir John Stewart of Bonkyl who died in the Battle of Falkirk in 1298. He was ancestor to the Stewart Earls of Buchan, the Lords of Lorn, Garlies, Dalswinton, Darnley and Castlemilk. His fourth son, John, was ancestor of the original Castlemilk line and died with three of his brothers at the Battle of Halidon Hill in 1333. The title later passed to the family of another of the sons of Sir John of Bonkyl, from whom both the Darnley and later Castlemilk lines stem. Sir William Stewart of Castlemilk and his younger half-brother, Sir John of Darnley, fought for the Dauphin, later Charles VII, and Joan of Arc at the siege of Orleans in 1429. The brothers died at nearby Rouvray in a conflict known as the Battle of the Herrings, where they were trying to disrupt supplies to the English besiegers. The 19th century oak fireplace mentioned above commemorates their part in the siege.

It is thought the Stewarts built Castleton c.1460, some say on the site of a 13th century castle. They sold their Dumfriesshire estate in 1579 to Lord Maxwell and transferred the name to their new home. Castlemilk was one of the houses which claimed to have provided lodging for Mary, Queen of Scots, the night before the Battle of Langside in 1568. A room in the house was named Queen Mary's Room and was decorated to commemorate the alleged event. The house had been burned in the aftermath of Langside.

Given their close relationship to the Darnley Stewarts and Mary's marriage into that family, the Castlemilk family saw themselves as close kin to future generations of Stewart monarchs. It has been suggested that this provided the impetus behind the purchase of the remaining portions of the parish from the Hamiltons and the extension of the house into a grand mansion, befitting their status as royal cousins. Additionally the suggestion is that it was a desire to re-emphasise their earlier connections to the Stewarts which prompted the change of name of the property and a later change in the spelling of their name to Stuart.

In 1662, James Stewart, the 2nd son of the Castlemilk laird, foreclosed on the debts of Hamilton of Torrance. His descendant, Andrew Stewart, united both estates when his uncle, John Stewart of Castlemilk, died without an heir and Andrew inherited. A noted genealogist, he was Rector of Glasgow University from 1777-79. He wrote a genealogy of the House of Stewart, through which he hoped to stake a claim for his family as the senior representatives of the Royal Stewarts.

It was the 18th century before the name Castlemilk was used confidently in local records as the name of the estate, though the family had consistently used that title. By this time the church at Carmunnock was now regarded as being dependant on the goodwill and financial support of the family. Their burial vault remains a feature of the present church.

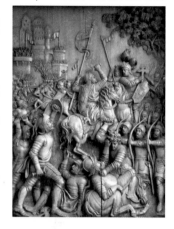

In 1706 they inherited the large estate of Milton on the north of the City. This inheritance was dependant on them including the name Crawford in their own and, since by this time, they had adopted the French style of their surname and had married into the family of Stirling of Keir, their name had become Crawford Stirling Stuart.

The Milton estate was large, including the modern areas of Balornock, Barmulloch, Milton, Hyndland, Possil and Cowcaddens. It was particularly rich in coal and was feud to the city, much increasing the wealth of the family.

In 1938 the last laird died. The estate was sold to the city and from 1948 the castle was used as a children's home. This closed in the early 1960s, after much public and media protest, the castle was demolished in 1969. Lady Helen, a surviving daughter of the last laird, died in a nursing home in Carmunnock in the 1970s.

The recently renovated stables and a bridge are 'B' Listed. The woodlands which remain in the area are the remnants of the park surrounding the house and abound in supernatural tales. There were reported sightings of a 'White Lady' near a bridge over the burn, a 'Green Lady', and an ancient Scottish soldier, who allegedly fired a ghostly arrow into the back of the head of a local, causing stitches to be inserted!

Then there was the 'Mad Major', who was said to ride at speed in the moonlight up to the doors of the house. This apparition was believed to represent the return of Captain William Stirling Stuart from Waterloo. It is reported that the Major's horse was buried in the grounds. Compare Carmunnock.

Other references: Cassiltoun, Castleton

CASTLE SEMPLE

Renfrewshire   Ruin or site   OS 63   NS 377601

2 miles northeast of Lochwinnoch, on minor roads west of A737 and Howwood, just east of Semple Collegiate Church, and just west of Low Semple.

Site of a medieval castle. 'Castle Semple, the principal messwage of a fair lordship of the same denomination'. Originally known as Castleton, the castle was demolished in about 1730 to clear the site for Castle Semple House, a classical mansion built in 1735 and itself mostly demolished in the 1960s. The remaining structures are the mansion's stable block and peripheral walling with gates and lodge. Castle Semple appears as a massive tower complex at the head of Castle Loch on Pont's map of the late 16th century.

The Semples lived at Elliston, though built 'Castleton' either in 1492-3 or 1550; sources differ and either date may indicate an extension since Castleton appears in a charter as early as 1474. Crawfurd described it as a large court, part of which seemed to be 'a very ancient building'. The foundations were uncovered in 1836 when a drain was being dug.

The Semple, Semphill, Sempie or Sempill family owned the estate from at least as early as the 14th century. They were recorded as being Stewards of the Barony of Renfrew. Sir Robert Semple appears as a charter witness in 1246 and later as Chamberlain of Renfrew.

James III granted William Semple a charter, probably a confirmation, of the lands of Elliston and Castleton in 1474. Some sources indicate that Sir Thomas Semple fell at the Battle of Sauchieburn in 1488. Crawford, however, says that Thomas died in 1486, and that his son John was at Sauchieburn, having been created Lord Semple in the same year. He founded the nearby Collegiate Church in 1505 and was killed at Flodden in 1513. His tomb can still be seen within the ruins of the church. His son William extended the family estates, adding Leven, Glassford and numerous others to their landholding. He was one of a group summonsed for treason by James V in 1526, having allegedly been involved in the murder of the servant of Robert Douglas of Lochleven. He is also said to have murdered William Cunninghame of Craigends in 1533. Robert, 3rd Lord, became known as the 'Great Lord

Semple'. He was captured after the Battle of Pinkie in 1547. In 1560 the castle was besieged and captured by reformers due to Robert's firm adherence to Mary, Queen of Scots. After the murder of Darnley he switched his support to the infant James VI, being one of those who signed a bond to protect the young king. Robert was against Mary at Carberry Hill in 1567. He led the vanguard for the Regent Moray at Langside in 1568 and was granted the forfeited Paisley Abbey estates of Lord Claud Hamilton as reward. Hamilton regained these at a later date. Robert was succeeded by his grandson, another Robert. He was tutored by the Regent Morton and became a Privy Counsellor to James VI and Ambassador to Spain.

The family opposed the Jacobites and fought with the Hanoverians in the risings of 1715 and 1745, appearing at Culloden in 1746 where the 12th Lord, a brigadier general, commanded the left wing.

By 1727 the castle had passed to the MacDowell family. Colonel William MacDowell ordered the demolition of the old castle to clear the site for his new mansion and in 1791 obtained plans from Robert Adam to remodel it. This plan was never executed as the family ran into financial difficulties. The estate was gradually broken up and the house fell into disrepair. It burned down in 1924 and survived as a shell until finally demolished. A wing and a few subsidiary buildings survive, including an ice house and a stable block. These were later used as farm buildings. A number of these make up a group of 'B' listed buildings, while the Collegiate Church is 'A' listed and an ornamental well is 'C' listed.

The site and other buildings now stand within Castle Semple Country Park.

Other references: Castleton, Castle Tower

CATHCART CASTLE

City of Glasgow   Ruin or site   OS 64   NS 587601

2 miles southwest of Rutherglen, off minor roads south of B767, west of Old Castle Road, and east of White Cart Water, at head of Linn Park.

Sited on a hilltop precipice above the White Cart, Cathcart Castle survives only to a height of 3ft. The castle originally consisted of a simple oblong keep of 51ft by 30.75ft within a courtyard, which extended a further 10ft on each side. There were four round corner towers on the perimeter wall. The original entrance to the courtyard was in the east, opposite the main entrance to the keep. This was of four storeys and probably a garret, the basement being vaulted. A door at ground-floor level entered a small corridor. Opposite was the entrance to the basement, to the north was a turnpike stair within the walls accessing all floors above and to the south was a small chamber of 5ft by 6ft, which may have acted as a prison since there was access from above. The main chamber at this level was illuminated by three slot windows.

The hall on the first floor measured 32.5ft by 17ft and had several larger windows, one of which had stone seats. That in the east wall may have been the original entrance and recent reassessment of photographic evidence suggests that this was guarded by a machicolated projection supported by three corbels set a few feet below parapet level. There was a large open fireplace in the south wall. In common with the floors above there were various mural chambers within the walls. The floors above had originally consisted of large single rooms, though that on the second floor had been subdivided to give two disproportionate rooms and a link corridor. The castle was demolished to its present height by Glasgow City Council around 1980 due to its deteriorating and dangerous condition. The remnant is now overgrown and daubed with graffiti.

The Cathcarts held the estate from the 12th century, though the site of their original seat is not known. Some suggest the ancient earthworks at Camphill within Queens Park, others identify the site of the present ruin as that of a possible ringwork.

The Cathcarts took their name from these lands and first appear in 1179 when Rainaldus de Cathcart witnessed a donation of the church of Cathcart to Paisley Abbey by Allan, the son of Walter the High Steward. Alan Cathcart appears in 1387 when he inherited the baronies of Sundrum and Auchincrew from his uncle, Sir Duncan Wallace. Another Alan was made Lord

Cathcart in 1447 and received a charter of confirmation of the barony. He built the castle in 1450. In 1546 a further Alan alienated Cathcart to Gabriel Semple, a younger son of John, 1st Lord Semple. Alan died a year later at the Battle of Pinkie.

Robert, Lord Semple, and his adherents opposed Mary, Queen of Scots, at nearby Langside in 1568, but

despite this a legend persists that she watched proceedings from a knoll known as 'the Court Knowe', immediately west of the castle. It is also alleged that she may have stayed in the castle the night before the battle. Both tales are unlikely.

In 1725, Maxwell of Williamwood and Maxwell of Blawarthill, jointly inherited Cathcart. The Williamwoods appear to have taken up residence, building Cathcart House just to the south and abandoning the castle in 1740. It was unroofed and sold for building material but the contractor found the project uneconomic and walked away. Five storeys remained in situ in 1866.

Cathcart House has long since been demolished. It may have been bought by a Major Morrison before being purchased by the soldier William, Viscount Cathcart, who became Earl of Cathcart in 1814. He died on the estate in 1843.

CATHKIN HOUSE

South Lanarkshire   Ruin or site   OS 64   NS 628589
2 miles south of Rutherglen, west of A749 East Kilbride Road, north of B759 Cathkin Road on Menteith Place, at Cathkin House.

The present mansion dating from 1799 replaced earlier buildings, which may have been fortified. This is almost certainly the site of one of two castles within the parish of Carmunnock owned by the Douglases in the early 15th century. In 1710 an earlier form of the mansion was described as one of the principal houses of Lanarkshire.

The estate of Cathkin was formed from a collection of smallholdings, including some Templar lands. It belonged to the Douglases by the early 15th century. In 1414 Archibald the Grim, Lord of Bothwell and Galloway, added Cathkin to his endowment to the Collegiate Church of Bothwell. In 1452 an exchange of lands took place which was ratified by James V in 1455. This saw Carmunnock and Drumsagard pass to the Hamiltons and Bothwell return to the Earl of Douglas.

The Hamiltons had an early house here, which was the centre of an estate separate from their other lands in Carmunnock. At the close of the 17th century the estate was divided between the families of three heiresses. The house was then occupied by Dunlops and then the McLae family. In 1790 it passed to the Ewings, who assumed the name McLae on inheriting. They pulled down the old house and built the present mansion in 1799. Having been used as a nursing home, the building has now been converted into apartments. Compare Carmunnock.

CATTER CASTLE

The Lennox & East Dunbartonshire   Private   OS 57   NS 473871
0.5 miles south of Drymen, just southwest of junction of A811 and A809, in garden of Catter House.

An impressive motte remains of an early castle of the Earls of Lennox. Catter guarded the ferry point over the River Endrick which allowed access to the lands east of Loch Lomond from the south. It was of further strategic importance due to its position at the meeting of the main routes through the area to Glasgow, Dumbarton and Stirling.

The castle was apparently abandoned in the 14th century and replaced by Inchmurrin Castle. However, there is evidence that a 'manor house' once occupied the site and that it still existed in 1505. The present house has a small spiral staircase leading from the basement and very small windows in this same section of the building. There was also an extensive area of cobble stones to the rear of the house all of which, it has been suggested, survive from the 'manor'.

The motte stands 11ft above the garden of the house and 40ft above the low lying ground between it and the river. The southern approach had faint remains of a ditch in 1955. It has a roughly oval summit, of 100ft by 115ft. Resistivity survey by archaeologists suggests that the summit supports the remains of a large rectilinear building, perhaps a hall house of the Earls of Lennox. There is also a very large flat stone, described by some as a cup-marked stone and by others as the socket for the earl's gallows.

Catter House is a two-storey Georgian mansion of 1767, built over what may be an earlier basement. It is now owned by the Grahams, but was once part of the Buchanan estate from which that family took their name.

CHATELHERAULT HUNTING LODGE

South Lanarkshire   South Lanarkshire Council   OS 64 NS 737540
1.5 miles southeast of Hamilton, southwest of A72 (Carlisle Road) Ferniegair, in Chatelherault Country Park.

No castle, but an impressively grand building nonetheless. Chatelherault was the hunting lodge, kennels and summer house of James, 5th Duke of Hamilton.

Designed and built in 1723-24 by William Adam, it has been restored and acts as a visitor and exhibition centre for the 500-acre park.

Within the park are the ruins of Cadzow Castle, miles of country walks, 18th century gardens, and the centuries-old Cadzow Oaks. The gorge of the River Avon provides particularly scenic views, particularly when at the Duke's Bridge. There are displays on both the history and natural history of the area, which abounds with wildlife including roe deer, kingfishers, dippers and badgers (www.visitlanarkshire.com/attractions/child-friendly/Chatelherault-Country-Park/).

CLAIRINSH

The Lennox & East Dunbartonshire   Ruin or site   OS 56   NS 413899
By boat, 0.75 miles southwest of Balmaha and B837, on Clairinsh island, Loch Lomond.

'Clairinsh' was the battle cry of Clan Buchanan, reflecting the importance of this island as their early stronghold.

The curiously fish-shaped island faces northeast into the bay of Balmaha and just off the northeastern tip is a crannog, equally curiously named 'The Kitchen'. Island strongholds without defensive buildings seem to be common among the clans in this region, as with the MacNabs at Eilean Rowan near Killin, or the MacGregors at Eilean Molach on Loch Katrine.

In 1935 foundations were identified on the island of a rectangular building 37.5ft long by 19ft wide. The ground floor was equally divided into two rooms, one of which had a corn drying kiln built into the north wall. Other ruins were also located, possibly those of a round house and another rectangular building 'of no great antiquity', measuring 46ft by 23.5ft close to the northern shore. Archaeological finds indicated occupation as far back as the Iron Age, possibly connected to the crannog. In 1973, the remains of a total of five rectangular buildings were observed, though no evidence of the apparent round house.

Later studies of the remains of seven buildings in 1980-81 suggested agricultural and domestic uses for the buildings but no firm dating evidence, though a speculative range of 16th-19th century was made.

There have been no excavations of the Kitchen although it is obviously a crannog. In the early 19th century one writer referred to it as a ruined castle below the water.

In 1225 Maldouen, Earl of Lennox, granted the island to his Seneschal, Absalom, for a pound of wax to be paid annually. Absalom is said to be the progenitor of the Buchanans. The grant was made on the island itself and was confirmed by a charter of Alexander II in 1231. It is thought that the Kitchen may have acted as a 'council isle', in the same way that the Council Island of Finlaggan was used by the Lords of the Isles. It is a well known use of artificial islands in that period. The family may have left the island for the more convenient base at Buchanan Pele.

CLEGHORN CASTLE

South Lanarkshire   Ruin or site   OS 72   NS 898461
2 miles north of Lanark, on minor roads west of A706, just south of railway, and north of Mouse Water.

Cleghorn House was a mansion which incorporated part of a castle. Cleghorn was a distinct estate from as early as 1220 when William de Hertford held part or all of it from his superior, Robert of Carmitely (Carmichael).

Alan Lockhart, 1st of Cleghorn, appears as a charter witness in 1441. In 1476 his son Stephen succeeded and became Armour Bearer to James III. In 1484 he won a decree against Patrick Cleland and Richard Hastie for wrongfully withholding the profit from the ferryboat at Crossford. In 1488 he was charged with treason, having supported James III at the Battle of Sauchieburn; however he seems to have been quickly pardoned by the young James IV. Sir Stephen's eldest son, Alan, inherited Cleghorn, while his second son became the 1st Lockhart of Waygateshaw. Alan died at Flodden in 1513. His son Mungo was knighted by the young James VI in 1569. In 1572 he was one of many accused of the murder of Henry, Lord Darnley. He was cautioned for supporting the Hamiltons in 1579. In 1580 both Mungo and his son Alan served on the assize of Hamilton of Bothwellhaugh for the murder of the Regent Moray. The family descended continuously in the male line until the 18th century when the heiress, Marianne, married into the Elliott family and adopted the surname Elliott-Lockhart. Her eldest son John Elliott-Lockhart died at the battle of Waterloo in 1815.

The castle was destroyed by fire in 1747 and a remaining portion incorporated within the mansion which replaced it. This was demolished in the 20th century. The family still live in Cleghorn and the estate gardens are available for functions and events (www.cleghornestategardens.com).

CLELAND HOUSE

North Lanarkshire   Ruin or site   OS 64   NS 783578
1 mile southeast of Carfin, 1 mile southwest of Cleland on north bank of South Calder Water, off minor roads, south of B7029, at Dalziel Park Golf and Country Club.

Site of a castle of the Cleland family. It was replaced by or incorporated within a mansion, itself demolished in the 20th century. A modern hotel now occupies the site.

The name Cleland, originally Kneeland, first appears on record with Alexander (sometimes mentioned as Adam) Kneeland of that Ilk, who is said to have married the sister of Sir William Wallace. The family were hereditary foresters to the Earls of Douglas.

Alexander's son James fought alongside the great patriot from 1296 at Loudounhill, Stirling in 1297, Falkirk in 1298 and continued to serve Wallace in France. He supported Robert I at the Battle of Bannockburn with his son John. Bruce awarded James a charter of East Calder for his efforts. In 1450 the marriage of another James Cleland to a Somerville produced the cadet branches of Monkland, Faskine and Gartness. In 1513 Alexander Cleland of that Ilk died at the Battle of Flodden with his cousin, William of Faskine. Members of the family were eminent at the courts of James V, Mary, Queen of Scots, and James VI. William Cleland of that Ilk was one of those accused in the murder of Henry, Lord Darnley. In the reign of James VI, William Cleland married the sister of the first Lord Blantyre. His successor married the daughter of Lord Bargany and their eldest son sold Cleland to a cousin, taking the main branch of the family to Laird Braes in Ayrshire.

In 1689 William Cleland, a son of the gamekeeper to the Marquis of Douglas, died as he commanded the Cameronians for the Government Army at Dunkeld. Wounded in the early part of the conflict, he apparently crawled away and died of wounds to his head and liver. It is said the he did not want his men to see him die and that it was his leadership qualities which led to the repulsion of the Jacobite attack on the town.

In 1702 Alexander of Cleland sold the estate to William and Archibald Hamilton in order to pay off his debts. They then sold it in 1711 to Gavin Hamilton of Inverdovat, a sale which included 'the five pound land of Clelandtown with the tower and fortalice etc'.

In 1786 Alexander Inglis Hamilton of Murdostoun sold the estate to Captain Hew Dalrymple of Fordal. His nephew, Sir William Dalrymple served in South America, helping to capture the fort of San Fernando de Omoa and the port of Omoa in Honduras. On his return to civilian life having achieved the rank of colonel, he founded the Omoa Iron Works at Cleland.

A large cave once existed below the house within which William Wallace was supposed to have hidden with his men. It is said to have been guarded by a door and yett, and had room for 50 men. There are mentions of it having its own fireplace and chimney, features still visible in the 18th century. Land slippage has left little of the cave, which now is said to be a featureless indentation in the cliff face. (www.dalzielpark.co.uk).

Other reference: Kneeland

CLOAK CASTLE

Renfrewshire   Ruin or site   OS 63   NS 344606
1.5 miles north of Lochwinnoch, off minor roads west of B786, west of Meikle Cloak, above Knockan Linn on the River Calder.

Site of a castle, which stood on a high precipice. Nothing remains. It was a property of the Montgomeries, possibly from as early as the 14th century. It was demolished in the early 18th century for building materials. Sometime thereafter, a 'cave' was discovered below the site, wherein were found two querns. Both Nether and Over 'Klook' appear as small properties on Pont's map of the late 16th century and in Blaeu's *Atlas Novus* of the 17th century.

In John Ainslie's map of c.1800 the name Shin Castle appears on a hilltop to the north of Meikle Cloak and this is repeated in Thompson's map of 1832. However, it consistently appears to the west on Ordnance Survey maps from the 19th century as 'Site of Cloak Castle'. It is possible that the alternative names have transferred from another site.

Other references: Shain Castle, Shin Castle, Shine Castle

CLOBERHILL TOWER

City of Glasgow   Ruin or site   OS 64   NS 497742
Off Towerhill Road, close to junction of Cloberhill Road and Knightswood Road, Knightswood, Glasgow.

Site of a tower, owned from 1567 by the Crawfords. 'Clebarhill' appears as a double-towered structure in Blaeu's *Atlas Novus* of the mid 17th century. Cloberhill House was a mansion dated 1666 on the same site, which was apparently renamed Cowdenhill Mansion in 1716 by John Spreull, after his ancestral home of Cowdenhall in Neilston.

In 1612 Hew Crawford of Cloberhill assisted a kinsman, possibly his son or brother, Crawford of Possil to assail Corslie Castle. Hew Crawford of Cloberhill was appointed to the Committee of War for the Shire of Renfrewshire in 1644, by an Act of Charles I. He appears again as a Commissioner of the Presbytery of Dumbarton in an Act of Charles II in 1649.

In 1716 John Spreull married Isabel, the Crawford heiress, and gained the property on condition that he adopted the Crawford name. He then became John Sprewll Crawford.

The estate passed to the child of his eighth daughter, who again had to adopt the Crawford name, and the family became the Hunter-Sprewll-Crawfords. This line died out in 1837, and the estate passed to a nephew, Sir William Alexander.

Although listed in RCAHMS as Clobar House, this is a quite separate property from the now demolished 18th century Clobar House which stood on the bank of the Allander to the northwest of Milngavie.

Other reference: Cowdenhill Mansion

CLOWBURN

South Lanarkshire   Ruin or site   OS 72   NS 941405
4.5 miles southeast of Lanark, on minor road just east of the A73 at Clowburn.

Site of a tower illustrated on Pont's manuscript map of 1596, and in subsequent maps as both Clonburn and Cloburn.

This was church land, assigned to the canons of Dryburgh Abbey. At the Reformation ownership passed to the Weirs. Hugh Weir was in possession in 1617 and John Weir of Clowburn was fined £600 for nonconformity as a Covenanter in 1662. It passed by marriage to Sir Andrew Kennedy. He became Baronet Clowburn in 1698, having been a 'Conservator of the Scots Privileges at the United Provinces'. He was descended from the Kennedys of Bargany.

COCHNO HOUSE

The Lennox & East Dunbartonshire   Private   OS 64   NS 497532
Off minor roads, north of Duntocher, and A810, at Cochno House.

Site of a tower house with 16th century origins. The present Cochno House is a large classical mansion built by John Adam in 1757 for the Hamiltons of Barns. It was extended in 1842 to provide a lower kitchen block, and had replaced the 16th century tower. Since 1956 it has been owned by Glasgow University, and is used as a centre for veterinary medicine and astronomy. It was refurbished in 2002-03.

The lands of Cochno were given to Paisley Abbey by Alwen, Earl of Lennox, in the 12th century. The first Hamilton of Cochno is Andrew, apparently descended from the Hamiltons of Torrance and Ardoch. He acquired Cochno in 1550. He was Provost of Glasgow and Governor of Dumbarton Castle, until losing that position due to his support of Mary, Queen of Scots, at Langside in 1568. Following the battle, he was charged to give up the 'tour and fortalice of Cochno', when Lord Semple was ordered to take possession for the Crown. Andrew was dead by 1573 and Cochno was restored to his heirs by the Treaty of Perth. He was succeeded in turn by his sons, John, then Claud, whose own son Claud succeeded and sold the estate to the Earl of Abercorn in 1617. His son in turn granted it to the Hamiltons of Barns in 1647.

The Hamiltons of Barns were descended from Gavin Hamilton, 9th of Raploch, who settled the lands of 'Bornis and Culbowie' on his son Claud in the early 17th century. His descendants are recorded as a Sheriff, Commissioner for Supply and then MP for Dunbartonshire in the late 17th century, then Burgess and Guild Brother of Glasgow in the 18th century. Claud Hamilton, the 7th of Cochno, fought in the Battle of Cartagena in 1741 during the War of Jenkins Ear. In the 19th century the male line expired and the estate passed to a nephew, Claud Hamilton Brown, on condition the he adopted the Hamilton surname. This line ended with Grace, the 11th Hamilton of Barns and Cochno. She died unmarried in 1887, and was succeeded by her cousin, Claud Hamilton. The last on record is Claud Archibald McKenzie Bruce Hamilton, 13th of Barns and Cochno, who died c.1954.

COCHRANE CASTLE

Renfrewshire   Ruin or site   OS 64   NS 418616

1 mile southwest of Johnstone, 1 mile east of Black Cart Water, on minor roads south of A737, east of Auchengreoch Road, in the grounds of 'The Red House'.

Site of a castle of the Cochrane family, now marked by miniature rubble built keep dated 1886.

The Cochrane family held the lands from at least as early as the 13th century, taking their name from the lands. In the 13th century Waldenus de Cocheran witnessed a charter of the lands of Skipnish to Walter Earl of Menteith. In 1296 William de Cocheran gave homage to Edward I. The family appear regularly in charters in the following centuries. William Cochrane was confirmed in the manor of Cochrane in 1556 and added a tower to his 'manor'. Thereafter it was known as Cochrane Castle.

In 1603 the heiress Elizabeth Cochrane took the estate to her husband, Alexander Blair, who adopted the name and arms of Cochrane and in doing so gained a charter of the lands of Cochrane. In 1623 he also received a charter of the lands of Cowden in Neilston. Their son, Sir John Cochrane, was an active Royalist and surrendered his estates at his death to his brother William Cochrane of Cowden. He had received a charter of Cowden in 1634, and in 1638 was granted a charter of Dundonald. Knighted in 1641, he became Baron Cochrane of Dundonald in 1647. He became Lord Paisley in 1653, having purchased the lordship and barony from the Earl of Angus. In 1658 he sold the superiority of the town to the magistrates of the burgh. He was awarded the title Earl of Dundonald in 1669. William, 7th Earl, was an army officer who died at the siege of Louisbourg in 1758. Thomas, 8th Earl, supported the Hanoverians in 1745 and it is said that his horse was shot from under him by Jacobite forces in Edinburgh. He later gave evidence at the trial of Archibald Stewart, Provost of Edinburgh, who had surrendered the city to Prince Charles Edward Stewart. His line continues to the present day in the person of the 15th Earl.

The Cochrane estate was sold in 1760 to the Johnstones. Ruinous by 1771, the vaulted basement of the castle was still in use as a cart shed in 1782 but by the mid 19th century the site was vacant.

The Cochranes had another stronghold nearby, once called Easter Cochrane and now Johnstone, which was sold to the Houstons during the reign of James V. George Ludovick Houston built the small tower at Cochrane to commemorate the castle site and incorporated an armorial stone with the Cochrane arms, dated 1592. Nothing else remains.

Other references: Cocheran, Coueran, Coveran

COLGRAIN

The Lennox & East Dunbartonshire   Ruin or site   OS 63   NS 326804?

On A814, 2.5 miles northwest of Cardross, and 3 miles southeast of Helensburgh, at or near Colgrain.

Site of a manor or old or fortified house of the Dennistouns. In 1351 Donald, Earl of Lennox, confirmed a grant by his brother Maldouen of the lands of 'Keppoch, Culgrayne and Kameskanys' and others to Walter of Faslane.

By 1377 the Dennistouns had possession. Originally Danzielstoun, they were a family who hailed from a property of that name in Renfrewshire. Hugh de Danzielston is on record as having paid homage to Edward I in 1296 and was head of one of the most eminent families in the west of Scotland. His daughter married Mure of Rowallan and their daughter Elizabeth married Robert II, resulting in the Dennistoun's proud boast that:

'Kings have come of us, not we of kings.'

Hugh's son, John de Danzielston, was Sheriff of Dunbartonshire and hereditary Keeper of Dumbarton Castle. His son Robert gained the keepership of Dumbarton and the bulk of family estates. It was he who left only heiresses dividing their father's estates and taking them to their husbands Cunninghame of Kilmaurs and Maxwell of Calderwood.

Walter the second son was a churchman who, on his brother's death, claimed his right to Dumbarton Castle and took it by force. Robert III apparently offered him the Bishopric of St Andrews in exchange, which he accepted.

William, the third son, was progenitor of the Colgrain branch, having received it from his father before 1377. This became the senior male line. William is thought to have held office at the courts of both Robert III and his ill-fated son, David, Duke of Rothesay. When William died in 1393, his widow Marjory received a pension from the Exchequer.

In the 16th century Robert Dennistoun of Colgrain was forfeited for being in association with the treasonous activities of the Earl of Glencairn, who had been in league with Henry VIII.

In 1546 Robert was given a remission under the Great Seal for all his treasons and crimes. His son, James, took the family into such debt that his son, Walter, had to sell off parts of the estate, including Cameron. Colonel John Dennistoun, Walter's son, was a Royalist during the Civil War and eventually died of wounds incurred fighting alongside the Earl of Glencairn. He left an heiress, Margaret, who married her cousin, William Dennistoun of Dalquhurn. By that time the estate was much reduced, partly due to the debts incurred by John's backing of the losing side in the Civil War. In the end Dalquhurn was lost. William and Margaret had 16 children, of whom only John survived his parents. He managed to eliminate the debt before his death in 1796 and was succeeded by his son, then grandson, both James. The latter was Convener of Dunbartonshire for over 30 years, Vice Lieutenant of the Shire, and commander of the local militia. The next in line was another James, who took the designation 'of Dennistoun'. In 1836 he sold the estates of Colgrain and Camis Eskan and purchased Dennistoun Mains in Renfrewshire, the original estate of his ancestors. The Campbells of Breadalbane established a cadet branch here.

Archaeological assessment in 2000 of the present complex at Colgrain found no evidence of any structure earlier than 1800 and no sign of the medieval manor. Camis Eskan House seems to have become the Dennistouns' main residence once built in 1648, though it was unfinished in 1667. There have been additions to the north and southwest c.1840. It is likely to have been unfortified, although it does have vaulted basement rooms and walls 4ft thick. It may be that it is built upon the site of or incorporates the older house of Colgrain, although the two properties appear as separate entries on Blaeu's *Atlas*, albeit the names appear to have been transposed. Culgren appears on Charles Ross's map of 1777, which indicates a large house which appears to sit on the present site of Camis Eskan, with the latter name marking the burn. Camis Eskan House came into use as a hospital and was subsequently converted into luxury flats in the late 20th century.

Other reference: Camis Eskan

COLLINS BURN

South Lanarkshire   Ruin or site   OS 72   NS 951187

0.75 miles north of Elvanfoot, west of M74, and west of A702, by foot on north bank of Collins Burn.

A large oval earthwork sits on a knoll above the Collins Burn, in an area protected on all sides by peat bog. It is surrounded by a ditch, with both interior and exterior ramparts. It measures some 200ft by 161ft, and the ditch varies between 10ft and 18ft wide. This is now badly silted up, and the ramparts much diminished. There are entrances on both the west and east sides, the gap on the inner ramparts reaching as much as 120ft wide. The interior is featureless.

The site appears in one list of medieval sites, while elsewhere as an unclassified earthwork. It is certainly sited in a strategic position, overlooking the meeting of two main thoroughfares through the hills of the upper Clyde Valley and close to the junction of two Roman Roads.

A medieval origin cannot be discounted and this could be a Norman ringwork, but such a layout in this area is more suggestive of an earlier origin. The area is rich in archaeological sites from all periods.

Other reference: Elvanfoot

COLTNESS HOUSE

North Lanarkshire   Ruin or site   OS 64   NS 798564

In Wishaw, 1 mile north of A722, 1 mile southeast of Cleland, west of Coltness Road, just west of Ballater Crescent opposite junction with Letherton Drive.

Site of a tower house which developed into an extensive mansion around 1800, which was demolished in the 20th century. Coltness was originally part of the extensive estates of the Somervilles of Cambusnethan. It is said to have passed to the Logans of Restalrig in 1553. It was later purchased by John Hamilton of Udston, becoming his principal residence.

His descendants sold it in 1653 to Sir Walter Stewart of Allanton, who gave it to his younger brother Sir James. It was described at that time as, 'a convenient little tower house...consisting only of a vault and two rooms, one above the other, with a small room on top of the turnpike stair and a garret'. Sir James added 'a good kitchen, cellar, meat room or low parlour, a large hall or dyning room, with a small bedchamber and a closet over these, and above that two bedchambers with closets, and yet higher in the fourth storey, two finished roof rooms'. Sir James was Lord Provost of Edinburgh in 1648 and 1658. He died in 1691.

His elder son, Thomas Stewart of Coltness, was a Covenanter, who was forfeited in 1685 for his part in the murder of Archbishop James Sharp and the burning of 'his majestie's lawes' at the mercat cross in Rutherglen in 1679. He received a remission for this and was knighted in 1687.

He died in 1698 and was succeeded by his brother, Sir James of Goodtrees, who adopted the Steuart spelling of their surname. He was a lawyer who, in 1669, had published what was considered a treasonable pamphlet defending people's rights. He had to flee the country on no less than three occasions. He returned after 1681 to receive a pardon and become the first Baronet of Coltness and Lord Advocate. His son, James Steuart of Goodtrees and Coltness, became Solicitor General. His son took on the additional surname of Denham on gaining the estate of Westshield. As Sir James Steuart Denham of Coltness and Westshield, he was a political economist who travelled extensively around Europe. He was courted by the Jacobites before returning to Scotland in 1740. He was in Edinburgh when Prince Charles took the city and fled to Germany after Culloden in 1746, having been implicated as a Jacobite. He was a prolific writer on politics and economics, who returned to Scotland in 1763 to continue his work. His son, General Sir James Steuart Denham of Coltness and Westshield, was a career soldier who served the county of Lanark as MP. By the time of his death at Cheltenham in 1839 he had become the army's most senior General.

Coltness House was extensively remodelled and extended in 1800, and is said to have had a picture gallery 200ft long. In 1840 it came to the industrialist Houldsworth family, before becoming a Barnardo's children's home in the 1950s. It was later used as a resettlement centre for Vietnamese refugees until demolition in the 1980s to make way for a housing development.

COLZIUM CASTLE

The Lennox and East Dunbartonshire   Ruin or site   OS 64   NS 729788

0.5 miles east of Kilsyth, north of the A803, by driveway through Colzium Lennox Country Park, just northeast of Colzium House.

A section of wall 47.5ft long by 16ft high by 3.5ft thick is now integrated as a gable for a cottage and its garden wall. This is all that remains of this 15th century L-plan tower and its extension. The outline of a vaulted roof is evident on the wall, as is an arched recess and a walled up entrance. There is an ice house of 1680 within the gorge to the east. It is essentially intact. Colzium House is a mansion of the 18th century.

Colzium Castle was constructed in the mid 15th century upon a platform at the edge of the ravine of the Colzium Burn. A large hall house was added in 1575 and it is a remnant of this which survives. The foundations of the original tower were excavated in 1977 prior to being covered in tarmac to create additional car parking. In the courtyard of the house an inscribed stone from the castle is on display bearing the arms of Livingston of Callendar and the date 1575. A larger collection of stones from both Colzium and Kilsyth Castles are displayed inside. Stone from the castle ruins was used in the construction of the house.

These lands belonged to the Earls of Lennox and were granted to the de Callendar family. They were Thanes of Callendar, descended from the Earls of Lennox through the female line. Sir John de Callendar rendered homage to Edward I in 1296, and his grandson, Sir Patrick de Callendar, was forfeited for supporting the English around the time of Edward Balliol's campaign for the throne of Scotland. The Callendar estates including Colzium were granted to William Livingston in 1346, who then married Christian de Callendar, Patrick's daughter and heiress.

His son, John, died at Homildon Hill in 1402. In 1436 following the murder of James I, Sir Alexander Livingstone of Callendar, Governor of Stirling Castle, became Guardian of the young James II. He utilized his possession of the young king to further his own aims, effectively ruling Scotland. It is thought that in coalition with Sir William Crichton, they eliminated their main rival for power the 6th Earl of Douglas, by having him arrested and executed for high treason at the notorious 'Black Dinner' of 1440. Douglas had been invited to Edinburgh Castle to dine with the young king. After the meal, it is said that a black bull's head was served, a traditional sign of an impending death. Douglas was arrested and following a mock trial, was dragged of to be beheaded on Castlehill. Douglas had been accompanied by Sir Malcolm Fleming of Cumbernauld, who was also executed. In an ironic turn of events, Fleming's granddaughter married Alexander's great grandson some 32 years later.

Alexander's son James succeeded and adopted the same role, achieving the position of Great Chamberlain. When the king came of age in 1449 James was forfeited and imprisoned but quickly released. By 1454 he was again Chamberlain and in 1458 became 1st Lord Livingston of Callendar. His son James, 2nd Lord, was unkindly designated 'an idiot'. It is thought that the estate was managed by his brother Alexander, whose son James succeeded as 3rd Lord. It was he who married Beatrice Fleming, daughter of the 1st Lord Fleming in 1472.

Sir William Livingstone, 4th Lord, inherited in 1503; however in 1509 he resigned his entire estate to his son Alexander. He became guardian to the young Mary, Queen of Scots, and his daughter Mary became lady-in-waiting to the young queen, one of her 'Four Maries'. His son, James, Master of Livingston, died at the Battle of Pinkie in 1547 and, since he had no heir, his brother William inherited on Alexander's death in 1553. William fought at Langside in 1568 and was a staunch supporter of the Mary. He was succeeded by his son Alexander, 8th Lord Callendar, who supported the cause of her son James, capturing Stirling Castle on his behalf in the 1580s. A trusted confidante of the king, he was one of those who rescued him during the Gowrie Conspiracy. This support earned Alexander the award of an earldom, that of Linlithgow. In 1641, his younger son was awarded the title Earl of Callendar, the titles merging in 1695.

George, 3rd Earl of Linlithgow, was a Royalist during the Civil War and in 1650 received a remission for his part in the Engagement for the rescue of Charles I. From 1677 he served as Major-General of the forces in Scotland during the Wars of the Covenant. Following the Battle of Drumclog in 1679 he recalled Claverhouse to the main army and they fell back on Edinburgh where he was relieved of command by the Duke of Monmouth. Following the Battle of Bothwell Bridge, Claverhouse and Linlithgow were sent to London to encourage more severe measures against the Covenanters. In 1684 he was appointed Justice General, and he died in 1690.

His son, George, became 4th Earl of Linlithgow and his second son, Alexander, was 3rd Earl of Callendar. George died in 1695. James, 5th Earl of Linlithgow, held both titles, but was charged with High Treason after the 1715 rebellion and was forfeited.

At some point, Colzium came to the Livingstones of Kilsyth, (they had added an 'e' to their name to differentiate themselves) who are known to have owned it in the late 17th century. William, 3rd Viscount Kilsyth, ordered the demolition of the castle in 1703, prior to inheriting estate from his brother in 1706.

In 1783 the Edmonstones acquired the estate, on their return from Ireland, and built Colzium House. The house was extended by the addition of two wings in 1861. The family later restored and occupied their ancestral home at Duntreath. In 1930 the house and gardens were purchased by W. MacKay Lennox, former Town Clerk of Kilsyth, who presented them to the burgh in 1937 in memory of his mother. The council demolished part of the old house after World War II, due to dry rot. The space is now occupied by the interior courtyard. The walled garden is well maintained and very attractive. Colzium House is apparently haunted by a 'Blue Lady'.

The house and gardens are now operated by North Lanarkshire Council and are available for hire as a conference and event venue (www.kilsyth.org.uk/colzium.htm).

COLZIUM MOTTE

The Lennox and East Dunbartonshire Ruin or site OS 64 NS 735783
0.5 miles east of Kilsyth, north of the A803, by the eastern driveway through Colzium Lennox Country Park, southeast of Colzium House, at southwestern bank of Banton Loch, at Castlehill.

A motte represents the earliest fortification on the Colzium Estate. It was built in the 12th century by the Earls of Lennox as one of a series of strongholds strung across Scotland from Dumbarton to Stirling.

A tower illustrated on Pont's Manuscript map of 1596 and subsequently in Blaeu's *Atlas Novus* of the 17th century appears to indicate continued development of this site, which may have included a stone building. Archaeological examination showed no trace of any wooden structure or otherwise on the motte; however a well is indicated a little to the west on large scale OS maps, on the raised ground which supports the modern house, now known as Castlehill. This area would be the natural site for, and may represent the remains of the bailey. The two parts of the site are now divided by a driveway, which leads along the periphery of the park to the loch and then Colzium House.

Banton Loch is a man-made reservoir used to supply water to the Forth and Clyde canal. When flooded, the waters drowned the battlefield of Kilsyth where in 1645 Montrose scored an important victory over a Covenanting army led by General William Baillie. The names of a variety of hills around commemorate the event: Slaughter Knowe, Baggage Knowe etc. Following the battle Baillie's army were scattered and some perished in Dullatur Bog to the south. Peat rich, the bog preserves. On the digging of the Forth and Clyde Canal c.1770 several bodies of the Covenanting soldiers were uncovered in remarkably good state, one apparently still mounted on his horse.

COMYN'S CASTLE

South Lanarkshire   Ruin or site   OS 64   NS 628562

1 mile north of East Kilbride, west of Stewartfield, 50yds north of Mains Castle, off minor roads north of B783.

Only earthworks and traces of foundations remain of a castle. There appears to have been a stone keep in the southeast corner of the site. A double ditch and bank surrounds a round cornered quadrilateral site. The double ditch has led one commentator to surmise that this may indicate earlier origins than generally supposed. Part of the outer ditch has been eroded due to its use as a farm track, while another section has been filled in.

The barony of Kilbride was granted to Roger de Valence, de Valognes or Valonis, in the 12th century. He apparently built the castle in 1182 and the nearby hamlet of Rogerton is named after him. The estate was inherited by Roger's daughter, Isabelle, who took it by marriage to David Comyn in the late 12th century. In 1250 as 'Lady of Kilbride', Isabelle granted her forest of Dalquhairn to Glasgow Cathedral 'for the soul of her husband David Comyn'.

The estate apparently came to John 'the Red' Comyn before 1290. In his redistribution of the Comyn lands after 1306, Robert I is said to have awarded Kilbride to the High Steward. Following the death of David II, the High Steward succeeded to the throne as Robert II. In 1382 he granted the estate to Lindsay of Dunrod. They apparently used the castle until the 15th century, when they built Mains.

Other reference: Kilbride Castle

COREHOUSE CASTLE

South Lanarkshire   Ruin or site   OS 72   NS 882414

1.5 miles south of Lanark, on minor roads south of A72, on west bank of River Clyde above Corra Linn waterfall.

Standing on a promontory and protected on three sides by precipitous drops to the River Clyde below, Corehouse is a ruined 16th century tower house of the Bannatynes.

The main building is protected on three sides by a 100ft drop to the river and on the fourth and northern side it was guarded by a deep ditch 15-20ft wide cut into the rock. This is now mostly filled. Originally there would have been a drawbridge, though a stone walled bridge now carries a road to the site. There are the remnants of a 65ft by 33ft courtyard across the ravine to the west, though this is of later date.

A 6ft-thick wall with arched gateway protects the approach once across the ditch. At the end of the bridge, this angles off to the southeast terminating in the remains of a round tower, which may have housed a stair. On the interior and within the original courtyard, it can be seen that this stood at one end of a secondary block with oven and drain.

The western end of the perimeter wall acted as the gable of the main block. This runs the length of the western ravine and contains four vaulted chambers, two of which are

linked and entered by one doorway. Both of the other chambers have their own doors from the courtyard. Above this, the hall utilised two thirds of the floor space, while a private room occupied the northern-most third. Above this room was a further floor surmounted by a garret, as illustrated in a painting of Corra Linn by Paul Sandby, dated c.1753. This additional floor housed a bedroom. There do not appear to have been other floors above the hall. At the southern end of this block are the remains of a small square stair tower. Nothing now remains above the floor level of the hall.

The original name of this estate was Corrocks, which being similar to the Irish Curragh means 'rough swampy ground'. The estate belonged to Lesmahagow Priory in the early 12th century. Sometime between 1160 and 1180 the Abbot granted an eighth part of Corrocks to Waldeve son of Bodin, *homino nostro*, 'our man'. By 1203, the estate had been granted to David son of Peter, Dean of Stobo. In 1315 the monks exchanged the lands of Kype with Reginald de Currokis (Corehouse) for his land at Fincurrokis. Reginald's son Andrew resigned Kype to the monks in exchange for a pension of four silver merks.

Corehouse was granted to William Bannatyne before 1400, when an inquest was held to determine if his son John Bannatyne was entitled to the estate. In 1476 Richard Bannatyne of Corehouse was one of a jury found by the Lord Auditors of giving a wrong verdict in a trial. In 1527 John Bannatyne and 63 others were accused of the mutilation of Walter Weir. By 1536 he did not need quite so many henchmen to slaughter John Graham of Westhall and his company, his brother Thomas and 19 others sufficed…

Mary, Queen of Scots, is said to have spent the night here after her defeat at Langside in 1568. In 1572 John Bannatyne was one of those accused of complicity in the murders of Henry, Lord Darnley, and the Regents Moray and Lennox. He had to find £3,000 security for his behaviour.

In 1596 William Bannatyne of Corehouse was indicted as 'art and part in the away-taking and the reifing of Margaret Hamilton, dochter of John Hamilton of Auchnaglen, furth of James Weir's house of Dargavill'. His son gifted 20 merks to the library of Glasgow University in 1631 and inherited the estate the following year. In 1643 John Bannatyne of Corehouse had not yet inherited, but was a Commissioner appointed to raise a tax by the Convention of Estates. He was on the Committee for War for the county in the same year, then again in 1647 and 1648. He narrowly escaped the battlefield at Dunbar in 1650 when his father's tent was cut down while he was inside. He was appointed Local Commissioner of Excise in 1661, a Justice of Peace in 1663 and Commissioner of Supply in 1667. In 1682 this or another John was one of those outlawed and imprisoned as a rebel for his support of the Covenant. His name appears on the Covenanter Monument in Lanark, where he was later appointed as minister.

The Bannatynes sold Corehouse to the Somervilles of Cambusnethan in 1695, apparently in order to resolve their debt problems. The current Sir John had married an heiress of estates in Cumberland and moved there in 1694. By 1773 it had been sold to a family named Dixon, then to the Edmonstones. By the 19th century it had passed to George Cranstoun, who was raised to the bench as Lord Corehouse in 1826. By 1827 he had built himself the Elizabethan mansion nearby designed by Sir Edward Blore. Blore later enhanced his career by completing Buckingham Palace, following the dismissal of John Nash. He returned to extend the palace in 1847, providing it with the current facade. Corehouse was visited by William and Dorothy Wordsworth, who described the modern house as 'a neat white lady-like house'.

Corra Linn is one of the famous Falls of Clyde. It, with the castle and house, are said to be named after 'Cora', a princess who allegedly leapt the fall on horseback.

Access to the castle is prohibited since it is an important roost for Daubenton's Bats. It is a Scheduled Ancient Monument.

Other references: Corra Castle, Corrocks

CORMISTON TOWER

South Lanarkshire   Ruin or site   OS 73   NT 001372

2 miles west of Biggar, by minor roads north of A72, and north of the River Clyde at Cormiston Towers Farm.

Site of a tower house, of which nothing remains. It stood on the site of the present farm. From an early date the Somervilles were feudal superiors in this part of Quothquan Parish, which in 1660 was annexed to Libberton Parish and is now apparently within Biggar Parish. It appears as a small tower on Pont's map of the late 16th century. 'Tower' is depicted on William Forrest's map of 1816 and again on Thompsons map of 1832. By 1857 all traces of 'the old fortalice' had gone.

There is considerable ambiguity regarding ownership of the estate. In 1229 Ralph of Cormiston appears in a grant by Hugh of Biggar to the monks of Lesmahagow. Later it is described as 'an old possession' of the Chancellors of Shieldhill. In 1533 William Chancellor was designated of Quothquan, Shieldhill and Cormiston, and in 1535 stood as surety for Hugh, Lord Somerville, at the Justice Aires in Lanark. Curiously only a year later he, his brother Robert, and James Chancellor stood trial for the murder of Thomas Baillie, Laird of Cormiston, at which Lord Somerville reciprocated by standing as surety for their behaviour. There is also a William Baillie of Cormiston during the reign of Mary, Queen of Scots, who seems to have been forfeited then restored to his estates.

The estate has obviously been divided at a later date, since in the 19th century a house called Cormiston Towers was built and owned by the Collyer family and then sold in 1910 to Mr Peter MacLellan. The farm of Cormiston Towers seems to have been under different ownership since in 1857 James Gibson was in possession and by 1933, J.A. Brown. Sir Wyndham Charles James Carmichael MP was designated of Cormiston Towers in 1874–80. Other local properties are Cormiston, which belonged to the Somervilles in the 19th century, and Cormiston House, which contemporaneously belonged to a family named Thompson. There is also mention of an Alexander Johnston of Cormiston in 1853.

CORSLIE CASTLE

Renfrewshire   Ruin or site   OS 64   NS 545593

2.5 miles east of Barrhead by A726, just northeast of junction with B769, at or near Crosslees House.

Site of a castle of the Montgomerie Earls of Eglinton. It had a walled courtyard.

In 1710 Crawford in his *History of the Shire of Renfrew* named it Eastwood and described it as 'the principal Manour of that Barony…an ancient possession of the family of Eglinton'. Pont illustrates a small un-named three-storey tower, just north of 'Estwood' church in a position which approximates to that of Crosslee House.

It is said that on the death of the 5th Earl in 1612, he left an outstanding debt payable to Crawford of Possil. Crawford became frustrated at a lack of payment from the Earl's executors due to a dispute over the succession. He elected to take the law into his own hands. On the cloudy night of the 5th of September, he attacked Corslie, scaling the walls using ladders. Assisted by Hew Crawford of Cloberhill, he evicted the caretaker Gabriel Montgomerie at gunpoint. Montgomerie was grievously wounded. Tried and imprisoned, Crawford of Possil spent the following two years in Edinburgh Castle. Corslie was last occupied at the end of the 17th century.

The Barony of Eastwood had been the property of the Montgomerie Earls of Eglinton from the 15th century, excepting the larger portion of it which belonged to the Maxwells of Pollok. This included Auldhouse, Nether Pollok and latterly Darnley. The Montgomerie portion known as Eastwood proper was sold in 1812 to John Anderson. He sold it off in portions excepting Mains of Eastwood, which was retained by Lady Montgomerie. An alternative site has been suggested in Eastwood Park.

COT CASTLE

South Lanarkshire   Ruin or site   OS 64   NS 739457

2 miles northeast of Strathaven, 1 mile southwest of Stonehouse, 0.25 miles northeast of Bridgeholm Farm, just north of A71, and south of Avon Water.

Nothing remains of Cot Castle, occupied c.1500 by the Hamiltons. The castle stood on a mound at the edge of a precipice above the Avon, which may have originated as a motte. In 1838 the remains of two mortared walls and traces of two others were uncovered. These formed a square, the remains of the wall being about 7ft thick. Part of the site was used as limekilns in the 19th century. Two arched draw holes with projecting buttresses set into a bank remained of these. Cot Castle Farm was built on the site, but was abandoned in the 1970s and fell into disrepair. In 1955 the mound was described as being about 6.5 ft high, oval shaped, and about 92ft east-west by 66ft north-south. Nothing else remains.

The Barony of Stonehouse belonged to the Ross family at an early date, and in 1362 David II confirmed a charter by Godfrey de Ross to Alexander Elphinstone of the lands of Kythumbre. Godfrey was forfeited and the king granted William son of Maurice Moray the barony. It then came to the Douglases and Archibald the Grim, Earl of Douglas, granted Kythumbre to one of his prebendaries of Bothwell Kirk. On the forfeiture of the Douglases in 1455, the Hamiltons gained ownership, half went to Lord Hamilton and half to the Laird of Stonehouse. In 1512 Alexander Hamilton of Catcastle delivered sasine of the lands of Woodland and Brownland 'by his own hand' to James Wynzet. This may be the same Alexander Hamilton designated of Silvertonhill who was the ancestor of the Hamiltons of Newton. It has been suggested that Lord Somerville then gained Catcastle and Tweedie through his marriage to the daughter of Sir James Hamilton of Finnart. He then granted them to John Hamilton of Newton, Alexander's grandson, a grant confirmed under the Great Seal in 1531. Another charter under the Great Seal in 1581 granted Tweedie, Catcastle and Goslington to Sir Robert Hamilton of Goslington, who had inherited the latter from his father, Sir Andrew of Goslington. Andrew had various charters of other properties, notably of

Provan in 1599 following his marriage to the heiress of William Baillie. In 1666 Sir Robert Hamilton of Silvertonhill inherited Catcastle from his father Edward Hamilton.

The Hamiltons sold it c1700 to Lord Lee, who sold it on to his son. It then passed to a daughter and her husband, Lady Castlehill and the Sinclair Laird of Stevenson. By then the castle was ruinous and the couple were living at Cambusnethan in 1710.

Other references: Cat Castle, Coul Castle, Kat Castle, Kot Castle

COUTHALLEY CASTLE

South Lanarkshire   Ruin or site   OS 72   NS 972482

1.5 miles northwest of Carnwath, east of B7016, south of Woodend, west of main Edinburgh-Carstairs railway.

Only fragments remain of this castle of the Somervilles. It is thought to have originally consisted of a courtyard castle within a moat and accessed by drawbridge. Excavations in 1913 showed that the moat was in fact a series of three concentric ditches of little more than 1.5ft deep, but 16 to 23ft wide. These become waterlogged due to the surrounding boggy ground and at such a shallow depth could not be considered a true moat, but would nevertheless have presented an obstruction to would be assailants.

The walls varied in thickness from 5 to 6.5ft. There was an L-plan tower, a rectangular gatehouse and another tower at the main points along the wall. Once added these structures took up almost all of the available wall space, giving the remaining enceinte the proportions of a barmkin wall. The entire structure measured 59 by 70ft and, it is said, faced an avenue which apparently stretched for over a mile to Carnwath.

The castle was first recorded in the mid 12th century. The family had moved here from their motte and bailey castle at Carnwath. Couthalley was burnt by the English in 1320 and rebuilt in 1375. The structure was enlarged in 1415.

Thomas Somerville, Lord Justiciar of Scotland, is thought to have been created 1st Lord Somerville in around 1430, but his son William was the first clearly designated as such when mentioned in 1445. The references do not agree and presents one of several ambiguities in records for this family. This confuses the lineage since the 4th Lord is often listed as the 3rd and so on. The numeration allocated by *Burke's Peerage* designates William as 2nd Lord.

John, 3rd Lord, was with the Scots army who defeated the English at Sark in 1449. In 1451 he had Carnwath erected into a Burgh of Barony. He was also at the siege of Roxburgh in 1460 when a cannon exploded killing James II. He participated with the Boyds when they abducted the young James III, effectively giving control of the king and country to Robert, 1st Lord Boyd, who became Governor. John attended the Parliament of 1469 at which Lord Boyd's brother and accomplice, Alexander, was condemned to death for treason.

He was succeeded by his grandson, John, to whom James IV provided a grant of the lands of Carnwath 1508. The annual Red Hose Race commemorates this, since the charter demands that the laird provides 'one pair of hose containing half an ell of English cloth at the feast of St John the Baptist, called Midsummer, upon the ground

of the said barony, to the man running most quickly from the east end of the town of Carnwath to the Cross called Cawlo Cross'. John died in 1522-3 and was succeeded by his brother Hugh, 5th Lord.

Hugh made extensive additions and alterations to the castle in 1524-28. It then consisted of a square tower to the north, a round tower to the east and the new tower to the south. This latter is described as 'square, twice walled, and double battlemented'. The towers were quite separate, linked only by sections of the old enceinte of about 9ft high. Each tower was of four storeys, with one room to each floor. In 1520 he benefited from the forfeiture of his father's half brother, John 'Red Bag' Somerville of Cambusnethan. Losing a legal battle over the properties by 1528, Hugh sought the backing of Sir James Hamilton of Finnart. His son James married Finnart's daughter Agnes in 1536 and James V is alleged to have attended the wedding at Craignethan. He is thought to have visited Couthalley around the same time. Hugh was on the jury which condemned Finnart to death for treason in 1540.

The castle was besieged and partly destroyed in 1557, which is said by one source to have been carried out by Lord Somerville. It is said that his brother was holding the castle against him. James signed a bond with other nobles to promote the Reformation in 1560. Despite this he was loyal to Mary, Queen of Scots, and she is said to have visited Couthalley in 1563. He was severely wounded fighting for Mary at Langside in 1568, and in the aftermath signed several letters from Scottish lords to Queen Elizabeth requesting Mary's release. He died a year later.

The family moved to Drum but rebuilt Couthalley in 1586. The 8th Lord, Gilbert, entertained James VI at Couthalley in some splendour. James jokingly christened the castle 'Cow-thalley' since Gilbert had to slay a cow and ten sheep a day due to feed the attendant court. The name persists in some quarters today. To alleviate his debts, Gilbert conveyed the estate to John Erskine, Earl of Mar. He died in 1618 leaving only daughters and the title passed to his brother Hugh Somerville of Drum.

Hugh opted not to assume the title and it fell into abeyance until his descendant James decided to dispute a secondary claim to the title. He won his case and parliament appointed him 13th Lord in 1723. He was a Hanoverian during the 1715 Jacobite rebellion and was appointed aide-de-campe to General Cope at the Battle of Prestonpans, then General Hawley at the Battle of Falkirk.

There were still substantial remnants of the towers in 1815 but these burned down in 1820. The line ended in 1870 on the death of Aubrey John Somerville, 19th Lord.

St Mary's Aisle at the west end of the Carnwath dates from 1386. It was converted to a collegiate church by the Somervilles 1425. The existing remnant is the former north transept which became the mausoleum of the Somervilles, the Dalzell Earls of Carnwath and the Lockharts. It contains rare effigy style memorials, including that of Hugh, 5th Lord, and his wife Janet Maitland, daughter of Maitland of Lethington.

Other references: Couthally, Cowthalley

COVINGTON CASTLE

South Lanarkshire   Ruin or site   OS 72   NS 975399
6 miles east and south of Lanark, 2 miles north of Thankerton, on minor roads north of A73, just north of Covington.

Set on raised dry ground within what was once marshland and surrounded by the complex earthworks and the ditches of an predecessor, Covington Castle is a ruinous 15th century tower house. There is a partly restored 16th century circular doocot of 500 boxes a few yards away. This probably stood at one corner of a courtyard with gardens. A short section of the linking wall remains. The tower is built of coursed rubble, which once had dressed ashlar blocks around the features, though these are now robbed out. The village retains the classic medieval grouping of castle and church.

The upper floors and parapet have long since gone, though it was probably a four-storey structure and measures approx. 47ft by 38ft. Built upon walls 11ft thick, there were numerous slot windows, with slightly larger examples lighting the upper apartments.

The ground floor was vaulted and had a loft. There remains a stone sink and conduit drain within a recess in the west wall. There was probably a well, long since blocked. Entry from the courtyard was via a door centrally placed in north side and from this a short straight stair led to a turnpike and the floor above.

The hall utilised the whole of the first floor and had large window recesses with stone seats and dressed ashlar arches. The fireplace was in the east wall, with mural chambers either side. Above these additional long slot windows improved the lighting. A pit prison is built within the walls.

The ditches may represent the remains of the *villa Colbani*, the early moated manor house of the Flemish/ Norman lord Colbin. Colbin witnessed the deed of David I which founded what became Kelso Abbey at Selkirk. He was succeeded by his son, Merevin, who witnessed the charter by which David founded the Benedictine Abbey at Dunfermline and similarly the foundation of Dryburgh Abbey. Colbanston in its various spellings came

to be used as the surname of their successors, who appear as charter witnesses in the 12th and 13th centuries. In 1265 the barony was taken by the Crown for non payment of a fine of 100 merks and in 1288 the exchequer paid for repairs to the house of Nortun belonging to the sisters of Colbanston. Margaret and Isabelle with Edmund de Colbanston rendered homage to Edward I in 1296, after which Margaret was granted restoration of the estate by the Sheriff of Lanark.

Covington was granted by Robert I to Robert Keith, the Earl Marischal. In 1324 he resigned his position and estates to his grandson Robert, among other heirs. In 1406 William, Earl Marischal, granted the Barony and Church to his son, Robert Keith of Troup. It has been said that the barony was granted around this time to John Maitland, nephew of the Keith owner.

By 1420 it had come to the Lindsays and they built the tower in 1442. They had been vassals of the Keiths since early in their tenure and may have been at Covington since 1368, when John Lindsay laid claim to the former Hospitaller property of Warrenhill. John had married a Covington heiress and probably gained the estate as her dowry. Another John Lindsay of Covington was a witness to a charter of Shieldhill in 1460. In 1468 John Douglas raided the lands of Covington, robbing and burning the town.

John Lindsay seemed fond of a day or two in court. In 1473 he became involved in an action against James Somerville, Parson of the Church at Covington, then in 1478 had to defend himself against a charge of independently taking on the role of Baillie of Crawford and collecting the rents. In 1489 he sued Robert Lockhart of Lee and then from 1471 to 1486 was engaged in a prolonged case against Livingston of Belstane and his superior Robert Maxwell regarding ownership of the lands of Warrenhill. In the early 16th century John Lindsay of Colbanston and his brother Roland were given a nineteen year remission for the murder of Weir of Stonebyres in Edinburgh. The estate was held as security and in 1534 was granted to Malcolm, 3rd Lord Fleming. John Lindsay had his lands restored before 1541, when he was charged with treason for abstaining from a Scottish raid on Wark. He died in 1550 and was succeeded by another John, who was involved in a violent feud with John Somerville, the Rector of Libberton, and various others of that family. In 1554, with 200 others including his brother John, James Somerville and Alexander Lindsay of Northflat, he attacked the rector's barn and grievously wounded his servant. In retaliation, James, Lord Somerville, and his men attacked and seriously wounded John Lindsay's half brother, also John. Lindsay then attacked and killed Lord Somerville's brother, John, at Gaitsyde. In 1563 John helped Carmichael of that Ilk attack the officers of the Sheriff of Lanark, then held one of them as prisoner in Covington for three days. In 1582 he was imprisoned in Edinburgh Castle for two years for treasonably burning the cereal stocks of the advocate John Sharp at Horstoun in Midlothian. John died in 1602 and was succeeded by his grandson, who unsurprisingly was named John. His brother George and their uncle Gavin were among those accused of the murder of Alexander, Lord Spynie, in 1607. The Lindsays were obviously a belligerent lot, and a local rhyme echoes the sentiment of a rhyme associated with their namesakes at Dunrod:

'Who rides so fast down Coulter brae, The Devil or a Lindsay?'

In 1679 William Lindsay of Covington, ironically a Justice of the Peace, sold the estate to Sir George Lockhart

President of the Court of Session in order to pay off his debts. William died that year. It is said that he had squandered so much of the family wealth that his descendants were employed as farm labourers. Extensive gardens are mentioned as having existed within the grounds of the castle and the complexity of earthworks may reflect this.

Other reference: Colbanstoun

COWDEN HALL

Renfrewshire   Ruin or site   OS 64   NS 467572
South of A736 Lochlibo Road, Neilston, Renfrewshire.

Site of a castle of the Spreulls of Dalmuir. Now a ruin, Cowden Hall had origins in the early 14th century. A portion of wall in the corner of a field is all that remains of two roofless buildings at opposite corners of a rectangular courtyard shown on OS maps of the mid 19th century. A 19-20th century mansion of the same name stood 0.3 miles to the northeast.

Described as a 17th century laird's house and farmstead with 18th century additions, the two buildings noted within the courtyard stood 65ft apart, that to the northwest was an L-plan range and that to the southeast being rectangular. The former measured about 100ft long with a wing or 'outshot' in its southwestern corner measuring about 20ft by 17ft. This was probably a thatched single storey structure. The other range was about 37ft long, and divided into two unequal apartments on the ground floor.

The remaining fragment stands in the corner of a field. In 2007 it consisted of a gable reaching 21ft high, with wall sections measuring 22ft and 30ft which are between 3 and 4 ft thick. The gable contains the remains of a fireplace and chimney. The building was of coursed rubble and there is evidence that it was covered in pink harling.

Sir Robert Croc is thought to have had an early castle in Neilston. In the late 12th century he was granted the lands of Kilbride in the parish by Alan the High Steward as 'a land of 100s which he owed to Robert' and in 1163 granted his church at Neilston to the monks of Paisley Abbey. The later Stewart Earls then Dukes of Lennox became superiors of the Barony of Neilston.

In 1305-6 Walter Spreull of Dalmuir, Seneschal to the Earl of Lennox, was given a grant of the estate of Cowden. He witnessed the 1316 charter to John of Luss by Robert I. Later members of the family received grants of confirmation in the estate in 1481 and 1515. In 1572 Thomas Spreull, Laird of Cowden, attended parliament in Edinburgh.

James Spreull sold Cowden to Alexander Blair of that Ilk in 1622. Alexander married the Cochrane heiress and adopted her name, their descendants becoming the Earls of Dundonald. Cowden passed to the Marquis of Clydesdale in 1725. The Mures of Caldwell obtained it in 1766.

In 1860 Robert Orr, the owner of Crofthead Mill, built the mansion, but was demolished in the 1960s. It had been used as a convalescent home during World War I. The gate piers and sections of the walled garden are some of the few remnants that remain.

Other reference: Cowdon Hall

COWGLEN

City of Glasgow   Ruin or site   OS 64   NS 535612
West of the M77, south of the B762, on east bank of the Brock Burn, just south of Silverburn Shopping Centre.

Site of an old or fortified house of the Maxwells of Pollok. In the 16th century, John Maxwell, son of George Maxwell of Cowglen, married the heiress of Pollok, his first cousin . In 1558 he inherited the Pollok estate from her father. John was knighted by Mary, Queen of Scots, and was a loyal supporter. In 1568 she wrote to him requesting that he meet her at Hamilton, 'boden in feer of Weir'. He accompanied her to fight at the Battle of Langside. He died ten years later.

By the 19th century the estate had been divided into two farms, West and East Cowglen.

CRAIGBARNET CASTLE

The Lennox & East Dunbartonshire   Ruin or site   OS 64   NS 593790
2 miles west of Lennoxtown, just north of the A891, at Craigbarnet.

Once a large and important castle of the Stirlings, nothing remains of Craigbarnet Castle. It was replaced by a mansion and then another, of which the walled garden and an ornate barn remain. The castle site is adjacent to the modern farm, the remains having been cleared and planted as woodland by developers. The second Craigbarnet House was demolished in 1953.

Gilbert, the first Stirling of Craigbarnet, appears on record in 1434, the year of his death. He was the son of William of Cadder and is supposed to have gained the estate by marrying the heiress Alicia de Erth (Airth). The name Craig-Barnet is a corruption of Craig Bernard and is allegedly a throw back to Alicia's great grandfather, Bernard de Erth.

On Gilbert's death, the estate passed to his son, who was still a minor. This is the Johannes (John) de Strivelyn de Craigbernard mentioned in an instrument of Sasine in 1468. His grandson, John, was appointed Keeper of Dumbarton Castle by James III, a position he still held under James IV. This king stayed in at Craigbarnet and is recorded as having received 24 shillings from the treasurer to play cards 'that nicht in Craigbernard', the 9th of February 1507. His second son William was the progenitor of the Glorat branch of the family.

Another John became involved in a feud with Sir William Edmonstone of Duntreath in 1531. The Stirlings managed to withhold Duntreath from Sir William for three years. By 1563 they had an established feud with the Kincaids. James, the heir of Kincaid, and his brother, Malcolm, were attacked by a group of Stirlings in Glasgow, the younger brother losing the use of his left arm through mutilation. Both escaped with their lives. The feud with the Kincaids continued during the tenure of the next John, and in 1581 he, with accomplices, attacked the Kincaids killing Malcolm Kincaid, whom his father's party had so badly injured. Malcolm was avenged when his brother Thomas killed Stirling of Baldoran, one of the group involved in Malcolm's death.

John, 9th of Craigbarnet, was a close friend and comrade in arms of the Marquis of Montrose, his near neighbour from Mugdock. After Philiphaugh in 1645 he was captured by General Leslie. His fellow prisoner was Mungo Stirling of Glorat, who later became his father-in-law. Sir John was nicknamed 'Burrie' due to a speech impediment. In 1662 he decided to replace the old castle with a new mansion. He had apparently chosen an altogether different site at Keirhill, on an ancient burial ground, and whatever he constructed by day was destroyed at night. One night he heard a voice say:

'Burrie build your house in a bog, and you'll ne'er want a fou' cog'

John apparently conceded and built his house to the south of the present farm on an artificially raised area in what was a peat bog. A similar tale has also been told of Ballindalloch Castle on Speyside. The new house was said to be square on plan with pepper pot turrets and a wet ditch with drawbridge.

John was succeeded by his son, Mungo, who married the Glorat heiress. By 1731 the estate was so encumbered by debt that it was purchased by Stirling of Keir 'to preserve the estate of Craigbarnet to Mungo Stirling and his heirs'. There are no records on which side Mungo took in the Jacobite rebellion of 1715, but it has been suggested that support for the Pretender was the cause of his debts. Mungo died aged 73 in 1733, followed by his wife 11 days later. Their son James inherited and occupied Craigbarnet as a tenant. He also had a speech impediment, and so the 'Burrie' nickname was reused. James was 'out' in the 1745 rebellion and it is said that Bonnie Prince Charlie stayed at Craigbarnet. He later apparently presented his friend with a sword, and with a waistcoat embroidered by Flora McDonald. The family retained these treasures at least until the 19th century. James was taken prisoner by the Hanoverians in the aftermath of the rebellion and escaped from Dumbarton Castle after about a week. He went on the run in home territory and often hid in a house at the Kirklands of Strathblane or at Glorat. He had many narrow escapes, often in disguise as an old woman, and fled to either the thick woodland around Woodhead, or the copses around Strathblane. It is even said that the Prince himself once hid with him in the Kirklands. James died in 1773 and was succeeded by his son, John, who built a new house on the site of the present farm in 1776, adjacent to the old castle site. He demolished the old house in the bog and incorporated armorial stones from it in the new build. In 1805 John died childless and the estate passed to Alexander Gartshore-Stirling and then to Major Charles Campbell Graham Stirling. Through the marriage of his posthumous daughter, it came to her husband Lt. George H. Miller R.N.

The estate was sold in the 20th century and the site of the house and original castle became a woodland development. The adjacent ground, including the barn and walled garden, were developed as the present farm.

Other reference: Craigbernard Castle

CRAIGBET

Renfrewshire Private OS 63 NS 370655
1 mile west of Bridge of Weir, by minor roads south of A761, east of Quarrier's Village.

Site of a castle. Craigbet is a harled Renaissance-style house, consisting of a basement and two upper storeys which probably dates from the mid 18th century. There is a flight of 14 steps to the entrance on the east side. The garden contains a sundial which was removed from Giffen Castle and placed here in 1968.

A tower with barmkin and secondary tower are sketched on Pont's map of the late 16th century. Craigbet was a property of a cadet branch of the Semples, who were descended from David, a younger son of the 2nd Lord

Semple. They held the property from at least as early as 1550 when William Semple was in possession. By 1800 it belonged to Curry Esq. and in 1818 by Alexander Graham. Later in the 19th century it belonged to the McCullochs.

Other reference: Kraigbar

CRAIGEND CASTLE

The Lennox & East Dunbartonshire Ruin or site OS 64 NS 545777

2.5 miles north of Milngavie, on minor roads between A81 and A809, 0.25 miles northwest of Mugdock Castle, at Craigend.

Craigend Castle was a large mansion built in 1812. It stood within a large estate, and possibly replaced or incorporated an earlier castle or tower, which may at some point have belonged to the Inglis family.

Formerly known as Gallowhill, this had been part of the Graham's Mugdock estate until 1660 when the 2nd Marquis of Montrose had to sell this portion to reduce his debts. It was purchased by his tenants, the Smith family, who were merchant burgesses and later booksellers in Glasgow. They had a house here, which may have been incorporated in the later buildings. They built a plain square late 18th century house on the site, before incorporating parts of it within the present mansion in 1812. Designed by the family, it was completed by Alexander Ramsay.

It was purchased in 1851 by Sir Andrew Buchanan GCB, former British Ambassador to Vienna, and son of Buchanan of Ardenconnel and Blairvadick. He leased the castle to Harold Yarrow, son of the famous shipbuilder, who lived there until the 1920s. In 1949 it was sold to the Wilsons, a father and son zoologist family who operated it as a zoo until 1955. The house is now a roofless empty shell, which stands as a feature within Mugdock Country Park. The Visitor Centre is located within the former stable block (www.mugdock-country-park.org.uk).

CRAIGENDS CASTLE

Renfrewshire Ruin or site OS 64 NS 419662

1 mile east of Kilmacolm on minor roads south of B790, and east of B789, on south bank of River Gryffe, just north of Cunninghame Gardens, Craigends.

Demolished before 1889, the mansion of Old Craigends House may have contained an earlier structure. A large castle is illustrated at the site and is named 'M. Kragas' on Pont's map of 1596. In 1857 it was described as an excellent mansion, over 300-years old, whose very strong walls were perfectly preserved. Another source indicates that portions of it dated from 1477.

Early owners of the estate may have included the Knoxs of Ranfurly. It is said that they continued to use the designation 'of Craigends' long after the estate came to the Cunninghames in the late 15th century. William Cunninghame, a younger son of the 1st Earl of Glencairn, was given the estate by his father in 1477. His descendants founded the cadet lines of Robertland, Cairncurran, Bedland, Auchinharvie and Suthook. It is said that his eldest son, William, was murdered in 1533 by William, 2nd Lord Semple. Gabriel Cunninghame of Craigends died at the Battle of Pinkie in 1547. He left two sons: William, who succeeded, and James, who founded another cadet branch at Auchinyards. William died in 1568, the year of the Battle of Langside. His son Alexander inherited as 5th Laird and it is said that in 1594 a group of 54 people were bound over not to harm him. In 1854 William, 15th Laird, sold the estate to his uncle Alexander and retired to Belmont in Ayrshire.

In 1857 Alexander demolished the old house and built a new mansion designed by David Bryce on a site to the southeast. His son John was the last of the line and died in 1917. His widow stayed in the house until her death in the late 1950s. In 1961 the contents of the house were auctioned off by a nephew. The estate was sold and the house fell victim to vandals. The ruins were demolished in 1980.

Other reference: Old Craigends House

CRAIGHEAD

South Lanarkshire Ruin or site OS 72 NS 815407

Just north of Lesmahagow and east of M74, by minor roads west of B7018 east of River Nethan at or near Craighead.

Site of a large tower depicted on Pont's manuscript map of Clydesdale of the late 16th century, and subsequently in Blaeu's *Atlas Novus* of 1654.

A disused water driven corn mill dating from the 18th century and in use until 1974 now bears the name. The rear wall of the building is thought to be earlier. There is also evidence of a 'medieval farmhouse' at Craighead.

Robert Weir 'of Craighead' is recorded in the 16th century. He was the 3rd son of James Weir of Blackwood, and married the sister of the alchemist, Sir David Lindsay. Robert apparently so offended the Marquis of Hamilton,

Lord High Commissioner, that he sold his estate in 1610 and emigrated to County Fermanagh in Ireland, establishing a cadet line of the family there. He changed the name of Monaghan House to Hallcraig. By 1625 the Duke of Hamilton had possession of Craighead and gifted it to David Hamilton of Auldton. The Craighead referred to in references is described as 'on the Clyde'. It is possible that this relates to a different property of the same or similar name, perhaps Hallcraig.

Other reference: Fairholm

CRAIGIEVERN CASTLE

The Lennox & East Dunbartonshire   Ruin or site   OS 57   NS 493910
2.5 miles north of Drymen, off minor road north of A811, just south of Muirpark reservoir, near Craigievern.

Craigievern consists of a three-storey T-plan 18th century lairds' house, with a small 20th century addition in a farm complex. This house is thought to have been built using stone from an older castle, probably on the same site.

A tower appears here on Pont's maps of the late 16th century and a large complex as 'Kragivairn' in Blaeu's *Atlas Novus* of the 17th century. There are the remains of what is now thought to be a broch, 0.25 miles to the southeast. In the 1960s some authorities had identified this as the barmkin for the original castle. In 1963 the remains were described as 'a ruinous and grass grown stone wall measuring between 8 and 10ft thick…75ft in diameter'. There is evidence of stone robbing. The broch occupies the highest point of a low ridge west of the Altquhur Burn.

The old house belonged to a cadet branch of the Buchanans, and it is said that they purchased the estate from the Napiers probably in the late 16th century. The Napiers had a grant in 1494-5 which included the 'fishings on the Endrick and Altquhur' which were within their barony of Edinbellie-Napier.

CRAIGMADDIE CASTLE

The Lennox & East Dunbartonshire   Ruin or site   OS 64   NS 575766
2 miles northeast of Milngavie, on minor road east of A81, just east of Craigmaddie House.

All that remains of Craigmaddie is a vaulted basement and the lower portions of the gables. It is a 16th century tower house, which stands in a D-shaped fort. One authority believes the fort to be a medieval ringwork castle. The straight side of the D is formed by the crest of a steep drop from the ridge which the site occupies. The curved side of the site is bounded by the remains of two unmortared stone ramparts, one of which was 12ft thick. The site measures 135ft by 110ft. The entrance seems to have been at the eastern end of the straight side.

The only internal feature of the 'fort' is the ruin of Craigmaddie Castle. It comprises a rectangular tower of a little over 22ft by 24 ft, with walls 5ft thick. There was a single room on each floor and the surviving basement is vaulted with a slit window in each gable. The northwest gable reaches a height of 10ft and a fragment of the southwest gable slightly higher. Other wall fragments survive only to foundation level.

Craigmaddie stands within the parish of Baldernock, which Maldouen, Earl of Lennox, granted to Maurice, son of Galbraith, as 'the lands of Cartonvenach', an early name for the parish. In 1238 Maldouen, Earl of Lennox, granted 'the two Baldernocks' and Kincaid to William son of Arthur son of Galbraith.

Early in the 15th century, Baldernock passed by the marriage of an heiress to John (sometimes recorded as David), the 5th son of David Hamilton of Cadzow. Duncan, Earl of Lennox, confirmed John's ownership by grant. A later John Hamilton was confirmed in his estate of Bathernock by James IV in 1505. The Hamiltons left for their new castle at Bardowie before 1526.

The tower at Craigmaddie is traditionally associated with the Galbraiths, but is reckoned to have originated in the 16th century, when it would have been Hamilton property. Earlier medieval use of the ringwork would be contemporary with the Galbraith era. It has been suggested that Baldernock is derived from 'place of the druids', and Craigmaddie from 'the rock of god'.

Other reference: Kraigin Castle

CRAIGNEITH CASTLE

South Lanarkshire   Ruin or site   OS 64   NS 663553
1.5 miles northeast of East Kilbride, by minor roads and foot south of A725, west of Auchentibber, and above the Avon Gorge.

The ruinous stump which remains is the remnant of an accommodation block, which had a small round stair tower at one end. It was apparently built in the early 18th century by the Maxwells of Calderwood as accommodation for their servants. It was demolished in the late 20th century.

A large castle next to a bridge in this vicinity is illustrated and named as 'Kalder' in Blaeu's Atlas. This undoubtedly represents Crossbasket.

CRAIGNETHAN CASTLE

South Lanarkshire   His Scot   OS 72   NS 816464

4.5 miles northwest of Lanark by the A72, 2 miles west of Crossford, 1 mile northeast by track from Tillietudlem.

Craignethan consists of a large 16th century tower house within a walled courtyard with supporting towers at strategic points of the perimeter. A second walled courtyard protecting the approach and a sophisticated arrangement of a ditch and gun-ports around all provides further defence. It is sited upon a spur that is protected by a ravine on three sides, the fourth and west side being the heavily defended approach.

The main tower, or keep, of the castle is sited close to the point of the spur and is separated from the awkward approach by several strong lines of defence. It is a parallelogram of around 63 by 50ft and 33ft high. There were once two storeys plus an attic, now lost, above a vaulted basement below ground level. There were four large vaults here, and one smaller, which was possibly a prison. One of these contained the well, and another had a hatch leading to the kitchen above for supply purposes. A cramped stairwell, also accessing the kitchen, supplemented this. The building is divided into two halves by an interior wall stretching the entire length of the east-west axis of the structure. An unusual feature is that the main rooms are on the ground floor as opposed to the usual first floor arrangement.

The main door is in the west wall at this level, leading to a very large reception area. From this a wide stairway leads to the first floor, with another below to the basement. There is a small guardroom containing a mural stairwell leading to the parapet. The main hall is entered from here, it measures 20ft by 40.5ft. It had a high vaulted ceiling and two large windows on the south wall. A fireplace was incorporated within the central wall, but has now gone. A stair in the southwest corner leads to a musician's gallery high on the west wall. A private chamber with fireplace and garderobe is entered from the northeast corner, as is a private stair to the first floor. A kitchen with large fireplace and a private suite of rooms for the lord take up the remainder of the floor. Above this section was an additional floor at the level of the vaulting in the hall, and it was supported by wooden flooring. There is an altered serving hatch from the kitchen to the reception area. The upper floor is ruined, though it appears to have had four rooms with individual garderobes and fireplaces. There remains decorative string coursing and corbelling atop the walls. It is thought that the keep was battlemented, and stone roofed. There are open bartizans at each corner and machicolations over the entrance.

Towers at each corner and a gate tower strengthened the inner courtyard wall. The western wall reached 16ft in thickness, in illustration of the design of the castle as principally for defence against artillery. It once supported

artillery batteries and had a battlemented parapet. Much of it is now demolished. The southeastern tower is larger than the others and is the least ruinous. It is believed that this was the chapel, but has acquired the by-name of the 'Kitchen Tower'. This has three storeys and is unusually proportioned, 34ft by 31.75ft. Its basement is at ground level outwith the perimeter of the castle, while within the ground reaches the first floor. Subterranean vaults support the courtyard to this level within the yard, these being accessed from a door and stair in the south wall. The vaults of the keep may have been entered from these at one time. Each of the towers supported auxiliary accommodation, either for guests or servants. The ground floors would have provided service areas, for bakery, brewhouse and so on.

Access to the inner yard from the outer was via a drawbridge, thence a narrow gateway, which led into one of the towers. A ditch supplemented the western defences. At 30ft wide and 12ft deep it presented a formidable barrier. In 1962 a unique feature was excavated at the southern end of this ditch. The caponier is a defensive structure which traversed the width of the ditch, with gunloops allowing fire along the base of the ditch. This added a major obstacle to an attacking force. The caponier was accessed via a stair from within the west wall. At the northern end of the ditch, a wall provides gunnery positions from which crossfire could be given. It was similarly accessed from the west wall.

The outer courtyard was a larger area, and may once have been centred by gardens. It is of later date than the inner courtyard. The walls here were not as strongly built, though could still have prevented smaller assaults. A tower which functioned as the 'Dovecote Tower' strengthens the northeast corner, while in the southeast corner the wall carries a fireplace and blocked door of a former room betraying the position of a lost tower. Adjacent to this is a postern gate. The gatehouse is situated midway along the outer western wall.

In the southwestern corner stands a later house of 1665. It is known as Andrew Hay's house and has two storeys and an attic. There is a round stair tower off-centre, and it is built against the perimeter wall. It incorporates parts of an earlier tower. Lean-to subsidiary buildings probably surrounded this entire courtyard, and in many places on the interior wall, projecting corbels can be seen which would have supported their roofs.

Formerly known as Draffane, this was a Douglas property until their forfeiture in 1455. It was granted to the Hamiltons and in about 1530 was given to Sir James Hamilton of Finnart, 'the Bastard of Arran'. He was the illegitimate son of the 1st Earl of Arran, legitimized in 1513. As a young man he had toured Europe and had studied the defensive architecture of several countries, possibly even meeting Leonardo Da Vinci when he was in France. On his return, Hamilton gained popularity at court and, with his continental experience, became Master of Works to James V. He was a ruthless, dangerous and acquisitive character who frequently appears as a short-term owner of properties in the 1530s. He was willing to trade property with anyone, if the deal suited his personal ambitions at the time.

He began work on Craignethan about 1531, building it as a showcase for his talents and as the most sophisticated example of a castle designed for defence with and against artillery. Some argue that this is the irony, given that the land on the west is high enough to provide an artillery platform from which cannon could strafe the entire site. In fact the former great height of the west wall and the squat nature of the keep would have prevented this, the parapet of the wall providing an artillery platform from which the approaches could be bombarded. The castle provides a unique example of what could be achieved given a talent such as his. James, Master of Somerville, married Finnart's daughter Agnes in 1536, and James V is thought to have attended the wedding at Craignethan. In 1540 Finnart was beheaded for treason, after having been charged with conspiracy against the King, including 12-year-old charges of firing guns and missiles at James V and his company in Linlithgow.

The castle was regained by the Hamiltons from the Crown in 1542. Arran added the outer court prior to the coronation of Mary, Queen of Scots, when he gained the French title Duke of Chatelherault. He became Regent for Mary during her infancy, but later lost Craignethan and Cadzow to the Crown as he opposed her marriage to Darnley. He returned to regain both and support her after her enforced abdication, helping her escape from Lochleven Castle in 1568. Lord Claud Hamilton may have had her as a guest at the castle and the next day led her forces at Langside. He lost the battle, Cadzow and Craignethan to the Regent Moray. He recaptured the castles in the same year. Hamilton of Bothwellhaugh assassinated Moray two years later.

The animosity between those who controlled the young James VI and the Hamiltons continued and in 1579 they were again proclaimed outlaw. They fled to France and both castles surrendered without a fight. Craignethan's massive west wall was pulled down along with the northwest tower.

The noted Covenanter Andrew Hay purchased Craignethan, and built himself the new house in the outer courtyard. The castle was bought by the Duke of Douglas in 1730. Along with Bothwell, it passed through his descendants until in 1949 the Earl of Home gave them into the care of the state.

Sir Walter Scott is said to have used Craignethan as model for 'Tillietudlem' in his novel *Old Mortality*, though he habitually denied such links. He did consider restoration of the castle as his own home, but opted to build anew at Abbotsford. The railway companies followed their tradition of naming stations after places invented by Scott, and named the local station 'Tillietudlem'. The castle has since acquired Scott's invented name as an alias.

A headless spirit is said to haunt the castle and it is suggested that this apparition is of Mary. Andrew Hay's house is also reported to have spectral visitations.

Open daily April to October (tel: 01555 860365) Historic Scotland.

Other references: Draffane, Tillietudlem

CRAWFORD CASTLE

South Lanarkshire   Ruin or site   OS 72   NS 954213

0.5 miles north of Crawford, on minor roads east of the A74, just north of the River Clyde, and just south of Castle Crawford Farm.

Crawford Castle sits upon the large motte of its predecessor, which retains traces of a silted-up ditch and large bailey. A causeway crossed the ditch from the east. The motte stands 18ft high. The tower was ruinous by 1864.

The castle consisted of an almost square enclosure within a curtain wall 5ft thick and measuring some 80ft by 70ft. Plans drawn by MacGibbon and Ross show a remnant of a semi-circular round tower in the northwest corner of the enceinte. Similar towers at the other corners may have existed. The gateway was probably in the south wall, now mostly gone. The northeast corner of the court was once occupied by a vaulted building of one storey. The northern two thirds of the western wall was formed by a large rectangular block of three storeys and a garret, of which only the once vaulted ground floor remains. There may have been a defensive wall to the west of the main block outwith the main enclosure. Much of what remains probably dates from the extensive rebuilding programme of the Marquis of Douglas in the 17th century. A number of armorial stones presumably from the castle, one dated 1649, are built into the walls of Castle Crawford House.

The castle at Crawford was first recorded in c.1175 when the Bishop of Glasgow granted the 'chapel of the castle', which was dedicated to St Thomas the Martyr, to Holyrood Abbey. It is said that from an early date the hereditary keepers were the Carmichaels of Meadowflat. They retained the office until at least 1595, despite changes in ownership.

From at least the early 12th century the barony and castle were the property of the Lindsays. From an early

date it was known as Crawford Lindsay, distinguishing it from Crawfordjohn. The family made regular grants of land to the church and in 1170 William de Lindsay made just such a donation to the monks of Newbattle. It records that he owed service to the king and to 'Swein son, of Thor', his feudal lord. William de Lindsay was Justiciar to William the Lion and was designated 'of Crawford, Ercildoune and Luffness' in 1227. In 1239 his grandson David de Lindsay granted Glengonnar and Glencaple to Newbattle Abbey. John de Lindsay of Lanarkshire rendered homage to Edward I in 1296. During the Wars of Independence, Crawford was held by Henry de Pinkney, an adherent of Edward I, who may have been married to a Crawford heiress.

Sir William Wallace captured the castle from the English in 1297, and the Lindsays were reinstated in the Bruce era. Sir David Lindsay of Crawford was one of an impressive gathering of nobles at the signing of the Treaty of Edinburgh in 1328 by which Edward II renounced all rights of sovereignty in Scotland. David's son, James, was granted a safe conduct by Edward III as he was to be a hostage for the release of David II after the battle of Neville's Cross. His son, the next Sir James Lindsay of Crawford, was a close associate of Robert II and in 1372 was briefly awarded the earldom of Wigtown. It was quickly reassigned to Archibald the Grim, Lord of Galloway and later Earl of Douglas.

His nephew David Lindsay inherited and became Earl of Crawford in 1398. He married the daughter of King Robert II and is thought to have been the organiser of the 'Battle of the Clans' in Perth in 1396. He was a renowned jousting champion and famously defeated the English champion, Lord Welles. Having easily unhorsed Welles, he was accused of nailing himself to his saddle. His response was to leap out of and then back into his saddle, no mean feat in full armour.

His grandson David died in 1445 at the Battle of Arbroath while attempting to broker a truce between the Lindsays and the Ogilvies. Next up was Alexander, the 'Tiger Earl', an ally of the Douglases. As a result of refusing to abandon his treaty with Crawford, the 8th Earl of Douglas was stabbed to death by James II at Stirling Castle in 1452. James's forces finally caught up with the Tiger Earl and defeated him at the Battle of Brechin, after which he submitted to the king. Also known as 'Beardie', Alexander's ghost is said to haunt Glamis Castle, where he is said to play cards with the Devil in a walled up room.

His son David achieved high office under James III and had Crawford erected into a Burgh of Barony in 1467. As Lord High Admiral, Master of the Royal Household, Great Chamberlain and Justiciar, he was created Duke of Montrose in 1488, the first non-royal to receive a dukedom. He fought alongside James III at the Battle of Sauchieburn that year and as a result James IV declared him forfeit. Sometime later the new king reinstated the dukedom for David's lifetime only. The Crawford earldom continued through the descendants of his son John who became Earls of Lindsay then Earls of Balcarres.

The castle and estate of Crawford was granted to Archibald Douglas, 5th Earl of Angus. He was known as 'Bell the Cat' due to the manner in which he planned the removal and execution of Thomas Cochrane, the overly influential favourite of James III. Bell the Cat held the positions of Chancellor and Warden of the East March and was head of the Red Douglases. They had actually benefited from the demise of their Black Douglas cousins in 1455. Their main residence was at Tantallon Castle. Archibald changed the name from Crawford Lindsay to Crawford Douglas. He was not at the Battle of Flodden in 1513 which saw the death of his two eldest sons.

On Archibald's death c1513-14, Crawford and the earldom passed to his grandson, also Archibald. He married Margaret Tudor, the widow of James IV, a marriage which caused resentment among the other nobles and ultimately cost Margaret the regency. In the political machinations of the minority of James V, he became Chancellor and filled most of the important positions in government with Douglases. He resisted armed attempts to relieve him of the custody of the young king who, as he approached maturity, became increasingly disenchanted with his stepfather. In 1528 Margaret divorced him, and the King escaped to Stirling where he took refuge with his mother and the Earl of Arran. James forfeited Archibald almost immediately, who went into exile in England.

Thereafter Crawford became a favoured hunting seat of the king, who repaid the keepers hospitality by making his daughter pregnant (see Boghouse). On the king's death in 1542 the forfeiture was revoked. Angus returned from England and reclaimed his estates.

Archibald, 8th Earl, was Warden of the West March, Privy Counsellor, and twice Lieutenant-General of the Realm. He was in league with his uncle the Earl of Morton during the minority of James VI and attempted to rescue him from imprisonment. Angus was convicted of treason in 1581 having persistently plotted against the Regent Arran. In 1585 he invaded Scotland then overthrew Arran. The king restored his estates. The following year he was granted the Earldom of Morton.

In 1588 he was succeeded by his cousin, William Douglas of Glenbervie, whose death in 1591 was attributed to witchcraft at the North Berwick trials. Barbara Napier was found guilty and burned on the Castlehill in Edinburgh.

His son William, 10th Earl of Angus, visited the French Court, returned as a Roman Catholic and fought against the reformist government. Imprisoned in Edinburgh Castle, he escaped and joined the revolt of the Earls of Huntly and Errol, attacking Aberdeen. With his allies, he was given the opportunity to renounce Catholicism or go into exile, he chose the latter and was forfeited in 1593. In 1597 he proclaimed himself a Presbyterian, and was restored to his estates and titles. He became a Privy Counsellor and the King's Lieutenant in the south. In 1608 he again fell out with the government following the award of a marquisate to Huntly. He went into exile in France, where he died in 1611.

His son William, 11th Earl of Angus, was also a Catholic. He supported King Charles I in the Civil War and in 1638 became Marquis of Douglas, taking the title from his main residence. His sons gained a number of honours, Archibald became Earl of Angus and later Earl of Ormonde, William, Earl of Selkirk, later gaining the Dukedom of Hamilton, and George became Earl of Dumbarton. Archibald's son James became the next Marquis of Douglas and a privy Counsellor to Charles II and James VII. The family sold their Crawford estate to Sir George Colebrooke in the 18th century. He was a wealthy and influential merchant banker from England with diverse business interests. He bought up a number of Lanarkshire estates as part of an investment in land.

Other references: Castle Crawford, Crawford Lindsay, Crawford Douglas, Tower Lindsay, Lindsay Tower

CRAWFORDJOHN CASTLE

South Lanarkshire   Ruin or site   OS 71   NS 879239

In Crawfordjohn, just east of the B740, at its junction with minor roads, on knoll in centre of village.

This is the likely site of Crawfordjohn Castle, of which nothing now remains. One 19th century source speculates that it was a peel tower and another says that the ruins were still visible in the 18th century. It is said that stone from Crawfordjohn Castle was used in the construction of Boghouse and that it had a semi-circular moat.

The origins of this estate begin in the 12th century when John, the stepson of Baldwin of Biggar, built the motte near Abington. Another John of Crawford died in 1259 and his heirs were in dispute with William of Douglas over a portion of their inheritance. It is said that a John of Crawford had died leaving two daughters and that one of these married Thomas Randolph, nephew of Robert I. He married Isabel, the daughter of Sir John Stewart of Bonkyl. The other heiress married a Barclay, whose portion became known as Crawford Barclay.

Thomas Murray was in possession of one portion in 1359, when taxes were raised for the king from Crawford Barclay, but none from Sir Thomas who had been granted it 'so long as he should be hostage for the king'. In that same year a castle at Crawfordjohn came into Royal possession. In 1366 it was granted to the Douglases, who were forfeited in 1455. It was then granted to the Hamiltons.

Sir James Hamilton of Finnart obtained half of the barony from his father in 1528 and was granted a licence to build towers here. He received a grant of confirmation in 1530-31. The other half of the barony had come to the Crawfords, who before 1537 exchanged it with Finnart for his properties at Kilbirnie and Drumry. Finnart then exchanged Crawfordjohn with James V for the Boyds' forfeited estate of Kilmarnock. In the exchange, he reserved to himself 'the Auld Castle' and two acres of land, the office of Parish Clerk, and the right to appoint priests to the kirk. Hamilton himself was declared forfeit and executed for treason in 1540. Crawfordjohn, but not Kilmarnock, was returned to his heirs in 1543 and remained with them until 1693.

Like neighbouring Crawford, the estate was bought up by the Colebrookes in the 18th century and the local public house is still the 'Colebrooke Arms'. The family continued to use nearby Gilkerscleugh House as a shooting lodge until the early 20th century.

Some early map references have Boghouse as Crawfordjohn Castle, though the two sites were separate. They are recorded a few hundred yards apart on the first edition six inch OS map of the mid 19th century.

CROGALS CASTLE

North Lanarkshire   Ruin or site   OS 64   NS 770624
3 miles south of Airdrie, 0.5 miles west of Chapelhall, by foot south of Calderbank, just east of B802, above ravine on south bank of Calder Water.

Crogals Castle is an earthwork of unknown date built upon a high promontory above the confluence of the Calder Water and Kennel Burn. The ravines of each watercourse run some 50ft deep and only allow access to the summit from the east. This approach has been strengthened by the use of a ditch and bank. This provides a triangular platform measuring about 200ft by 260ft. The site has not been excavated and so is undated.

CROOKEDSHIELDS

South Lanarkshire   Ruin or site   OS 64   NS 652575?
1 mile southeast of Cambuslang, by minor roads, north of the A726, north of Nerston, at or near Crookedshields.

Possibly the site of an early, old or fortified house, which lay close to the boundary of the baronies of Drumsagard, Carmunnock and Kilbride. Originally spelt 'Cruiketshiel', this property probably got its name from the Crocket family, who are on record locally in the 13th century. 'Shiel' or 'Shield' is from the Old Norse for a shelter. An indistinct building is denoted as 'Kruketshile' on Pont's map of the late 16th century and it appears in Blaeu's *Atlas*, as 'Kruketshil.' It is absent on Roy's map of 1747-55, but is denoted on Richardson's map of 1795.

Huwe Croket of 'Kameslank' and William Croketa of Kilbride gave homage for their lands in the Ragman Roll of 1296. William may have been in possession of neighbouring Letterick which seems at times to have been within Kilbride Parish. Their seals survive, though the heraldry seems to indicate that they were not related.

There is little information regarding later ownership of the property and it may be that, like neighbouring Letterick, it had been granted to the Church. By 1622 it belonged to John Small, then his son John. Compare Kirk Burn Motte

CROOKSTON CASTLE

City of Glasgow   NTS/His Scot   OS 64   NS 526627
3 miles east of Paisley, on minor roads east of the A736, on south bank of Levern Water, just off Tower Avenue.

Sited upon the summit of a hogback ridge and surrounded by the modern housing estate of Pollok, Crookston was thought to date from the thirteenth century, but more modern estimates date it to the decade 1390-1400. Roughly X-plan, it consists of a massive rectangular central block, once supported by a tower at each corner. Only one of these remains intact and of two there is little evidence.

It stands within a wide and deep ditch, the remnant of an earlier ringwork. This is entered from the southeast adjacent to the keeper's cottage. The hill on three sides is steep, and on the north is an almost precipitous drop to the Levern Water.

The main block of the castle measures 60ft by 40ft, and sections of the walls reach 13ft in thickness. There is one entrance to the castle, in the main block at the re-entrant with the northeastern tower. A machicolation above provided protection. The entrance was defended by two doors and a portcullis, the sockets for drawbars can still be seen. This was cleverly designed, the first door opened outward and when the bar was drawn back it would have prevented access to the stair. The straight stairway rises westward within the wall to the first floor. The passage directly facing the main door enters a rib vaulted basement. This consists of a large single room with mural stairs leading to the floor above at various points and a recess within the wall contains a well. There are several arrow slot windows, which provide light and enhance the defensive features of the castle. A recess within the wall at first floor level also allows access to the well. The first floor contained the great hall, also vaulted, which has a large fireplace and windows with stone seats.

The basement of the northeastern tower contains a guard room, which is entered from just within the main door. This room contains a hatch which opens to reveal a pit prison. The upper floors were accessed from the hall. There is a single room to each floor and access to the upper floors is by using modern wrought iron ladders to the centre of each floor. There are four storeys above the basement, each illuminated by long slot windows. The upper storey, containing the lord's bedroom, has a larger window to the east. The corbelling which supported a parapet and bartizans at the open sides is continuous, though it is likely that this has been added in the renovations, which were undertaken to commemorate Queen Victoria's visit to the city in 1847. The view from the roof is well worth the trauma of the climb.

Little remains of the southeastern tower other than a vaulted basement. Archaeological investigation of the site suggests earlier use, and traces of a circular enclosure predating the ringwork have been found just out with the site perimeter. This contains traces of a circular structure with a wall about 3ft thick, thinner than, though similar to that of a Dark Age dun. Within the ringwork a mortared structure was found just northwest of the castle, which may represent a subsidiary building of the 15th century, which had gone out of use by the 16th century.

The original ringwork defences were constructed by Sir Robert de Croc of Neilston in the 12th century. He was in the area before 1163, when he granted his church at Neilston to the new abbey at Paisley, for which he witnessed the foundation grant. Around 1180 he founded a chapel within the ringwork, the remains of which were excavated to the east of the castle in the 1970s. Robert was a follower of Walter the High Steward, who was brought to Scotland by David I. His descendants were active throughout the 13th century. By 1330 the line had apparently ended in an heiress, possibly named Marion. She is said to have sold the estate to Sir Alan Stewart of Darnley, however Crawford in his *History of the Shire of Renfrew* states that the Stewarts gained the estate by marrying her.

Alan died with his three brothers, including John of Castlemilk, at Halidon Hill in 1333. His descendants built the present castle around 1390-1400. They gained the Earldom of Lennox in 1488. The family and the Lyles of Duchal went into rebellion against the young James IV. His reply was severe. Bringing the great bombard Mons Meg from Edinburgh, he destroyed the western end of the castle forcing its submission. He then successfully attacked Duchal, and moved on to besiege Dumbarton where Lord Darnley, the Earl's heir, was in command. In 1544 the Regent Arran and Cardinal Beaton laid siege to the Crookston while the Earl of Lennox was holding Glasgow Castle against other assailants.

A later Lord Darnley, Henry, was to become the husband of Mary, Queen of Scots, and it was allegedly below an ancient yew tree at Crookston that they became betrothed. This tree was cut down in the 19th century and its wood used to create a carved model of Crookston, which can now be seen in Pollok House.

The castle is said to have passed through various hands until in 1757 it was sold by the Duke of Montrose to the Maxwells of Pollok. In 1797 a large coin hoard was discovered in the vicinity of the castle. Mostly English groats of Henry IV, V, VI and Edward IV, two were Scottish from the reign of James I.

Sir John Stirling Maxwell was a founder of the National Trust for Scotland and gifted them Crookston as their first property in 1931. It is still owned by the trust, though administered by Historic Scotland.

CROSSBASKET CASTLE

South Lanarkshire Private OS 64 NS 667565

2 miles southwest of Blantyre, 1 mile northeast of East Kilbride, on minor road west of A725 and B7012, above east bank of River Calder, at Crossbasket.

Crossbasket is a harled 16th century tower house of three storeys and a garret with a corbelled out parapet. The superstructure remains essentially intact other than enlargement of the windows and blocking of the original doorways. The interior has been completely rebuilt on the addition of the 19th century mansion adjoining its north side. The continuous corbelling of the parapet may have been renewed at the rebuilding. There are numerous water spouts to drain the wallhead and a square caphouse at the southeast corner. The garret storey has large

dormer windows. The hall was originally on the first floor and the basement is vaulted.

The lands of Crossbasket apparently belonged to the Hamiltons until the 15th century. They came to the Lindsays of Mains who built the castle in the 16th century and used it as a jointure house. Alexander Lindsay of Mains and Dunrod ran into serious debt due to an extravagant and apparently cruel lifestyle. He sold both Mains and Crossbasket in 1640.

In c.1661 the house was purchased by the lawyer James Kincaid. By the early 18th century it had been sold to Thomas Peter, a Dean of Guild in Glasgow. His son General David Peter is commemorated by the adjacent 'B' Listed General's Bridge. It was built in 1790 to carry the new turnpike road from Hamilton to East Kilbride across the Calder. He later moved to Craigmaddie House.

Crossbasket was purchased by Charles Macintosh, the inventor of the famous raincoat. Later it was owned by Alexander Downie then James Cabbell before being purchased by the Glasgow merchant, James Clark, and his son, John. They are credited with the building of the adjoining mansion in the 19th century. In 1891 they sold it to George Nielson, who sold it in 1919 to the East India merchant Thomas Dunlop Findlay. In 1932 it was acquired by James Little, who sold the three cottages on the estate.

It came to the Roosevelt Memorial Trust and was used as a residential training centre for the disabled under the operating title of James Little College. From 1981 it became a depot and children's nursery operated by the 'Missionaries of The Latter Day'. It was sold sometime after 2003 to developers, who gained planning consent for conversion into 18 homes, of which the old tower was to comprise the largest single unit. However, the project did not proceed. The property has again come onto the market and is presently lying vacant. It is a category 'A' Listed Building.

As 'Kalder', Crossbasket appears in both Pont's map of the late 16th century and in Blaeu's *Atlas Novus* of the 17th century, adjacent to an earlier bridge across the Calder.

CULCREUCH CASTLE

The Lennox & East Dunbartonshire   Private   OS 57   NS 620877

0.5 miles north of Fintry, by minor roads north of B822, 0.25 miles north of Endrick Water, Culcreuch Castle Hotel.

Culcreuch consists of a late 15th to early 16th century keep, extended to the east and north at the end of the 17th and 18th centuries.

The keep measures 41ft by 28.75ft, and is of four storeys including a garret. The walls average about 5ft thick through which there was a door into the basement at the northern end of the eastern wall. In the northeast corner what is now the 'Cellar Bar', a remnant of the original stairway is still visible. The basement has two connected vaulted chambers, originally lit by slot windows. There were a number of gunloops. There was a main entrance on the first floor immediately above the basement door, the former being accessed by removable ladder. The hall had a fireplace in the southern wall which has been replaced in the 19th century. There is an aumbry with moulded ogee arched frame in the west wall. The windows are larger than on the basement floor and those in the east wall have been opened up to provide access to the mansion. There remain two windows each in the west and south walls. The remnants of a garderobe chute have been discovered in the west wall.

The plan of the second and garret floors are similar, having been divided into one small room and one large with access corridor. Each room had its own fireplace and enlarged windows. The floor of the garret is 3.5ft below the level of the wall-walk outside. The parapet is supported on chequered corbelling with a single continuous corbel supporting all. There are many water spouts which drain it. The upper part of the parapet wall has been replaced. The stairway between the floors has now gone, access to each is now via the mansion.

The entrance to the mansion on its southern facade is decorated by worn armorial stones. One of these is dated 1721 and supports the initials of John Napier and his wife. The alteration to the windows of the tower and other internal changes were probably made when this first extension was added. It comprises a four-storey block with attic, which rises to the same height as the tower. Further later extensions were added to the rear of the building in the 19th century.

Culcreuch was a major stronghold of the Galbraiths. The surname is derived from the Gaelic words for Briton and stranger, or foreigner. With strong legendary links to Dumbarton and early intermarriage with local magnates, it is conjectured that they descend from the old kings of the Strathclyde Britons and in Gaelic they are known as *Clann a Bhreatannich*, children of the Britons.

The first chief, Gilchrist, is on record in 1193. He was married to a daughter of the Earl of Lennox. In 1320 Maurice Galbraith, the 3rd son of the 6th chief, was designated of Culcreuch. At this point the chiefly line was represented by his elder brother, Patrick of Gartconnel. By 1425 Maurice's grandson, James, was designated of Culcreuch. He assisted in the sack of Dumbarton Castle supporting the deposed Regent Albany and the Earl of Lennox. It is said that he and his family then fled to Gigha and Kintyre; however his son James inherited but died before 1455. In 1489 the 12th chief, Thomas of Culcreuch, was defeated at Talla Moss during his support of the rebellion of Lord Lyle and the Earl of Lennox. Thomas was hanged and forfeited. The following year his brother, James, was restored to the family estates as part of a general amnesty.

His son, Andrew, 14th chief, was present in 1526 when the Earl of Lennox was captured near Linlithgow, following a failed attempt to release the young James V from the clutches of his stepfather, the Earl of Angus. Having surrendered, Lennox was murdered in cold blood by Sir James Hamilton of Finnart. James, 16th chief, was Sheriff Depute of Dunbartonshire. In 1592 his son Robert was granted a Commission of Justiciary to pursue the outlawed MacGregors, but misused his powers to continue a feud with the Colquhouns and MacAulays. He burned their homes on the pretext of hunting MacGregors. He continued his belligerency, was outlawed on numerous occasions and imprisoned in Edinburgh Castle. He got himself into severe debt and in 1619 wadset his estates, including Culcreuch, to his brother-in-law, Alexander Seton, whom he later attacked. Seton became a judge and took the title Lord Kilcreuch. Having been denounced as a rebel Robert surrendered his estate to Seton in 1622. During the colonisation of Ulster by James VI, he emigrated to Ireland with his family, never to return.

In 1632 Seton sold Culcreuch to Robert Napier of Edinbellie and Merchiston. It remained with that family until purchased by Alexander Speirs in 1796. He built a large and successful cotton mill on the estate. It was sold to Sir William Menzies in 1901 and descended to a nephew of his heirs in 1970. From that point the estate developed as a business and is now a hotel.

Culcreuch is said to have supported a garrison of Cromwell's troops in the 17th century and is allegedly haunted by a harpist. The story originates in 1582 when a Buchanan was fatally wounded by Robert Galbraith, the future 17th Laird. The dying man was accompanied by his mistress and when he died she began to play a clarsach, a wire strung harp. It is said that sometimes in the dead of night her playing can still be heard. There are also said to be other manifestations.

CUMBER

South Lanarkshire   Ruin or site   OS 73   NS 779341
By minor roads 3.5 miles west of M74 at Lesmahagow, at South Cumberhead

Site of a substantial tower, also recorded as Cumberhead, which appears on Pont's map of c.1596 and subsequently in Blaeu's *Atlas Novus* of the 17th century. It belonged to Hamilton of Raploch in 1630, but before the end of the 17th century had come to the Weirs of Stonebyres. In 1896 a stone implement was found on the farm of South Cumberhead at a location known as Castle Dauphin.

Other references: Castle Dauphin

CUMBERNAULD CASTLE

The Lennox & East Dunbartonshire   Ruin or site   OS 64   NS 773759
In Cumbernauld, off minor roads south of A80, east of Cumbernauld Village, at Cumbernauld House.

Cumbernauld House is partly constructed of stone from the late 14th century castle of the Flemings. The courtyard now acts as car park for the house. It contains portions of the original wall and subsidiary buildings, including two vaulted chambers. There is a renovated 16th century doocot at the east gate. Excavations of 1963-64 uncovered the remains of a 15th century rubbish chute, a prison, and a 17th century well-house to the northeast of the house. The excavation was filled in.

Cumbernauld was originally part of the Comyns' great barony of Kirkintilloch. Robert the Bruce granted it to the Flemings of Biggar in 1306. About 1371 the family decided to move their main seat from Kirkintilloch to Cumbernauld, this being more central for involvement in national affairs. They built a tower and later extended it by adding several buildings including a large hall house. They replaced the castle by commissioning Cumbernauld House, a mansion by William Adam, in the early 18th century.

Robert Fleming was the son of the Lord of Biggar. He was one of the Bruce's strongest friends and allies. He died just prior to Bannockburn, but Bruce had shown his gratitude by knighting his son Malcolm and rewarding him with this portion of the Comyns' vast lowland estate. Later Sir Malcolm became Sheriff of Dunbartonshire and Keeper of Dumbarton Castle. Finding it simpler to manage his duties as one domain, it was he who arranged that Cumbernauld and the estate become part of the Shire of Dunbarton, albeit detached. This curious anomaly persisted in local government organisation until recently.

In 1440 another Sir Malcolm of Cumbernauld was one of the companions of the Earl of Douglas when they were murdered at the 'Black Dinner' in Edinburgh Castle. Douglas and his companions were accused of treason. Sir John Fleming protested his father's innocence for many years thereafter and James II may have visited Cumbernauld during his investigations. The outcome did not change events, but at some point Sir John was made a Lord of Parliament and gained the title Lord Cumbernauld.

In the reign of James IV, John, 2nd Lord, married Euphemia, a daughter of Lord Drummond. James had a poorly concealed relationship with this lady's sister, Margaret. He made frequent trips to Cumbernauld with the excuse that he was hunting the famous wild white cattle of the area. It is supposed that meetings with Margaret Drummond were the real reason for his visits. The relationship led to tragedy, as Euphemia, Margaret, and their sister Sybilla died after dining at their father's house of Stobhall, each suffering an agonising death with severe abdominal pain. Poison was suspected but never proven. For political reasons James subsequently married Princess Margaret Tudor, the sister of England's King Henry VIII. She was the choice of James's counsellors, though it is said that James had wanted to make Margaret Drummond his queen. In the end James marriage to the Tudor led to the Union of the Crowns.

The Flemings importance at court was maintained and Mary Fleming, daughter of Lord Fleming, was one of Mary Queen of Scots's 'Four Maries'. These girls accompanied Mary in her flight to France as an infant and subsequent upbringing at the French court. James, Lord Fleming, was one of a party of commissioners sent to arrange Mary's marriage to the French Dauphin, though he died with his companions on their return journey. Again poison and English desires for another Anglo-Scottish royal marriage were suspected.

Later Mary visited Cumbernauld and during the feasting the roof of the great hall collapsed. The next Lord James was Mary's Governor of Dumbarton, who escaped the 'daring raid' of 1571. He had fought for her at Langside in 1568 and assisted her flight to England.

In 1606 James VI granted the title Earl of Wigtown to John Fleming. The first Earl married Lilias, daughter to the Earl of Montrose. His son, the next Lord Cumbernauld, was therefore friend, ally and cousin to the 1st Marquis of Montrose. This led to the original covenant being signed at Cumbernauld, the document becoming known as the Cumbernauld Bond. In due course, Montrose reverted to the side of the monarchy as the aims of the Covenanters became more extreme and war ensued. Following a brilliant campaign Montrose was finally defeated at Philiphaugh, his entire bodyguard died to ensure his escape. Among his immediate staff who escaped with him was Lord Cumbernauld, who subsequently became the Earl of Wigtown.

It is said that the castle was destroyed by Cromwell's troops in 1651; however it seems to have remained in use, at least in part. It was used as stables following the construction of Cumbernauld House by William Adam for the 6th Earl in 1731. During the 1745 rebellion, the old building was burned down by dragoons, leaving only the remnants described.

In 1747 the last male heir died, and the title passed by marriage to the Elphinstones. They left to make Carberry their main seat, though a grandson added Fleming to his name in order to gain the title. He was Admiral Charles Elphinstone-Fleming and was a much revered parliamentarian for Stirling. He died at Cumbernauld House.

In the 19th century the title moved south of the border by inheritance and eventually the estate was broken up and sold. Cumbernauld House was purchased by Lord Inverclyde, but the house burned down in 1877 before he could move in. Internally the building required reconstruction and so only the exterior remains of Adam's work.

It became the headquarters for the Cumbernauld Development Corporation and was then owned by the local council. They sold it to an engineering firm, who used it as office space until they went into liquidation in 2007. It lay vacant for a time but has been purchased by a developer. The house is being converted into flats with additional housing in the car park area. Objections were raised by the local community, who set up a charitable trust whose aim is to purchase and retain the house for community use.

It is a category 'A' Listed Building, and behind it stands a 'B' listed 18th century sundial, which was formerly at the front of the house until moved in the 1930s.

The remainder of the grounds remain accessible. Cumbernauld Glen is managed as a wildlife reserve by the Scottish Wildlife Trust. Within the park stands 'the Mote' which is widely accepted as an original Comyn seat, but is described by one 19th century source as having been erected to commemorate Lord Elphinstone's appointment as Governor of India c.1820. There is a 'B' Listed doocot about mile to the northeast in Crow Wood. This seems to have reconstructed from ruin sometime in the 19th century.

DALDOWIE

City of Glasgow   Private   OS 64   NS 674618

1 mile west of Uddingston, off minor roads south of M74, west and south of Daldowie Crematorium.

Site of old or fortified houses. Daldowie was part of the extensive landholding of the Diocese of Glasgow and was occupied by tenants until the Reformation. Thereafter the occupiers became proprietors. Daldowie existed as two distinct properties, Wester Daldowie and Easter Daldowie or Daldowie proper. Both appear on Pont's manuscript map of c.1596. Both again are in Blaeu's *Atlas* of the mid 17th century, although by this time Daldowie is denoted within a park, implying some importance.

'Jame' Scot is recorded as being in possession of Wester Daldowie in 1518. The site of a subsequent farm is now occupied by the former quarry at Greenoakhill, now a land-fill site adjacent to the M74.

The family most associated with Daldowie proper is that of Stewart. The Stewarts of Allanton and Daldowie claimed a proud lineage, citing descent from Sir John Stewart of Bonkill, who died at the Battle of Falkirk in 1298. He granted Daldowie to his 6th son, Sir Robert, in 1290. He is said to have been companion-in-arms and son-in-law to Sir James Douglas, to have fought at Bannockburn in 1314, and then at Dundalk for Edward Bruce in 1318.

This line continued with his son Alan who earned the nickname 'Alnwickster' for his part in the storming of Alnwick Castle. In 1385, and at over 60 years old, Alan was still active enough to lead a party of men assembled from Daldowie and Rutherglen to fight against an invading force of Richard II. En route to meet with the Scots army, they routed an English cavalry force at McMorran Moor, but the engagement cost Alan his life. He was succeeded by his son, a second Alan, who also distinguished himself against the Auld Enemy. It was claimed that he was knighted by Robert III and that he appeared as witness to a charter granted to Mure of Rowallan in 1393. In 1421 he was apparently granted the lands of McMorran (or Morningside) and changed the name to Allanton. The Stewarts of Allanton named him as the first of their line. Both Daldowie and Allanton were used as either a single or double designation by later heads of the family. It has been suggested that these early connections to Daldowie relate to another place of the same name outwith Lanarkshire, though no alternative location is given. There is a place named Dallowie near Patna in Ayrshire.

Dubiety and controversy surrounds this story, most notably in an outbreak of hostility in the pages of *Blackwood's* magazine in the early 19th century. The argument became known as the 'Saltfoot Controversy' and dates back to c.1680 with Lord Somerville's attack on the Allanton family in his *The Memorie of the Sommervilles*. Saltfoot refers to a quote by Lord Somerville who wrote in acerbic tone that Sir Walter Stewart of Minto's predecessors:

'...until that man, never came to sit above the saltfoot when at the Laird of Cambusnethane's table'

The argument flared up in a series of letters to *Blackwood's* Magazine in 1807 when it was alleged that the Allanton lineage was fictitious. A heated exchange of views followed between the correspondents 'JR' and 'Candidus'.

It is known that in 1521 Robert Stewart was the rentaller in Daldowie, since he appears in the diocese rental records. He was one of a number of the Stewarts of Minto who became Provosts of Glasgow and major landholders around the city.

In 1553 Robert's son Alan Stewart died to be succeeded by his son, Gavin. One source suggests that it was this Alan who was the true progenitor of the Allanton family. Gavin's son, James, may be the James Stewart of Daldowie who inherited Allanton from an uncle. He also owned Wester Daldowie from 1598.

In 1649 an Act of Parliament was passed in order to resolve the disputes between Sir Walter Stewart of Minto, his son Ludovick, and their creditors. By the act, the rents of Daldowie were reserved to provide Ludovick with 'present sustinence'. In 1653 he gained permission to convey the lands to the Woddrops of Dalmarnock. Later the estate passed by inheritance to the Muirheads of Bredisholm. In the early 18th century it was conveyed to the Bogles. Around 1730 George Bogle built a mansion on the site, removing the old house in the process.

In 1745 following the theft of some horses and cattle by the passing Jacobite Army, a letter was issued on behalf of Prince Charles Edward Stewart in response to a complaint from George. The letter required the officers of the army to protect and defend the estate.

The Bogles were a well-known tobacco merchant and landholding family in Glasgow. They retained the estate for a little over 100 years when it passed to a nephew, George Brown of Langside. Thereafter it was sold to John Dixon of Calder Ironworks, who extended the mansion. He sold it in 1830 to the McCalls, another well-known merchant family, who gifted the estate to the city. The house was demolished in the 1960s.

The City utilized the site to build Daldowie Crematorium and that part of the estate to the north of London Road became Glasgow Zoo, now sadly closed. Of the house, only the doocot survives. Dating from c.1745, it originally stood near the Clyde and later became enclosed within the bounds of a sewerage treatment work. It was dismantled and restored on a new site providing a more accessible and prominent position adjacent to London Road. It is a category 'A' Listed Building.

DALMARNOCK

City of Glasgow   Ruin or site   OS 64   NS 615628
2 miles southeast of Glasgow Cathedral, west of A749 north of River Clyde at Dalmarnock.

The lands of Dalmarnock were part of the estate of the Grays of Carntyne, with a lesser portion owned by their near relatives the Woddrops. The Grays sold their portion to the Buchanans of Ardoch, who built Dalmarnock House shortly after 1784. It is said to have been the only house on the whole property at the time. There is no evidence of an earlier house, and the name does not appear on early maps.

DALMOAK HOUSE

The Lennox & East Dunbartonshire   Private   OS 63   NS 384771
1 mile west of Dumbarton, south of A82 and west of A812, at Dalmoak.

Dalmoak is a castellated mansion dating from 1866-69, which was built for James Aitken. The house is adorned by ornamental battlements, machicolations, and gunloops but appears to have no earlier origins. It has been suggested that there had been a building here since the mid 15th century and a minor property called 'Dalmowack' does appear in Blaeu's *Atlas*. John Semple of Dalmoak secured Dumbarton Castle for the Covenanting army in the 17th century. In 1684 he and John Yuill of Darleith were convicted and fined – with numerous others – for holding Conventicles.

DALMUIR CASTLE

The Lennox & East Dunbartonshire   Ruin or site   OS 64   NS 481713
In Dalmuir, Clydebank, on Castle Street, at or east of Castle Square.

Site of a castle of the Spreull family, which sat close to the Duntocher Burn near its confluence with the Clyde. The name was also spelt Dalmure.

Some time between 1234 and 1244 the Earl of Lennox gave a grant of confirmation of the lands of Dalnottar and Blairmore (Dalmuir) to Sir Hugh Fleming. In 1280 the lands were resigned by Roger de Dundener and granted to Walter Spreull by Earl Malcolm. Walter was Seneschal of Lennox at the time. About 1286 he was granted the lands of Dalquhurn and rendered homage to Edward I in 1296. By 1306 he also held the estate of Cowden in Renfrewshire and in 1316 witnessed a charter to John of Luss by Robert I. There were a series of Walters as heads of the family, though the dates of succession are not distinct.

Walter's descendants occupied Dalmuir for centuries, building a castle on the estate. John Spreull was a descendant via the Cowden branch of the family and a leading light in the Covenanting movement of the 17th century. He suffered a harsh imprisonment on the Bass Rock for his beliefs. Cadet lines of the family at various times held estates at Linthouse, Milton, Blochairn and Castlehill (Renfrewshire). In 1907 a stone hammer or pounder was removed from the castle ruins. It was donated to Paisley Museum in 1951.

In the 19th century the estate belonged to the Glasgow paper-making family of Collins. Robert Collins built a mansion known as Dalmure House (NS 484716) on an eminence in what is now Clydebank Public Park. His house was known locally as Collins Castle but was demolished in 1905.

Other references: Collins Castle

DALSERF

South Lanarkshire   Ruin or site   OS 64   NS 801506

2 miles south of Overton, east and north of A72 by minor roads, to east of Dalserf village.

Site of a large tower, illustrated on Pont's manuscript of 1596 and subsequently in Blaeu's *Atlas Novus* of the 17th century.

Dalserf was a Hamilton property, granted by Robert I in 1312. In the reign of Robert III it was granted by Sir John Hamilton, 4th of Cadzow, to his son David. The family became the Campbell-Hamiltons of Dalserf, one of whom is remembered by a stained glass window of 1890 in St Mary's Episcopal Church in Hamilton. The house was demolished in the 20th century. The family also had nearby houses at Milburn and Auldton. They were closely related to the Hamiltons of Broomhill.

DALZELL HOUSE

North Lanarkshire   Private   OS 64   NS 760550

1.5 miles southeast of Motherwell, on minor roads south of A721, west of Muirhouse and south of Motherwell College, 0.5 miles north of River Clyde, at Dalzell.

Dalzell has a variety of spellings, Dalziel, Deeyell, Dalyell, Dalyiel, Deill and many others. It is normally pronounced DL. The name means white or 'bright field or dale' in Gaelic.

Situated on the western edge of a treacherous ravine, Dalzell is a much altered and extended castle, the earliest portion of which probably dates to the 15th century. It was added to at various times, eventually enclosing a courtyard. There remains a section of moat guarding the western approach to the main entrance, though it has been suggested that this may be an ornamental representation of an original moat which had previously been filled in.

The oldest section is a three-storey keep of the late 15th century, which some authorities attribute to the early 16th century. It has a corbelled parapet and modernised garret. Measuring 39ft by 32ft, and 48ft to the wall head there is an unusual buttress like projection in the southwest corner. This was 2.75ft deep and 17ft wide and had the original entrance at its centre. There was a portcullis guarding the door for which the grooves remain.

The basement was vaulted, as was the hall on the first floor above. This has corbels projecting from the wall indicating an intermediate wooden floor dividing the room into two storeys. The second floor had chambers and galleries within the walls.

A straight mural stair from the entrance led up to the first floor, and a turnpike continues from there to the storeys above. The parapet has chequered corbels supporting open rounds at the corners. The entrance now leads to a large hall which takes up the entire ground floor.

In the 17th century, extensions were added to the north and south of the keep and westward from the southern end of the south extension. This completed two sides of a rectangle, the remainder completed by a wall, parts of which remain. The extension provided a vaulted kitchen with similarly vaulted cellar space below. There are shot holes throughout. There is said to have been a passageway from the terraced garden into the house.

Sometime between 1200-30 Richard 'personna de Dalzell' witnessed a grant of the villa of Smeaton by Ness of London. Various other charter entries mention a Baron of Dalzell around the mid 13th century but do not name the incumbent until Sir Hugo de Dalzell was recorded as Sheriff of Lanark in 1288. Sir Thomas de Dalzell gave homage to Edward I in 1296 and fought at Bannockburn in 1314. Sir Robert de Dalzell is then said to have been forfeited for staying in England without the king's permission.

DALZELL HOUSE

David II granted Dalzell to Sir Malcolm Fleming 'and others'. These others included the Sandilands, Cathcarts and Colquhouns. This portioning of the estate creates a complexity of ownership, as illustrated by various grants of Dalzell over the next few decades. By 1352 one portion was held by Robert Stewart, later Robert II. Duncan Wallace held part in 1368 and was given a grant of Dalzell and Motherwell in 1373. With John de Nisbet he is described as co-proprietor by the time Robert became king in 1371.

In 1364 a Sir William de Dalzell is said to have become a Sergeant of Lanark with a fee of £5. He fought at Otterburn in 1388, where he lost an eye, and accompanied Sir David Lindsay to London for the famous joust with Lord Welles. Robert II made a grant of Dalzell to his daughter's husband, James Sandilands, Lord Torphichen. In 1395 James resigned it in favour of William's son George Dalzell who married his daughter. A grant of confirmation in the barony was given by the king in the same year.

The family built the present castle around the end of the 15th century, although some authorities date it to the early 16th century and it is likely that there was an earlier structure. In 1568 Robert Dalzell fought for Mary, Queen of Scots, at the Battle of Langside. In 1628 his son, also Robert, became Lord Dalzell. In 1639 the 3rd Robert became Earl of Carnwath and by 1641 was a member of the king's council. In 1643 he was accused of treason by the Scottish Convention. Found guilty, Robert was sentenced to death but on appeal was fined £10,000 instead. He fought for the Royalists at the Battle of Naseby in 1645. As a result of the fine he sold Dalzell to his nephew, James Hamilton of Boggs in 1649. By then the Dalzells were living in Carnwath.

Hamilton of Boggs was a second son of the Orbistan family who had amassed a large personal fortune by supplying Cromwell's army during the Civil Wars. He carried out the first major extensions to the house in the 17th century. The grounds were used for Conventicles and a large tree is known as the 'Covenanters Oak'.

For three years from 1857 the famed architect R.W. Billings lived in the castle. He had received a commission to extend from John Hamilton of Dalzell. Hamilton was a Liberal politician in Gladstone's government and became Baron Hamilton of Dalzell (the title Lord Dalzell was still in use by the Earls of Carnwath). Billings designed and built the northern wing. This was designed to be sympathetic with the older structures, which Billings greatly altered in the process. His adaptations included enlarging the windows of the keep, moving the main entrance to a central position on the west wall and building out a wing from the south wall to overlook the terraced gardens. He also added a wall along the edge of the ravine and from there along the southern front encasing the gardens until reaching the 'moat' at the western approach. A well was introduced within the courtyard.

Gladstone visited his former government colleague here on several occasions, and the Prince and Princess of Wales visited in 1888. The north wing was used as a hospital in World War I. When the 2nd Baron, Gavin George Hamilton, died in 1952, the estate was sold. The castle became a school for boys, until it was purchased by the local council in 1967. It stood empty for a number of years, and was then renovated and converted for use as private flats. The family and title continue in the person of the 5th Baron, who lives in Surrey.

The castle apparently has several ghosts. A 'Grey Lady' in a nurse's uniform is said to haunt the north wing. The 'Green Lady's Room' is named after a ghost who haunts the piper's gallery. She is associated with the strong smell of exotic perfume, flashing lights, footsteps and other noises. A maidservant is allegedly buried within one of the walls and may be the 'White Lady', the ghost of a pregnant and unmarried servant girl who threw herself from the battlements in despair. There is also reputed to be a young man buried below the courtyard. A 'Brown Lady' has also been reported.

Other references: Dalzell Castle, Dalziel Castle, Dalziel House, Dalyell Castle, Dalyell House

DARGAVEL CASTLE

Renfrewshire Private OS 64 NS 433693
1 mile south of Bishopton, on minor roads south of A8, within the Royal Ordnance Factory, Dargavel, Bishopton.

Dargavel House is a large Z-plan structure of three storeys and an attic. Dating in part from 1574, it was altered and extended in 1670. It was remodelled by David Bryce in 1849 and modernised in 1910.

The original building consists of a main block with two round towers projecting at diagonally opposite corners. From the entrance in the south wall a corridor led to the southwest tower. This contained a turnpike stair to first floor level. From there an angle turret was corbelled out in the re-entrant. This carried a turnpike to the floors above and is illuminated by a small window, surmounted by a sundial of 1670. A similar stairway existed within the northeast tower.

The ground floor of the main block was vaulted and contained a kitchen and two cellars. The first floor had the hall with a large fireplace in the east wall. There were two private rooms. The second floor consisted of two rooms, one larger than the other. A mansion wing has been added to the southeastern corner, producing an L-plan. A dated armorial stone of 1584 in the east gable confirms the construction date and the builders as Maxwells.

For centuries Dargavel was the property of the Earls of Lennox. In or before 1516, Earl John gave a charter of the estate to Patrick Maxwell, the eldest son of George Maxwell of Newark. There was another Dargavel in Kirkcudbright which was burned in 1591 when owned by another branch of the Maxwells. This has confused some antiquaries.

It is known that this house was built by Patrick's great grandson, another Patrick, who appeared twice in 'bonds of caution' in 1591. By the 18th century the estate had been inherited by John Hall, a nephew of William Maxwell, who died unmarried. John was descended from the Halls of Fulbar and adopted the surname Hall-Maxwell. He reconstructed and extended the old house in 1849, to designs by David Bryce. The family were still in possession in 1873. By 1937, construction of the ordnance factory had begun on the estate. The house has survived intact despite being enclosed by the factory grounds. It was put into use as offices. The now diminished factory is in the hands of BAE Systems, who operate Dargavel as a meetings and conference centre.

DARLEITH HOUSE

The Lennox & East Dunbartonshire   Ruin or site   OS 63   NS 345806
3 miles north of Cardross, on minor roads north of A814, at Darleith Farm.

This once ruinous neo-classical mansion of the 18th century incorporated a much altered rectangular 16th century tower house with a round bartizan. It has been suggested that it was originally built around 1510 when Matthew Earl of Lennox granted sasine of the 'Black Third of Darleith' to John Darleith. It was subsequently extended to the north at both its eastern and western ends in 1616 and 1684. The arms of John Darleith and his wife and the 1678 arms of John Yuill, with the motto 'Gods Providence is my inheritance', adorn the building. Further extensions were added to the south toward the close of the 18th century, which provided a Palladian entrance, and then to the southeast in 1903. The 16th and 17th century portions were originally identified for demolition in 2004, with plans to convert the remainder into dwellings. Partial restoration was completed and the buildings occupied by 2006. By 2009 the 16th century tower had been consolidated and retained as a ruin. There are stable blocks and a walled garden of the 18th century.

The principal family associated with the estate are the Darleiths of that Ilk, who took their name from the estate. Their history, like many a Lennox family, is shrouded in debate, myth, and the inventiveness of early genealogists, though the common origins of each thread links them to families who claim descent from the fabled King Arthur.

There were apparently MacArthurs of Darleith, who may be descended from the Campbells, the MacAulays of Ardincaple, or alternatively from the MacArthurs of Inistrynich on Loch Awe. It is said that they adopted the name Darleith when they were granted the estate with the lands of Garmoir by the Earl of Lennox. This was said to be as a reward for their services as his falconers. They are recorded as early as 1489 when an Arthur Darleith was granted a remission for his part in holding Dumbarton Castle against the king. This probably refers to the Lennox/Boyd rebellion against the young James IV.

In 1519 John Darleith of that Ilk was in dispute with the widow of Malcolm Darleith of that Ilk and following arbitration through Colquhoun of Camstraddan she provided John with a silver belt in settlement. Another Arthur Darleith of that Ilk is recorded in 1567, and a John Darleith of that Ilk appears as a charter witness in 1591. They are known to have allied themselves with the MacFarlanes during a feud with the Buchanans in 1619.

In 1670 John Darleith sold the estate to John Yuill, (alternatively spelt Zuill). He had been a merchant and solicitor in Inveraray, a town with which his family had links dating back to at least the 16th century. He was a zealous Covenanter who was fined £1,000 in 1685 for holding Conventicles. On refusing to pay he was imprisoned in Dumbarton Castle for two years. His family developed in business as merchants and burgesses of Glasgow from the late 17th century. Following the Act of Union in 1707, they branched into the tobacco trade and became very wealthy indeed. They held properties at Darleith, Glasgow, London, Halifax (Virginia) and very probably elsewhere. They retained possession into the 20th century.

Despite sitting so close to the modern village of Cardross, Darleith was within Bonhill Parish, and so many of the Yuill family were christened or buried in that church and are therefore recorded as being born or dying in Bonhill. Near to the house is the ruined medieval Darleith Kirk which was restored around 1685 in order that the imprisoned John Yuill could have his wife Ann (Agnes) Fisher interred there.

In 1946 the seminary St Peter's College moved into the house following a fire at Bearsden College. In the 1960s it moved onto the Kilmahew Estate, leaving Darleith House to become ruinous. The house is a category 'B' listed building. The Buildings at Risk Register lists it as 'Currently Under Restoration', the entry was last updated in 2009.

DARNGABER CASTLE

South Lanarkshire   Ruin or site   OS 64   NS 729501
About 6 miles southwest of Hamilton east of the A723 and west of the A72 by minor roads and foot, east of Crookedstone.

Nineteenth century references report that only foundations remained of the castle of Thomas, sometimes named Walter, the third son of John Hamilton of Cadzow. He lived around the turn of the 14th century and is named as the progenitor of the Torrance, Dalserf, and Raploch branches of the family. The lack of further Hamiltons using the designation 'of Darngaber' suggests that the castle had a short life.

Denoted as a motte, this promontory site is surrounded by steep slopes on all but the southwest side where it runs onto level ground. The summit is almost circular with a diameter of about 55ft. Small cellar vaults were discovered which had been proposed as possible Iron Age structures. It has been quarried into, and there are a large number of flat stones scattered around the site which are thought to be traces of foundations. Both these and the original remains were described as being unmortared. Some rubble banking on the north side may be evidence of later dumping. The site is badly overgrown.

DARNLEY CASTLE

City of Glasgow   Private   OS 64   NS 529596
At Darnley Toll, south of A726, at The Mill.

Early histories of Renfrewshire reinforce a local tradition that this is the site of a castle of the Lords Darnley. Local legend asserts that part of it survived in use as a doocot, which was then incorporated within a mill complex, part of which is now in use as a restaurant. A round stair tower and adjoining room survive as part of the renovated complex of buildings.

This was the ancestral home of the Stewarts of Darnley. They were descended from Alexander, 4th High Steward, via his son Sir John Stewart of Bonkill. Sir Alan Stewart of Darnley died at Halidon Hill in 1333. Robert the High Steward (later King Robert II) gave them a grant of the Darnley estates in 1356, although they had obviously been in possession for some time before that. In 1429, John Stewart of Darnley died fighting for the French in their attempt to relieve Orleans. He had been awarded the French lordship of Aubigny-sur-Nère. This passed to his second son, John, while the elder son, Alan, inherited the Scottish estates.

Alan's descendants became Earls of Lennox in 1488 and the Darnley title became that of the eldest son. Matthew, 2nd Earl, died at Flodden in 1513. Mary's husband, Henry Stewart, Lord Darnley, was the son of Matthew, 4th Earl who, as a descendant of two royal families, had a claim to the thrones of both England and Scotland.

In 1579 James VI granted the Earldom of Lennox to his cousin Esme Stewart of the Aubigny line, and in 1581 the title was raised to that of duke. At the same time the Lordship of Darnley was promoted to the status of earldom. In 1623 Esme's son Ludovick was awarded the additional title Duke of Richmond. All of the family titles became extinct on the death of Charles, 6th Duke, in 1672. His third wife and widow was the famed Frances Theresa Stewart, who modelled as 'Britannia'.

Darnley may then have come to her cousin, Sir Ludovick Stewart, the son of Walter of Minto (a cousin of the 1st Lord Blantyre). Ludovick had differences with his father which led to Walter receiving a number of injuries. In 1649 an order of protection was issued by parliament to allow both to appear before them in Edinburgh to answer one another's counter charges. Sir Ludovick was in the interim forbidden from meddling in the 'rents, mails, duties and others pertaining to Sir Walter Stewart, his father'. In 1679 Ludovick was summonsed for a debt of £11,146 and lost most of the estates.

In 1689 the Duke of Montrose purchased Darnley, which was allowed to fall into ruin. It was then sold to the Maxwells of Nether Pollok, who demolished most of the structure, apparently only leaving the remaining portion which was roofless. Later it was developed for the other uses mentioned.

The building has been rebuilt with cleansed original stone, though with some concession to modern requirements. The undressed section of the building represents the castle remains, the other buildings having been whitewashed. It is a 'B' Listed building.

Recent archaeological investigation did not confirm the site, stating that the remains are likely to be those of the once large mill complex, albeit that the buildings had gone through 'a slow and complicated metamorphosis'. No foundations remained which were substantive enough to have supported a tower house, but dating evidence did suggest origins in the 15th century. This presents the possibility that the site lay elsewhere. One 19th century reference states that the ruin stood on an eminence adjacent to the Mill of Darnley. On older cartographic references as far back as Pont in the late 16th century, the name seems to be centred around the site later occupied by Darnley House, at NS 523 588. Darnley House first appears on map references after 1800. All of the buildings in that complex were demolished in the 20th century.

DAWSHOLM

City of Glasgow Ruin or site OS 64 NS 551694
In Glasgow, 1 mile north of Anniesland Cross, east of A739, at southern end of Dawsholm Park, below railway embankment.

Early map references show a building known as 'Daushoom'. By 1823 the property on site was denoted as 'Castle' on John Thompson's map of Dunbartonshire. By the later 19th century the site had been covered by a railway embankment.

DENNISTOUN

Renfrewshire Ruin or site OS 63 NS 364673
2 miles south of Kilmacolm, south of A721, north of Gryffe Water, at or near Craigends Dennistoun.

Probable site of an old or fortified house of the Dennistoun family. Milton Bridge Motte, a few yards to the northwest, may represent the original family seat. The main branch of the family ended with heiresses around the turn of the 15th century, taking the Renfrewshire and other estates to their husbands. The Colgrain branch of the family continued the name.

The property appears on Pont's map of the late 16th century and appears continuously until the turn of the 20th century. It was denoted as 'Laigh' or 'South' Dennistoun in the 19th century . Although there is no entry in Canmore for the site other than for Milton Bridge Motte, there remain substantial foundations of a large T-plan building, which support low wall sections throughout. The well for the complex remains patent and is covered by a flagstone for safety reasons.

The Dennistoun family took their name from the lands, originally called Danzielstoun. In 1836 following his father's death, James Dennistoun of Colgrain lost his Dunbartonshire estates and repurchased the family's original Renfrewshire seat. He thereafter took the designation 'of Dennistoun'. A member of the family gave their name to an area of the City of Glasgow.

DOLPHINTON HOUSE

South Lanarkshire Private OS 72 NT 100467
On A702, 7 miles southwest of West Linton, west of Dolphinton.

Probable site of a fortified house, held by the Brown family.

Despite its remote location, the Barony of Dolphinton had been part of the lordship of Bothwell since the time of Walter Olifard in the 13th century. By the close of the 16th century the Douglas Earl of Angus had superiority over the occupants, but did not own the land. The family of Brown of Carmaben, 'heritors of Dolphinton', held the majority of the barony. From the early 17th century they were designated 'of Dolphinton', but may have been in possession since as early as 1517. They were succeeded through marriage by the family of the advocate Kenneth McKenzie in 1755. Dolphinton House was apparently built in 1801, probably on the site of an earlier manor house. It was certainly in existence by 1816 when Forrest confirms it in the possession of the McKenzies.

The barony did not comprise the entire parish, the lands of Roberton and Newholme being annexed to the Barony of Skirling in Peebleshire, although now within Lanarkshire. At an early date the Knights Templar held the lands of Thriepcroft.

Other reference: Kirkhouse

DORMANT

City of Glasgow   Site or ruin   OS 64   NS 524633
In Pollok, at western end of Dormanside Road, at or near Bonnyholm Primary School.

Site of a tower house which appears in Blaeu's *Atlas Novus* as 'Dormant'. It appears as a smaller structure named 'Dormanside Piel' or 'Hall' on Pont's original manuscript of 1594.

This was a Cleland property and in the late 17th century, Alexander Cleland of 'Dormondsyde' was the brother of Cleland of Faskine. His son John inherited the Faskine estate in 1686, fought with Bonnie Dundee in the Jacobite rebellion of 1689 and was forfeited in the following year.

References to George Weir, alias Laurie of Dormoundsyd, relate to a property in Lesmahagow parish.

DOUGALSTON HOUSE

The Lennox & East Dunbartonshire   Private   OS 64   NS 565740
East of A81, just north of junction with A807, near Milngavie, at Ewing Walk.

Dougalston House was demolished in c.1976 on the laying out of the golf course. It possibly replaced or may have incorporated part of an older structure. Dougalston appears as a small tower in Blaeu's *Atlas Novus* of 1654.

The estate of Dougalston is said to date from the 13th century. The Grahams were its earliest recorded owners, though their lineage is uncertain. It seems most likely that they were a branch of the Grahams of Mugdock and Kincardine. It is said that in 1591 Walter Graham of Dougalston became the latest in a long series of local lairds to seriously quarrel with his neighbour Hamilton of Bardowie. On this occasion the outcome does not appear to have been fatal, though several Hamiltons had lost their lives in disputes with other neighbours. John Graham built a house here in 1707. In 1767 the merchant John Glassford purchased the estate and extended the house. His descendants occupied it for almost 100 years but by the mid 19th century it belonged to the Glassfords, then the Kers. There is mention of Crawfords being in possession in 1797.

In the 1950s the estate was donated to the city with a view to it becoming home to the Burrell Collection; however plans by the National Coal Board to put down mines in the area caused Sir William Burrell to reject the idea. He died in 1957 and his collection was eventually housed in a specially designed museum in Pollok Park.

DOUGLAS CASTLE

South Lanarkshire   Ruin or site   OS 72   NS 843318
0.75 miles north of Douglas, on minor roads west of the A70, east of the Douglas Water, and 1 mile south of M74 in public park.

A round corner tower and vaulted cellars are all that remain of the castle. A later mansion of the Dukes of Douglas on the adjacent site designed by the Adam brothers is long since gone. The round tower which remains is thin walled and of later date, possibly 17th century.

The family took their name from Douglas Water, or 'black water' as the Gaelic *dubh glas* translates. This was their original estate before they reaped the rewards of Sir James Douglas's unfailing support of Robert the Bruce, though it is said that their original seat was at Ladle Knowe. They may have been close kin to the Murrays, as suggested by similarities in early coats of arms. They were descended from Theobold the Fleming, who was granted the Douglas estates by the Abbot of Kelso in 1147. His son, William, inherited and he appears to be the first to have adopted Douglas as a surname.

Apparently on record in 1288, the castle was held by the English in 1307, and recaptured by stratagem by Sir James while the garrison were at worship in the village Chapel. It became known as 'Douglas's Larder' since he had the garrison put to death and the castle razed. Sir James died in battle in Granada in Spain while carrying Bruce's heart on crusade.

The family became increasingly powerful and were

awarded the title Earl of Douglas. As the most important magnates in the south of Scotland, they developed their role as the principal protection against English hostility and by the reign of Robert III virtually ruled Scotland south of the Forth. This brought them into conflict with the Crown and those who wished to control the young king, particularly in the reign of James II. Sir William, 6th Earl, was executed at the Black Dinner in Edinburgh Castle in 1440, when Sir Alexander Livingston and Sir William Crichton had deceived him into

attending a reconciliatory dinner with the 10-year-old king. The pair had believed that Douglas power was a threat to their own powerful positions within the Royal Household as Governor of Stirling Castle and Chancellor of the Realm respectively. James struggled to curb the Douglas power as he entered his majority, and in 1452 he murdered the 9th Earl at Stirling Castle. Douglas Castle had been rebuilt by 1455 when James had it sacked after the Battle of Arkinholm at which the Black Douglases were defeated then forfeited. Their cousins, the Red Douglases, Earls of Angus, then gained the estate and probably rebuilt the castle soon afterwards.

The castle was allegedly rebuilt again by Henry Clifford, Earl of Cumberland and English Warden of the West March, during the 'Rough Wooing' of the mid 16th century. This was a campaign conducted on behalf of Henry VIII to encourage the Scots to betroth the young Mary, Queen of Scots, to his son, Prince Edward (later Edward VI). The castle thus gained the by-name 'Harry's Tower'. It was destroyed by fire in 1758 and the surviving fragment is alleged to be the corner tower of either a tower house, or surrounding wall.

In 1707 the family were created Dukes of Douglas. In 1757 they had the Adam brothers begin construction of a large scale castellated mansion, with various round towers and turrets. The building was not completed as the Duke died in 1761. There followed a legal dispute over the succession, with a claim by the Hamiltons eventually being displaced by the Duke's nephew. Both Playfair, in 1791, and Gillespie Graham, in 1826, were commissioned to produce plans to finish the building. The Earl of Hume inherited the estate in 1877 and it was he who finally finished the house to a design by Wardrop and Reid, with a chapel by Henry Wilson.

The mansion was demolished in 1937 due to the expected effects of subsidence caused by the opening of a new coal mine which was to follow a seam below the house. The offending Rankine Mine was closed in 1959.

The park was used as a base for both the British and Polish Armies during World War II and the foundations of many Nissen huts remain in the vicinity. There is a memorial to the Poles at the entrance to the park from the village. A further memorial closer to the tower was erected to commemorate the Cameronian Regiment, who had their origins in the Covenanting wars.

In recent times a historical theme park was proposed within the parkland around the site, including replicas of a crannog and a motte and bailey castle. Nothing seems to have materialised.

The castle was used by Sir Walter Scott as a model for 'Castle Dangerous' in his last novel. Information boards around the park describe the tower as a folly and it had been retained as such when the mansion was built. The window apertures appear to have been altered to match those of the mansion. A sundial which originally stood in the centre of the ornamental garden is now sited in Aitkenhead Park, Glasgow.

St Bride's Kirk, in the village of Douglas, contains the stone effigy of Sir James and several of his family who were laid to rest in the crypt. Access is via the Douglas Heritage Centre and Museum, which is open on Saturdays and Sundays from 2-5pm during the tourist season.

Other reference: Castle Dangerous

DOWANE

South Lanarkshire Ruin or site OS 71 NS 815405
Northeast of Milton and Lesmahagow, east of M74, by minor roads east of Nethan Water and north of confluence with Galrig Burn.

Site of a 13th century house or castle and a later successor.

Between 1180 and 1203 the lands of Dowane were granted by the Abbot of Kelso to Constantine. He took the name 'de Dowane' and was said to be the son of a priest at Lesmahagow named Gilbert. He was granted the right to hold court in his lands. By 1240 Robert de Dowane had built a house on the property. The estate was the subject of litigation between the monks of Kelso and the de Dowane family, the monks claiming that some of the land had been taken illegally. The family retained both the Auchtyfardle and Dowane portions with concessions to the clergy. This involved the construction of a mill with a lade running through the Dowane lands close to the confluence of the Dowane (Devon) Water and the Nethan.

In 1301 the estate was formally divided into two. The family had come into debt, and had temporarily resigned part of their lands to the abbot in exchange for cash in 1294. They resigned Dowane 'in excambion' for 'Hautiferdale'. In 1311 Adam de Dowane the elder resigned his lands in Greenrig to Kelso Abbey. In 1326, John Dowane, son of Adam the younger, received a grant of Auchtyfardle and Auchrobert in exchange for half of Dowane and was appointed janitor at the gates of the priory.

It is possible given the vagueness of the references in describing the bounds of the properties to the south as having two hills, that the site at Moat (NS 846396) may be that described. Dowane became a property of the Weirs.

Other references: Devon, Auchtyfardle, Moat

DRIPPS

South Lanarkshire   Ruin or site   OS 64   NS 578553
1 mile south of Busby, west of Thorntonhall, by minor roads south of A727 and west and north of A726, at or near Meikle Dripps.

Possible site of an early castle or later fortified house.

Dripps means 'debateable land' or 'bone of contention'. It certainly lives up to its name. Originally included within the parish of Cathcart, then in 1725 transferred to Carmunnock, and now within East Kilbride, the lands of Dripps are recorded as part of the Barony of Mearns and then as a barony in their own right. A small tower at 'Druyp' is illustrated on Blaeu's Atlas of 1654 and in Pont's manuscript map of the late 16th century, but in both it is some way out of position.

'Le Drep' was part of the Renfrew based domain of the High Steward, who granted it to Paisley Abbey in the 12th century. The lands were rented out to William son of Maidus. By the 14th century they belonged to the Maxwells of Caerlaverock, who may have gifted them to the Maxwells of Pollok in 1371. In 1699 Meikle Dripps was occupied by a branch of the Robertons of Earnock. In 1710 it is recorded as a property of the Maxwells of Calderwood. There are a number of other properties in the area which carry the name, with a Township of Dripps, North Hill of Dripps and South Hill of Dripps, all within a radius of one mile or so indicating the full extent of the estate.

The centre of it all seems to have been near Meikle Dripps, where a large mound is suggested as the 'Moot Hill' or place of justice apparently mentioned in a charter by Lord Maxwell to his Nether Pollok namesakes. In this he is said to have reserved the Moot Hill to himself for holding courts. Another high point, the 'Hill of Birches' might also indicate a place of corporal punishment. Other authorities identify the Moot Hill as a large cairn. The foundations of a large rectangular building at NS 580556 have been suggested as the remnants of a long house or grange, though have not been investigated.

DRUID'S TEMPLE

Renfrewshire   Ruin or site   OS 64   NS 559575
On Cathcart Castle Golf Course, Williamwood.

A knoll once known as Druid's Temple is said to have supported the foundations of a building believed to have been an ancient keep. This structure apparently stood within what remained of a walled circular enclosure.

DRUMHEAD

The Lennox & East Dunbartonshire   Ruin or site   OS 63   NS 338792
1 mile north of Cardross, by minor roads north of A814, at Drumhead.

Drumhead House, which dates from the 18th and 19th centuries, may stand on the site of the old tower of Blairhenechan, which was recorded in 1552. The present house has a date-stone of 1700 and was extended in 1850.

Other reference: Blairhenechan

DRUMQUASSLE

The Lennox & East Dunbartonshire Ruin or site OS 57 NS 483869
1.5 miles southeast of Drymen on the north bank of the Endrick, at Park of Drumquassle

Site of a house or castle, also recorded as 'Drumquhassle', occupied in the 16th century by the Cunninghames. This estate had been part of the vast estates of the Dennistoun family and probably passed by marriage to the Cunninghames in the late 14th century. In 1572 Sir John Cunninghame of Drumquassle was keeper of Dumbarton Castle. He had been appointed joint commander of the small force which took it in the 'Daring Raid' of 1571. By 1577 he was Master of the King's Household. Sir John was executed in 1584, in the aftermath of the Ruthven Raid when James VI was taken and detained in Ruthven Castle for a year. It was alleged that Cunninghame was involved in a plot to kidnap the king and hold him in the Lennox. By 1615 the estate was badly burdened with debt and John's son, also John, began to sell off large portions of it. Drumquassle belonged to the Buchanans by 1623 and may have become part of the Grahams 'Buchanan' estate. It eventually came to the Govan family.

DRUMRY PEEL

City of Glasgow Ruin or site OS 64 NS 515710
2 miles southeast of Duntocher, off minor roads north of A 82, off Drumry Place, Drumchapel, at Drumry Primary School.

Drumry, from *Druim Righ*, the 'king's hill' or 'king's fort'.

Drumry was a three-storey tower with a corbelled out turret in the northeast corner. It once had an extension to the east which was removed in 1959. The Peel survived until the late 1960s, when it was demolished. There were gardens and an orchard.

It was built in 1530–40 by Lawrence Crawford and probably replaced an earlier house. Originally a Callendar, then a Wemyss property, it passed to the Livingstones in 1338. Sir Robert Livingston of Drumry was Lord Treasurer of Scotland until executed in 1447. The last Livingstone Laird of Drumry was Sir Robert Livingstone of Drumry and Easter Wemyss, who died at Flodden in 1513. Sir James Hamilton of Finnart married his daughter, Margaret Livingstone. Hamilton did not keep it for long and he exchanged Drumry with the Crawfords in 1528. Crawford probably built the Peel before being accused of treason. It came to Lord Semple in 1545.

The Peel was a ruin by 1836 when it was restored and this may be when the extension was added as farm accommodation. It was apparently in good condition in 1951.

Other reference: East Kilpatrick

DRUMSAGARD CASTLE

South Lanarkshire Ruin or site OS 64 NS 666597
1 mile west of Blantyre, north of A724 by minor roads, 100yds southwest of Hallside village.

Drumsagard from *Druimsaigard*, 'hill of the priests'. There are many spellings of the name, including Drumsargard, Drumsburget, Drumsharg, Drumsharget and Drumsirgar.

Only a ditch and mound remain of Drumsagard Castle, a stone castle of probable 14th century date, which appears as a tower named 'Colsyd' on Pont's map. An earlier earth and timber castle probably occupied the same site. The mound is rounded, flat topped and 140ft in diameter. It is situated at the western end of a prominent ridge. It rises to a height of 20ft above the ground to the north and west and over 60ft above the lower ground to the south. A deep and wide ditch crosses the neck of the ridge, isolating the site from the approach. This has been accentuated by a modern road cut parallel to the ditch. There was presumably a drawbridge. Mid 20th century aerial photography illustrates that the present landscaped area to the west of the ridge has always sat above the level of the low marshy ground around the site and would have been an ideal site for a bailey. Careful examination of early large scale OS maps also illustrate that the breadth of the mound has increased over the years, possibly the result of agricultural activity.

It is widely accepted

that Drumsagard, with Bothwell, was a property of the Olifard family. Drumsagard Castle, with the motte at Kirk Burn, has been assumed by different writers to be an Olifard seat. However, there seem to be no records to confirm their ownership. William the Parson of 'Drumsirgar' appears as a witness to charters of Bishop Jocelyn of Glasgow at the end of the 12th century. Other than that Drumsagard does not appear in records until the reign of Alexander II when it appears as a barony in the possession of William Murray, nephew of his namesake at Bothwell.

William Murray of Drumsagard was one of those appointed as an auditor when Edward I heard the cases of the competitors for the Scottish throne in 1291. He rendered homage to Edward in 1296. His son, John, was forfeited by Edward I in 1306 as penalty for supporting Robert the Bruce. John married the daughter of Malise, Earl of Strathearn, before 1320 and their descendants became the Murrays of Tullibardine. The Drumsagard line ended with Maurice Murray of Drumsagard, who died at the Battle of Neville's Cross in 1346. His daughter, Joanna, was apparently the widow of her cousin, Thomas of Bothwell. In 1362 she took both Bothwell and Drumsagard to her next husband, Archibald the Grim, the Douglas Lord of Galloway. As the illegitimate son of Bruce's companion Sir James Douglas, Archibald inherited the Earldom of Douglas following the death of his cousin at the Battle of Otterburn in 1388. Although already holding considerable lands and being a reliable and powerful ally to the Crown, this inheritance propelled him to prominence as the most powerful man in Scotland, excepting the king himself. That position was maintained by his descendants until the reign of James II, who was so concerned about such great influence being vested in one family that he resolved to destroy their power. The Douglases went into open rebellion and were defeated at the Battle of Arkinholm in 1455. However, the widow of the 5th Earl, Euphemia Graham, had been granted a 'terce', which included Bothwell. In 1452 she exchanged Bothwell with the 6th Earl, James the Gross, for the baronies of Carmunnock and Drumsagard. They came to her new husband, James Hamilton of Cadzow. This was confirmed by a royal charter in 1455, just prior to the forfeiture.

The name of the barony was changed to Cambuslang in the 17th century, matching that of the parish, which had taken that name by the 13th century. The castle was a ruin by 1796 and it is said that the remaining stone was used to build the adjacent Hallside Farms. Human bones were found on the site and occasional finds of early coins. The site now rises above a modern housing estate.

The Hamiltons retained superiority of the property until 1922, when all the land was sold off. Westburn House, built in 1685, had become the seat of the principal estate within the parish. It was demolished in the 20th century. There remains a doocot on Cambuslang Golf Course. The Hamiltons also had an 18th century 'lodge' on Dechmont Hill.

DUBS

Renfrewshire Private OS 64 NS 516591
0.5 miles northeast of Barrhead, east of B773, off Dubs Road, at Dubs Farm.

Site of an old or fortified house of the Maxwells. The defensive potential of this site is obvious, sited on a knoll, guarded by a burn and only approachable by a narrow looping drive. The present complex of buildings may disguise an older core. It appears as a relatively small property named 'Duby' on Pont's map of the late 16th century and in Blaeu's *Atlas Novus* of 1654. Some of the buildings at Dubs are said to have been constructed with stone taken from Tower Rais.

Dubs was a Maxwell property from 1271 until the 1830s. In the 1745 Jacobite rebellion Maxwell of Dubs went to fight for the Hanoverians. He trusted neither his family nor bankers and so hid his fortune high up in Darnley Glen. A local rhyme gives a clue to its whereabouts;

'Yont Capelrig and Lyoncross, and eke the auld harestane,

There a rowth o' siller lies, who finds a king will sain.'

He never returned to collect his hoard and occasional finds of gold and silver coins in the area give some credence to the legend.

DUCHAL CASTLE

Renfrewshire Ruin or site OS 63 NS 334685
1.5 miles west of Kilmacolm, by minor roads and foot south of B788, on a peninsula created by the confluence of the Burnbank (or Green) Water, and Blacketty Water.

Portions of curtain wall and fragments of a keep are all that remain of a large courtyard castle, probably dating from as early as the 13th century.

The curtain wall set apart all the high ground of the peninsula, giving an internal area of 210ft by 90ft. This could only be approached over the narrow neck of land at the western end. Precipitous 20ft drops guarded the northern edge above the Burnbank Water, while a high steep bank protected the east and south. The overgrown remnants of the wall remain on the north and incorporate a well or garderobe flue, which opens to the burn at the northeastern end of the site. This wall also supports the remnants of a number of gunloops. The entrance to the courtyard was assumed to be in the northwestern angle. A deep ditch was cut across the neck of the peninsula, guarding the approach. This can still be traced.

In the southeastern corner of the yard a 20ft high rocky knoll is surmounted by the overgrown foundations of a keep measuring 33ft by 39ft with walls 5ft thick. This was surrounded by a high curtain wall. The structures are impossible to date due to the poor quality of the remains. Although overlooked by higher ground, access to this would have been very difficult and therefore no threat.

Duchal was a property of the Lyle or de L'Isle family from the 13th century, and the family are on record as early as 1164 when William de Lyle was one of the witnesses to the foundation charter of Paisley Abbey. His son, also William, was taken prisoner at Alnwick with William the Lion in 1174. Ralph de Insula (a variation of Lyle) is designated 'of Duchal' in the reign

of Alexander II. Sir Robert Lyle was made Lord Lyle in the 1440s by James II. The next Sir Robert was a Privy Counsellor and Lord Chief Justice to James III but fought against the king at Sauchieburn in 1488. He then supported the Lennox rebellion of 1489 against James IV, who besieged Duchal in the same campaign which saw the fall of Crookston and Dumbarton. Despite this, he gained a second spell as Lord Chief Justice in 1492. Although Mons Meg was used at Crookston, there is no evidence to suggest that it was used at Duchal, though the legend persists. One of the cannon which was used at the siege was later named after the castle. It is claimed that Duchal may have been ruinous since then; however James IV returned to stay and liaise with one of his mistresses, Marion Boyd. They had a son, James Stewart, who became Archbishop of St Andrews and died with his father at Flodden in 1513. John, 4th Lord Lyle, died in 1544, but, with the consent of his son, had sold the estate to the Porterfields.

Thereafter the castle began to fall into ruin and in 1710 the Porterfields built a new mansion to the east, stripping materials from the castle. Human bones were apparently found within the walls during this process. The present Duchal House may date in part from this time, but is normally dated 1768. By the end of the 19th century, the estate was held by the Schaw Stewarts of Ardgowan and latterly by the Barons Maclay.

There is a tale regarding one Sir David Lyle, who is said to have battled the ghost of an excommunicated monk from Paisley Abbey. The monk apparently shouted profanities at anyone who came near and arrows melted when shot at him. Sir David was the son of the laird and was described as a godly youth. He cornered the spirit in the great hall and battle ensued. The hall was wrecked and David died. The spectral monk, however, departed never to return. One version of the tale suggests that the ghost was actually a baboon brought home from crusade.

This site is particularly overgrown and hazardous and, while access is open, sturdy footwear and utmost caution are recommended. This is particularly relevant when close to the edges of the site as vegetation disguises both the drop to the burn and crevices in the ground.

Duchal House gardens are occasionally open to the public (www.gardensofscotland.org).

DULLERS

South Lanarkshire Ruin or site OS 72 NS 828418
1 mile northeast of Lesmahagow, on B7018, at Dillars.

Site of a large tower, illustrated on Timothy Pont's manuscript map of the late 16th century and subsequently in Blaeu's *Atlas Novus* of 1654. In the 19th century a circular earthwork was noted on the summit of Dillarshill to the south, but no trace now remains at either site.

DUMBARTON CASTLE

The Lennox & East Dunbartonshire   His Scot   OS 64   NS 400745

On the north shore of the Clyde, south of Dumbarton town centre, off minor roads south of the A814, on Dumbarton Rock.

Dumbarton from *Dun Breatan*, 'fort of the Britons'.

Built upon a twin-peaked volcanic plug which rises prominently above the Firth of Clyde and the mouth of the River Leven, only a 14th century portcullis arch and the altered 16th century guardhouse remain of the medieval Royal castle of Dumbarton. The remaining structure is essentially a military fortress of the 18th and 19th centuries.

The higher western summit is known as White Tower Crag having once supported a medieval tower of that name. There remains a circular foundation thought to be that of an 18th century windmill. The second eastern-most summit is known as The Beak. From the main gate on the south of the rock, the castle walls spiral around and upwards to the west, then around the north side and on up to the summit on the eastern side. There are seven gun batteries at strategic points of the circumference. The entrance to the castle is by a steep climb through the southern end of the cleft which leads you past the Governors House, the guardhouse, and through the 14th century portcullis gate. This leads to a more level area between the two peaks at the northern end of which was the old northern gate and well. Here stood the 'Wallace Tower' which dated from c.1500 and was demolished when this entrance was closed in 1795. This site is now occupied by the Duke of York's Battery and the French Prison. On the summit of The Beak is the Powder Magazine, a sturdy thick walled hut within its own high-walled courtyard. The eastern end of the castle wall terminates in a platform, thought to have been the base for a crane used to hoist provisions up the rock and into the castle. In old rhymes regarding the Galbraith family there is mention of a 'Red Hall' which, it is said, underwent repair in 1460.

Dumbarton has been fortified since at least as early as the 5th century, when St Patrick wrote to the subjects of Ceretic, King of Alcluith, castigating them for a piratical raid on his Irish converts. It was the capital of the Kingdom of Strathclyde, the nation of the Britons, and was besieged on several occasions. In 756 a combined force of Picts and Northumbrians took the fort, only to be annihilated themselves a few days later. The buildings on the rock were burned in 780, though it is not certain whether this was a result of hostile activity.

In 870 a Viking attack led by Olaf the White of Dublin and Ivar the One-Legged led to a four-month siege. They severed the water supply and starved the occupants to submission. The fort was plundered for its wealth and people, 200 longships carrying the booty to Dublin. The Britons returned in strength in the 10th century and extended their territory southwards. In 1018 Owen the Bald, the last king of the Britons, died at the Battle of Carham. Malcolm II of Scots was able to set his grandson Duncan upon the British throne. When Duncan succeeded to the Scots throne in 1034, Strathclyde was permanently integrated into the Scottish kingdom.

Nothing is then recorded of Dumbarton until 1222 when the burgh charter mentions the new castle. Dumbarton at this time was of significant importance as it guarded the western approaches to the realm from the Viking territories of the isles and west highlands. Until their defeat at the Battle of Largs in 1263, the territory of the Norsemen came as close as Kilcreggan on the Rosneath peninsula, where it is likely that a Norse watch tower occupied the site of what is now Knockderry Castle.

From these early years it is evident that Dumbarton was a royal castle and as such was a target of Edward I in his invasion of 1296. He subsequently installed sympathetic Governors such as Sir John Mentieth, the captor of William Wallace. Legend asserts that Wallace was brought here as a prisoner prior to his departure for

London in 1305, though most authorities think this unlikely.

In 1333, in the aftermath of the Battle of Halidon Hill, the Scots sent the young David II and his queen, Joanna of England, to reside here for security. At this point Edward Balliol was attempting to regain his father's former realm for himself with English support. Dumbarton, although on the west coast, was then to become Scottish royalty's accustomed embarkation point for the safety of France and the young couple departed in early 1334.

In 1435 it was the port of departure for the 11-year-old Princess Margaret, the daughter of James I, who married Louis, the Dauphin of France. Ignored by her husband, she apparently died of homesickness, aged 20.

As a Royal castle under the care of the rebellious Earl of Lennox in 1489, it was again besieged by the young James IV himself, the castle being occupied by Lord Darnley, the Earl's heir. The siege failed as the garrison burnt the burgh, but James returned the same year and was successful. He may have utilised the great bombard Mons Meg in the second assault. James then put the castle to use as a base for his campaign against the Lord of the Isles.

In 1514 during the minority of James V it was held by the Lord Erskine for the Queen Mother. The Earl of Lennox captured it on behalf of the opposing faction, led by the Earl of Arran. The assailants had tunnelled below the north entrance and stormed the garrison.

A year later the Duke of Albany arrived at the castle from France, to take up his duties as Governor of the Realm. As the late king's cousin, he had been invited to take up the role as a neutral and immediately arrested Lennox, installing a garrison of Frenchmen. He thereafter used Dumbarton as his regular port of departure to France. In 1523 he arrived with a large French force with the intention of invading England, but the plan was never

followed through, due to inconsistent support from the Scots. He left the following year with his troops and never returned. The divided Scots nobles squabbled over the castle and control passed among the various parties until it was regained for James V.

In 1548 it again had a royal resident as the young Mary, Queen of Scots, was brought to the castle to protect her from the 'Rough Wooing' of Henry VIII. She left for France within five months, where she married the Dauphin. She returned to visit in 1563. Her governor of the castle was Lord Fleming of Cumbernauld, who had fled with her after Langside in 1568. He returned in 1570 to be besieged in the castle by the Regent Moray. The arrival of a French fleet and the murder of Moray relieved him within a few weeks. Fleming held the castle for Mary until 1571, when Captain Thomas Crawford of Jordanhill took it for the young James VI. His assault was recorded in detail.

Leaving Glasgow an hour before sunset on the evening of the 31st March, Crawford and about a hundred men carried ladders and ropes with iron hooks. They were armed with muskets. By 1am they halted a mile from the castle, bound their guns to their backs and crossed what was then marshland to the highest point of the curtain wall. Climbing by stages they reached the base of the wall at dawn and as the first of the assailants crossed the parapet a sentry raised the alarm. The garrison awoke and were attacked by Crawford's men. Three died and the remainder fled. Crawford established his forces on The Beak and when no counter attack developed he used the castle's own artillery against the remaining strong points. Most of the garrison fled and some were captured, but the Lord Fleming made his escape by sea. Archbishop James Hamilton of St Andrews was captured. He was one of the exiled Mary's staunchest supporters, and was tried and executed. Thereafter the castle was used mostly as a state prison, hosting noble inmates such as the Earl of Morton, Archibald Dubh McDonald of Gigha and the Earl of Orkney.

The castle changed hands several times during the Covenanting period and the Civil War. It sustained repeated damage and required extensive repair by the time extension and improvement work was begun in 1675. It regained strategic importance as a military installation in the Jacobite years. From then on the construction of military buildings and gun batteries obliterated what remained of the medieval castle. The role as a fortress continued through the Napoleonic wars and into the 19th century. It was used as a military prison throughout this period. The constructions of that time represent the bulk of what can be seen today. It remained in use as a military installation until World War II, when two bombs were dropped on it during bombing raids on Clydebank.

Archaeological investigation found the remains of a rubble, earth and timber bank on the eastern spur of The Beak which had been destroyed by the fire of 780 or during the Viking raid of 870. It is likely that all habitable portions of the rock were utilized in the dark ages as the rock functioned not only as a fort, but as a substantial settlement. Excavations in the area of the Governor's House uncovered the foundations of an earlier gatehouse which had been demolished when the house was built.

In the town is the 17th century town house of the Earl of Glencairn known as his 'Greit House' or the 'Glencairn Tenement.' It was built in 1623 and was acquired by the town council in 1923.

Dumbarton Castle: open to public year round, Apr-Sep daily 09.30-17.30, Oct-Mar, Sat-Wed 09.30-16.30, closed Thurs & Fri. last entry 30 mins before closing, closed on 25/26 Dec and 1-2nd Jan (tel 01389 732167)

Other references: Alcluith, Alt Clut, Clyde Rock

DUNGAVEL

South Lanarkshire   Ruin or site   OS 72   NS 659373
6.5 miles southwest of Strathaven, east of the A71 and just east of the B743, at or near Dungavel.

There are Hamiltons of Dungavel on record in the early 16th century and the farm of Peelhill just to the west at NS 645368 may indicate the site of a small fortified tower. James Weir of 'Dargavel' is recorded in the late 16th century.

The present Dungavel House was built in the early 20th century for the Duke of Hamilton and has no earlier origins. Formerly used as a prison, it is currently a detention centre for the Home Office. In 1941 it was the intended destination of Hitler's Deputy Fuhrer, Rudolph Hess, when he crash landed at Floors Farm, near Busby. He was apparently attempting to broker peace by making contact with the Duke of Hamilton. His reasons for choosing the Duke appear to have been spurious and led to a libel case. Having strayed off course, it is thought that Hess may have mistaken Eaglesham House for Dungavel House. He was taken prisoner and after a short stay in Buchanan Castle, eventually become the sole prisoner in Berlin's Spandau Prison. He remained there for the duration of the Cold War. He committed suicide in 1987.

DUNGLASS CASTLE

The Lennox & East Dunbartonshire   Private   OS 64   NS 435735
2 miles east of Dumbarton, south of the A82 just west of Bowling, on north bank of Firth of Clyde, within Oil Terminal grounds.

Little remains of a 14th century castle with a sea gate, other than a portion of courtyard wall and an incorporated round tower. A turreted house of the late 16th century stands within the northeastern corner of the yard. This was extended and remodelled in the 19th century. There is a 17th century doocot.

For centuries Dunglass was the main stronghold of the Colquhouns, who took their name from the parish. They later inherited the Luss estates by marrying the heiress. From 1439 to 1478 this was the home of Sir John Colquhoun, Chamberlain of Scotland. The present house is thought to have been begun by Humphrey Colquhoun of Luss toward the end of the 16th century. Although the house is much altered, the round turret corbelled out from the northwest corner is thought to be from his time.

The Edmonstones gained Dunglass in 1738, but it fell into ruin soon afterwards. In 1783 the castle began to be used as a quarry in the building of a new quay. This process was halted by Buchanan of Auchentorlie, who purchased, extended and restored it.

In the 19th century the graphic artist Talwin Morris lived in the house and commissioned Charles Rennie Macintosh to redesign the interiors, although many of his fittings have now been removed. His work here led to his commission for the Hill House in Helensburgh.

Derelict in 2000, limited restoration work has taken place within the last decade and the building appears to be wind and watertight. Much of the oil terminal facility has been demolished though work has still to be done before the site is useable.

Within the grounds, just west of the house, is a tall obelisk erected to the memory of Henry Bell, the steam boat pioneer who lived in Helensburgh. His *Comet* was the first passenger carrying steamboat in Europe and initially plied trade between Glasgow, Helensburgh and Greenock.

The terminal site remains under 24–hour security. Access is denied and the house has been fenced off. The terminal owners apparently intend to renovate the house.

DUNROD CASTLE

Renfrewshire   Ruin or site   OS 63   NS 223731

3.5 miles southwest of Greenock, on minor roads east of A78, west of railway at Dunrod.

Site of the original stronghold of the Lindsays of Dunrod. By 1856, only a grassy mound remained, but now there is no trace. The castle apparently 'disappeared' between 1619 and 1650, only to be rebuilt before 1710. This building had been demolished by 1782, though the Old Place of Dunrod still appeared on a map of the Greenock Railway in 1823. Dunrod had gone completely by 1890.

James Lindsay of Dunrod was the companion in arms of Robert the Bruce, and was one of those who ensured the death of the Red Comyn when he was stabbed by The Bruce in Greyfriars Kirk Dumfries in 1306. His son, John, was granted the former Comyn estate of Mains of Kilbride by Robert II in 1382 for 'his good and faithful service'. The family seem to have preferred Mains as a residence, though they maintained the Dunrod estate.

In 1619 Dunrod was sold by Alexander Lindsay to Archibald Stewart of Blackhall. Lindsay died in poverty sometime after 1627 and is described as a haughty, oppressive, depraved character who indulged in 'every sort of wickedness'. Perhaps these old rhymes reflect the common opinion of him better than any description:

'In Innerkip the witches ride thick,
And in Dunrod they dwell,
But the greatest loon among them a',
Was auld Dunrod himsel.'

And in another:

'Auld Dunrod he stack a pin
A bourtrie pin in the wa',
And when he wanted his neighbour's milk,
He just gaed the pin a thraw.'

By 1890 the barony of Dunrod was a part of the Ardgowan estate of Sir Michael Stewart of Blackhall.

DUNSYRE CASTLE

South Lanarkshire   Ruin or site   OS 72   NT 071476

At or near Dunsyre, 6 miles east of Carnwath, by minor roads north of A721 near Newbigging, west of A702 north of Dolphinton.

On the banks of the Medwin, 300yds from the church stood a three-storey tower with vaulted basement and mural turnpike stair.

It is said that William Somerville of Carnwath gained Dunsyre by marriage to the Gourlay heiress of Newbigging in 1147. Later in the 12th century, a donation of the church at Dunsyre was made to Glasgow Cathedral by Fergus Macabard (Baird?). Bishop Jocelin thereafter managed to obtain Dunsyre for his brother Elias, who granted the church to Kelso Abbey c.1186. In 1299 John, son of Adam of Dunsyre, sold Hills to Alan Denholm.

By 1367 William de Newbygging was in possession. The property came to the Earls of Douglas, who in 1444 granted half of the estate to Hepburn of Hailes. This half consisted of the Easter and Wester Towns of Dunsyre, Netherhill, and Stoneypath, as confirmed by royal charter in 1452. The Black Douglases were forfeited in 1455 and the Red Douglas Earls of Angus gained possession of their portion. In 1475 Adam Hepburn, son of Lord Hailes, received a charter of the barony. In 1492 the Hepburns were involved in a complex temporary exchange of properties involving Hermitage Castle, Bothwell Castle and Dunsyre, among others. Dunsyre went to Angus, but by 1511 the estate had returned to Hepburns. From around this time about half of the estate was feued out creating a number of smaller estates. In 1540 Dunsyre was granted, with Weston and Todholes, to Robert Maxwell of Caerlaverock.

In 1542 the estate was temporarily annexed to the Crown during a complex legal dispute over the king's right to alienate properties without parliamentary consent. The Hepburns were again forfeited and the estate returned to the Earl of Angus in a ratification of 1567. A subsequent Angus forfeiture saw the property granted to the Earl's wife, though was restored to the 10th Earl of Angus in 1603. The superiority of the whole of Dunsyre and the unfeued property was purchased by Sir George Lockhart, President of the Court of Session. In 1690 it passed to his son George Lockhart of Carnwath, whose heirs gradually bought outright ownership of every property, excepting Stoneypath.

The castle was the seat of the barony and, despite its ruinous state, court was still held there until 1740. At that time it retained its 'instruments of torture'. Medieval jougs are still visible at the parish church.

DUNTERVY CASTLE

South Lanarkshire Ruin or site OS 72 NS 828401
1 mile east of M74 and Lesmahagow, off minor roads south of B7018, just north of Brocketsbrae, at Dumbraxhill.

Site of a 15th century castle, occupied in the 16th century by the Durham family. The name is also spelt Duntervie Castle, Duntarvet Castle, and Dunterby. The head of this family built part of Lesmahagow's first post-Reformation church. This was known as the Durham Aisle. A Thomas de Durham appears as Prior of Lesmahagow in 1315. He was also Abbot of Kelso at that time and may have been an English appointee. Durham of 'Dunterby' is on record as paying five merks feu duty per annum to Kelso Abbey for his £100 lands in Lesmahagow.

The castle ruin was drawn on Forrest's map in the early 19th century and is described by others at the time of being 'of more than usual size'. The *Name Book* of 1856 records that 'Nothing remains but a single gable of great thickness. Traditionally the date of erection is given as 1400.' It appears on the OS 25 inch map of 1858, a few yards south of Dumbraxhill Farm. There are now no remains.

Other reference: Dumbraxhill

DUNTREATH CASTLE

The Lennox & East Dunbartonshire Private OS 64 NS 536811
4 miles north of Milngavie, 1 mile north of Blanefield, just west of A81, and east of Blane Water, at Duntreath.

Duntreath, pronounced 'Duntreth', lies in the Blane Valley close to the lofty conical mound of Dungoiach. It guards the southern approaches to the heartland of the earldom of Lennox. This was therefore a position of great strategic importance in early centuries forming a gateway to and from the highlands. It consists of a large keep of the 15th century, once with extensive additions of the late 16th and early 17th centuries which created a quadrangular courtyard castle, with external measurements of 120ft by 100ft. Much of the 17th century structure has gone, replaced in part by a mansion of the 19th century.

The western wall of the courtyard was broken centrally by an arched gatehouse of three storeys with round corner towers defending the outward approaches. These had turnpike stairs to the upper floors. The gateway was adorned with a heraldic panel, bearing the arms of Edmonstone.

The keep stands in the northwestern corner of the former courtyard and is of three main storeys and a garret. Measuring 48ft by 26.5ft, it is an excellent example of a 'double tower', each floor being divided by a thick central wall providing two rooms to each. The parapet is crenellated and is supported by a single course of corbelling 39ft above ground level. The entrance at the eastern edge of the south front has an unusual projecting porch. This is on a small scale, allowing space above for a turnpike stair. This projection of the wall recedes to merge with the wall as it rises and the width of the stair narrows. Rather than creating a stair tower, the impression is given of a buttress. There is a round caphouse above this, dating from Victorian renovations. The garret and roof were rebuilt around the same time. There is a further stair in the northwestern corner which

accessed each floor. There are machicolated projections in the southern and northern fronts, which may have served as garderobe chutes. The keep represents all that remains of the older buildings.

To the east of the keep the northern perimeter was continued by a large ruinous chapel of the 17th century, which may have been created from an earlier hall block, perhaps of the 14th century.

From the northeastern corner and running southward, stood a long two-storeyed utility range, containing three rooms per floor. The ground floor contained the kitchen. This building culminated with the 'Dumb Laird's Tower' of the early 17th century. This had two floors above the basement and contained a scale-and-platt stairway to first-floor level. Access to the upper floor was via a stair turret corbelled out from the re-entrant with the kitchen block. The entrance to this tower was on the north front within the courtyard and was surmounted by a heraldic panel. The south side of the courtyard may never have been completed, and the site is now occupied by a mansion dating from the 19th century.

Duntreath was part of the estates of the Earls of Lennox. In 1360 Earl Donald granted the estate to his brother, Murdoch. In 1425, when Earl Duncan was executed for treason, James I granted the estate to his sister Princess Mary and her husband, William Edmonstone of Culloden. The castle was gradually enlarged by this family until creating the complex described.

In 1578 the Earl of Argyll, acting as Justice General of Scotland, granted Sir James Edmonstone the power to hold justice courts at Duntreath. Sir James died in 1618, by which time he had added the gatehouse. William, 9th of Duntreath, was titled the 'Dumb Laird', being deaf and not able to speak since birth. It was in his honour that the tower was named. This was his residence, although his handicap meant that he could not take up his full title. He was, however, reported to have exceptional intelligence and overcame his handicap, communicating his will to others and administering the estate with some skill. He died toward the end of the 17th century.

Thereafter the family removed to their Irish estates at Redhall and Duntreath fell into ruin. Possibly during their absence, the chapel suffered 'a crash' during a service. The family sold Redhall and returned to live at Colzium House, which they built for themselves in 1783. About 1863 Sir Archibald Edmonstone, 13th of Duntreath and 3rd Baronet, had the castle renovated and extended. The family reoccupied it soon afterward. In 1958 all of the older work, excepting the original keep, was demolished. The keep and mansion are what remain today. The family remain in occupancy and are believed to have been descended from a branch of the Seton family, who were granted the estate of Edmonstone in Midlothian around 1248.

DYKEBAR HILL

Renfrewshire   Ruin or site   OS 64   NS 497623

2 miles southeast of Paisley, by minor roads and foot, south of the A726 at Dykebar.

Site of an early earthwork or 'clay' castle.

In the 19th century, ditches and ramparts were noted on the summit of Dykebar Hill, though the site was being ploughed on a regular basis. It is said that stone from the buildings within was regularly being carted away for dyke building. In 1968 the site was measured at 185 ft by 110ft to 162ft, and is described as heart shaped. In 2004 the site was buried below 10 ft of boulder clay as the ground nearby was prepared for residential development.

Finds from the site included spears, swords and 'curious chain links' in the 19th century, then green glazed pottery, a coin and a brooch in 1964. In 1987 a hoard of 221 Edwardian coins was uncovered within the grounds of the adjacent Dykebar Hospital.

An 18th century landscape feature and World War II heavy anti aircraft gun emplacement are also on record on the hill, which has been considerably disturbed over the years.

DYKES

South Lanarkshire   Ruin or site   OS 72   NS 661390?

5.5 miles southwest of Strathaven, 1 mile east of Drumclog, east of A71, and west of B743, at or near West Dykes.

This is the probable site of the castle of the Forsyths of Dykes. 'Dyks' appears in this location in Pont's manuscript map of the late 16th century and in Blaeu's *Atlas Novus* of 1654. The estate comprised the lands around the confluence of Dykes Burn and the River Avon.

Legend asserts that the Forsyths were granted these lands in the 14th century, having defeated an English force in the area and successfully defending an existing castle named Dykes. However, it is more likely that they were involved in the defence of Stirling Castle, since Robert Forsyth then his son and grandson in succession were Governors there in the second half of the 14th century. They are said to have been awarded the family motto *Instaurator Ruinae*, restorer of ruins, as a result.

Many of the family records were destroyed by Cromwell in the 17th century, and therefore very little of their history can be verified. David Forsyth of Dykes is on record in 1488, since his seal of that date was recorded by the Lord Lyon. This discredits one account which states that the family gained Dykes in exchange for the lands of Gilcamstoun in Aberdeenshire in 1519. They did sell these lands to the Gordons around that time.

There are a variety of Dykes names in the area, which mark out the extent of the lands: West Dykes, East Dykes, High Dykes, Dykes Bridge and the Dykes Burn among them.

The family are strongly associated with Glasgow, holding office in the cathedral, city and the university from the 15th to the 17th century. The Forsyths of Dykes are said to have been opposed to the Union with England, despite the apparent involvement of the main branch of the family in the initial steps to promote it.

The family were still in possession at the beginning of the 17th century when another David Forsyth of Dykes is recorded as a Burgess of Glasgow. In 1623 both he and Alexander Stewart were sued by Lord Ley at the Court of Session for the recovery of debts.

The family permanently moved to their other property of Inchnock, possibly in 1654, but more likely earlier. No trace of the castle remains at Dykes.

EAGLESHAM CASTLE

Renfrewshire   Ruin or site   OS 64   NS 572519

On Eaglesham Common (The Orry), in Eaglesham, 4 miles southwest of East Kilbride by the B764, and by minor roads through village.

Eaglesham means the 'hamlet of the church', and there may have been an early Christian chapel here.

A mutilated motte remains on The Orry. This flat-topped mound represents the remains of what is probably the earliest castle of the Montgomeries on their Eaglesham estate. Now measuring 130ft by 59ft at the base, the construction of an 18th century cotton mill on the site necessitated the removal of a large section of the mound. The Mill has now gone and the burn which powered it remains in a culvert below the site. It would once have enhanced the defences of the motte. The mound projects from the side of the burn valley and is thought to have been defended on that side by a semi-circular ditch. There are slight traces of a ditch around the southwestern base. The summit once measured 50ft in diameter, but is now around 50ft by 33ft. It stands to a height of 13ft above the surrounding ground.

To the northwest of the village, the farms of Castlehill and Boreland (a term indicating the mains or home farm of the castle) may indicate another early castle site. Near these is 'Deil's Hill', a man-made mound of early origin once also thought to have been a motte and later considered to be a moot hill. Informed opinion now identifies this as a cairn.

To the southeast the late 14th century castle at Polnoon was built upon another motte.

From the 12th century Eaglesham was the seat of the Montgomerie family. They were vassals of the High Stewards based at Renfrew and received a grant of the lands upon the marriage of Sir Robert to the daughter of Walter Fitz-Alan, the progenitor of the Stewarts. Robert was the grandson of the 1st Earl of Shrewsbury. He had accompanied Walter when he came north to take possession of the extensive properties granted to him by David I. He witnessed Walter's foundation charter of Paisley Abbey. His great grandson, John, fought at the Battle of Largs in 1263. Another John is on record as having rendered homage to Edward I of England in 1296.

In the 1360s another Sir John Montgomerie married the heiress of Sir Hugh Eglinton. He gained the baronies of Ardrossan and Eglinton on Hugh's death in 1374. He captured Henry 'Hotspur' Percy at the Battle of Otterburn in 1388 and held him for ransom, using the funds to build himself a new castle at Polnoon. The two became firm friends, and Hotspur is said to have helped design Polnoon.

The Montgomeries became Earls of Eglinton in 1508.

The present village was laid out in 1796 by the 12th Earl of Eglinton to provide accommodation for the workforce of his new cotton mill. No trace remains of the original village, which is thought to have stood a little to the northeast.

Eaglesham House, which once stood north of the village, was a grand sprawling mansion with no fortified core. It was built in 1859 for Allan Gilmour, a ship owner and importer of timber.

It was used as barracks for Polish troops during World War II, although locals often say that it housed German captives. The local POW camp was actually at Patterton. A serious fire led to the demolition of the Eaglesham House in the 1950s.

In 1960 Eaglesham was the first village in Scotland to be designated a place of special historic interest.

EARNOCK HOUSE

South Lanarkshire   Ruin or site   OS 64   NS 699546

1 mile south of Hamilton, west of B755, in Earnock, above west bank of Earnock Burn, at or near Rederech Crescent.

Site of a fortified house, replaced or incorporated within a mansion, which was extended by William Leiper in the 19th century. The site has been developed as a housing estate.

Two properties carried the name Meikle Earnock, which is described here, and Little Earnock, a later and lesser property belonging to a branch of the Hamiltons with whom the Robertons had intermarried. 'Meikeirnock' appears in Blaeu's *Atlas Novus* as a small tower.

This was the property of the Roberton family from as early as 1390, who claimed to be chiefs of the name in the early 18th century. The estate may originally have been granted to Robert of Roberton by Malcolm IV in the 12th century. His descendant, Stephen of Roberton, signed the Ragman Roll in 1296. As a supporter of the Balliol faction, he was forfeited by Robert I in the early 14th century.

The family were granted the Earnock estates in 1390, as vassals of the Hamiltons, with whom they made numerous marriages. In the 17th century they were noted Covenanters.

The Roberton lairds of Earnock held the lands of Motherwell in the 15th century and substantial properties in Avondale Parish in the 18th century.

The last Roberton laird sold the estate to a Mr Semple at the turn of the 18th century, who in turn sold it to a Mr Miller in 1810. By 1889 the property was held by John Watson, coal master. He became Sir John Watson, Baronet, and held the most extensive mining operation of his time in Scotland.

Sold again in 1925, the house was demolished only a year later.

EASTEND HOUSE

South Lanarkshire   Private   OS 72   NS 949374

7 miles southeast of Lanark, and 1.5 miles west of Thankerton, on minor road south of A73, just south of Glade Burn, at Eastend.

Eastend incorporates a 16th century tower house, to which tall corbiestepped gabled wings of 1673 have been added. There is also an 18th century bow-fronted range encasing one side of the tower and a castellated extension designed in 1855 by David Bryce.

The tower is of three storeys and a garret. There is a corbelled-out crenellated parapet with open corner rounds. It once had a vaulted basement but this was removed on the complete reconstruction of the interior.

This was a Carmichael property from early times and a cadet line was apparently established at Eastend c.1500. In the 19th century they were reckoned to be the senior of the two Carmichael families in the parish. The family records were accidentally destroyed in 1677, the earliest surviving document being the marriage contract of a daughter in 1568.

In 1682 Thomas Carmichael of Eastend was found guilty of coercion and fined 5,000 merks. He had induced the dying Daniel Mure of Gledstanes to leave him his entire estate, effectively disinheriting Mure's brother, Francis. In order that a disposition of this kind was legal, Mure had to appear before a solicitor at 'kirk and market' to prove his mental aptitude. Carmichael dressed his servant as the dying man and convinced the doubtful lawyer that this was indeed poor Daniel in full health. Following Mure's death, Francis objected to being disinherited and discovered the deceit. Taking the case to the Court of Session, he was granted the Gledstanes estate and 2,000 merks of the fine for his inconvenience.

Eastend passed from father to son continuously, excepting inheritance by a nephew in 1789. His mother was a Hay of Restalrig whose ancestor, Sir John Hay of Alderston, was secretary to Bonnie Prince Charlie. This led to a lock of the prince's hair and a pair of diamond knee buttons being preserved in Eastend. In contrast to their cousins of Carmichael who supported the Hanoverians, the Carmichaels of Eastend were Jacobites.

From c.1870 they were known as Thomson-Carmichael.

In 1921 the male line ended and the estate was inherited by the MacNeil-Hamilton family. They retained it until the death of the spinster Miss Millicent MacNeil-Hamilton in the late 1980s.

At that point, her cousin Richard Carmichael of Carmichael exchanged Eastend with her heirs for other local properties. He is the current clan chief, and operates the Carmichael Estate and Visitor Centre (www.carmichael.org).

He and his family are resident in Eastend House.

EASTER GREENOCK CASTLE

Renfrewshire Ruin or site OS 63 NS 293749

1 mile west of Port Glasgow, east of Greenock, by minor roads south of A8, just northwest of junction of Castle Street and Bridgend Road, Greenock.

Site of a castle, the ruins of which were marked on the OS 25 inch map of 1857. The site was destroyed on construction of the railway in 1886.

Easter Greenock, or Easter Kilbirny Castle, belonged to the Crawfords of Kilbirnie, and the estate was considered to be a detached part of that barony. It is said that Malcolm Crawford of Loudoun gained the estate through marriage to the daughter of a Galbraith c.1400. His descendants became the Crawfords of Kilbirnie and held the estate until 1667 when, burdened with debt, they sold it to the Schaws of Wester Greenock. This sale excepted Cartsburn, which was portioned off to create a separate estate. The castle is illustrated as a large and impressive structure on early cartographic references.

EASTERTON BURN MOTTE

South Lanarkshire Ruin or site OS 72 NS 992310

0.75 miles east of Lamington, east of A702 by track from 'Smithy'.

A high narrow ridge formed between the confluence of the Easterton Burn and a tributary, has been divided by the cutting of a ditch to create a motte. A further ditch isolating a possible bailey was recorded in 1955, but appears

to have been filled in by agricultural activity. The motte occupies the end of the ridge, and has a diameter of 66ft. The summit is flat and 10ft above the ground across the ditch. It shows evidence of occupation, though no building remains are evident on the surface. The curving ditch, which separates it from the rest of the ridge, measures 11.5ft deep and 33ft wide. Agricultural activity has created a ramp to this area which carries a track toward the summit. The material for this may have been taken from the motte, which is badly damaged on its western side. This has caused some erosion, which is exposing large stones suggestive of a structure.

The site is isolated from other areas of occupation in the area, being some distance from the 12th century Lamington Church and the Roman road which passed through the area. This has raised questions regarding the dating of the motte and has been taken to indicate that it is unlikely to date from the period of Norman settlement of the area. It is therefore unlikely to be the seat of Lambin Asa, who gave his name to Lamington.

There is a tradition that the English Sheriff of Lanark, Sir William Hazelrig, stormed a castle at Lamington belonging to Hugh Braidfute. The story continues that Hugh's daughter, Marion, was rescued by Sir William Wallace, and later became his wife. Hazelrig had intended to marry Marion to his own son, but on discovering her marriage to Wallace, he killed Marion at Lanark as she protected Wallace's escape through her house. Wallace took his revenge, storming and burning Lanark Castle, then executing Hazelrig. There are a number of variations to this tale, which is normally associated with Lamington Tower. The Baillies of Lamington claim descent from Marion and William's daughter. It is also said that Hazelrig himself had a castle at Lamington.

Other reference: Loanhead Mill

EASTSHIELD TOWER

South Lanarkshire Ruin or site OS 72 NS 960500
2.5 miles northwest of Carnwath, at the junction of the B7016 and a minor road, at Eastshield.

The remains of the north wall and a lofty round stair tower at what was the northwest angle represent the remains of a large tower house of the Inglis family. A doocot is built within the upper storey of the tower. A section of walling, about 3ft high and 18ft long, is built into the field dyke running southward from the tower. It stands to a height of about 30ft and is about 10ft in diameter. The north wall extends from the tower to the east for about 10ft; it is 4ft thick. A date-stone carrying the name Thomas Inglis and the date 1567 is now in use as a door lintel in a barn. There is mention of a peel here in the 15th century and a William Inglis of Eastshield is mentioned in the records of the Scottish Parliament in 1491.

The Inglis family were closely associated with the Somervilles and were most active in the 16th and 17th centuries.

EDDLEWOOD CASTLE

South Lanarkshire Ruin or site OS 64 NS 720520
1 mile northwest of Quarter Iron Works, on banks of Meikle Burn.

An 1879 reference notes a mound of 'rubbish' and a fragment of wall which mark the site of Eddlewood Castle.

This was a Carpenter property in the early 14th century. Legend tells that Robert I was travelling to meet Sir John Menteith at Dumbarton Castle, when Roland the Carpenter stopped him in the woods of Colquhoun. He informed the king of an intended ambush on his arrival. Aware of the danger, he turned the tables on his intended attackers, then awarded the lands of Eddlewood to the informant. It is said that David II confirmed his father's grant to the Carpenters. An Oliver Carpenter was resident in the mid 14th century.

In 1368 David Fitzwalter was granted a confirmation of his lands at Cadzow with the additional estate of Eddlewood, lands and tenants. The castle was probably dismantled by the Regent Moray in the aftermath of the Battle of Langside.

Eddlewood House was built on the site of the chapel, though Mains of Eddlewood became the main residence. A family named Alston were in possession of the Mains from 1657 and purchased a further portion in 1672. They were merchants and coal masters, and held estates throughout this part of Lanarkshire. The rest of the estate remained Hamilton property, until sold in 1750, possibly to the Cochrane Earls of Dundonald. In 1770 the estate was known as Annsfield. It passed to Captain James Gilchrist on his marriage the Earl's daughter. When he died, it returned to his widow, who subsequently married Boyes of Wellhall. There seems then to have been a long-running legal dispute over the inheritance until at some point it became home to the Erskine-Cochrane family. Eddlewood House may have served as a prison around 1862.

EDINBELLIE CASTLE

The Lennox & East Dunbartonshire Ruin or site OS 57 NS 576890
2 miles east of Balfron, on minor roads north of B818, north of Endrick Water, south of Ballindalloch Moor, at Edinbellie.

Site of a tower house or 'old mansion'. This was a property of the Napiers of Merchiston, gained on the division of the Lennox estates following the execution of the Earl of Lennox by James I in 1425. In 1509 it was erected into a free barony called Edinbellie-Napier, for Archibald Napier of Merchiston. It is one of the properties suggested as the birthplace of John Napier in 1550, famed for his invention of logarithms. Merchiston is a more likely site for his birth.

By the end of the 16th century it seems to have been occupied by Galbraiths. The ruins of the 'old mansion' were still visible when the second *Statistical Account* was written in 1841. An armorial stone was recorded on a wall at this time.

In 1750 the sons of Rob Roy forcibly abducted Jean Kay from the house. She was a young widow and heiress to the estate. She was forced to marry Robin Og. She soon died and three years later Robin was tried and executed.

Inspection of the site in the 1950s found no trace of the castle, though some of the farm buildings were noted to be of an earlier date than the others. There was a United Presbyterian Church of Scotland building on this site in the 19th century, which is partly occupied by the present farmhouse.

EDMONSTON CASTLE

South Lanarkshire Private OS 72 NT 070422

4 miles northeast of Biggar, off minor road south of A721 and north of A702, 1.5 miles south of Elsrickle, at Edmonston, just west of the Candy Burn.

Edmonston consists of a small ruined 15th century tower and adjoining courtyard. It was complete, other than a few missing slates, until 1872, when the tenant was afraid that it would collapse. Intending to demolish the tower, he set charges of dynamite, but was only partially successful. The western corner of the building has gone above first floor level, as has the roof, and a gaping hole now exists in the vaulting of the basement. Of the courtyard wall, only a small section adjoining the centre of the northeastern wall remains, this framing an arched gateway.

Measuring 26ft by 20.5ft, the tower consisted of three storeys. A round turret which projects from the northern corner may have been added at a later date. It housed a turnpike stair which accessed all floors. The original entrance to the first floor sits above the main entrance.

From the re-entrant, the main door enters into a small lobby. From here access is gained to the stair and a door leads to the vaulted chamber. A small spy hole in the basement chamber watches the lobby. This chamber is illuminated from a slot window set high upon the northeastern wall. There is a shot hole in the wall opposite the door.

The first floor is entirely occupied by the hall. A window gave a view of the exterior of the main gate to the courtyard. Two other windows in the southwestern wall provided light. There was a fireplace in the southwestern wall, though this has since fallen apart. There is also a small recessed cupboard within this wall.

The top floor contained a single room. There is a large cupboard and the remains of a fireplace on the southwestern wall. The windows are above those in the hall. No detail remains of the parapet.

A second house was built within the courtyard, the demolition of which, in 1815, destroyed any evidence of the courtyard detail. At this time a new mansion was built a little further down the hill. This was designed by James Gillespie Graham.

In 1322 the estates of Edmonston and Candy were resigned by William son of Haldwine of Edmonston in favour of Sir James Douglas. This was done with the consent of his superior, Gilbert Fleming of Biggar. The Flemings retained the superiority throughout the centuries that followed. In 1382 Robert II issued a charter confirming the property in the hands of Douglas of Dalkeith. This family later became the Earls of Morton. The tower is believed to have been built between 1450 and 1500. Around this time, Sir John Herring is mentioned as being in possession of Edmonstone in Clydesdale, and Gilmerton in Lothian.

The 4th Earl of Morton was active in national politics during the reign of Mary, Queen of Scots, and the minority of James VI. He was a reformist sympathiser, who was involved in the murder of David Rizzio, Mary's Italian secretary. Afterward he fled to England, but was pardoned and returned to take a leading role in her forced abdication. He led the vanguard of the army which opposed her at the Battle of Langside in 1568, and became regent for the young king. In 1581 he was found guilty of complicity in the murder of the king's father, Henry, Lord Darnley, who had been murdered in 1567. Morton was executed using 'The Maiden', an early guillotine, reputedly of his own devising.

The Earls of Morton retained Edmonston until they sold it to Baillie of Walston in 1650. By the start of the 18th century it had passed to Lawrence Brown, whose descendants held it until 1867, when it was purchased by the Woddrops of Elsrickle and Dalmarnock.

The 'High House' is both a Scheduled Ancient monument and 'B' Listed Building. Edmonston House is also 'B' Listed. A medieval brass cauldron was unearthed on the laying out of the tennis courts in 1881.

Other reference: High House of Edmonston

EILAN I VHOW CASTLE

The Lennox & East Dunbartonshire Ruin or site OS 56 NN 331127

About 5 miles north of Tarbet, and 2 south of Ardlui, just east of A82, on Island I Vhow, Loch Lomond.

Eilan I Vhow means 'island of the cows', although the island was also known as Eilean Bhannaomh, Eilean Mhore and Island I Vhow. The MacFarlane owners were notorious cattle thieves and it is said that they held their plunder on the island. A legend of a nunnery on the island may mean that the name is corrupted from Eilean Bhannaomh, the 'Island of the Women'.

Eilan I Vhow is a ruined 16th century Z-plan tower house, which occupies the southern end of Loch Lomond's most northerly island. The main building measures 34 ft by 24ft. The northern wall has collapsed to ground-floor level and deterioration of the west wall suggests a risk of further collapse. Of what remains, there is a vaulted cellar, the south wall with a window at first-floor level and the eastern wall. The latter supports the remnant of a fireplace at second-floor level. The entrance is thought to have been on the north and stairway from the northeast corner led to the first floor. Later fireplaces and window adaptations suggest remodelling at some stage. A jetty, portions of a courtyard wall and the remains of a number of low rectangular buildings complete the site.

A tower house with two wings is illustrated on the island on Pont's 1583-96 map of Loch Lomond. The castle was built by Alexander MacFarlane in 1577, and by 1581 the dowager of the family was granted the island for the duration of her life. James VI is said to have visited the castle. The family made their main residences here and at Tarbet when their other island stronghold at Inveruglas was destroyed by Cromwell's forces in the 17th century. In 1697 the MacFarlanes moved to Arrochar and this house is said to have come into use as a store, though it was still inhabited in 1743 when it was described as 'a pretty good house with gardens'. The MacFarlanes sold their estates in 1784 to pay off debts and the castle was in a ruinous condition by the time William Wordsworth visited in 1814. At that time the remains apparently provided a roof for a recluse, giving it the by-name of 'The Hermits Cave'.

In recent years the island has been the subject of a number of 'a non-domino title' claims to ownership, as the owner could not be identified and the island was claimed by individuals who wished to add it to their own property. The island became a Scheduled Ancient Monument in 2005 and the castle is a 'B' Listed building.

Other reference: Island I Vhow

ELAN ROSSDHU

The Lennox & East Dunbartonshire   Ruin or site   OS 56   NS 360894
On an island in a deep bay off Rossdhu Point, Loch Lomond, east of A82 at Rossdhu.

Elan Rossdhu means 'island at the dark headland'.

Upon a crannog there are remnants of a substantial building. It is believed that this was an original seat of the Colquhoun Lairds of Luss prior to the building of Rossdhu Castle, which was completed before 1541. The island consists of two parts, the northern being an oval mound of stone measuring about 60ft by 66ft to a height of about 7ft above water level. The southern section appears to consist of natural silting covering an area 50ft by 70ft rising to about 1.5ft above water level. The stone mound to the north consists of both well-worked ashlar blocks and un-worked stone. These are the remains of a structure measuring about 30ft square, which seems to have been systematically robbed. There are wall footings built from well-dressed sandstone blocks and a particularly large section of mortared masonry. Vegetation makes the outline indistinct in places, though one eastern corner is visible. The most prominent sections stand to a maximum height of 3ft. Some internal walling can be made out, including an internal rectangular structure some 13ft by 12ft. The site has not been excavated. There is a jetty at the northeastern corner of the island, though this may be comparatively modern. The site is now very overgrown and the island is gradually becoming attached to the mainland at its southern end due to severe silting. There may have been a causeway to the mainland.

Alwyn, 2nd Earl of Lennox, granted the island to Maldouen of Luss before 1220, and it was then confirmed to Gillemore of Luss by Maldouen, 3rd Earl, in 1225. The Colquhouns gained the Luss estates by marriage in 1368 and they remained in possession of the site until the opening of Loch Lomond Golf Club, of which it now seems to be part. The island appears as Inchfriethillane in the 1541 charter of the Barony of Luss, the name becoming Rossdew in a later charter of 1602. It is thought that stone from the site was used in the construction of the new castle at Rossdhu.

ELLISTON CASTLE

Renfrewshire   Private   OS 63   NS 392599
3 miles southwest of Johnstone, on a minor road between the A737 and B776, 0.5 miles south of Howwood, in private garden.

Only one high section of wall and an overgrown mound of rubble survive of Elliston (also recorded as Ellieston or Eliotstoun), a 15th century tower within a courtyard. The tower originally measured about 42ft by 33ft over walls 6.5ft thick. There was a vaulted basement and there may have been mural chambers and a stair within the thickened southeastern wall. There were opposing arched openings in the east and west walls, which apparently had the dimensions of windows rather than doors. The shorter end walls of the tower were 9ft thick. The castle had been adapted at some point when gunloops had been inserted into the walls. It was partly demolished about 1735. In 1836 the walls stood to a height of 20-30ft, but within 20 years only the north and south walls stood to that height. Further demolition took place in 1950 due to the unstable nature of the building. The remaining structure is again in a dangerous condition.

This was the seat of the Semple family, who apparently abandoned it to move to their other residence at Castle

Semple in 1550. The Semples held this estate from at least as early as the reign of Alexander III. Robert Semple, Seneschal to the Barony of Renfrew, witnessed a charter by James the High Steward sometime between 1283 and 1306. In 1318 this, or another, Robert Semple witnessed the grant of the Church of Largs to Paisley Abbey by Walter the High Steward in memory of his wife Marjorie Bruce. As Barons of Elliston they again appear in the charters of Paisley Abbey in 1367, 1392 and 1402.

ERSKINE CASTLE

Renfrewshire Ruin or site OS 64 NS 453724

0.5 miles north of Erskine, on minor roads north of A726, and southeast of Erskine Bridge, on south shore of River Clyde, at Erskine Hospital.

Site of a castle of the Erskine family. Erskine gave its name to the family who owned the estate from 1266 or earlier. It is said to be an old Brythonic name meaning 'green rising ground'. Some less-likely sources suggest that this situation is reversed and that the family gave their name to the place, Erskine apparently meaning 'dagger man'. The family were close associates of the High Stewards based at nearby Renfrew and the families are said to have fostered each others' children.

The first on record was Henry de Erskyn, who witnessed a grant of the chapel at Rosneath to Paisley Abbey by Maldouen, Earl of Lennox, in 1225. John Erskine appears in numerous charters from about 1260 to 1300. Like many Scottish nobles, he swore allegiance to Edward I in 1296. His son William supported Robert I during the Wars of Independence. Sir Robert Erskine became heritable keeper of Stirling Castle during the reign of David II and later Sheriff of Stirlingshire. His son, Thomas, was one of the hostages for the release of King David from English captivity following the Battle of Durham in 1348. By 1370 Robert was governor of the royal castles at Edinburgh, Stirling and Dumbarton. The family by this time held large estates throughout the country and had established several cadet branches. They made generous grants of land to a variety of ecclesiastical institutions including Cambuskenneth Abbey.

Thomas succeeded and was followed by his son Sir Robert, who laid claim to the vacant earldom of Mar. It became the subject of dispute when it was retained by the crown in adherence with an agreement with the previous earl, Alexander Stewart. However by 1467, James II apparently felt that such a major earldom should be in the hands of a Stewart and annexed the title to the crown by court order. The title was then awarded to a series of royal sons. Robert was granted the title Lord Erskine in recompense. In 1513 another Robert, 4th Lord Erskine, died at Flodden with James IV. His grandson, Robert Master of Erskine, died at the Battle of Pinkie in 1547.

John, Lord Erskine, received the earldom of Mar from Mary, Queen of Scots, in 1562 and the grant was confirmed in parliament in 1567. Following Mary's forced abdication and the subsequent assassinations of the Regents Moray and Lennox, John became Regent of Scotland for the young James VI in 1571. His son John, Earl of Mar, became Lord High Treasurer and Comptroller of Scotland for James VI. In 1601 he was James's ambassador to Elizabeth I of England and was apparently instrumental in securing the English succession for James. He accompanied James to London for his coronation in 1603 and was invested into the Order of The Garter. The 22nd earl, the 6th Erskine to hold the title, was forfeited in 1716, following his leading role in the Jacobite uprising of the previous year. The Earldom was held in abeyance for a century. He was awarded the title Duke of Mar in the Jacobite peerage and had earned the nickname 'Bobbing John' because of his tendency to alternately support opposing factions.

The family had sold Erskine to Sir John Hamilton of Orbistan in 1638 and his family then sold it to the Stewart Lords Blantyre in 1703. They extended the castle by adding a western wing, but by 1828 had commissioned the present sprawling mansion. The castle was still standing a little to the east of the mansion in 1838, but had disappeared by 1856. Since 1916 Erskine House has served as the Princess Louise Scottish Hospital for Limbless Sailors and Soldiers, now better known as Erskine Hospital.

FAIRHOLM

South Lanarkshire Private OS 64 NS 754515

4 miles southeast of Hamilton and 1 mile west of Larkhall, on west bank of Avon, by minor roads east of A723, at Fairholm.

Site of a castle or fortified house which belonged to the Hamiltons of Millburn and Auldton. Beautifully situated on a peninsula created by a loop of the Avon and set amidst mature woodland, the present house is a 'B' listed building mostly of the 18th century with 19th century extensions. It may incorporate portions of a house of 1650.

The first Hamilton designated of Fairholm was Allan who is on record in 1471. He was the grandson of Thomas Hamilton of Darngaber and 2nd cousin to the Hamiltons of Cadzow. Allan is also recorded as the proprietor of the lands of Newton at Strathaven in 1492. In 1539 John Hamilton conveyed his lands at Fairholm to his brother Robert of Auldton and Millburn. His son, Matthew 4th of Fairholm, was described by John Knox as a 'rank and incorrigible papist'. He achieved the positions of Gentleman and Squire to the King's House and captain of both Linlithgow Palace and Blackness Castle.

In 1570, following the assassination of the Regent Moray, an English force under Sir William Drury laid waste the Hamilton properties in Clydesdale. Fairholm was one of many Hamilton houses he destroyed. Robert, 9th laird, apparently began the present mansion in 1650. Charles Hamilton fought against the Jacobites at Culloden in 1746. The estate fell to an heiress, Eliza, designated 15th of Fairholm. She married Stevenson of Braidwood in 1866. Since then the family have had the surname Stevenson-Hamilton. They apparently still live in the house.

FARME CASTLE

South Lanarkshire   Ruin or site   OS 64   NS 620623

In Rutherglen, off minor roads north of A724, 100yds northeast of Farme Cross (the junction of A724 & A730), east of Baronald Street, and just west of Farme Castle Court, on industrial site.

Farme Castle was a simple keep of the 15th century, possibly with an older core. Later it became one corner of a courtyard formed by an extension in the form of a castellated mansion built by the Farie family. High walls and subsidiary buildings completed the court. There was an ornate arched battlemented gateway to the courtyard

adjacent to the keep. The keep was of three storeys and a garret above a corbelled out parapet with machicolations and water spouts.

Farme was part of the royal estate in Rutherglen until the time of Robert I. He granted the Farme estate to Walter the Steward sometime before 1327. The lands extended along the river from Dalmarnock to Cambuslang. In the reign of David II it passed to the Douglases. The estate was divided, and from 1482 to 1599 Farme belonged to the Crawfords, becoming known as Crawford's Farme.

The eastern portion of the estate had become Hamilton property sometime before 1425 and was then known as Hamilton Farme. This passed to the Bogles, and was occupied by William Somerville in the early 17th century. It later became the site of a steelworks. Hamilton Farme may also have supported a fortified house. A further portion of the estate was called Castle Vallie, which was granted to Robert Hall by Robert III. This may be the same portion which is mentioned as Noble's Farme in 1661, being owned by the Nobles of Ferme and Ardardan.

Farme passed by marriage to Sir Walter Stewart of Minto in 1611 and, following the disputes between himself and his son Ludovick, it was reserved to give sustenance to Sir Walter until the case was resolved. It came to Sir William Fleming, Commissar of Glasgow, and passed through two generations of his family. It then went, via the Earl of Selkirk, to the Duke of Hamilton. It was sold to local industrialist James Farie in the mid 18th century.

In 1792 an old ceiling was removed by Farie's colliery manager, who was resident in the house. This revealed the ancient wooden ceiling. On the sides of the beams, a number of verses of old poetry were discovered. These were in single lines, black writing on a white background, and proclaimed the virtues of good breeding and manners:

'Faire speiche in presence, with guid report in absence;
And maners in to fellowschep, obtian grait revrence.
....Gyf thou heiniousnes vois or Vice also;
for schame remains quhen pleisour is ago.
He that sitis doun to ye hend for to eite,
Forgetting to gyf God thankis for his meite,
Syne rysis upe and his grace oure pass,
Sitis doun lyk ane ore, and rysis upe lyk ane ass.'

Some lines had been obliterated, but two lines alluded to the Crawfords:

'Thir armes that is heir, that ar abuine pented; are the nobill howses that the laird of this hows is descendit, JC, AH written 1325.'

Hamilton of Wishaw had described these in the early 18th century and pointed out that the rhymes were of more recent origin and provided an example from elsewhere. He suggested a more likely date of c.1595 and gave the initials as those of James Crawford and his wife Annabel Hamilton.

The Farie family later lived at Baronald House, now the grade 'A' listed Cartland Bridge Hotel near Lanark. This had been designed for the family c.1890 by Sir John James Burnett. The old ceiling at Farme was removed in 1917 and the house remained Farie property into the 20th century. It was finally demolished in the 1960s to make way for a factory. By that time it was in use as a repository for redundant mining equipment. The foundations were still visible in 1984 and the site is now marked out by a grassy area within a factory yard.

Other references: Crawford's Farme, Ferm

FASKINE HOUSE

North Lanarkshire   Ruin or site   OS 64   NS 760631

2 miles south of Airdrie, north of the A8, and south of the B802, on the north bank of Calder Water, northwest of Calderbank, at Faskine.

Site of an old or fortified house of the Cleland family, which was demolished in 1900 to make way for the present farm buildings. It probably originated in the late 15th century. A square doocot was also demolished at this time. Pont illustrated it with a wing on his manuscript map of c.1596. Descriptions written in the 19th century describe a two–storey building of great antiquity.

A younger son of Cleland of that Ilk obtained Faskine toward the end of the 15th century. The second laird, William Cleland, died at Flodden in 1513. John Cleland of Faskine, with other members of the family, is believed to have fought on the side of Mary, Queen of Scots, at Langside in 1568 and is mentioned in the remission of 1571. John and his brothers Gavin, Robert and James, seem to have been a quarrelsome lot and there are numerous instances of them being at the centre of unrest. In 1599 Gavin and James were denounced as rebels at a hearing of the Privy Council for 'houghing' a horse belonging to James Crawford at Dundyvan. They did not appear at the hearing, but John of Faskine did. They are said to have acted on his instruction and then he 'setted' them in his house. He had to pay security of £1,000 to 'underlie the law before the justice'.

The younger brother, Robert, was a merchant in Glasgow and is named in a complaint regarding sedition and rioting in Glasgow. These were provoked by changes made to the election process for the Provost and City Council around 1607.

In 1627 John Cleland of Faskine sold the estate to his second son, James of Monkland. In 1641 the portion known as Cairnhill was sold to John Moir of Shawheid. Faskine was then sold to a cousin, George Cleland of Gartness, in 1658. William Cleland of Faskine was a captain in the royal army which helped quell Argyll's forces during the Monmouth Rebellion of 1685. He was killed in a skirmish at Muirdyke by Sir John Cochrane. His nephew, John Cleland of Faskine, was one of a 'brilliant staff of officers' who followed James Graham, Viscount Dundee, during the 1689 Jacobite Rebellion. He was mentioned by name in the proclamation of treason issued by King William and Queen Mary against those who had supported Dundee. John was officially forfeited in 1690 and the property gained by his sister, who was the wife of Cleland of Glenhove.

A further sale occurred in 1700 when it was bought by Dr W. Wright. This may have been the result of an action by creditors of the estate, Hamilton of Wishaw and Muir of Cairnhill. In 1710 Hamilton took out a legal suit at the Court of Session against Muir's heir to test an agreement made 25 years previously regarding the allocation of moneys between them.

The estate came to the Stirlings and in 1782 Admiral Sir Walter Stirling of Faskine was Commander of the Fleet at the Nore, a major anchorage in the Thames estuary. He was offered a baronetcy by George III but declined. Both of his sons became admirals and in 1800 the eldest, also Walter, accepted the baronetcy offered to his father. The title has since become extinct. In 1832 a John G. Muirhead of Faskine is recorded as a Deputy Lieutenant for the Shire of Lanark. By 1900 Faskine belonged to the Watsons.

Faskine was apparently the execution place of witches in the 16th and 17th centuries. A tree near the house was known as the 'Bell Tree' or 'Witches Tree'. Another local legend alleged that the three local Cleland houses of Gartness, Monkland and Faskine were linked by underground passages.

Other references: Foskane, Foskan

FASLANE CASTLE

The Lennox & East Dunbartonshire Ruin or site OS 56 NS 249902

East of A814 and Gareloch, 0.5 miles northeast of Faslane Port, under railway line just southeast of Greenfield by minor road and foot.

In 1851 only a motte remained of this 12th century castle of the Earls of Lennox. The mound was destroyed on the building of the West Highland Railway around 1890. In the mid 18th century it was said that the ruins still provided shelter for 'the last representative of a once powerful family'. It is apparently mentioned in documents dating from 1543 to 1693.

A short way to the south there are the ruins of a medieval chapel dedicated to St Michael where, it is said, Henry, Lord Darnley, was christened. The earls moved their main seat to Balloch in the 13th century. The Faslane and Ardincaple estates were granted to Aulay, progenitor of the MacAulays of Ardincaple. The lands later came to the Colquhouns of Luss.

FATLIPS CASTLE

South Lanarkshire Ruin or site OS 72 NS 969340

5 miles southwest of Biggar, by minor roads and foot west of A73, just northwest of Tintoside, high on Scaut Hill, north of Lanimer Burn.

This tower of the 16th century survives only at basement level and is as curiously sited as it is named. The structure is of coursed rubble with a basement, which appears to have had two chambers. One of these has a fireplace and chimney and was probably the kitchen. It had walls 6ft thick and measured about 37ft by 26ft, which stand to a maximum height of 6ft. The southeastern corner is rounded and unquoined. No other detail is discernible.

There are no charter records to confirm its ownership and the site, on a shelf high on the flank of Tinto Hill, is secretive and seemingly remote. It would nevertheless have provided an excellent vantage point from which to observe any movement along this strategically important stretch of the Clyde Valley where the Rivers Clyde and Tweed almost meet. This was a crossroads on the invasion routes from England with access to both west and east coast routes. Fatlips may have functioned as a peel tower, akin to those of the borders, with a brazier to hold a warning fire

One unconfirmed legend tells that it was built by Symington of that Ilk in order that he could continually observe his deadly enemy, Baillie of Lamington, at his home in the valley below. Symington taunted Baillie that he would not even be able to water his horses in the Clyde or that his wife could not go outside for her 'nightly motions' without him watching. Unable to live with this level of intrusiveness, Lamington apparently left his home and built Windgate House where he could live in privacy and be aware of any approach by his enemy.

FERGUSLIE

Renfrewshire Ruin or site OS 64 NS 467637

About 1 mile west of Paisley Abbey, on minor roads north of A737 at Ferguslie

Site of a castle, a portion of which survived until the 19th century. A mansion was built nearby, but it was demolished in 1920. Some decorative stonework from this later house was used in the renovation of Blackhall.

The property was part of the estates of Paisley Abbey. It was granted to the Hamiltons of Orbistan in 1544. In a long-running dispute, which lasted from 1643-47, the 'Goodwife of Ferguslie', Margaret Hamilton, was repeatedly summoned to the church at Paisley to explain her non attendance and subscribe to the Covenant. Pleading infirmity and accused of pretending illness, her non attendance initiated an inquiry. Eventually the poor woman had to be carried on her bed to the church before the ministers were satisfied.

The estate passed to a nephew John, the younger son of Wallace of Elderslie, who had to adopt the Hamilton name. In 1701 it was Cochrane property and William Cochrane of Ferguslie was the brother of the Earl of Dundonald. He was sued by the captain and crew of the frigate *The Mary* for payments of arrears and the return 'of the money extracted from them' at Bo'ness.

In 1747 the estate was purchased by the town of Paisley, though a portion was in the hands of a merchant named John Cochrane. In 1798 part of the estate was purchased by Thomas Bissland, who built a new house. Ferguslie became the property of the Wilsons in 1837. The estate was purchased by the thread barons, the Coats family. They built the mansion to a design by Hippolyte J. Blanc. The former stables buildings have been restored and converted into flats. The lairds had mills at Ferguslie, Paisley and Neilston.

Other reference: Ridfurd

FINGALTON CASTLE

Renfrewshire   Ruin or site   OS 64   NS 508558?
3 miles west of A77, and 1 mile west of B769, by minor roads southwest of Newton Mearns, and southeast of Neilston, south of Glanderston Road, at or near Duncarnock Farm.

Site of a castle or fortified house. In 1710 the house of Fingalton was said to have stood to the south of Balgray. Alternative sites include Craigton, Middleton and Langton. Pont's map of the late 16th century illustrated a tower named 'Duncarnock' in this location.

Robert Croc de Fingaldon appears on the Ragman Roll in 1296. Presumably he was related to the Robert Croc of Crookston who gained the barony of Neilston in the 12th century. In 1359 David Fitzwalter of Cadzow granted the once extensive estate of Fingalton to his uncle, John Fitzgilbert of Rossavon. John's descendants were therefore the most senior of the many cadet branches of the Hamiltons. Being within the parish of Mearns, the superiority of Fingalton is said to have been held by the Maxwells of Nether Pollok, and Hamilton is supposed to have sought the agreement of his nephew before taking up feudal agreements and submitting himself to Maxwell. John died c.1345 and was succeeded by his son, another John. He married an heiress and gained the East Lothian estate of Preston, which then became their primary residence. In 1503 John, a second son, established a cadet branch of Hamiltons in Airdrie, when he acquired the estate from Newbattle Abbey. In 1568 Sir David Hamilton of Fingalton was forfeited for his part in supporting Mary, Queen of Scots, at the Battle of Langside. In 1650 the family records were destroyed when Cromwell burnt their tower at Preston.

Sir Robert Hamilton was a noted Covenanter and commanded their forces at the battles of Drumclog and at Bothwell Bridge in 1679. In the aftermath he escaped to Holland. He was brother to Sir William, who at that time owned the Preston and Fingalton estates. William was created a baronet of Nova Scotia in 1673 but later sold his estates, including Fingalton, to his brother-in-law, James Oswald. William retired to Holland but returned for the Monmouth Rebellion of 1685, an attempt to dislodge James VII and II from the throne. Back in Holland he found favour with William of Orange and was one of the ranking officers in the invasion of England in 1688. He died of a sudden illness during the march to London. Robert returned to inherit his brother's title but died in 1701. The baronetcy and representation of the main line of Hamilton of Fingalton and Preston passed to the Hamiltons of Airdrie. When they died out in 1799 the title went into abeyance. In 1812 a 'Logan of Fingalton' is on record.

In 1816 the philosopher Sir William Hamilton went to court to prove his descent from the family and successfully claimed the title. He was cousin to the deceased Hamilton of Airdrie. He had no claim to the property, which in 1838 Fingalton was purchased by Adam Gilmour of Eaglesham, a ship owner and trader in timber.

Other reference: Duncarnock

FINLAYSTONE HOUSE

Renfrewshire   Private   OS 63   NS 365738
3 miles east of Port Glasgow, and 2 miles west of Langbank off minor roads just south of the A8, at Finlaystone.

Finlaystone House is an 18th century mansion by John Douglas, extended and remodelled between 1898 and 1903 by J.J. Burnet. It incorporates a tower, which it is claimed dates from the 14th century. This was described in the 18th century as 'a noble and great building around a court'. This now constitutes the northeast wing. It appears in Pont's map as a sprawling courtyard castle with five roofed structures of similar height to the enceinte.

Finlaystone was within the Dennistouns' Renfrewshire estates in the late 14th century, and is said to have been their principal seat. It passed by the marriage of an heiress to the Cunninghames in 1404, and Finlaystone may have been established at this time.

Alexander Cunninghame was created Lord Kilmaurs in 1450 and 1st Earl of Glencairn in 1488. He died fighting on the losing side for James III at the Battle of Sauchieburn in the same year. His son was unable to take up the title due to the Act Recsissory of 1488 but Alexander's grandson, Cuthbert, was restored to the title by James IV's Act Revocatory of 1503 to became 3rd Earl. William, 4th Earl, was a 'notorious intriguer'. As Lord Kilmaurs, before inheriting the earldom, he was in receipt of a pension from Henry VIII of England. In 1524 he was one of a party who tried to snatch the young James V from the Mary of Guise at Edinburgh. He became Lord High Treasurer of Scotland for a brief period in 1526 and inherited the earldom in 1542. In the same year he was captured by the English at the Battle of Solway Moss, and then released for a ransom of £1,000. He was a pro-English campaigner during the 'Rough Wooing' of Mary, Queen of Scots. Leading a force with the Earl of Lennox, they were attacked and defeated 'with great slaughter' by the Earl of Argyll at Glasgow Muir. Changing sides he received a pardon from the Regent Arran, but by the end of the year was again in negotiation with the English and is said to have been party to the assassination of Cardinal David Beaton.

Alexander, 5th Earl, was a zealous reformer and in 1556 had John Knox 'ministrat the Lordis Table' at Finlaystone. Knox is said to have preached under a yew tree in the garden. The Earl became one of the leaders of the Reform Party and a member of the Privy Council by 1560. He was against Mary, Queen of Scots, at the Battle of Carberry Hill in 1568 and was one of those who defaced the Chapel Royal at Holyrood once Mary was imprisoned in Lochleven Castle.

James, 7th Earl, was also a political activist, and Privy Councillor to James VI (and I of England). He became involved in a dispute over precedency with the Earls of Eglinton, Caithness, Montrose and Cassillis. The dispute rumbled on, and was finally found in favour of his grandson William, 9th Earl, in 1648. He led a rising for Charles II in 1654, but the rebellion failed. After the restoration, Charles made him Chancellor of Scotland.

Robert Burns was a great friend of the 14th Earl, and scratched his initials on a window pane in the library at Finlaystone. He named his son 'James Glencairn' in his honour. On Glencairn's death in 1791 Burns wrote a lament, and in his own words:

'In loud lament bewailed his lord,
Whom death had all untimely taen
But I'll remember thee Glencairn,
And a' that thou hast done for me'

Finlaystone and the right to the arms of the earl passed to the Grahams of Gartmore. This was via a deed of entail by the 9th Earl dating from 1709. They were sued for bankruptcy on two occasions. In the first in 1826, Robert Cunninghame Bontine sued his father William Cunninghame Graham for the rents and profits of Robert's estate of Ardoch, which his father had held in trust for him until his majority. This money was not forthcoming, and the case settled in court for £40,000. This appears never to have been paid, though the sum was reduced by the transfer of a life rent of Finlaystone to the son. William was declared bankrupt but his other creditors later sued. They argued that the transfer was illegal because it gave the son preference over them and had not been concluded before his bankruptcy. They lost the case, despite appealing it to the House of Lords in 1836. Finlaystone became one childhood home of Robert Bontine Cunninghame Graham of Ardoch, adventurer, gaucho and early socialist and nationalist politician.

By 1901 the house was home to the Glasgow merchant G. F. Dixon, then passed to the MacMillans. General Sir George MacMillan had the grounds opened to the public. There is a visitor centre with Clan MacMillan exhibits, a doll museum and Celtic Art display.

Tel. 01475 540285; gardens and grounds open year round, house open on Sundays from April to August.

FINTRY CASTLE

The Lennox & East Dunbartonshire   Ruin or site   OS 57   NS 641863

1 mile northeast of Fintry, north of Endrick Water, by foot 0.5 miles north of the B818 at Broomhole Bridge, in Fintry Hills.

Little remains of Fintry Castle, other than some rubble sitting on the summit of a high knoll. The outline suggests a rectangular building lying on an east-west axis with a possible tower at the northwest. The walls appear to have been about 4ft thick and the main block measured roughly 26ft by 45ft. On the north and east sides are traces of a courtyard wall. A description of 1841 complains that so much stone had been robbed from the site that it was thought that within a few years nothing would remain. Various early descriptions indicate that there had been a ditch around the site. The castle was said to be ruinous by 1724 though appears in Roy's map of 1747-55 as 'Fintray Hall'.

The Grahams of Fintry were descended from Robert Graham, who was granted the estate by his nephew, Patrick, Lord Graham, in 1460. The castle probably dates from this time. In 1529 and 1541 William Graham, 4th of Fintry, obtained charters of his lands at Fintry, Perthshire and Forfarshire from James V, when they were erected into free baronies in his favour. He was married to the sister of the assassinated Cardinal David Beaton. He was strongly Catholic and supported the French party during the regency of Mary of Guise.

David, 5th laird, was knighted by James VI. His son, also David, was beheaded in Edinburgh for involvement in 'a popish conspiracy' with the Earls of Huntly and of Errol. The next David Graham of Fintry was a devoted Royalist and fought in the Civil War with Charles I. His financial support for the cause reduced the family's fortune. At some point in the 17th century the family exchanged these lands with the Duke of Montrose for an estate near Dundee, apparently taking the Fintry name with them.

Based thereafter at Mains of Fintry in Angus, James, 9th of Fintry, was offered a knighthood by Charles II but declined on the basis that he had insufficient funds. The 10th laird, another David, was a well known Jacobite who was 'out' in the rebellion of 1715, and supported the rebellion of 1745. Baron Fintry became one of numerous titles held by the Dukes of Montrose. The family sold their estates in the 19th century and emigrated to South Africa.

FINTRY MOTTE

The Lennox & East Dunbartonshire   Ruin or site   OS 57   NS 612866

In Fintry, 0.25 miles southwest of the junction of the B822 and B818, in Fintry Wood.

This motte is situated on a steep sided ridge protruding from the flank of a hill 150ft above the River Endrick. The oval mound is overgrown with bracken, grass and trees, and stands to a maximum height of 16ft above the bottom of its ditch. On the west the minimum height reached is 9.5ft. The summit is around 120ft by 100ft, but the ditch has been damaged by water erosion on the north side. In 1965 a number of stones were visible in the slopes of the mound.

Maldouen, 3rd Earl of Lennox, issued charters from Fintry in the middle of the 13th century and it is likely that this motte was his residence here. It is said that in later times it became the residence of the Grahams. The motte is a Scheduled Ancient Monument.

FLATTERTON

Renfrewshire   Ruin or site   OS 63   NS 228747

2.5 miles southwest of Greenock, and 1.5 northeast of Inverkip, by minor roads west of A78, at Flatterton.

Site of an old or fortified house of the Crawfords. In the 15th century Flatterton and Spango belonged to William Park of that Ilk. When he died, his estates were divided between three heiresses. Christian, the eldest, retained the family home at Park of Erskine. Half of Spango went to another daughter, who had married Alexander Cunninghame of Drumquhassle. The third sister married George Stirling of Craigbarnet, who gained Flatterton and the other half of Spango. He exchanged their inheritance for Kilwinnet in Stirlingshire with James Crawford of Sydehill, a cadet of the Crawfords of Kilbirnie.

In 1623 James Crawford of Flatterton was one of several local lairds who were raided by Godfrey MacAllister of Tarbert, for whom a bond of caution of £1,000 was pledged by John Lamont of Auchnagill. Godfrey was ordered to abstain from molesting the lairds in question. The family had held the estate for six generations, then they sold them to Stewart of Blackhall during the reign of Charles I. In 1890 Flatterton and Spango were still part of the Stewart's Ardgowan estate, by which time a corn mill had been built at Flatterton. The present farm is the site of a World War II anti-aircraft battery.

FOLKERTON

South Lanarkshire   Ruin or site   OS 71   NS 866364

About 4.5 miles southeast of Lanark, 1 mile west of Douglas Water, by minor roads north of the A70, at or near Tower Farm.

Probable site of an early castle, which was replaced by a tower house. Tower of Folkerton appears on General Roy's map of the mid 18th century.

Between 1208 and 1218, Abbot Henry of Kelso Abbey made a grant of confirmation to Richard, son of Solph of 'Folcardistune, which his father and his ancestors had possessed'. Adam seems to have taken illegal possession of the neighbouring lands of Poneil, for which he was excommunicated. In 1269 his son William issued a grant of these lands back to the Abbey for their own use, in response to the possibility of his own excommunication. By 1295 he was again in dispute with the Abbot, this time over ownership of Folkerton. He seems to have won his case, since Sir Alexander of Folkarton appears as a charter witness for the abbey in 1311. In 1316 he claimed Poneil as part of his inheritance, but the abbot pointed out that he had not paid his duties for nine years. Alexander settled for a liferent of Poneil at a reduced rent.

The Folkarts were still in possession in 1484, when two brothers, Adam and Robert, are recorded with their wives. Robert died, and a complex dispute arose regarding ownership of parts of the estate. The case was brought before parliament by Catherine and Beatrix, heiresses of John Folkart, against Alexander Folkart, John Symonton of that Ilk, Sir William Knollis the Preceptor of Torphichen, and many others. An agreement was reached by 1495 and the estate seems to have gone with an Elizabeth Folkart to her new husband, Carmichael of Balmady.

By 1628 the estate was in the possession of the Menzies of Castlehill. Before 1696 the Menzies incumbent had died, but parts of the estate were by then the property of the Kennedys of Auchtyfardle. The whole property later came to the Dukes of Douglas and then to the Earls Home.

FULBAR

Renfrewshire Ruin or site OS 64 NS 456624

1 mile southeast of Elderslie, by minor roads south of the A8, in Foxbar, near junction of Spey Avenue and Don Drive.

Site of an old or fortified house of the Halls of Fulbar. Stephen son of Nicholas is said to have been granted the estate by James, 5th High Steward, in the late 13th century. A charter was confirmed by Robert II to Thomas de Aula in 1370. The estate remained with the direct male line until 1550 when it passed to a cousin, Adam Hall of Tarquinhill. His grandfather had died at Flodden in 1513.

In 1591 James VI forfeited and denounced as rebels James and William Hall, the sons of Adam Hall of Fulbar, for the slaughter of John Montgomerie of Scotstoun. The estate temporarily came into the hands of the Stewarts of Rossland. A remission for the murder was granted in 1595 and the Halls restored to their estates. In 1633 Robert Hall of Fulbar was Commissioner to parliament for the Burgh of Renfrew, and in 1643 was a representative for the Sheriffdom of Dumbarton. Thereafter Fulbar remained a possession of the family at least until the early 18th century, when Robert Hall of Fulbar inherited the Dargavel estate through the right of his wife. His younger son inherited Dargavel and adopted the surname Hall-Maxwell. His descendants came to represent the senior line of the Halls.

The estate was acquired by Alexander of Newton, who sold it before 1818 to Alexander Speirs of Elderslie.

It appears as 'Foulbar', a small property on both Pont's manuscript map and in Blaeu's *Atlas Novus* of 1654. A mansion known as Fulbar was standing on the site by 1854 and remained extant on OS maps of the 1920s. The Halls apparently held several properties in Glasgow, one of which was a tower or fortalice which stood on the west side of 'Stockwellgait', just outside the port. This was taken down at the end of the 19th century.

GAIRDWOODEND

South Lanarkshire Ruin or site OS 72 NS 993515

4 miles north of Carnwath, by minor roads west of A70, at Girdwoodend.

Site of a tower house with barmkin illustrated on Pont's manuscript map of 1583-96. Andrew and William Proudfoot were 'at Gairdwoodend' in a record of 1596. The locality seems to have been the source of the common local surname Girdwood.

Other references: Card Woodhead, Eardwood, Girdwoodend

GALLOWHILL HOUSE

Renfrewshire Ruin or site OS 64 NS 493654

About 1 mile south of Renfrew, on minor roads east of A741, off Gallowhill Road, near Arkleston Road, Paisley.

Possible site of an old or a fortified house. Gallowhill Cottage is marked on the 1864 OS map. This may be the old house demolished to make way for a mansion in 1867.

In 1553 John Hamilton, the Commendator of Paisley Abbey, granted his position and the lands of the abbey to his 8-year-old nephew. The boy, Lord Claud Hamilton, is said to have built one of his houses at Gallowhill. Over and Nether Gallowhill merged to become one property at this time.

Claud Hamilton was a younger son of James, 2nd Earl of Arran. He was a hostage of the English following the Treaty of Berwick in 1560. A staunch supporter of Mary, Queen of Scots, he assisted her escape from Lochleven Castle in 1568 then fought for her at Langside. He was forfeited as a result. He was implicated in the murders of the Regents Moray and Lennox, but managed to recover his estates by 1573. A few years later the Privy Council ordered his arrest for past deeds and he escaped to England where he was used by Elizabeth I in her political manoeuvrings in Scottish affairs. He then spent some time in France before returning to Scotland in 1586. He was briefly imprisoned in 1589 for his involvement in the promotion of the Catholic cause on behalf of the imprisoned Mary and Philip of Spain. He was back in favour by 1587, when he became Lord Paisley, but quietly retreated from public life and was declared insane. His eldest son became Lord Abercorn in 1603, then Earl in 1606. Gallowhill was later sold to the Earl of Dundonald. The 6th earl gave it to his daughter on her marriage to Captain William Wood.

The estate then passed through various owners and was divided into the original portions in 1866. A mansion was built on this site in 1867. Gallowhill House was a French baronial mansion, sometimes described as Gothic. It was designed by James Salmon and Son for Peter Kerr, a Paisley thread manufacturer. It was used as an auxiliary hospital during the World War I. The house was still standing when the 1925 OS map of Glasgow was published, but was later demolished.

GARRION TOWER
North Lanarkshire Private OS 64 NS 796510
2.5 miles south of Wishaw, on minor roads east and south of A71, on north bank of River Clyde, at Garrion.

Garrion (or Garrien) Tower is a small 16th century fortified house, which had become ruinous. It was restored and extended to the north by the addition of a mansion in the 19th century. There was probably an earlier house which was used as a summer residence by the Bishops and Archbishops of Glasgow in the 15th and early 16th centuries.

The tower is an L-plan structure with a main block measuring 25ft by 19.5ft. This sits on an east-west axis and is of three storeys plus an attic. Access to all floors is by a turnpike stair within the small wing, which sits on the eastern end of the north wall. The entrance was originally via the base of the stair tower through the re-entrant; however the extension was built within this angle and a new entrance was opened from the east wall, where a porch was added. The stair rises within a square cavity to first floor level and above this within a rounded cavity. There are shot holes below the sills of the stair tower windows. A link corridor provided access to two vaulted ground floor rooms which gained light from slot windows.

The hall occupied the entire first floor, which was illuminated by two windows in the south wall, opposite which were a fireplace and an aumbry. The second floor has been subdivided to provide two bedrooms, which are now entered from the extension and no longer have access to the stair tower. Each has a window in the south wall above those of the hall. There is an aumbry in the western wall of the west room, with the east room mirroring this arrangement. The attic has also been divided into two rooms, one entering from the other. The eastern room is accessed from the stair tower.

Ralph de Clare granted the land of Garrion to Paisley Abbey before 1226, and it remained with the monks until at least 1265. At some point it was transferred to Glasgow Cathedral and a house of the Bishops of Glasgow is said to have been rebuilt in 1424. It may have been let to the Forrest family, but by 1530 'Garyn' was owned by Sir James Hamilton of Finnart and it is possible that he built the present tower. In 1605 a grant was issued under the Great Seal to another 'James Hamilton of Garrion and Elizabeth Haye, his spouse, and the longest liver of them, and to their heirs, of the lands of Garrien, held of the Archbishop of Glasgow'. The later Episcopalian bishops may have used the house for a time. The seniority passed from the archbishops to the Duchess of Hamilton during the reign of William and Mary. In 1710 it was the property of Hamilton of Wishaw and by 1820 of Lord Belhaven.

In 2000 a planning application was made to develop it into a tourist centre. The plans went to a public enquiry and were refused. The house is 'B' Listed and was added to the Buildings at Risk register in 2008. It was vacant at that time and had been used as a commercial address. It went up for sale in October 2011 and was being marketed as a ten-bedroom home in need of a great deal of renovation. It was described as 'not a project for the faint hearted'.

Other reference: Garyn

GARSCADDEN CASTLE
The City of Glasgow Ruin or site OS 64 NS 523710
1.5 miles southwest of Bearsden, on minor roads north of the A82, Drumchapel, 0.5 miles north of Garscadden Road.

Garscadden was a 15th century tower incorporated into or replaced by a mansion of the early 18th century. It was apparently destroyed by fire in 1959 and the last remnant demolished in the 1970s.

Until 1369 this was a property of Patrick, second son of Malcolm Fleming of Biggar. He exchanged it for the lands of Board, near Croy, with Sir Robert Erskine. In 1444 the Erskines passed it to the Galbraiths of Gartconnel, who retained it until 1611. Garscadden was apparently then held in turn by the captains of Dumbarton Castle. This arrangement lasted until 1655 when it came to the Glasgow writer, William Colquhoun, descended from a Colquhoun of Camstraddan. It passed by inheritance to the Colquhouns of Killermont, uniting the estates. The artist Henry Colquhoun of Kilermont extended it into the Georgian mansion known as Garscadden House. In the 19th century the line ended in an heiress, who married the Campbell Lord Provost of Glasgow. Their son adopted the surname Campbell-Colquhoun.

The south gates to the estate were known as 'the Girnin Gates' and were of such an outlandish design that they were known locally as the ninth wonder of the world. The story goes that when it rained, water ran down the faces of two decorative cast iron lions giving the illusion of tears.

Toward the end of the 18th century, at the end of a drinking session in Law, the laird of Kilmardinny remarked on the pale appearance of the laird of Garscadden. To this their host replied that Garscadden had been dead for over two hours, but he had not mentioned it for fear of disrupting such good company. This event is reputedly responsible for the Glaswegian phrase, 'as gash as Garscadden', meaning deathly pale. His epitaph apparently read:

'Beneath this stane lies auld Garscad. Wha loved his neebors very bad. Noo how he fends and how he fares. The deil ane kens an' the deil ane cares.'

GARTCONNEL CASTLE

The Lennox & East Dunbartonshire   Ruin or site   OS 64   NS 537732

In Bearsden, close to junction of the A810 and A809, south of Gartconnel Avenue, in grounds of Bearsden Academy.

Site of a 14th century keep of the Galbraiths of Culcreuch. The ditch was evident in the 18th century and traces of it survived into the 20th century.

Around 1238 Maldouen, Earl of Lennox, issued a grant of the lands of Cartonvenach (Gartconnel) to Maurice, son of Galbraith. Gartconnel became the principal seat of the Galbraith clan, the incumbent normally being the chief. Arthur Galbraith paid homage to Edward I in 1296. This branch of the family ended with the death of William Galbraith c.1390. William is recorded as a man 'of good account' during the reign of David II. He left three heiresses, one of whom married Logan of Balvie and took Gartconnel to her husband. The other sisters passed Bardowie and Mains to the Hamilton and Douglas families.

John Logan of Gartconnel was the subject of litigation in 1530 and was a Sheriff Depute for Dumbarton.

GARTLEA

North Lanarkshire   Ruin or site   OS 64   NS 766648

In Airdrie, 3 miles north of A80, and 1 mile west of A73, at junction of Gartlea Road and Gartleahill.

A small tower labelled 'Gartly' appears in Blaeu's *Atlas Novus* of 1654. It was a property of Crawford of Rochsolloch.

GARTNESS CASTLE

The Lennox & East Dunbartonshire   Ruin or site   OS 57   NS 502865

2 miles northeast of Drymen, on minor road west of A81, south of Endrick Water, at or near Gartness.

Nothing remains of this 15th century castle of the Napiers. They gained the estate in 1495, and a stone used as a lintel in the mill was reportedly taken from the castle. It carries the date 1574. Another date-stone of 1684 with the initials R G and I S is said to have lain in the garden of the mill. Other stones have apparently been used at Park of Drumquhassle.

Gartness was granted by a charter under the Great Seal to Archibald Napier in 1495. It is one of a number of possible sites considered as the birthplace of the inventor and innovator John Napier of Merchiston, who is most famous for his logarithms. However, in the biography of Napier, it is said that he and his wife, Elizabeth Stirling, built the castle following their marriage in 1572, but rebuilding or extending are more likely. They had two children before she passed away, and he remarried in 1579. When his father died in 1608, John inherited Merchiston and moved there. Before the turn of the 18th century, Gartness came into the possession of the Govane family of Park of Drumquhassle.

In 1957 a low rectangular mound with discernable wall fragments remained. Disturbed ground seemed to indicate the remains of a ditch and possibly a courtyard. By 1973 the mound had gone.

Adjacent is the Pots of Gartness, a waterfall on the Endrick Water, famed for leaping salmon.

GARTSHERRIE HOUSE

North Lanarkshire Ruin or site OS 64 NS 721663

In Coatbridge, 2.5 miles east of A752, north of Gartsherrie Road and east of Lomond Road, at the northwestern corner of the former Freightliner Terminal.

Site of an old or fortified house. An indistinct though substantial building here is illustrated as 'Gartshary' on Pont's map of the late 16th century, and appears again as a large building in Blaeu's *Atlas*. Later cartographic references show this as the site of the 18th century Gartsherrie House.

Gartsherrie was part of the vast Monklands estate, which had belonged to the monks of Newbattle Abbey since the reign of Malcolm IV. It is said that in 1565 Gavin Cleland was granted the estate of Gartsherrie by the Archbishop of St Andrews. In 1587 the lands and barony were gained by Mark Ker, 1st Earl of Lothian, a son of the Abbot of Newbattle. His son Robert became 2nd Earl, and he is alleged to have consulted witches and magicians. He barred himself in a room at Newbattle, stabbed himself several times and then cut his own throat. He was said to have accrued great debts at the time. The Monklands estate was later divided among lesser land owners and the superiority gained by the Marquis of Hamilton.

The Starks of Auchinvole occupied Gartsherrie from at least as early as 1629 until 1789, when the Colts of Auldhame and Inveresk purchased them. The Colt family built a bridge over a local stream and inadvertently gave Coatbridge its name, or so the story goes.

The house was a property of the Whitelaw family in the 19th century, but the lands had been feud and developed by the Baird family. They were industrialists and were at the forefront of the iron and steel industry in the Monklands. Their foundries stood close to the house, the last of them closing in 1967. The site was later developed as the container base.

GARTSHORE HOUSE

The Lennox & East Dunbartonshire Private OS 64 NS 692737

3 miles southeast of Kirkintilloch, off minor road south of B8048, 1.5 miles west of Drumgrew Bridge.

Probable site of a castle of the Gartshores of That Ilk. The site was later occupied by subsequent mansions named Gartshore House. The house depicted in MacGibbon and Ross dated from the 17th century. It represented an example of the transitional phase when the need for defensive features diminished and domestic comfort became more important.

Consisting of a double tenement block, each with corbiestepped gables, sitting side by side creating a V shape, the blocks were joined on their longest sides and internally were separated by a thick central wall, effectively creating two houses in one. The entrance was centrally placed below the V of the roof. There was a large heraldic panel above the door. Each block was of two storeys and an attic with dormer windows. Each floor had a series of large windows. A smaller two-storey T-plan structure adjoined one of the blocks centrally on one side of the structure. The gables of this structure were also corbiestepped. The house was rebuilt in c.1880 as a large Scots baronial mansion which was used as an auxiliary hospital during World War I. It was demolished in 1963. Within the vicinity there remain a dooot, the stables and at Wester Gartshore a Quaker's cemetery, all of which are 'B' Listed. The walled garden survives but is not maintained.

The family of Gartshore took their name from the estate, and are said to have been in possession since the reign of Alexander II in the 13th century. At that time William Comyn, Earl of Buchan, made a grant to John, son of Geoffrey, of the 'half land of Gartshore which had belonged to Cristin Crummunketh'. In 1491 William Gartshore of that Ilk appeared before the Lords Auditors. In 1553 a life rent of Easter and Wester Gartshore was sold by charter of the Duke of Chatelherault to his eldest daughter Barbara Hamilton. This contract was witnessed by James, Lord Fleming, the feudal superior.

By 1579 John Gartshore, alias Golfurd, was in possession when he was cautioned by the Privy Council. In 1594 he acted as surety for 'certain burgesses of Kirkintilloch'. In the 17th century various Alexanders, as Gartshore of that Ilk, held positions as MPs for Dunbartonshire, Commissioner of Supply, Commissioner of Loans and Taxes and on the Committee of War in 1647-8. Members of the family appear in parliamentary records until the Act of Union in 1707.

In the 18th century the estate is said to have come to the Starks of Auchenvole. However, the Gartshore family persisted until the 19th century when the estate was inherited by the second son of Murray of Ochtertyre, who adopted the Murray-Gartshore surname. By the 19th century, Gartshore belonged to the Whitelaws. Willie Whitelaw was of this family. He later became Secretary of State during the Conservative government of Margaret Thatcher, then Viscount Whitelaw. It was he who had the house demolished.

GEILSTON HOUSE

The Lennox & East Dunbartonshire   Private, gardens NTS   OS 64   NS 340783
3.5 miles northwest of Dumbarton, by the A814, just east of Cardross, at Geilston.

Site of a tower house of the Woods family. Geilston house is a two-storey L-plan house of 1766 with later extensions. It was thought to incorporate work from as early as the 16th century. The walls are harled and it has corbiestepped gables. There is a beautiful walled garden dating from 1797.

In the late 16th century this was a property of the Woods family, who had a tower here. It passed through the hands of the Bontines in the 17th century, and the Buchanans of Tullichewan and Donalds of Lyleston in the 18th century. It was purchased by the Geils in 1825. In 1925 it was sold to the Hendry family, who held it until 1983 when the gardens were granted to the National Trust for Scotland. A small entry fee is payable.

The house was gifted to the NTS in 1997 and a survey of the structure at that date indicated that the present building had originated as a modest thatched laird's house of c.1666 or earlier. It was developed to become a villa and then a cottage. From 1770 the stables, doocot and estate buildings were added. The garden and grounds were planted at this time. The house, gardens, stables and doocot form a group of 'B Listed' buildings. (www.nts.org.uk/Property/Geilston-Garden/).

GILBERTFIELD CASTLE

South Lanarkshire   Ruin or site   OS 64   NS 653587
2.5 miles northwest of East Kilbride, off minor roads southeast of Cambuslang and south of A724, on north side of Dechmont Hill at Gilbertfield Farm.

Gilbertfield is a ruined late 16th or early 17th century L-plan house of three storeys and an attic. It seems likely that an earlier house occupied the site and a building here appears as an indistinct sketch on Pont's map of c.1596.

The house consisted of two blocks, the larger running east to west joined at the western half of its north side by the other, which has the door in the re-entrant. This leads to a small lobby, which provides access to a turnpike stair within a square well. To the left, a door leads into a larder with service stair in the southwestern corner leading to the dining room or hall on the floor above. A door in the east wall accesses the kitchen within the southern wing. This has a window with gunloop which guarded the entrance, a large fireplace with oven and seat, and a stone sink with conduit drain. To the right of the lobby, another door leads to a chamber possibly used as a wine cellar. This has two small slot windows in the north and east walls. There were only a few small windows at ground-floor level. These had been secured by iron bars. All chambers on the ground floor were vaulted.

The first floor of the southern wing was entirely composed of the dining room or hall, which measured 27ft by 17ft and 14.25 ft to the ceiling. There was a fireplace in the north wall which at some point had been reduced in size. A corridor led past the stair well to a parlour in the north wing. The entire floor is illuminated by a series of larger windows on all sides, many with gunloops. Access to the stair is from the northwestern corner of the hall. The plan on the floors above was similar, with three bedrooms to each.

Externally there was a heraldic panel above the door, which once carried the date 1607. It has been assumed that this dated the building of the house, though it may commemorate the granting of a knighthood to Sir Robert Cunninghame. There were originally two round corner turrets at the southeastern and northwestern corners. Of these only the supportive corbelling of the latter survives. The roof and corbiestepped sections of the gables have now gone, though the stepping itself was adapted to accommodate the corner turrets. The attic rooms were lit by five dormer windows. The gables for two of these supported a complex monogram below crowns, as opposed to the earl's coronets suggested in one source. This probably represents James, Marquis of Hamilton, and his wife, Anne Cunninghame, who may have contributed to the construction of the house for a loyal servant, Robert

Cunninghame. The other three windows apparently carried a monogram of the letters R.C. Several of the upper storey windows had gunloops below them. There was no parapet or wall-walk, access to the turrets was gained through the rooms of the attic storey. There is no visible evidence of a ditch or courtyard.

The estate stands within the barony of Drumsagard. It has been suggested that the name Gilbertfield dates from the 13th century and that the lands may have been given by the de Moravia family to their kinsman Gilbert, Bishop of Caithness. Around 1410 the lands were granted to the Parks family by the 4th Earl of Douglas 'for services done and to be done'. James Park of Gilbertfield was a charter witness in 1531 by which time the Hamiltons held superiority of the barony. In 1534 Thomas Park enrolled at Glasgow University. He is recorded as the son of the laird of Gilbertfield. James Park, also the son of a laird of Gilbertfield, served on an assize in 1543. This is the last mention of the family.

A letter by Sir James Stewart of Coltness credits the building of the present house to Sir Robert Cunninghame in 1607, possibly based on the armorial stone mentioned. It has been suggested that the Cunninghames may have held the estate from as early as 1550. A charter of entitlement was issued by the Marquis of Hamilton in 1611, which illustrates that the lands of Gilbertfield also included the lands of Easter Moffat in Monklands Parish.

Robert Cunninghame was a long-standing loyal servant and envoy of Lord John Hamilton during his periods of exile in France and England. He held appointments as freeman of Dundee, Captain of Dumbarton Castle and may have been Chamberlain to the Hamiltons. He appears in a charter of James Marquis of Hamilton in 1606, was married to Dame Janet Hamilton and died in 1628. His heirs resided at Gilbertfield for almost the next 100 years and all of the elder sons were also named Robert. In 1657 the laird signed his lands over to his son and by 1683 was described as being mad. In 1701 a grant to the Cunninghames of their estates was confirmed by Anne Duchess of Hamilton. In June of that year Robert Cunninghame sold them to Archibald Hamilton, the minister of Cambuslang. He in turn sold on to Hamilton of Carmunnock, later of Westburn. For a few years afterward, Robert Cunninghame continued to use the designation 'of Gilbertfield' and is recorded as such in 1704. One of Robert's daughters, Barbara, provides Gilbertfield with its first literary connection since she was the mother of the novelist Tobias Smollett, who was born in 1721. His father had married Barbara without his father's consent or knowledge.

By 1708, when his son was born in the house, Gilbertfield was occupied by the retired soldier turned poet William Hamilton. He was responsible for the translation of Blind Harry's epic poem *The Wallace*. This work of 1477 provides a partly mythic biography of Scotland's national hero and Hamilton's edition brought it back to the national audience. The screenplay of the film *Braveheart* was based upon it. As a poet Hamilton was admired by Burns.

'And would'st thou have me dissipate my grief;
While Scotland weeps, weeps out her dearest blood,
And floats to ruin down the crimson flood.'

With Westburn, Gilbertfield became the property of the Grahams of Fereneze. The gable and northern wall of the main block collapsed in the 1950s. The roof and internal floors have now gone. Gilbertfield is a Scheduled Ancient Monument and category 'B' Listed Building.

GILKERSCLEUGH HOUSE

South Lanarkshire Private OS 72 NS 903230
2 miles west of Abingdon, on minor road south and west of M74, south of B7078 and east of B740, 2 miles east of Crawfordjohn, at Low Gilkerscleugh.

This is the site of an L-plan tower of three storeys, reputed to be of the 17th century, but more likely to have had mid 16th century origins. It is illustrated on Pont's map of 1596.

The original building was a rectangular structure running north-south with a projecting round stair tower at the northwest corner. There were round corner turrets and corbiestepped gables. It had been extended at various times, and date-stones of 1668 and 1696 are recorded. Altered and modernised in 1907 for use as a shooting lodge, wings extended to the west and north. It was demolished in 1958 after a fire, and only a stump of the stair turret and buried foundations survive.

Crawfordjohn belonged to Sir James Hamilton of Finnart, who was executed for treason in 1540. His estates were declared forfeit, though his son Sir James Hamilton of Avondale and Crawfordjohn was reinstated by Act of Parliament in 1543. Avondale's second son, Sir John Hamilton, inherited Gilkerscleugh with other lands in Crawfordjohn. He was forfeited for supporting Mary, Queen of Scots, at the Battle of Langside in 1568, but regained his estate in the settlement of 1573.

In 1682, another John Hamilton of Gilkerscleugh held a grievance against Weir of Newton. He reported to the authorities that Weir had allowed Covenanting ministers to baptise children in Newton and had also provided horses and succour to rebels escaping after the Battle of Bothwell Bridge. Weir was admonished, but feeling that his life, estates and reputation had been put at risk by a malicious charge of treason, he sued. In 1683 Hamilton was fined 2,000 merks because his wife had attended Conventicles when he had previously put himself forward as security for her good behaviour. He died in 1700 while Weir's lawsuit was still being heard. Determined to be compensated, Weir redirected his claim toward John's son, James, and won. James's descendants continued to hold the estate until the 19th century, when they sold all their properties in Crawfordjohn to the Colebrookes of neighbouring Crawford.

In the 1920s the estate was purchased by the tobacco merchant family of Mitchell, one of whom had previously bequeathed the Mitchell Library to the City of Glasgow. It was again sold in the 1950s to the Brzygrodzki family. They were the owners when the house burned down.

GILLBANK HOUSE

South Lanarkshire Ruin or site OS 71 NS 859432
Above the south bank of the River Clyde, 2 miles west of Lanark, off minor roads south of the A72, near Linnville, at Kilbank.

In 1852, the last vestiges of an old tower were removed due to their 'dilapidated condition'. For centuries this was the property of the Auchinleck family, one of whom was an uncle of William Wallace. According to the early histories, they raided Lanark from here. Legend asserts that because of the friendly welcomes at Gillbank, Wallace frequented the area when fugitive. A cave in the hills to the north of the Douglas Water bears his name.

Other properties of the same name exist on the east bank of the Clyde at Rosebank and south of Strathaven, but neither of these is the site referred to. The tower appears in Pont's manuscript of the late 16th century as 'Kilbanck'. Roy's map shows another property known as Auchinleck, now Affleck, close by. In the 17th century James Bruce of Kilbank was fined £240 Scots for being a Covenanter. By the 19th century Gillbank belonged to the Thompsons.

Other reference: Gilbank; Kilbank

GLADSTONE

South Lanarkshire Ruin or site OS 72 NT 030428
4 miles southeast of Carnwath, by minor roads south of A721 and north of B7016, at East Gladstone.

The present farmhouse stands adjacent to the site of a square tower, roughly 24ft each side and 25ft high. Its walls were 4ft thick. The tower had been replaced by the present building by 1911 and, although the date of origin is not known, the barns carry re-sited date-stones of 1619 and 1778. Nearby is Gladstone Boreland, originally the home farm of the estate. The ruined castle appears at one corner of the farmyard of East Gladstone in the OS 25inch map of 1864.

The name derives from 'gled' an old name for the red kite, a raptor. It was the property of the Gledstane family as vassals of the Somervilles from the 13th century until the late 1600s. Herbert de Gledstane signed the Ragman Roll in 1296, pledging allegiance to Edward I. William Gledstanes (Chevalier), an adherent of the Earl of Douglas, was a charter witness for David II in 1354. He was present at the Battle of Poitiers in 1356. His son of the same name gained lands near Peebles, which he called Cocklaw, apparently transferring the name from a hill near Gladstone. He then acquired lands near Roxburgh by marrying a Turnbull heiress. As their estate dwindled in the 17th century, the family moved to nearby Arthurshiels. In the 18th century they went to Biggar, where they made a living as merchants. It was from about this time that the name developed from Gledstane to Gladstone. They were the ancestors of William Ewart Gladstone, four times Prime Minister in the mid 19th century. He lived at Fasque in Kincardineshire. By 1710 'Gledstane' belonged to Sir William Menzies.

Other reference: Gledstanes

GLANDERSTON CASTLE
Renfrewshire   Ruin or site   OS 64   NS 500563
2 miles south of Barrhead, on minor roads south of A736, on west side of Duncarnock Hill, southeast of Glanderston Mains.

Glanderston Castle was demolished in 1697 and replaced by Glanderston House, a tall castellated mansion, which is now also demolished. Part of the old building may have been incorporated within the new. The mansion was a ruin by 1890, and all that remains is an overgrown rubble platform near the farm and just below the dam of the reservoir. Some worked stone, believed to have come from Glanderston House, has been used to build the spillway for the dam.

This was a property of the Mures of Caldwell, which apparently resulted in a 50-year feud with the Maxwells of Nether Pollok, who disputed ownership. They held a charter of Glanderston issued by John, Lord Darnley, in 1477. Over the period it is said that there were many skirmishes, law suits, and even a riot in Paisley in 1490. The property fell within the influence of the Stewart Earls of Lennox, who held the superiority from about 1507. Glanderston was granted to William, second son of John Mure of Caldwell, during the reign of James V. When the Caldwell line died out c.1700, William Mure of Glanderston succeeded his cousin. He was succeeded by his nephew, William Mure of Duncarnock. His son, William, sold Glanderston to Alexander Wilson before purchasing Wester Caldwell and Cowden, then building Hall of Caldwell. Glanderston may then have come to Speirs of Elderslie.

Latterly it provided a home for the gamekeeper, before being rented out. One family of tenants were the parents of E.A. Walton, a well-known Renfrewshire watercolour artist. He was born in the house in 1860.

GLASGOW CASTLE
City of Glasgow   Ruin or site   OS 64   NS 601655
In Glasgow city centre, at Cathedral Square, within the space framed by Glasgow Royal Infirmary, St Mungo's Museum and Glasgow Cathedral.

A plinth bearing a brass engraving illustrating the castle stands at the centre of the square formed by the cathedral, hospital and museum. This marks the position of the Bishop's Palace, though the castle was more extensive. The plinth is of stone taken from the castle itself, and other decorative stones from the castle are on display within the crypt of the cathedral.

Archaeological excavation in the 1980s revealed that the castle had probably originated as a low widely spread motte or earthwork with a ditch, within which were found traces of timber buildings. A stone hall and solar building were added at the western end of the site. In the 1430s a five-storey tower was built by Bishop Cameron, which was centred on the spot marked by the plinth. In the early 16th century Archbishop James Beaton constructed the curtain wall and built a 'great' tower at the southwestern corner on the site now occupied St Mungo's Museum. In 1544 a magnificent gatehouse flanked by round towers was built on the southern wall by Archbishop Gavin Dunbar, adjacent to the present location of the gate to the Necropolis. In 1853 the mound was removed revealing the silt-filled ditch and a drawbridge constructed of 12 beams of pegged oak. On the site of the gatehouse four oak piles were discovered with a variety of silver coins, cannon balls, and 'a stone used for fixing the gallows'. The castle well was nearby. The remnant of a structure, thought to be stables, was also found on the southeast of the site.

The early history of the castle is vague, but it may have originated with the granting of burgh status to the town in the 1170s. It has been said that Glasgow was a Royal Burgh, but in fact it was a Burgh of Barony erected in the name of the bishop, then from 1450 a Burgh of Regality.

In the 13th century the Bishop's Palace had been a separate entity and was first described in charters of 1258 and 1268 as being 'without' and 'beyond' the Castle of Glasgow. The palace was to be assigned as a residence for the canons whose own accommodation was insufficient. The sites seem to have merged and became the seat of the Bishops of Glasgow before the Wars of Independence. The castle was reputedly sacked by William Wallace following the unconfirmed 'Battle of the Bell o' the Brae', when he is said to have taken all the furniture and fittings belonging to the English bishop Anthony Beck. Edward I garrisoned the castle

in 1301. It changed hands six times during the various conflicts between the reigns of James V, Mary, Queen of Scots, and the minority of James VI. During this period the castle was besieged twice. The first siege was conducted in 1544 by the Regent Arran after the Battle of Glasgow Muir, when it was held by the men of the Earl of Lennox. The surrender of the castle was negotiated with the condition that the garrison would be allowed to walk free without harm; however Arran set up a gallows and hanged the leaders. The second occasion was in 1571 when the Hamiltons tried to regain it for the imprisoned and exiled Mary. On this occasion 24 inexperienced men supporting the Regent Lennox apparently held out until relieved by the approach of English troops.

The castle then became ruinous until Archbishop Spottiswoode restored it 1611. It was still in use in 1659 when Mary, Duchess of Lennox and Richmond, granted a commission to George Maxwell of Pollok to attend the Castle of Glasgow and represent the young duke at the election of the Provost of Glasgow. It was described in the mid 17th century as 'fenced with an exceeding high wall of hewn stone', but derelict by 1689. It became a prison and held 350 prisoners during the 1715 Jacobite rebellion. The castle was again in ruins by 1727 and was soon being used as a quarry. It was demolished in 1789 to clear the site for Glasgow Royal Infirmary.

The nearby cathedral was saved from the ravages of the Reformation by protests from the craftsmen's guilds. It was then brought into use as the parish church. It contains the shrine of St Mungo and the tomb of Bishop Robert Wishart, a leading player in the Wars of Independence. Sadly the head of his effigy was removed. Glasgow is the only intact pre-Reformation Scottish cathedral, St Magnus in Kirkwall having been built by the Norsemen.

Other references: Bishop's Castle, Glasgow; Castle of Glasgow

GLASSFORD

South Lanarkshire   Ruin or site   OS 64   NS 729471
2 miles west of Stonehouse, on minor roads north of A71, just east of Glassford, and just east of Hallhill House.

Site of a castle which stood near the church, also recorded as 'Glassart'. The castle is mentioned in 1710 as being ruinous, and was demolished in 1828 when it was said to have 'contained an arch so spacious that a hundred men could be arrayed beneath it'. As recently as 1954 the site was identifiable as a level platform on slightly sloping ground within a field. This can still be traced on aerial photographs. The castle is denoted on Pont's manuscript map as 'Hoomhead', and similarly in Blaeu's *Atlas Novus* where it is shown in close proximity to the church. The location may explain one reference to a castle at Quarter.

The Glassford family held the estate in the 1296, when John de Glasford and his son, Aleyn, paid homage to Edward I. John, Earl of Carrick, (later King Robert III) granted it to John, son of Thomas, Lord Semple, in 1375. In 1710 the Semples sold the estate to the Stewarts of Torrance. A cluster of buildings named 'Castle' appear on Roy's map of 1747-55.

Other references: Quarter

GLENANE CASTLE

South Lanarkshire   Private   OS 71   NS 812420
East of M74, off minor roads east of B7078, 1 mile north of Lesmahagow at Kerse.

The Elizabethan-style mansion of Kerse replaced a tower house known as Kerse or Kerrs. Originally called Glenane, it appears in Blaeu's *Atlas Novus* as 'Kemp Castle'. 'Kerse' is simply an old version of the Scots word 'carse', a fertile plain beside a river.

Between 1180 and 1203 Osbert, Abbot of Kelso, granted a part of the lands of Glenane to his 'servant' Radulphus and his heirs. This is probably the Radulphus or Ralph de Vere who is the first of the name Weir recorded in Scotland. He was captured with William the Lion at Alnwick in 1174. Around the same time he donated a bovate of land to Kelso Abbey and seems to have been a regular charter witness.

In 1607 George Weir of Stonebyres was served as heir to his father in the lands of Kerse. There was a disposition by Thomas of Thomastoun (or Thompson) in favour of Ralph Weir, 'portioner of Auchtygemmil' in 1612. Ralph later became superior of Poneil (Saddlerhead), Daldaholm and Clannachyett, other local properties. The Weirs of Kerse and Auchtygemmil were cadets of the Stonebyres family. They ended with an heiress who married a Cunninghame in the late 18th century. In 1793 Kerse was sold to James Ferrier, 'late of Jamaica'. An old house was demolished in 1893 and is said to have been about 200-years old at that time. It was replaced by the present mansion. This was purchased by the Gilchrists of Arthur's Craig (Hazelbank) in 1912. The family moved out in the second half of the 20th century and the house fell into use as farm storage. At some point it had burned down and was rebuilt at a lower height.

In 1987 it was purchased by the Singh family, who renovated it and by when it was known as Little Castle. Mr Singh commissioned the first known 'Asian Tartan'. As a Robert Burns enthusiast, he renamed his uninhabited Hebridean island of Eilan Vacsay as 'Burns Island'. Mr Singh purchased the title Lord of Butley Manor.

Other references: Kerse, Kerrs, Kemp Castle, Little Castle

GLENDORCH BASTLE

South Lanarkshire   Ruin or site   OS 71   NS 871189
3.5 miles south of Crawfordjohn, by minor road and track south of B740, west of Glendorch Burn, at Glendorch.

Enough remains of this 16th century bastle house of the Foulis family to show that it was occupied by a family of at least moderate means. The laird at Glendorch was known to have been involved in the mining of gold and lead. The remains of a lead smelter (possibly medieval) are recorded nearby. They are said to have been Edinburgh goldsmiths, who had a licence to mine here.

The ruin comprises a rectangular building measuring 54ft by 22ft with walls 3ft thick. A ground-floor room had a vaulted basement and cobbled floor with a trough. This room is said to measure about 16ft by 7ft and is separated from the main room by a wall 2ft thick. The highest portion of walling stands to a height of about 11ft, but most of the exterior walls are now overgrown and about 3ft high. Medieval glass and slates with peg holes were recovered on excavation, but the site has been much disturbed. There was a small splayed window in the south wall of the basement and a centrally placed doorway. Part of the building was incorporated within a barn until the 1950s. The ruin was formerly interpreted as a tower.

GLENGEITH

South Lanarkshire   Ruin or site   OS 71   NS 947166
4 miles northeast of Leadhills, by track and foot south of B7040, at Glengeith.

The foundations and lower parts of the wall, including the springing of a vault, support what is now a sheep shelter with corrugated iron roof. It was most likely a typical 16th century bastle house, though once thought to have been a peel. It measured approximately 30ft by 15ft.

In the mid 17th century Glengeith was tenanted by John Willison. A Covenanter, he found his remote home an ideal location to give shelter to his persecuted friends. It is said that he built a secret room within his house and hid its entrance within the cow shed by hanging an old plaid. By 1713 Glengeith was occupied by a family named Moffat.

By 1858 all that remained was a vaulted basement of rough whinstone slabs. The springing of the vault is still visible in the present structure. A metal detection sweep of the area recovered 69 items including coins, lead shot and buckles. Most were of 17th century date.

The bastle, enclosures, earthwork and field systems of Glengeith form a Scheduled Ancient Monument.

GLENGONNAR

South Lanarkshire Ruin or site OS 78 NS 899201

About 4 miles northeast of Leadhills, 0.5 miles south of Lettershaws, immediately east of B797 by foot.

Glengonnar is the site of a 16th century bastle house of the Bulmer family. The property appears on Forrest's map of 1816 at the confluence of Glengonnar Water and the Cleuch Burn. A level platform beside a ford marks the site. It is illustrated as a wide complex of two linked towers in Pont's map of the late 16th century. The site had been cleared by 1899.

'Gonnar' is alleged to mean 'gold bearing' and the glen seems to have lived up to the description. From the 13th century Glengonnar and nearby Glencaple belonged to Newbattle Abbey, the donation having been made by David de Lindsay of Crawford. The monks worked for gold and lead here for centuries, predominantly funded by the Crown. Foreign miners are noted in the area, even from as far as Germany. These worked under licence and had to pay a share to the exchequer as payment.

Sir Bevis Bulmer was a well known English courtier, prospector and metallurgist. There are many old gold and lead workings on Bulmer Moss as elsewhere in the surrounding valleys, an area once known as 'God's Treasure House in Scotland'. Glengonnar was predominantly a source of lead, and the Elvan Valley over the hill the main source of gold.

Bulmer is said to have presented a gold porringer (a small dish) to Queen Elizabeth of England, engraved with:

'I dare not give, nor yet present,
But render part of that's thy own,
My mind and heart shall still invent,
To seek out treasures yet unknown'

Over the lintel of the door of his house at Glengonnar were the words:
'In Wanlock, Elwand, and Glengonnar
I won my riches and my honour'

He is said to have been liberal with his generosity and often gave gold to 'unthankful persons...and such as he was liberal to, were ready to cut his throat.' He searched for gold in the highlands in 1609.

GLENHOVE

North Lanarkshire Ruin or site OS 64 NS 773724

2 miles southwest of Cumbernauld, east of A73 by minor roads, at Glenhove.

Site of an old or fortified house, now occupied by a farm. The name appears on Pont's manuscript map of the late 16th century as 'Glenhoof'.

Glenhove belonged to Robert Cleland, a merchant Burgess in Glasgow. It passed to his brother James, and then to John Cleland of Faskine. George Cleland of 'Glenhoof' was John's brother. He was an adherent of Mary, Queen of Scots. In 1577 his widow and second son George held a charter of confirmation of 'Glenhoiff', which had been signed in 1562. This George appeared as a charter witness in 1595 and is mentioned in the records of the Privy Council in 1603. Another George succeeded him and is mentioned in 1627 as a custodian of James Cleland of Faskine. He died in 1647 and the inventories of his effects 'were given up by John Cleland in Banheith'. The estate passed to his daughter Agnes, who married John Cleland of the Manse of Stobo.

By 1710 Glenhove was jointly owned by Hamilton of Wishaw and James Somerville. In 1816 it was the property of a Mr Marshall. Nearby is an 18th century tomb which carries the initials WM. By the mid 19th century Glenhove belonged to the Findlay family of Castle Toward and Glenhove, who are recorded as Land Tax Commissioners.

GLENOCHAR

South Lanarkshire Ruin or site OS 78 NS 944140

2 miles south of Elvanfoot, by foot west of the A702, west of Daer water, near Glenochar Farm.

Gleannn Ochar means the 'glen of shoes'. Glenochar is a late 16th century/early 17th century bastle house, and enough remains to show a vaulted ground floor and internal stair to the floor above. The site has been excavated to reveal the remains of nine buildings within the complex, of which at least two were byres adapted for later uses including a smithy. The entire site may represent the development of a 17th century fermtoun, complete with cobbled road centred upon the bastle. At least one of the structures may be older than the main house. An abundance of coins and other artefacts were uncovered during eight seasons of excavation, including five Elizabethan sixpences.

The bastle itself measures approximately 31ft by 21ft with walls 3ft thick. The entrance to the ground floor was in the west wall and the stairway rose internally just to the left of the door. There is a gutter running across the floor which emptied through a drain in the south wall. The building had been altered, including the addition of an 18th century fireplace in the ground floor room and the cobbling of the road outside. The finds dated from the 16th, 17th, and 18th centuries.

Early ownership of Glenochar is not documented, but it was a Graham property during the 17th century. Wills survive of a John Graham of Glenochar in 1623, James in 1635, Adam in 1655, and Walter in 1667. In 1681 John Williamsone was in Glenocher, then in 1702 John McQueen. John Hope is recorded as the farmer in 1836 and William Hope later in the same century. By 1864 it is described as being tenanted by non-residents.

Within the vicinity there are a number of Bronze Age platformed homesteads. Finds include a flint dagger recovered from within a cairn. The range of archaeology indicates regular periods of occupation throughout the ages. Glenochar was noted for its production of slate and there is an old quarry to the south of the site. The entire fermtoun with field system is a Scheduled Ancient Monument. The site has been prepared for visitors as a trail, including the provision of a car park. (www.biggararchaeology.org.uk/ht_glenochar.shtml).

GLENRAE

Dumfries & Galloway   Ruin or site   OS 71   NS 833185
5 miles northeast of Sanquhar by the B740, 0.5 miles southeast of Nether Whitecleugh, 0.25 miles by foot along Glenrae Burn.

Possible site of a castle. Boundary changes since the 19th century now put this site within Dumfries and Galloway, but when the ruin was first recorded it was just within Crawford Parish, hence its inclusion here.

The foundation lines of a 'baronial castle' here were still visible in the 19th century. When these were removed a carved stone head carrying the initials RW was discovered. This was taken to a garden in Kirkland near Tynron. It is said that the lower steps of a strongly built staircase were also revealed.

The outline was still discernible on aerial photographs taken in 1978, and is marked out by a level sub-rectangular platform, measuring about 65ft across. The site is marked on the OS maps of the area from the 19th century, but on no earlier maps. Nothing is known of its history or ownership.

GLORAT HOUSE

The Lennox & East Dunbartonshire   Private   OS 64   NS 642778
1 mile northwest of Milton of Campsie, and 1 mile northeast of Lennoxtown, about 0.75 miles north of A891 by minor roads, at Glorat.

Glorat House is a late 19th century mansion, which incorporates part of an early 17th century house within the thick west gable. A date-stone of 1625 with the initials MS is visible on the wall. The foundations of a 16th century tower house of the Stirlings were reported a little to the northwest in 1892 but apparently cannot now be found.

The Stirlings of Glorat are descended from William, second son of Sir John Stirling, 3rd of Craigbarnet. John resigned his rights to Glorat allowing Matthew, Earl of Lennox, to grant it to William in 1508. William acted as deputy to his father as Governor of Dumbarton Castle until it was handed over to Lord Erskine in 1510. In 1514 custody of the castle became essential to rival parties as they jousted for position in the minority of the newly crowned James V. William led some of the leading men of the region to successfully recover Dumbarton for the Earl of Lennox. As a reward William was appointed Captain and Keeper of the castle for his lifetime. He also gained the Kirklands of Strathblane, formerly owned by the Collegiate Church of Dumbarton. These included the lands of Ballagan. In 1534 he was murdered by Humphrey Galbraith and accomplices while travelling from Stirling to Dumbarton. They are said to have been among those whom William had 'hounded' from Dumbarton. He was succeeded by his son George, who was also captain of the castle. In 1544 the Earl of Lennox was acting in English interests when he arrived with English troops and demanded the surrender of Dumbarton Castle. George refused, counterattacked and forced Lennox to withdraw. He died in 1547 as the result of wounds received at the Battle of Pinkie. His son John inherited the estate as the 3rd of Glorat.

The Stirlings of Craigbarnet, Glorat and Ballagan were involved in a long-running feud with Kincaid of that Ilk. John was present in 1581 when the Stirlings killed Malcolm Kincaid. He was imprisoned in Blackness Castle but released on a bond of caution for 5,000 merks put up by John, Earl of Montrose. His grandson Mungo was a staunch loyalist and fought at Philiphaugh in 1645 with Montrose. He was captured and imprisoned in Glasgow and as a result accrued substantial debts. He petitioned Charles II for compensation following the Restoration, but a baronetcy given to his son George was scant reward for his loyal service and financial discomfort. George inherited impoverished estates, causing him to sell the Kirklands of Strathblane to his cousin, Stirling of Law and Edinbarnet.

By 1886 Sir Charles Elphinstone Fleming Stirling was baronet. It was he who rebuilt Glorat in its present form. The house remains occupied by the family, who are now chiefs of the original Cadder line. Glorat House is a 'B' Listed building.

GOSLINGTON

South Lanarkshire   Ruin or site   OS 72   NS 747423
4 miles southeast of Strathaven, south of the A71, and north and east of the B7068 by minor roads, just east of Goslington.

Site of an old or fortified house of the Hamiltons. The property appears on Pont's map of c.1596.

In the early 16th century Alexander Hamilton, 'tutor of Silvertonhill', received a charter of the estate of Goslington from his father, Andrew Hamilton of Silvertonhill. His son, Andrew, fought for Mary, Queen of Scots, at the Battle of Langside in 1568 and was forfeited as a result. Restored in the settlement of 1572, he was succeeded by his son, Robert. Robert married the heiress of Baillie of Provan, and gained Provanhall. His son, Edward Hamilton of Balgray, acquired some of the estates belonging to Francis Hamilton of Silvertonhill during his financial difficulties and subsequently inherited the remainder of his estate when Francis died without an heir. He took the designation 'of Silvertonhill' and inherited Provan at a later date.

GOUROCK CASTLE

Renfrewshire   Ruin or site   OS 63   NS 244770
In Gourock, off minor roads south of A770, about 0.25 miles south of Kempock Point on Bath Street, at Castle Brae/Castle Mansions.

Site of a small castle which was the seat of the Barony of Finnart-Stewart. It was demolished in 1747, but some remnants survived until 1875. Finnart was a property of the Earl of Douglas until his forfeiture in 1455. This western portion was granted to the Stewarts of Castlemilk and became known as Finnart-Stewart. The Stewarts retained it until they sold it to a family named Darroch sometime after 1710. Gourock House, a plain mansion of 1747, was built just to the southeast. The castle site was apparently marked by a small flat-topped mound but has since been developed. The site was marked on OS maps until as recently as 1970.

GRAHAM'S CASTLE

The Lennox & East Dunbartonshire   Ruin or site   OS 57   NS 682859
5 miles east of Fintry, just north of B818, by Forestry Commission track at western end of Carron Valley Reservoir, Carron Valley.

On the point of a high steep sided spur of Cairnoch Hill is an almost square mound, measuring 77ft by 75ft, defined by a dry moat 10ft deep and 30ft wide. Classified as a motte, it is very possible that the mound represents a talus or the lower courses of a large keep which have subsequently become overgrown. Access was probably via a drawbridge on the north.

The site is approached from the hillside to the northeast where there is a hint of a ditch across the approach, though this may be the result of forestry planting. There are fragmentary remains of what may be a later house on the left as the mound is approached through, what is described as, the bailey. This building is now badly deteriorated and consists of an overgrown rubble mound which is held in place by lengthy portions of the exterior walls of its southern face. The structure is about 130ft long. A short portion of the western wall also survives. The walls stand to a height of about 4ft and are roughly 3.5ft thick. Lower sections of the west and north walls stand to about 2ft. Evidence of a garderobe chute has been recorded in the northeastern corner. This building probably formed one side of a rectangular court, which is hinted at by faint undulations in the grass which suggest building remains on the northwestern side. Flanking towers on either side of the ridge are possible.

The castle appears on Pont's manuscript map of the late 16th century. His sketch seems to denote a large tower on a talus or splayed plinth, with a secondary tower behind. Later references describe the ruin as having very thick walls.

Sir David Graham had been granted charters of Strathcarron and Dundaff by Patrick, Earl of Dunbar, early in the 13th century. He is confirmed in possession in 1237. The site is usually associated with his grandson, Sir John de Graham, who fought alongside Wallace at Stirling Bridge in 1297 then died at the Battle of Falkirk in 1298. His

elder brother, Patrick, was killed at the Battle of Dunbar in 1296. John's tomb lies in Falkirk Kirkyard close to the grave of another fallen hero of Falkirk, Sir John Stewart of Bonkyl.

The Graham's epitaph reads:

'Here lyse Sir John the Graham, baith wight and wise,
Ane of the chiefs who saved Scotland thrise,
Ane better knight not to the world was lent,
Nor was gude Graeme of truth and hardiment.

A second inscription translated from the Latin reads:

'Of mind and courage stout,
Wallace's true Achates,
Here lies Sir John de Graham,
Felled by the English baties (dogs).'

Early local histories suggest that both Fintry and Graham's Castles were destroyed by Edward I in the aftermath of the Battle of Falkirk in 1298, though it is unlikely that the present Fintry Castle existed at that time. In 1460 Sir Robert Graham of Dundaff granted the lands of Fintry to his uncle, Patrick Graham, who is thought to have built the now ruinous castle a few miles to the west. Sir John's descendants became Viscounts Dundaff and eventually Marquises of Montrose, who feature in Scottish history on a regular basis. Perhaps the most famous Graham is James, 1st Marquis of Montrose and Viscount Dundaff, who through the Civil War years remained loyal to Charles I. He fought a dramatic campaign across Scotland with victories at Tippermuir, Inverlochy, Auldearn, Alford and Kilsyth, before defeat at the hands of Leslie at Philiphaugh in 1645.

The valley itself was once a very fertile and productive place, now bleak since the reservoir dam was built and the water has drowned much of it. It nevertheless retains a rugged and remote beauty, accentuated by a number of forestry plantations. This lends a hint of surrealism given its proximity to the industrial heart of Scotland.

The site itself had strategic importance, lying west of the meeting place of the few roads that allowed a crossing of the hilly barrier of the Campsie, Touch and Kilsyth Hills. Before the construction of the reservoir, the courses of the Carron and Endrick Rivers passed within a few yards of one another just below the hill. This again emphasises the strange atmosphere of the place as one emptied via Loch Lomond into the Clyde on the west coast and the other into the Firth of Forth on the eastern seaboard. This is well worth a visit if only to absorb the views and enjoy a wilderness within the central belt of industrial Scotland.

Other references: Dundaff, Sir John de Graham's Castle

GREENEND PRECEPTORY

Renfrewshire Ruin or site OS 64 NS 481693

In Inchinnan, by minor roads north of A8 and Old Greenock Road, at Northbar House.

Site of a Preceptory of the Knights Templar.

The present Northbar House is a three-storey corbiestepped farmhouse of about 1742. It carries the arms of the Gilchrists above the door. Until the 19th century it was called House of Hill. It is believed that Northbar House stands on the site of the Preceptory of Greenend, held by the Knights Templar, then by the Knights of St John of Jerusalem. It is also believed that stone from the preceptory was used to build the house.

Most of Inchinnan Parish belonged to the Templars, and then the Hospitallers. With other Hospitaller lands, Greenend was granted to Sir James Sandilands, the last Preceptor of Torphichen. A nearby farmstead bears his surname. The estate then came to the Earls of Lennox, and under their superiority was given to the Graham Duke of Montrose. It was sold to the MacGilchrists in 1672 and passed by marriage to the Balfours. There was a previous Northbar House to the north, on the south shore of the Clyde, where Donald MacGilchrist built a house and harbour in 1646.

Nearby is Teucheen Wood, recorded as being the site of the bloodiest episodes in a battle of 1164, fought between the armies of Somerled, Lord of the Isles, and Walter Fitzalan, the High Steward. Somerled died here and the battle is variously known as Renfrew, Bloody Mire and Knock. In 1905 a mound in the wood was said to have revealed fragments of bone and armour when the summit was ploughed.

In 1977 the Old Parish Church of All Hallows at Inchinnan was demolished to allow extension work to Glasgow Airport, the church being in the flight-path. It stood on the site of the ancient church of St Conval. Several Templar gravestones and a stone shrine cover presumed to be that of St Conval were transferred to the new parish church in order that they were retained locally.

Other references: Northbar, House of Hill

GREENOCK MANSION HOUSE

Renfrewshire Ruin or site OS 63 NS 282760

0.5 miles east of Greenock, 0.25 miles south of Firth of Clyde, south of A8, east of Well Park, just west of Terrace Road.

Only a well carrying a monogrammed date-stone of 1629 and gate piers of 1635 remain of this much extended L-plan tower of the late 15th or early 16th century. The original entrance is believed to have been in the re-entrant as was usual, this giving access to a stair tower and vaulted basement.

Numerous extensions were added, including an 18th century mansion block designed by James Watt, the father of the steam pioneer. Some of the extensions and door lintels were dated 1635, 1637 and 1674. The mansion block was of the 1730s. MacGibbon and Ross looking retrospectively at plans and drawings supplied by Lord Cathcart, described the older part of the building as 'a picturesque assemblage of crowstepped gables and chimneys'

The histories of the local estates can be a little confused, with a variety of names denoting the later portioning of Gourock and Greenock. Greenock of old had been the property of the Galbraiths, and it is thought that the Hugo de Grenock, who subscribed to the Ragman Roll in 1296, was a Galbraith. During the reign of Robert III, Malcolm Galbraith died and seems to have left two heiresses. One married Malcolm Crawford of Loudoun and took Easter Greenock to her husband. The other married a Schaw, bringing him Wester Greenock in about 1420. The family gained their Sauchie estate by marriage about 1431.

It would seem that Gourock was originally a Douglas estate known as Finnart. When the Earl of Douglas was forfeited in 1455 the western portion was granted to the Stewarts of Castlemilk, which became the Barony of Finnart Stewart. The eastern portion including this site became known simply as Finnart and was granted to Lord Hamilton. In 1510 his successor, the Earl of Arran, granted it to his illegitimate son, Sir James Hamilton. He took the designation 'of Finnart' and is also known as 'the Bastard of Arran'. Sir James was executed and forfeited for treason, and his Finnart property was granted to Sir Alexander Schaw of Greenock and Sauchie in 1540. Alexander gave Greenock to his eldest son John in 1542. The grant to Alexander included the 'auld castellsteid, castell, tour and fortalice and manor place new buildit'. This indicates that the oldest structure on site was already of some antiquity and had recently been extended. This is probably the Greenock Castle which appears in Blaeu's *Atlas Novus* of 1654 and on Herman Moll's map of Renfrewshire compiled before 1732. By 1679 the house is said to have become partly ruinous and a section had collapsed. In 1702 plans were put in place to rebuild and renovate. The death of Sir John Schaw prevented the work being carried out. His son and his wife lived at Carnock in

Stirlingshire and did nothing to the house at Greenock. The property passed to a descendant, Lady Cathcart, who commissioned Watt to add the mansion before 1740.

The family moved to Ardgowan in 1745 and let the property to various tenants. The basement was used as a prison. It was demolished on the building of the Caledonian Railway in 1886, and a tunnel for the railway passes directly below the site.

Other references: Wellpark, Wester Greenock, Wester Greenock Schaw

GRYFFE CASTLE

Renfrewshire Private OS 63 NS 385663
0.5 miles north of Bridge of Weir, on minor road north of A761, just west of junction with B790, at Gryffe.

Possible site of a castle. Gryffe Castle is a small asymmetrical mansion of 1854 which may be built on the site of an earlier castle, also known as Grief's Castle. The mansion was built by Robert Freeland, but became a property of the Barbours of Auldhame. In the early 20th century it was occupied by William Alexander Campbell, who was the cousin of the Prime Minister, Sir Henry Campbell Bannerman. It passed through various owners, including the Coats family of thread-makers, until requisitioned by the Army in World War II. In the 1950s it belonged to the Corporation of Glasgow and has been used as a children's home ever since.

There is no firm evidence of an earlier structure on the site. It has been suggested that the slight eminence nearby may have been a motte. Law Hill immediately to the north supports the remains of a possible fort.

The name Gryffe Castle first appears on record in 1474 when it was granted by James II to Uchtred Knox, son of John Knox of Ranfurly and Craigends, who later resigned the property. In 1619 it was apparently in the possession of Hugh de Montford, but the greater portion was still in Knox hands when they sold it to Lord Cochrane in 1665. Gryffe Castle is described as a farmstead in 1797, when Thomas Pott and his accomplice were tried and hanged for robbing it. It appears as a small farmstead on early 19th century maps, but there are apparently no earlier cartographic references.

The house is a 'B' Listed Building.

GRYMM'S CASTLE

Renfrewshire Ruin or site OS 63 NS 375678
2 miles southeast of Kilmacolm by the A761, and 1 mile north by minor roads, at or near Barlogan Farm.

Site of a small tower, which appears on Pont's map of the late 16th century and again in Blaeu's *Atlas Novus* of 1654.

HAGGS

North Lanarkshire Ruin or site OS 64 NS 722622
3 miles south of Coatbridge, by foot, south of A8, west of A725 on former Douglas Support Estate, just north of Calder Water.

Site of a large tower house, subsequently replaced by a Flemish-style mansion, which has since been demolished. A tower here appears on Pont's map of 1596 and subsequently in Blaeu's *Atlas Novus* of the 17th century. Thomas Pettigrew of Haggs is on record in the late 15th to early 16th century. His daughter Janet took the property to her husband, Gavin Hamilton, son of the Provost of Bothwell. It then seems to have passed to his nephew, Alexander Hamilton, the third son of John Hamilton of Orbistan. Sir Alexander Hamilton, 7th of Haggs, became a baronet of Nova Scotia in 1670. The line ended with his death in c1691.

By then ruinous, Haggs was acquired by Archibald Hamilton, brother to the laird of Barncluith. He built a mansion and renamed the property Rosehall. His daughter and her husband, James Hamilton (of the Orbistan family), inherited. Their grandson sold it to the estate of Margaret Duchess of Douglas. In c.1774 she bequeathed funds for the purchase of land in Scotland, thereafter to be called Douglas Support or Mains Support. This was for the benefit of her nephew Archibald Douglas, the heir of Mains.

In 1868 the property was owned by Brigadier-General Sir Thomas Monteith Douglas, who died in that year. It was inherited by the Reverend Sholto Douglas Campbell-Douglas. He was the second son of Douglas of Mains and in 1908 succeeded his brother as Lord Blythswood. Only a month before, Douglas Support had been devastated by fire. The damage totalled about £100,000 and artefacts of Robert Burns were destroyed. It is said that the family also held relics of Robert I and Sir James Douglas in the house. It was rebuilt and occupied by his brother and heir, General Barrington C. Douglas. The estate was sold in 1933.

In 2003 a planning application was submitted to use the site for commercial purposes. This was later withdrawn.

There are a wide variety of antiquities on this land, including former garden features, old coal mines, a mineral railway, and the sites of Iron Age cists.

Other references: Rosehall, Douglas Support

HAGGS CASTLE

City of Glasgow   Private   OS 64   NS 563627
In Pollokshaws, just northeast of junction of B768 and B769 with St Andrews Drive.

Haggs Castle is a much altered 16th century L-plan house of three storeys and an attic. There are a plethora of both square and round gunloops. There is much decorative moulding, particularly around the door and windows. The building has corbiestepped gables and corbelled-out stair turrets above first floor level.

The small wing contains a turnpike stair which is accessed from an entrance at the re-entrant in the east wall. A door from the base of the stair leads to the vaulted basement of the main block. A passage runs west to east, two thirds of the length, terminating at a door which opens into the kitchen. In its east wall was a centrally placed fireplace, measuring 19ft by 5ft. From this a large chimney stack rises within the walls. To the north of the passage are two other rooms. Within these there are a few small recesses within the walls. Originally this floor was illuminated by slot windows, of which a few remain, the others having been enlarged.

The main stair terminates at first-floor level, where access is gained to the former hall. This had three windows and a large fireplace in the south wall. From the in-shot of the large west window access is gained to a mural chamber measuring 10ft by 4ft, from which a private stair led to the cellar below. At the eastern end of this floor a dividing wall created a private room. This was accessed via a porch like structure which was formed by a corbelled-out staircase turret at the southwestern corner of the hall. Within the private room was a garderobe in the north wall, the chute for which serviced similar closets on the floors above. A further round stair turret was corbelled out in the western wall at the southwestern corner of the hall. The dormer windows of the attic appear to have been enlarged and retain some of the original elaborate decorative moulding. Similarly the cornicing at the eaves is highly detailed.

Until restoration in the 19th century the floors above were completely ruined, and so a fair assessment of the internal plan cannot be given. The exterior walls above have been much altered, including the addition of more modern windows. A small half-octagon extension was added out of the south wall just east of the stair turret. This provides another door at ground level and a new main stair to all floors. Above the original main door a highly decorative heraldic panel declares:

1585

Ni Domino

Aedes Strvxe

Rit Frustra Strvis

Sr Jhon Maxwell of Pollok Kny

ght and D. Margaret Conynghame

His Wife Beggat This Hows

The first section is said to be a representation of Psalm 127:1, 'Unless the Lord builds the house, those who build it labour in vain'. 'Sir John Maxwell Knight and Dame Margaret Cunninghame his wife began this house'.

Sir John Maxwell built Haggs to replace the Laigh Castle to the west. In 1586 he apparently had to demand the return of his mason, Robert Boyd, from his neighbour Stewart of Minto. Boyd had left to work for Minto without completing the contract for Haggs. In 1587 Sir John borrowed 300 merks from his father-in-law to finish the internal work. For many years the family were involved in Lord Maxwell's feud with the Johnstones of Annandale. This led to Sir John's death at the Battle of Dryffe Sands in 1593 where the Maxwells suffered a heavy defeat.

His son, another Sir John, was created a baronet of Nova Scotia in 1630. When he died, the estate passed to his distant cousin, George Maxwell of Auldhouse. George was known as the 'Bewitched Baronet', and his story is told in the entry for Auldhouse. Despite the nickname, he did not inherit the baronetcy. The family were Covenanters and held a Conventicle in Haggs in 1667. This became the subject of an inquisition by the Episcopal Presbytery of Glasgow. Refusing to pay a fine of £8,000, Sir John Maxwell was imprisoned. Despite this, he was awarded a new baronetcy in 1682. A further hefty fine may have been avoided only because of the Glorious Revolution in 1688, the overthrow of James VII and II which brought William and Mary to the throne. He became the longest serving Rector of Glasgow University, having held office from 1691 until 1718. On his death the baronetcy and estate passed to his cousin, John Maxwell of Blawarthill. The latter commissioned the building of Pollok House.

Haggs was abandoned following the completion of the mansion around 1753, initially becoming a dower house and then falling into ruin. By 1840 the ground floor was being used as a smithy for the local mine. It was restored by another Sir John Maxwell in 1860, and a low northern wing was added. It became home to the estate factor, Mr Colledge. By 1878 the Crum family of Thornliebank were resident.

The house was requisitioned for military use in 1943 and then converted into four flats in the years after World War II. It was acquired by the City of Glasgow and in the 1970s the north wing was brought into use as the Museum of Childhood. It was sold to a private developer in the late 1990s, and was restored and refitted. Haggs is again in use as a private residence, and is a grade 'B' Listed Building.

HALLBAR TOWER

South Lanarkshire Private OS 72 NS 839471
2 miles south of Carluke and 0.5 miles southwest of Braidwood, on minor road just east of B7056.

Commanding a hilltop site above the Fiddler's Burn, Hallbar is a tower of the 16th century which is often said to be as ancient as the 11th century. A courtyard once measured 93ft by 40ft, with walls 4ft thick. The tower has four storeys and a garret, over walls 5ft thick. Each floor consists of a single room. The garret is gable ended and is flanked on the east and west sides by crenellated parapets with walks supported on corbels. There is square caphouse in the southeastern corner. Although its barmkin has gone, it does retain a few unusual features.

Square in plan, each side measuring 24.75ft, the entrance is centrally placed on the southern wall, atypically at ground floor level. This gives entry to a vaulted chamber for which light is provided by an arrow slot in the north wall.

From the door a steep straight stair rises eastward within the wall to reach first floor level at the southeastern corner of the building. From here a mural corridor leads northward in the eastern wall to its midpoint. Doors open to the hall on the left and from the right to the exterior. This once accessed a wall-walk around the barmkin wall.

The hall measures 14ft square and has the only fireplace in the house. This sits on the northern wall in the northeast corner. Light is provided by a single window in the south wall, which enhances the defence of the main door below. A mural chamber was accessed by a short stair in the southwest.

A similar straight mural stair rises from the doors in the eastern wall to enter the second floor room from the northeast corner. This floor had a second hall with a garderobe in the southwestern corner. This projected to the exterior on machicolated corbels.

From the northwest corner another straight stair rose southwards in the western wall to the third-floor bedroom. At the stair head was a slot window. Within the bedroom a deep window recess provided further space. This floor was vaulted to support the weight of the stone flagged garret and roof. The door was set along the south wall, a mural corridor having wound around the southwest corner. The stair continued to the garret.

At roof level the stair terminates in the caphouse, which once had a pyramidal roof. A door gives access to the eastern battlement, and midway along this a door opens into the garret room. This has a vaulted ceiling. The western battlement is entered by a door midway down that side of the room. Centrally from the south wall, a small oriel window projects to the exterior and was supported on three large machicolated corbels. On the exterior of the north gable, nesting boxes for a doocot are built into the wall itself. The walls of the doocot and the service walkway formed a brattice, a projecting timber tower. Access to this was via a door from the northeast corner of the garret. This brattice may also have had a defensive function. The garderobe and battlemented parapet are thought to have been added in a 19th century restoration.

Hallbar was the stronghold of the important Barony of Braidwood. This first appears in 1326–27 as a grant to Sir John de Montfode by Robert I. It became a property of the Earls of Douglas, then James, Earl of Morton, and the Earl of Angus, each of whom were forfeited. In 1581 Harie Stewart of Gogar received a grant 'of the heretable gift of all and haill the landis and baronie of Braidwod, the toun of Braidwod, Langshaw, mylne of Masthok,

extending in the haill to ane xx lib. land, with toure, fortalice, maner place, orcheardis, yairdis, woddis, mylnis, fishingis, outsettis, partis, pendicles, tennentis, tenandreis, service of frie tennentis, coillis, coilhewchis thairof, and all the landis adjacent thairto, with all thair pertinentis, lyand within the schirefdome of Lanerk.'

Harie was the brother of the infamous James Stewart, Earl of Arran, who was Chancellor to James VI, not Harie as is sometimes erroneously claimed. James was murdered in 1586, and Hallbar passed to his rival, Maitland of Thirlestane. He had developed his own notoriety and also rose to become Chancellor. The Marquis of Douglas held the property before selling to the Lockharts of The Lee in 1861. The tower had fallen into ruin following the building of Braidwood House nearby. The tower was restored for Sir Norman Lockhart McDonald, when the entire upper structure was rebuilt, slates replacing the old flagstones of the roof. It was tenanted until 1984 when, left vacant, it fell victim to the weather and vandalism. By 1998 Hallbar was again semi ruinous. It was purchased and restored by the Vivat Trust, a charitable foundation who restore historic properties. Funding came in the form of grants by the National Lottery and Historic Scotland, among many others.

Hallbar is available as a holiday let (www.vivat-trust.org/properties.php?pid=107). It is a Grade 'A' Listed Building and Scheduled Ancient Monument.

Other reference: Tower of Braidwood

HALLCRAIG HOUSE

South Lanarkshire   Ruin or site   OS 72   NS 829500

1.5 miles west of Carluke, off minor road west of A73, in woodland southwest of Carluke Golf Club, by foot on north bank of Jock's Burn.

Site of a castle. A large tower, apparently named Nether Shielhills, appears in Blaeu's *Atlas Novus* of 1654. This name, however, seems to have been transposed from a small property across the burn, a distinction which is clearer on Pont's manuscript of the late 16th century. On this, the name of the tower is indistinct, appearing as 'Clcraig', or perhaps 'Glentig'. Hallcraig House, which subsequently occupied the site, was an 18th century mansion which possibly incorporated part of the castle. This was demolished in the 1950s.

The estate belonged to the Weirs in 1572, when Alexander Weir of Hallcraig was one of several Lanarkshire lairds indicted for the murders of Henry, Lord Darnley, and the Regents Moray and Lennox. It is possible that this is the property known as Craighead, which appears in the story of Robert Weir (see Craighead). In 1632 Alexander Hamilton of Hallcraig is mentioned as a debtor of the late Bishop of Glasgow. The family were Covenanters, John Hamilton of Hallcraig and his sons being among many fined or imprisoned without charge or hearing c.1650. His heir, Sir John, became a Lord of Session with the title Lord Hallcraig. In 1697 he was involved in the investigation and trial of 24 people suspected of witchcraft in Renfrewshire, seven of whom were burned. His son benefited from a grant of estates in Renfrewshire following the forfeiture of two Porterfield brothers in 1671. Before 1695, Lord Hallcraig purchased the neighbouring estate of Milton, which became the family home. In 1710 Hamilton of Wishaw described Hallcraig as an ancient house belonging to Sir John Hamilton, 'the inheritance of his predecessors'.

The combined estate of Hallcraig and Milton passed to Lord Hallcraig's daughter, Lady Isabel Gordon, wife of William of Invergordon. General William Roy, the cartographer, was born at Miltonhead on this estate. His father was factor and gardener for the Gordons. In 1748 Hallcraig and Milton became the subject of a legal dispute between their sons, Sir John Gordon and Charles Hamilton Gordon. The inheritance had depended upon adoption of the Hamilton surname and arms. Charles had taken possession in 1740, and met the conditions; however John was older, and claimed not to have adopted the surname since his ownership had never been confirmed. Charles won, and his descendants continued in possession as the Hamiltons of Hallcraig and Milton.

In 1793 parts of the old hall were still evident, 'on the very pinnacle of the rock' upon which the modern house stood. Walls, vaults and a causeway were still visible in the garden. By 1839 Hallcraig belonged to a Colonel Robertson and by 1862 to Lt. James G. Lindsay. Compare Craighead.

HALL OF FINNART

The Lennox & East Dunbartonshire   Ruin or site   OS 56   NS 242951
2 miles north of Garelochhead, east of A814, within BP Oil terminal, at Finnart House.

Hall of Finnart is a small tower house marked on Pont's map of Gare Loch, Loch Long and Holy Loch of the 16th century. Finnart House now appears to stand on the site, but is in a poor state of repair.

In the second half of the 13th century Malcolm, Earl of Lennox, issued a charter and 'eased all suits which Arthur Galbraith and his heirs are bound to make, according to the terms of their charters in return for the lands of 'Banchorane', 'Keangerloch', and 'Fynnard', and of 'Buchmonyn' and 'Kilgerintyn', and 'Auchincloich', to the performance of one suit by one man at his and his heirs' court of Lennox, when Arthur and his heirs should reasonably be summoned for this reason.' In other words, the previous terms of their charters had been altered and they now held these estates for one knights service. The Finnart mentioned may refer to his estates at Greenock but mention of Keangerloch (Garelochhead) gives this grant a local proximity.

Finnart House was built in the 1830s by the architect William Burn for the shipbuilder, John MacGregor. It was purchased by the philosopher, Edward Caird, relative of John Caird, principal and professor of Glasgow University. Since the 1950s it has been enclosed by the oil terminal, and has gone out of use. It is on the Buildings at Risk Register and is a 'B' Listed Building.

HAMILTON MOTTE

South Lanarkshire   Ruin or site   OS 64   NS 727566
In Palace Grounds, Hamilton, on southern edge of M74, just east of Hamilton Services.

Now covered by woodland, a mound on low-lying ground has spread and diminished in height. To the north the site is bounded by the M74, to the west by landscaped ground, and on the south and east by soft marshy terrain. The mound now reaches a maximum height of 8ft with a summit averaging about 60ft in diameter. The ditch is no longer obvious.

This may be the remains of the royal hunting lodge at Cadzow used by David I in the 12th century. Alternatively it may have later origins and originate from the Comyn, Fitzgilbert or even the Seviland 'of the Orchard' periods of ownership. It became a Scheduled Ancient Monument in 2003 and is described as the remains of a motte and bailey castle with buried archaeology.

Other references: Mote Hill, Netherton Motte

HAMILTON PALACE

South Lanarkshire   Ruin or site   OS 64   NS 726557
In Hamilton Low Parks, 100–200yds south of mausoleum, Hamilton.

This luxurious mansion was demolished in 1921. There are references to earlier buildings on this site dating back to at least the 15th century. The award of a lordship of parliament to James Hamilton in 1426 states: 'the manor house of the said James, now called the Orchard, situated in the Barony of Cadzow, shall in future be the principal messuage of the lordship and be stiled Hamilton'.

In 1368 this portion of the Cadzow estate was in the hands of Hugh Seviland who was recorded as 'Laird of the Orchard' in 1368. He made a grant of wax to the church of Glasgow to which he affixed the borrowed seal of David of Cadzow.

Until about 1590 this castle is consistently referred to as 'The Orchard'. Later it became known as 'The Palace'. The building of this time is often described as being fortified and on demolition to allow mining, the foundations of one wing of the 17th century palace were found to have been supported by much older work, with walls up to 10ft thick. It is possible that this was the castle at Hamilton dismantled by the Regent Morton's forces in 1579, though Cadzow is also a candidate. It is more likely both were destroyed.

In 1695 the 3rd Duke of Hamilton had the architect James Smith build him what was to become one of the grandest mansions in the country. In 1730, the 5th Duke commissioned William Adam to redesign the north

front; however the Duke's death and monetary considerations caused this project to be shelved. Further work took place for the 10th Duke in the 19th century, most notably with a new facade for the north front by the architect, David Hamilton. He utilized the Adam design, and this was completed in 1842. The lands around the palace were purchased and cleared, creating a vast landscaped environment with a grand tree-lined avenue, leading from Chatelherault to the far end of the Palace grounds. The Netherton (low town) disappeared and the High Town was developed. This still boasts a variety of estate buildings, including the stables, which are now a museum.

During the construction of Strathclyde Park, within which the palace grounds were incorporated, vaulted cellars were discovered. These were thought to belong to the original house. They were infilled with rubble.

Clustered around the palace site various other locations from the old town are recorded. These include the Bishop's Gate, Tollbooth and the Collegiate Church. Other adjacent antiquities include the massive Hamilton Mausoleum and Mote Hill.

The RCAHMS website hosts a 'Virtual Reconstruction' of the palace: http://hamilton.rcahms.gov.uk/rediscover.html

HARPERFIELD

South Lanarkshire   Private   OS 72   NS 892397
3 miles south of Lanark, on west bank of River Clyde, by minor roads west of A70.

Harperfield is a mansion house dating from the 17th century, to which a new front was added in the 18th century, with further additions to the rear in the 19th century. It stands on or near the site of a tower which appears in Pont's map of the late 16th century. On Forrest's map of 1816 and Thompson's map of 1832, a 'castle in ruins' appears 0.5 miles to the west of the present location, close to the farmstead of Netherhall.

This is thought to have been part of the Bannatyne's estate of Corehouse, which passed to the Menzies family in or before the 17th century. In 1662 John Menzies of Harperfield was excluded from the 1660 Act of Indemnity when forfeited Royalists were restored to their estates. He was required to pay a fine of £1,000 Scots.

Following a legal dispute in 1694, the property passed to the Carmichaels and then via an heiress to the Dundas family. In the 18th century it was sold in turn to the Hamiltons, Carmichael of Bonniton, the Cochranes, Carmichaels of Eastend and then to the Gordons of Pitlurg.

Harperfield is a category 'B' Listed Building and the stable block is category 'C'.

Other reference: Netherhall

HAWKHEAD CASTLE

Renfrewshire   Private   OS 64   NS 508624
1 mile east of Paisley, on minor roads north of the A726 and south of the A737, east of Hawkhead Road, just east of Ben More Drive.

Site of a castle of the Ross family. A large keep was extended by ranges to form a quadrangle in 1634, and remodelled in 1782 by James Playfair, though his plan was only partially carried out. This was demolished in 1953.

Originally part of the Steward's great estates of Renfrewshire, Robert II continued to divide these and granted this portion to the de Ros family in 1367. The family became hereditary keepers of the royal castle of Renfrew.

John de Ros is said to have had the by name 'palm my arm', a wrestling term. He is supposed to have won a fight to the death with a giant of an Englishman, the fight taking place between a moat and an inferno. As a reward for retaining the honour of Scotland, he is said to have been reluctantly granted the King's Inch in Renfrew. With James II in the audience, John fought against the Burgundians in a tournament at Stirling in 1449, drawing his bout. He was knighted the following year, and in 1489 he became Lord Ross of Hawkhead.

His grandson John, 2nd Lord Ross, died at the Battle of Flodden in 1513. The 4th Lord Ross, James, was a strong adherent of Mary, Queen of Scots, and signed the Ainslie Bond, an agreement to allow her marriage to the Earl of Bothwell. He fought for her at Langside in 1568 but was captured. In 1578 he is recorded as still being an adherent of the queen, who by now was a prisoner in England. He was Roman Catholic and was excommunicated in 1573. Robert, 5th Lord Ross, is known to have been in rebellion against James VI, and in 1591 James wrote to Mure of Caldwell asking him to use his influence and bring him to heel. It appears not to have been effective and Lord Hamilton was directed to bring him to justice.

In 1681 Hawkhead was visited by the Duke of York, who later became James VII. The 12th Lord Ross was supported the Act of Union and was given a place in the House of Lords. He became Lieutenant of Renfrewshire in 1715. In the late 18th century the line ended with a daughter, the wife of the Boyle Earl of Glasgow. Her son, George, inherited and became Lord Ross of Hawkhead and Earl of Glasgow. In 1815 he was given the additional title Baron Ross of Hawkhead.

Hawkhead stayed with the family until 1866, when the estate was sold to William Stevenson, a quarry master. Thereafter it passed through various hands until 1914, when the grounds were used as the site of Hawkhead Asylum, now Leverndale Hospital. Hawkhead Infectious Diseases Hospital was opened in the western end of the estate.

HAZELSIDE

South Lanarkshire   Ruin or site   OS 72   NS 816288
Off minor road, just north of A70, 1 mile east of Glespin, and 3 miles southwest of Douglas, at or near Hazelside Mains.

Site of a large castle, which appears on Pont's map of 1596, and subsequently in Blaeu's *Atlas Novus* of the 17th century. This was a property of the Symington family. William, Lord Douglas, is said to have had a servant, named Richard, whose son Thomas became known as Dickson and assumed his father's role. He was apparently captured at Sanquhar Castle in 1295 while fighting alongside William Wallace. In 1306 he is said to have provided food and shelter to the young Sir James Douglas during the English occupation, and to have been central to the ploy which saw Sir James retake Douglas Castle. The story is recounted by Sir Walter Scott in 'Castle Dangerous'.

Thomas received a grant of Hazelside from Sir James and then a grant of Symington from Robert I. His descendants then assumed the Symington surname. They became hereditary Baillies of the Barony of Douglas and keepers of the castle there. In 1605, John Symington of that Ilk was served heir to his grandfather in the Barony of Symington, as Baillie of Douglas and captain of its castle. Hazelside is recorded as part of that inheritance.

By 1710 Hazelside was occupied by Samuel Douglas. Nothing remains of the castle.

HILLS CASTLE

South Lanarkshire   Ruin or site   OS 72   NT 049481
At or near East Hills, 4 miles northeast of A721 at Newbigging, off minor roads.

Site of a tower house. It was apparently still standing in the early 19th century, though all trace has now gone. It was 'a fortalice of the Scottish tower and peel type with a vaulted lower storey'.

In the 12th century Fergus Mackabard (Baird?) had ownership of the barony of Dunsyre. It came to Elias, the brother of Bishop Jocelin of Glasgow. Thereafter ownership seems to have been with a family who took their name from the lands and in 1299 the lands of Hills were sold to Allan de Denume by John the son of Adam of Dunsyre.

Hills became one of the properties within the parish which was feued out by the Barony of Bothwell. It was owned by Baillie of Lamington in 1638, then by the Hamiltons of Udston. It was purchased outright by Sir George Lockhart of Carnwath, President of the Court of Session, in the late 17th century.

Other reference: East Hills

HOUSEHILL

City of Glasgow   Ruin or site   OS 64   NS 525612

In Pollok, Househillwood, by minor roads south of B762, just south of Levern Water, near Levern footbridge.

Site of an old or fortified house. The old house of Howsle was replaced by a mansion at the beginning of the 19th century, which was itself demolished in 1939.

Sir Thomas Stewart of Minto gained Wester Partick and Househill by marrying Isabel, the daughter of Stewart of Arthurlie. His possession was confirmed by a charter dated 1477 from John Stewart, Lord of Darnley, (Earl of Lennox from 1488). This was again confirmed by Royal charter in 1489. This may be the property for which Robert Boyd the mason left his work at Haggs in 1586. The Stewarts held it until 1646, when financial difficulties forced the sale of Sir Ludovick Stewart's Glasgow properties. Househill was purchased by Thomas Dunlop, son of Dunlop of that Ilk. By 1682 it had been sold to the Blackburns and in 1750 was purchased by Robert Dunlop, son of Dunlop of Garnkirk.

Other reference: Howsle

HOUSTON HOUSE

Renfrewshire   Private   OS 64   NS 412672

3 miles northeast of Bridge of Weir, just northeast of Houston, on minor roads north of B790, and east of B789.

Site of a castle of the Houston family, dating from the 12th century, considerably developed, altered and then rebuilt as a mansion in the 18th century. The present building has been converted into flats.

Houston takes its name from Sir Hugh of Padvinan (Pettinain), who was gifted the lands of Kilpeter by Baldwin, Sheriff of Biggar, in the 12th century. As was often the case with Baldwin's associates, it is thought that Hugh was related and may have been his son-in-law. He is said to have been associated with the Knights Templar and to have died while with them at the Battle of Hattin in 1187. Hugh is also known as an adherent of his superiors, the High Stewards, and witnessed Walter Fitzallan's foundation charter of Paisley Abbey. His descendants became the Houstons of that Ilk, and Sir Finlay Houston submitted to Edward I in the Ragman Roll of 1296. Sir Peter Houston fought and died alongside the Earl of Lennox at the Battle of Flodden in 1513. His son Sir Patrick was slain in 1526 at the Battle of Linlithgow Bridge, while fighting for the Earl of Lennox in his attempt to gain control of the young James V. His grandson, also Patrick, was knighted by Mary, Queen of Scots, and allegedly accompanied her during her visit to see Henry, Lord Darnley, in his sick bed in Glasgow.

Houston House is said to stand on the site of Hugh's original castle. The family obtained a substantial barony in West Lothian, where they built a castle upon the site of a former Cistercian Abbey. John Houston of that Ilk died in 1609 and appointed the Earl of Lennox as governor of his eldest son. In 1688 Sir Patrick Houston received a baronetcy from Charles II. Many of the family are buried at St Peter's Church in the village.

According to MacGibbon and Ross, Houston House was thought to be a 16th century courtyard castle of the Earls of Lennox, but they admit that little is known of its early history. However, Patrick's son, Sir John Houston of that Ilk, was in possession in 1710, suggesting that the confusion may have arisen from the Earl's governorship.

By the late 19th century all that remained was a block of 1625, which once formed the east side of the yard. There was originally a high-arched gateway in the south front of the courtyard. The block had an entrance in the northern end of the west front giving access to a wide stair within a square well. To the south of this a door opened into the smaller of two large rooms, the second of which is subdivided into several smaller rooms. There was a secondary entrance in the south gable with service stair to the first floor. The floor above was similarly divided, the smaller of the rooms acting as a bedroom and the divided room providing a dining room and a drawing room. The exterior walls were about 5ft thick, where they formed the outside of the former courtyard. They reached a width of 3ft on the west within the yard. The 5ft thickness continued on the main interior dividing wall. Drawings of the mid-18th century show the remains of massive corbelling along the top of the eastern wall. The building had corbiestepped gables at the north and south ends. A high square tower once stood at the northwest corner of the 'Palace', as the house became known.

In 1740 the Houston estate was sold to Sir John Schaw of Greenock. He sold it on to Sir James Campbell of Jamaica. His heirs sold it to Captain McCrae, a former Governor of the East Indies. He modernised the house, removing three sides of the courtyard. He also funded the reconstruction of the village on the present site, considerably further from the house than originally.

From 1782 the property belonged to Alexander Speirs of Elderslie, who used it as a shooting lodge. In 1872 the house was substantially rebuilt, but only the eastern wall of the tower seems to have been incorporated. The

1625 date stone survives, set into this part of the wall. During the rebuild many original outbuildings were removed. Further changes were made in 1893-95.

The house is a category 'B' Listed Building. There remains a walled garden, a sundial, and a raised square mound which supported a bowling green. This has been suggested as a modified motte.

HOWGATE

South Lanarkshire   Ruin or site   OS 72   NS 920352
3 miles northwest of Wiston, west of A73 by track north of B7055, at Howgate.

The present farmhouse is said to retain a vaulted basement, possibly a remnant of a bastle house. The Baillies held Howgate, probably from before 1500. In 1541, Archibald Baillie of Howgate was involved in a feud with John Livingstone of Warrenhill. In 1541 he killed his adversary and was in turn slain by his victim's kinsman, James Livingstone. By 1681 Howgate was held by Thomas Alexander, in 1695 by the Sandilands, and by 1824 by Robert Greenshields. By 1863 it was occupied by the Carmichaels.

HYNDFORD

South Lanarkshire   Ruin or site   OS 64   NS 906416
2 miles southeast of Lanark, west of the A73, off minor roads north of the River Clyde, and northwest of Hyndford Bridge, at Hyndford.

Site of a small tower of the Carmichaels, which is illustrated on Pont's map of 1596. From 1701 the Carmichaels took their title as earls from this property. It became a farmstead, which was owned by the Howieson family by 1816. A 'Mote' to the northwest, which is denoted on OS maps, has been excavated and shown to be the remains of a crannog.

INCH CASTLE

Renfrewshire   Ruin or site   OS 64   NS 515675
0.5 miles east of Renfrew, north and west of the M8 and north of the A877, 100yds north of Merlinford Drive.

Elderslie House, a long vanished 18th century mansion, was said to have been built about 40yds from the ruin of this place marked on Blaeu's *Atlas*. Walter Fitzallan, High Steward of Scotland, built a wooden castle here. It is said to have been constructed upon stone foundations and may have been a motte. This was abandoned when his descendants, the Stewarts, built Renfrew Castle, hence King's Inch (island).

Sir John Ross of Hawkhead was granted the estate and built a 'new' Inch Castle before his death in 1474. It was a four-storey keep with corbiestepped gables and a centrally placed round stair tower corbelled out from first-floor level. The last Ross occupant died in 1732.

The castle was ruined by 1770 when Alexander Speirs of Elderslie purchased it. He built Elderslie House, apparently removing the old building, although his house was demolished later and nothing now remains.

Speirs was an incredibly wealthy merchant and banker based in Glasgow. From 1745 onwards, he purchased a great many estates in the area, including Elderslie, Houston, Neilston, Inch and Culcreuch. At the latter, his family established a cadet line. On completion of Elderslie House, he had his diverse properties erected into a barony, after which the house was named. A William Wallace enthusiast, he is said to have owned at least two of the patriot's double-handed swords. His land holding company, Elderslie Estates, continues to this day, and it is owned by the Crichton-Maitland family, his direct descendants. Their major land holding is an area of 4,000 acres situated between Houston, Kilmacolm and Bridge of Weir.

Archaeological assessment of this site prior to development, uncovered the footings of Elderslie House. These had some features which may have been consistent with a 15th century building. The site is no longer an island, and was occupied by a power station and farms.

Other reference: King's Inch

INCHGALBRAITH CASTLE

The Lennox & East Dunbartonshire   Ruin or site   OS 57   NS 369904
On the island Inchgalbraith, Loch Lomond, 1.5 miles southeast of Luss, and 0.5 miles east of A82 at Bandry.

Only fragments survive of a 15th century or earlier castle of the Galbraiths of Bandry. The present structure is said to have originated c.1542, but is probably considerably older. The ruin covers almost all of a small circular island,

82ft in diameter. This was once considered as a possible crannog, which is now known to be a natural glacial deposit.

The largest portion is of the castle is the northern tower, which stands to the base of the second floor. It reaches a maximum height of 23ft on the north, with lower wall remnants reaching only 4ft high on the south and east. It measures 34.5ft by 41.5ft overall, and seems to have been built within a courtyard measuring 49ft by 39ft with walls 4.5ft thick. There is evidence of a portcullis groove within 'a fine entrance' on the eastern wall. There are also signs of early restoration work, particularly around a window or doorway in the north wall. There is a blocked, arched doorway at ground-floor level in the north wall, possibly a postern. There do not appear to be any arrow slots or gunloops. There may have been an external stair to first floor level, possibly added at a later date.

At the western end of this tower, a round-ended wall projects for some 6.5ft. This is thought to have been associated with a pier or landing place which may have been enclosed. The south wall of this tower had two doorways at ground floor level which led directly to the shore. The eastern of these has evidence of sockets for an iron yett.

There may have been as many as three buildings, with definite traces of a southern block. The remainder of the island is overgrown and strewn with rubble and so the remaining layout cannot be determined without clearance and investigation. Parts of the building are at severe risk of collapse due to tree growth.

The ruins were apparently home to a family of ospreys during the 18th and 19th centuries. They were shot, and the species never returned to nest on the island. Happily, the species has been returning to the loch annually since the late 1980s.

The castle appears as 'Yle na Castel' on Pont's map of Loch Lomond of the late 16th century, in which he describes it as being old and wood-bound, though he clearly sketches a tower and courtyard. In 1832 it appears on John Thomson's map as 'Galbraith Cas. In Ruins'.

The Galbraiths anciently owned the Bannachra estate, Inchgalbraith being their stronghold. In the late 16th century the property passed to the Colquhouns of Luss, who built Bannachra Castle. They left the island stronghold to fall into ruin, in which state it is recorded by the early 18th century.

Inchgalbraith was said to be the home of a 'brownie', or mischievous goblin, which apparently had a daily habit of stealing the roast from a spit at Rossdhu Castle. Another version of the story blames the Galbraith proprietor of the island, who apparently swam to Rossdhu for his dinner. The Colquhoun laird was unable to catch him, but becoming determined to do so, he set up nets in the water to trap the thief. Caught like a fish, Galbraith was taken ashore and promptly hanged.

The ruin is a category 'C' Listed Building.

Other references: Galbraith Castle, Yle na Castel

INCHINNAN CASTLE

Renfrewshire   Ruin or site   OS 64   NS 482697

1 mile southeast of Erskine, 0.5 miles north of Inchinnan, by minor roads north of the A8, at or near Flures Place, Garnieland.

Stone from this castle was evident in dykes throughout the area and the ruins were substantial in 1710. The castle appears as a large tower on Pont's map of 1583-96 and, similarly, within a park in Blaeu's *Atlas Novus* of 1654. It had disappeared by the time of General Roy's map of the 1750s. The site became a stockyard for Garnieland Farm, but is now occupied by modern housing.

A manor house here was held by the High Steward in 1151 but passed to the Stewart Earls of Lennox. It was superseded by a 'palace' built by Matthew, 2nd Earl, in 1506, which passed to the Crown in 1571. It returned via several members of the Stewart family to the Earls of Lennox and Richmond. They sold it to the Campbells of Blythswood.

An inscribed stone, supposed to have come from the castle, was recorded in the wall of a corn mill at Garnieland. It was then moved to the old Inchinnan churchyard in 1905. It read 'DD ISL KCL 1631'. Another reference states that an inscription over the door of the palace commemorated its building by Matthew, 1st Earl of Lennox, and his wife, Helen Hamilton. This is both misleading and erroneous, since Matthew was the 2nd Earl and his wife was Elizabeth Hamilton. Matthew died at the Battle of Flodden in 1513.

Inchinnan, with nearby Govan, was an early Christian site, both producing a variety of ancient coffins in various styles from archaeological digs. See also Oldbar.

Other reference: Palace of Inchinnan

INCHMURRIN CASTLE

The Lennox & East Dunbartonshire   Ruin or site   OS 57   NS 373863

3 miles north of Balloch, at the western edge of Inchmurrin Island, Loch Lomond

Inchmurrin means 'Mirren's Island', a reference to a monastery established here in the 7th century, dedicated to St Mirren. The castle ruin sits on a high knoll at the western end of the island, allowing effective control of boat traffic on Loch Lomond. Inchmurrin was the property of the Earls of Lennox, and is said to have superseded the castles at Balloch and Catter. The construction of the castle was completed in 1393.

The ruin occupies a rocky knoll in the southwestern corner of the island. This provided defence by virtue of a precipitous fall on two sides, while ditches were dug on the northeastern and southwestern sides. The first of these has apparently been filled at the eastern end to carry a path to the modern house, though in 1956 was measured at 10ft deep and 24ft wide, while the latter was deeper at 13ft deep, but of similar width. This has been almost completely removed by modern landscaping and now appears only as a slight depression in the ground.

A non-invasive archaeological survey of the ruin was carried out in 1995, a task hampered by a thick growth of brambles and bracken. The castle comprised of what may have been a tower or gatehouse, a main block and an enclosure wall. This was 1.5ft thick and protected the southwestern boundary of the site. No trace was found of an enclosing wall on the northeastern side, or on the northwestern side, though it is suggested that this may have collapsed down the slope.

The main block now comprises the most prominent part of the ruin. It consists of the remnants of three rooms at ground floor level, any structure above has now gone. The varying thickness of the walls, from 1.5ft to 3ft has given rise to the idea that there may have been three stages of construction. The building measures 34ft by 118ft.

The northeastern room measured 24ft by 22.5ft and had a window 3ft wide on the exterior, which tapered to 4.5ft internally. There is a thickening of the wall to the south of the window, suggestive of the site of a fireplace. The entrance to the building is via this room, on the northeastern wall.

The central room measures 22ft by 8ft. It has a slot window in the northern corner, which may have been a later feature. Protruding stonework and alterations to the lay out suggest that this room may have housed the original entrance. Adjacent, on the southeast wall, are traces of a 5ft wide circular stair tower, which also abutted the southwestern room.

This third room measures 28.5ft by 22ft which, with walls 4ft thick, appears more substantial than the others. There are arched windows in the northwestern and southeastern walls, though the latter has been blocked up. There is an arrow slot below the northwestern window, which puts the originality of the latter into question. Further adaptation of the structure has been noted in this general area, suggesting a join in the building and a possible former entrance. The surviving height of this section of the building, with a floor level higher than that of the central room, prompted the suggestion of a fourth room below.

There was an entrance in this room, which led to what may have been a gatehouse, though dense vegetation hampered the assessment. The archaeologists found a rounded tower base on the northwest side, and a hint of a room at the southeast.

The foundations of a dry-stone building were found on the southern side of the northeastern ditch and adjacent to it was a remnant of a circular corn drying kiln. Another platform to the east is thought to be modern and the result of landscaping for a golf course. The castle is said to have had a remote watch tower at Tom Bay, at the northeastern end of the island.

Robert I is said to have established a deer park on the island in the early 14th century. It has been suggested that the castle was built as a hunting lodge for Duncan, 8th Earl. In 1425 James I executed the Earl of Lennox and his male heirs with Murdoch Stewart, 2nd Duke of Albany. Each had played their part in Albany's corrupt regency during the king's imprisonment in England. Murdoch's widow, Isabella, the daughter of the executed earl, became dowager Duchess of Lennox. For her part she was imprisoned in Tantallon for eight years. Following the death of James I, she was released, and from 1437 lived out her retirement on Inchmurrin. Sir John Colquhoun and his retinue were murdered by highlanders in the castle in 1439. Isabella died in 1458.

The executions of 1425 brought about a division of the Lennox estate, one portion going to the Napiers of Merchiston, another to the Haldanes of Gleneagles. The remaining estate and title, including Inchmurrin, was retained by the Duchess. This was granted to the Stewarts of Darnley in 1488.

James IV visited in 1506 and in 1585 James VI stayed. In 1617, 13 years after the Union of the Crowns, he visited again. This was to be his only return trip to Scotland. He was the guest of his cousin, Ludovick Stewart, to whom he had granted the earldom.

In the early 18th century this part of the Lennox passed to the acquisitive Dukes of Montrose who, it is said, built a hunting lodge on the island. The Earldom of Lennox is now one of the titles held by the Duke of Richmond and Gordon.

Other reference: Lennox Castle

INCHNOCK TOWER

North Lanarkshire Ruin or site OS 64 NS 718693
Off minor roads, 2.5 miles east of A752, east of Marnock, north of Glenboig south of Inchneuk Farm.

All that remains of Inchnock (or Inchneuk) Tower is some rubble and a short stretch of wall 4ft thick and 2.5ft high. The site is known locally as 'the rocks'. The tower was built in the late 16th century by the Forsyths of Dykes, well known as office bearers and merchants in the City of Glasgow. In 1710 it was described as 'an old house, situated in the midst of woods, surrounded by moss, and most difficult of access'.

At the Reformation Lord Boyd gained the parish of Medrox and divided it into four portions. Inchnock was feud to the Forsyths. It is said that the Scots garrisoned Inchnock against the army of Cromwell during his campaign of 1650-51.

Inchnock apparently passed to Hamilton of Dalzell. By the mid to late 17th century, it was in the possession of Andrew Hay, son of Reverend John Hay of Renfrew. Andrew's son, John, inherited and was styled 'of Inchnock and Gayne', the latter being another local property. John was an Episcopal minister and was incumbent at Yester, then Dunlop and finally New Monkland. On being deposed from the latter in 1692, the Kirk Session had to write to him requesting the return of the baptismal basin and session registers. The former was promptly returned; however the Kirk Session had to take out a case against him at the Commissary Court of Hamilton for the return of their records.

A family named Steele gained it before 1836, when John Steele of Inchnock was a Commissioner for Land Tax. His family had a private tomb 100yds to the southeast of the ruin. They continued to use this, at least until 1857, by which time the tower was in ruins and may have been replaced by a new house at, what is now, the farm to the north.

INVERKIP CASTLE

Renfrewshire Private OS 63 NS 205728
5 miles southwest of Greenock, and 0.5 miles north of Inverkip, on minor roads west of A78, south of Ardgowan House.

Standing on a cliff overseeing the Firth of Clyde, Inverkip is a restored 15th century square keep of three storeys and formerly a garret. It measures 30ft by 23ft and stands to a height of 40ft. The tower has a double course of chequered corbelling supporting a crenellated parapet with open rounds at three corners. The basement is vaulted and entered by a door below the original main entrance at first floor level. This is now reached by a later external stone stair. There is an arrow slot guarding the basement door.

A 13th century castle here was held by the English during the Wars of Independence, and it was to the castle that Sir Philip Mowbray fled, after being routed by Sir James Douglas. In 1306 the castle was besieged by Sir Robert Boyd on behalf of Robert I.

In 1390 Robert III granted the Renfrewshire estate of Auchingoun to his natural son, Sir John Stewart. Sir John was then granted Blackhall in 1396, before gaining Ardgowan in 1404. The combined estates were erected into a barony for James Stewart of Ardgowan in 1576. In the 17th century, Archibald Stewart was a Commissioner to Parliament. He was knighted when he became a member of the Privy Council to Charles I. In 1667 his grandson, another Archibald, was created a baronet by Charles II. Marriage alliances saw the family gain estates at Scotstoun and Pardovan.

In the early 18th century the castle was extended. The scars of this remain on the tower, the extensions having been removed. It was superseded by nearby Ardgowan House in the 19th century, falling into ruin thereafter. It was restored in 1936 though left roofless. Ardgowan remains with the same family, now named Schaw-Stewart of Ardgowan. The tower is a category 'B' Listed Building, while Ardgowan House is 'A' listed.

Other reference: Ardgowan Tower

INVERSNAID GARRISON

The Lennox & East Dunbartonshire   Ruin or site   OS 56   NN 349096

2 miles east of Loch Lomond, 1 mile west of Loch Arklet, west of B829, just north of minor road, at Garrison Farm.

Not a castle or residence, but a place of strength worthy of note. Two barrack blocks for government troops were built in 1718, a response to the Jacobite rising of 1715. The garrison was built to quell the MacGregors, whose territory this was. Before it was completed Rob Roy is said to have led an attack on the construction workers.

The garrison was apparently destroyed in 1745, and then rebuilt. The remains are incorporated into barn walls. The height of the remains varies from foundation level to 17.5ft in one block. A number of gunloops are still evident.

General James Wolfe was a commander here early in his career, before making his name in the wars against the French in Canada. The Garrison was abandoned by 1800 and came into use as an inn. It was partly demolished in 1828.

INVERUGLAS CASTLE

The Lennox & East Dunbartonshire   Ruin or site   OS 56   NN 323096

3.5 miles north of Tarbet, east of A82 at Inveruglas, on Inveruglas Isle, Loch Lomond.

Site of a castle of the chief of the MacFarlanes, which was burnt to the ground by Cromwell's troops in the 1650s. This was the principal and earliest confirmed home of the MacFarlane chiefs. The remains are those of a Z-plan castle, a sub-rectangular main block having round towers at the southwestern and northeastern corners. The surviving walls stand to a maximum height of 11ft and are 5ft thick. Overall the building measured 40ft by 16.5ft. The corner towers are of unequal size and appear to be later additions to the original main block. There are a number of square and rectangular gunloops at first-floor level, with evidence of wall thickening at this level, perhaps indicating a mural passageway or stairwell. There are also two fireplaces on the first floor, one in each of the north and south walls. The interior is so full of rubble that it is not possible to suggest a ground floor layout, or even whether there was vaulting. The destruction caused by the attack is described as comprehensive.

Nearby are foundations of two large rectangular buildings, which may be part of the castle complex or of a later date. In the southeastern corner of the island are the inaccessible remains of a substantial landing stage.

The clan claimed descent from the old Celtic Earls of Lennox and fought with Robert I during the Wars of Independence. When, in 1425, the last of the original line of the Earls of Lennox was executed for treason, the chief of the MacFarlanes submitted a claim to the title. He lost out to the Stewarts of Darnley. The 11th chief died at Flodden in 1513 and Duncan, 13th chief, led 300 men to defeat at the Battle of Glasgow Muir. He died at the Battle of Pinkie in 1547. They were in the Regent Moray's army at Langside in 1568.

Following the destruction of this castle, the chiefs moved to Eilan I Vhow and Tarbet. They fought with Montrose at Inverlochy, where they helped defeat Archibald Campbell, Marquis of Argyll.

The ruin is a Scheduled Ancient Monument, the scheduled area covering the entire island.

JERVISTON HOUSE

North Lanarkshire   Private   OS 64   NS 758582

1 mile northeast of Motherwell, by minor roads north of A723, and west B799 of on north bank of Calder Water, at Colville Park.

Jerviston was an L-plan house of the 16th century, with a corbelled out stair turret above first-floor level within the re-entrant. It had corbiestepped gables and once had bartizans in the northwest and southeast angles. Of these only the corbels remained. The entrance was in the north face of the wing in the re-entrant. A wide spiral stair led from here to the first floor. Above the door was a heraldic panel, which once held the initials RB and EH. The basement of the main block was vaulted and contained the kitchen and a cellar. Above this on the first floor was the hall. The top floor provided private apartments or bedrooms. On each floor of the wing were further bedrooms. These were entered from the stair turret. This originally had a conical roof, as had the bartizans.

The property belonged to the Baillies, the initials representing Robert Baillie and his wife, Elizabeth Hamilton. He was possibly the brother of Baillie of Carfin. Robert Baillie, grandson of a laird of Jerviston, was chaplain to Lord Eglinton's regiment in the Covenanting Army. He was sent to London in 1640 as a commissioner to argue the case against Archbishop Laud's impositions on the Scottish Church. In 1649 he was one of those sent to Holland to negotiate with Charles II over his restoration to the Scottish throne, ensuring his acceptance of Presbyterianism. In 1651 he became Professor of Divinity at Glasgow University, then Principal in 1661.

The house was abandoned in favour of a mansion built by Robert Adam in 1782. Old Jerviston, as it was then called, fell into use as a garden store. The estate became the property of the Colvilles, iron and steel magnates. By 1953 the old house was described as still roofed and complete, though dilapidated and subsiding due to mine workings. The old house, new house, or both were demolished in 1966, and an ice house was then demolished in 1967. The mansion has been replaced by a modern country club and the estate occupied by a golf course.

Despite this, both houses still appear on more recent OS maps.

JERVISWOOD HOUSE

South Lanarkshire Private OS 72 NS 884455
1 mile north of Lanark, off minor road north and west of A706, on east bank of Mouse Water.

Defensively sited high above the Mouse Water on the east side of a ravine, Jerviswood is a 17th century L-plan house of three storeys and a garret, below a steeply pitched roof. MacGibbon and Ross drew the ruins of an older castle adjacent to the house in the late 19th century. Part of this was demolished c.1950 when the house was improved by the addition of bathrooms. Foundations measuring 26ft by 23ft and a wall fragment 11ft high survive.

The lower sections of the walls show signs of having originated in a much earlier period than the remainder of the house. The basement was not vaulted and contains the original kitchen fireplace and oven within a 12ft arch. A square stairwell rises to the floor above. Much of the original interior was destroyed as the house was converted to house farm labourers. Of the remaining external features, an arrow slot in the north wall, heraldic panel above the door, and the generally fine workmanship of the building are notable.

The earliest records of a castle at Jerviswood are dated 1513. The older castle would have been constructed by the original Livingstone owners. It was purchased in 1636 by George Baillie of St John's Kirk. He rebuilt the house and a later extension was added to the east.

He was succeeded by the Covenanter Robert Baillie, who hid in a recess within the walls before being captured. Implicated in the Rye House Plot to assassinate Charles II and his brother, James, Duke of York, he was hanged, drawn and quartered for high treason in 1684. The parts of his body were displayed in Edinburgh, Lanark, Ayr and Glasgow. The Lanark folk rescued their part of his body and gave it a decent burial. Before his death he wrote to his son George saying, 'if ye have a strong heart ye may go and see me nagled; but if ye have not the heart for it, ye may stay away.'

George fled to Holland, returning in the reign of William and Mary. He had his estates restored, then married

the daughter of the Earl of Marchmont. They eventually inherited Mellerstain. In 1859 another George Baillie of Jerviswood inherited the Earldom of Haddington from his second cousin, Thomas Hamilton. He adopted Hamilton as a second surname becoming known as George Baillie-Hamilton.

A heraldic panel bearing the arms of George Baillie is built into the wall of the Mains Farm. The house has been restored and reoccupied as a private home, and received a Civic Trust Commendation in 1984. It apparently retains several 'magnificent' original fireplaces. Jerviswood is a category 'A' Listed Building.

Other references: Geriswood, Jarviswood

JOHNSTONE CASTLE

Renfrewshire Private OS 64 NS 425623
In Johnstone, on minor roads south of A737, just south of Quarrelton, in Tower Place.

Johnstone is an altered L-plan tower house of the 16th century. It appears as 'Eliebanck' on Pont's map of the late 16th century, and this was misinterpreted to appear as 'Lugbanck' on Blaeu's *Atlas Novus* of the 17th century.

The tower consists of a main block of three storeys and a garret with a smaller altered wing, which now rises to an additional storey. This wing has been gothicized. A two-storey bartizan crowns the gable of the main block and a massive chimney stack dominates the east gable. There is a watch house in the re-entrant, corbiestepped gables and many arrow slits.

There is a porter's lodge within the door, which sits in the re-entrant. This was protected by a machicolated projection from the floor above. The door leads to a vaulted passage, from which the two basement rooms are reached. A bricked-up portion of this passage probably led to the stair. The eastern room is the kitchen, which has a wide-arched fireplace. The room to the west was a wine cellar and had a service stair to the hall above. Although much altered, the hall retains a garderobe and a deep window recess. There is a decorated heraldic panel high on the wall below the watch house.

Originally named Easter Cochrane or Quarrelton, Johnstone was a property of the Cochranes, who in 1669 became Earls of Dundonald. The Houstons of Johnstone ('Milliken') bought it in 1733, and changed the name to Johnstone, bringing the name from their previous castle. They extended in 1771 and in 1812 had the building remodelled, possibly by James Gillespie Graham. Frederick Chopin apparently visited in 1848.

The last of the Houstons of Johnstone died in 1931 and the tower was briefly tenanted by the Watsons of Linwood Paper Mill. The estate and mansion were then taken over by the local council, and in 1950 they ordered the demolition of the mansion. This left only the old core with some modifications to the wing.

It now stands within a housing estate and was used as a store by the council. Work was begun in 2005 to restore the tower as a private dwelling, and it is a 'B' Listed Building.

Other references: Easter Cochrane, Eliebanck, Lugbanck, Quarrelton

JOHNSTONE CASTLE

Renfrewshire Private OS 64 NS 430622
1 mile east of Kilbarchan, just west of Barochan Interchange on A737, 150 yds southeast of White House of Milliken.

Site of a tower house. Originally named Johnstone, Johnstoun or Johnstoune, this was a property of the Nisbet family, which passed to the Wallaces of Elderslie by 1561. When the last of the Wallaces died, the property passed to the Houstons of Houston in the 17th century. This is the tower named 'Johnstoun', which appears on the west bank of the White Cart in Blaeu's *Atlas Novus*.

In 1733 the Houstons purchased Easter Cochrane, selling this property to James Milliken, a merchant with a large estate on St Kitts in the Caribbean. They renamed Easter Cochrane as Johnstone, while Milliken named his new property after himself. He pulled down the tower house and built himself a 'rustic' mansion, which burnt down in 1801. In 1776 the estate had passed to a grandson of the third Milliken, Colonel Robert John Napier. He was a direct descendant of the Culcreuch family and so of John Napier of Merchiston, inventor of logarithms. This may explain the name Merchiston appearing as that of a local hospital. The Napiers built a new mansion on the site, which was itself demolished in the 1930s.

A little to the south is a 'tower', which is in fact a cylindrical doocot with 1000 nesting boxes. This is a 'C' Listed Building. The present house on the estate, known as the White House, is 'B' Listed, and was restored in 1915. The remains of a walled garden sit to the west. The site of Milliken House remains as a level platform to the southwest.

Other reference: Milliken House

JORDANHILL

City of Glasgow   Ruin or site   OS 64   NS 538683

South of A82, and west of A739, 0.5 miles south of Anniesland, on an eminence in the grounds of Jordanhill College, Glasgow.

Site of a tower house, built in 1562 by the Crawfords. It was later replaced by an 18th century mansion of the Houstons, and then a college. Jordanhill, although north of the Clyde, was once within a detached portion of Renfrewshire.

In 1546 Lawrence Crawford of Kilbirnie founded a chaplainry at Drumry and granted it the £5 land of Jordanhill as financial support. Recovering it at the Reformation, he granted it to his son, Thomas, who built his tower house upon an eminence in 1562.

On 31 March 1571, with Cunninghame of Drumquassle, he jointly led a small force against Dumbarton Castle. The stronghold was being held against the Regent Lennox by Lord Fleming, for the exiled Mary, Queen of Scots. His 'Daring Raid' was successful and the young James VI wrote to Crawford to express his gratitude:

'Captain Crawford,

'I have heard sic report of your guid service done to me from the beginning of the wars against my unfriends, as I shal sum day remember the same, God willing, to your greit contentment: In the mein quhyle be of good comfort, and reserve you to that time with patience, being assured of my favour. Fareweil. Your guid friend, James Rex. 15 Sept 1575.'

In 1577 Thomas was Lord Provost of Glasgow and built the first bridge to Partick across the River Kelvin. He died in 1603, the year in which his 'guid friend' assumed the English throne.

In 1750 the estate was purchased by Alexander Houston, a Glasgow merchant and partner in the Ship Bank. His son built a new mansion on the site of the old house.

The house and estate were purchased by Archibald Smith, a West Indies merchant, in 1800, who extended the house. The family remained in possession at least until the death of the noted barrister and mathematician Archibald Smith in 1872.

The estate was purchased in 1911 as the site for a new teacher training college. The Scottish Education Board had decided that teacher education could not be left to the churches and took over the role. They built new colleges at four locations in Scotland. Jordanhill College was established here and this was completed in 1919.

It is now the Faculty of Education for the University of Strathclyde.

KELLY CASTLE

Renfrewshire   Ruin or site   OS 63   NS 198685

2 miles south of Inverkip, on minor road east of A78 and Wemyss Bay Pier, on north bank of Kelly Burn, south of Kelly Mains.

Site of a castle of the Bannatynes. In the 15th century James Bannatyne received a grant of these lands from James III. He was descended from the Bannatynes of Kames on Bute and founded a cadet line at Kelly. Their castle was destroyed by fire in 1740 and never rebuilt, and the Bannatyne line ended with heiresses during the 18th century.

In 1792 the estate was purchased by John Wallace of Neilstonside and Cessnock. He constructed a new house in 1793, which was extended by his son, Robert. He enhanced the value of the estate by land exchange, increasing the arable land, planting woodland, and introducing pheasant and grouse. By 1818 Kelly House was described as being one of the finest seats on the Firth of Clyde. It was later occupied by Sir James 'Paraffin' Young, pioneer of oil technology. This house was demolished and replaced by another new house, designed by William Leiper, for the Stephen family in 1890. This was burned down in 1913, probably by suffragettes.

By the 19th century only a smooth grassy knoll was evident at the site of the castle; however there is now no trace. It lies in woodland overlooking a waterfall from the north bank of the Kelly Burn. The mansion sites are situated to the northwest within a caravan park.

Other references: Old Place of Kelly, Old House of Kelly

KEMP KNOWE

Renfrewshire Ruin or site OS 64 NS 494661

2 miles south of Renfrew, 1 mile north of Paisley, north of M8 and west of A741, by minor roads, at Marjory Road near Ross Avenue, Knock, Renfrew.

Site of a mound with ditch, recorded as a probable motte. In the late 18th century it was described as being about 20yds in diameter with a moat 5yds wide. The moat was about 4ft deep in 1710. In 1782 it was flattened and the ditch filled during agricultural improvements. The site is now covered by a housing estate.

The Knox family took their name from the lands of Knock, and had a manor house in the vicinity. The 18th century traveller Thomas Pennant was told that the Kempe Knowe was traditionally the site of the death of Somerled.

It was near here that Marjorie Bruce, daughter of Robert I and wife of Walter the High Steward, was thrown from her horse while heavily pregnant. She died, but her son was born by caesarean section and grew up to become Robert II, the first of the Stewart kings of Scotland. Robert was born with an eye deformity, possibly due to the caesarean cut, and became known as King Blearie.

A stone cross known as Queen Blearie's Cross was said to mark the site.

KENMUIR

City of Glasgow Ruin or site OS 64 NS 660622

On south side of M74, 1 mile east of Carmyle, 0.25 miles north of River Clyde, off minor roads east of A763.

Site of a tower, which appears in Blaeu's *Atlas Novus* of the 17th century. The site is now occupied by ruined farm buildings, and are now surrounded by a land-fill site, sewerage works and the M74. The site has the ruin of a later house, which burned down in recent years.

Carmyle and Kenmuir were parts of a parcel of land gifted to the monks of Newbattle Abbey by the Bishop of Glasgow in the 12th century. From that time, these lands lay within Monkland Parish, though ownership seems periodically to have reverted to the bishops.

A property known as Kenmure was held by the Colquhouns but this is more likely to have been elsewhere. In 1681 this estate belonged to John Millar, who was still in possession in 1710. Later in the 18th century two houses at Kenmuir were occupied by Messers Scot and Corbet, though one of these was newly built. By 1816 the remaining house was occupied by the Balfours. Both the Scots and the Balfours had married the Corbet heiresses. A third heiress married William Wilson. In 1820 the estate was at the centre of a legal battle over inheritance and Corbet trustees seem to have been in possession. Even at this late date, it is recorded that the Duke of Hamilton was the feudal superior.

A tale is told of a boy from Kenmuir and his closest friend and neighbour from Carmyle. The boys were inseparable life-long friends, but both fell hopelessly in love with a young maiden who had recently moved into the area. She preferred one to the other, tensions grew, and the boys decided to battle for the girls' affections. The resultant sword fight was fatal to both and their families buried the boys together, inseparable even in death. The spot where their duel and burial took place was once called 'Bloody Neuk'.

A spring in the area naturally produced a brownish-red deposit of iron oxide, which for many years the locals believed was associated with the burial.

In the 20th century Kenmuir was the property of a family named Wilson, possibly the descendants of the heiress mentioned above. The last occupant constructed a display of building facades built from restored sandstone recovered from the landfill. This originated from demolished tenements in Glasgow. They still provide a conspicuous landmark adjacent to the motorway.

A modern housing estate is said to be in the planning stages for the former farmlands around the site. The landfill is to be closed and apparently planted with up to one million trees.

KEPPOCH

The Lennox & East Dunbartonshire   Ruin or site   OS 63   NS 330798
North of A814, 1.5 miles west of Cardross and 3 miles southeast of Helensburgh, at Keppoch.

Site of a building, described variously as a fortalice, peel tower or tower house, which was recorded in 1545 as being a property of the Stirlings of Glorat. It passed to the Ewings in the 17th century.

Nothing remains of the original building and the site is now occupied by a mansion. This dates from 1820 when it was built for Alexander Dunlop. In the 19th century it was owned by the Baird family. There is a walled garden, which may predate the mansion, and both are 'B' Listed.

KERSEWELL

South Lanarkshire   Ruin or site   OS 72   NT 008472
2 miles northeast of Carnwath, 1 mile northwest of Newbigging, off minor road east of A70 and north of the A721 at Bertram House.

Site of a tower, depicted on Pont's manuscript map of the late 16th century, later replaced by a mansion.

Since the 12th century this had been part of the Somerville's Carnwath estate. It is said that Robert I granted the lands of Kersewell to Andrew Douglas, and that they had formerly belonged to Henry of Winton, 'deceased'. The estate was then held by Sir John Herring of Edmonstone, before being repurchased by Sir John Somerville in 1461-2. It devolved to the Cambusnethan branch of the family. In 1524 the estate was granted to Sir James Hamilton of Finnart.

By 1617 Kersewell was in the possession of John Chiesly, minister of Quothquan. His son, Sir John, inherited in 1636. At the Scottish Parliament of 1649, he was appointed Master of Requests to King Charles I. His son, another Sir John, was a man of notoriously bad temper. In 1689 he gained lasting infamy as the man who killed Sir George Lockhart of Carnwath, President of the Court of Session, following a decision against Chiesly in court.

Sometime in the early 18th century Kersewell was purchased by the Bertrams. They built the mansion known as Kersewell House, called on the OS map Bertram House. The family retained it until the 20th century.

By 1947 it was an agricultural college and was used to house refugees from Vietnam in the 1980s. It then came into use as commercial premises, hosting a variety of business ventures. In 2005 an archaeological assessment of the estate was conducted in advance of plans to construct a golf, spa and leisure facility. A number of sites of archaeological interest were identified.

Both the house and the walled pheasantry are 'B' Listed Buildings.

Other references: Bertram House, Carsewell

KILALLAN HOUSE

Renfrewshire   Private   OS 63   NS 382689
1.5 miles east of Kilmacolm, on minor roads east of A761, 0.5 miles southeast of Lawfield Dam, at Killallan.

Killallan (or Kilellan) House is a stout 17th century two-storey house with attic and corbiestepped gables. There is a projecting round tower with turnpike stair. The slate roof is steeply pitched, and there are later single-storey extensions from both east and west gables.

The rectangular main block runs east west. At the eastern end the stair tower projects to the north. The entrance is in the south wall, opposite the stair tower, an unusual arrangement. Some of the windows have been enlarged, though a few retain their original moulded recesses. The door is similarly set within mouldings. From the entrance, a door to the left gives access to an un-vaulted basement. The kitchen has been converted into a public room, with a smaller moulded fireplace than the original. This has been reset from a room on the floor above. There is an aumbry in the northern wall. Beyond the kitchen is a private room. The plan on the first floor is similar. Above the kitchen was the hall, with a bedroom beyond. The attic contains two further rooms, a large dormer window having been built into the roof for one of these.

The house was renovated and extended in 1783, 1921, and again in 1962-3. Kilallan was originally the manse of the parish of the same name, until its amalgamation with Houston in 1777. It is now used as a farmhouse.

In 1659 the Reverend Alexander Jamieson was ordered to remain in the house by the Privy Council. He was alleged to have suffered at the will of the 'Witches of Pollok', being possessed or cursed, and was compelled to harm himself or others. The house is a 'B' Listed Building.

The ruined church of St Fillan stands just to the southwest of the house, and originated in the 8th century. A hollowed stone nearby is named St Fillan's Seat in his honour. There is also a spring known as St Fillan's Well, which was thought to have healing properties. Infirm children were brought to the well and pieces of cloth left until the end of the 17th century. The water is said to have been used in baptisms in the church. The well now provides water for cattle. The church and churchyard are a Scheduled Ancient Monument and grade 'B' Listed building.

KILLEARN HOUSE

Stirlingshire   Ruin or site   OS 57   NS 505847
1.5 miles southwest of village of Killearn, to west of A81 and to east of Blane Water, at Killearn House.

Killearn House is a once ruinous 19th century mansion, which stands on the site of an old or fortified house known as 'Croyleckie'.

From as early as mid 15th century, Croyleckie was the property of the Leckie family. John of Croyleckie is said to have married the sister of Rob Roy MacGregor in 1677. He and Rob Roy fought together for the Jacobites in the 1715 rebellion and were involved in the Battle of Sheriffmuir. As a result, John had his estates forfeited and he fled into exile. Croyleckie became the property the Muirhead family, merchants in Glasgow. Afterwards it came to Professor William Richardson of Glasgow University, upon whose death in 1814 the estate was sold.

In 1816 Killearn House was built on the site for the Glasgow sugar merchant, John Blackburn, who had purchased all the estates in the parish outright. He was descended from a third son of Blackburn of Househill. His family remained in possession at least until the end of the 19th century. It has recently been restored as a complex of executive dwellings.

Other references: Croy, Croyleckie

KILMACOLM CASTLE

Renfrewshire   Ruin or site   OS 63   NS 361693
South of old part of Kilmacolm, near A761, east of Gryffe Water. The position given is that indicated in Blaeu's *Atlas Novus*.

Site of a castle which appears as 'Kilmakobam' in Blaeu's *Atlas Novus* of 1654 and on Herman Moll's map of 1745. This, however, may be a transcription error from Pont's map, which clearly shows a large tower to the north of the town. This coincides better with place name evidence such as Old Hall, Wateryetts and Plaintreeyetts, which lay as a local group on Roy's map. There was also a later property known as Castlehill to the west of the town.

Kilmacolm was within the Renfrewshire estates over which the Dennistouns and then Cunninghames held superiority. It was also within the Barony of Duchal, which was held by the Lyles until the 1540s, when it was purchased by the Porterfields. Their family tomb dated 1560 was repositioned within the graveyard on the rebuilding of the old Kirk in 1831.

KILMAHEW CASTLE

The Lennox & East Dunbartonshire   Private   OS 63   NS 352787
1 mile north of Cardross by minor roads north from A814, 0.5 miles east of Kirkton, just northwest of Kilmahew House.

Kilmahew consists of a ruined 15th century keep of five storeys and a garret. The south and west walls were rebuilt in the 19th century, with a view to incorporating the keep in a gothic mansion, which was never completed. Only the north and east walls survive of the 15th century building. These stand to their wallheads. The northern-most portion of the west wall includes the entrance. Some of the internal features of the ruin were also altered, including a fireplace in the west wall and a variety of recesses.

The keep measured 46ft by 25ft, the main door on the ground floor being guarded from above by a machicolated projection at parapet level. The parapet itself was projected upon corbels. The lintel above the door once carried the inscription 'The peace of God be herein'. The stair originally rose from just within the doorway and the basement rooms do not appear to have been vaulted. The kitchen fireplace remains in situ on the north wall. The hall, as usual, was on the first floor. Some of the parapet corbelling survives.

The estate was held by the Napiers of Kilmahew from the 13th to 19th centuries. John Napier 'of the county of Dunbarton' appears in the Ragman Roll of 1296. He is said to have received a grant of the estate from the Earl of Lennox c.1290. In 1304 he was one of several knights who were punished and fined by Edward I for being members of the garrison who held Stirling Castle against him.

Charters of the estate were issued to William Napier and then to John Napier by David II and Robert II.

Various Napiers of Kilmahew appear as witnesses in documents issued by the Earls of Lennox in the 14th, 15th and 16th centuries. Peter Napier of Kilmahew was killed by the MacGregors at the Battle of Glenfruin in 1603. His heir, John, was one of the jury at the subsequent trial.

The castle became ruinous at some point and was partly rebuilt in gothic fashion. It is widely accepted that it was to be integrated within a never-completed mansion. It has been said that this was planned by George Maxwell Napier, who was virtually bankrupt by the time of his death in 1744. Parallels have been drawn with the original design details drawn by Roger Morris for Inveraray Castle. His project for the Duke of Argyll dates from 1744. George was a Maxwell of Newark, who had inherited Kilmahew from his maternal grandfather. He adopted the Napier surname on gaining the estate.

In 1820 the family sold off the estate in portions and the castle was given to Alexander Sharp in lieu of gambling debts. He is widely credited with the rebuilding work mentioned, though there are no records to confirm this. The original portions of land were then bought up by John Burns to reform a single estate before 1859. He built a new mansion, retaining the castle a folly. His Kilmahew House was subsequently incorporated within the buildings of St Peter's Seminary, which opened in 1948. These were derelict by 2007. The castle remains as he left it.

Kilmahew takes its name from an ancient chapel on the estate, dedicated to St Mahew or Mochta, who died in 535. Inscribed standing stone fragments uncovered there suggest that it may have originated as early as the 6th century. The surviving structure dates from the 15th century.

The castle is a Scheduled Ancient Monument and category 'B' Listed Building.

KILMARDINNY

The Lennox & East Dunbartonshire   Ruin or site   OS 64   NS 550727

In Bearsden, west of A81 Milngavie Road, south of Kilmardinny Loch, on Kilmardinny Avenue.

Site of a tower, which appears in Blaeu's *Atlas Novus* of 1654, though the name Mains has been transposed from a nearby property. Parts of the old house may be incorporated within the present Kilmardinny House.

Kilmardinny was anciently a portion of the Earldom of Lennox, which was divided c.1425. There was an 'early mansion' recorded on the site. The larger portion of the estate on which this developed was granted to Sir John Colquhoun of that Ilk, the remainder went to the Lennoxes of Balcorrach. The Colquhouns retained the estate at least until the early 18th century. It then became the property of a cadet line of the Grahams of Dougalston. The laird of Kilmardinny played host to the notorious drinking session, at which the laird of Garscadden died.

The old house was variously extended and remodelled before coming to John Leitch sometime before 1833. He had his own company which traded with the West Indies and spent his profits by extensively remodelling and extending the building to create the edifice which exists today. Leitch and his successors gradually purchased other portions of the original estate, until by the end of the 19th century about half of it had been acquired. It eventually became the property of East Dunbartonshire Council and now houses the Kilmardinny Arts Centre. It is a category 'A' Listed Building.

KILMARONOCK CASTLE

The Lennox & East Dunbartonshire
Ruin or site   OS 57   NS 455877
1 mile west of Drymen, north of A811,
on south bank of Endrick, at Kilmaronock.

The ruin of this 14th century keep stands
to second-floor level. Vaulting remains in
the basement and partially at first-floor level.
The walls vary in thickness from 7 to 8ft.

Formerly of four storeys, this large
keep had its entrance by removable ladder
on the east side of the second floor. This
led directly into a vaulted hall of 27ft by
19ft. A stair in the southeastern corner led
to the floors below, while another in the
northeastern corner led to the floors above.
In the hall above the main entrance, and
entered from the rising stairway, was a
musicians' gallery. There was a large
fireplace in the western wall. Either side of
this in the north and south walls were two
large transom and mullion windows, an
unusual feature in a secular building of this
date. Both windows have stone seating
within their recesses.

The basement was vaulted and
consisted of two chambers of unequal size.
The smaller, narrow chamber was accessed
only by a small stairway from the kitchen
above and may have been the prison. The larger was probably a wine cellar and was illuminated by three small slit
windows.

The first floor also had two differently sized chambers. The smaller vaulted room was very narrow and had a
fireplace. This appears to have been the kitchen and had no windows. At one of its narrow ends was the base of the
staircase from above, which at its head had a passage to the prison. A doorway from the kitchen led to a larger
vaulted chamber with three small windows and the stairway down to the wine cellar.

The third floor also had transom and mullion windows, this time with arched heads. The single large room of
this floor had many mural chambers and recesses. On the southern exterior, the wall projected to provide further
chamber space from the first floor upwards, possibly as garderobes.

The base of the keep slopes outward on all sides. This feature was known as a talus, which provided extra
stability on soft ground and allowed missiles dropped from above to ricochet into assailants. There may have been
a moat supplied with water from the River Endrick a few yards away.

The lands were anciently part of the Earldom of Lennox, but were granted to Sir Malcolm Fleming in 1329.
The estate became the dowry of his daughter, who married Sir John de Danyelston, or Dennistoun. His son, Sir
Robert, was one of several hostages given to the English as ransom for David II in 1357. As reward the family were
granted the hereditary keepership of Dumbarton Castle, large grants of land and the Sheriffdom of Lennox. The
Dennistouns built the keep, and their coat of arms adorned the wall above the door. Sir Robert died toward the
end of the 14th century and the estates were divided between his two daughters. The male line continued through
the Dennistouns of Colgrain. Kilmaronock passed to Margaret, wife to Sir William Cunninghame of Kilmaurs,
whose descendants became Earls of Glencairn.

They passed the Barony of Kilmaronock to the first Earl of Dundonald in the 17th century. He granted the
property to his second son, William Cochrane. The estate was broken up and let to various tenants, the keep going
to John M'Goune in the 18th century. The castle thereafter deteriorated and was ruinous by the mid 19th century.

The remains stand within the grounds of Kilmaronock House, a 19th century mansion, modernised in 1901.
The tower is a Scheduled Ancient Monument and both the tower and house are category 'B' Listed Buildings.

Other reference: Mains of Kilmaronock

KILSYTH CASTLE

The Lennox & East Dunbartonshire Ruin or site OS 64 NS 717787

North of the A803, northeast of Kilsyth, and south of Allanfauld Farm, on Allanfauld Road, above the banks of the Garrel Burn.

Kilsyth lay within the great central Scotland estates of the de Callendar family. The estates came to the Livingstons by marriage, and a cadet line was established at Balcastle by Sir William Livingston, who died in 1459. He built a substantial tower house on this site. His descendants distinguished themselves from other branches of the family by adding an 'e' to the end of their name. In 1500 his son or perhaps grandson, William, built a court with kitchens and an L-plan corner tower. He died at Flodden in 1513. Another Sir William was knighted in 1565, when Lord Darnley was created Duke of Albany. The next Sir William, his son, was part of an embassy to France led by the Duke of Lennox. His infant son was knighted at the birth of Prince Henry in 1595. William added a three-storey domestic range to the castle in 1600. Appointed as Lord of Session in 1609, he became a Privy Councillor and Vice Chamberlain of Scotland in 1613. His knighted son inherited, but this next Sir William's heir died in infancy.

The estate passed to his uncle, James Livingstone. He garrisoned and strengthened the castle against Cromwell, who spent the night in the castle after its capture in 1650, before blowing up the main tower and burning the rest. It was subsequently used as a quarry providing stone for many of the field walls in the area. In 1661 James was created Viscount Kilsyth and Lord Campsie by Charles II, but his second son William, the 3rd and last Viscount, was forfeited for backing the Jacobites in the rising of 1715. He fled to exile in Holland and died in Rome.

The site was excavated in 1976 as a part of it was prepared for house building. A rocky outcrop supported a rubble mound which covered wall remnants and foundations, reaching a height of 4 ft. This structure was dated to c.1500 and was the remnant of a small L-plan tower with a double garderobe chute in the re-entrant. There was a postern door in the smaller southern wing. Courtyard walling ran through into the next field, where there was evidence of further buildings. The remains extended to the gully of the Garrel Burn. Artefacts recovered included a coin of Charles I, a green-glazed pot, a bronze spoon and the basket hilt from a broadsword. These have gone to various museums, including Colzium House, the Hunterian Museum, Kelvingrove Museum, and to Castle Cary. Some of the more interesting blocks of masonry from the site have made their way to the Colzium House Museum. In 2002 wall remnants standing to a height of about 3ft were recorded and drawn at the site, one of these still had plaster rendering.

Other reference: Allanfauld

KINCAID CASTLE

The Lennox & East Dunbartonshire Private OS 64 NS 650760

Just south of Milton of Campsie, and just west of B757, and south of Glazert Water, at Kincaid House Hotel.

Site of a castle, which may have stood some way to the west, possibly at Castlehill (NS 632753).

The lands known as Kincaid, Kincaith or Kyncaid, lay between the Glazert Water and the River Kelvin. They were Galbraith property and were tenanted out to Patrick Graham sometime after 1273. In 1290 the estate was sold to a local family, who adopted the name Kincaid as their own. The origins of the family are not known, but some references claim a descent from the old Celtic Earls of Lennox. Their coat of arms bears a triple towered castle. They had been appointed hereditary Constables of Edinburgh Castle following an ancestor's 'valiant efforts' in recovering it from Edward I during the Wars of Independence.

In 1461 John of Kincaid was Keeper of Linlithgow Palace, and Patrick of Kincaid was squire to James IV. Seven Kincaids are said to have been in the retinue of Lord Fleming when he accompanied James V to France for his marriage to Madeleine de Valois. Cadet branches of the family held lands in Perthshire, Linlithgow, Leith and at Warriston in Edinburgh.

In 1563 as part of an ongoing feud, James and Malcolm, the sons of Kincaid of that Ilk, were attacked in Glasgow by Stirling of Glorat, Stirling of Craigbarnet and 19 others. James received a head wound and was 'put in peril of his life', while Malcolm's wounds were so severe that he lost the use of his left arm. In 1581 Stirling of Glorat, the son of Stirling of Craigbarnet and their accomplices were tried for 'the crewell slaughter' of the same Malcolm. His brother Thomas avenged him by killing Luke Stirling of Baldoran, one of the original assailants. Luke left a widow and 'ten faderles bairnis'.

In 1690 the family abandoned their original castle and built Kincaid House. In the early 19th century, despite an ancient feud between the families, John Kincaid of that Ilk married Cecilia Lennox, the heiress of Woodhead. They adopted the joint surname of Kincaid-Lennox. Their son built the grandiose mansion of Lennox Castle to impress his remote claim to the Earldom of Lennox, a claim which failed. The family mausoleum is one of several ancient graves in the church yard at Clachan of Campsie. The house was extended in 1712 and then rebuilt by the architect David Hamilton in 1812. It is now the Kincaid House Hotel (www.kincaidhouse.com). It is said that the Kincaids were in possession of an old broadsword engraved with their arms and the motto, 'Wha' will persew, I will defend, my life and honour to the end'. The hotel is a grade 'A' Listed Building.

Other reference: Kyncaid

KIRK BURN MOTTE

South Lanarkshire   Ruin or site   OS 64   NS 639585

1 mile south of Cambuslang, north of the A749, and east of the B759, in a small wood adjacent to Kirkhill Golf Course.

Protected on the east by the gully of the Kirk Burn and on the south and north sides by ditches, this motte has a diameter of 120ft at the base and 50ft on its summit. There is no evidence of a ditch on the west, where it reaches a height of only about 7ft above the adjacent ground, whist the maximum height above the burn to the east is 28ft. A ramp to the summit was evident around the north side in the first half of the 20th century. This is now difficult to discern. Descriptions of the 1920s tell that terraced medieval cultivation was evident on the slopes nearby. The site is wooded and the east side overgrown by gorse.

The motte sits within the boundaries of the old barony of Drumsagard, the church of which has always been referred to as Cambuslang. The name of the barony was changed to match that of the church at a later date. It is widely assumed that the Olifards built this motte, but there is no evidence to show that they actually owned Drumsagard, even though it was owned at a later date by the Murrays who had inherited Bothwell from them in the mid 13th century. Hugh Crocket of Cambuslang rendered homage to Edward I in 1296.

The motte has not been excavated and remains undated. The site is a Scheduled Ancient Monument. Despite this there is recent evidence of digging by people with metal detectors on the mound.

Other reference: Greenlees Motte

KIRKHOPE TOWER

South Lanarkshire   Ruin or site   OS 72   NS 968065

6 miles south of Elvanfoot, off minor roads east & south of A702, below waters of Daer Reservoir near Kirkhope Cleugh.

Low-water levels in 1995 allowed partial excavation of the ruins of a 20ft square tower with walls 4ft thick. There were roll moulded window and door frames, a vaulted basement and a projecting stair tower. A byre drain was recorded through the mid line of the basement. What remains is now perceived to be a bastle house. Another period of low water in the reservoir allowed further examination of the site in 2001. There appear to be further buildings within the complex, the foundations of which produced pieces of green-glazed medieval pottery. A cobbled road surface and an open drain were also noted.

In 1449 one of the sons of James Hamilton of Cadzow had a charter of Quhitecamp (Silvertonhill) and Kirkhope from the Earl of Crawford. By 1615 Kirkhope was held by Sir Robert Hamilton of Grinleys. The Barony of Daer was created in 1646 for the Douglas Earl of Selkirk and it passed to the Duke of Hamilton in 1885. During that period, Kirkhope is known to have been rented by a non-resident farmer.

Other references: Daer, Daerhead

KIRKHOUSE

South Lanarkshire   Ruin or site   OS 72   NT 098463

On A702, 7 miles southwest of West Linton, southwest of Dolphinton Churchyard, at Kirkhouse Farm.

Site of a small tower of the Browns of Dolphinton, which was occupied by James Brown in 1695.

KIRKINTILLOCH PEEL

The Lennox & East Dunbartonshire   Ruin or site   OS 64   NS 651740

In Kirkintilloch, south of A803, in Peel Park, southwest of the confluence of Luggie Water and River Kelvin.

Nothing remains of a 13th century castle of the Comyns, known as Kirkintilloch Peel or Castle, other than a large rectangular platform. This measures 56ft by 98ft and has the remnants of a ditch on the south and east sides. In 1732 it was reported that it had a double rampart made of lime-mortared stone which was in the process of being quarried away. The ditch is said to have been 30ft wide and there were also reported to have been earthen ramparts of 40-50ft thick surrounding all sides. Given the location on the line of the Antonine Wall, early historians assumed that the site was Roman in origin and there is archaeological evidence of a fort in the vicinity. It seems to have been this which led to the use of the term peel, implying a palisaded enclosure. Medieval records consistently use the term castle for the stronghold at Kirkintilloch. The hill beside Lenzie railway station has been suggested as a likely site for another early castle within the barony.

In the 12th century Thorald, Sheriff of Stirling, was lord of the manor of Kirkintilloch. His son William granted the church to the monks of Cambuskenneth in 1195. These are probably the same individuals mentioned as progenitors of the Stirlings of Cadder. It then seems to have become the property of the king for a brief period.

Lenzie, including Kirkintilloch, was granted by William the Lion to William Comyn for one knight's service shortly before 1200. The extent of the land was decreed as being the same as that which the king had held. It is from this period that the castle is first mentioned.

Comyn was a great grandson of Donald Ban, twice King of Scots in the 1090s. Like his father, William became Justiciar of Lothian, which was all Scotland south of the Forth. In 1212 he married Marjory, the heiress of the Earl of Buchan and immediately adopted that title. His sons from a previous marriage became Lords of Badenoch and his elder son by Marjory, Alexander, continued the Buchan line. Alexander was succeeded by John, who became Robert the Bruce's main rival for the throne.

In the aftermath of the Battle of Dunbar in 1296, Kirkintilloch was surrendered to James the High Steward, who had recently pledged allegiance to Edward I. It was garrisoned and strengthened for Edward, but the archers and crossbowmen of the garrison are known to have petitioned the parliament in England for arrears of wages in 1305.

In 1306 Bruce killed John's cousin, John 'the Red' Comyn, at Dumfries. He snatched the throne then forfeited the entire family during a campaign which destroyed their lands and power. John fled to England and became the English Warden of the West Marches. He died in 1308.

In 1306 Bishop Wishart of Glasgow used mangonels in a successful siege of Kirkintilloch. These siege engines were allegedly built from wood granted by Edward I for the repair of the spire at Glasgow Cathedral. The castle was in English hands in 1309-10 when Sir Phillip de Mowbray was the English appointed constable. Sir Philip's mother was the daughter of the Red Comyn. By 1314 Philip was Governor of Stirling Castle and it was he who made the deal with Edward Bruce which led to the Battle of Bannockburn.

Robert I, Bruce granted the barony, by then known as Kirkintilloch, to Malcolm Fleming. This was again for one the service of one knight. The family preferred a site at Cumbernauld and founded the castle there. Kirkintilloch seems to have fallen out of use or, as seems likely, did not survive either the wars or Bruce's harrying of the Comyn lands.

John Kennedy of Dunure is said to have married the daughter of Sir Malcolm Fleming and probably came into possession of Kirkintilloch as a result. In 1384 the Flemings, as superiors, confirmed a tailzie of the 40 merk lands of Kirkintilloch from John to his son Gilbert. In 1466 his grandson, Gilbert, Lord Kennedy, won a legal case reclaiming the lands from Lord Fleming. The tailzie document was the decisive evidence. The Flemings regained the estate at a later date, possibly by default when the Kennedy's were forfeited. In 1526 Kirkintilloch was erected into a Burgh of Barony for another Malcolm, Lord Fleming.

The castle site lies within a Scheduled Ancient Monument which encompasses both the Roman antiquities and the castle site.

Other references: Lenzie Castle, Peel of Kirkintilloch

KIRKTONHOLME

South Lanarkshire Ruin or site OS 64 NS 633547
0.5 miles northwest of East Kilbride town centre, just south of B761, at East Kilbride railway station.

Site of an old or fortified house. In 1559 James Hamilton received a charter of the lands of Kirktonholme, although the name suggests that the estate had previously belonged to the church. The Hamiltons retained possession until 1666, and in 1710 it belonged to a younger son of Montgomerie of Skelmorlie. About 1760 the old house was destroyed by lightning. The estate passed by marriage to the Montgomerie-Cunninghame family of Corsehill, who built an elegant new mansion on the site. Various members of the family styled themselves Lord Lyle. The Montgomerie-Cunninghames continue as Baronets of Corsehill and have a claim to be Earls of Glencairn. The property does not appear on any maps after the building of the railway in the mid 19th century. Nothing remains.

KIRKTON OF CARLUKE

South Lanarkshire Ruin or site OS 72 NS 842503
0.25 miles west of Carluke, on minor roads west of A73, northeast of railway station, southern side of Station Road.

This mansion was demolished before 1970. It had as its core an altered three-storey tower house. The older section had a projecting tower with narrow turnpike stair, although it had replacement windows and a new roof. There was a vaulted basement and the hall was as usual on the first floor. A date-stone of 1600 had been re-sited on the newer part of the building, while the eastern gable supported a date of 1618. Excavation in 2007 revealed that the earliest building had been rectangular. Sandstone foundations were discovered of a building which had twice been extended to the south in the 19th century. The archaeologists report that examination of photographs of the former building suggested a medieval origin and that it would have been unusual for such a structure to have originated as late as the 17th century.

The lands of Kirkton anciently belonged to Kelso Abbey. They became the property of the Weirs of Kirkton, cadets of the Weirs of Stonebyres. A son of Weir of Kirkton, Major Thomas Weir, was a renowned soldier who had fought in Ulster during the Irish rebellion of 1641. He signed the Solemn League and Covenant in 1643 and was an anti-Royalist during the civil war years. Retiring from the army, he commanded the Town Guard of Edinburgh. He reputedly mocked and abused the Marquis of Montrose while he was in custody awaiting execution. Weir's mother, Lady Jean Somerville, had a reputation as a clairvoyant and Thomas developed a reputation as one of Scotland's more notorious wizards.

While ill and possibly delirious in 1670, he began confessing to a life of sin and vice. He and his sister were taken to the Tollbooth of Edinburgh and interrogated. His sister gave an even more detailed account, alleging acts of witchcraft, sorcery and vice. A witness came forward who said that Weir's walking stick had been observed moving ahead of him as he walked down a street. The corroboration was damning and brother and sister were tried and condemned for execution by strangulation and burning. Before the sentence was carried out he made further confessions of fornication, adultery, bestiality and incest with his sister. His story has been cited as one of the influences for Robert Louis Stevenson's *Strange Case of Dr Jekyll and Mr Hyde*.

The property passed to the Lockharts of the Lee in 1662, and by 1891 was held by the Hamiltons of Fairholm.

Other reference: Carluke

KNIGHTSWOOD

City of Glasgow Ruin or site OS 64 NS 530695
At or near Knightswood Cross, Glasgow.

Possible site of a 15th century tower house. The knights were the Knights Templar, who in early days kept this ground as their hunting forest. They had their Temple at what is now Anniesland where the name Temple survives. It is possible that mention of a tower here referred to Cloberhill.

KNOCKDERRY CASTLE

The Lennox & East Dunbartonshire Private OS 56 NS 218836
1 mile north of Cove, on minor road just off B833, on east shore of Loch Long, at Knockderry Castle.

Perched on a rocky outcrop, Knockderry Castle is a mansion of 1855 which was enlarged in 1886. It is said to be built upon the foundation of a Norse watchtower of the 13th century and is alleged to be haunted by ghosts associated with its dungeons.

KNOWNOBLEHILL

North Lanarkshire   Ruin or site   OS 64   NS 794589
1 mile southeast of Newarthill, off minor roads south of A723, 0.5 miles west of Knownoble, at Knownoblehill.

Site of a tower house, also recorded as Knowhoblehill, of the Cleland family, of which the vaulted basements were still visible just prior to 1880.

Arthur of Knownoblehill was the first of this cadet branch of the Clelands. As a son of James Cleland of that Ilk, he inherited the estate from his father in 1547. He was accused of complicity in the murder of Henry, Lord Darnley. Like his brother, he was a devoted follower of Mary, Queen of Scots, and as a result was accused of treason against James VI in 1572.

In 1662 John Cleland of Knownoblehill was accused of being a Covenanter and fined £200. From about 1720, the family seem to have moved to the nearby property of Auchinlea and taken their designation from there. This may have been due to the sale of the Cleland estates in 1711. From about that date the Clelands of Auchinlea claimed to be the senior line. They held Knownoblehill until about 1800, but they sold Auchinlea to the banker Robert Carrick in 1820.

KYPE

South Lanarkshire   Ruin or site   OS 71   NS 708417
3 miles south of Strathaven by minor roads south of the A71, west of the B7086, at Hall of Kype.

The name Hall of Kype is suggestive of a fortified house. It is likely that there were a number of old or fortified houses on the lands and numerous property names appear in the records. Some of these may refer to the same place.

Richard Bard or Baird held Avondale from the de Bigres (Biggar) family until 1228, when he granted Little Kype and the tithes of Meikle Kype to the monks of Lesmahagow. In 1315 they exchanged it with Reginald de Currokis (Corehouse) for his land at Fincurrokis. Reginald's son Andrew resigned it to the monks in exchange for a pension of four silver merks. Little Kype came into the possession of the Hamiltons, and in 1511 John Hamilton of Broomhill was given a tack of the lands of Langkype by Andrew Stewart, Bishop of Caithness and Commendator of Kelso Abbey. In 1520 the Earl of Lennox granted a charter at Glasgow to James Stewart of Tweedy for the lands of Kype, at that time occupied by various tenants. There are then references to a number of Hamiltons owning different portions of Kype. Alexander Dalzell of Kype is recorded in 1572 when, among many others, he was charged with complicity in the murders of Henry, Lord Darnley, and the two Regents. Sir James Hamilton stood security to the sum of 500 merks.

Gavin Hamilton of Kype is recorded in 1648-9. In 1650 his son John inherited West Kype and James, possibly a second son, received a charter of Longkype. In the same year Cromwell is alleged to have stayed overnight at Hall of Kype, en route to Ayr following the Battle of Dunbar. Robert Burn's friend, Gavin Hamilton of Mauchline, to whom he dedicated his *Kilmarnock Edition*, was the fifth son of John Hamilton of Kype.

A senior ancestry is claimed for the Hamiltons of Kype, via the branches of Preston and Fingalton, to David Fitzwalter, 2nd of Cadzow. This perhaps explains the reported comments of a laird of Kype, who was asked by the Duke of Hamilton from which branch of the family he descended. He replied, 'It would be needless to seek the root amongst the branches', implying his own seniority.

There is a tale that, in 1335, an English army led by John of Eltham, Earl of Cornwall, put Avondale to the sword. It is said that Eltham packed St Bride's Chapel with locals, and burned both. His brother Edward III was said to have been so furious at this act of malice, that he stabbed Cornwall to death when they met at Perth. The same story is told of Lesmahagow Priory by John of Fordoun. Cornwall did lead the army through this part of Scotland, burned the Abbey, and died at Perth, though probably of a fever. He was buried in Westminster Abbey.

Other references: Hall of Kype, Lang Kype, Little Kype, Meikle Kype, St Bride's Chapel, West Kype

LADLE KNOWE

South Lanarkshire   Ruin or site   OS 72   NS 826294
1 mile southwest of Douglas, north of A70, and immediately south of Douglas Water near confluence with Moss Burn.

This descriptively named oval motte stands to a height of 12ft and measures 100ft by 85ft at the base, and 60ft by 45ft on the summit. About a third of the motte has been lost due to erosion by the river. There is no obvious evidence of a ditch or a bailey. It is now hidden below a conifer plantation.

Local legend tells that this was the original stronghold of the Douglas family.

LAMINGTON TOWER

South Lanarkshire   Ruin or site   OS 72   NS 980320
5 miles southwest of Biggar, on minor roads north and west of A702 at Lamington, just east of River Clyde.

Tall portions of the south and west walls remain of Lamington Tower, a late 16th century tower house of the Baillies. The almost square plan may indicate an earlier origin for the building and there was certainly an older house on the estate.

The remains are sited upon a gravel knoll, which sits above the flood plain of the Clyde. This was a rectangular keep of 38.75ft by 31.75ft with walls 6ft thick and bartizans on at least two corners. One of these remains, though it has been repositioned on the southeast corner – and was not present when the ruin was examined by MacGibbon and Ross in the late 19th century. This has been reset on top of a semi-ruinous wall and so sits at a lower level than its original position. The northwest bartizan, which was recorded as being in situ by the intrepid architects, now lies broken within a field to the east.

The north and east walls survive only to foundation level and must have contained the entrance, stair and hall fireplace, since no trace of these remain. The basement was vaulted, but only traces of this are visible on the southern wall. The hall was on the first floor and had a window within an arched recess in carefully dressed stone. On the rim of the south wall is a date-stone of 1589 which may have been re-sited. The uppermost courses of this wall have seemingly been rebuilt and the date-stone has the proportions of a keystone for an arch. Below the date-stone is a round gunloop which appears to be in situ. There are remnants of a garderobe, and a mural chamber has been partly built up to strengthen the ruin. A heraldic stone bearing the arms of the Baillies was removed to the Episcopal Chapel at Lamington. An engraving there states that it was removed from 'Wallace's Tower'.

The approach to the castle from Lamington Mains Farm is across a narrow area of raised ground which may have been built as a causeway across a notoriously flood prone area of ground. This tendency to flood makes the castle knoll a seasonal island.

Lamington takes its name from Lambin Asa, the original Flemish settler granted the barony by Malcolm IV. In 1266 Robert 'the Frenchman' was in possession when he acknowledged before the king that he had no rights to the lands of Ardoch, which were the property of Kelso Abbey. He was described as the son and heir of Henry, who was the son and heir of William of Ardoch. Robert's son William, 'an esquire of Scotland', pledged allegiance to Edward I in 1296, but was imprisoned by Edward in Fotheringhay Castle from April to October 1299.

In 1329 Lamington was the property of Alexander Seton, whose daughter Margaret received a grant from David II confirming her rights to the estate as her dowry. It has been suggested that the estate was then managed by Margaret's brother, Sir William Seton, and that his daughter inherited. She is then thought to have married William Baillie of Hoprig, who was granted the estate in 1368.

Later versions of Blind Harry's *The Wallace* tells that Baillie gained the estate by right of his wife, the supposed daughter of Sir William Wallace and Marion Braidfute. Marion was said to be the heiress of Sir Hugh Braidfute of Lamington. There is no factual evidence to confirm that Wallace married and none at all that he had children. Sir Hugh does not appear in any contemporary references and his designation 'of Lamington' appears to be at odds

with evidence of 'the Frenchman' and his heirs. Hazelrig is said to have held a castle at Lamington for Edward I. There are enticing possibilities, if it was not on the present site. Easterburn Motte is one obvious potential candidate, a second is the earthwork on Whitehill, to the northeast.

William Baillie was one of the hostages sent to England to secure the release of David II. David knighted him in 1357 and later awarded him the estate. Another William Baillie of Lamington was a favourite of James III, yet another was Master of the Queen's Wardrobe to Mary, Queen of Scots. She visited Lamington in 1565, and William was forfeited after supporting her at the Battle of Langside in 1568. It is possible that the older house was destroyed or damaged in one of the campaigns by the Regents during the minority of James VI.

William died in 1580 and the estate passed to his daughter, Margaret. Her husband, Edward Maxwell, was the younger son of Lord Herries. He adopted the Baillie arms and surname. The initials EB adorn the date-stone on the present ruin. He may have built the tower at this time, or perhaps repaired and remodelled an older structure. Inheritance through an heiress became a recurrent pattern, with marriages into the Carmichael, Ross, Dundas and Cochrane families, who each in turn adopted the Baillie surname.

The Parish of Lamington was combined with the Parish of Wandel in the 17th century. This led to a quarrel about the appointment of the minister, since Wandel was under the patronage of the Duke of Douglas, and Lamington of the Baillies. It led to lengthy litigation at the General Assembly of the Church of Scotland which resulted in the 1642 appointment of the Douglas candidate. Lady Lamington and others of the parish then occupied the pulpit in protest claiming that 'no dog of the house of Douglas should ever bark here!' Lady Lamington was sent to the Tollbooth in Edinburgh, and her husband fined 1,000 merks. The argument continued, and was finally settled at the Court of Session in 1821 when, after a vacancy of five years, Lord Douglas and Baillie of Lamington finally agreed to joint patronage, with alternate appointments.

The tower was still occupied in 1750, but was blown up in 1780 by the estate factor to free the stone to build dykes and farm buildings. It is said that, by the time an unhappy Lady Ross Baillie became aware of the demolition work, the damage was too severe to be remedied.

Alexander Cochrane Baillie inherited in 1833. A Conservative politician, he was appointed to the House of Lords in 1880 as Lord Lamington. He built the Elizabethan-style mansion known as Lamington House. Charles Wallace Alexander Napier Cochrane-Baillie was the 2nd Baron Lamington. He became Governor of Queensland, then Governor of Bombay at the dawn of the 20th century. He was assistant Private Secretary to the Prime Minister, Lord Salisbury. He gave the Lamington name to the famed Australian chocolate and coconut cake. He died at Lamington House in 1940. From 1902-10 his mother, Lady Mary Cochrane Baillie, held the position of Lady of the Bedchamber to the Princess of Wales, later Queen Mary. In World War II, Lamington House provided a safe home for children evacuated from cities to escape the bombing. The mansion was, however, demolished in the third quarter of the 20th century.

Lamington Tower is a Scheduled Ancient Monument and category 'A' listed Building.

Other reference: Wallace's Tower

LANARK CASTLE

South Lanarkshire   Ruin or site   OS 72   NS 879433
In Lanark, 0.75 miles south of A73, off minor roads, at Castlebank, at Lanark Thistle Bowling Club, Castlehill.

A huge motte remains of this 12th century earth and timber castle, which is now topped by the greens of a bowling club.

This was a royal castle, which existed during the reign of David I, and a number of charters were issued here by the kings of the Canmore dynasty. It is thought to have been built upon the site of an old fort, but the promontory has been scarped and shaped to accommodate the castle. The mound measures 300ft in diameter at the base and has a summit diameter of 165ft. The site has supported a bowling green for over two centuries and on construction the summit was levelled and possibly lowered. An imposing ditch to the north was filled in to provide access. The slopes around the edges of the mound are precipitous in places and there is recent evidence of minor landslip, particularly on the west. The slopes are now covered by mature woodland.

The castle hosted sittings of the Scottish Parliament in 1293, 94 and 95. It may have been used as a prison around this time. It was garrisoned and held by the English during the Wars of Independence. Sir William Wallace massacred the garrison and torched the castle after killing the English Sheriff, Hazelrig. It was presumably rebuilt, since it was recaptured from the English by Robert the Bruce in 1310. He then had it pulled down as part of his policy of rendering major strongholds indefensible by his enemies.

Coins of Edward I and of the Roman era have been found on and around the site. General Roy certainly believed that it was the site of a Roman fort; however it would not be typical as a choice of location. It is thought that the site may have been occupied by the local populace in that era. Recent excavation produced pottery of the 12th to 14th centuries, and 17th to 18th centuries. The site is a Scheduled Ancient Monument.

Other reference: Castlehill, Lanark

LANGTON

Renfrewshire Ruin or site OS 64 NS 501541
3.5 miles southeast of Neilston, and 3.5 miles southwest of Newton Mearns, off minor roads west of B769, 1 mile south of Craigton, and 0.5 miles south of Middleton, at Langton.

Possible site of a castle. Rectangular foundations measuring 50ft by 38ft, of walls 6ft to 15ft thick, were reported on the summit of a rocky outcrop. There was apparently evidence of an entrance on the west side, a ditch to the west and south, and there are steep drops to the east. A lintel stone from an old barn carrying the date 1610 with the monogrammed letters BMH is said to survive above a modern fireplace in the present house. The site was occupied by farm buildings in the 19th century. Compare with Fingalton and Middleton.

LANRIG

Renfrewshire Ruin or site OS 64 NS 535546
Off minor roads east of A77, and south of Newton Mearns, in woodland behind the former site of Mearnskirk Hospital.

This wooded knoll is a possible site of an early castle, which had been suggested as the Maxwell's original site at Mearns. They built their new castle and vacated the old site in 1449. An alternative site suggested as the 'new manor' of 1300 is on the hill now occupied by Paidmire Gardens, which was recorded in 1791 as being known as Castlehill. One assessor identified that these lands had been owned by the Templars and thought that the site may have been the remnant of a grange.

The site has been examined on several occasions and was first described as a rectangular enclosure, defended by crags and steep slopes augmented by ditches. The abutment for a wooden bridge was apparently visible over the southern ditch in 1982. There are surviving remnants of medieval rig and furrow in the vicinity.

A recent reassessment of the site identified the ditches, but no architectural fragments as originally described. The stone abutment originally noted was thought to be natural or the result of quarrying.

The Maxwells of Caerlaverock gained the estate of Mearns by marriage to the Pollok heiress c.1300. James II granted a licence to build the new castle in 1449. One of the family died at Flodden in 1513, another was imprisoned in the Tower of London while Ambassador to France in 1542. He was ransomed. The Maxwells of Nether Pollok inherited in 1648, and the lands later came to the Schaw-Stewarts of Ardgowan and Inverkip.

LARABANK CASTLE

Renfrewshire Ruin or site OS 63 NS 328586
1.5 miles west of Lochwinnoch, by minor roads west of A760, just west of Glenlora.

A natural knoll has been shaped to form a motte-like platform, from which the foundations of a castle were removed in the 19th century. 'Larabanck' appears as a diminutive property on Pont's map of the late 16th century. In the 19th century it was the property of the Orr family.

The surviving motte measures about 65ft in diameter. The site is a Scheduled Ancient Monument.

Other reference: Lorabank Castle

LAUCHOPE HOUSE

North Lanarkshire   Ruin or site   OS 64   NS 781617

3.5 miles northeast of Motherwell, off minor roads, north of A8 and south of B799, south of Chapelhall and southeast of Lauchope Mains.

Site of a strong tower house of the Muirheads, which was later incorporated into a mansion, now demolished. Lauchope appears on Pont's map of c.1596 as a particularly large and important tower house of two blocks within a courtyard and an enclosed park. The tower is said to have had very thick walls.

The name 'Chappel' is prominent on Blaeu's *Atlas Novus* of 1654, but the name 'Lauchob' also appears. The chapel in question was ancient and dedicated to St Larsach. It was ruined by the 18th century but had become the burial place of the family. Although in modern times this area is included within Monklands, it was part of the vast parish and barony of Bothwell, though became part of Bertram Shotts when the parish was divided just after the Reformation.

In the reign of David II, Thomas de Moravia granted a charter of Over and Nether Lauchope to William Balyston. By the end of the 14th century, the Muirheads were in possession. In 1393 a William Muirhead was knighted by Robert III and as Sir William Muirhead of Lauchope appeared as a charter witness in 1401.

This first Muirhead of Lauchope was renowned as a hero nationwide, if the legend of the notorious robber baron Bertram of Shotts is to be believed. Bertram was a giant among men, deemed capable of fighting a dozen men at once, and winning! The crown was so concerned by his piratical antics that they offered a substantial reward for his removal. Muirhead was their man. Dumping a cart load of heather close by a well that the giant was known to use, Muirhead lay in wait for his victim. Sure enough Bertram came to drink, and after examining the curious pile, he bent over to sup from the well. Muirhead emerged from below the heather and struck the giant a fatal blow to the head with his sword. The story continues that Robert II was so grateful that Muirhead was granted the Lauchope lands as a result. This same hero supposedly died at Flodden, 140 years later! The existence of a Bertram of Shotts has never been shown in fact, though the legend warranted a mention in Sir Walter Scott's epic, 'The Ballad of the Battle of Flodden Field'. Other versions of the story place events in the reign of James IV.

There is another legend that John Muirhead, a younger son of Muirhead of Lauchope, became known as Stark after saving James III from an attack by a wild bull. He is said to have been granted lands and become the progenitor of the Starks of Auchinvole. James Muirhead of Lauchope is said to have died at the Battle of Flodden in 1513 while serving in the bodyguard of James IV.

The tower gave refuge to Hamilton of Bothwellhaugh in 1570, after his assassination of the Regent Moray in Linlithgow. Lauchope was burned in retaliation and the family papers destroyed. James Muirhead of Lauchope was Hamilton's brother-in-law and was imprisoned in Edinburgh Castle in the aftermath. In 1679 another James Muirhead and his brother, John, fought at the Battle of Bothwell Bridge for the Covenanters. Captured and tried, they refused to pledge allegiance to Charles II and were banished to the English colonies in America in 1685.

There is mention of a long-running feud between the Muirheads of Lauchope and the Clelands of that Ilk. The Muirheads died out in 1738 and the estate passed to a cadet branch, the Muirheads of Bredisholm. The property came into the possession of a branch of the Robertons of Earnock before 1816, and they are credited with building the mansion in 1839. This family were still in possession when the house was demolished in 1956.

LAW CASTLE

The Lennox & East Dunbartonshire   Ruin or site   OS 64   NS 515737

Off minor roads north of the A810, 1 mile west of Bearsden, and east of Duntocher, 100 yards south of Law.

Site of a 16th century tower of the Stirling family. The old tower of Law is said to have been demolished in 1890 to provide stone for offices at nearby Edinbarnet House. In 1981 the site was identified just to the south of the present farm. It is a low flat-topped mound, which is denoted as a possible motte by the RCAHMS. There are a number of worked stones within the dykes in the area.

Law was part of the Drumry estate of the Livingstones, which passed by marriage to Sir James Hamilton of Finnart after 1513. He sold Law to the Stirlings of Glorat about 1528, when he exchanged the remainder of his Drumry property with the Crawfords for their Kilbirnie and Crawfordjohn estates.

Andrew, the first of the Stirlings of Law, was the son of William, the first of Glorat. There were five Stirlings of Law before the line ended with an heiress. She was married to John Campbell of Succoth. Their son, also John, adopted the Stirling surname to inherit and became John Campbell-Stirling of Law, Edinbarnet and Kirklands, the latter being the family estate in Strathblane. John was a Hanoverian during the 1715 Jacobite rebellion and was one of the instigators of a plan to harness all the boats on Loch Lomond to prevent their use by the rebels. His son,

James, sold the Kirklands to his cousin of Craigbarnet and alienated other parts of the estate. By 1885 the Edinbarnet portion belonged to the MacKenzie family. They had J.J. Burnet design them the present Edinbarnet House, which is now a residential care home. It is a category 'B' Listed Building.

LAW'S CASTLE

North Lanarkshire   Ruin or site   OS 65   NS 826611
1 mile south of the B7066 at Salsburgh, by foot, or 0.5 miles by foot east of minor road at Jersay, on summit of the hill known as Law's Castle.

Site of a large castle, which appears on Blaeu's *Atlas Novus* of the 17th century. A complex of buildings is recorded on the site in General Roy's map of 1747-55. It appears as a ruin in Forrest's map of 1816, and again in John Thompson's map of 1832. There are no remains.

By 1880 it was said that 'there did not appear to have been a building on it'. The RCAHMS record this as a natural feature with a scatter of stones on a rocky knoll. In the 1930s these stones were known as the 'Cups and Plates' and the 'Giant's Stone'.

LEE CASTLE

Renfrewshire   Ruin or site   OS 64   NS 577585
5 miles south of Glasgow city centre, on the east side of the B767 (Clarkston Road), in Beechgrove Park, Netherlee.

This is the site of the 14th century castle of Lee. It was a property of the Cochranes of Lee in the 15th century, but in the 16th century was acquired by David Pollok, a grandson of Pollok of that Ilk. By 1603 he had also gained the estate of Balgray from the Park family. There were many marriages between the Pollok cousins, and the Balgray line eventually inherited Pollok Castle. Lee Castle was abandoned in the mid 17th century.

A large tower house appears as 'Overly' on Pont's map, though as a less prominent entry on Blaeu's *Atlas Novus*. In 1840 the foundations were removed and revealed a number of human bones which the *New Statistical Account* described as 'of almost superhuman magnitude'. The description indicated that the tower was square in plan. The site produced a large amount of pottery of the 14th and 15th centuries from among the roots of a fallen tree in 1985.

The location is within the

later estate of Williamwood, which became home to a cadet line of the Maxwells of Auldhouse. The traces of their house (NS 573587) on the estate were described in the 19th century as being 'in the style of Saxon architecture.' It existed before 1678 when ejected ministers were given shelter in the house. The Maxwells had developed their estate at Williamwood from those of Lee and Bogton in the 1660s.

It passed to the Stewart family, who held it until the 1930s. They built the second Williamwood House (NS 575587) in the 19th century, shortly before the *New Statistical Account* was written. The present and third house (NS 574586) was built in the 1930s, and is now a residential care home.

Other references: Overlee, Williamwood

LETHAME

South Lanarkshire   Ruin or site   OS 62   NS 687446

By minor roads north of A71 and west of A726, 1 mile west of Strathaven, just west of Lethame House.

Site of an old or fortified house of the Hamilton family. The present Lethame House is a large mansion of 1813, and is a 'B' Listed Building. The adjacent ruin is of an old cottage.

Archibald Hamilton was given a grant of Nether Lethame in 1531. In 1542 he gained a grant of Little Kype and St Bride's Kirk. His son and heir, Andrew, was Captain of Dumbarton Castle in 1546. He was involved in the Raid of Stirling in 1571, when supporters of the exiled Mary, Queen of Scots, tried to take control of the young James VI. The family held other estates at Drumcross and Kittiemuir. The 7th of the line, James, died without issue. The estate passed to his nephew, John Knox, who held it in 1816. He sold it to the Nisbets, from whom it may have passed to a family named Struthers.

LETTERICK

South Lanarkshire   Ruin or site   OS 64   NS 669572

1.5 miles southeast of Cambuslang, by minor road and track south of the A724, at Mid Letterick.

Site of an old or fortified house, also known as Lethrig. These lands were probably owned by William de Croketa or Hugh de Crocket in the 13th century, both of whom paid homage to Edward I in 1296. These two gentlemen were probably unrelated.

Later, the Hamiltons came into possession and donated the lands to the church in 1507. At the Reformation, they repossessed them, granting the estate to Sir John Hamilton of Lettrick, an illegitimate son of James Hamilton, Earl of Arran, who had him legitimized in 1600. Sir John gained the estate of Carriden, near Bo'ness, and built himself a tower there, which became his main residence. His son John became Lord Bargany in 1639, having purchased the Ayrshire estate from Thomas Kennedy.

In 1751 William Hamilton of Gilbertfield died at Letterick 'at an advanced age'. He was the soldier poet who translated Blind Harry's *The Wallace* into Scots, bringing it once again to the attention of the national audience. The screenplay for the film *Braveheart* was (loosely) based upon his work.

The overgrown and ruinous buildings at the eastern end of the site are of the Victorian farm complex.

Mention of Sir John de St Clair of Lethrig, who witnesses charters in the 15th century, refers to a property in the Lothians.

Other reference: Cambuslang Town

LICKPRIVICK CASTLE

South Lanarkshire   Ruin or site   OS 64   NS 617527

In East Kilbride, 2 miles south of A726, 1.75 miles east of B764, south of Troon Crescent just west of Lickprivick Road.

A castle here was said to have been 'no contemptible building', with 'towers, battlements etc'. It was in ruins by the 1733 and only 'some scattered rubbish' remained by 1793, then nothing at all by 1840. One source suggests that the castle dated to the early 17th century, but was said to have incorporated an earlier keep which, some say, may have been built by Sir James Hamilton of Finnart. A large tower appears on Pont's map of the late 16th century and in Blaeu's *Atlas Novus* of 1654.

The Lickprivick family are said to have been well known before the reign of Robert I and they were given a grant of the estate in 1397. 'For singular services' they were given the Sergeantcy and Coronership of the Lordship of Kilbride and apparently received grants of confirmation from James I, James IV and James VI. In 1569 Robert Lickprivick was printer to the General Assembly of the Church of Scotland. Reverend David Ure stated in 1793 that the last of the name died in Strathaven a few years previously.

Andrew Hamilton of Lickprivick, Shawfield and Midhope is mentioned in the Records of the Scottish Parliament as a Burgh Commissioner for Glasgow in 1546. It has been suggested that he was a natural son of Sir James Hamilton of Finnart and was forfeited for his part in supporting the cause of Mary, Queen of Scots, and fighting for her at the Battle of Langside in 1568. In 1572 he was returned to his estates by the Treaty of Perth. Robert Hamilton of Lickprivick was among another collection of forfeited landowners who were restored to their estates by Act of Parliament in 1584. By 1669 Lickprivick was the property of Anne, Duchess of Hamilton.

By 1793 the estate belonged to the Stewarts of Torrance. The Lickprivick name had moved to the farms of North and South Lickprivick, which formerly stood either side of Lickprivick Road at Greenhills shopping centre.

Other reference: Lekprevick

LICKPRIVICK MOTTE

South Lanarkshire Ruin or site OS 64 NS 616525
In East Kilbride, 2 miles south of A726, and 1.75 miles east of B764, west of Lickprivick Road and Greenhills Shopping Centre.

A mound on top of a small hill is associated with the 14th century castle of the Lickprivicks of that Ilk. In the 18th century it was described as 14ft in height, with a square summit, and measuring 36ft on each side. In 1954 it was measured at just 8ft high, with a summit measuring 23 ft by 23 ft. Modern landscaping or adjacent quarrying appear to have altered the mound, which now has an almost circular summit and a diameter of 79 ft. It is surmounted by a triangulation pillar.

LITTLE CALDWELL

Renfrewshire Private OS 64 NS 414550
1.5 miles west of Uplawmoor, west of A736 by minor roads, at junction of B775 and B776, at Hall of Caldwell.

A tower house here was illustrated on Pont's 1596 manuscript map of Renfrewshire. It was a property of Caldwells of that Ilk and was replaced or developed into a hall house known as Hall of Caldwell. The hall was on the first floor and is now divided into two rooms. It has a slate roof and corbiestepped gables.

The Caldwells of that Ilk had given much of their estate to the Mures through marriage in the 14th century. They continued to live here, the line ending with John Caldwell of that Ilk at the turn of the 18th century. The estate belonged to the Earl of Dundonald before 1710. In 1725, with Cowden, it passed by inheritance to the Hamilton Marquess of Clydesdale, who as Duke of Hamilton sold the estate to Mure of Caldwell in 1766.

Hall of Caldwell was subsequently extended and altered, notably in 1905-27. The present structure is a category 'B' Listed Building. The listing dates it to the 17th century and an arched gateway to a walled garden carries the date 1684.

Other references: Hall of Caldwell, Hall House, Wester Caldwell

LITTLE CLYDE

South Lanarkshire Ruin or site OS 78 NS 994161
3 miles southeast of Elvanfoot, by minor roads and track east of A74, opposite Beattock Summit, at Little Clyde.

Site of a tower of the Weirs, possibly of the Newton family. William Weir of Little Clyde died in 1603.

The farm midden marks the site of a large tower, which was demolished sometime before 1856. It is said to have stood within a group of trees to the west of the house and was described as a peel tower of the type found in the borders.

The entire site is scheduled as it is within the confines of the remains of a large Roman fort and above the major Roman road through Clydesdale. A fine steel sword was uncovered at the demolition.

Other reference: Little Clydeshead

LITTLEGILL

South Lanarkshire Ruin or site OS 72 NS 943261
1 mile north of Abington, east of A702 at Littlegill.

Site of a tower, illustrated on Pont's manuscript map of the late 16th century. No trace remains. Evidence of a settlement and rig and furrow cultivation has been found in the immediate vicinity. In 1710 Baillie of Littlegill lived in a house known as 'The Moat' in Roberton parish. The name was due to a 'tumulus' above the bank of the Clyde. This was in fact was the motte now known as 'Moat'. There was no house at Littlegill by that time.

Other reference: The Moat

LOCHWINNOCH MOTTE

Renfrewshire Ruin or site OS 63 NS 347582
0.5 miles southwest of Lochwinnoch, just east of the A 760, and northwest of Barr Castle.

A high rectangular mound, protected by depressed ground to the east and accessed by a rampart on the west, has been suggested as an earthwork predecessor to Barr Castle.

186

LOGAN'S RAIS

Renfrewshire   Ruin or site   OS 64   NS 505605
1 mile northwest of Barrhead, Off minor roads east of B 771 Grahamston Road, at Logan's Raes.

Site of a tower of the Logans, which was illustrated on Pont's map of c.1596 and in Blaeu's *Atlas Novus* of the 17th century.

John Logan of Rais witnessed the resignation of the lands of Fulton by William de Urry in 1409. Another John Logan of Rais was an arbiter between the Burgh of Renfrew and the Abbey of Paisley in 1488. John Logan of Rais, both elder and younger, appeared regularly in the records of Glasgow between 1613 and 1622.

By the early 19th century was a property of the Lords Ross, Earls of Glasgow, by which time 'there was no house on it'.

Other references: Rais, Raiss, Raith

MAIDEN CASTLE

The Lennox & East Dunbartonshire   Ruin or site   OS 64   NS 643785
3.5 miles northwest of Kirkintilloch, and 1 mile northeast of Lennoxtown, on lower slopes of Campsie Fells, 0.25 miles north of Glorat House.

A small, traditionally pudding-bowl shaped motte remains of a 12th century castle.

The motte is surrounded by a ditch 12ft wide and has a bailey. A burn protects the eastern side though this has caused some erosion, removing around a third of both mound and ditch. On the south, it reaches a height of 18ft from the base of the ditch, with a drop of 43ft to the bed of the burn on the east. The summit is 57ft in diameter.

The bailey was originally oval, 170ft by 140ft, but has been eroded by the action of hillside springs. It is marked out on the south and west by an overgrown stony bank, 12ft thick and 2ft high, possibly a collapsed wall. The eastern section of this has again been eroded by the burn. Parts of the boundary bank have also been destroyed by ploughing. On the north another long stony mound approximately 8ft high marks out an inner boundary. There is an 8ft gap which may mark an entrance. A similar structure marks an outer boundary.

Maiden Castle was probably one of a series of motte and baileys commissioned by the Earls of Lennox to guard traffic ways from north to south. It protected the southern end of the drove road through Campsie Glen to Fintry.

Other reference: Garmore

MAIN CASTLE

East Ayrshire   Ruin or site   OS 71   NS 612346
2 miles southeast of Darvel, by track and foot south of the A71.

Standing on the west bank of the infant River Avon, this site qualifies for inclusion as being within the watershed of the rivers Avon and Clyde.

Said to be the site of a 15th century castle, this motte-like mound has been interpreted as an Iron Age homestead by the RCAHMS and discounted as a motte only because of its isolation. It is said to be a natural knoll, which has been adapted to form a defensive site. It is oval in shape, and surrounded by a ditch. In the 19th century the summit was said to measure '25 paces by 10 paces' and was described as a fort. At that time foundations were visible on the summit. These were said to be of later date and measured 16 paces by 12. They ran over the top of the mound and through the ditch, and these were interpreted as a sheepfold.

MAINS

The Lennox & East Dunbartonshire   Private   OS 64   NS 539742
1 mile northwest of Milngavie, on minor road east of A809, just south of Mains housing estate, at Old Mains Farm

Site of a tower house of Douglases of Mains. Old Mains Farm incorporates portions of the original buildings. A square building with corbiestepped gables is thought to have been a doocot, while an adjacent house contains fragments of a much older building. This is now coated in cement render. The buildings are 'B' Listed.

This was a property of the Galbraiths of Culcreuch, and passed by marriage to Nicholas, a son of Douglas of Dalkeith in 1373. John, 5th Douglas of Mains, was killed at the Battle of Flodden in 1513. In 1562 the Regent Arran accused Malcolm Douglas and his father-in-law, John Cunningham of Drumquhassle, of participating in the Raid of Ruthven when the young James VI was taken prisoner. They were both beheaded for treason in 1585. In 1571 Matthew Douglas, Malcolm's father, assisted Crawford of Jordanhill in his 'Daring Raid' on Dumbarton Castle.

Malcolm's second son, Robert, became Page of Honour to Henry Stewart Prince of Wales, and upon the prince's early death was appointed Gentleman of the Bedchamber to James VI and I, then Master of the Household to Charles I. He was awarded the title Viscount Belhaven on being appointed to the Privy Council.

The 10th laird, Archibald, was the last in the direct line. The title passed to John Douglas of Ferguston, a descendant of the 4th laird. On his death, the estate went to his nephew, James Campbell, of the Blythswood family. He adopted the Douglas name. His daughter Margaret married the 1st Duke of Douglas and bequeathed money to purchase lands to be known as Douglas Support as an aid to the debt-ridden Mains estate. The 14th laird became Lord Blythswood in 1767.

Douglas Academy stands on the site of the old mansion of Balvie, ancient home of the Logans. In the early 19th century, this was purchased by the Douglases, who moved in and changed the name to Mains. Old Mains then became a farm. They retained the property until the 20th century

Other reference: Old Mains

MAINS CASTLE

South Lanarkshire   Private   OS 64   NS 628560
1 mile northwest of East Kilbride, and just west of Stewartfield, off minor roads north of A726, and south of A749, just south of Comyn's Castle.

Mains is a plain rectangular keep of the 15th century, built upon a mound. It once had a courtyard and substantial outbuildings. It has three storeys, a garret and a square cap house above a corbelled-out parapet.

The structure measures 37.5ft by 26.8ft and reaches a height of 41.25ft to the parapet, the garret adding a further 12ft. The entrance is at the western end of the south wall and takes the form of a round-arched doorway. This gives access to a mural turnpike stair which accesses all floors. At the head of the stair, the square caphouse has corbelled supports for the roof. It opens onto a wall-walk along the parapet, which was once crenellated. The roof is stone flagged, and the garret had corbiestepped gables which supported chimney stacks at each end.

Internally, the basement is vaulted, consisting of a single chamber with loft. The lower section was illuminated by two arrow slits and the loft accessed by a passage from the stair. Also from this passage, an opening led to a dungeon within the walls. This access was about 1ft square and has been sealed for many years.

The hall on the first floor had a garderobe in the north wall and a plain fireplace in the east. There are two windows with stone seats. The hall probably doubled as the kitchen, and there is a stone sink with conduit drain in the access passage from the stair. There is a mural chamber in the west wall. The floor above has been subdivided into

two rooms, each with a fireplace, a garderobe and mural chamber above those in the hall.

The entire site was surrounded by a deep ditch, which remained visible 200 years ago and was crossed by a drawbridge to the east. This was guarded by an arched gateway bearing a stone with the royal arms. This stone was taken to Torrance House.

The estate belonged to the Comyns, but was granted to John Lindsay of Dunrod in 1382. Sir James Lindsay had been present at the murder of the Red Comyn in Dumfries Kirk, the famous altercation with Robert the Bruce. This is another castle which claims to have provided shelter for Mary, Queen of Scots, on the eve of the Battle of Langside in 1568. A later Lindsay was angered by one of his servants while curling on the nearby pond. He ordered a hole to be cut in the ice and the man was held under until he drowned. The spot became known as Crawford's Hole.

Lindsay of Dunrod sold the property to the Stewarts of Castlemilk in 1619 to pay off debts. In 1695 an Act of Parliament granted the Mains of Kilbride to William Cunninghame, the brother of Cunninghame of Gilbertfield. It was unroofed in 1723 and fell into ruin. Some repairs were carried out in the 1880s, but a fierce storm caused the roof to collapse. In 1976 it was fully restored and remains a private house. The restoration work won two prestigious Saltire Awards, one for the best restoration, the other for excellence in reconstruction. It is a category 'A' Listed Building.

The castle is reputedly haunted by a variety of ghosts, one of which is reputed to be the spirit of a woman strangled by her jealous husband.

MASHOCK MILL MOTTE

South Lanarkshire   Ruin or site   NS 72   NS 836468
1 mile northeast of Crossford and A72, south of B7056, 100yds east of Mashock Mill.

A mound, at one time thought to be entirely natural, has been partly eroded to reveal that while the lower half is natural, the remainder appears to be man made. It has been interpreted as a small motte.

The portion of mound which remains is about 33ft in diameter at the base, 12ft high, and has a flat circular summit 9ft across. A line of stones 6ft long indicates that it once supported a building on the summit. A hoard of 21 German dollars of the 17th century was discovered here, and it is thought that the find occurred during the digging of a water channel feeding the mill. The position of the find and subsequent erosion due to construction of a new lade has led to the suggestion that the motte was at one time considerably larger than now and that the hoard had originally been concealed within the building.

The mill itself has been destroyed, probably in 1872, when the mills lade was diverted around the mound. The mill house carried a date-stone of 1601, with another of 1666 bearing the initials EF and WG. These are now located within a newer building. The mill house was described as a three-storey structure with a thatched roof. In 1998 there was a surviving fragment of a building contemporary with and subsidiary to the original mill.

MAULDSLIE

South Lanarkshire   Ruin or site   OS 72   NS 808504
3 miles west of Carluke, by minor roads south of A73, and south and west of B7011, at Mauldslie.

Site of a substantial tower which appears on Pont's manuscript map of c.1596.

Mauldslie or Maudsley, or Forest Kirk as it was sometimes known, was royal demesne land until the Wars of Independence. Portions of it were granted away by Robert the Bruce, and Mauldslie came to the Dennistouns at some point in the 14th century. John Dennistoun received a grant of confirmation from Robert II. In about 1400, it passed via one of the co-heiresses to Maxwell of Calderwood. They had a substantial tower here, which they retained until about 1640.

They sold the property to Arthur Erskine of Scotscraig. By this time, further portions of the estate had been sold off. Erskine developed financial problems and Mauldslie went to his kinsman, the Laird of Alva, in payment of the debts. This Erskine sold it to Sir Daniel Carmichael, second son of Lord Carmichael. When he died childless, he left it to his namesake and grand nephew, the son of the Earl of Hyndford. He improved and extended the castle.

It passed through the family to the 5th Earl of Hyndford who, in 1793, commissioned Robert Adam to build a new mansion, also named Mauldslie Castle. The old building seems to have been removed in the process and Roy's map shows that it stood in approximately the position adopted by the new house. In 1850 the estate was obtained by James Hozier, grand father of the diplomat Lord Newlands. Extensions were added by the architect David Bryce in 1860 and again by James Bryce, but the mansion was demolished in 1935.

MEARNS CASTLE

Renfrewshire Private OS 64 NS 552553
3 miles southwest of Barrhead, just east of Newton Mearns, and 0.25 miles north of Earn Water, off minor roads
south of A77, at Mearns Parish Church.

Sited on the edge of a precipitous drop, Mearns is a 15th century rectangular keep of three storeys, which is now
connected to a modern church building for which it serves as a church hall. Lord Maxwell already had a castle on
this estate but on the building of his new house, moved the village, and possibly the kirk. It may be that the site was
occupied by a previous structure, since the wall to the head of the basement door is of rough rubble, while the
structure above is of dressed ashlar block.

The building stands on a level platform, defended on the west and north sides by a severe drop. There were
once a wall and ditch protecting the remaining sides. A drawbridge provided access across the ditch. It has been
suggested that the site was once that of a fort.

The tower measures 44ft by 29.5ft, and reaches 45ft in height to the corbels of the parapet. At ground-floor
level the north wall is as much as 10ft in thickness and the others 8ft. They thin to 6.5ft at the top storey. An
entrance at ground-floor level in the north wall is now closed. Immediately above this, the arched outline of the
original main entrance to the hall has been adapted to create a window. A connecting corridor has been built from
the church and enters the castle in the west wall.

From the ground-floor entrance, a straight stair rises within the wall to first-floor level. Within the northwest
corner a turnpike stair rises to the floor above.

The vaulted basement room was illuminated by splayed arrow slots in the west and south walls. The hall
occupied the whole of the floor above, and internally measured 27.75ft by 16.5ft. It reached 21ft to the vault,
allowing the introduction of a musicians' gallery or entresol high on the north wall. This was entered from the
turnpike stair by a passage and was illuminated by a window above the door. The hall had a closet in the north wall
adjacent to the main door, and the fireplace was centrally sited on the south wall. Two arrow slots, in the closet and
on the west wall, plus larger windows with stone seats in the west and east walls, provided illumination.

The top storey was similar in plan to the hall, though from the closet a machicolated projection from the east
wall allowed use as a garderobe. The supporting corbels remain.

The stair to the parapet and probable caphouse has now gone, though there remain impressive machicolated
corbels at the wall head around the entire structure. Internally there are sockets for the support of massive roof
beams, though it is not now possible to say exactly what form the roof took.

A licence to build the castle was granted by James II to Herbert, Lord Maxwell, on the 15th of March 1449.
The document permits Lord Maxwell 'to build a castle or fortalice on the Barony of Mearns in Renfrewshire, to
surround and fortify it with walls and ditches, to strengthen it by iron gates, and to erect on top of it all the warlike

apparatus necessary for its defence.' It has been suggested that this implied that the castle was supplied with mangonels or similar weapons, possibly indicating a flat roof from which they could operate. Alternatively, it may simply refer to the machicolations at the wallhead.

In 1188 Helias of Partick, a son of Fulbert de Pollok, held Mearns and granted the church to Paisley Abbey. The estate passed by marriage to Maxwell of Caerlaverock, possibly as early as the reign of Alexander II in the first half of the 13th century. In some sources the bride is given the surname McGeachin. In 1424 Sir Herbert Maxwell of Caerlaverock and Mearns was awarded a Lordship of Parliament, becoming 1st Lord Maxwell. It may have been this improved status which prompted the building of Mearns.

Lord John Maxwell died at Flodden in 1513. His son Robert, an Ambassador to France, was captured at the Battle of Solway Moss in 1542. He was imprisoned in the Tower of London until ransomed. John, 6th Lord Maxwell, was appointed Warden of the West March. From 1581 he held the Earldom of Morton, following the execution of his brother in-law, the Regent Morton. He had to relinquish this title in 1585, when it was claimed by Morton's nephew, the Earl of Angus. The family also inherited the titles Lord Herries and Earl of Nithsdale, though the three titles were often held by different branches of the family. In 1589, James VI addressed a letter from Craigmillar to the Roman Catholic William, 5th Lord Herries. James demanded the surrender of William's castles at Caerlaverock, Threave, Morton and 'the place and fortalice of Mearns.' The 6th Lord was killed by the Johnstones at the Battle of Dryffe Sands in 1593. In that same year in an act of retaliation, John, 7th Lord Maxwell, murdered Sir James Johnstone. He went into exile, but on his return in 1613 was betrayed, tried and beheaded. These were the latest events in a long-running feud between the families over dominance in the West Marches and appointment as Warden.

In 1648 the Earl of Nithsdale sold the estate to Sir George Maxwell of Nether Pollok. It then passed to the Stewarts of Blackhall, later the Schaw-Stewarts of Ardgowan and Inverkip. It was abandoned and fell into ruin until renovated and incorporated into the present Church of Scotland building in 1971. The castle is a category 'A' Listed Building.

MIDDLETON

Renfrewshire   Ruin or site   OS 64   NS 495545
3 miles southeast of Neilston, and 3 miles southwest of Newton Mearns, off minor roads west of B769, 0.5 miles south of Craigton, just south of Middleton.

Possible castle site. A rocky outcrop extended by a platform was said to support the ruin of an L-plan building, of which a 6ft thick section of wall was reported to be standing in 1984. Recent archaeological assessment found nothing except field clearance debris. Compare Fingalton and Langton.

MILTON

South Lanarkshire   Ruin or site   OS 72   NS 812493
2 miles west of Carluke, by minor roads west of the A73, and south of the B7011, on east bank of Clyde at Milton Lockhart.

Site of a substantial tower, which appears on Pont's map of c.1596.

The estate belonged to the Whiteford family as early as 1496. In 1576 Adam Whiteford of Milton and his nephew, John Semple of Beltrees, were tortured when charged with conspiracy to assassinate the Regent Morton. Semple was found guilty of the apparently false charges, but later pardoned. Whiteford survived, despite persistently denying the charges, though his body 'was cruelly mangled'. He was declared forfeit when he failed to answer a summons to trial in 1577. His son, John, must have been restored to the estates, since his brother, Adam, inherited from him c.1606. Adam's son John was a 'persecutor' of Covenanters. He is alleged to have murdered several as they flew the battlefield at Rullion Green in 1666 and then to have informed upon Gavin Hamilton of Park of Mauldslie, who was tried and executed as a result. These actions prompted the prediction that 'the world would see his house a desolation, and nettles going in its close'. A few years later, Sir John ran into serious financial difficulties and his house was sequestrated and orders given for his arrest. He apparently defended himself and his house by throwing stones from the battlement.

It is said that the estate changed hands several times before the house became derelict. The property was purchased by the Hamiltons of Hallcraig before 1695. Sir John Hamilton of Hallcraig, a Senator of the College of Justice, obviously found it habitable since Milton became his principle residence. It was described as an old house in 1710.

In c.1726, the cartographer General William Roy was born in Miltonhead, a small house on the estate where both his father and grandfather were employed as gardeners to the Hamilton family. Roy's maps inspired the establishment of the Ordnance Survey.

In 1816 Milton was owned by a Miss Jeffray. The architect, William Burn, was commissioned to build a new house by John Gibson Lockhart, the son-in-law and biographer of Sir Walter Scott. This was built in the period 1829-36 and was named Milton Lockhart. This stood on a site a little to the east of the old tower, which seems to have been removed in the process. In 1987 Milton Lockhart was dismantled, then reassembled on Hokkaido Island, Japan, where it is now known as Lockheart Castle.

Other references: Mylntoune, Milton Lockhart

MILTON BRIDGE MOTTE
Renfrewshire   Ruin or site   OS 63   NS 358683
1 mile southeast of Kilmacolm, west of the A761 and just south of the B788.

This motte stands prominently on the end of a slight ridge above the east bank of the Gryffe Water. It measures 92ft in diameter at the base and the sub-circular summit measures 46ft by 43ft. On the east it reaches a height of 6ft above the approach, but 12ft on the west. The surrounding low ground is soft and wet, though there is now no evidence of a ditch.

The mound was excavated in 1894, a trench being dug across the summit from east to west. At about 4ft down, four rows of boulders were found, and below this a layer of ash. The mound consisted of clay, thought to have been taken from an adjacent hollow.

In 1992 a German-style of counting piece and a shard of medieval pottery, both dating from the 15th-16th centuries, were recovered from an erosion scar on the northern side of the motte. This was taken to indicate continued use of the site into this period.

Just to the east, extensive rubble foundations remain of a large rectangular building. Nearby is an old well, which has been covered by a flagstone. These are the remains of the farm of Laigh Dennistoun, which appears on maps from the 16th century onwards.

These were the lands from which the family of Dennistoun took their name. The motte may represent the remains of their original 12th century seat. The family returned when James Dennistoun of Colgrain sold his Dunbartonshire lands and purchased Dennistoun Mains in 1836.

Other references: Dennistoun, Duchal Motte, Kilmacolm Motte

MOAT, Lesmahagow
South Lanarkshire   Ruin or site   OS 71   NS 846396
At Moat, off minor roads 3 miles east of M74, at Lesmahagow.

A tower in this position is denoted as 'Mote' on Pont's map of c.1596, and 'Kreddes' in Blaeu's *Atlas Novus* of 1654, though this may be a transcription error. On subsequent maps it appears only as the farm 'Moat', with no indication of a ruin on the site.

A description of 1864 records that a building here measured 30ft by 15ft and could be surrounded by water to resist Annandale thieves. It was vaulted and had loopholes in 'the lower part'.

In 1955 a 'low marshy tract' was evident around the northwestern corner of the rectangular platform upon which the farm stands. This had the appearance of being man made. Nothing else remains. Moatyetts and Moat Mains are other nearby properties, each indicative of a castle site.

Moat is listed as one of the farms of the Weir's Stonebyres estate in the early 18th century and the castle may have been the seat of the Hawksland estate of Weir of Blackwood. Compare: Devon, Dowane.

MOAT, Roberton
South Lanarkshire   Ruin or site   OS 72   NS 940271
At Moat, 2.5 miles south of Roberton, on A73.

The motte here has been excavated and shown to have been constructed during the 14th century. The ground below surrendered pottery of this date, negating the theory that this had been the seat of Robert the Fleming in the 12th century. Moat is now thought to have been constructed by Mary of Stirling, who supported the Balliol faction during the reigns of Robert I and David II. She had been compelled to provide herself and her followers with a fortified base in this area. She resigned her lands at Roberton in 1346 in the hope of a pardon from David II. By 1710 there was a house here known as 'The Moat', which belonged to Baillie of Littlegill. He apparently had

a bridge over the Clyde, across which he could access his estate.

The mound is now a horseshoe shape, the centre and one side having been removed during the creation of a silage clamp before 1958. Excavation in the 1970s confirmed that the motte had once stood within a ditch. In 1955 this was recorded as being 2ft deep and 16ft wide. Post holes were found which would have supported a wooden structure and a palisade. The motte has a diameter of 75ft, with a circular summit 40ft across. The steep sides reached a height of 10ft, except on the south, where it sits on the edge of a precipitous drop to the River Clyde. There is no evidence of a bailey, but the natural position for one is now occupied by the adjacent farm buildings.

MONKLAND HOUSE

North Lanarkshire   Ruin or site   OS 64   NS 774638
2 miles south of Airdrie, 1 mile north of Chapelhall, on minor roads west of A73, just west of Monkland Bridge, above ravine on north bank of Calder Water.

Monkland House has been demolished, though it had been an impressive L-plan house of the early 17th century. It was built against a slope, so that the main entrance at ground level on the north actually entered at the first-floor proper. A later porch had been added at the entrance. There was no entrance at ground-floor level.

The building consisted of a long main block, running east to west, with round towers at both southern corners. On the north side against the slope, a square wing was joined by half its length at the western corner. In the re-entrant, a round tower carried a turnpike stair from the door. This led downwards to the basement of the main block and upwards to third-floor level. The main block rose to three storeys and an attic for two thirds of the eastern end. An additional storey rose above the western third. The wing had three storeys, and supported a wide chimney flue on the northern wall. All of the gables were corbiestepped and topped by chimney stacks. The windows on each floor had been enlarged in the 18th and 19th centuries, and dormers provided for the attic rooms of the lower section of the main block. There were many gunloops around the building.

All of the ground floor rooms were vaulted and protected by external walls reaching 5ft thick. The kitchen occupied the basement of the wing and from there the three chambers of the main block were accessed via the stair tower.

Each floor of the wing appears to have had a single room. On the first floor of the main block was a drawing room, a dining room and a smaller connecting room between the two. The rooms of the round towers were continuous with those into which they opened. Access to the room in the wing was via a door in the northern connecting wall, behind the stair tower. The private chambers would have occupied the floors above.

There is said to have been a wall surrounding the whole property and, apparently, a moat. A doocot survived until its removal before 1952.

The extensive Monklands estates of Newbattle Abbey were acquired by the Kerrs of Ferniehirst at the Reformation. The Hamiltons then obtained them before this portion was purchased by James Cleland, who built the house.

James was the second son of Sir John Cleland of Faskine. He appears as a complainer to the Privy Council in 1606. In 1607 he received a grant of the lands of Petersburn, Airdrie, Caldercruix and Brownside from James VI, upon the resignation of Thomas Hamilton of Binnie. Sometime before 1612, he was knighted and in 1615 he witnessed a charter by Ludovick, Duke of Lennox. In the same year he was charged with resetting Jesuits and hearing Mass. The charges were dropped.

In 1624 he became involved in a dispute with Lord Boyd over the patronage of Monklands Kirk. Boyd gained a warrant from the Archbishop of Glasgow to appoint his own nominee, Reverend James Fullerton. Cleland found this objectionable and garrisoned the kirk on the Saturday night before the arrival of the minister. His men were 'boddin in feare of warre', dressed and armed for the occasion. They were also well supplied with ale and tobacco! On Sunday morning, the new minister arrived to take his first service, but was turned away despite his production of the warrant. Charged before the Privy Council, Cleland was found to be within his rights in barring the archbishop's intrusion in a civil matter. He was, however, bound to provide 5,000 merks security for the safety of the Rev. Fullerton. In 1627 the case was finally found in favour of James. His son, Ludovick Cleland, sold the patronage to the Duke of Hamilton in 1639. Ludovick died childless leaving the estate to his uncle, George Cleland of nearby Gartness. In 1694 the estate passed to his grandson, George Weir.

The house was ravaged by fire in 1700 and apparently substantially rebuilt. In the 1950s it belonged to J.V. Sassoon. It was then converted for use as the Monkland House Hotel. It lay derelict for a number of years following another serious fire in the 1960s and was then demolished. A housing development now covers the site.

Other reference: Petersburn

MOOT HILL, Govan

City of Glasgow   Ruin or site   OS 64   NS 555658
On south bank of River Clyde, by minor roads north of the A8, east of Govan Kirk at Water Row.

The Moot or Doomster Hill of Govan has long since disappeared, but is believed to have been a place where judgement was pronounced and oaths of fealty taken. Recent evaluation has suggested that it was a actually a castle motte. Although the area has been subject to numerous excavations, the precise location of the Doomster Hill is still not known. The discovery of a 'ditch' has now been dismissed as in-filled water courses and the traces of sand-quarrying work.

In 1795 the mound was described as conical and 17ft high, with a diameter of 150ft at the base and 108ft at the summit. By 1895 the summit was in use as a reservoir for a dye works. Work to deepen this revealed some blackened oak timbers, bone fragments, and a layer of what were thought to be decayed bulrushes. At that time it was supposed to be a tumulus.

A sketch of early Govan shows a massive motte-like mound with stepped slopes and a ditch, towering above the river bank and the surrounding settlement. The accuracy of this sketch, however, has been called into question in regard to the depiction of both the stepped slopes and the ditch. The Moot Hill appears on Ainslie's 1800 map of Renfrewshire as a large conical hillock.

Govan is known to have been an early Christian site, contemporary with, or perhaps even slightly pre-dating, Glasgow, and is associated with the 6th century Christian martyr, Constantine, to whom the early church was dedicated. The present church has a collection of Viking-style hogback grave stones, a high-status sarcophagus, and fragments of stone crosses that have been found around the kirkyard. Having such early origins, Govan may have had associations with Dumbarton, the capital of the ancient Kingdom of Strathclyde.

The sarcophagus is elaborately carved with Celtic motifs, including a hunting scene, where one of the horses has an emblem carved into its rump. To some, this appears to be the letter A, and evidence of King Arthur. The plinth supporting the sarcophagus, however, claims that it is the coffin of Constantine. He is believed to have been buried at Govan and to have established a monastery here, although current opinion dates the sarcophagus to the 10th or 11th centuries, too late for the saint's burial. The Moot Hill may have been connected to the Strathclyde kings, but a castle motte would date from much later.

David I granted the church at Govan to the Bishop of Glasgow in 1147. It seems to have been given out of the Royal demesne, since the grant was given with the consent of his son, Henry. In c.1153 Govan was made a prebend of the cathedral, keeping it fully within the control of the bishop. This variety of Dark Age and medieval associations provides many possibilities as to the function, location, date and ownership of the Doon or Doomster Hill, which cannot currently be resolved.

MOSS CASTLE

South Lanarkshire   Ruin or site   OS 71   NS 845227

3 miles west and south of Crawfordjohn, on minor roads north of B740, 1 miles west and north of Eastertown Farm, at Mosscastle.

A large tower is illustrated at Mosscastle on Pont's map, then on Blaeu's *Atlas Novus*. It is depicted as a ruin by the time William Forrest published his map in 1816. The ruin had disappeared before the first edition OS maps were published in the 1850s. The name Glespin appears in the same area, and the site is close to the head of the Glespin Burn. It is highly likely that the ruin is the old house of the MacMorran family.

Glespin was a substantial holding of this family. Their old house was of 'considerable extent', and their estate encompassed the neighbouring farms of Netherhill, Stonehill, Sheriffcleugh, Shawhead and Greenburn. William MacMorran is on record as having held lands named Glespin in Douglas Parish in 1538. These were situated at the foot of the Glespin Burn where it enters Douglas Water. In 1609 John MacMorran of Glespin was accused of the murder of Andrew Hamilton, a saddler in Sanquhar. By 1654 James MacMorran is recorded as laird of Glespin and Cairncurrishaw in Crawfordjohn Parish. His father had possessed these estates before him. It has been suggested that their lands encompassed the full length of the Glespin Burn, straddling both parishes, hence the duality in the record. The lairds and their sons feature prominently in the parish records of Crawfordjohn during the 17th and 18th centuries, mainly as the fathers of numerous illegitimate children. The Laird of Glespin was a Hanoverian during the 1745 Jacobite rebellion and was one of a gathering at Lamington who were assembled to harass the movement of the Jacobite Army during their retreat north. The family had a reputation of being alternately miserly, then spendthrift.

They died out at the beginning of the 19th century and their properties were purchased by a Glasgow merchant. He sold them on to the Edinburgh legal firm of Inglis and Wood, who developed the estate as a shooting venue. Before demolishing the old house, they erected outhouses, stables and barns for the horses and their attendants. This was probably on the site named Glespin, a little to the west, which is denoted on maps from 1816 onwards. By 1858 the estate was in the possession of Lady Montague-Douglas, the sister of Lady Home.

The name Glespin is now more commonly associated with a mining village of that name, some way to the north.

Other reference: Glespin

MUGDOCK CASTLE

The Lennox & East Dunbartonshire   Friends of Mugdock Castle   OS 64   NS 550772

1.5 miles north of Milngavie, on minor roads west of A81, 0.5 miles west of Mugdock village, in Mugdock country park, on west side of Mugdock Loch.

Mugdock Castle is sited upon a narrow level ridge some 320ft long, which once formed a steeply banked peninsula into a now partly drained loch. Before drainage, the loch would have protected the west, north and eastern sides of the castle, but now sits only on the east. The complex was gradually extended to fill the whole of this peninsula.

There remains a fairly intact slim tower at the original southwestern corner and, adjoining this, the western end of the southern wall and the gateway. This is 8.3ft wide, and retains the marks of a pair of folding doors, one outside a portcullis, and one inside. A small portion of the gatehouse survives. A section of high courtyard wall runs northward from the tower. This terminates in the vaulted basement of the remains of the northwestern tower. There was probably a wide ditch with a drawbridge and rampart guarding the entrance. This portion of the castle is thought to date from the 14th century.

The tower is an irregularly shaped structure of four storeys and is 24ft wide. It reaches a height of 59ft to the parapet and represents one of several lesser towers of a very ruined large courtyard castle. The ground floor room contains a mural garderobe, which probably drained via a conduit to the ditch. It had no internal access to the floor above. The first floor is rib vaulted and supports the main entrance, formerly entered by way of a removable ladder and now by external stone stair. From here a turnpike stair within the wall at the southeast corner leads to the second floor. The second floor stands at the same height as the top of the courtyard wall. A straight stair within the east wall led to the floor above and to the battlements. The parapet wall is plain and not crenellated. The roof is a replacement thought to be similar in form to the original.

In the 15th century the castle was extended by the addition of another large courtyard, filling the western portion of the peninsula. At the northern end of the ridge are the remains of what is thought to have been a chapel. This and an attached latrine tower are thought to be of the same period as this second courtyard. This western side is now entered by a large gateway attached to the north side of the tower. It gives access to an open area occupied by a range of buildings constructed in 1655.

Ruins to the east of the tower fill the site of the original courtyard and represent the remnants of the mansion house of J. Guthrie Smith, an eminent local historian of the Victorian era. A stone arched bridge over the gateway joined the first floor of the tower to the mansion, into which it had been incorporated.

Mugdock was a Graham property from the early 13th century. The castle is first mentioned in 1372 when an agreement between Sir Patrick Graham and Angus Hawinroyss over the lands of Boclair was signed here. It may have been the birthplace of James Graham, 5th Earl and 1st Marquis of Montrose. He succeeded his father in 1626 and joined the Covenanters in 1638. As they became more extreme, he opposed Scottish intervention in the English Civil War and the anti-Royalist sentiment that engendered. Lord Sinclair sacked Mugdock during Montrose's imprisonment in 1641. Montrose was released and came to live at Mugdock. He then went on to conduct a remarkable campaign against the Covenanters in 1644–45. He won the battles of Tippermuir, Aberdeen, Inverlochy, Auldearn, Alford and Kilsyth. He was, however, defeated at Philiphaugh by David Leslie but escaped to the continent. During his campaign, the Buchanans harried the castle and after this the northern portion and that facing the loch were allowed to become ruinous. Montrose returned in 1650 and was defeated at Carbisdale, being betrayed, captured and then hanged at Edinburgh. The family was forfeited, and Mugdock was gained by Montrose's greatest enemy, the Campbell Marquis of Argyll. The 2nd Marquis of Montrose repurchased the castle for £50,000, but retrieved the money in 1661 when the Campbells were ordered to repay it. Argyll was himself executed. The Grahams moved to Buchanan Castle in the 18th century.

The castle remained occupied until J. Guthrie Smith built his castellated mansion in 1875. He damaged or destroyed much of the old castle in the process. The mansion became derelict after being used by the government in World War II, then it passed to the local council who turned the estate into a country park.

The site is a Scheduled Ancient Monument and category 'A' Listed Building.

Grounds open all day, southwest tower open to visitors Sat & Sun 14.00-17.00 (last weekend in May to last weekend in September each year); www.mugdock-country-park.org.uk

MUIRHALL

South Lanarkshire Ruin or site OS 72 NS 994528
6 miles north of Carnwath, west of A70, by minor road, at Muirhall.

Site of a tower, illustrated on Pont's map as 'Moorehall', but in Blaeu's *Atlas Novus* the name has strayed from the site and been transcribed as 'Moorehead'.

There was reputedly an ancient chapel dedicated to St Mary Magdalene on an adjacent site. The chapel is said to have been endowed with £60 Scots annually from the lands of Carnwath, which seems an overly large donation for a small chapel. It had a chaplain, Sir Thomas King, who at the Reformation returned the value of the revenues as 16 merks 5 shillings and 6 pence. It is likely that the large donation from the Somervilles afforded the building of a tower as a residence for their chaplain. No trace remains of either chapel or tower.

MUIRHOUSE OF LIBBERTON

South Lanarkshire Ruin or site OS 72 NS 981431
3 miles south of Carnwath, by track west of B7016, 1 mile northwest of Libberton, east of River Clyde at Muirhouse.

Site of a tower, illustrated on Pont's map of 1596, which was much altered by 1970.

In 1564 Muirhouse of Libberton was granted by Lord Somerville to Sir James Hamilton, son of Hamilton of Crawfordjohn. Sir James was thereafter known as Hamilton of Libberton. His family held Libberton until the early 17th century when it was sold to the Earl of Carnwath. In 1662 Hugh Roxburgh of Muirhouse was fined £240 for nonconformity with the prelacy. By c.1690 the Denholms of Westshield owned the property.

Other reference: Murrays

MURDOSTOUN

Renfrewshire Ruin or site OS 63 NS 274748
2 miles southwest of Greenock, south of A8 and B7054 by minor roads, at High Murdieston.

Site of a small tower and courtyard illustrated on Pont's manuscript map of the late 16th century, and in Blaeu's *Atlas Novus* of 1654.

Other reference: Murdieston

MURDOSTOUN CASTLE

North Lanarkshire Private OS 65 NS 825573
1 mile north of Newmains, east of the A73 and north of the A71, by minor roads, on north bank of South Calder Water, at Murdostoun.

A much altered L-plan tower, which dates from the 15th century, forms the rear half of the southeastern wing of a large mansion, which is now a specialist care home. The tower is built of sandstone rubble, and has a parapet and simple cornice. It was originally extended around a central court, which was then enclosed by further extensions of the 1860s and 1900s.

It is said that Alexander III granted the Barony of Shotts to the Scotts. In 1296 Sir Richard Scott married the Murdostoun heiress and gained the estate. He pledged allegiance to Edward I in the same year, and is said to be the ancestor of the Scotts of Buccleuch and of Sir Walter Scott. Sir Michael Scott, the heir of Murdostoun, is reputed to have distinguished himself at the Battle of Halidon Hill in 1333, although he died at the Battle of Neville's Cross in 1346.

The Inglis family gained the estates of Murdostoun and Hartwood in 1446 in exchange with the Scotts for the estate at Branxholme in the borders. The Inglises built the tower. In 1696 Thomas Inglis, the last of the line, sold the property to the Edinburgh merchant, Alexander Inglis. When he died in 1719, Murdostoun passed to a nephew, Alexander Hamilton. He had to adopt the Inglis name to inherit, becoming Inglis-Hamilton. Colonel James Inglis-Hamilton of Murdostoun died at the Battle of Waterloo in 1815.

The estate was purchased in 1856 by the former Glasgow Provost, Robert Stewart, who was responsible for the introduction of Glasgow's Loch Katrine water supply. His descendants remained in residence until the last of the line died in the 1970s. The estate was broken up and sold in portions in 1979. The castle was again on the market in 1988 and came into use as a specialist hospital dealing with brain injury.

There is a walled garden, a doocot and an old well head within the grounds. With the castle, the well head and doocot form a group of category 'B' Listed Buildings.

NEMPHLAR

South Lanarkshire Private OS 72 NS 856444
2 miles west of Lanark, on minor roads south of A73, north of River Clyde, at Hall Road, Nemphlar.

This bastle house is virtually complete, though it has been modernised and extended at various periods. The original entrance was in the south gable, which gave access to a barrel-vaulted basement where there is a blocked stairwell. The upper floor has been modernised and is occupied as a home. A dormer window has been inserted for the attic room and there is an 18th century stone fore-stair and a 19th century extension to the north. A date-stone is recorded in the garden. It carries the date 1607, a shield and the initials DF and DL: it is thought to be a marriage stone of the Forrest and Lockhart families. It may once have been used as a lintel for a fireplace.

John Forrest of Halltown of Nemphlar is on record in 1636. By 1664 James Lockhart is described as the portioner of Halltown of Nemphlar. Thereafter are consistent references to Lockharts of Mid-town, Middle Town or Mid-Tower of Nemphlar throughout the 17th to 19th centuries. It is likely that these refer to this property since East and West Towns of Nemphlar appear distinctly in the records. All three properties appear on Pont's map of 1596 and appear to be of equal importance. It is therefore probable that further bastle houses once existed at the other the other two properties. Nemphlar is a 'B' Listed Building.

Other references: Halltown of Nemphlar, Middleton of Nemphlar, Midtown of Nemphlar, Mid-Tower of Nemphlar

NETHERPLACE

Renfrewshire Ruin or site OS 64 NS 520556
2 miles west of Newton Mearns, west of M77 and A77, west of B769, 0.25 miles south of Caldcoats.

An entry in Canmore, the data base of the RCAHMS, provides information that a castle stood at Nether Pollok. The position is that given above, the former site of Netherplace House. It has been allocated on the basis of the 'place' element of the name. The information given, however, describes the development of the Laigh Castle, near Pollok House (Nether Pollok) as opposed to this site (Netherplace) near Pollok Castle. See Pollok House.

'N:place' appears on Pont's map, but the building is given little importance.

NEWARK CASTLE

Renfrewshire His Scot OS 63 NS 328745
In Port Glasgow, on north side of A8, on south shore of Firth of Clyde, at Newark.

Newark consists of a complex of buildings of the 15th, early 16th and late 16th centuries, forming three sides of a courtyard. The wall, which once completed the court, is long gone. It is a remarkably well-preserved structure and well worthy of the care of Historic Scotland.

The oldest section stands at the southeast corner. It is a four-storey keep, dated to about 1484. It measures 29ft by 23ft and reaches a height of 48ft to the present parapet. This is a storey higher than the original construction, an extension having been built up from the single corbels of the wall-head. The entrance to the keep was at the northwest corner. The original doorway remains and is accessed from a lobby within the late 16th century range. The ground floor is vaulted and had two entresol floors built high within the vault, each illuminated by widely splayed arrow slot windows, though these may be a later adaptation. A mural turnpike stair in the northeast corner leads to all of the floors above. At these levels renaissance windows have replaced the originals in order that it reflected the style of a later extension. Each of the upper floors had a single room, sharing a collection of garderobes, mural chambers and fireplaces. The timber floor has gone at second floor level, but the corbels which once supported it remain.

Midway down the west side of the former courtyard is a gatehouse of the early 16th century, measuring 23.5ft by 20ft. This features an arched pend running west-east. Within this are a stone seat and a door leading to a vaulted guard chamber. Two gunloops provided defence of the approaches from the west and south either side of the entrance. A turnpike in the northeastern corner led to the two floors above. These have a single room to each, with stone seats within the window recesses. These rooms display similar features to those of the keep, and are thought

to have provided a hall and bedchamber for the castle steward. Adjacent to a garderobe on the first floor is an ogee-arched aumbry. The attic is framed by corbiestepped gables topped by chimneys. A later adaptation of this room was the insertion of a dormer window to the west. The entire north face of this structure adjoins the western end of a late 16th century block.

The north and east sides of the yard were enclosed by the construction of this long L-plan block of three storeys. It has a projecting central section on its north side. Each of the four northward facing corners has a round turret corbelled out from second-floor level and a matching stair turret is centrally placed on the projecting wing. A door in the re-entrant at the east side of the courtyard gave the only access. Above this an engraved stone gives the date 1597, and the hopeful inscription, 'The blissings of God be herein'. A dormer window carries a date of two years later.

A long corridor ran around the courtyard side of this block. Directly opposite the door, a wide scale-and-platt stair ascends to the first floor. Turning southwards from the door, the ground floor contained a bakehouse, whose ovens and chimney stack are built outwith the exterior wall. Above this at first-floor level is a bedchamber, still with the original built-in timber wardrobes and a fold away 'press' bed. There is a fireplace and stool cupboard. The survival of these fittings is exceptional. The floor above would have contained a further bedroom, though it is now bare. Southward, the ground-floor corridor leads to the door of the old keep. Within the northern and longest side of this range, the corridor terminates at each end with small vaulted chambers. The western of these was adjacent to a small stair leading to a service room on the floor above. On the northern side of the corridor, doors open to the kitchen, a store, and a buttery or wine cellar. The kitchen has a wide fireplace with recess in the northern end, and the wine cellar has a small service stair to the hall above.

On the first floor, the central block of the projecting wing is completely occupied by the hall. The room measures 37.25ft by 20.75ft. There are a number of Renaissance-style windows on all sides, and a wide decorated fireplace in the north wall. This measures 8.6ft wide by 7.5ft high. Adjacent on the east side of this is a door to the round stair turret. There is a small closet of about 2ft by 3ft in the southeast corner, from which a spy-hole or gunloop guards the entrance to the block from the yard. The wing to the west of the hall contains the service room mentioned.

The second floor contained a single massive room, a 'gallery' used as a function suite on grand occasions. The area could be divided by use of removable screens or doors, which separated the area within the projecting wing. A further possibility is that screens were used to subdivide this area into bedrooms, since a fireplace is available for each. The gallery was illuminated by a series of four dormer windows along its southern wall and two either side of the central stair turret on the north side. All of the walls of this block support a number of gunloops.

Before construction of the northern block, the courtyard perimeter would have come south from the gatehouse. Initially further buildings formed the boundary, for which the outline of a roof can be seen on the south wall of the gatehouse. A wall would have marked out the remainder, running eastward beyond the keep. It then ran northwards, to meet a now isolated round corner tower at the northeastern extremity of the site. Formerly a defensive feature, this was converted for use as a doocot. It retains two gunloops and a garderobe with chute. It originally had two rooms above the ground floor. These floors have gone, allowing access to the numerous nesting boxes. The courtyard wall would then have gone westward then south to enclose the courtyard. There may originally have been other corner towers which, with a great hall and other buildings within the courtyard, have now gone. There was a chapel within the barony which stood either within the courtyard, or on a nearby site.

The estate was a property of the Dennistouns, sitting within their barony of Finlayston. When the Dennistoun laird died, his vast estates were shared between his two daughters who took them by marriage to the Maxwells of Calderwood and to the Cunninghames of Kilmaurs. Robert Maxwell granted this estate to his second son George. He built the keep, though the Dennistouns' original castle is thought to have been at Finlayston, which became home to the Cunninghames.

The Maxwells were distantly related to royalty through the Dennistouns, and so James IV visited on several occasions. In 1495 he lodged here on his way to quell disturbances in the Western Isles. In 1497 he paid four shillings and eight pence for 'ane bote fetch wine fra the schip twys, quhen she lay at New Werk'. A year later he paid another boatman six shillings to take his gear to Newark from the Royal Castle at Dumbarton, across the river.

In 1593 Maxwell of Newark was among many of the name killed in the Battle of Dryffe Sands, where they fought with their enemies the Johnstones.

His heir, Sir Patrick Maxwell of Newark, was a confidant of James VI and by reputation a gentleman. On the other hand he was a murderer and wife beater, who used his position at court to avoid punishment. He was involved in long-running feuds which led to his implication in the murder of his cousin Patrick Maxwell of Stanely in 1584. In 1596 he killed Montgomerie of Skelmorlie and his heir. In 1595 his own mother had written to the king to complain about his behaviour. He mistreated his wife, Margaret Crawford, over a long period of time, often assaulting her or confining her to her bedchamber. In 1632 he assaulted her in front of their guests and became so violent towards her that she was bedridden for six months. She recovered only to be beaten with a sword. Again confined to her room and given only a little water and half a loaf per day, her son tried to intervene but was ejected from the house. She became fit enough to escape and he was called to trial. However, he became ill, never travelled to Edinburgh and apparently died soon afterwards. Margaret provided him with 16 children in 44 years of marriage. Patrick built the northern block in 1597. His initials, with Margaret's, appear in a monogram which decorates the dormer windows of the south facade. Her ghost is said to haunt the castle.

In 1668 another Patrick Maxwell sold the surrounding land to the Magistrates of Glasgow, allowing the building of a new port for the city. At this point the name of the hamlet changed from Newark to Port Glasgow. The castle itself passed to the Schaw-Stewarts and in the 18th century fell into partial ruin. Part of the building remained habitable and in the 19th century was the residence of several poorer families, while the roofless portions were used as a midden. The castle came into State care in 1909 and has been restored, although the floors of the attic rooms have never been replaced.

Newark is a Scheduled Ancient Monument, and category 'A' Listed Building.

Historic Scotland; open April to September (tel 01745 741858).

NEWBIGGING

South Lanarkshire Ruin or Site OS 72 NT 013460

2 miles east of Carnwath, on A721, at or near West Mains.

Possible site of an early castle. In the vernacular, 'Newbigging' meant simply to build new or a new build. As such it is a common enough name with no less than 14 places of that name in Scotland.

Pont's map of c.1596 illustrates a tower at the western end of the village and there is a 19th century report of a small farm named Moat of Newbigging in the vicinity. East Mains and West Mains farms still exist.

Walter de Newbigging is on record in the parish of Carnwath, when Newbigging appears to have been a separate barony. The lands passed by the marriage of his heiress to the Somervilles of Carnwath in the middle of the 13th century. The knight of Newbigging was one of the supposed leaders of a Scottish army which William Wallace led to victory at Biggar in 1297. It is said that Robert I united Newbigging and Carnwath into a single barony in favour of John Somerville. In 1468 John Livingstone inherited a 'third part' of the lands of Newbigging from his father.

NEWHOLME

South Lanarkshire Ruin or site OS 72 NT 081477

6 miles east of Carnwath, by minor roads north of A721, west of A702 north of Dolphinton, 0.25 miles southeast of Dunsyre.

Site of a tower, which appears on Pont's map of c.1596 as 'Newhaim'. Newholme, with Roberton, belonged to the Cockburn family and then the Hamiltons. By the 17th century it had passed to the Learmont family, one of whom was a noted Covenanter.

In 1666 having fought at Rullion Green, where he had commanded of the left wing of the defeated Covenanting army, Major Joseph Learmont went on the run. He was declared forfeit and his brother-in-law, Hamilton of Wishaw, paid compensation to retain the estate for the family. Learmont is said to have hidden in Ireland, within his own house at Dolphinton, and in the surrounding hills. He is even said to have had a vault built by the banks of the Medwin, where he could hide without fear of discovery. He apparently reappeared to fight at Bothwell Bridge in 1679, after which he was captured and condemned to death. By that time he was an old man and so his sentence was commuted to life imprisonment on the Bass Rock. He was released some five years later, to go home to die.

By the time William Forrest compiled his 1816 map, Newholme was a Cunninghame property. The present house dates from the 19th century and is a category 'B' Listed Building.

NEWHOUSES

South Lanarkshire Ruin or site OS 71 NS 686438

1 mile west of Strathaven, on north side of A71, at Newhouses.

Site of a keep or strong tower, which appears in Blaeu's *Atlas Novus* of the 17th century. This appears to have been a Hamilton property until the 20th century.

NEWTON

South Lanarkshire Ruin or site OS 71 NS 701433

1 mile southwest of Strathaven, on minor road west of A721, at Newton.

Site of a substantial tower of the Hamiltons. Allan Hamilton of Fairholm owned this estate in 1491. In 1541, Andrew Hamilton of Silvertonhill was given a grant of the lands in the parish of Avondale. This consisted of Newton, Overton, Braconrig and Maidenburn. By the 19th century, the property had been divided into East Newton and West Newton, the latter being the property of Miss Brown. This branch of the Hamiltons also held Newton near Cambuslang.

NEWTON, Elvanfoot

South Lanarkshire Ruin or site OS 78 NS 954176

0.25 miles east of Elvanfoot, on east bank of the Clyde, just west of Newton House.

Site of a castle, which belonged to the Weirs, or Veres, of Newton, cadets of the Weirs of Blackwood. The family were established here in or before the 15th century, and they held an old castle 'with much lodging in it' and 'a house of size and pretension', which stood above the bank of the Clyde.

In 1512 William Weir of Newton served upon an assize. In 1528, his widow and son John submitted a protest to parliament that they should not be disadvantaged by the forfeiture of the Earl of Angus, superior of the Barony of Crawford. In 1662 John Weir of Newton received £320 as compensation for his forfeiture, imposed as a result of fighting for the Royalist cause during the civil wars. In 1682 John received a further pardon, as he had apparently kept the company 'of one who was in rebellion'. The story goes that his sister was the wife of Irving (Irvine) of Saphock, a privy councillor. He gained access to the council chamber for his wife. She pled unsuccessfully for her brother's life but, being heavily pregnant, the strain apparently put her into labour. She refused to be removed until a pardon was granted. Seeing her in obvious pain and the birth imminent, the Chancellor ordered the granting of the pardon in order that she could be removed. Weir was so grateful that he declared that the child would inherit his estates. In order to ensure this, he transferred them to his sister and her husband.

A new house was built in the early 19th century by Alexander Irving, Lord Newton, Chancellor of the Court of Session. This apparently caused the diversion of the old coach road. He had inherited the property from his father George. Alexander died in 1832 and it passed to the lawyer and antiquary George Vere Irving, author of *The Upper Ward of Lanarkshire, Described and Delineated*. He died in 1869.

NEWTON HOUSE

South Lanarkshire   Ruin or site   OS 64   NS 663613
1 mile north of A724, 1 mile east of A763, north of Westburn Road at north end of Newton Avenue.

Site of an old or fortified house of the Hamilton family. The first Newton House was probably fortified and may have occupied a site closer to the River Clyde to the north. The Hamiltons of Silvertonhill are said to have gained the estate by marriage to a Douglas heiress in the 15th century.

A house built in 1602 burned down in 1694, causing the loss of the family records. It was replaced by a mansion which passed to an heiress, the wife of Colonel Montgomery of the 51st Regiment of Foot. Their descendant built a new house in 1825. This house was later occupied by Archibald Glen Kidston; however the Montgomerys still owned the property until the 20th century. They may have been living in Stobo Castle by 1873.

The house appears on maps compiled as recently as the 1970s. It was said to form one side of a quadrangle, the stables and offices which made the other four sides were said to have an 'old world quality', while the house retained a modern appearance. Only the gate posts remain.

NEWTON MEARNS

Renfrewshire   Ruin or site   OS 64   NS 537559
In Newton Mearns, off minor roads west of A77, off Capelrig Road, opposite northern end of School Road at Robshill Court.

Eighteenth century estate maps apparently show this to be the site of the 13th century 'Nova Villa' of Sir Herbert Maxwell of Mearns. The castle was probably of earth and timber construction, and a charter to build it was granted in 1273. A flat-topped rectangular mound was said to be visible on a bluff at Rob's Hill in the 1970s. The site has been built over, and there may have been a later fortified house nearby.

'The Newton' was the seat of the Barony of Mearns and came into the possession of the Rankins. It passed by marriage to Matthew Stewart, a descendant of the Stewarts of Blackhall. His family were still in possession in 1710. Compare with Lanrig.

OGS CASTLE

South Lanarkshire   Ruin or site   OS 72   NT 031446
4 miles east and south of Carnwath, 2.5 miles west of Elsrickle, off minor roads north of A721, just east of South Medwin Water, at Ogs Castle.

Site of a castle, of which there were remnants in the 19th century, also spelt as Oggs. The site lies just south of the front of the present house. Having been described as a small square tower in the 19th century, it was demolished and the site cleared in 1808. On excavation in 1968, the rubble foundations were found to measure 35ft by 15ft, with walls 3ft thick.

The castle is illustrated by Pont in his map of c.1596, and it is marked on Roy's map of 1747-56 as a complex of three buildings. From 1773 to 1822, Ross, Ainslie, then Thompson illustrate it a large and imposing structure known as Haig or Heg Castle.

Ogs Castle sits within the portion of Libberton Parish, which was part of the estate sold by Robert Dalziel, 4th Earl of Carnwath, to Sir George Lockhart, President of the Court of Session. Following his assassination in

1689, his family retained it until the 19th century, although is not known if this portion of the estate was feud out. In 1816 the owner is named as Linning Esq, while by 1825 the property belonged to the Patersons, then by 1837 the Blackwoods, and in 1864 by the Griersons.

The present house is a single-storey pavilion-style house with a sunken basement. It apparently dates from 1817 and is a category 'B' Listed Building.

Other references: Haig Castle, Heg Castle, Ugs Castle

OLD BALLIKINRAIN

The Lennox & East Dunbartonshire Private OS 57 NS 559880
1 mile southeast of Balfron, east of the A876 and north of B818, south of River Endrick, at Old Ballikinrain.

Now much altered and having an 18th century facade and some 19th century features, Old Ballikinrain incorporates a 17th century fortified house. It retains a drawbar, known as 'Rob Roy's bar', to defend the entrance.

This was a Napier property from as early as the 15th century. In 1741 James Napier of Ballikinrain was one of many local lairds who contracted themselves into the provision of a mutual watch of their highland borders. On the death of John Napier, the 16th of the line in the late 18th century, the property passed to his grandson. He was the son of the marriage between John's only daughter and Robert Dunmore of Kelvinside. Robert was a well-known tobacco merchant and John's business partner. He built a cotton mill at Balfron and his son adopted the surname Dunmore-Napier. By 1886 this family also ended with an heiress, who was married to Graham-Stirling of Craigbarnet. Old Ballikinrain is a category 'B' Listed Building.

Nearby is Ballikinrain Castle, a 19th century Scots baronial castellated mansion, designed by David Bryce in 1864 for Sir Archibald Orr-Ewing. He was MP for Dunbartonshire, and purchased the estate in 1862. The house was built around a steel frame, but was burned out in 1913. It was rebuilt in 1916 and operated as a hotel, gave temporary residence to a private school during World War II, and now operates as a Church of Scotland Residential School for boys. This is also a 'B' Listed Building.

Other reference: Ballikinrain

OLD DALQUHURN HOUSE

The Lennox and East Dunbartonshire Ruin or site OS 63 NS 390778
2 miles northeast of Dumbarton, east of the A82 by minor roads and foot, east of Renton, at Dalquhurn Point.

Site of an old or fortified house. The house was described as being of three storeys, with a single storey wing at the western end. It was 'of plain architecture' and stood on a knoll above the west bank of the River Leven.

In 1286 the estate of Dalquhurn was granted by Malcolm, Earl of Lennox, to his Seneschal, Walter Spreull. In 1620 John Spreull of Cowden sold it to his son-in-law, John Dennistoun of Colgrain. It was sold again in 1669 and then in 1692 to Archibald Smollett. He was the father of the novelist Tobias Smollett, who was born here in 1721. There is a monument in his memory in the town and the family mausoleum is in the kirkyard of St Andrew's Church in Renton. Renton itself is named after Cecilia Renton, a daughter-in-law of the family. The Stirling family had a large bleachfield at Dalquhurn, which developed into a substantial dye and print works. The site has now been cleared, but the industry occupied much of the ground around the site of the house.

Other references: Dalchurn, Dalchurne, Dalquhurn

OLD PLACE, Kilsyth

The Lennox & East Dunbartonshire Ruin or site OS 64 NS 690780
1.5 miles west of Kilsyth, off minor roads north of A803, just north of Queenzieburn at Old Place Farm.

Site of a hall house of the Livingstones of Kilsyth which was in ruins by 1740. It appeared on Pont's map of the late 16th century and on General Roy's map of 1747-56.

ORBISTON HOUSE

North Lanarkshire Ruin or site OS 64 NS 735587
1 mile northwest of Motherwell, off minor roads, west of the A721, on Bellshill Golf Course.

This is the site of a tower house, also known as Osbornstoun, of the Hamilton family, the last remnants of which were demolished around 1830. Orbiston House, an 18th century mansion and the 19th century successor, stood some way to the south at the northern edge of Strathclyde Park.

Opinions vary as to the date of the old tower, suggesting 15th to 16th century or a little later. A 15th century date is most likely, coinciding with the beginning of the Hamilton tenure. It is likely that this original house was badly damaged in the aftermath of Langside of 1568, when the troops of the Regent Moray conducted a persecutory raid on Hamilton properties across Lanarkshire. Only a small portion of the northeast wall with stone sink and conduit drain to the outside survive below the surface of the first green at Bellshill Golf Course.

The ruin of the mansion indicates possible origins in the 17th century. There were vaulted chambers on the lower and possibly second storeys. A ruinous 18th century doocot and icehouse remain. The mansion ruins and doocot are category 'C' Listed Buildings.

The Barony of Bothwell consisted of all land between 'the two Calders', which included the lands of Orbiston. They were originally owned by Walter Olifard, Justiciar of Lothian. He granted £10 annually from the lands of Orbiston to the founding of a chapel there dedicated to St Catherine the Virgin. He died in 1242 and his son-in-law, Walter de Moravia, inherited. Bothwell then passed to Archibald the Grim, Earl of Douglas, who had married the heiress, Johanna of Bothwell. He donated Orbiston to the Collegiate Church of Bothwell in 1398.

In 1468, Gavin Hamilton, a 4th son of Hamilton of Cadzow, was Provost of Bothwell. With the consent of the relevant parties, he gifted Orbiston to his sons of whom the third, John, founded the line of Hamilton of Orbiston. A later John Hamilton of Orbiston was killed at Langside in 1568. Two years later his cousin, James Hamilton of Bothwellhaugh, assassinated the Regent Moray in Linlithgow. Another John Hamilton of Orbiston was granted charters of Orbiston, Carnbroe, Unthank, Stevenstoun, Alderstoun, Carphin, and Jerviston in 1604. His son, unsurprisingly also named John, was Lord Justice Clerk, and further extended the family's lands by gaining a charter of the lands of Provan and purchasing Erskine from the Earl of Mar in 1638. The property was inherited by Hamilton of Dalzell and the estates were combined.

In 1800 the family sold Orbiston due to insurmountable debts. It was purchased by Gilbert Douglas, a West India merchant. He renamed the mansion and estate Douglas Park. His widow purchased the nearby estate of Boggs and adopted the name Orbiston for the combined estate.

Other references: Orbistan; Urbanstoun

OVERTOUN

The Lennox and East Dunbartonshire   Private   OS 64   NS 424761
1.5 miles northeast of Dumbarton, off minor roads north of the A82 at Milton, at Overtoun.

Overtoun House (or Castle), also sometimes known as Overtoun of Colquhoun, is a large Scots baronial mansion, designed in 1860 by the architect James Smith for the chemical manufacturer, James White of Overton. James Smith was the father of the unhappy Madeline Smith, who was tried and acquitted for the murder of her French lover in 1857.

Overtoun was part of the extensive Colquhoun estates of Umfridus de Kilpatrick in the 13th century. In 1695 the lands of Chapelton, Chapelcroft, Middleton and Meikle and Little Overtouns were sold by Sir Humphrey Colquhoun of Luss to John Colquhoun of Garshake. The Garshake estate belonged to James Duncanson, Town Clerk of Dumbarton, during the Jacobite rebellions of 1715 and 1745. Gabriel Lang of Greenock then purchased Overtoun from the Garshake Estate in 1762 and apparently built a cattle farm on the property. White purchased Overtoun in the 1850s, having lived in the neighbouring property of Crosslet. His son became Lord Overtoun in 1907 after a successful political career.

The house was acquired by Dumbarton Town Council in 1939 and came into use as a maternity hospital until 1970. It is now used as a Christian Centre for Hope and Healing. The estate, nature trail and formal gardens are open to the public (www.overtounhouse.com).

PALACERIGG

The Lennox & East Dunbartonshire   Ruin or site   OS 64   NS 783733?
Palacerigg Country Park, Cumbernauld.

The exact site of a lesser house of the Flemings has not been located. As the name implies, it is believed to have been a hall house. It is recorded in the early 17th century, though may have been older. In the 17th and 18th centuries it is thought to have been occupied by tenant farmers. The name 'Palacerigg' appears in Blaeu's *Atlas Novus* of 1654 and in General Roy's map of the mid 18th century. It disappeared from map references in the 19th century, but by the turn of the 20th century the City of Glasgow had established a 'farm colony' at Palacerigg, an attempt to deal with their unemployment problem. In the 1970s it became home to a Country Park, well known for its collection of rare breeds and wildlife sanctuary.

http://www.visitlanarkshire.com/attractions/garden-and-parks/Palacerigg-Country-Park/

PARISHOLM

South Lanarkshire Ruin or site OS 71 NS 762280
5 miles southwest of Douglas, to southeast of Glenbuck Loch, just south of A70, southwest of near Parish Holm.

The remains of a small tower were still visible close to the foot of Cairntable in 1864. In 1993 the site was identified to the southwest of the present farm, where earth-fast stones and a level platform were formerly identified as a sheep fold. The building is thought to have been an L-shaped tower with vaulted basement and an enclosing bank. It is listed as a possible bastle house.

A small tower is marked on Pont's manuscript map as 'Parrok Hoom', and as 'Parrchoom' on Blaeu's *Atlas Novus* of 1654.

The name may be explained by records of a chapel in the vicinity. This was founded during the reign of James IV and dedicated to the Virgin Mary. It stood on the banks of Monks Water. In 1513 James IV granted the four merk land of Parroch-holm *in mortmain* to the chaplain of the chapel, Sir George Eirmair.

Other references: Paris Holm, Parroch-holm, Parrockholm

PARKGLEN

Renfrewshire Ruin or site OS 63 NS 400707
2 miles northeast of Houston, 3 miles north of Bridge of Weir, by minor roads and foot north of A761, north of Haddockton in Parkglen Wood.

Mortared rubble and foundations of various outbuildings sit alongside a more substantial structure, thought to have been a tower house. The ruins are hidden below dense vegetation. Some sections of stone wall are visible along a cliff edge on part of the site. The south side of what is thought to have been the tower are marked out by a stony mound measuring 18ft wide and 5ft high. The walls may have reached 3ft thick. A reference from 1961 records that 'The site of Park Castle situated on the Formaken Burn, near Bishopton, after a long search have now been traced'. There is no such water course marked on the OS maps. The reference probably relates to the Parkglen Burn, which runs below the ruin and then through Formakin Park to the east. Also related is: 'The foundations show that it was a place of considerable strength.'

Place-name evidence supported by early cartographic evidence suggests that Parkglen is the remnant of the Castle of Park which originated in 13th century. It appears in Pont's map of 1596 and subsequently in Blaeu's *Atlas Novus*. The site is denoted as 'ruins,' adjacent to 'Parkside', on General Roy's map of 1747-56. In 1710 the estate was known as Park of Erskine and the site is just south of a farm known as Park Erskine.

This was the seat of the family of the same name, which ended with the death of William Park of that Ilk during the reign of James IV. William left three heiresses. Christian, the eldest, inherited Park and married Cunninghame of Auchenharvie. This couple also left an heiress, who married George Houston and founded the family of Houston of Park. The line died out shortly before 1710 with another George.

Other references: Castle of Park, Nether Glens, Park Castle, Park of Erskine

PARKHEAD

South Lanarkshire Ruin or site OS 72 NS 863305
1 mile east of Douglas, east of the A 70, and just west of the M74 and B7078, at Parkhead.

A large tower named Parkhead appears here on Pont's map of the late 16th century.

There were Douglases of Parkhead as early as 1527 when Sir James Douglas of Parkhead was Captain of the Royal Guard. His daughter, Mariota, married George Douglas, the illegitimate son of Douglas of Pittendreich. George was the nephew of the Earl of Angus, and half brother of James, Earl of Morton. He is said to have been Provost of Edinburgh and captain of its castle in 1556 and 1577. His second son was Sir George Douglas of Mordington, Gentleman of the Bedchamber to James VI. The elder son, James, extended his estate by marrying Elizabeth Carlyle, heiress of Torthorwald. He murdered James Stewart, Earl of Arran, in 1595 and was himself murdered in revenge by Arran's nephew in 1608. His son, also James, inherited the estates and became Lord Torthorwald. The estates were acquired by William Douglas, Earl of Queensberry, in 1638, in whose favour James resigned his title.

PARTICK CASTLE

City of Glasgow   Ruin or site   OS 64   NS 559663

In Partick, on west bank of River Kelvin, and north of River Clyde, off minor roads south of A814, at east end of Castlebank Street.

Partick Castle has long gone, though it stood on the site of an ancient manor of the Bishops of Glasgow. There may also have been an ancient seat of the Kings of Strathclyde at Partick. David I granted the lands to the Bishop of Glasgow in 1136.

Despite the ruins being given the name of 'Bishop's Castle', the castle was from the early 17th century. The contract for its construction survives and describes the structure in detail. It was commissioned by George Hutcheson, the well-known city benefactor. He employed William Millar, 'the masoun in Kylwynning', as his builder. The contract dates the castle to 1611. It was an L-plan building, 33ft high. It had two storeys plus a garret and a vaulted basement. The contract states that some of the foundations and walls were previously built and that these were to be removed, new walls to be erected of sufficient thickness as to serve a vaulted house.

The work requested was as follows: 'a mayne hous and ane jamb, turnpykis, and all other easiments', the walls of the mayne hous being maid thrie futtis and ane half of the said George's awin fute' longer than the gables already laid. The jamb or wing was to be 16ft between walls, and to contain an arched fireplace. The turnpike was to be at the northeast re-entrant. The doors were to be arched and the passageways of the basement vaulted. There were to

be cellars and a kitchen in the basement, and a pantry on the first floor with service stair to the east cellar. A variety of small windows were to be inserted providing plenty of light. The room in the wing off the hall on the first floor was to be called the 'chalmer of daiss' and a variety of gargoyles and water spouts were to adorn the corner angles of the building. The mason had to provide a high arch built in the north wall so that a gallery could be formed above the hall and serviced from the room over the 'chalmer of daiss'. Alternatively this was to be an independent room for use as a wardrobe room for Mrs Hutcheson. Dormer windows were to provide light for the top floor bedrooms.

The house came into the possession of John Crawford of Milton. It was vacated by 1770 and unroofed in 1783. It survived as a ruin until removed in 1837. A large structure named 'Parthick' is denoted in a park on the east bank of the River Kelvin on Pont's map of c.1596. This is probably 'Bishop's Mills', which stood in this location.

PATRICKHOLM

South Lanarkshire   Ruin or site   OS 64   NS 756500

0.5 miles southwest of Larkhall, off minor roads and track west of B7078, above west bank of Avon Water.

A ruinous T-plan two-storey 17th century farm house contains vaulted cellars from a previous building on this site. There was also an undated armorial panel over the door, bearing the arms of Hamilton. A property known as Patrickholm appears in Blaeu's *Atlas* and is known to have belonged to the Hamiltons of Raploch. From the beginning of the 17th century, it was held by the Hamiltons of Lethame. The property later returned to the Hamiltons of Raploch by marriage, and thereafter it appears to have been occupied by a variety of tenants.

Local legend asserts it to have been a rendezvous for Royalists during the 17th century 'Killing Times' when Covenanters were persecuted. It was occupied in 1954 but by 1959 was vacant and falling into disrepair. It appears as a ruin on modern maps.

PENNYTERSAL MOTTE

Renfrewshire   Ruin or site   OS 63   NS 337712

2 miles west of Houston, by minor roads and foot south of the A761, west of Auchenbothie Mains, and east of Priestside.

This slightly oval motte stands on high ground and has the traditional Christmas-pudding profile. It measures 88x75.5x10ft and has been partly damaged on the north side. In 1955 slight traces remained of earthworks to the west, east and south which were assumed to be the outline of the bailey. The terrace to the west is now thought to be natural and the earthworks of the east and south sides are no longer visible.

The motte lies near to Auchenbothie Mains, a name associated by Blind Harry with Sir Malcolm Wallace, the father of Sir William Wallace. He was said to be designated 'of Ellerslie and Auchenbothie'.

PENWOLD HOUSE

Renfrewshire   Ruin or site   OS 63   NS 400642

1 mile southeast of Bridge of Weir, and 0.5 miles north of Kilbarchan, off minor roads south of A761, at Penwold House.

The foundations of a castle were barely visible in 1856, though the stones survived in situ until dug up early in the 20th century to provide material for a garden.

A large portion of the Parish of Kilbarchan consisted of the estate of Penwold, once Penneld, Pannell or Penuld. It was held by Henry St Martin in the 12th century, one of the knights who owed service to Walter the High Steward. In 1177 Walter granted the lands to the monks of Paisley Abbey. The castle was reputedly built by a man named Haic, who never completed it.

In the 17th century it was a property of Lord Semple, who granted the estate to James Cunninghame of Weitlands, a descendant of the 3rd Lord Semple. In the 1950s several roughly hewn stones were excavated at the site, and these were said to be similar to those removed to make a rockery at Penwold House.

Other references: Pannell, Penneld

PETTINAIN

South Lanarkshire   Ruin or site   OS 72   NS 955429

2 miles south of Carstairs Junction, by minor roads south and east of the A70, and north of A73, at Pettinain.

A possible motte is listed in the Scottish Sites and Monuments Record. It was identified during a review of Norman settlement in Upper Clydesdale in 1978. The location given is in the churchyard, though this seems to be based on the traditional grouping of medieval church and manor rather than any structural evidence. The location given in Canmore is imprecise. The church at Pettinain was granted to Dryburgh Abbey in 1150 by David I.

In the 12th century Hugh of Pettinain (also known as Padvinan) was granted the lands of Kilpeter in Renfrewshire by Baldwin of Biggar. The village and family of Houston take their name from him. He was a regular charter witness, notably for Walter the Steward in 1165 and 1173.

It seems that at least part of the estate was crown property, since David I granted a portion of the land with the church to monks of Dryburgh. In 1249-86, for 'his lands of Pettinain which he held of the king', Adam 'of the livery' was found to owe the service of two bowmen and one 'serviens' on horseback for the making of livery.

Eustace Maxwell was granted the estate of Pettinain by Robert I. It had been forfeited by John, son of Valdeve. It was then forfeited by Herbert Maxwell before David II granted half of the barony to Herbert Murray. In the aftermath of the Battle of Arkinholm in 1455 the Earl of Ormonde, brother of the Earl of Douglas, was captured by Carlyle of Torthorwald and Johnstone of that Ilk. They were rewarded with one half each of the £40 land of Pettinain. Through Elizabeth Carlyle, her estate passed by marriage to Douglas of Parkhead, later ownership mirroring that estate, while the Johnstone half became the estate of Westraw.

PLACE OF KILLEARN

The Lennox and East Dunbartonshire   Ruin or site   OS 57   NS 522852

0.5 miles southwest of Killearn, west of the A875, and east of the A81, south of the B834, in Killearn Glen.

Place of Killearn was an 18th century laird's house, which probably replaced earlier houses.

Killearn was a Graham property for centuries, but the first to be designated of Killearn was William, Rector of Killearn. He was the fourth son of the second Earl of Montrose, who died in 1571. His descendants retained possession until the 18th century. John Graham of Killearn is best known as the Duke of Montrose's notorious factor in the tales of Rob Roy, and he was Sheriff Depute of Dumbarton.

Killearn passed to the Scot family and by the 1790s it belonged to the Montgomerys.

In 1994 non invasive archaeology revealed the outline of a rectilinear building, 49ft long.

PLACE OF PAISLEY

Renfrewshire   Ruin or site   OS 64   NS 485639
In Paisley, just south of the A726, at Paisley Abbey.

Place of Paisley is a large complex building of several periods, attached to the structure of Paisley Abbey. It originated in the late 16th and early 17th century, but has had several additions and modifications. It stands around the former site of the abbey cloister to the southwest of the complex.

St Mirren's Chapel, which projects from the southern face of the abbey, abuts the wall of the northeastern block of the Place. The upper floor of the chapel was accessed from the Place, and was incorporated into its accommodation. The northeastern block reaches four storeys and an attic. There are dormer windows on the south wall, which has no windows at all on the ground floor. Adjoining this, by overlapping the southwestern corner, is a long block running east-west, and built in 1675. This has a small wing at the southeastern corner. There is a fore-stair projecting from the eastern side of this block in the re-entrant, giving access to first-floor level. The east gable has one small window per floor and the west gable has a number of small windows on each. Square corner towers projected at both ends of the west wall. Adjoining the northern of these, and running north to enclose the former cloister, was a long western block. This had contained the oldest parts of the building. With the northern tower, it was removed in 1864. A new northern tower was built in 1961-62. The southern tower rises to only two storeys. There is a fine 17th century painted ceiling in one of the rooms and several of the chambers retain wooden panelling.

Founded by Walter Fitzalan, High Steward of Scotland in the 12th century, Paisley Abbey is the burial place of all six High Stewards of Scotland as well as King Robert III. Other notable burials include both wives of Robert II and his mother, Marjorie Bruce, the daughter of Robert I.

Lord Claud Hamilton was created Commendator of the Abbey at the tender age of eight years old. He was created Lord Paisley in 1587 and his descendants became Earls of Abercorn. He or his son built the Place as their own residence. It passed to the Semples and back to the Hamiltons before coming into the hands of the Earl of Angus. It was purchased by the 1st Earl of Dundonald. Later it provided a number of dwelling houses and then contained a public house before badly deteriorating. It has been restored and functions as the manse for the abbey church.

Both the Place of Paisley and Paisley Abbey are category 'A' listed buildings.

PLOTCOCK CASTLE

South Lanarkshire   Ruin or site   OS 64   NS 741502
2 miles west of Larkhall, by minor roads and foot, 3 miles west of A723 and 0.5 miles east of Thinacres, above east side of the Powforth Burn just east of Plotcock Bridge.

On a promontory above a sharp bend in the gully of the Plotcock Burn, scant ruins survive of a 16th century rectangular tower house, apparently measuring only 18ft by 14ft. This was presumably an internal measurement. The lower courses survive of rubble built walls, which reach about 6ft thick. There was a ditch to the east, isolating the promontory. The site is very overgrown and appears as a mound from the exterior due to the build up of soil against the walls. It was partly destroyed in 1828.

It is possible that this is the seat of the estate of Kittiemuir. In 1529 this was sold by James Hamilton of Kincavel to his cousin, James Hamilton of Stonehouse. In the 1530s it belonged to Sir James Hamilton of Finnart and was identified in his charters as the inheritance of his son, Alexander. The tower was reputedly used as a prison.

By the 19th century the tower probably stood within the bounds of the Broomilton estate, the property of the Aikman family of Ross.

Plotcock is an old Scottish name for Satan. As a result the area is rich in tales of witches and ghosts inspired by the site. One 19th century supernatural tale tells of a bull hide full of treasure buried below the castle and guarded by the Devil himself.

The name Plotcock does not appear on early maps. On Pont's map the tower is shown as Burmelstone, an early name for Broomilton. By the time of Forrest's map of 1816, the castle was ruinous.

Other references: Brumilton, Burmelstone, Kittiemuir

POLLOK CASTLE

Renfrewshire Ruin or site OS 64 NS 524569

1 mile west of Newton Mearns, and 2 miles southeast of Barrhead, east of Balgray reservoir, by minor roads west of B769, on Pollok Castle Estate.

Pollok Castle was a renaissance mansion dated 1686 and 1687, which incorporated a keep of the 15th century. It burned to a shell in 1882 and was restored in the baronial style. It was demolished in 1947 and only traces of foundations remain. Sited on the edge of a crag high above the valleys of Clyde and Cart, the house provided extensive views reaching beyond distant Ben Lomond.

The castle was described in 1710 as having been 'a handsome old tower, according to the ordinary model, with a large battlement'. When Sir Robert Pollok decided to build himself the mansion house in 1686-93, he demolished the east and south walls, using the remainder to form part of the southwest corner of his stately C-plan mansion. A few original features survived, such as a straight mural stair in the north wall from ground floor to first, then a turnpike within the northwest corner wall to the floors above. A few small windows and a mural chamber also survived.

The mansion was a large four-storey house, much decorated with fancy stonework, with numerous stone garden features such as sundials, pavilions, and ornate gateways. It was notable because of the careful dating engraved on successive additions and alterations in 1706, 1708 and 1710. This included the addition of stable blocks and other peripheral buildings. The remains of a motte were recorded within the bounds of the garden. This has apparently vanished with extensive earthworks required by the construction of the M77.

The Pollok family originated with Fulbert in the 12th century. His son, Peter de Pollok, was the first laird to appear on record when he donated land to Paisley Abbey in the reign of Malcolm IV. He also witnessed a charter by King William in 1190. Another Peter of Pollok gave homage to Edward I in 1296, and in 1372 Robert Pollok of that Ilk received a charter of his lands from Sir John Maxwell, his grandfather. In 1568 Sir John Pollok fought for Mary, Queen of Scots, at Langside. In 1593 his son, also John, was killed at the Battle of Dryffe Sands while supporting his Maxwell cousins in their feud with the Johnstones. The Polloks were a belligerent lot and crop up in reports of feuding throughout this area.

Sir Robert Pollok, who built the mansion, was a made a baronet in 1703 for his service during the Glorious Revolution of 1688, when William of Orange and his wife Mary Stewart replaced her father James VII and II on the throne. Pollok was the first MP for Renfrewshire in the Westminster Parliament following the Act of Union in 1707 and commander of the government garrison at Fort William during the 1715 Jacobite rebellion.

Pollok Castle was used as an ammunition store during World War II and was last occupied in 1944.

POLLOK HOUSE

City of Glasgow NTS OS 64 NS 549618

Off minor roads in Pollok Country Park, north of Haggs Road and west of Dumbreck Road, 0.75 miles south of M77 at Dumbreck Interchange.

The remains of the Laigh Castle of the Maxwells may constitute part of the garden wall near the stable block of Pollok House. The Maxwells had at least two earlier castles somewhere nearby, one possibly just south of the White Cart, on what is now a golf course. One of these was built in about 1367. The sites were destroyed when the gardens were laid out. The Laigh Castle may have been built upon the site of the other.

In the original state there was a ditch with drawbridge, the river supplementing the defences to the south. The Maxwells abandoned the site in favour of their new castle at Haggs in 1585, but returned in 1753 when Pollok

House was completed. This was extended in 1890 by the architect Sir Robert Rowand Anderson.

The Maxwells of Pollok were a branch of those who gained Mearns by marrying a Pollok heiress in the 13th century, Nether Pollok being a division of the original estate. The first of the name was John Maxwell of Pollok, who witnessed a charter by his brother Herbert Maxwell of Caerlaverock to Paisley Abbey c.1273. In 1676 Sir George Maxwell took part in a Witch Trial in Gourock. Shortly afterwards he believed himself bewitched, suffering a 'hot and fiery distemper'. A local dumb girl disclosed that his effigies were to be found stuck with pins at the house of Janet Mathie, widow to the miller of Shaw Mill. Janet, her son John Stewart (an alleged warlock), her daughter Annabel, and another three women were tried in Paisley in 1677. Annabel was only 14 years old and was released, the others were burned at the stake. Sir George recovered, but lived for only a few short months. Janet Douglas, the dumb informant, recovered her speech. The story has been dramatised for the stage. George's son died childless and the estate was inherited by his cousin, Maxwell of Blawarthill.

In 1966 after many years of selling portions of the estate off for development, the daughter of Sir John Stirling Maxwell gifted the house and park to the city. The house is used as a museum and exhibition centre for local events. There is a hand carved model of Crookston Castle, fashioned from a branch of 'the Crookston Yew' under which Mary, Queen of Scots, is reputed to have pledged her troth to Henry, Lord Darnley. The famous Burrell Collection is situated within the park and displays a fraction of Sir William Burrell's collection of artwork, armour, weaponry and other antiquities. The collection is so large that it could not conceivably be displayed at one time, and so is frequently changed. The park also contains a highland cattle enclosure, the Strathclyde Police Dog Handling School, Mounted Division, and other items of interest.

Pollok House and several of its associated structures are category 'A' Listed Buildings. Numerous others are 'B' listed.

Visiting (NTS): open daily all year 10am-5pm, closed on 25/26th Dec., and 1/2 Jan. (tel 0141 616 6410).

Other references: Laigh Castle, Nether Pollok

POLNOON CASTLE

Renfrewshire   Ruin or site   OS 64   NS 585513
3 miles southwest of East Kilbride, 1 mile southeast of Eaglesham, off minor roads south of the B764, on the west bank of the White Cart at Polnoon.

The name Polnoon is said to be a corruption of the Scots word 'poinding', where a debtor's moveable property is seized to pay their creditor. It is more likely that the 'pol' name element indicates a deep pool or bend of the burn.

Polnoon Castle is the ruinous remnant of a strong 14th century castle of the Montgomeries. It consists of a motte surmounted by the remnants of a strong castle, protected by precipitous drops on the north and west sides. On the west, the approach is protected by the gully of the Polnoon Water, and on the east are the silted remnants of a deep ditch. The approach from the south is across a level field. Mature trees cover the mound, which hosts several massive though shapeless lumps of mortared rubble, while grass covered smaller fragments make the going treacherous on the slope of the east side. Along the southern base of the motte, erosion by cattle and rabbits has exposed lengths of a revetment or the lower courses of a courtyard wall. The summit appears grass grown and featureless, but again masses of rubble below the grass create difficult walking terrain. At the northwest corner of

the summit, a few inches of well-finished ashlar blocks protrude from the soil, marking out the corner of a keep. A second outer court is thought to have stood between the ruin and the present farmhouse to the east. From burn to battlement the keep is thought to have reached a full height of about 100ft, an impressive stronghold. An armorial panel above the door of the Cross Keys Inn at Eaglesham is said to have been removed from the castle, as the best stone provided

building material for the planned village that exists today.

Sir Henry 'Hotspur' Percy was captured by Sir John Montgomerie of Eaglesham at the Battle of Otterburn in 1388. Held for ransom, Hotspur befriended Montgomerie and helped design his new castle. He paid for it with his own funds, or so the legend goes. Sir John is said to have commissioned a carving of a spur to be placed above the door of the castle in commemoration of his capture of Hotspur.

In the 1360s Sir John had married the heiress of Hugh Eglinton and gained that family's large Ayrshire estates of Ardrossan and Eglinton. The family took the designation 'of Ardrossan', and in 1430 Sir Alexander Montgomerie was Governor of Kintyre and Knapdale for James I. In 1445 he became Lord Montgomerie, and in 1454 his son of the same name acquired the Heritable Bailliary of Cunninghame from his nephew Cunninghame of Kilmaurs. His son, Hugh, was created Earl of Eglinton in 1503 by James IV. In 1520, John Master of Eglinton was killed in Edinburgh at the skirmish known as Cleanse the Causeway, a conflict between the Earls of Arran and Angus. Hugh's grandson, also Hugh, succeeded him. He was one of those appointed Governor of Scotland while James V went to France to arrange his marriage in 1536-7. The Earls of Eglinton had a long-running feud with the Cunninghame Earls of Glencairn and the 4th Earl was murdered by Cunninghame of Clonbeith near Stewarton in 1586. The Montgomeries took their revenge when Cunninghame was found hiding up a chimney in Hamilton. He was cut to pieces by Hugh's brother, Robert.

Polnoon was the principal residence of the Montgomeries until they removed to Eglinton Castle at the beginning of the 16th century. Polnoon fell into decay, but was refurbished for use in 1617. It was again in a ruinous state by 1676.

The site is a Scheduled Ancient Monument.

PONEIL

South Lanarkshire   Ruin or site   OS 71   NS 836343
Off minor roads, 1.5 miles west of M73, 3 miles north of Douglas, at Midtown of Poneil.

Site of a tower house, which appears on Pont's manuscript map of 1596, and subsequently in Blaeu's *Atlas Novus* of the 17th century. It is said that in 1147 the lands of Poneil were granted to Theobold the Fleming, ancestor of the Douglases, by the Abbot of Kelso. One source, however, indicated that there may have been a transcription error in a later copy of the charter and that the grant was only of the lands of Douglas.

In 1269 William son of Adam de Folkart issued a document in favour the Abbot of Kelso, admitting that his father had illegally held the lands of Poneil, which rightfully belonged to the abbey. This was to avoid implementation of a threat of excommunication, a sentence which had already caused his father to leave Scotland. In 1270 the Abbot of Kelso granted Poneil to William de Douglas. The estate was won back in litigation by the Folkarts. The case began in 1295, and was concluded before 1311, when Alexander de Folkart was in possession. It was again in dispute in 1316, when Alexander had not paid his feu duties to the abbot for nine years. In his defence he pointed out that the estate had been devastated by war. The abbot agreed that the feu duty should be reduced for the next three years and that Alexander would hold them in liferent. The family disappeared from the area in about 1495 (see Folkerton).

By 1587 the Weirs of Blackwood were in possession. In that year John Weir of Poneil was murdered by Weir of Stonebyres, part of an on-going feud between the families over seniority. As a result, the latter signed a bond of manrent to Blackwood, effectively acknowledging him as his chief.

PORTERFIELD

Renfrewshire   Ruin or site   OS 64   NS 498670
0.75 miles west of Renfrew, on east bank of White Cart Water, by minor roads west of A741 and south of A8, at Porterfield.

Site of an old or fortified house of the Porterfields of that Ilk.

In 1262 John de Porter witnessed the donation of the Kirk of Dundonald to Paisley Abbey by Alexander the High Steward. Walter de Porter submitted to Edward I in 1296 and about 1362 Stephen de Porter obtained a charter of his lands of Porterfield from Robert, Earl of Strathearn. By 1460, when John Porterfield gained a charter of the estate from James III, the family were calling themselves the Porterfields of that Ilk. In 1544 another John Porterfield purchased the estate of Duchal from Lord Lyle. The line died out in 1815 when Alexander Porterfield died unmarried.

POSSIL

City of Glasgow   Ruin or site   OS 64   NS 591682
2 miles north of Glasgow, east of Balmore Road, south of Mansion Street, near Saracen Street.

Site of an old or fortified house of the Crawfords. The estate of Possil was church land until the Reformation. This was divided into Over and Nether Possil, the latter subsequently being divided again to form Nether Possil and Easter Nether Possil. It was the former which was acquired by Hew Crawford of Cloberhill in 1595 for his second son Robert. In 1612 Crawford of Possil was imprisoned in Edinburgh Castle for taking the law into his own hands. With the aid of his uncle, Hew Crawford of Cloberhill, he tried to recover a debt owed to him by the late Earl of Eglinton by attacking his castle at Corslie.

The Crawfords held Possil until 1638, but by the end of that century it had passed through various hands until in 1697 the writer John Forbes built a new house on the estate.

In 1749 one William Crawford of Birkhead purchased the estate and subsequently bought the old Easter Nether Possil lands to reunite the estate. In 1808 Possil House was sold to the Campbells. Over Possil had become part of the estate of Milton, which in 1828 came to the Stewarts of Castlemilk, causing them to add Crawford to their surname in order to inherit.

Possil House has since been demolished, the site occupied by the Possilpark Trading Estate.

PRIORHILL

South Lanarkshire   Ruin or site   OS 71   NS 750400
4 miles southeast of Strathaven by B7086 and minor roads, south and east of Kype water, southwest of Deadwaters at Priorhill.

Site of a large tower, depicted on Pont's map of 1596. It was subsequently illustrated in Blaeu's *Atlas Novus*, though the name Birkwood had been transposed to it. A large house here is illustrated on Forrest's map of 1816. By the mid 19th century the property had been divided into two farms, North Priorhill and South Priorhill.

This may have been a residence of the Prior of Lesmahagow. The lands of the priory were apparently sold off to former tenant farmers at the Reformation, Hamilton of Priorhill was one of these. In 1662 John Hamilton of Priorhill was fined £300 for supporting the Covenanters.

PROVAND'S LORDSHIP

City of Glasgow   Glasgow Museums   OS 64   NS 605655
In Glasgow, on the west side of Castle Street opposite Glasgow Cathedral, and St Mungo's Museum.

Provand's Lordship is the oldest house in the City of Glasgow. Sited at the centre of the medieval city, it was set within the vicinity of the cathedral, castle and the original university site. It is said to date from 1471, though its fireplace has been firmly dated to 1460. It was initially part of St Nicholas's Hospital, constructed by Bishop Andrew Muirhead. It became the town house or manse of the Lord of the Prebend of Provan(d), hence the name. During its ecclesiastical ownership, it was held in common ownership with Provanhall. While there is no evidence that it was fortified, it provides a worthwhile visit and gives a sense of medieval high-status domestic living. The medieval garden and cloisters were designed to illustrate a shift from medicinal to recreational purposes. The house features medieval furniture donated from the Burrell Collection, and is a category 'A' Listed Building.

Open all year: Mon–Thu & Sat 10.00-17.00, and Fri & Sun 11.00-17.00. This property has disabled access and there is public car parking nearby.

PROVANHALL

City of Glasgow   NTS   OS 64   NS 667663
50yds West of Auchinlea Road, Easterhouse, in Auchinlea Park.

Described by the National Trust for Scotland as '...probably the most perfect pre-Reformation mansion house in Scotland', they claim a 15th century origin for this house, while other sources suppose it originates from the 16th century. This certainly poses a question over the Provand's Lordship claim to be the oldest house in Glasgow, though they seem to be contemporary. It was sketched by Pont on his late 16th century map, though it is unclear whether this represents a single tower within a courtyard, or a complex of three buildings.

The house and a later successor form the north and south perimeters of a square courtyard, which originally stretched to the shore of Provan Loch, long since drained and now represented by a duck pond to the south. The more modern house is probably late 17th century and was renovated by Dr John Buchanan in the form of a

plantation house, reflecting the source of his wealth in the tobacco trade. This part of the property is properly known as Blochairn House, though picked up a by-name of Coach Mailing, as it was a rest stop for the Glasgow-Stirling mail coach. The lower courses of the walls of this building are thought to be those of an earlier structure, probably of the same date as the 'old house'.

The older house contains a huge fireplace in the kitchen. Another, on the first floor, is very similar to one dated firmly at 1460 in Provand's Lordship. The house is of two storeys and a garret, the ground floor having three vaulted rooms. The vaulting in the kitchen runs east to west and that in the dairy and hallway north-south. This unusual feature gave added strength to the floor above and the vaulting in the kitchen is reckoned as one of the finest surviving examples in the country. The hallway provided access to the round 'stair tower' in the northeast corner of the building, though no there is no longer evidence that a stair existed. It has been suggested that access to the floor above was by removable ladder. In the base of the round tower are two styles of gunloop, which protected against attack from the blind side of the house. There are other loops at first floor level.

The first floor contains two rooms, each with fireplace. The room to the east was the main living room and was supplied from the dairy below by a primitive form of dumb waiter. This room was at the exit from the stair tower, though a later external stair and door now provide direct access from the courtyard. A curious hollow in the floor, just off centre, puzzled observers for many years, until it was realised that this was the resting-place of the ladder that originally led to the garret space. The room to the west provided sleeping quarters and contained a later stair to the attic and servant's quarters, possibly via a long vanished turret.

The small courtyard has an unusual feature in that the gateway is protected by a lookout window above the gate in the eastern wall, this being accessed by a flight of stairs which is flush to the wall. The stair also provides access to a gunloop, which could provide covering fire across the approaches. A later gate in the western wall leads to a walled garden.

There is much evidence of rebuilding at Provanhall, and some features may have been wrongly located at the 1930s restoration or earlier. The present boundary wall is thought to date from 1647, but it also carries signs of adaptation. The lookout window above the gate has possibly been re-sited from elsewhere and the presence of different styles of gunloop in the 'stair' tower, imply different eras of construction. The scars of development and repair work are also evident on the west gable, where a blocked doorway at first floor level and the stumps of the original courtyard wall are obvious.

The lands of Provan were originally granted to the church of Glasgow by David, Earl of Cumbria, before his accession to the throne as David I. It became part of the Prebendary of Barlanark, a division of the Bishopric of Glasgow. William Turnbull, who later became the bishop, held the prebendary from 1440 and so was probably responsible for building the oldest parts of the house c.1460. The next incumbent was James IV, who chose church duties as penance for his part in his father's death at the Battle of Sauchieburn in 1488. By this appointment he provided himself with some of the best wild-fowling grounds in the west of the country. James became one of Scotland's most effective monarchs, uniting the country by a combination of force and diplomacy. His policies were so effective in gaining him universal respect that when he died at the disastrous battle of Flodden in 1513, it is

said that every noble family in the country lost at least one member.

In 1522 William Baillie held the prebendary and then it was granted to Thomas Baillie by personal Papal Bull in 1528. In 1549 Sir William Baillie, President of the Court of Session, was in possession. In 1562 he was granted a feu charter by the crown. Sir William is widely credited with the building of the house, though rebuilding is more likely. It is claimed that Mary, Queen of Scots, stayed here and either planted or sat under an old yew tree which stood just a little way from the stair tower.

Baillie's daughter Elizabeth married a Hamilton of the Silvertonhill family in 1593. By 1647 Provan Hall belonged to Sir Robert Hamilton, and his initials appear with the date 1647 on a much weather-worn stone above the gate. Sir Robert was a Royalist in the Civil War and the house was attacked as a result, but in 1667 he sold it to the City, as his fortunes waned. The house was rented out and gradually fell into decay. In 1729 the estate was divided, and in 1760 the superiority of Provan was purchased by William MacDowell of Castle Semple, who had West Indies plantations and achieved some notoriety for his use of slaves. The council retained the right to appoint a Baillie of Provan and their rights as Lords of Provan.

In 1788 the estate was purchased by Dr John Buchanan, who built Blochairn House, and renovated the old house with monies earned from his Jamaican plantations. His son inherited, and after his death the estate was managed by the accountant, Alan Fullerton. His daughter married Reston Mathers, a farmer from Budhill. The last resident owners were her sons, William and Reston Mathers, famed for the beauty of their gardens and wild parties. The pair died in 1934, leaving no heirs. The house was then purchased by a group of interested local businessmen, who restored the property and donated it to the National Trust for Scotland in 1937. A variety of outbuildings once stood to the west and north. These were removed, presumably in the 1930s' restoration.

Provan Hall seems to have provided the last residence and employment of Harold Sydney Bride, the young radio operator who helped send distress calls from the Titanic in 1912. Seriously injured when rescued by the *Carpathia*, Bride and his family later moved to Glasgow to escape the negative attentions of the national press. After working as a salesman, he apparently gained employment with the National Trust for Scotland as resident custodian. Sadly he seems to have died of cancer at Ruchill Hospital within months of his appointment.

The house is said to be the most haunted in Glasgow, the apparition of Reston Mathers apparently having been seen and heard on various occasions in Blochairn House. It is also said that one of the lairds murdered his wife and son in the first floor bedroom and allegedly her image as the 'White Lady' has been seen and heard at the garden gate calling for her son.

The property had a small secondary house at Ruchazie (Rough Hazy). That site developed as Craigend House, and vaulted basements and a well could be seen in Croftcroighn Park.

Provanhall provides local community facilities and is impressively decorated annually at Halloween, when it is transformed into a chamber or horrors for the local children. The 'Friends of Provanhall' organise a series of annual events and guided tours are available. They are attempting to raise funds for a community archaeology project with the support of the NTS. Provanhall is a category 'A' Listed Building.

Note: visiting arranged via Steve Allen, caretaker, tel 0141 771 4399.

Closed on 25/26th Dec., and 1/2 Jan., and when special events in progress.

Other references: Blochairn House, Coach-Mailing

QUOTHQUAN

South Lanarkshire   Ruin or site   OS 72   NS 995395
2.5 miles northwest of Biggar, off minor roads north of A72, south of B7016, east of River Clyde at or near Quothquan.

Site of an old castle of the Chancellor family. The Chancellors are said to have arrived in Scotland in the 12th century with the Somervilles of Carnwath. The first confirmed record of them is in 1432, when George Chancellor received a grant of Quothquan and Shieldhill from Lord Somerville. In 1536 William Chancellor and his brother Robert were charged with the murder of Thomas Baillie of Cormiston. They were fined 300 merks for non appearance at court. When they finally did appear, they were acquitted. William supported Mary, Queen of Scots, at the Battle of Langside in 1568, and the castle was destroyed by the Regent Moray as a result. The Chancellors subsequently moved to their other property at Shieldhill.

RALSTON HOUSE

Renfrewshire   Ruin or site   OS 64   NS 511638
2 miles east of Paisley centre, off minor roads south of Paisley Road.

A mansion here was built about 1810, and extended in 1864. It replaced earlier structures, probably fortified.

The Ralston family claim descent from the MacDuff Earls of Fife. Their progenitor, Ralph, settled here and gave his name to the lands, Ralphston. His descendants took the name of the estate as their surname. They first appear as charter witnesses when Nicholas de Ralfstoune is recorded in 1272. Hew de Ralston subscribed to the Ragman Roll in 1296. In 1445 John de Ralston was Secretary to James II and witnessed the charter which promoted James Hamilton of Cadzow to Lord Hamilton. John's political career had seen him hold the positions of Keeper of the Privy Seal, Bishop of Dunblane, Lord High Treasurer and Ambassador to England. Hugh Ralston died at the Battle of Pinkie in 1547. About 1551, the family moved on a permanent basis to their other estate of Woodside in Ayrshire and neglected Ralston.

In 1704 Ralston was sold to the Earl of Dundonald, then passed by marriage to the 5th Duke of Hamilton. About 1800 it was sold to William Orr, a Paisley merchant. He built a mansion which was demolished in 1934. The stable block has been converted for use as a golf club house, and both east and west lodges survive. The west lodge is a category 'B' listed building, the east lodge and club house, are category 'C.'

RANFURLY CASTLE

Renfrewshire   Ruin or site   OS 63   NS 383652
0.5 miles west of Bridge of Weir, on minor roads south of A761, on Ranfurly Golf Course.

Ranfurly consists of a ruined 15th century tower, with later additions which partly enclosed a courtyard. The original tower survives only to the second storey, though without the west wall. It measured 20ft square and had walls 5ft thick. The eastern wall had a door and a wide splayed arrow slot. Extending from the southeast corner are the overgrown foundations of a later extension, about 43ft long, which had two rooms in the basement. Protruding centrally from the south wall of this was a semi-circular stair tower. Facing the south side of the tower and enclosing a courtyard about 15ft wide, are the remains of another block with three vaulted chambers on the ground floor. A courtyard wall between this and the keep is traceable.

It is said that the tower was constructed c.1460 and that the eastern block was built around 200 years later. The southern range originated at some date between the two. One interpretation is that the tower ruin was adapted when incorporated into a farm steading comprised of the eastern block. The tower may have been built to supersede the nearby motte at Castlehill.

The estate belonged to the Knox family from the 15th century or earlier. They took their name from the lands of Knock near Renfrew and claimed descent from the 10th century Earl Uchtred of Northumberland. They appear as regular charter witnesses in the reigns of Alexander II and III, but are not recorded with the 'Ranfurly and Craigends' designation until 1474.

The reformer John Knox was apparently a grand-nephew of Knox of Ranfurly. Andrew Knox, a younger son of John Knox of Ranfurly, became Episcopalian Bishop of the Isles. He then transferred to Raplo in Ireland in 1622. His son, Thomas, was then appointed Bishop of the Isles but died shortly after his inauguration.

Having only an heiress, Uchter Knox sold the barony to William Cochrane, 1st Earl of Dundonald, in 1665. It was later bought by the Aikenhead family.

A cadet line of the Knox family were living in Ireland by 1818 and using the designation 'of Ranfurly'. The honourable Thomas Knox of Ranfurly was created Lord Northland in the Irish Peerage. In 1826 he was created Baron Ranfurly, and in 1831 was granted the title Earl of Ranfurly. The family still hold the title and the 7th Earl lives in Suffolk.

The ruin is a Scheduled Ancient Monument.

RAPLOCH CASTLE

South Lanarkshire   Ruin or site   OS 64   NS 757510
North of Larkhall, near B7078, east of Avon Water at Raploch.

Site of a castle of the Hamiltons. This was part of the Comyn property of Machanshire until they were purged by Robert I, and in 1312 he gave the lands to the Hamiltons. The Hamiltons of Raploch are said to be descended from John Hamilton, 4th of Cadzow, through his third son Thomas (also recorded as Walter) Hamilton of Darngaber. His son, James, is said to be the first of the Raploch line, who lived c.1440. They were the progenitors of the Hamiltons of Stonehouse, Torrance, Woodhall, Dechmont and Barns among others.

The castle was destroyed after the Battle of Langside in 1568 because of the family's support for Mary, Queen of Scots. Gavin Hamilton, 6th of Raploch, was Commendator of Kilwinning Abbey until 1555. He then became Coadjutor of St Andrews and then Archbishop of St Andrews in 1571, but died in a skirmish a few months after his appointment. Another Gavin Hamilton of Raploch was forfeited in 1579 for his support of his Hamilton cousins during the minority of James VI, but was restored by Act of Parliament in 1585.

Hamilton of Raploch was the captor of Colonel Robert Rumbold at Lesmahagow. Rumbold was a conspirator in the Rye House Plot to assassinate James VII and II, and was executed in Edinburgh in 1685. The family died out and seniority passed to the Hamiltons of Barns.

The park for the house is marked as 'Roplock' on Pont's map of c.1596, but by that time the castle had gone. There was a later mansion here, owned by a Mr McNiel. By 1858 all that remained was a doocot and an old yew tree. A coal pit occupied the site of the house. Nothing remains.

Other reference: Roplock Castle

RENFIELD

Renfrewshire   Ruin or site   OS 64   NS 501684
Northwest of Renfrew, by minor roads north of the A8, on east bank of White Cart Water at the confluence with River Clyde.

Site of an old or fortified house, which was replaced by a mansion.

In 1568 James Stewart, Earl of Moray, granted a charter of the estate to Canon Andrew Hay of Glasgow, who later became Parson of Renfrew. In 1654 John Hay, another Parson of Renfrew, sold the estate to Provost Colin Campbell of Glasgow. Sixteen years later, Campbell purchased the estate of Blythswood from the Elphinstones. His family took the name of this second estate as their designation, becoming the Campbells of Blythswood. The family died out in 1767, and Douglas of Mains inherited. He adopted the Campbell surname and his descendants became Lords Blythswood.

In 1810 they abandoned the old house and built a new mansion further from the river. Blythswood House was demolished in 1935 and both sites are now occupied by a golf course.

The original house appears as 'Ronnise' in Blaeu's *Atlas Novus* of 1654. On Roy's map of 1745-46 it appears as a complex of three buildings within a park. In Ainslie's map of 1796 it is Renfield, but by Thompson's map of 1832 it is 'Renfield or Blythswood'.

Other references Blythswood, Ranfield, Ronnise

RENFREW CASTLE

Renfrewshire   Ruin or site   OS 64   NS 510684
In Renfrew, south of River Clyde just west of A741, just north of Renfield Street.

Site of the 12th century castle of Walter Fitzallan, progenitor of the Stewart dynasty, and High Steward of Scotland. An attack on the castle was planned by Somerled, Lord of the Isles, in 1164, but Somerled was assassinated at Knock before the castle was taken.

Walter, 6th High Steward, married Marjorie Bruce, daughter of Robert I. Marjorie died at Knock when she fractured her neck. She fell from a horse while heavily pregnant and their son, Robert, was born by emergency caesarean section. The child grew up to become Robert II in 1371, the first of the Stewart kings. Possibly as a result of a birth injury to his eye, he had the nickname King Blearie.

Ross of Hawkhead was made hereditary constable of the castle and retained the rights to collect the duties of the fairs at Renfrew for centuries. About 1404 Robert II disjoined the Barony of Renfrew from Lanarkshire, thus creating Renfrewshire.

The castle, orchards and meadows were rented out to Robert Lord Lyle from 1468. The ditch was still visible in 1775, and was said to be stone lined, with a stream running through it. The stone from the castle was quarried to build a soap works, before the site was used for Castlehill House. Excavation of the site found the footings of the bay window of Castlehill House, but only fragments of pottery from the castle.

RIDFORD CASTLE

Renfrewshire   Ruin or site   OS 64   NS 455635?
Off minor roads north of A761, south of A737, 2.5 miles west of Paisley, 0.75 miles west of Ferguslie Park.

Site of a tower house, known as Ridforf, Reedford or Ridforf, which appears on Pont's map, Gordon's map and Blaeu's *Atlas Novus* of the 17th century. It may have been a Hamilton property and it is possible that this is the same site as Ferguslie, though on all three maps Ferguslie is denoted as a lesser property to the east.

Other references: Ferguslie

RINGSDALE CASTLE

South Lanarkshire   Ruin or site   OS 64   NS 764493
2 miles south of Larkhall, on minor roads north of A71, on west bank of Avon Gorge.

Ringdale is a defended promontory site on the west bank of the Avon Gorge. The pear-shaped summit measures 33ft by 20ft and rises 6ft above the base of the ditch, which isolates it from the approach. There has been considerable erosion and it may once have supported a motte. In 1959 a few large undressed stones were recorded as being embedded in the north face of the mound, but otherwise is recorded as having no signs of a building.

The adjacent property of Kittiemuir, or Kythumbre as it was once known, was a benefice of one of the Prebends of St Bride's Church at Bothwell.

ROBERTON

South Lanarkshire   Ruin or site   OS 72   NS 942287
3 miles north of Abington, by minor road, just west of A73, just northwest of the church and old mill at Roberton

The edges and western end of the flat summit of a long and narrow, isolated hill is marked out by earthen banks, with a prominent knoll at its northwestern corner. The earthwork is badly mutilated, though still traceable. This has been recorded as a fort in the past, but is now accepted as 'almost certainly' medieval. An entrance gap is recorded at the eastern end and a square platform just within this. It has been described as a 'medieval earth and timber castle of some size, with a commanding and defensible position'.

Castledykes is now thought to be the seat of Robert, the brother of Lambin Asa. He is on record here in the 12th century and gave his name to the settlement. His descendants became the Robertons of that Ilk, later known as the Robertons of Earnock.

In 1312, Robert I granted the estate to John de Montfode, but in 1372 Sir James Douglas of Dalkeith granted his 20 merks of land in Roberton to William of Cresseuyle for the duration of his life. In 1411 Sir James Douglas of Roberton, the son of Douglas of Dalkeith, was the proprietor. In 1634 Roberton became a Burgh of Regality and in 1710 the entire parish, with the exception of Moat, was owned by the Marquis of Douglas.

ROBERTON

South Lanarkshire   Ruin or site   OS 72   NT 096473
By minor road, 0.5 miles west of A702 at Dolphinton, at Roberton Mains.

Site of an old or fortified house, which appears on Pont's manuscript map of the late 16th century. Roberton, with neighbouring Newholme, belonged to the Cockburn family and then the Hamiltons. In the 17th century it passed to the Learmont family, one of whom was a noted Covenanter. Having fought at Rullion Green in 1666, where he was in command of the left wing of the defeated Covenanting Army, Major Learmont went on the run. His family paid compensation to retain the estate. He is said to have hidden in Ireland, within his own house at Dolphinton and in the surrounding hills. He is even said to have had a vault built by the banks of the Medwin where he could hide without fear of discovery. He reappeared to fight at Bothwell Bridge in 1679, after which he was captured and condemned to death. However, by that time he was an old man, and so was sent to the Bass Rock for the remainder of his life. He was released some five years later and allowed to go home to die.

ROBROYSTON HOUSE

City of Glasgow   Ruin or site   OS 64   NS 634692
1 mile east of Bishopbriggs, and 3 miles southwest of Kirkintilloch, off minor roads 0.75 miles north of junction with M80 with B765, at Robroyston Mains.

Site of an old or fortified house. The mansion house of the ancient estate of Robroyston has long been demolished and all that remains are the ruins of the Mains Farm. The older parts of the mansion had walls up to 5ft thick, indicative of defensive intent. The house bore a date-stone, which was illegible by 1857, though a sundial was dated 1623.

The property is recorded in the early 14th century as the scene of the betrayal and capture of William Wallace by the 'False Mentieth'. The site of the barn in which he was resting is now marked by a monument erected in the 19th century. Nearby is a natural spring consolidated by walling and named 'Wallace's Well'. This provides further commemoration of the event and is commonly identified as the hero's source of fresh water during his short stay on the site. He was taken to London and tried for treason against the English king, Edward I. Found guilty, despite his declaration that he had never sworn allegiance to Edward, Wallace was hanged, drawn and quartered. His head was put on a spike on London Bridge, and his four quarters were displayed at Berwick, Newcastle Upon Tyne, Perth and Stirling.

Robroyston was the property of the Bishops of Glasgow from the 12th century until 1587, when it was annexed to the Crown. In 1594 it passed into private ownership. In 1670 it belonged to Reverend Robert Landess, but by the 19th century it was owned by the Lamonts. In the early 20th century it was purchased by the City of Glasgow for the construction of a smallpox hospital. An adjacent part of the site developed later as a maternity hospital, but in the 1980s the hospital site was developed for housing.

ROCHSOLES HOUSE

North Lanarkshire   Private   OS 64   NS 756677
1 mile north of Airdrie, 0.5 miles east of Glenmavis, 1 mile west of A73, south of the B803 at Rochsoles.

Probable site of an old or fortified house. Rochsoles was part of the Monklands estate of Newbattle Abbey. It may have come into the possession of the Crawfords after the Reformation. From at least as early as the mid 17th century, this was Cochrane property. In 1829 William Cochrane of Rochsoles was Sheriff Depute of the Upper Ward of Clydesdale. The property went to the Gerard family, who had a mansion house here, of which the stable block survives. It is a category 'B' Listed Building, dated 1839. A large tower named 'Ruchsols' appears indistinctly in Pont's map of c1596, and in Blaeu's *Atlas Novus* of 1654.

ROCHSOLLOCH CASTLE

North Lanarkshire   Private   OS 64   NS 754649
0.5 miles southwest of Airdrie town centre, south of A89, near Rochsolloch Road, at Rochsolloch Farmhouse, Victoria Place.

The renovated 19th century Rochsolloch Farmhouse stands on the site of earlier structures, and it is very likely that one or more of these were fortified. It appears as 'Reybillach' on Pont's map of c.1596 and in Blaeu's *Atlas Novus* of 1654.

The church owned the lands as part of the Monkland property. Rochsolloch was leased to a Crawford, who from 1547 was granted the powers of Baron Baillie in this Parish. His seat was at Rochsolloch, using his own dungeon as gaol and holding courts in the house. The family retained these powers after the Reformation. In 1647 the estates and baronial authority passed to James Hamilton of Dalzell. The estate changed hands in 1685, going to John and Walter Aitchieson and then by marriage to Mr Alexander of Kentucky.

ROSNEATH CASTLE

The Lennox & East Dunbartonshire   Ruin or site   OS 56   NS 271822
1 mile southeast of Roseneath, on minor roads east of B822, at south end of bay at Castle Point.

Site of a 15th century castle of the Campbells of Argyll. Rosneath is said to have had a royal castle in the 12th century, which was burned by William Wallace in the 13th century. He is said to have evaded his English pursuers by making a death-defying leap into the Gareloch from a precipitous rock, known as Wallace's Leap. He apparently swam the Rhu Narrows and made his escape through the wilds of the Lennox.

The lands were held by the Earls of Lennox, but came to the Campbells in 1489. They became in turn Earls, Marquises and Dukes of Argyll. In 1633 the castle was extended and remodelled as a more commodious house, but was burned down in 1802. In the 17th century it was apparently used by the Duke to provide shelter for Covenanters.

A large elegant mansion of 1806 replaced the old house, and this was sold on the death of Princess Louise, Dowager Duchess of Argyll, in 1939. It came into use as an administrative centre for the American Navy, who were based here during World War II, but was abandoned before being blown up in 1961. The site is now a caravan park.

ROSSDHU CASTLE

The Lennox & East Dunbartonshire   Private   OS 56 NS 361895
2 miles south of Luss, on west bank of Loch Lomond, on peninsula to east side of Rossdhu Bay, east of A82, on Loch Lomond Golf Course.

Rossdhu means the 'black or dark headland'.

A single high section of wall remains of a plain 16th century tower of the Colquhouns of Luss. It is thought to have replaced the earlier castle on Eilan Rossdhu, which stood on a crannog in the bay, just to the southwest. It was superseded by the 18th century Rossdhu House.

Rossdhu Castle is said to have been built in 1541. The remains consist of the south gable, with short portions of the west and east walls. The gable is 33ft long and reaches a height of 40ft with walls 7.5ft thick. The remaining portion of the west wall has a maximum length of 10ft and the east wall 6ft. The south wall contains a round arched doorway, slightly off centre. An arrow slot to its left guards the approach. Above it is a window aperture and above that there is a serious fissure in the wall. On the interior are the remains of a pointed arched doorway and a window at ground floor level, with a fireplace at first floor level. The ruin was stabilized by concrete underpinning to prevent its collapse in the 1990s. Prior to this, archaeologists investigated the area around the structure. They found traces of a building running southward from the western end of the south wall.

Rossdhu was inhabited until 1770 and was used as a source of stone when Rossdhu House was built in 1774. The archaeology seems to confirm that the south wall of the tower had been retained as a garden folly, while the remainder of the building was stripped of materials to build the house. The remnants of the east and west walls were left to buttress the south wall.

Rossdhu was visited twice by Mary, Queen of Scots, who knighted Sir John Colquhoun of Luss. He was apparently mentioned in the possibly forged 'casket letters', which were said to be her private love letters to Bothwell. The letters, if genuine, would have proved her complicity in the murder of her second husband, Henry, Lord Darnley. The letters were apparently destroyed by her son, James VI.

In 1603 Alexander Colquhoun of Luss led his men to annihilation against the MacGregors in the Battle of Glenfruin. In the aftermath, the MacGregor name was proscribed and their leaders tried and executed. Another Sir John Colquhoun of Luss was said to have been a necromancer and skilled in black magic. He married the sister of James Graham, the Marquis of Montrose, but fell in love with his wife's sister. The pair eloped, and Sir John died in Italy. His son, also Sir John, was known as the 'Black-Cock of the West', because of his haughty manner.

In 1654 Rossdhu was attacked and captured by Cromwell's troops. Sir John had supported the royalist cause and was fined £2,000.

Dr Samuel Johnson and James Boswell visited Rossdhu House during their Tour of the Hebrides, though Lady Helen Colquhoun found the doctor boorish and his manner insufferable. Her ghost is said to haunt what were the servant's quarters.

In woodland, a little to the north of the castle, are the remains of the 12th century Chapel of St Mary, or Our Lady's Chapel of Rossdew. This may have been rebuilt when the castle was constructed. It contained an effigy, said to be of St Kessog, which is now in the church at Luss. The floor consists of a number of slate grave slabs.

To the south is the Adam-style Rossdhu House, mentioned above. The design is attributed to John Baxter with contributions from Sir John Clerk of Penicuik. It was extended by the addition of wings in the early 19th century and altered in 1910. The architects William Leiper and W. Hunter MacNab were involved.

The castle and chapel are Scheduled Ancient Monuments, and category 'B' Listed Buildings, while the house is 'A' listed and its outbuildings form a cluster of 'B' and 'C' listings.

Rossdhu House is now the club house for Loch Lomond Golf Course, and accommodation is available. Tel. 01463 655555 (www.lochlomond.com).

Other references: Rosduy, Rossdew

ROSS HOUSE

South Lanarkshire   Private   OS 64   NS 739558
North of M74, 1 mile east of Hamilton, immediately southeast of meeting of the Rivers Clyde and Avon.

A tower here appears on Pont's map of 1596 and in Blaeu's *Atlas Novus* of 1654. The property was part of the royal hunting forest of Cadzow in the reign of David I, but was granted to the monks of Kelso Abbey in 1222. In 1339

it was granted to John Hamilton, second son of Gilbert, the progenitor of the Hamilton family. The Hamiltons of Rossavon were therefore the most senior cadet line of the family. They gained further estates at Fingalton, then Preston in East Lothian in the 14th century.

David Hamilton of Rossavon, Fingalton and Preston had an important role in the passing of the Act of Reformation, his chief, the Earl of Arran, being at the forefront of the Lords of the Congregation who voted it through Parliament in 1560. David bound himself to 'defend the evangel of Christ against all persecution', but despite this, he maintained his allegiance to Mary, Queen of Scots, and fought for her at Langside in 1568.

Sir John Hamilton was one of the first to speak out against the Five Articles of Perth of 1618, which imposed Episcopalian worship on the Scottish Church. The family maintained his Covenanting stance and Robert Hamilton was a commander at the Battles of Drumclog and Bothwell Bridge in 1679. Robert was forfeited in 1684.

Ross came to the Aikman family before 1705. A Georgian mansion was built on the site in 1783, which was extended in 1830. In 1889 Colonel H.H. Robertson-Aikman commissioned Alexander Cullen to adapt and modernise it, creating a massive Scots baronial mansion with a six-storey corner tower. This remains occupied as a private residence and is a category 'B' Listed Building.

Other references: Rossavon, The Ross

ROSSLAND

Renfrewshire   Ruin or site   OS 64   NS 439709
Off minor roads west and south of M8, east of A8, 1 mile east of Bishopton, in Rossland, at or near Castle Crescent.

Site of a tower house, which appears on Pont's map of Renfrewshire, and on Blaeu's *Atlas Novus* of the 17th century. It was depicted on map references until the early 19th century, but was ruinous by 1821 and nothing remained by 1863.

In 1591 a family named Stewart of Rossland are recorded. Before the end of the 16th century, Hannibal Brisbane received a charter of Rossland from his father, John Brisbane of Brisbane. Hannibal was succeeded by his son, also Hannibal, who in 1636 sold the estate to his cousin, John Brisbane of Bishopton. The estate was divided and Easter Rossland, which was the site of the castle, was sold to the Patersons of Craigton. In 1706 Wester Rossland and Bishopton were purchased by the Walkinshaws of that Ilk.

Other references: Rostad, Roslin

ROSS PRIORY

The Lennox & East Dunbartonshire   Private   OS 56   NS 415876
3.5 miles northeast of Balloch, on southern shore of Loch Lomond, 1 mile north of Gartocharn, by minor roads north of A811, at Ross Priory.

Ross is said to have been the site of a 14th century castle of the Buchanans. A high-roofed mansion with wings was built on the site in 1693, and may incorporate earlier work. It was remodelled in 1810-16 by James Gillespie Graham. Sir Walter Scott was a frequent visitor when writing *Rob Roy*, and the mansion is now owned by the University of Strathclyde.

The Priory is a category 'A' Listed Building, while the outbuildings are category 'C'. Nearby is the 18th century Buchanan burial ground, which is category 'B'.

Ross Priory is available as a function and conference centre, accommodation is available, and the gardens are open occasionally as part of the Scotland's Gardens scheme (www.rescat.strath.ac.uk/prioy_accom.html / www.gardensofscotland.org: 0141 548 3565).

ROUGH HILL

South Lanarkshire   Ruin or site   OS 64   NS 608554
2 miles west of East Kilbride, north of A726, east of Stewartfield Way, in grounds of Centre 1, on south bank of Kittoch Water.

A motte, which once supported a later tower, stands on the edge of a precipice 60ft above the Kittoch Water.

Rough Hill supported the remains of a building measuring 73ft by 63ft, which was being used as a source of stone for local dyke building in the late 18th century. During this work, labourers exposed a subterranean vault, which they cleared of rubbish in the hope of finding something of value. They were disappointed and filled the void.

Rough Hill stands on land which may once have been part of the nearby farm of Philipshill. This is apparently named after Philip de Valognes, who was Chamberlain to William I. He owned land in Kilbride, which he gifted to Paisley Abbey and for which the monks received a rent of one merk. This is mentioned in confirmations of Papal privilege in 1226 and 1265. His brother, Roger, was Lord of Kilbride, probably based at the site now occupied by Comyn's Castle. Nothing is known of the later history, though it probably followed similar ownership to Comyn's Castle. A Dreghorn of Roughill referred to in the 18th century refers to the estate of Ruchill in the north of Glasgow.

RUTHERGLEN CASTLE

South Lanarkshire   Ruin or site   OS 64   NS 615618
In Rutherglen, 0.25 miles west of A749, and 0.25 miles east of A 730, north of Main Street, just northwest of junction of Castle Street and King Street.

Once a large and important royal fortress, the last remnants of the foundations of Rutherglen (or Ruglen) Castle were removed in 1759. It was a 13th century castle of enceinte with several towers, the walls being 5ft thick.

The English held the castle during the Wars of Independence. It was while at mass in the nearby Old Kirk of St Mary, that Sir John Mentieth was informed of the Wallace's hiding place at Robroyston and set off to make his infamous capture in 1305. The castle was taken by the Scots for a while in 1309 and hosted a sitting of Parliament. It was then recaptured by the English, before being retaken in 1313 by Edward Bruce, the king's brother and future short-lived King of Ireland.

The 'Castle Vallie of Rutherglen and the King's Isles' are said to have been granted to Robert Hall by Robert III. The castle was in the hands of the Earls of Douglas, until their forfeiture in 1455. It was then granted to Alexander Hamilton, the second son of James Hamilton of Cadzow, and brother to James, 1st Lord Hamilton. At that point only the great tower was standing. Alexander's descendants had the designation 'of Elliston' and then 'of

Shawfield'. Alexander's third son, James, is said to have become Hamilton of Silvertonhill, probably inheriting his Uncle John's estate.

Andrew Hamilton of Shawfield supported Mary, Queen of Scots, and as a result the castle was burned in 1569 by the Regent Moray. Several abortive attempts were made to restore the building, but it fell into ruin. By 1611 the estate had passed to Sir Claud, the son of Lord Claud Hamilton. By the middle of the 17th century, his son James was in financial difficulties and moved to Ireland. Shawfield passed through several owners until it was purchased by the Campbells.

David Campbell of Shawfield, MP for Glasgow had a mansion by the Clyde, but also owned the Shawfield Mansion on Glasgow Green. On the day of the imposition of the Malt Tax, the populace rioted and David became the target of their anger. They attacked his home by the green and completely demolished the interior.

The last remnants of the old keep at Rutherglen were removed in 1759 to create space for a vegetable plot! An excavation prior to a housing development just west of the site produced only a few shards of pottery.

Other references: Castle Ru

SANDILANDS

South Lanarkshire   Ruin or site   OS 72   NS 885379
About 3.5 miles southeast of Lanark, east of Douglas Water and west of A70, at Sandilands.

Probable site of an early castle of the Sandilands family. In 1348 William, Earl of Douglas, granted the lands of Sandilands and Redmire to James Sandilands of that Ilk. It has been said that he had held them since 1334, when they were granted as a reward for distinguished service during the Wars of Independence. While there is no cartographic evidence of a castle here, the estate was important enough for Sandilands to be 'of that Ilk' when he had held other estates in Peebleshire since 1336.

In 1350 he married Lady Eleanor Bruce, widow of Alexander, Earl of Carrick, Douglas's sister. By this marriage he obtained the Barony of West Calder in Lothian. The family thereafter took the designation 'of Calder' and quartered their arms with those of Douglas.

SHANDON

The Lennox & East Dunbartonshire   Site or ruin   OS 56   NS 257878
4 miles northwest of Helensburgh, by minor roads and foot east of A814, 1 mile northeast of Shandon.

Shandon means 'old fort'. It is said to have been an early seat of the Earldom of Lennox and is currently interpreted as a dun.

A mound sits at the foot of gradual slopes from the north, where the site is protected by a deep natural gully. Deep ditches have been cut to protect the south and east sides. The summit measures 105ft by 56ft, and in 1977 the traces of a strong, rubble-built, encircling wall could be seen around it. The site was thickly overgrown with bracken and gorse. Earlier records of the wall describe it being about 6ft thick and 1ft high.

SHIELDHILL

South Lanarkshire   Private   OS 72   NT 006404
About 3 miles northwest of Biggar, on minor roads west of B7016, north of Quothquan at Shieldhill.

A massive square keep, allegedly dating from as early as 1199 but probably of the 16th century, has been incorporated into a sprawling building of various dates. It was extended in the 17th century, in 1820, and later. Within the keep, there is a mural stair rising from the entrance to the southwest corner. There was a chapel on the second floor, the altar and a piscina having been uncovered during the restorations of 1820. Parch marks on the lawn indicate the rectangular foundations of another structure.

This was a property of the Chancellor family. They moved here from their other house at Quothquan when it was destroyed in the aftermath of the Battle of Langside in 1568. The family lived here until the 1920s, after which the building has been used as a hotel.

1630 saw a long-running dispute between the presbytery of Lanark and John Chancellor come to a head. He was 'convick of contempt of word, of railing against his pastor', and 'wes injoined to make his publick repentance, in his awin claithes, only one day, if he maid a guid confessione, and so to be absolved'. The minister at Quothquan was not content, and made an accusation against John's wife and daughter, accusing them of resorting to charms to restore the health of a sick child. His daughter attended the presbytery, and kneeling before them had to confess her guilt. In 1639 John was charged with breaking down the door of Quothquan Kirk, in order to bury his wife within. He was censured by the kirk session.

Robert's son, James, joined the cause of the Covenanters, and was imprisoned for aiding those fleeing from defeat at the Battle of Bothwell Bridge in 1679. He then took 'violent possession' of the lands of Parkholm, which had belonged to Carmichael of Bonnyton, until a violent storm had altered the course of the River Clyde. The land lay neglected, but eventually Carmichael crossed the river and cultivated the land for several years. When Carmichael died in 1688, the estate passed to a minor. Chancellor and his neighbours belatedly claimed that, since the river had anciently been the boundary between the estates, the land was rightfully theirs. They reaped the crop and carried it off for use as silage and bedding. During the harvesting, they confined local inhabitants to their homes under guard. Chancellor was charged with riot, but the case was not proven. In 1695 the Lords of Session decided that Parkholm should remain Carmichael property. James was made to pay 300 merks in recompense.

Shieldhill is said to be haunted by the ghost of a daughter of one of the Chancellor lairds. She was raped by soldiers returning from battle and became pregnant. It is said that the child was taken from her and in an act of even more cruelty, was left to die. She wept herself to death and her ghost has allegedly been seen in recent years. There are other versions of the story.

It was at a fort nearby that William Wallace is said to have addressed his men before the Battle of Biggar.

The house, doocot and stable block are category 'B' Listed Buildings.

(shieldhillcastlehotel.co.uk)

SILVERTONHILL

South Lanarkshire   Ruin or site   OS 64   NS 725546
1 mile south and east of Hamilton, off minor roads east of A723, in Larch Grove Silvertonhill, just east of Aspen Place.

Site of a tower, which is in Blaeu's *Atlas Novus*. The tower was replaced or incorporated within a mansion, which was demolished in the 20th century. The old tower was ruinous by 1710. This was the seat of the Hamiltons of Silvertonhill, from which they took their title.

One of the sons of James Hamilton of Cadzow received a charter of 'Whitecamp' and Kirkhope from the Earl of Crawford in 1449. It is said that Quhitecamp, or Whitecamp, was the original name of this estate and the family thereafter adopted the designation 'of Silvertonhill'. In the next generation, James Hamilton of Silvertonhill is said to have married a daughter of the widowed Countess of Douglas and gained Newton in Cambuslang. James's son, John, thereafter took the designation 'of Newton', though he owned both estates. In 1531 John gained the estates of Tweedie and Cot Castle by grant from Lord Somerville. His son Andrew gained a charter of the Barony of Stonehouse and the estate of Goslington. He resumed the 'Silvertonhill' designation. In 1541, Andrew received a further charter of Overton and Maidenburn. It is likely therefore that he is the same Andrew Hamilton who held Lethame. By this time the family was also in possession of Newton in Strathaven and later gained Provanhall. Andrew's grandson, Francis, apparently believed that he was bewitched by Lady Boyd and made several representations to parliament on the subject. He squandered the family estates and died childless. The title fell to his cousin, Edward Hamilton of Balgray, who thereafter used the 'Silvertonhill' designation. In 1646 his son Robert received a baronetcy of Nova Scotia from Charles I.

Other references: Quhitecamp, Sillerhill, Whitecamp

SMITHWOOD

South Lanarkshire   Ruin or site   OS 72   NS 959092
5 miles south of Elvanfoot, by minor roads and foot east of A702 , south of Wintercleugh, west of Daer Reservoir, on northwestern flank of Hitteril Hill, on the Old Town Burn.

The ruin of this bastle house has been excavated and consolidated. The rubble-built structure measured about 46ft by 18ft. It is thought to have had a barrel-vaulted basement. The walls appear to have been about 1ft thick, except on the north where the wall reaches 5.5ft thick and there is evidence of a doorway. There was a paved floor with central drain in the basement and possibly an internal stair in the southeastern corner. There are remnants of a number of ancillary buildings, sheep folds and field boundaries around the site. Outside there was a cobbled area and the building appears to have been adapted for use as a sheep fold once it had fallen into ruin.

In 1725 Smithwood was occupied by William Veatch.

Other reference: Helm Hill

SNAR

South Lanarkshire   Ruin or site   OS 71   NS 863200

3 miles southwest of Crawfordjohn, on minor roads and track south of B740, on east bank of Snar Water, at or near Snar Farm.

Site of a 16th century house of the Douglases. The ruins were very dilapidated, making interpretation difficult. Two square rooms at ground-floor level were recorded as being vaulted and inhabited in 1813. By 1858 all that remained was a wall about 3ft high, which had been incorporated into a sheepfold. Partial excavation revealed the foundations of a building measuring 26ft by 19ft, with walls 4ft thick and rising to 4ft above the floor. There was a possible entrance in the southeastern corner and the floor was the natural bedrock. It had been extended by the addition of another room to the south measuring 13ft by 16ft, with walls 3ft thick, which survive to a height of 4ft. This room had a cobbled floor and a drain leading through the west wall.

It is noted on earlier maps as the ruin of a tower, but has more recently been interpreted as a bastle. The property appears on Pont's manuscript map and is depicted a small tower.

Douglas of Snar made his money from mining gold and lead and was apparently celebrated for his exploits during 'the border warfare'.

SOUTH GIBBALSTON

Renfrewshire   Ruin or site   OS 63   NS 352661

4 miles west of Bridge of Weir, south of A761, immediately west of B786, at South Gibbalston.

Site of a mound, which is thought to have been a motte. By 1856 very little remained, the farmer having levelled the site for cultivation. It appeared on the 1857 OS map as 'Mote Hill' and was described as 'a ring of slopes'. It was approximately 80ft in diameter. Nothing remains

STANEBYRES

Renfrewshire   Ruin or site   OS 64   NS 598495

2 miles southeast of Eaglesham, by Strathaven Road and minor road, at Stonebyres.

Site of a tower, depicted on Pont's map of c.1596. The present farm buildings are category 'C' listed and date from the late 18th–early 19th centuries, with mid 19th century alterations. There is medieval rig and furrow cultivation in the vicinity and a stone mace head has been found on the farmland. Stanebyres sits within the Barony of Eaglesham, and would therefore have been owned by or tenanted from the Montgomerie Earls of Eglinton. Stonebyres was occupied by a family named Gilmour throughout the first half of the 20th century.

STANELY CASTLE

Renfrewshire   Ruin or site   OS 64   NS 464616

1 mile southwest of Paisley, on minor roads west of B775, in Stanely Reservoir.

Originally surrounded by marsh and now standing in the water of a reservoir which has flooded its basement, Stanely is a ruined L-plan keep of the 15th century.

Internally the building is completely gutted and was formerly of four storeys and a garret. The entrance is in the re-entrant and the ground floor has several gunloops with circular eyelets at the base. There is a continuous corbel around the wall-top which once supported the parapet and rounded bartizans at each corner. At parapet level above the door the corbelling is machicolated. There are a variety of small windows on each floor.

The estate of Stanely was a property of the powerful Dennistoun family. With Newark, it passed by marriage to the son of Maxwell of Calderwood in 1402. The Maxwells built the castle, and about 1477 Archibald Maxwell, a son of George of Newark, founded a cadet branch of the family.

There is evidence that at least portions of the estate had been sold and let to tenants. In 1560 James Hamilton of The Peel surrendered his rights in the estate to David Lindsay of Dunrod, his superior. The estate consisted of Mains of Stanely and the manor of the same name.

In 1584 Patrick Maxwell of Stanely was killed in Paisley by Sir Robert Montgomerie of Skelmorlie. Montgomerie was engaged in a long-running feud with the Cunninghames of Glencairn, to whom Maxwell was allied.

The family of Maxwell of Stanely flourished until 1629, when John Maxwell sold their estate to Lady Ross of Hawkhead. The family continued to use the designation, since in 1633 John Maxwell, the younger of Stanley, was

in debt to James Hamilton, Provost of Glasgow. Stanely passed by marriage to the Boyle Earls of Glasgow in about 1750. In the early 19th century it was abandoned and in 1837 the surrounding marsh was flooded to create the reservoir. A rise in water level since then has submerged the basement and the island upon which the castle stands.

The castle is a Scheduled Ancient Monument and category 'B' Listed Building.

ST JOHN'S KIRK

South Lanarkshire   Ruin or site   OS 72   NS 983360
0.5 miles northwest of Symington, immediately south of the junction of A72 and A73.

Site of an old or fortified house of the Baillies. The family were descendants of John, second son of William Baillie of Lamington and Hoprig. John lived around the turn of the 16th century and became the ancestor of the Baillies of Walston and of Jerviswood.

Baillie of St John's Kirk fought for Mary, Queen of Scots, at Langside in 1568, and as a result his lands were ravaged by the Regent Moray in the aftermath of the battle. In 1572 he was charged with the 'slauchter of James Ballayne and others' at that battle. The charges were dropped. His family were still in possession during the reign of James VII and II when the laird's wife supported the Covenanters. By 1816 it belonged to the Howiesons. The present Victorian mansion is said to retain a vaulted basement from its predecessor.

STOBCROSS

City of Glasgow   Ruin or site   OS 64   NS 570655?
2 miles west of Glasgow Cathedral, on north bank of the Clyde near A814, at Stobcross.

Site of an old or fortified house, which dated from the late 16th century. The house consisted of a main block with two right angled wings, and stair towers in the re-entrants. These framed a courtyard. The house appears on Pont's map of c.1596.

Stobcross was a property of the Andersons in the 16th century, until sold to the Orrs of Barrowfield in 1735 or 1747. By 1816 it belonged to Phillips Esq.

The expansion of the city gradually overtook the estate and the house was demolished c.1850.

STONEBYRES HOUSE

South Lanarkshire   Ruin or site   OS 72   NS 841437
2.5 miles west of Lanark, on minor roads west of B7018, and south of A744, just east of Stonebyres Holdings.

Stonebyres House was a large castellated mansion of 1850, which was further extended by the addition of wings in the early 20th century. It encased a 15th century five-storey tower. It was demolished in 1954, but in 1962 the foundations were still visible to a height of about 1ft.

The old keep occupied one end of the rectangular main block and had been considerably modified to match its extension. In 1850 it may have been extended upwards, re-roofed, given corbelled out corner turrets and a centrally-placed round stair turret in the gable from the second floor upward.

The walls of the keep were 8-9ft thick and it measured 34ft by 29ft, compared to the 34ft by 70ft of the completed mansion. The entrance was at ground level with an adjacent turnpike within the wall leading to the second floor. Across a landing, another turnpike led to the floors above. Each floor had a single room, excepting the third, which was unevenly divided into two. The ground and second floors had small fireplaces, while the hall on the first floor had a larger example. The basement walls were pierced by gunloops and the hall was famed as one of the finest in the country.

Stonebyres was the seat of the Weirs or Veres of Stonebyres. Rothaldus de Vere was granted a confirmation of his estates in 1400. It is thought that he divided his extensive estate between his two sons, so founding the dynasties of Weir of Blackwood and Weir of Stonebyres.

In 1524 William Weir, younger of Stonebyres, with his nephew and namesake were proclaimed as rebels for the murder of James Halyburton, a burgess of Edinburgh. Weir's father, the laird of Stonebyres, stood security for their good behaviour. William was himself murdered in 1525, and the following year John Lindsay of Covington received a remission for the crime.

In the late 16th century the family were involved in a feud over seniority with their cousins of Blackwood. It culminated in 1587 with the murder of John Weir of Poneil, James of Blackwood's son. In the aftermath, William Weir of Stonebyres gave his bond of manrent to the grieving father and promised to serve under his banner. This agreement was ratified by parliament in 1592. In the 18th century the family began to use the Vere spelling of their surname, but in 1845 they sold the estate to the Monteiths.

STONELAW TOWER

South Lanarkshire Ruin or site OS 64 NS 619609
Off Stonelaw Road, south of Greystone Avenue, Rutherglen.

An L-plan tower of four storeys, which is alleged to have originated in the 16th century, but also credited to the 19th century. It was supplemented by a T-shaped single-storey mansion, the supporting leg of the T extending out from the re-entrant, the remainder at right angles on either side of the main block. Canmore, the database for RCAHMS, states simply 'Built 1835'; however the house appears clearly on Forrest's map of 1816, although it does not appear on earlier maps.

The tower was built by the Spens family, one of whom, General John Spens, planted the surrounding woodland. Several members of the family became Provosts of Rutherglen and had been in possession of the estate for centuries. In 1927 the tower was purchased for use as a Masonic Lodge. The last resident was a local nationalist councillor, Alan Titson, who owned it from the 1930s until 1963, when it was taken over by the Power Petroleum Company. It was thereafter badly vandalised and the company had it demolished in 1965. A rear gate and a large part of a tall, thin enclosing wall are all that remain. A filling station and a block of flats now occupy much of the site.

STRATHCASHEL

The Lennox & East Dunbartonshire Ruin or site OS 56 NS 393931
2.5 miles northwest of Balmaha, by minor road and foot, west of B837 on east bank of Loch Lomond, at Strathcashell Point.

'Row Cashel' is marked on Pont's map of the late 16th century, traditionally the site of an early stronghold of the Buchanans.

Strathcashell Point lies on the east shore of Loch Lomond. There are the remains of both an Iron Age fort and a crannog here. The fort sits on the tip of the peninsula and the crannog a short distance offshore to the south. There are no defensive ditches across the approach.

The fort retains the footings of a rectangular building which, according to reports, does not appear to be of 'great age'. However, in 1724 Alexander Graham of Duchray described them as standing to a height of 9 or 10ft and in the following year the ruin was described as of two buildings, which seemed to be joined by sloping roofs 'to each side' of the enclosing wall of the fort. This wall is circular and about 6ft thick. Of dry-stone construction, it had an entrance from the eastern side. The ruin of a further large rectangular building to the east was recorded in the 1960s. The term cashel normally indicates a religious establishment of the dark ages.

One story is that Clan Buchanan descends from Sir Anselm O'Kyan, the son of an Irish king, who apparently assisted in the fight against the Danes. In return for his services, he was awarded the lands of Buchanan to the east of Loch Lomond by the Earl of Lennox. However, grants to Absalon, the Earl's Seneschal, in 1225 and to Gilbert, a subsequent Seneschal, in the mid 13th century, seem more trustworthy. Gilbert and his descendants are known to have adopted Buchanan as their surname. Their original patronymic is given as MacAuslan.

Other references: Row Cashel

STRATHAVEN CASTLE

South Lanarkshire   Ruin or site   OS 71   NS 703445
Just south of the A71, east of junction with A726, in Strathaven.

Standing upon a largely artificial mound above the village, Strathaven Castle consists of the remains of a large rectangular block with a round tower at one corner. Much of the north wall remains with fragments of the others.

The building was rubble built and measured 70ft by 38ft running east to west. It was three-storeys high and retains a few original features, including a fragment of corbelling in a style dated to the 15th century. The four-storey round tower sits at the northwest corner and there was a projecting wing at the southeast corner. The round tower retains a selection of widely splayed gunloops, which allow a wider angle of fire. The basement was vaulted. Excavations at the site uncovered part of the foundations of a surrounding wall and portions of the rest of the structure. It is described in the *Statistical Account*, as being 'surrounded by a strong wall, with turrets at certain distances, and the entrance secured by a drawbridge'.

Superiority of the Barony of Avondale is first recorded with the de Bigres family in the 12th century. From at least as early as 1228, the lands were held by the Bairds, who were forfeited in 1340. They probably established the earliest castle on the site. It came to Alexander Stewart, who resigned the estate in favour of Maurice Murray of Bothwell and Drumsagard. This was confirmed by a grant by David II. It thereafter went with the superiority to James Douglas, 'the Gross', who became 1st Earl of Avondale in 1437 and 7th Earl of Douglas in 1440. In 1450 the 8th Earl had Strathaven erected into a Burgh of Barony. It remained with the Douglas earls until their forfeiture in 1455 when the castle was surrendered to James II and sacked.

In 1456 the king granted Avondale to Andrew Stewart, the illegitimate grandson of the Duke of Albany. He

became Lord Avondale in the following year and built the present castle. He was Chancellor of Scotland for James III. In 1534 his son exchanged Strathaven for Ochiltree with Sir James Hamilton of Finnart, the legitimised 'Bastard of Arran'. He was an immensely wealthy character and a close confidant of James V. He had amassed a huge personal fortune and extensive estates and paid for the construction of the Royal Palace at Stirling Castle from his own pocket. He was issued a grant in 1539 by which, 'for services at the palaces at Linlithgow and Stirling', he had all of his Lanarkshire properties placed under a single charter for the Barony of Avondale. He was executed for treason and forfeited in 1540. Two years later, Sir James Hamilton of Avondale and Crawfordjohn, his eldest son, had his father's estates restored by an act of parliament. By that time the infant Mary, Queen of Scots, was on the throne and Sir James's uncle, the Earl of Arran, was both heir to the throne and Regent. In 1617 the estate was sold to his cousin, the Marquis of Hamilton. The last resident was Anne, Duchess of Hamilton, who lived there until her death in 1716. The Hamiltons then abandoned the castle and it became ruinous.

A skeleton was found bricked up within the walls when part of the structure collapsed in the 19th century. A plaque adjacent to the castle tells that, 'According to tradition, the wife of a past lord so greatly displeased her husband that she was walled up alive in part of the castle wall. Nothing is recorded of her crime, yet it is said that she was led into a small purpose-built niche, blessed by a priest, given some food and water, and then walled up forever. When a portion of the walls fell down in the middle of the 19th century human bones were discovered, giving some credence to this story.' Local tradition also asserts the existence of tunnels leading to various points in the village, including the tower at Udstonhead.

The castle is a Scheduled Ancient Monument, and category 'B' Listed Building.

Other references: Avondale Castle, Gavler's Castle

SYMINGTON PLACE

South Lanarkshire   Ruin or site   OS 72   NS 998350
4 miles west of Biggar, east of junction of A73 and A72, 100 yds south of A72 by minor road and foot, on east side of Main Street, 0.25 miles north of Symington.

Nothing remains of a small knoll in a field to the north of the village, which was recorded as a moated site. In 1710 the old house of Symington was described as ruinous. Building debris was reported in the 19th century and mortared rubble was said to have been ploughed up at that time. By 1858 the moat had almost been levelled.

This was said to have been the site of the manor of Simon Loccard, which developed into the home of the Symingtons of that Ilk from the early 14th century. It has also been suggested that the earthwork at Castlehill, to the southwest of the village, may have been an early seat of the barony. There is evidence of ring ditches of indeterminate age at Broadlees and Westside and a variety of uninvestigated enclosures in the area.

In the early 12th century the manor of Wice encompassed what are now the parishes of Wiston, Roberton and Symington. Wice granted his original church to Kelso Abbey and two new chapels sprang up on the lands of Roberton and Symington. By the end of the century, both Roberton and Symington had established their own independence as parishes and baronies. Simon was in dispute with the monks of Kelso in 1189 over the patronage of his church. The outcome was that he gave up his rights to the church, while the monks conceded that it was independent of Wiston and appointed his nominee as priest. His descendants are recorded in possession in 1300.

After the Wars of Independence, Thomas Dixon received a grant of Symington from Robert I. His descendants then assumed the Symington surname. They became hereditary baillies of the Barony of Douglas and keepers of the castle there. John Symington is on record as depute Sheriff of Lanarkshire in 1478 and 1490. In 1605 John Symington of that Ilk was served heir to his grandfather in the Barony of Symington, as Baillie of Douglas and captain of its castle.

The Barony of Symington was held by John Mure of Annieston in 1646, and he is confirmed in possession in 1649. It is said to have passed to the Baillies of St John's Kirk and then to Lockhart of The Lee. By 1710 it was owned by George Lockhart of Carnwath.

TANNOCHSIDE

North Lanarkshire   Ruin or Site   OS 64   NS 716620
2 miles south of Coatbridge, on minor roads east of the A752 and north of the A721, south of the North Calder Water, in Viewpark.

'Tennoksyid' appears as a substantial low building on Pont's manuscript map of c.1596. It is the site of a later mansion, said to have been built at the beginning of the 17th century, and which carried a date-stone of 1683 above the door.

In the 17th century Tannochside was home to the Rae family, merchant burgesses of Glasgow. The family were bankrupted in 1795, having been heavily involved with the Houstons, whose financial collapse was said to have been the greatest financial failure the city had ever seen. The Rae estates raised £70,000 when sold and it is said that, had they been able to hold on to them, they could have been among the wealthiest families in the kingdom due to their coal reserves.

By 1816 it belonged to Ironside Esq. In about 1840 Tannochside became home to the soldier and politician, William Hozier, 1st Baron Newlands. He changed the name of the house to St Enoch's Hall. William was the second son of Hozier of Mauldslie. The estate passed to his son James, 2nd Baron, who was also a politician and a diplomat. He was Grand Master Mason of Scotland from 1899-1903 and Lord Lieutenant for Lanarkshire from 1915-21. He died childless in 1929. The house was demolished and no trace remained by 1953. By that time the estate had been developed as Viewpark housing estate.

Other references: St Enoch's Hall, Viewpark

TARBET CASTLE

The Lennox & East Dunbartonshire Ruin or site OS 56 NN 329054
At north end of Loch Lomond, east of A82, on Tarbet Island, 0.75 miles northeast of Tarbet.

This is the site of a 14th century castle of the MacFarlanes, also known as Claddach. Pont sketched a small tower with barmkin on 'Yle Terbert' on his map of Loch Lomond in the late 16th century.

The island is overgrown with trees and scrub, but the foundations of a sandstone building of unknown provenance are still discernible. It measures 46ft north to south by 18ft east to west. It is possible that it had rounded corners and possibly had timber walls. This has been suggested because of the lack of rubble within, but stone robbing could also explain this. The ground floor is divided into two rooms, the southern-most of which is smaller and suggestive that the building tapered toward that end. It has been proposed that this portion was a watchtower.

Other reference: Claddach Castle

TARBRAX

South Lanarkshire Ruin or site OS 72 NT 025551
Off minor roads west of A70, 7 miles north of Carnwath, at or near Lawhead House, Torbrex.

Site of a tower house of the Somervilles, which had passed to Lockhart of Cleghorn by 1649. A tower with barmkin appears at this location on Pont's map of the late 16th century and the present 'C' listed 19th century doocot is constructed of reused stone, which includes an entrance dated to the late 16th or early 17th century.

William Somerville of Tarbrax is said to have been a son of John, 3rd Lord Somerville, and is recorded in the mid 15th century. It is said that in 1558 Alexander Somerville of Tarbrax acted as judge for Cardinal David Beaton in the heresy trial of Walter Milne, the last Protestant martyr to be executed in Scotland. In one account, Alexander was described as being 'devoid of all honesty, religion or fear of God.' In 1603 John Somerville of Tarbrax inherited his father's estate of Cambusnethan. By 1649 George Lockhart, a younger son of Lockhart of Cleghorn, acquired the estate. Norman Lockhart of Tarbrax is recorded in 1836.

Other reference: Torbrex

THE LEE

South Lanarkshire Private OS 72 NS 854465
2.5 miles northwest of Lanark, on minor roads south of A73, north of the Auchenglen Burn, at Lee Castle.

The Lee is a 19th century mansion, which incorporates an earlier house and possibly portions of a castle of the Lockharts. The present house was designed by James Gillespie Graham in 1834-35. A very substantial tower named 'Lie' is depicted on Pont's manuscript map of c.1596.

The family held the lands from as early as the 12th century. Legend asserts that they gained their name because Sir Simon Loccard carried the key for the casket containing Robert the Bruce's heart when Sir James Douglas took it on crusade. However, the family were already known as Loccard in the 12th century when their ancestor Simon and his brother Tancard gave their name to the villages of Symington and Thankerton. It has also been suggested that they altered the spelling of their name to honour Sir Simon's exploits.

In 1491 Gilbert Lockhart was found to be in the wrong by occupying and cultivating lands which rightfully belonged to Christian Maxwell, the widow of Alan Lockhart of The Lee. Gilbert was ordered to pay three years rent in recompense. In 1494 a legal dispute arose over 'certain stuff and stones' sold by James Lockhart of The Lee

to a dyer named David Henderson. Sir Steven Lockhart of Cleghorn agreed to defend and protect William Murray of Touchadam who possessed the items. Alan Lockhart of The Lee was killed at the Battle of Pinkie in 1547. In 1568 James Lockhart of the Lee was one of a number of landholders who protested to parliament that they should not be prejudiced against because they held some lands from the outlawed Earl of Glencairn. James was declared forfeit, but restored to his estates in 1585. The Lockharts were Royalists during the civil wars of the 17th century and James, Lord Lee, a member of the Court of Session, commanded a regiment at the Battle of Preston in 1648. His son Sir William, fought on the Royalist side but, after marrying Cromwell's niece, he became a Parliamentarian and was appointed Commissioner for the Administration of Justice in Scotland.

The estate passed to James's grandson, George, the son of Lockhart of Carnwath. He became a spy for the Jacobites and published evidence of the bribes paid by the English Treasury to secure the passage of the Act of Union in 1707. He was deeply implicated in the preparations for the 1715 Jacobite rising and was imprisoned in Edinburgh Castle as a result. Once freed, he resumed his activities as a Jacobite spy. In 1727 his correspondence was intercepted and he fled into exile. He was allowed to return the following year, but retired from public life before being killed in a duel in 1731. The property passed from the family in the 20th century.

'The Lee Penny' is a healing amulet, consisting of a dark red gemstone set within a silver groat of Edward IV. It was apparently acquired by Sir Simon Loccard while on crusade. It is said, when dipped in water, to heal bleeding, fever, animal ailments, and the bites of 'mad dogs' and (perhaps) Englishmen. It inspired Sir Walter Scott's story, 'The Talisman'. The Lee and the doocot are category 'B' Listed Buildings.

Other reference: Lee Castle

THE PARK

South Lanarkshire   Ruin or site   OS 72   NS 863325

2.5 miles northeast of Douglas, on minor roads and foot south of A70, 0.75 miles south of junction with M74, on east bank of Parkhall Burn.

Parkhall, a modern farm, stands to the north of the site of an old castle of the Douglases. A tower named 'The Park' appears here on Pont's map of c.1596, and the site is identified by that name in the 19th century. Is occupies the southern end of a high spur defended by steep drops to the burn on the west and south. Only traces remain of an L-plan structure, the longer part of which measured 54ft by 40ft.

The Douglases are said to have held a strong early castle here. In 1329-30 Sir James Douglas is reported to have signed a charter in favour of Newbattle Abbey at The Park, just prior to his departure to the Holy Land with Bruce's heart. The lands of Park came into the possession of the Carmichael Earl of Hyndford before 1710.

Other reference: Parkhall

THE TOR

South Lanarkshire   Ruin or site   OS 64   NS 650526

1 mile south of East Kilbride, just east of A726, just north of southern exit from Calderglen Park.

This motte, also known as the Torran, sits in woodland at the end of a ridge and is defended on its northern, western and eastern flanks by a deep stream gully. It has been formed by scarping of a natural mound which sits 6ft above the surrounding terrain and 50ft above the bed of the stream. It was recorded as having a moat in the 1950s, though a broad dry ditch is more likely given the surrounding topography. The course of the ditch can be identified with difficulty around the southern side of the motte, though in places sections of the mound and ditch have been buried below waste from landscaping activity. This includes rubble deposits. The summit is oval, and measures 20ft by 25ft. It is now covered by mature woodland, though this is sparse enough to allow easy access to the summit and examination of the site. Some areas of the summit have been disturbed by tree planting and other intrusive activities by both humans and an industrious rabbit population! (www.visitlanarkshire.com/attractions/garden-and-parks/Calderglen-Country-Park/)

THINACRES

South Lanarkshire   Ruin or site   OS 64   NS 737503?

1.5 miles west of Larkhall, on minor roads 3 miles southeast of A723 and Meikle Earnock, at Thinacres.

Possible site of a tower house of the 16th century. It may be that references actually describe the ruinous tower at Plotcock, 0.25 miles to the southeast.

Other reference: Plotcock

THORNTONHALL

South Lanarkshire   Ruin or site   OS 64   NS 591550

2 miles west of East Kilbride, by minor roads south of A727 (formerly A726), and west of new A726, at Thorntonhall.

A low building with courtyard is named 'Thorntoun' on Pont's map of c.1596. Thornton with Dripps, Jackton, Newlands and other properties are said to have comprised the Barony of Calderwood, which was granted to Sir Robert Maxwell by his parents in 1401. Thornton is said to have been held for several centuries by the Ross family, and later by the Nivens, under the superiority of the Maxwells.

The site developed into a farm which was purchased by a grocery magnate named Cooper in the 19th century. He built Thorntonhall House, known locally as 'The Hall', around which the present village developed. The Hall was demolished in the 20th century.

Other reference: Thorntoun

THORRIL CASTLE

South Lanarkshire   Ruin or site   OS 72   NS 865310

2 miles east of Douglas on the east side of the A74, north of Maidengill, on east bank of Parkhall Burn.

The foundations of a building, interpreted as a two-storey bastle house, were discovered during the 1990 M74 Fieldwork Project. There was a rectangular block within a courtyard comprised of at least three buildings. The wall fragments vary in height between 1ft and 6ft. Several pieces of reused roll moulded masonry are incorporated into the walls of a nearby sheepfold, which suggest a date of the late 16th to early 17th century. The quality of this stonework suggests a high-status building, though one 19th century source records that Thorril stood 'a few yards' from the ruined tower of Parkhead.

A substantial building named Maidengill appears close to this location on Pont's manuscript map of c.1596 though may be a separate site.

The Douglases of nearby Parkhead were lairds here and the name Thorril is thought to be a derivation of Torthorwald, a property near Dumfries, which was also owned by this branch of the family. The site is a Scheduled Ancient Monument.

Other reference: Maidengill

TIGHVECHTICHAN TOWER

The Lennox & East Dunbartonshire   Ruin or site   OS 56   NN 312045

At or near Tarbet and Arrochar railway station, on minor road north of A83 at Tighvechtichan.

Traditionally, this is said to be the site of a tower of the MacFarlanes, which was manned to exact 'mail' or tolls from traffic on the drove road that traversed the glen.

TODHOLES CASTLE

South Lanarkshire   Ruin or site   OS 72   NT 038461
4 miles east of Carnwath, on minor roads north of A721, south of Weston, at or near Todholes.

Site of a tower measuring 20 ft by 15ft within a ditch. It was described as a typical Scottish peel tower, a place of strength which stood until 1810. It was demolished due to its dangerous condition and the stone used to build local dykes.

In 1540 Robert Maxwell of Caerlaverock was given a grant which included Todholes, Dunsyre and Weston. Todholes was occupied by a family of Douglases in 1572, when the proprietor is recorded as standing security that Alexander Weir of Hallcraig and Thomas Weir of Kirkton would attend the Justice Ayre at Lanark to face charges of complicity in the murders of Henry, Lord Darnley and the Regents Moray and Lennox. James Douglas of Todholes was one of numerous adherents of the Earl of Angus who were forfeited by James VI in 1584 for their part in the Raid of Ruthven.

Todholes had passed to the Baillies by 1645 when William Somerville the minister at Dunsyre was so concerned by 'the cruel and barbarous carriage' of James Baillie, younger of Todholes, and by his threats to kill him, that he sought the protection of the Marquis of Douglas. In 1649, James was one of many given local responsibilities in an act of parliament which put 'the kingdom in a posture of defence'. He did not comply and in 1662 he was excluded from the Act of Indemnity, which pardoned those who supported the Parliamentarians in the Civil War. He was expected to pay a fine of £360 for his part.

TOLLCROSS HOUSE

City of Glasgow   Ruin or site   OS 64   NT 636636
North of A74, south of A89, just north of Tollcross Road, in Tollcross Park, Glasgow

The architect David Bryce built the present mansion for James Dunlop in 1848, replacing an earlier house which may have had origins in the defensive period.

The Grays of Carntyne are said to have held Tollcross until John Gray put the estate up for sale in the late 16th century. It is said that his brother James, a lawyer, had 'distressed him with litigation' which necessitated the sale. By

the beginning of the 17th century the Corbett family appear as owners of the estate, although some 19th century sources state that they had been in possession of Tollcross for over 500 years. In 1810 the estate was sold to James Dunlop, who commissioned David Bryce to build the mansion mentioned. It was acquired by the Corporation of Glasgow in 1897 and housed a children's museum from 1905. It now provides supported accommodation for the elderly. It is a category 'A' Listed Building, and its conservatory is category 'B'.

TORRANCE HOUSE

South Lanarkshire   Private   OS 64   NS 654526
1.5 miles southeast of East Kilbride, off A726 in Calderglen Country Park.

Torrance House is an 18th century mansion which incorporates an early 17th century L-plan tower which may have 14th century origins. The first residence on this estate was a motte a little to the west of the house, known as The Tor. Later, a stone castle existed at Torrance, which was destroyed in 1570. The L-plan tower was built to replace it and was apparently completed in 1605. A small tower named 'Torrans' appears on Pont's map of c.1596.

Torrance is an L-plan tower house of four storeys and a garret with a tall square stair tower within the re-entrant. This contains a left-handed turnpike stair to all floors with a small room to the east on each floor. Many alterations have taken place, including enlargement of the windows. On the southern face this gives the building a Georgian style. A porch with an arched entrance has also been added at the main door. This supports an armorial stone displaying the Royal Arms of Scotland, which was reset from Mains Castle. On the north side of the courtyard the wall carries another armorial stone bearing the arms of Lindsay of Dunrod. This presumably was also removed from Mains. There is apparently a stone tablet within the house bearing the inscription 'Built 1605, restored 1875' with the coat of arms of Stuart of Torrance.

The estate was the property of the Torrance family. It passed by marriage to Thomas Hamilton prior to 1465. He was the grandson of Sir John Hamilton of Cadzow. In 1492 George Hamilton, brother of the then laird, was murdered by Lindsay of Mains and Dunrod. James Hamilton of 'Torrens' was Provost of Glasgow in 1548-49. He seems to have founded the line of Hamilton of Peill, having gained that property in the previous year. In 1568 his elder brother, Robert Hamilton of Torrance, was forfeited for taking the side of Mary, Queen of Scots, at the Battle of Langside.

In 1570 Torrance was burned to the ground by a contingent of English troops. They had been sent by Elizabeth I of England to assist the Regent Lennox in his destructive raid against Hamilton properties following the assassination of the Regent Moray. In the 1650s another James Hamilton of Torrance was sued for a variety of debts. These were bought up by James Stewart, the second son of the Laird of Castlemilk. He foreclosed in 1652 and set up home at Torrance. In 1740 the Stewarts commissioned William Adam to plan extensions to the house. This project never materialised, but by 1774 two wings, a coach-house and courtyard had been added.

The debts incurred by James Stuart's descendants forced them to relinquish the estate in 1947. The house was then used to house the offices of the East Kilbride Development Agency. In 1965 the east wing was seriously damaged by fire and then demolished, causing the agency to vacate. The house was considered for demolition, but was renovated in 1982. The west wing became the offices and shops of the new country park and the remainder converted to provide private residences. There are the remains of a 17th century doocot 100yds to the north of the house. This is in a poor condition.

A rectangular earthwork on a high promontory to the northeast has been reported as a motte, with some masonry evident where it has collapsed. This is more likely to be the site of the old parish church of Torrance, closed when the parishes of Torrance and Kilbride were amalgamated in 1589.

The house, its outbuildings, bridge and a statue of Sir John Falstaff form a cluster of category 'A', 'B' and 'C' Listed Buildings.

TOUR OF MAUCONLY

South Lanarkshire Ruin or Site OS 72 NS 960138

2 miles southeast of Elvanfoot, east of Daer Water and the A702, south of M74 by foot, on summit of Brown Hill.

Pont's manuscript map of c.1596 very clearly illustrates a substantial tower in this location. There are no visible remains on the ground. The structure appeared in Blaeu's *Atlas Novus* of 1654 and on Herman Moll's map of 1745, but not on the contemporary map by General Roy. There are no other records of the tower and nothing is known of the history. It has been suggested that this was a watch tower giving a view of the junction of two major thoroughfares through the hills from south to north. The routes have been used since Roman times and the modern roads follow or overlie the Roman roads.

TOWER

The Lennox & East Dunbartonshire Ruin or site OS 64 NS 613741

0.25 miles west of Torrance, north of A807 Balmore Road east of Tower Road, and just east of Tower Farm.

This is thought to be the site of a tower house. Some foundations remained in the late 18th century, but had been dug up prior to 1860. Traces of outbuildings remained in 1890 and silver coins have been found at the site. The same commentators also described an earthwork at the site, which they believed was a Roman camp. It was described as a 'large square encampment' with a single rampart 11ft thick and measuring about 1500ft, though did not say if this was in circumference, area, length or diameter. Nothing remains of either structure.

The site has been referred to as Broken Tower and one antiquarian of the late 19th century believed that the tower had existed before 1400. This name seems also to have been used on at least one 18th century map to depict Cadder, though consensus indicates that the name had 'travelled' from this site.

Blaeu's *Atlas Novus* of the 17th century shows a tower named 'Badhindrocht' in the vicinity.

In a 1526 charter following the forfeiture of Sir John Stirling of Keir, the superiority of Bardowie, 'Bawchindrowch' and other local lands was granted to Sir James Hamilton of Finnart.

Other references: Badhindrocht, Bawchindrowch, Broken Tower

TOWER RAIS

Renfrewshire Ruin or site OS 64 NS 509595

0.25 miles north of Barrhead, just northeast of B773/A736 junction.

Rais is an old Scots word for 'rise'. This small square tower with very thick walls and a vaulted basement is said to have been constructed between 1437 and 1449 by Alexander Stewart. In 1484, another Alexander Stewart received a grant of Halrig and Rais upon the resignation of Hector Stewart, his father. It is said to have guarded a ford over the Levern Water and to have been used as a hunting lodge by the Stewarts of Darnley, from whom the Stewarts of Halrig are said to be descended. In 1538 Edward Stewart, son of Hector Stewart of Rais, was granted a charter of Robertlone and Schiels in Ayrshire. In 1543 Hector appeared as a charter witness for the Earl of Lennox. Local romanticists named it Queen Mary's Castle, associating it with the local romance of Henry Lord Darnley and Mary, Queen of Scots. The couple are said to have courted in the vicinity before being married in 1565.

The tower was ruinous by the time Richardson's map of Glasgow was published in 1796. It became a source of stone for building, some of which was used in farm buildings at Dubs. It remained a familiar local landmark until a reluctant Burgh Council demolished the remains in 1932 to preserve the safety of the local children, for whom it represented a romantic play area. At the time regret was expressed that the funds could not be raised to preserve the building. Parts of the foundations were exposed during work to construct a cycle path in 1999. The path was diverted to avoid the remains.

A house to the east known as Tower Rais is a 19th century mock-Tudor mansion. It is also known by the name Montford House, and is a category 'B' Listed Building.

Other references: Old Rais, Queen Mary's Castle, Stewarts Rais, Rais Tower, Wraes

TRESMASS

The Lennox & East Dunbartonshire Ruin or site OS 64 NS 428752

2 miles east of Dumbarton, on minor roads north of A82 and Milton, north of Loch Bowie, at Middleton.

This is said to have been the site of the original castle of the Colquhouns. The parish was known as Colquhoun long before the family adopted the name as their own. They gained the Luss estates when one of them married the heiress of Luss. A branch of the Colquhouns is said to have moved from here to Barnhill House in 1543. The Lorane family then became tenants for several centuries.

The castle was a ruin by 1810 when a wall 3ft thick and 7-8ft high section of wall was extant to the northeast of the farmhouse. By 1868 only foundations remained, excavation revealing a 10ft length of wall 3-4ft thick. Nothing now remains. Middleton was the Middle Town of the parish and the remains of a 14th century chapel were recorded nearby in the 19th century.

Milton village, as the name suggests, was the Mill Town of Colquhoun Parish and the remains of a large 18th century mill complex sit high above the village as a picturesque Gothic-style ruin.

Other references: Mains of Colquhoun, Middleton of Colquhoun, Milton of Colquhoun

TULLICHEWAN

The Lennox and East Dunbartonshire   Ruin or site   OS 63   NS 382811
Just west of the A82 and Alexandria, east of Tullichewan Farm.

The estate of Tullichewan, or Tully Colquhoun, was sold by the Colquhouns to James Buchanan in 1792. In that year the architect Robert Lugar built a castellated mansion at this location. It was sold to the Horrocks family in 1817 and again in 1843 to William Campbell, a Glasgow merchant. In 1930 it was purchased by J. Scott Anderson, and he owned it until the house was requisitioned by the Royal Navy in World War II. Mr Anderson returned after the war but found the costs of upkeep excessive. The house lay vacant for several years before being blown up in 1954. The surviving stables, cottage and the gate piers are category 'B' Listed Buildings.

These lands are said to have been part of the Royal hunting ground of Robert I during his residence at the manor of Cardross. This, combined with remnants of vaulted basements and a part of the tower of the mansion, has led to a local legend that these are the ruins of his castle.

TWEEDIE

South Lanarkshire   Ruin or site   OS 71   NS 721440
1 mile southeast of Strathaven, off minor roads east of the B7086, south of the A71, at Tweediehall.

Site of a substantial tower, known as Tweedie or Tweediehall, which appears on Pont's map of c.1596 and subsequently in Blaeu's *Atlas Novus* of 1654. On General Roy's map of the mid 18th century, 'Tweedyhaw' appears a little to the west of a small settlement known as Tweedy. The history of this tower may have been shared with, or translated to, the site at 'Tweedieside'.

Tweediehall is ideally located to guard crossings of the River Avon to its north, and Kype Water to its west.

TWEEDIESIDE

South Lanarkshire   Ruin or site   OS 71   NS 727427
2 miles southeast of Strathaven, off minor roads east of the B7086, south of the A71, at Tweedieside.

The upper storey of the present farmhouse dates from 1900, though the building is recorded as being of a single story until then. It is said to stand on the site of, or incorporate parts of a castle of the Hamiltons of Silvertonhill and Goslington. A Stewart of Tweedy is on record here in 1510.

It appears as a small tower with barmkin named 'Tweediehill' on Pont's map, and was apparently also known as Silvertonhill. These references to Tweedie and Silvertonhill may be confused with a more substantial tower named 'Tweedie' which appears on Pont's map at what is now Tweediehall.

By 1710 Tweedieside belonged to Lady Castlehill and her husband, the Sinclair Laird of Stevenson. Hamilton of Wishaw names the estate 'Tweedieside, Goslington', but he does not clarify whether they were separate houses or alternate names. The Stevensons lived at Cambusnethan. By 1900 Tweedieside was the property of the Lockharts of Castlehill. A family named Tweedie owned the estate in the 12th and 13th centuries.
Other reference: Silvertonhill

UDSTON

South Lanarkshire   Ruin or site   OS 64   NS 697558
In Udston, Hamilton, 1 mile east of A725, off minor roads, at or near Udston Hospital.

Udston House has long gone, but it succeeded or incorporated older and possibly fortified houses.

The site was home to an important early branch of the Hamilton family. The original line was descended from Andrew Hamilton, 3rd son of Sir David Fitzwalter, 2nd of Cadzow. Andrew is designated the first of Udston and is on record in the period 1390–1406. His elder brother became 3rd of Cadzow, while his other brothers were the progenitors of the Bardowie and Bathgate lines of the family.

Andrew's son Robert inherited the estate but seems to have died without an heir. In 1444 Udston was resigned by William Baillie of Lamington in favour of his son, also William. A grant of the transfer was made by James Hamilton of Cadzow and ratified by James II in 1451.

By the end of the century the property was held by Patrick, designated 3rd of Udston, a son of Hamilton of Broomhill. Patrick's daughter, Elizabeth, took the property to her husband, Hamilton of Neilsland. Their son John Hamilton of Udston was killed at the Battle of Langside in 1568 while fighting for Mary, Queen of Scots. In 1579 James VI issued a grant confirming the sale of Udston and other properties by John Hamilton of Stonehouse to James Hamilton, the grandson of Sir David Hamilton of Fingalton who provided the funds.

The sons of a later Hamilton of Udston founded the families of Hamilton of Wishaw, and Barncluith. The senior representation of the Udston line eventually descended via the female line to the Lords Belhaven. In 1627–29 another John Hamilton of Udston left 200 merks to the hospital of Hamilton 'and the poor there'. In 1649 his grandson, also John, received ratification of various deeds of 'Clare Constat'. This ensured his possession of numerous parcels of land in and around the Hamilton area.

The family had moved to Coltness by the early 17th century which became their main residence for a few decades. By 1710 the Udston estate had been acquired by the Hamiltons of Barncluith. In the early 19th century the house belonged to a Mr Jackson. It was resold in 1850 and in 1919 became an infectious diseases hospital. Udston Hospital still exists, but the house has been demolished.

UDSTONHEAD

South Lanarkshire Private OS 71 NS 740470
On western side of the A723, 2 miles north of Strathaven, at Udstonhead.

The present building is a plain rectangular structure, rubble built of two storeys and an attic with corbiestepped gables. There are a few carved decorations embellishing the eaves of an otherwise plain and unfortified structure, a carved rose and a gargoyle are easily noticeable above the southern wall. There are sash widows at both ground and first floor level and a door enters the ground floor in the eastern gable.

The tower originated in the 16th century and appears as a substantial tower on Pont's original manuscript of c.1596.

Udstonhead is mentioned in an exchange of lands between Sir James Hamilton of Finnart and Andrew Stewart, Lord Avondale, in 1534. In 1541 James V granted the estate to Gavin Murray, with the 'land and cottages'

and superiority which had formerly belonged to the forfeited and executed Finnart. Gavin didn't hold it long, since only four months later the king granted the lands of Udstonhead, Whitecamp and Overton to John Mure, the heir of Patrick Mure of Annieston. In the following year the king issued a second grant, which put the property into the joint ownership of John and his wife, Margaret Hamilton, with whom it appears to have remained. None of these charters mention the tower and so it seems to have been built by the Mures after 1541.

Known simply as 'The Tower' in the 19th century, it was presumed to have been built by Finnart's descendants, the Hamiltons of Avondale, to resist the depredations of Annandale thieves. Local legend asserts that there is a tunnel between Strathaven Castle and The Tower, a highly unlikely scenario given the distance involved.

By 1880 it had been reduced from the original three storeys. Restoration had removed the upper storeys, included the insertion of larger windows and the addition of a modern roof. The ornaments on the gables described above, may be original though re-sited from the original roofline. A single storey 19th century wing has also been added to the southwest wall and a modern bungalow-type farmhouse to the northeast.

Other references: Hiddinstounheid, The Tower, Tower of Udstonhead, Udistounheid

WALKINSHAW HOUSE

Renfrewshire   Ruin or site   OS 64   NS 464668
2 miles northwest of Paisley, east of M8, west of A726, just east of the confluence of Black Cart and Gryffe Waters, 0.5 miles north of Blackstone Mains Farm.

There was an early 16th century tower here, which is said to have been extended. It appears on Pont's map of c.1596. In 1791 a unique triangular mansion by Robert Adam replaced it. This was extended and renovated in 1825 but was demolished in 1927.

In 1235 Dungallus, Justice of Lennox, conducted an exchange of property with Paisley Abbey. He surrendered his estate of Knoc and gained lands beside Walkinshaw. It is said that his descendants became the Walkinshaws of that Ilk, who were hereditary foresters to the High Steward of Scotland. The main line of the family was not continuous. In the early 15th century the estate was divided between heiresses. Easter Walkinshaw became the property of the Mortons, later of Levan. Wester Walkinshaw passed to Walkinshaw of Fulwood who adopted the designation 'of that Ilk'. The family appear in charter records in 1464, 1511 and 1532. In 1636 the estate was inherited by Walkinshaw of Garturk, another cousin. In 1683 Gavin Walkinshaw of that Ilk sold the estate to John Walkinshaw of Barrowfield, a cousin who was a merchant in Glasgow. In 1715 he was an envoy for the Jacobites to Vienna, but lost a fortune supporting their cause. He was captured at the Battle of Sheriffmuir, declared forfeit and imprisoned in Stirling Castle. He escaped by simply walking through the gates in his wife's clothes. He received a pardon in 1717 and returned to Glasgow. His Barrowfield estates were purchased by the magistrates of Glasgow, but John's wife was allowed a modest income from the coal pits on the Barrowfield estate and made her home at Camlachie.

Their tenth daughter was Clementina Walkinshaw, the famed mistress to Prince Charles Edward Stewart, the famous Bonnie Prince Charlie. Called to the exiled Jacobite court in 1752, Clementina had a daughter with Charles. He soon became a violent and possessive drunk, from whom she sought the protection of his father, James Stewart, the 'Old Pretender'. He granted her a pension, while mother and daughter enjoyed safety from Charles by moving between various convents in France. Charlotte was legitimized in 1783, but when Charles died her uncle, Cardinal Henry Stewart, forced her to sign a quitclaim which allowed him the principle claim to the throne. Charlotte died a year later.

By the 1860s Walkinshaw House belonged to Alexander Cunninghame and was described as one of 'the pleasantest seats in the county'.

WALLACE'S BUILDINGS

Renfrewshire   Ruin or site   OS 63   NS 442631
In Elderslie, near A727, on south side of Main Road, 1 mile east of Black Cart.

Foundations, and a monument to Sir William Wallace, are all that remain on the site of a 17th century building with vaulted kitchen and associated farm buildings. A castle here is mentioned in 1710 when it was described as 'decayed'. The remaining buildings were demolished in the 1970s.

Archaeological and early map evidence suggests that the site was previously occupied by a rectilinear moated structure with stone walls and corner bastions. It may have had a collection of buildings in its northeast corner. The moat was described as flat bottomed, 15ft wide and 4ft deep. Pottery finds suggest a 13th–14th century origin for the structure. Some evidence of a probable rock cut ditch was also found. The later buildings evidently contained sculpted stones of an earlier date.

Ellerslie, later Elderslie, was a property of the Wallace family from the 13th century until 1850. This is alleged to be the birthplace of Sir William Wallace. His father, Sir Malcolm, is said by Blind Harry to have been to have been styled 'of Auchenbathie and Ellerslie'. A 17th century society claimed the family seat was at Ellerslie in Ayrshire, now remembered only in name. The Ayrshire claim is maintained to this day.

Sir William was the prime instigator and leader of the resistance movement in late 13th century Scotland.

Their aim was to free the country from the English, who had invaded in 1296. Wallace led the Scots to victory at Stirling Bridge in 1297, but his army was heavily defeated at Falkirk the following year. He travelled in Europe, seeking assistance from the Pope, before returning to resume the fight for independence. He was betrayed, captured and executed before leadership of the country was taken up by Robert the Bruce, who was crowned king in 1306.

Toward the end of the 14th century Elderslie was granted to a younger son of the Wallaces of Craigie. They appear on record in 1398 when Thomas Wallace was granted the lands of Auchenbothie by his father, John Wallace of Elderslie. His descendants retained the estate until 1678 when it returned to the Wallaces of Craigie. In the 18th century the estate was purchased by Alexander Speirs.

Other references: Elderslie, Ellerslie, Moat House

WALLANS

South Lanarkshire   Ruin or site   OS 72   NS 812487
3 miles southwest of Carluke, near A72 and River Clyde, near Overton.

Possible site of a castle of which one wall was extant until 1845, but of which there was no trace by 1954. The site was reputedly once an island; however a change in course of the river left it on the west bank of the river.

Local legend tells that this was a refuge for William Wallace while he was active in the area.

Other references: Castle Wallans, Overton, Temple Walls

WALSTON

South Lanarkshire   Ruin or site   OS 72   NT 060457
At Walston, 3 miles north of Elsrickle, off minor roads north and east of A721.

Site of a castle. It was described as a square tower, which was in use as a hunting lodge for the Earl of Mar in 1601. It was demolished in the early 1800s to make way for cow sheds. Denoted as Walston Mansion and Walston Place to the east of the church on later maps, it appears as a large square tower beside the names Boreland and Walston on Pont's map.

Like neighbouring Dolphinton, the small parish and barony of Walston was the property of the Lords of Bothwell. It passed through the hands of the Olifards and Murrays. It was then separated from the Bothwell lordship when it was granted by Sir Thomas Moray of Bothwell to Sir Robert Erskine in the reign of David II. It seems to have returned to Bothwell ownership with the Douglases, then via Sir John Ramsay to the Hepburns in the 15th century.

On the forfeiture of James Hepburn, 4th Earl of Bothwell, in 1567, Walston was retained by the crown. In 1581 it was returned by grant of James VI to Sir Robert's descendant, James Erskine, Earl of Mar. The grant was challenged by Francis Stewart, Earl of Bothwell, and he was awarded the estate at parliament later in the same year. He was forfeited and in 1593 the Earl of Mar became undisputed owner of the estate. At the beginning of the 17th century, Mar sold it to an Edinburgh merchant named Robert Baillie whose family owned the entire parish until the early 18th century. He was the son of Baillie of St John's Kirk.

At this time the 'manor' is described as 'one old house seated near to the church and well planted with barren timber'. John Baillie sold Walston to Lord Lee of Carnwath in 1709. From 1722 he divided up the Elsrickle portion, which sat to the south of the Black Mount, and sold it to various proprietors. Elsrickle itself was occupied by James Harper in 1747, but by 1840 it belonged to the Woddrops of Dalmarnock. They held the superiority of the whole of Elsrickle and are known to have feued out a number of properties at this time.

Other reference: Elsrickle

WATERSIDE

South Lanarkshire   Ruin or site   OS 73   NS 790371
By minor roads west of M74, 2.5 miles southwest of Lesmahagow, just north of Waterside Bridge and Logan Water, at Waterside.

Site of a substantial tower of the Weirs, which appears on Pont's map of 1596, and in Blaeu's *Atlas Novus* of 1654.

The Weirs of Waterside appear to have been tenants of Lesmahagow Priory, and obtained ownership of their lands at the Reformation. The family were Covenanters and Thomas Weir of Waterside died at the battle of Drumclog in 1679. Apparently his horse bridle snapped and the animal carried him into the midst of the enemy. In the same year his son Gavin was proclaimed a rebel and imprisoned for his part in the Battle of Bothwell Bridge. He was released in 1684 and in 1705 became an elder of the parish church.

WAYGATESHAW HOUSE

South Lanarkshire   Private   OS 72   NS 825484

4.5 miles northwest of Lanark, and 2 miles southwest of Carluke, on minor roads west of B7056 and east of A73, on east bank of River Clyde, at Waygateshaw.

Waygateshaw House is a 16th century courtyard castle, consisting of a small L-plan tower house with 17th century wing. It has a more modern block and a 12ft wall which encloses the fourth side of a small courtyard. The entrance to the yard is through a moulded arched gateway, which is guarded by gunloops. Over the entrance gateway stood sculptures of two dog-like animals and a re-sited sundial, as described by MacGibbon and Ross. These have been replaced by a pair of lions. Another pair in the form of a lion and lioness, but in an alternative style, sit above an arched entrance of later date on the southern side of the yard. These are said to once have been the supporters of a large sundial which stood in the garden.

The tower house is rectangular, of three storeys with a small stair wing. There was possibly another floor then a parapet above with garret, though these have gone. It now has a modern roof. The walls have gunloops, one guarding the entrance to the yard, a second in the northern wall and a third guarding the entrance at the re-entrant. There are a few small windows. The basement is vaulted and consists of two chambers. In the wing a particularly steep turnpike stair reaches all floors. The hall on the first floor is vaulted. Above this the room has been rebuilt to form a garret, lower than the original, though the original fireplace has been remodelled to form a window. The extension of the 17th century is of three storeys and an attic. There is no vaulting in this building, and an original fireplace survives on the second floor.

It is said that Hugo Polay obtained a charter of half the lands of Waygateshaw from Robert I in 1327-28. By 1455 it belonged to Andrew Murray, who is said to have received a grant of the estate from his father. He was one of the Murrays of Touchadam and an heiress is said to have taken the property by marriage to Alexander Lockhart in 1539. However, it may well have come to the Lockharts of Cleghorn as early as 1490, and Alexander Lockhart is on record in 1534 designated 'of Waygateshaw'. In that year he sold the estate to Sir James Hamilton of Finnart, a sale confirmed by a charter of James V. Later in the same year it was one of the properties absorbed into Finnart's Barony of Avondale by a charter of James V. In 1536 it was occupied by tenants in a charter of confirmation to Finnart. At some point, probably at Finnart's forfeiture in 1540, it returned to the Lockharts. In 1572 Stephen Lockhart of Waygateshaw was indicted in the murder of Henry, Lord Darnley. William Lockhart was forfeited for taking part in the Pentland Rising of 1666, but later regained the estate. It is said to have provided a home to the (reputed) necromancer Major Thomas Weir and his sister, who were closely related to the Lockharts.

Waygateshaw was sold to the Weirs in 1720 and then passed to the Steel family. In 1959 it belonged to Miss Willis and has since passed through various owners. It had been restored in the 1980s, though was burnt to a shell about 1990. Repairs were made, but the house still required restoration in 2000. This has now been completed. There are the remains of a doocot to the north, of which only the north wall stands to its full height. The other sides have collapsed to within a foot or two of the ground.

Waygateshaw sits within the famous fruit growing region of Clydesdale and early in the 19th century boasted the largest fruit tree in the area. This ancient tree apparently produced no less than 3000lbs of pears in 1809. The house and doocot are category 'B' Listed Buildings. (waygateshaw.com).

Other reference: Wicketshaw

WESTHALL TOWER

South Lanarkshire   Ruin or site   OS 72   NT 048473

5 miles east of Carnwath, on minor roads north and east of the A721 from Newbigging, 0.5 miles east of Weston, at Westhall.

Also known as Westhall of Dunsyre, the ruin of this small L-plan tower of the 16th century was badly mutilated when it was converted for use as a pigsty about 1900. It has now been cleared and wall fragments on the north and east stand to a maximum height of about 15ft. In the 1950s the internal dimensions of the tower were estimated at 27ft by 15ft, with walls of varying thickness to a maximum of 4ft. These were recorded as reaching a maximum height of 8ft in 1864 and sections of this have clearly been added during the adaptations mentioned. The springing for a basement vault, the base of a spiral staircase, a slit window and evidence of the fireplace can still be seen.

It was probably built by the Grahams, who acquired the lands before 1477, when John Graham of Westhall appeared as a charter witness. In 1536 John Graham of Westhall and his company were slaughtered by John Bannatyne of Corehouse, his brother Thomas and 19 others. In 1670 Westhall was inherited by John Baillie of

St John's Kirk from his brother, Thomas. It may at various times have passed to the Hepburns, Hamiltons, Douglases, and the Lockharts, though these references probably relate to the superiority of the Barony of Dunsyre.

The ruin is a category 'C' Listed Building.

WESTON

South Lanarkshire   Ruin or site   OS 72   NT 043476
5 miles east of Carnwath, on minor roads north and east of the A721 from Newbigging, at Weston.

Probable site of a castle, the second of two towers mentioned as having stood at Westhall. Weston was granted with Dunsyre and Todholes to Maxwell of Caerlaverock in 1540.

WESTRAW

South Lanarkshire   Private   OS 72   NS 947430
3 miles east of Lanark, 2 miles south of Carstairs, 3 miles north of A73 by minor roads, 1 mile west of Pettinain at Westraw Mains.

The present house dates in part from the 15th century, though has lost all of its defensive features during modifications and extensions. The top storey was removed in the 18th century.

The lands of Westraw were included in a grant of lands, which had been forfeited by John Fitz-Waldeve, to Eustace Maxwell, during the reign of Robert I. It became a property of the Johnstones, who (legend tells) was granted the estate when the progenitor of this branch of the family captured the Earl of Douglas at the Battle of Arkinholm in 1455. The Earl of Douglas, however, was safe in England at the time, although Johnstone did assist in the capture of Hugh Douglas, Earl of Ormonde, the Earl's brother.

In 1555 Johnstone of Westraw was allied to Lindsay of Covington in a feud with the Somervilles. In 1624 the family sold Westraw to Sir James Carmichael, later Lord Hyndford.

The house and associated farm buildings are category 'B' Listed Buildings.

Other reference: Westerhall

WESTSHIELD

South Lanarkshire   Ruin or site   OS 72   NS 946494
5 miles northeast of Lanark, on minor roads north of A70, east of A706, west of B7016, just north of Mouse Water at Westshield.

Westshield was a rectangular 16th century keep, extended by two 17th century gabled wings and a square stair tower in the re-entrant. Additional low wings were added though later partly removed, but it was demolished late in the 20th century due to its ruinous state.

The keep represented the eastern portion of the main block, having been extended length-wise by one extension, while another lay at right angles along the east gable, creating an L-plan. All had corbiestepped gables and enlarged moulded windows.

The original keep was built of rubble and had four storeys and a garret. It may originally have had a parapet and wall-walk, though in keeping with the later extensions the roof was extended to the wall head, creating eaves. The wall head was decorated by a cornice and there were a variety of chimney stacks with string coursing. The ground floor consisted of three vaulted chambers and one un-vaulted room within the western extension. A turnpike stair, within the wing, rose from the entrance to all floors. On the first floor of the keep, the hall occupied the entire floor. Bedrooms and private rooms occupied the floors above.

An apparently poor example of a heraldic panel displayed the arms of Denholm, the family who built the castle. In 1685 William Denholm of Westshield supported the rebellion of the Earl of Argyll and was with him in Amsterdam prior to his attempted invasion of Scotland in support of the Duke of Monmouth's rebellion. In his absence he was tried, forfeited and sentenced to be executed. He evaded capture and was restored to his estate after 'The Glorious Revolution'. William died before 1714, when his widow married Daniel Campbell of Shawfield. Westshield passed to the Lockharts of The Lee sometime after 1771.

WHITECASTLE

South Lanarkshire Ruin or site OS 72 NT 011416
4 miles southeast of Carnwath, just south of B7016, by foot west of White Castle.

A small tower appears here in Pont's map of 1596. The circular earthwork with a double rampart recorded on the summit of the hill is a fort. Whitecastle was owned by the Muirheads in 1710 and the Dicksons in 1777.

WHITEFORD

Renfrewshire Ruin or site OS 64 NS 498633
1 mile southeast of Paisley, on north bank of White Cart, south of A761, north of A726, and west of A736, and just west of Hawkhead Road, at factory site.

Whiteford Tower belonged to the family of the same name. It stood on the north bank of the Cart until the early 18th century. It appears on Pont's map of c.1596 and in Blaeu's *Atlas Novus* of 1654.

The progenitor of the family is said to be Walter, who so distinguished himself at the Battle of Largs in 1263 that he was given a grant of the lands of Whiteford by the High Steward. In 1584 John Whiteford of that Ilk was charged with seven others of the murder of Patrick Maxwell of Stanely. Of the eight, Whiteford was the only one to stand trial. He was acquitted.

The Whitefords of that Ilk held the estate continuously until it became the property of the Earl of Dundonald in 1689. They also held estates at Blairquhan (Ballochmyle) in Ayrshire and at Milton in Lanarkshire. Walter Whiteford, a son of the laird, became Bishop of Brechin during the return to Episcopacy in the reign of James VI.

A circular crop mark close to the location given by RCAHMS (NS 506622) was visible in aerial photography in 1957 and was scheduled as an ancient monument in 2011. Neither has been positively identified as the site of the tower; indeed early cartographic references, including General Roy's map, place the property of Whiteford some way to the west at the location given above. 19th century maps place 'Old Mill' at the RCAHMS location.

WHITEHILL

South Lanarkshire Ruin or site OS 72 NS 998327
1 mile northeast of Lamington, north of A702, just east of Overbarns.

A series of three earthworks, consisting of banks and ditches, sit at the end of a long narrow ridge above low lying ground beside the River Clyde. The first lies to the northeastern end of the site and is an oval platform defined by a ditch with a rampart of stone and earth. These reach a height of no more than 2ft on the internal side, while the enclosing ditch is almost entirely filled. To the northeast are traces of a broad ditch, 25ft wide, thought to have been an outwork. The enclosed area measures almost 90ft by 250ft. Within this, at its western end, is a poorly defined circular platform of later date, which measures about 68ft in diameter. At the western extremity of the promontory is a third earthwork, where the bank reaches an internal height of 4ft at its highest point on the south. To the east there is another broad ditch of slightly broader proportions to the outwork of the northeastern earthwork. The enclosed area measures 190ft by 98ft. Plough damage has significantly altered the proportions of the ramparts and ditches.

There has been no excavation of these sites and so they remain undated. The only opinion ventured is that they are not typical of Iron Age sites, though they do appear on a list of prehistoric sites in Lanarkshire. Superficially the site has the appearance of an earthwork castle.

WINDGATE HOUSE

South Lanarkshire   Ruin or site   OS 72   NT 016272

5 miles southwest of Biggar, on minor roads south of A702, on the bank of Fair Burn, at southeast of Cowgill Upper Reservoir.

Windgate House was thought at one time to be a similar structure to the Black Houses of northern Scotland, with no defensive elements to the building. However, relatively recent archaeological examination supports the opinion that this is small ruined bastle house of the 16th century with a vaulted basement. The ruin has been repaired and an interpretive plaque installed.

It is known locally as the vaults and is believed to have been a property of the Baillies of Lamington. It may have been built due to the sensitivities provoked by Lamington Tower being overlooked by Fatlips Tower. A spectral couple dressed in Victorian fashion allegedly appear here prior to a significant event in the lives of the Baillies. The site is a Scheduled Ancient Monument.

WINTERCLEUCH BASTLE

South Lanarkshire   Ruin or site   OS 78   NS 980114

4 miles southeast of Elvanfoot, on minor road and track south of A702, near Wintercleuch Burn, 1 mile northeast of Wintercleuch, east of Mid Height.

Only a basement survives of a bastle house. It was a rectangular structure measuring 34ft by 20ft with walls 3ft thick. Five steps of a turnpike stair remain in the northeastern corner. Excavation has revealed a drain running through the centre of the ground floor. It had been abandoned by the 17th century as the result of a serious fire, of which there is evidence. Other features associated with the house include earthworks and other buildings, one of which had been attached to the main structure. These show signs of habitation stretching into the 18th century. The site is a Scheduled Ancient Monument.

WISHAW HOUSE

North Lanarkshire   Ruin or site   OS 64   NS 787566

In Wishaw, north of A721, 0.5 miles northwest of railway station, in woodland on south bank of Calder Water.

Wishaw House was a sprawling mansion of the 19th century which, it is said, had a building of 1665 at its core. It had been improved and extended by James Gillespie Graham before 1839 but was demolished in 1953.

An earlier house stood on the site and is sketched on Pont's map of the late 16th century. It is possible that portions of this were also incorporated, although no earlier work was observed during the demolition.

This was a property of the Hamiltons of Wishaw, cadets of the Udston branch of the family. William Hamilton, a son of Hamilton of Wishaw, inherited the title Lord Belhaven in 1793. His son, eighth Lord Belhaven, was granted the title Baron Hamilton of Wishaw in 1831. It was he who contracted Gillespie Graham to build the mansion. Only the coach house remains, which is a category 'C' Listed Building.

WISTON MANOR

South Lanarkshire   Ruin or site   OS 72   NS 953314?

1 mile west of Lamington, by minor roads west of A73 southwest of Wiston at Wiston Mains.

The village of Wiston apparently takes its name from the Flemish immigrant Wice, who founded the church and settlement here in the 12th century. The location given denotes Wiston Mains Farm, though Wiston Place and Castledykes are other possible sites. It is highly probable that Wice had an earthwork castle somewhere in the vicinity. In 1159 he granted the church of his manor and its two chapels to the monks of Kelso Abbey.

The barony passed through the descendants of Wice, his son William, to Sir Walter then Sir Henry of Wiston, who was in possession in 1260. Henry had died by the outbreak of the Wars of Independence, when the wardship of the barony was granted to Walter Logan by the Guardians of Scotland.

In the reign of David II, the barony was resigned by William Livingstone in favour of Sir James Sandilands, whose descendants were recorded as still having possession in the 15th century. Thereafter the estate belonged to the Winram family, whose male line died out and the property was divided between three heiresses. The eldest married Alan Lockhart of Cleghorn, though the Sandilands still appear to have held the superiority. Thereafter portions of the estate were been feued out as smaller estates.

WISTON PLACE

South Lanarkshire   Ruin or site   OS 72   NS 957314
1 mile west of Lamington, by minor roads west of A73 southwest of Wiston at Wiston Place.

Reputed site of the castle of the barons of Wiston, and this is possibly a later site than the original manor. The present house is 'of indeterminate age'.

WOLFCLYDE MOTTE

South Lanarkshire   Historic Scotland   OS 72   NT 019363
1.5 miles west of Biggar, on east bank of River Clyde, just west of A72, at Coulter.

This traditional Christmas pudding-shaped motte lost its bailey during the construction of a railway station on the north side. The railway has now gone but the former station master's cottage occupies the site.

The motte stands to a height of 12ft and has a diameter at the base of about 75ft. The summit is oval, measuring 45ft by 38ft. There is no longer any evidence of a ditch.

This is probably the seat of Alexander de Cutir, who witnessed charters in the 13th century. In the 14th century the estate was divided in two. One half of the barony was the property of Walter Bisset, which he granted to William of Newbigging in 1367. By 1369 this half became the property of Sir Archibald Douglas. The other half of the barony seems to have belonged to the Menzies family and in 1431 David Menzies granted the lands of Wolfclyde to the monks of Melrose Abbey.

The site is a Scheduled Ancient Monument. Access is available at all reasonable times.

Other reference: Coulter Motte

WOODHEAD CASTLE

The Lennox & East Dunbartonshire   Ruin or site   OS 64   NS 606784
3.5 miles northeast of Milngavie, south of A891, in the grounds of the former Lennox Castle Hospital, just north of Lennox Castle.

Woodhead (or Woodheid) is a very ruinous 16th century tower house, set on the edge of a precipice. It is an L-plan tower, with a main block on a southwest to northeast axis and measuring 45.5ft by 25.5 ft. A small stair tower projects from the southern corner. Originally of three storeys and an attic, only the northeastern gable survives to full height. The other walls reach a maximum of 12ft. There is a small turret in the northern corner.

Woodhead was built by John Lennox, 6th of Balcorrach, shortly after succeeding his brother Duncan in 1572. The family were continually feuding with the Kincaid family. Ironically, they became one, when John Kincaid married Cecilia Lennox and adopted the name Lennox-Kincaid.

One example of the feud was a complaint registered with the Privy Council by the friends of John Lennox of Woodhead in September 1577: 'he being solitary at his prayers beside his dwelling place of Woodheid, belevit na evill of ony persoun bot to hav levit under God's peax and the Kingis; nonteles the sonnes and brethir of James Kincaid of that ilk upoun sett purpois cruellie invadit the said Johnne, and woundit and hurt him in diverse partis of his body to the effusion of his blude in great quantitie, and masterfullie and perforce tuke him to the place of Kincaid, quhair thay detaine him captive...'

The Lennox family claimed descent from Donald of Balcorrach, a son of Duncan, Earl of Lennox. The grandson of the couple mentioned above had staked a remote but ultimately unsuccessful claim to the earldom. To show that he carried the wealth to back up his claim he built the grandiose mansion of Lennox Castle in 1837. He left Woodhead as a picturesque ruin adjacent to his new house. It is now very overgrown with ivy and shrubbery, the result being a severe deterioration of the building. There are few features remaining. The ruin is a Scheduled Ancient Monument, and category 'B' Listed Building.

Lennox Castle became a nurses' home when the estate was gifted for use as a hospital. This closed and, after several vacant years, the mansion was seriously damaged by a fire in 2008. This has resulted in the collapse and demolition of sections of the building. There is a proposal to stabilise it and convert it into flats. It is a category 'A' Listed Building and is described as 'critical' on the Buildings at Risk Register.

GLOSSARY

Arch A self supporting structure, usually rounded, though occasionally curved to a point at the apex. Used to support loads.

Arrow slots Long vertical slots through a wall allowing use of a bow.

Ashlar Being of regularly sized dressed block of stone, squared and even faced.

Assize A criminal court, when someone was appointed to the assizes they were effectively a jury member.

Attaint /attainted/attainder To be 'tainted' by a conviction for a felony offence, such as treason. When placed under attainder the act effectively confiscates property and prohibits it from being passed onto entitled heirs. Often the process involved a ceremony where the heraldic arms of the accused were destroyed.

Attic Rooms within the roof space entirely below a gabled roof.

Aumbry Originally almry, a cupboard built within a wall, a recess usually above floor level; used to carry sacred vessels for mass then later used domestically.

Bailey A secondary defensible area enclosed by a ditch and palisade, usually containing subsidiary buildings. Usually larger than the associated motte.

Barmkin A small defensive courtyard framed by the buildings of a complex and a linking wall.

Bartizan A projecting corner tower with roof, usually corbelled out and providing a watch room with enhanced views of the approaches.

Basement The lowest storey of a building, occasionally below ground level.

Bastle house A small fortified building, usually with byre or barn on ground floor, and domestic rooms on the floor above. Usually the strongest building of a group within farmstead or similar settlement.

Battlement A fighting area at the wallhead, formed by a crenneled parapet and walkway.

Bay window A projecting window at ground level, with squared or sharp corners.

Boreland Another term for the mains or home farm, supplying provisions for the castle.

Broch An early drystone tower, with double wall and single narrow entrance. Had several wooden floors and a fighting platform or roof. Possibly used as a bolt hole when the community was under attack.

Caphouse A small watch chamber at a stair head, often providing access to a parapet walk, occasionally rising from within the parapet.

Caponier A stone shelter traversing a ditch from which covering fire could be given along its base, thus preventing it being crossed.

Caput The administrative and military centre of a barony, the seat of power, and residence of the local lord.

Castellations Battlements and turrets, this term usually applies when these features are added to enhance the appearance of a later unfortified mansion, and the features are purely decorative.

Castle In terms of this book, a building containing defensive features as part of the architectural design. Includes simple fortified houses to the fortress of a noble family or royalty.

Clare Constat A deed whereby a feudal superior confirms the rights of inheritance to a property.

Classical Having features of design associated with Greek and Roman buildings, such as pillars and pediments. An architectural style.

Conduit A channel through a wall, usually used as a drain for sinks or garderobes.

Conventicles Forbidden religious services held by the persecuted Covenanters.

Corbel A stone step projecting from a wall used to support another structure such as a turret or beam for an upper floor.

Corbiestepped From Scots corbie 'crow'. Squared stones forming a step sequence crowning a gable.

Cornice A decorative moulding filling the space below the eaves or at a ceiling/wall join.

Courtyard castle Usually built of stone, enclosed by a high wall which may be interrupted or surround the main buildings. In early examples the internal buildings were simple lean-to wooden structures. Later examples were normally large and politically important places.

Crenellated A battlement consisting of crenels and merlons, that is gaps and blocks spaced alternately giving the traditional appearance of a battlement.

Crowstepped	See Corbiestepped.
Curtain Wall	A high wall drawn around the area of a bailey or courtyard.
Demesne	Pronounced De Mains, lands held by a superior lord for his own support, the Scots term mains has devolved from it.
Diocese	The administrative area supervised by a Bishop.
Disponed	Legally transferred, a change of ownership.
Donjon	A large keep representing the central stronghold of larger courtyard castles, the English word dungeon is corrupted from this French word, since high-status prisoners were kept here.
Doocot	A Scots word for dovecote or pigeon house.
Dower house	Home of the dowager, or widow, of the previous owner of the estate.
Dun (doon)	A roofless fort with very thick drystone walls, usually round.
Eaves	The sheltered area below the overhang of a roof.
Emparked	Within a walled or fenced park or policies.
Enceinte	An older term for curtain wall.
Entresol	A secondary floor, often only partial, built out below ceiling or vault level to provide sleeping quarters, or a gallery for musicians.
E-plan	Describing the shape of the building when viewed from above, and the letter that resembles.
Excambion	In Scots law, where one property is taken away as warranty (eg for a mortgage or debt) on a superior property, the owner may demand its return for the surrender of the other on foreclosure.
Fair	A market held in a burgh, usualy on a date specified within the burgh's charter. The day of the fair became a local holiday.
Feu/feued	Where a property is held under the feudal superiority of another, and for which military service or a fee is due to the superior. A Scottish variation of the word fee. Feu duties were finally abolished in Scotland in 2000, though had been on the wane long before.
Fosse	A ditch.
Gable	The end wall of a building, usually with triangular shape at roof level when a sloping roof is used. Associated in Scotland's earlier architecture with corbiesteps.
Gallery	A long multi-purpose room often used a promenade area when conversing with visitors, used as a display area for family portraits and memorabilia, where visitors would be suitably impressed by the lineage and status of their host. Galleries became fashionable in the late 16th century.
Garderobe	A toilet or closet usually built into the thickness of the wall, and normally draining to the outside by a chute. The ammonia produced by stale urine was also known to repel moths, and so these rooms were also used as wardrobes, hence the name.
Garret	A small building upon the roof of a tower, separated from the wall head by a flat area or wall-walk. Usually set within battlements.
Gothic	A form of architecture characterised by narrow windows and pointed turrets, high pitched roofs and pointed arches. Lacking classical features.
Gunloop	A hole built through a wall to allow the firing of muskets or small cannon, and with some variation such as external splays to allow the aiming of the weapon.
Hall house	A long defensive building usually of two storeys with a hall above a basement. A hall house is longer than it is tall. Often called a palace, palis or place in Scots.
Harled	Roughcast and whitewashed with a slurry of lime mortar and sand. The sand used often provided a coloured tint, resulting in some buildings having a pink, yellow or red tinge, especially at sunset.
Heraldic panel	A stone frame containing a carved stone or wooden representation of the coat of arms of the occupying family.
Jougs	A medieval pillory.
Keep	The main tower or fortified building of a castle, the strongest building and final refuge, the administrative centre.
Knights Service	In feudal times grants of land were made in return for multiples of knights service, ie for the provision of a knight in times of war. Large portions of land could be granted to a major land holder for several knights service. Often smaller grants were made for a fraction or whole of a knights fee, ie several small landholders were together expected to maintain

and arm a single knight. Post Bruce, some lands were granted for archers, or even galleys of a specific size.

License to crenellate Granted by a monarch allowing the recipient to fortify his home, or build a castle or tower.

Listed Building Registered as a significantly important building with obligations upon the owner not to alter or damage the building without proper consents. There are three categories;

A listing is a building of national importance.

B listing for regional importance.

C listing for local importance.

L-plan Describing the shape of the building when viewed from above, and the letter that resembles.

Machicolation A slot or space between overhanging stone work, usually corbels, allowing liquids or objects to be dropped upon assailants at the base of the wall.

Main block The keep or tower, the primary residence or structure of the castle. Usually contained the private rooms and hall of the resident Lord.

Mains The home farm retained to supply the castle, see Boreland.

Marian Pertaining to Mary Queen of Scots

Moat Either dry or water filled, a deep surrounding ditch protecting the approaches to a castle or fortified enclosure.

Moot hill Literally a meeting place, though in practice the site of justice hearings. A court hill.

Mortmain A legal term where a grant of property is made to an institution, usually a religious one, in perpetuity, but where the sale or mortgaging of that property is prohibited. A grant of inalienable property.

Motte Corrupted to moat, though meaning the steeply sloped mound within a ditch upon which the main residence was sited in early timber and earth castles.

Motte and bailey An early defensive system originating in Roman times. Consisting of a large raised area within a ditch, within which a second ditch surrounded a motte. Both areas were normally protected by a timber palisade, or stout defensive fence.

Moulding Ornamental work of continuous cross-section.

Mullion A vertical spar dividing a window.

Mural Pertaining to or within the thickness of a wall.

Newel The centre post of a spiral or turnpike stair.

Of that Ilk Of a place of the same name, e.g. James Dunlop of Dunlop.

Ogee Shaped by a double curve, bending in alternate directions. OG, shaped as the interface of these letters following the lower half of the O and upper half of the G.

Oriel A projecting bay window.

Palace, palis, or place The Scots term denoting a hall house.

Palladian A style of architecture characterized by symmetry, with the use of both Greek and Roman motifs: columns and pediments. From the 16th century Italian architect, Andrea Palladio.

Parapet The wall preventing a fall from a sudden drop, as at a wallhead, usually in early Scottish architecture forming a defensive feature.

Parish The administrative area of the local church.

Peel Originally a court with palisade, later a small tower of wood and later of stone. In the border regions these were watch towers with a brazier for a warning fire to be lit during raids by reivers. The name came to be used for small fortified towers which were integral to many farm complexes. Also spelt peil or pele.

Pend A covered passageway which runs through a building, usually from the exterior, to a courtyard.

Piscina A small stone sink for washing holy vessels, usually sited close to the altar of a chapel.

Pit prison A cell within a wall, usually entered only from above by a hatch.

Portcullis A heavy wooden or iron gate which was lifted vertically to open, and guided by grooves in the wall.

Portioner The laird of a small property or of a portion of a larger one.

Postern A secondary or minor gate, allowing a rear or side exit.

Prebend The benefice or property which provided financial support for a canon of a cathedral.

Quoined Contrasting stonework used to create the exterior angle of a wall or other stonework, successive courses being stepped to add strength. Often ashlar is used where the rest of the building is of rubble.

Re-entrant	The internal aspect of a corner, where two buildings join at right angles.
Revetment	Stone walling put in place to retain and strengthen an artificially heightened section of ground, e.g. a motte or terrace.
Rib-vaulting	Where a vaulted ceiling is decorated or strengthened transversely by projecting stone in the form of ribs.
Ringwork	An earth and timber castle consisting of a continuous ditch enhanced by rampart and palisade and possibly a gatehouse, enclosing an area occupied by timber buildings.
Round	A roofless bartizan.
Royal castle	Property of the Crown, usually held by a Keeper or Constable. Often administered by a Governor.
Sasine	The handing over of feudal or immoveable property. Later the term came to be used for the actual documents or charters which confirmed this. To give sasine therefore meant to deliver the deeds of a property.
Scale and platt	A stair formed by short straight flights with landings at the corners.
Scheduled Ancient Monument	Protection under the law which prevents any disturbance of the site without permission from the Scottish Government.
Seneschal	A position in Gaelic household hierarchy similar to a steward, an administrator of an estate on behalf of its lord.
Shot hole	See Gunloop.
Solar	The private residential rooms of the lord.
Souterrain	An underground chamber constructed with flagstones, probably used as storage by peoples of the Iron Age.
Steading	(Scots) A group of buildings forming a small farm.
Stoup	A stone sink built into the structure of a wall. Normally used to hold holy water in a chapel.
Stool cupboard	A toilet, more modern than a garderobe, with no draughty drain to the outside. Instead a commode or other receptacle was used which would be regularly emptied.
String coursing	A projecting thin line of moulded stone work, decorative in nature, which runs around the external walls.
Superiority	See Feu.
Tailzie	A conditional deed of inheritance, the property cannot be sold except to the feudal superior.
Talus	A sloping plinth or outward sloping of the base section of the walls, providing a wider more stable base for buildings on softer ground and some protection against attacks by mining. The talus also helped ricochet projectiles dropped from the parapet into the faces of attackers.
Tower house	A self contained house with the rooms one on top of another. Usually there was a vaulted basement with the hall above, then private rooms on subsequent floors. A tower house is normally taller than it is long.
T-plan	Describing the shape of the building when viewed from above, and the letter that resembles.
Transom	A horizontal spar dividing a window.
Turnpike stair	A spiral stair formed around a central pillar or newel, usually very steep to give advantage to the defending swordsman at a higher level within. The direction of turn of the stair was decided so that the newel prevented a free swing of a sword when facing upstairs.
Turret	A small tower projecting from the upper storeys of a larger building.
Vault	A ceiling of stone use to prevent fire rising to the storeys above, and normally arched to bear the weight of the other floors.
Wadset	Given in security for a mortgage or other debt.
Wall-walk	A footpath along the top of a wall, usually protected by a parapet.
Watchroom	A room at a stair head used as a look-out point for the approaches to the castle, larger than a caphouse.
X-plan	Describing the shape of the building when viewed from above, and the letter that resembles.
Yett	Scots word for a strong hinged door made of interwoven iron bars.
Z-plan	Describing the shape of the building when viewed from above, and the letter that resembles.

SELECTED READING

The following is not a complete list of the resources used for this book, but comprises those which are most interesting or useful, and appear in no particular order of merit.

BOOKS

The Kingdom of the Scots, 2nd Edition, G.W.S. Barrow, Edinburgh University Press 2003
The Castles of Scotland, Editions 1-3, Martin Coventry, Goblinshead 1995/97/2001
The Castles of Scotland, 4th Ed, Martin Coventry, Birlinn 2006
The Castles of Glasgow and the Clyde, Gordon W Mason, Goblinshead 2000
The Blaeu Atlas of Scotland, Birlinn 2006
Origines Parochiales Scotiae, The Bannatyne Club 1851
The Queen's Scotland: The Heartland, Nigel Tranter, Hodder & Stoughton 1971
The Incomplete History of Castlemilk, Castlemilk Local History Group, Workers Educational Association 1993
The Fortified House in Scotland, Nigel Tranter, 5 vols, James Thin 1986
A Shorter History of Dunbartonshire, I.M.M. MacPhail, Spa Books 1962
The Castellated and Domestic Architecture of Scotland, MacGibbon and Ross, 5 vols, James Thin 1990
Scotland's Castles, Chris Tabraham, Historic Scotland 1997
Villages of Glasgow, Aileen Smart, John Donald, Vol. 1 1988, Vol 2 1996
The Black Douglasses: War and Warship in Late Medieval Scotland, Michael Brown, John Donald 1998
The Surnames of Scotland, George F. Black, Birlinn, 1999
Descriptions of the Sherrifdoms of Lanark and Renfrew, William Hamilton of Wishaw, Grimsay Press 2004
The History of the Shire of Renfrew, Crawfurd et al, Grimsay Press 2003
The Highland Clans, Moncreiffe of that Ilk, Barrie and Jenkins 1982
The Parish of Strathblane and its Inhabitants from Early Times, John Guthrie Smith, J McElhose and Sons 1886
Robert Bruce and the Community of the Realm of Scotland, Geoffrey W.S. Barrow, Edinburgh University Press 1988
Annals of Garelochside, WC Maughan 1897
The Book of Dumbartonshire, Joseph Irving, W. and A.K. Johnston 1879
Scotland: a New History, Michael Lynch, Pimlico 1992
The Castles of Scotland, Maurice Lindsay, Constable 1994
The Encyclopaedia of Scotland, Edited by J. and J. Keay, Collins 1994
Dumbarton Castle, I.M.M.MacPhail, John Donald 1979
The History of Rutherglen and East Kilbride, Rev D.Ure, Glasgow Press 1793
The Annals of the Parish of Lesmahagow, J.B. Greenshields, Caledonian 1864
Discovering: The River Clyde, I. MacLeod and M. Gilroy, John Donald 1991
The South Clyde Estuary, F.A.Walker, RIAS 1991
Glasgow's Rivers and Streams, Brotchie, 1914
Drumchapel, D.R. Robertson, John Wylie and Co. 1939
The Story of Bishopbriggs, J.A. Russell, Strathkelvin Dist. Libraries 1979
A History of the Scottish People From the Earliest Times, Rev. Thomas Thomson, Vols 1-6, Blackie & Son 1893–96
A History of Cambuslang, J.A. Wilson, Jackson and Wylie, 1929
Eastwood District: History and Heritage, T.C. Welsh, Eastwood Dist. Libraries 1989
Castles and Mansions of Renfrewshire, Millar, c.1899
Scotland's Lost Houses, Ian Gow, National Trust for Scotland/Aurum 2006
The Upper Ward of Lanarkshire: Described and Delineated, George Vere Irving, Thomas Murray & Son 1864
MacDonalds Rambles Around Glasgow, Edited by G.H. Morrison, A Smith & Son 1854
The Scottish Chateau, Charles McKean, 2001 Sutton Publishing
Domination And Lordship: Scotland 1070-1230, Richard Oram, Edinburgh University Press 2011
David I: the King Who Made Scotland, Richard Oram, Tempus 2008
East Kilbride: the History of the Parish And Village, Thomas Eric Niven, Wilson Guthrie and Lang 1965

A History of the House of Hamilton, Lt Col. George Hamilton, Skinner and Co 1933
Strathaven Reminiscences, Mary Gebbie 1880
A Contribution to the History of Lanarkshire, Wilson, J Wylie and Co 1937

The various individual castle guides published by Historic Scotland and many, many other books and local history publications.

INTERNET RESOURCES

The Records of the Parliament of Scotland to 1707, www.rps.ac.uk/
Pitcairn's Ancient Criminal Trials of Scotland, www.archive.org/stream/ancientcrim42pt202pitcuoft#page/n7/mode/2up
The Statistical Accounts of Scotland, edina.ac.uk/stat-acc-scot/
Paradox of Medieval Scotland 1093-1286, poms.cch.kcl.ac.uk/index.html
Burke's Peerage, www.burkespeerage.com/articles/scottish-barons.aspx
A Genealogical and Heraldic History of the Commoners of Great Britain and Ireland. John Burke via Google Books.
The Douglas Archives, www.douglashistory.co.uk/
University of Glasgow Special Collections, www.gla.ac.uk/services/specialcollections/
The Archaeology Data Service, ads.ahds.ac.uk/
Biggar Archaeology, www.biggararchaeology.org.uk/
RCAHMS Canmore Database, www.rcahms.gov.uk/
Pastmap, jura.rcahms.gov.uk/PASTMAP/start.jsp
NLS Map Collection, maps.nls.uk/counties/index.html
Scotlands People, www.scotlandspeople.gov.uk/
Glasgow Digital Library, gdl.cdlr.strath.ac.uk/
Internet Archive, www.archive.org/
The Scottish Nation Anderson 1863, www.archive.org/stream/scottishnation05andegoog#page/n8/mode/2up
The Family of Edmonstone of Duntreath, www.edmonstone.com/
East Renfrewshire's Heritage Collection, www.eastrenfrewshire.gov.uk/heritage/heritage_building.htm
British History Online, www.british-history.ac.uk/
Groome's 19th century Gazetteer for Scotland, www.scottish-places.info/

Et al.

INDEX